Implementing AI Tools for Language Teaching and Learning

Vu Phi Ho Pham
Industrial University of Ho Chi Minh City, Vietnam

Andrew Lian
Suranaree University of Technology, Thailand

Ania Lian
Charles Darwin University, Australia

Sandro R. Barros
Michigan State University, USA

IGI Global
Scientific Publishing
Publishing Tomorrow's Research Today

Vice President of Editorial Melissa Wagner
Director of Acquisitions Mikaela Felty
Director of Book Development Jocelynn Hessler
Production Manager Mike Brehm
Cover Design Phillip Shickler

Published in the United States of America by
IGI Global Scientific Publishing
701 East Chocolate Avenue
Hershey, PA, 17033, USA
Tel: 717-533-8845
Fax: 717-533-7115
Website: https://www.igi-global.com E-mail: cust@igi-global.com

Library of Congress Cataloging-in-Publication Data

Library of Congress Cataloging-in-Publication Data

Names: Phạm, Vu Phi Ho, 1971- editor. | Lian, Andrew, 1944- editor. | Lian, Ania, editor. | Barros, Sandro R., editor.
Title: Implementing AI tools for language teaching and learning / edited by Vu Phi Ho Pham, Andrew Lian, Ania Lian, Sandro R. Barros.
Description: Hershey, PA : IGI Global, 2025. | Includes bibliographical references and index. | Summary: "This book seeks to provide a thorough examination of the incorporation of artificial intelligence (AI) techniques in the field of language teaching and learning. The objective is to get a deeper understanding of the perspectives and experiences of educators and learners about AI technologies"-- Provided by publisher.
Identifiers: LCCN 2024052015 (print) | LCCN 2024052016 (ebook) | ISBN 9798369372609 (hardcover) | ISBN 9798369372616 (paperback) | ISBN 9798369372623 (ebook)
Subjects: LCSH: Language and languages--Study and teaching--Technological innovations. | Artificial intelligence--Educational applications. | LCGFT: Essays.
Classification: LCC P53.855 .I47 2025 (print) | LCC P53.855 (ebook) | DDC 418.0078/563--dc23/eng/20241214
LC record available at https://lccn.loc.gov/2024052015
LC ebook record available at https://lccn.loc.gov/2024052016

British Cataloguing in Publication Data
A Cataloguing in Publication record for this book is available from the British Library.

Table of Contents

Detailed Table of Contents

The use of artificial intelligence (AI) in language learning is a rapidly expanding field that has been gaining increasing interest since the 2000s. Despite its numerous advantages, its integration also poses challenges. This chapter explores these issues and emerging trends in language teaching, structured into three distinct sections. The first highlights the potential of AI to develop language skills. The second section examines how AI-based tools enhance the learning experience in terms of motivation, engagement, autonomy, and interactions, while addressing the main pedagogical, technological, and ethical challenges. The final section provides an overview of current research in this innovative field, presenting recent advances in AI-assisted language teaching/learning.

This chapter shed light on the students' perspectives on both pros and cons of the Grammarly application in English writing classes. To accomplish the research purpose, the chapter author used a closed-ended questionnaire and semi-structured in-depth interviews, with 120 participants from four English classes that the author directly taught. The findings show that students had a positive attitude towards the Grammarly tool, which might enhance the quality of their English writing in grammar knowledge and language style, and increase their motivation and confidence in writing. Besides the undeniable benefits, the Grammarly tool also caused students some difficulties in detecting tenses in sentences, accessing to premium features of Grammarly, and depending on the Internet connection stability. Despite these limitations, the growing popularity of AI-powered automated written feedback tools is indisputable. Thus, students should carefully consider incorporating Grammarly into their writing process to maximize the benefits that this tool can bring to learning English writing.

This exploratory qualitative study aims to explore the ChatGPT use of Van-Lang-University graduate students in a research writing course and the cognitive levels of their reactions to its responses. The data was collected from observations and interviews with twelve Vietnamese graduate students studying in a research writing class at this university. According to the findings, the participants opted for ChatGPT as a help-seeking strategy during their course due to several reasons including its convenience, instant feedback, and multifunction. Additionally, they had critical reactions to ChatGPT's feedback and advocated that ChatGPT could not replace lecturers' roles in future language classrooms. To develop the growth of critical ChatGPT use for research writing in Master's programs in English Language Studies at Van Lang University, actions from relevant stakeholders is required, including policymakers, lecturers teaching research writing, and MA students.

This primary research investigates the use of Poe AI, an AI-powered chatbot, in assisting Vietnamese EFL learners and teachers in learning and teaching lexical collocations. The study involved four teachers and twelve students in Ho Chi Minh City. The students were required to use Poe AI to complete a questionnaire consisting of a cloze task, a translation task, and a writing brainstorming task. The teachers were required to use Poe AI to prepare for a section of teaching lexical input to students. Open-ended questions about their perceptions regarding the use of Poe AI were included at the end of the questionnaires. The findings indicate that both learners and teachers were positive about the use of Poe AI in learning about lexical collocations and preparing materials for lexical input. It is suggested that Poe AI be introduced to learners to assist their collocation learning, while teachers should develop related skills to benefit from this tool. Simultaneously, more scientific research concerning their own teaching context should be carried out.

This research made use of an AI detector known as GPTZero to determine the proportion of each assignment that was written by humans and by AI. Based on the findings, it can be observed that the assignment receives higher marks when the percentage of the AI writing score is larger. One of the limitations of the research is that the use of ChatGPT for proofreading will also be identified as AI. There is a possibility that fairness will be a problem in the field of applying AI in education. The establishment of control mechanisms is necessary prior to the complete implementation of AI in educational settings to prevent AI from destroying human talents. The research aims to examine the frequency of student utilization of AI in writing tasks and to investigate students' attitudes towards AI tools in Mandarin writing. The research questions are: I) How to identify the ethnicity of an individual utilising AI ii) What measures should responsible AI use in the event of damage resulting from following AI recommendations and responses?

In today's digital era, the ability to efficiently process handwritten text has remained a significant challenge with the increasing demand for digitized historical records, forms, and handwritten notes. The Jaro-Winkler algorithm and big data analytics are used in this research to create an innovative approach to handwritten text recognition and spell check. Handwriting recognition, a challenging task due to its inherent variability, is achieved through the application of advanced machine learning techniques to vast datasets of text samples. We present the implementation of Optical Character Recognition along with the integration of the Jaro-Winkler algorithm for spell checking, demonstrating its effectiveness in rectifying errors. In comparison with existing methods, the experimental results demonstrate the performance of the system in both handwritten text recognition and spell check. Furthermore, this research explores the practical applications of our system across various domains, emphasizing its potential to revolutionize the way handwritten documents are processed and archived.

This chapter investigates the performance of Multilayer Perceptron (MLP) and Long-Short Term Memory (LSTM) models in the development of a high-accuracy chatbot for the NITH website. Tokenization and lemmatization are used for data preprocessing. LSTM model is used to interpret sequential data. MLP model used a 3-layer neural network with a bag-of-words technique for text representation. The experimental results reveal that the MLP model is more suitable for this specific application. The chatbot is successfully integrated with a web frontend using Flask and AJAX. The developed chatbot could respond to inquiries almost exactly like a human. Both models achieved over 97% accuracy on a dataset of predetermined patterns and responses.

This chapter explores the transformative impact of integrating artificial intelligence into writing instruction, emphasizing its potential to enhance students' writing performance. By utilizing artificial intelligence chatbots, educators can support specific sub-skills such as grammar, vocabulary, and sentence structure, while fostering creativity and engagement. However, the chapter cautions against over-reliance on artificial intelligence, advocating for a balanced approach that encourages critical thinking and discernment in evaluating AI-generated content. It underscores the importance of professional development for teachers to effectively incorporate these technologies while maintaining a focus on essential writing skills. Ultimately, this chapter argues that the thoughtful integration of artificial intelligence in high school education not only makes learning more relevant and engaging but also equips students with the necessary tools to navigate the evolving landscape of writing and communication in the digital age.

Preface

In an era where artificial intelligence (AI) is no longer a futuristic concept but a tangible force shaping education systems across the globe, the language teaching and learning landscape is undergoing a profound transformation. This edited volume, *Implementing AI Tools for Language Teaching and Learning*, brings together diverse perspectives from researchers and practitioners across Asia, Africa, Europe, and North America to explore how AI technologies are reshaping pedagogical practices, professional development, accessibility, and ethical considerations within language education.

Language education, by its very nature, is deeply rooted in human interaction, communication, and cultural exchange. The integration of AI challenges educators and learners alike to reconsider what teaching and learning mean in an increasingly digital world. From adaptive learning systems and intelligent tutoring platforms to AI-assisted writing tools and language processing applications, the opportunities presented are vast—yet so are the complexities.

This volume offers a comprehensive and nuanced exploration of the current AI landscape in language education. It captures the promise and pitfalls of integrating these technologies, not only through theoretical discussion and empirical research but also by engaging with the lived experiences of educators and learners navigating this shift.

Whether you're a language teacher looking to implement AI tools in your classroom, a researcher exploring educational technologies, or a policymaker shaping curriculum and access, this collection offers valuable insights and guidance for embracing AI in ways that are ethical, inclusive, and effective.

CHAPTER OVERVIEW

Chapter 1: AI Revolutionizing Education

This foundational chapter provides a sweeping overview of AI's transformative role in education, focusing on personalized learning, immersive technologies, and ethical challenges. It introduces key technologies like NLP and blockchain and emphasizes the need for interdisciplinary collaboration.

Chapter 2: Educational Transformation Through AI

Focusing on real-world implementation, this chapter discusses the potential of AI to streamline both teaching and learning. It outlines the dual role of AI in personalization and administrative efficiency while tackling concerns like algorithmic bias and data ethics.

Chapter 3: AI in Professional Development for Language Teachers

Here, the authors explore how AI tools support the continuous professional growth of language educators, particularly in higher education. They analyze platforms like ChatGPT, Grammarly, and intelligent tutoring systems, highlighting the impact on teacher skills and pedagogy.

Chapter 4: AI Tools: A Nostrum for Modern-Day Linguistic Educators and Learners

This chapter provides a historical context for AI in education and examines how modern tools enhance personalized learning, accessibility, and engagement, while critically addressing ongoing challenges like the digital divide and contextual limitations.

Chapter 5: Benefits and Challenges of Integrating AI Tools

This analysis centers on the ethical dilemmas and technical hurdles educators face when adopting AI in language education. The chapter highlights the tension between AI's benefits—like real-time feedback—and the risks of bias, privacy breaches, and reduced human interaction.

Chapter 6: Bridging Gaps: AI-Driven Accessibility

Focusing on inclusivity, this chapter examines how AI, especially NLP, can revolutionize language learning for students with disabilities. It advocates for inclusive design, cross-sector collaboration, and adaptive learning systems to enhance accessibility.

Chapter 7: Leveraging AI for Language Learning Activities

This chapter investigates how AI tools can elevate language learning by offering tailored learning paths, feedback, and contextual practice. It also discusses barriers to implementation, such as equitable access and teacher preparedness.

Chapter 8: Language Teaching in the Age of AI

Structured in three sections, this chapter explores the potential, pedagogical implications, and future directions of AI in language teaching. It offers a critical look at how AI affects learner autonomy, engagement, and the ethical landscape.

Chapter 9: Students' Perspectives on Grammarly

Through empirical research, this chapter examines how students perceive Grammarly in writing instruction. It reflects on the tool's motivational benefits, limitations, and the practical challenges of accessibility and dependence on internet connectivity.

Chapter 10: ChatGPT in Graduate Writing Courses

This exploratory study investigates how Vietnamese graduate students use ChatGPT during research writing. It highlights their critical engagement with the tool and argues for continued educator involvement in guiding AI usage in academic contexts.

Chapter 11: Poe AI and Lexical Collocations

Delving into the use of Poe AI, this chapter studies its role in helping learners master lexical collocations. The findings support the potential of AI to assist both learners and teachers in vocabulary acquisition and instructional planning.

Chapter 12: AI Writing Detection and Ethics

Here, the focus turns to the ethical landscape of AI-detected writing. The chapter raises important concerns about fairness, authorship, and control mechanisms in academic settings, especially in light of tools like GPTZero.

Chapter 13: Handwritten Text Recognition with Spell Checking

This technical chapter presents an innovative approach to recognizing and correcting handwritten text using small language models and the Jaro-Winkler algorithm. Its applications extend to digitizing handwritten educational content effectively.

Chapter 14: Chatbots Using LSTM for Educational Sites

Exploring chatbot development, this chapter compares LSTM and MLP models, showing how conversational AI can enhance student engagement and support. It details integration into a university website, achieving near-human response accuracy.

Chapter 15: Teaching AI in High Schools for Essay Writing

The final chapter explores the benefits of integrating AI into high school writing instruction. It highlights how chatbots can support grammar and structure while warning against over-reliance, advocating for balanced, critical use.

As the chapters in this volume demonstrate, artificial intelligence is no longer a distant possibility—it is actively reshaping the ways we teach, learn, and engage with language. While the promise of AI is vast, so too are the responsibilities we must embrace as educators, researchers, and developers. The insights and case studies presented here highlight not only the innovative use of AI tools but also the importance of ethical considerations, equitable access, and continued professional development. This book is a call to action: to thoughtfully integrate AI into language education while preserving the human connection at the heart of teaching and learning. As we move forward, let us embrace AI not as a replacement for educators, but as a powerful ally—enhancing our ability to foster meaningful, inclusive, and transformative learning experiences.

Vu Phi Ho Pham
Van Lang University, Vietnam

Andrew Lian
Suranaree University of Technology, Thailand

Ania Lian
Charles Darwin University, Australia

Sandro R. Barros
Michigan State University, USA

Chapter 1
AI Revolutionizing Education: Exploring Trends, Technologies, and Ethical Considerations for Future Learning Environments

Jyoti Rani
https://orcid.org/0000-0002-5577-7808
Lovely Professional University, India

Worku Tegegne Molla
https://orcid.org/0009-0006-2267-7241
De Montfort University, UK

Ramratan Guru
https://orcid.org/0000-0001-6142-2643
Mody University of Science and Technology, India

Jaswant Singh
https://orcid.org/0009-0003-4653-4972
Lovely Professional University, India

Sakthivel Santhanam
https://orcid.org/0000-0003-2856-7714
Presidency University, India

Sarishti Dutt
Lovely Professional University, India

ABSTRACT

AI is transforming education through personalized learning, adaptive assessments, AI-driven content creation, and immersive technologies like VR/AR. This study reviews AI's history and current trends, using expert interviews, case studies, and quantitative analysis to explore future developments. Emerging technologies such as NLP for interactive learning, machine learning for predictive analytics, and blockchain for secure credentialing are highlighted. Ethical concerns, including data privacy, bias, and equity, are examined. Future trends include fully personalized learning, AI-augmented teaching, and global learning communities. The study underscores the need for continued research, cross-sector collaboration, and ethical practices to create more effective, inclusive, and adaptive educational systems.

INTRODUCTION

Artificial Intelligence, or AI, is slowly and steadily becoming part of the educational systems while altering the way teaching-learning processes are modeled and implemented. AI in Education (AIEd) uses methods from AI and cognitive science to improve learning and learning processes, as well as help teachers with their work by integrating approaches to blended learning (Boulay, 2016). The use of AI

DOI: 10.4018/979-8-3693-7260-9.ch001

models in education works to meet the contemporary challenge by providing access to education using social Robots, Smart learning environments, and intelligent tutoring systems for the modernization of education techniques (Ahmad et al., 2021). The role of AI in education can be categorized into three main areas: Instructors and learners find AI shaping their connections through its role in teaching and learning (Xu & Ouyang, 2021). Various grades and courses in K-12 education incorporate AI with machine learning and tutoring systems as the leading techniques. These applications emphasize elevating student outcomes and instructing methods while examining student behaviors. Moreover, AI enhances research-informed teaching and learning practices by helping teachers produce and use contextualized evidence of their teaching practices, indicating that there is a symbiotic relationship between AI and education. In addition to facilitating the design of instructions as well as students' learning processes, this newly arising role of AI also mobilizes teachers in the creation of proofs regarding best practices of teaching in order to enrich the educational system. The regularity of the utilization of AI in education increases year by year, which means that new possibilities for learning personalization and better outcomes are anticipated in further improvements of this technology.

LITERATURE REVIEW

AI in education is revolutionizing the way in which learning is delivered and experienced. Numerous studies have addressed the potential of AI to personalize learning, automate assessments, and improve educational content engagingly and immersively. This section highlights key themes and findings from existing research on AI's implementation in education, from personalized learning and content creation to immersive technologies such as VR/AR and ethical considerations. Introduction to AI in education: Personalized learning AI systems can tailor learning processes to the specific requirements and learning styles of students, offering personalized educational experiences. Studies by (Luckin et al., 2016) also argue that AI-based technologies provide immediate feedback to students and can adapt learning materials in real time, leading to enhanced engagement and success in academic endeavours. AI systems like DreamBox and Knewton examine student data and tailor lessons and pacing to allow students to learn at their own speed. Research by (Pane et al., 2015) Such system allows tailoring the education in order to meet the expectations of each pupil, resulting in better outcomes. This is in line with cognitive and constructivist learning theories that stress active learning and learning at an individual pace. Within education, AI is also changing how we create and assess content. Automated systems are creating teaching materials, tests, quizzes and assessments that free up time for educators. Machine learning algorithm-based platforms like Carnegie Learning and Smart Sparrow act as Intelligent Tutoring Systems (ITS) offer real-time adaptive feedback on learners performance. Such systems can provide one-to-one tailored support, as effective as human tutors themselves (VanLehn, 2011). Also, AI tools automate grading so that teachers spend more time on interactive teaching instead of administrative work. YET the potential for AI to effectively assess one of the most complex tasks, such as creativity and critical thinking skills, is questionable, indicating the need for constant refinement of these systems. Virtual Reality (VR) and Augmented Reality (AR) are both examples of immersive technologies that have long gained popularity as effective learning tools. AI is at the heart of these technologies as it enables more interactive and personalised learning environment. Studies by (Mikropoulos and Natsis, 2011) cites studies indicating that VR and AR enhance engagement by offering hands-on experiential learning opportunities. Students can, for instance, virtually walk through historical events or calorimetry science experiments and make learning more vivid and memorable. AI can also adapt VR/AR experiences further still, manipulating the difficulty levels of tasks on-the-fly. While the potential for VR/AR is great, adoption has obstacles such as cost and lack of teacher training. Artificial intelligence is a promising technology that could significantly improve education. One of the most urgent concerns is algorithmic bias. If trained on such biased data, AI systems can reinforce existing biases, potentially resulting in unfair treatment of students. Research by (Noble, 2018) illustrates how biased AI systems can lead to discriminatory outcomes that further entrench educational inequalities. Another concern is data privacy, as AI systems need access to sensitive student data. Privacy laws like GDPR and FERPA on student information must be complied with all access must be restricted and monitored. Lastly, the digital divide presents a challenge, as not all students from low-income backgrounds may have access to the technology to study effectively.

PURPOSE OF THE STUDY

Hence, the role of the present study is to shed light on the complex impact of AI on learning settings and future teaching practices based on diverse contexts illustrated in the studies included in the present work. AI is redesigning educational interactions, personalizing the learning process, and automating many processes that directly influence student-environment interactions and their learning achievements (Seo et al., 2021). In specializing among Ambient Intelligent (AmI) environments that involve the use of AI, learners are able to get context-based as well as intelligent learning, which is more personalized and expected rather than being confined to specific settings. Furthermore, AI's role in education is categorized into three main functions: As a new subject, the first intermediary of so-to-speak mesonic relations between instructors and students, and a second, supplementary assistant affecting mesonic relations between students themselves, or between students and instructors. In the health workforce, AI education is crucial for preparing professionals to effectively integrate AI into clinical settings, emphasizing the need for understanding ethical implications, data suitability, and human-machine interactions. Thirdly, Intelligent Computer-Aided Instruction (ICAI) kind of Artificial Intelligence provides coached course imitation through improved student-computer interaction and increased control, which revolutionizes the conceptual mode of teaching-learning in universities. Altogether, these studies presented an unprecedented opportunity to improve existing educational practices and expertise with the help of artificial intelligence and discussed the possible problems that will have to be taken into account while implementing AI in education.

HISTORY OF AI IN EDUCATION

Early Developments in AI for Educational Purposes

AI for education in its initial stages refers to the use of AI in learning environments to improve the delivery of content through learning. AIED has applied both artificial intelligence and cognitive sciences to study learning processes and design systems that help learners get over to new knowledge and skills, with a call for teachers to create a mixed or integrated approach in which the systems themselves help learners together with completing some instructional actions that a teacher would usually carry out (Boulay, 2016). Another notable attempt at AI education is the development of Intelligent Computer-assisted Instruction (ICAI), which has been reviewed scientifically in science subjects particularly. ICAI incorporates the modeling of a student, teacher, and environment within `microworlds' that are used to support science education even though issues of Natural Language Processing and Machine (Ahmad et al., 2021; Chiu et al., 2022; Good, 1987; Woodward & Carnine, 1988)learning remain problematic (Good, 1987). Furthermore, (Woodward and Carnine, 1988) have mentioned that interest in ICAI has been of considerable interest, particularly in the field of special education, where it is envisaged as a modest enhancement of traditional computer-assisted instruction for importing structured antecedent knowledge to teach important concepts and strategies. This paper has also shown how AI has contributed to education by improving the pretertiary AI curriculum developed by the Chinese University of Hong Kong; throughout the curriculum the competencies and attitudes of the students were characterized as competent and favorable to AI learning while on the other hand, the teachers were equipped with the ability to incorporate the AI curricula into their practice (Chiu et al, 2022) In addition, AI applications in education have now gone beyond just ASSIST; covering social robots, smart learning environments, and intelligent tutoring system which addresses the modern education problems and the use of AI technology as an important tool in the contemporary learning (Ahmad et al., 2021). These are some of the early milestones in demonstrating how AI could revolutionize learning opportunities and ways of delivering education in the future.

Key Milestones Leading to Current AI Applications in Education

This paper aims to discuss various milestones that have made Artificial Intelligence (AI) what it is today in the education sector. The term Artificial Intelligence was first used in 1956 during a conference at Dartmouth College, which initiated the process of its invention and application in different areas, including education (Alqahtani et al., 2023; Hamal et al., 2022; Sanabria-Navarro et al., 2023; Wang et al., 2023)). AI has been a center of concern in academia for the last 30 years, bringing together education, psychology, and neuroscience to develop learning environments and tools in the process of formal and informal education (Hamal et al., 2022). AI's increasing presence in education has shifted to smartphone and tablet usage, mobile learning, educational gaming, and augmented reality due to the prominence of smartphones, tablets, and the cloud (Hamal et al., 2022). When it comes to public health education, AI has made a great contribution in theory and practice by helping the information overwhelming and data construction so as to strengthen the development of professional courses and improve the ability to handle public health emergency events (Wang et al., 2023). The adoption of AI in K-12 education has been substantial, and AI has been used on student outcomes, teaching, and behavior tasks, particularly in the STEM areas (Zafari et al., 2022). Machine Learning (ML) and Intelligent Tutoring Systems (ITS) have emerged as prevalent approaches in this sector (Zafari et al., 2022). Moreover, the advanced NLP methods and the LLMs such as GPT-4 and BARD have brought new supports in education, assessment, feedback, and even in the student's mental help (Alqahtani et al., 2023). These innovations show AI's possibility for enhancing learning and teaching practices and effectiveness while solving future problems, such as ethical issues and algorithmic prejudices, which help create an efficient and equitable learning futuristic environment (Alqahtani et al., 2023).

Initial Barriers and Breakthroughs in AI Integration

Artificial Intelligence integration with several domains, such as the healthcare and IoT domains, first comes with certain barriers and then breakthroughs. There is the opacity of these systems in question, mainly in healthcare, where clients and clinicians must work with the technology without necessarily comprehending how an ML model arrived at the final decision. This reticence inhibits the application of AI in healthcare environments, requiring advancement in algorithm explanation to enhance popularisation (Poon & Sung, 2021). The benefits of AI in applying new insights to physician and patient-centric processes in healthcare are clear. Still, issues like training ML systems, responsibilities, and requirements for stringent regulation remain. Frameworks are necessary to impose AI effectively and fairly(Aung et al., 2021). AI applied to breast imaging has demonstrated the potential to improve radiologist performance as well as organizational dynamics. Nevertheless, large volumes of datasets for testing and monitoring the AI models remain an issue, along with ethical, technical, legal, and regulatory concerns that should be resolved (Hickman et al., 2021). In the IoT context, the integration of AI brought the AI of Things (IoT) paradigm, where AI enhances IoT systems to be smarter and more effective. The problem is scattered and immense, including handling large volumes of dissimilar data and decision-making, which AI seeks to solve by improving perceiving, learning, reasoning, and behaving (Zhang & Tao, 2021). Third, the problem of commonsense knowledge, which is a necessity in order to create an automatic system similar to human intelligence, is still a challenge. The developmental approach that is based on the example of human infants is a type of approach that aims at the creation of knowledge through interaction with the environment. However, there are still several critical questions that remain unanswered(Guerin, 2011). The significant challenges exist within the integration of AI; however, research and development persist to push read optimization within the market.

KEY AREAS OF AI IMPACT IN EDUCATION

Personalized Learning

Flavored educational models present many advantages and numerous considerations, as stated in the research papers. It promotes the improvement of the learning experience in that students benefit from modified learning experiences that are more suited to their learning needs. This is achieved by using AI and machine learning techniques to dynamically map students' behavioral attributes to specific learning styles, thereby optimizing the learning process (Essa et al., 2023). Adaptive learning systems present material and tests according to the learner's knowledge and learning styles, which ensures that the learners are interested and that they will gain a better understanding, as stated by (Murtaza et al., 2022). When considered within the concept of sustainable development, personalized learning can help in adjusting the curricula in order to meet the needs of local education and support transformative learning experiences, as seen by (Zdravkova, 2023).

Further, students' learning systems have demonstrated that they help teachers increase their Technological Pedagogical Content Knowledge (TPACK), which makes it easier for them to incorporate technology into their instruction practices (Chaipidech et al., 2022). Nevertheless, some issues remain, including but not limited to the challenges brought by the data gathering and analysis process for differently-abled participants and the restricted environment for remote teaching and learning (Zdravkova, 2023). The existing challenges in practice also affect teachers in personalized learning plans, the connection between student progress and assessment practices, and engaging the community in project-based learning (Lee et al., 2022). Furthermore, there is a need for continuous research to address the gaps in the adoption and comparison of deep learning algorithms for classifying learning styles, which could enhance adaptability in personalized learning environments (Essa et al., 2023). Altogether, personalized models of education present a number of opportunities for enhancing educational outcomes that must nevertheless be accompanied by closer attention to these issues for their competent enactment and longevity.

ADAPTIVE ASSESSMENTS

Role of AI in Evaluating Student Performance in Real-Time

In this chapter, Artificial Intelligence (AI) has a great importance in analyzing the students' performance in real-time using the technologies and methodologies. Machine learning algorithms work best in certain cases of tracking students' performance in class in order to recognize learners who are in danger of producing substandard results hence mitigate the issue. For example, the applications of decision tree models have been applied in determination of student outcomes and instruction to help students facing challenges from the beginning of a course. Furthermore, in-class teaching and learning process is also evaluated by employing artificial intelligence-based components like computer visions to the teaching evaluation models and intelligent speech recognition. These models by employing ensemble learning methods are capable of assessing the level of student concentration and participation levels with high precision, hence afford real time information on dynamics of a class. Moreover, AI is not just an instrument of evaluation contributing to educational relationships, while also being a mediator and auxiliary in instructional and learning processes. This type of role is useful in increasing contact points between instructors and students as well as between students (Xu & Ouyang, 2022). Another significant subdivision of AI is Natural Language Processing (NLP); it is used to analyze student feedback, where a lot could be learned regarding educational practices and facilities. Real-time analysis of the feedback is made possible by natural language processing techniques including sentiment analysis and text summarization; to enhance understanding of student experience and expectations. In higher education, it uses machine learning models for approximating student performance, for the early identification of students at risk or potentially droppers and for predicting attrition rates. Accompanying these models are different evaluation metrics and demographic attributes to facilitate the execution of timely interventions by institutions (Fahd et al., 2022).

Immersive Technologies (VR/AR)

VAR systems are gradually being integrated into educational practice in order to increase their audience's learning ability during interactive lessons required by facility. These technologies enable the students to interact with environments and concepts that are otherwise out of reach because of the costs, the impracticality or lack of legitimate access. For example, with virtual reality (VR) educators can arrange situations and share situations and information that as accurately and fully represents the learners' real world context and requires the learner to engage with real reality-based environments (Schott & Marshall, 2018). In contexts of the higher education, the use of VAR technology is still innovative and, nevertheless, effective. A case study conducted at The University University of Sydney showed that a purpose built VR laboratory reconstructed a major learning advantage for the children, the lab has registered a healthy inflow of students in the following semesters of teaching, notifying giving this find, a 250% rise in enrollment (Marks & Thomas, 2022). Augmented reality (AR) encourages interactive learning that has personal, social, affective, and cognitive benefits that lead to greater student performance. True AR glasses permit full body engagement, allowing students to physically walk around their environments and engage in playful activities to learn scientific concepts. Extended reality (XR), which includes AR and VR, is helping math educators improve traditional pedagogy through immersive experiences that make complex concepts easier to grasp. More broadly, those kinds of VAR technologies transform education more generally through the ability to accommodate better instructional designs and unique and novel learning strategies providing new avenues in academic disciplines for meaningful and engaging learning opportunities.

EMERGING AI TECHNOLOGIES IN EDUCATION

New technology in AI enhances the learning and teaching sectors by employing the innovative technique of artificial intelligence and cognitive science. AIED is being used in order to design systems that will enable learners to rehearse until they achieve mastery, and where necessary teachers will implement a kind of blended learning whereby assigning certain tasks to AI systems will do (Du Boulay, 2016). Social robots, smart learning environments, and intelligent tutoring systems are amongst the AI applications which are helping to solve modern educational problems by enhancing educations accessibility and quality that led to the conclusion that educational organizations must consider AI technologies as the tool of contemporary learning (Ahmad et al., 2021). AI systems have improved the learning interaction in environments facilitating online learning, offer learner interfaces and automate task, offer formative and summative assessments, but the issues of social boundaries are raised due to surveillance (Seo et al., 2021). There is increasing interest in the incorporation of AI curricula for K-12 education including in the Asia-Pacific area, studies show that AI education can enhance students' knowledge, skills, and interest in AI while also shedding light on effective designs as well as standards of the curriculum (Sein Minn, 2022). A classification divides AI into curricular objects, direct mediators, and supplementary helpers regarding several educational relations and processes (Xu & Ouyang, 2022). Sarcasm and domain-specific language remain a challenge, while analyzing the precious feedback coming from the students – This is where Natural Language Processing (NLP), a branch of AI comes in handy (Shaik et al., 2022). Techniques in knowledge assessment made with the help of artificial intelligence are crucial for adaptive learning environments, machine learning and deep learning to create student models for providing unique learning experiences (Zafari et al., 2022). The integration of AI in K-12 education is particularly prominent in STEM courses, with machine learning and intelligent tutoring systems being the most common approaches, highlighting AI's significant impact on student performance and teaching practices is pending (Zafari et al., 2022). AI technologies are also being also used to track psycho-physiological states, which use neural networks to monitor head movements during learning tasks to evaluate students' abilities to learn informational content in education (Kataev et al., 2022). The work of such us Erica Melis has assumed the value of AI innovative and traditional systems in education, and need to keep researching and implementing AI technology in learning Mathematics and Science

(McLaren et al., 2014). Besides improving the effectiveness and availability of learning activities and materials, AI is making education more individualised, effective, and efficient.

ETHICAL CONSIDERATIONS IN AI-ENHANCED EDUCATION

The adoption of Artificial Intelligence (AI) in learning mechanisms has brought forth an elaborate set of concerning ethical questions that should be solved to make sure that this rising technology won't be misused. Introducing AI in Learning and Teaching context, known as AIEd, can improve the traditional teaching learning model and work as a subject, direct mediator and an indirect supporter, impacting learner instructor relations and learners' relations with each other (Xu & Ouyang, 2022). However, this advancement presents ethical dilemmas including; Concerns of bias, fairness and self- organization for decision making as well as socio-economic Justice problems that may feature or arise through bias in the system. It addresses issues to do with data privacy, consent and security since such systems call for the use of large quantities of personal data (Masters, 2023). In the domain of health professions education for example, AI is used in ways that force a harmonization between the strengths of the technology and ethical principles such as autonomy and beneficence all of which points to the fact that professionals are charged with the responsibility of being ahead and dealing with these vices (Masters, 2023). In addition, ethical concern of AI in education includes; accountability and comprehensible decision-making: Current form of machine learning algorithms applied is non-transparent, therefore the decision-making process of developing an AI is almost impossible to comprehend (Dorobantu & Wilks, 2019). Such opacity can erode trust and responsibility, meaning there is a need to build ways to increase the readability of AI solutions (Lewis & Stoyanovich, 2022). The effective use of augmented reality strategies in the classroom allows for the connection between ethical theory and practice more easily applicable by the students (Kwong et al., 2017). Further, teaching AI ethics, it is desirable to use the descriptive model in order that students could learn how to think critically about ethical problems and make proper ethical decisions (Goldsmith et al., 2020). In incorporated in medical education, health AI ethics is important as the learners who are future healthcare practitioners will encounter different ethical considerations of AI including consent and privacy of the patient (Katznelson & Gerke, 2021). Bearing in mind, the capability of AI to improve moral decision-making through virtual assistants that increases reflective autonomy and not the behavior of individuals form a positive line of ethical use of AI in education (Lara, 2021). Last but not the least, appearance of responsible data science courses which stress interpretability and fairness of algorithms will offer a solid groundwork for the vision of ethical problems in AI-enhanced education, thus preparing students for ethical entries of AI technologies (Lewis & Stoyanovich, 2022). Consequently, ethical concerns with reference to AI within learning contexts reflect the idea that an effective use of AI tools involves a broad approach that would encompass such aspects as the general idea of informational transparency, the fairness of outcomes, the privacy question, and the sensibility development regarding the core ethical ideas as applied to educational practice, always in order to create the augmentation of educational outcomes and not the opposite.

CASE STUDIES OF AI INTEGRATION IN EDUCATIONAL INSTITUTIONS

Examples of Successful AI-Driven Learning Initiatives

Nowadays, incorporation of AI in education has created unprecedented breakthrough as it brought innovative learning solutions to promote individualization, effectiveness, and availability. The above AI driven has been demonstrated in different levels of learning that include K-12, and also colleges and universities and has recorded decent progress in enhancement of learning. Here is the list of AI driven learning with success stories and impact of these efforts:

Intelligent Tutoring Systems (ITS)

- An example of AI used in education is the Intelligent Tutoring Systems, which offer the learner the flexibility of catering for his/her needs.These systems rely on the rule based AI to provide feedback and advice in addition to improving on the learning experience (Nagao, 2019; Zhou & Lawless, 2014).
- ITS has being applied successfully in many course areas such as, mathematics and science where the students use computers to learn concepts through engaging tutorials (Nagao, 2019).

Personalized Learning Platforms

- In addition, the development of personalized learning platforms with Artificial Intelligence in each system, including that under the project "X5GON" also enable a curriculum tailored to the needs of each student, the way they learn and their pace.. education these platforms incorporate Artificial Intelligence to gauge student data and modify the content and content delivery services for lifelong learning.
- In India, AI interventions were developed to design lesson plans based on intellectual performance and learning curve of students, for homeschooling establishments and learning curves to eradicate all prefixed formalities of the students as well as to enhance the performance of the learners.

Learning Analytics and Data-Driven Education

- Learning analytics as augmented by AI allows instructors to monitor and assess large amounts of information regarding student learning and performance. It serves the best platform for evidence-based practice in education, which provides the much-needed interventions and learning-accommodation strategies.
- The uses of AI systems may help track student's progress and inform educators on certain problems increasing the effectiveness of a learning process and students.

AI in Massive Open Online Courses (MOOCs)

- AI continues to support the creation and the dissemination of the MOOCs which offer education to a large number of people. These courses harness AI to coordinate the content, and tailor the learning experience while providing cost-effective educational solutions (Nagao, 2019) (Brown & Kauchak, 2013).

- New MOOCs applied artificial intelligence to improve teaching of subjects associated with the use of AI, including machine learning and processing of natural language (Brown & Kauchak, 2013).

AI-Enhanced Administrative and Support Systems

- AI assistance is also valuable in proctoring, grading assignments and syllabus creation, which should help to alleviate educators' workload and allow them to pay more attention to students and communication. This efficiency leads to more individual attention to students and in general, affects mostly the educational process.
- Virtual tutors come alongside the students and assist them in matters related to study such as simple mathematic problems and writing skills to engage the student in ways other than classroom lessons.

Lessons Learned From Institutions Using AI to Enhance Learning and Teaching

AI application in education system has contributed to tremendous progress in all domains related to teaching and learning. AI technologies have been applied in learning management to develop customized learning environments, to increase students' attendance and effectiveness and to raise learning achievement. Educational institutions all over the world have embraced different AI applications, including the intelligent tutoring systems, machine learning frameworks in attending to the different education requirements. The next sections describe the main lessons to be derived from such implementations, best practice, success, challenges, and future of AI in learning.

Personalized Learning and Intelligent Tutoring Systems

- It has been used in designing ITS which are computer-based systems that can deliver instruction. These makes these systems flexible so that they can take the student through content which is close to what he/she requires as well as feedback in real time thus increasing the chances of getting enhanced performance in the subject (Alam, 2023; Zhou & Lawless, 2014).
- The success of Yuanfudao in China, as well as Embibe and other Artificial Intelligence player in India, rightly show how Active Learning based on aid of Artificial Intelligence improves student performance and engagement (Sharma & Mohan, 2022).
- They enable the analysis of student's information and thus intelligent education that offers material in sequence with student performance and possibility (Alam, 2023).

Enhancing Engagement and Learning Outcomes

- In recent years, many technologies include virtual and augmented reality have applied in learning environments that enhance learners' involvement and passion (Alam, 2023).
- Gamification, powered by AI, introduces game-like elements into the learning process, making it more interactive and enjoyable for students (Alam, 2023).

- There are algorithms applied to student performance and pre-identified learning outcomes; hence, timely professorial interventions are useful in enhancing educational quality.

Global Best Practices and Frameworks

- Hence, there is adoption of AI in institutions across the world to favor educational practices. For instance, Ruangguru working in Indonesia, and Virti working in the United Kingdom have applied AI-Based solutions for learning to be efficient and effective (Sharma & Mohan, 2022).
- A brief taxonomy of AI in education has also been provided to help educators and developers to create the appropriate systems based on their learning requirements (Lameras, 2022).
- AI in higher education is a relatively emerging concept since there is an establishment of frameworks to facilitate AI integration in the higher education systems so as to optimize its effectiveness in improving learning experiences.

Challenges and Ethical Considerations

- Despite the benefits, the use of AI in education presents challenges, including ethical concerns related to data privacy and the potential for bias in AI algorithms.
- The constant development of AI technologies means that to solve these problems and to make sure that AI is being used appropriately in education it is necessary to carry out constant research.

Future Directions and Opportunities

- potential of AI in future of education is to contribute more innovations, like the appearance of more complex AI capable of recognizing and addressing students' moods and requirements.
- Academics and researchers are to carry on with the funding for AI Research to embrace its benefits and.ignore the present drawbacks inherited from AI use.
- New ethical framework for AI, development and integration in educational contexts need educators, developers and policymakers' cooperation.

Education institutions should work for improving technology while paying attention to ethical issues in a bid to make AI improve the experience of learning as opposed to degrading it. Emerging areas in artificial intelligence present exciting new frontiers for transforming education in profound ways. Quantum computing, for instance, holds incredible potential to revolutionize how vast troves of educational data are analyzed, enabling personalized and dynamic insights into learning progress. Integrating AI into evaluating social-emotional development offers another promising avenue, where systems could assess students' emotional wellness and interpersonal abilities, providing a more holistic perspective complementing traditional academic metrics. Furthermore, applying AI to enhance global online learning platforms such as MOOCs could personalize instruction at scale, tailoring entire courses and adapting content for individual learners worldwide. Exploration into these domains could illuminate how AI may address pressing future needs and challenges within education on a global scale, fostering discussion of how this technology could shape learning for generations to come.

Impact of AI Adoption on Student Outcomes and Educator Practices

AI integration in teaching or in learning systems has had a positive effect to the results of students and the behaviors of educators. AI applications have been embedded in different learning environments and can be used to improve approaches that are used in learning as well as personalizing learning processes. These effects are also the subject of this response based on the information and analysis of the research papers provided.

Impact on Student Outcomes

- *Enhanced Engagement and Effort:* Intelligent tutoring systems, which are a sub-type of the AI-based tools and applications, are considered to positively affect student's activity level as well as their task-related effort. For example, in a study of an AI tutor for geometry class, the researcher noted that students got more engaged and interested in class which he partly noted to increased competition from peers (Schofield et al., 1990).
- *Improved Learning Performance:* In this paper, authors have discussed how online AI systems has helped in customizing the learning process of a student and has also helped in enhancing the performance of the student. An AI-based learning style identification model for primary school learning style showed that learning material aligned to styles further enhanced learning.(Pardamean et al., 2022).
- *Positive Attitudes Toward AI Learning:* AI curricula implemented at the secondary education level have an effect of developing positive attitude and perceived self-competence. For instance, the AI4Future project implemented earlier in Hong Kong found that the subjects had a more positive attitude towards the AI learning via a set curriculum(Pardamean et al., 2022).

Impact on Educator Practices

- *Time Allocation and Teaching Strategies:* Machine learning and deep learning technologies have impacted on how teachers manage their time and\) resources. The study also found that the teachers who used the AI systems in classroom embraced more collegial attitudes and gave higher value to effort in grading (Schofield et al., 1990).
- *Professional Development and Autonomy:* The collaborative development of AI curricula has thus contributed to improving the authors' knowledge base and decision-making regarding AI teaching. The study also responded to the second research question, that explored the impact of training on the ability of teachers to adopt AI in Future Education teaching practice.
- *Support for Routine Tasks:* AI applications can often perform simple tasks in order to help teach assistants devote more time to students' individual communication. This has been especially helpful in technology-mediated learning, where the use of AI systems in can enhance timely information support as well as interaction quality (Seo et al., 2021).

While AI adoption in education offers numerous benefits, it also presents challenges that need careful consideration. The potential for AI to transform educational practices is significant, but it requires a balanced approach that addresses ethical, social, and technical issues. As AI continues to evolve, ongoing research and dialogue among educators, policymakers, and technologists will be vital to maximize its positive impact on education.

FUTURE TRENDS IN AI-DRIVEN EDUCATION

AI technology in education is the key to how education systems, schools, and colleges of the future will be like by implementing new Technologies, Customized learning experiences and new paradigms of learning. This transition is based on continuous development of AI in improving educational access, reach, and success, addressing student differences, promoting creativity, critical thinking and learning.

Integration of Intelligent Tutoring Systems and Multimedia

- ITS continued to be developed to provide enhanced controlled feedback and are now shifting in delivering context aware information or learning environment. These systems incorporate AI technology in order to facilitate instantaneous assessment and individual learning effectiveness and interest (Okamoto et al., 2001) (Ahmad et al., 2021).
- Another important trend is the use multimedia in learning environments. With the availability of higher bandwidth and different media types, the education delivery platforms can present more engaging and style-sensitive learning content (Okamoto et al., 2001).

AI Curriculum Development and Implementation

- It has been observed that, the AI curricula at the pretertiary level, as the AI4Future project shows, AI literacy is becoming more and more crucial.. Besides making a positive shift in the students' defined competence and perception related to AI, it helped the teachers to foster AI education in their classrooms(Chiu et al., 2022).
- The like programs are important in nurturing student to be fit for job markets that are expected to incorporate a lot of AI technologies.. The sharing process of these curricula also enhances the relationship between the academic institutions and industrial players(Chiu et al., 2022).

Adaptive and Personalized Learning Environments

- Another uniqueness of AI in learning environemts is that learning contents are personalized to suit the learner. These systems employ algorithms to evaluate student learning needs and progress; this gives education the optimal results (Sein Minn, 2022).
- AI also plays a key role in adaptive learning settings and includes the creation of advanced models for the student alongside psychological and machine learning elements that help to improve the assessment of knowledge (Sein Minn, 2022).

Service-Oriented and Ubiquitous Learning Ecosystems

- Dependency and the notion of services as a focus of AI in the context of learning experiences represent another change. This requires the ability to deconstruct AI educational platforms into

modular services that can easily be plugged throughout different devices and systems to make the learning process more open, adaptable and efficient(Nye, 2016).
- Such ecosystems also create new realms of user adjustment and testing for educational purpose, to redefine and redesign the educational methods and strategies (Nye, 2016).

IMPACT ON EDUCATORS, STUDENTS, AND POLICYMAKERS

Artificial Intelligence (AI) is seeping into the education system in ways that include availing weighty gears to both teachers and students as well as edging its ways into policies maker quarters. Various AI technologies are being implemented in education for students' benefit and to improve various academic processes as well as to support the development of the policies.

Impact on Educators

- *Automation of Routine Tasks:* With the help of AI systems educators can easily assign several routine tasks, for example grading and administrative works as these can be done without needing much effort can thus devote their efforts to matters that are more important and are centered on the learners (Seo et al., 2021). The main areas for achievement can include enhanced quality of teaching and increased student-teacher engagement.
- *Teaching Evaluation and Improvement:* Smarter proctoring solutions like; computer vision, and intelligent speech recognition are utilized in in class teaching evaluations to determine effectiveness of teaching as well as student attentiveness. It also means that these tools give back to educators information that helps improve the very methods employed in teaching the concepts (Guo et al., 2021).
- *Professional Development:* AI can assist the educators in their professional learning by furnishing them with information relative to teaching practices and student achievement as they progress towards meeting new standard as well as embrace new technology in their learning practices.

Impact on Students

- *Personalized Learning:* Some of the areas of AI use especially in education are Intelligent Tutoring Systems (ITS) where content is customized depending on a student's needs and the student's rate of learning. This can also make learning more attractive to the students besides improving the learning achievements on the course (Ahmad et al., 2021) (Minn et al., 2022).
- *Enhanced Interaction:* Through the use of AI in learning systems, students and instructors can; therefore, be able to interact and communicate effectively adaptively throughout their lessons especially with the emergence of e-learning and online teaching resulting from the COVID-19 pandemic. However, there remains privacy and breaking of the social barriers by the deployment of AI (Seo et al., 2021).
- *Skill Development:* AI lessons taught in K-12 curricula aim to teach students knowledge about AI and necessary skills to navigate technological environments in the future. Included in these is promotion of positive learning attitudes and interests in the fields of AI.

Impact on Policymakers

- *Curriculum Design and Implementation:* Policymakers are tasked with integrating AI into educational curricula, ensuring that it is age-appropriate and widely accepted. This involves setting educational standards and designing innovative pedagogical approaches.
- *Data-Driven Decision Making:* AI can assist policymakers in making informed decisions by analyzing educational data, such as student feedback, to identify areas for improvement in educational infrastructure and teaching practices.
- *Ethical and Privacy Considerations:* Policymakers must address ethical concerns related to AI in education, such as data privacy, surveillance, and the potential for bias in AI systems. Ensuring transparency and accountability in AI applications is crucial (Seo et al., 2021) (Xu & Ouyang, 2021).

Ethical Frameworks in Different Contexts

The adoption of artificial intelligence (AI) in education requires a strong ethical framework to deal with specific challenges and align responsible use. The document states that the UNESCO Recommendation on the Ethics of Artificial Intelligence represents a comprehensive worldwide framework that prioritizes equity, transparency and inclusivity in educational contexts, and encourages AI literacy and interdisciplinary cooperation to advance ethical use of AI In language education, risks such as privacy, data security, and algorithmic biases draw most attention. These biases can result from training data as well as design decisions, highlighting the need for transparency in AI systems, and strong privacy frameworks to safeguard student data and support human agency. The content covers the ethical implications of AI in the educational context, including issues related to AI in decision-making, student data privacy, and the effects of AI on pedagogical practices, as well as case studies that illustrate real-world ethical challenges through the perspective of educators and policymakers. In addition, the ethical implications of using AI in education require weighing advantages, including customized learning, against disadvantages such as violation of privacy and replacement of skills. This demands procedural transparency, accountability, and equality so that AI helps rather than hinders the achievement of educational objectives and the common good. Ensuring that digital technologies (including AI) in education is designed and used ethically, with safety, data privacy, and equity in mind is critical for all, and especially for vulnerable groups such as minors. Embracing this requires pluralistic dialogue alongside collaboration and strong legislation to protect students' online safety and privacy, while simultaneously supporting innovation in digital learning (White, & Stevens, 2024). Together, these frameworks and guidelines seek to address the ethical complexities surrounding AI in education and to ensure that its deployment results in a positive addition to learning spaces.

Real-World Case Studies

AI in Education Advancements Artificial Intelligence (AI) in Education is now making its way to educational settings with various applications. AI in Education Perhaps the hottest domain is in education due to creating independence and engaging students, as well as language learning, writing, new ideas, etc. This short synthesis pulses through a number of case studies that examine the diverse ways in which AI is being utilized in education, showcasing its transformative capacity, but also the challenges it entails.

AI in Language Learning

- *ChatGPT in Foreign Language Education:* ChatGPT has been used as a tool for foreign language learning, helping students to enrich their vocabulary, improve their grammar and writing. Its fun and appealing nature, along with its versatile and easily accessible, make it a great ally to language teachers who want to increase motivation and interest in their students.
- *Wordtune for Writing Skills:* Research evidence has demonstrated that the Wordtune application helps those learning English as a second language to produce better writing and engage more effectively with the feedback they receive. This AI tool allows students to master their writing while getting better results by offering personalized feedback (Rad & Jafarpour, 2023).

AI in Primary Education

- *ChatGPT and Student Autonomy:* ChatGPT was used in primary schools in Saudi Arabia to increase the students' autonomy in online classes. Although the application has encouraged students to have a better view on autonomy, it also leads to many adverse effects that must be address (Almohesh, 2024).

AI in K-12 Education

- *Systematic Review of AI Applications:* From a thorough narrative literature review of AI uses in K-12 education it became clear that the three main areas of AI applications for the largest share of uses in K-12 education are strongly related to student performance, teaching, and behavior tasks. The most prevalent AI techniques are Machine Learning and Intelligent Tutoring Systems, with a strong emphasis on science, technology, engineering and mathematics (STEM) courses areas (Zafari et al., 2022).

AI in Simulation-Based Learning

- *Simulation and Virtual Agents:* It is utilized in demonstration learning environments - both through the embodiment of virtual agents to lead students throughout situated learning experiences. These agents utilize affective computing technology that allow them to respond to the students' emotional states to optimize learning.

Ethical and Practical Challenges

- *ChatGPT in Education:* ChatGPT provides many educational benefits to students, but it creates ethical and practical challenges, including concerns around privacy, honesty, and misuse. To overcome these challenges, careful considerations are essential so that AI can be integrated responsibly and effectively in the education sphere.

Challenges in AI education

However, here are some of the challenges that merit consideration as teachers integrate AI into their work: A significant barrier to innovation is the complexity of teaching and learning, particularly in "softened" or "fuzzy" knowledge systems (Good, 1987). AI systems are often poorly equipped to deal with subjective or nuanced concepts like philosophy or creative writing. For example, AI tools that assign grades might rate a well-reasoned but atypically formatted essay too low because it didn't stick to the formats they are programmed to evaluate, disappointing students and teachers alike. Another big question is about the ethics and implications of AI. These raise issues of surveillance, responsibility and agency. Some AI systems used for classroom monitoring, including facial recognition cameras in some Chinese schools, have faced criticism for creating an environment akin to a "surveillance state" that can have a detrimental effect on students' autonomy and mental health. In order to overcome these problems, designing AI systems with principles of explainability and human oversight would be the way forward. However, then we encounter the problem of bias in AI systems that complicates their deployment (Figaredo, 2020). AI reflects the biases in its training data and does not treat students equally. For instance, some language learning applications promote the accents of native English speakers and find it difficult to recognize accent of non-native speakers; hence, the applications would disadvantage some learners. Universities may also use recruitment AI systems that, if trained on biased historical data, may favour candidates from certain demographics. Moreover, the use of data and privacy are still major issues. Information security — The volume of data generated in education increases the potential for breaches and misuse. One such incident is the 2021 data breach in which the sensitive information of millions of students was compromised, highlighting the need for strong data security measures like encryption and anonymization (Seo et al., 2021). Another challenge is the digital divide, as most AI-powered educational tools require advanced digital infrastructure. Generally, students from poorer or rural areas are often neglected due to lack of internet access, which was especially exposed during the COVID-19 pandemic. This inequality underscores the necessity of more inclusive technological solutions. Lastly, the adoption of AI in education is also hindered by a lack of teacher training. Most teachers are poorly trained to use these AI tools in their practices (Domínguez Figaredo, 2020). For example, (Howard et al., 2022) study revealed that only 30% of teachers felt confidence while using AI in classrooms, leading to its underutilization. The first and foremost step here is customized comprehensive training programs for the teachers. Some of these include; the formulation of sound policy frameworks, building inclusive infrastructure for the students and training of teachers and creating ethical guidelines for ensuring that the use of AI in education is equitable and effective.

RECOMMENDATIONS FOR FUTURE AI IN EDUCATION

Artificial Intelligence in education has become one of the dynamic domains, which is gradually being developed and implemented in order to transform teaching and learning processes. Recommendations for future use of AI in education are aimed at better curriculum development, teachers' preparation and AI accessibility. All these recommendations are based on the existing literature and best practices towards teaching AI.

Curriculum Design and Implementation

- *AI as a Subject and Tool:* AI must be adopted as a discipline of study and as a means of developing learning in inter-disciplinary subjects. This two-in-one method can assist college students in integrating AI into their daily lives as well as acquiring AI literacy from the related educational technologies (Xu & Ouyang, 2021) .
- *Age-Appropriate Curriculum:* It is therefore important to come up with an AI curriculum that will be acceptable and relevant for the learners at their age. This entails developing materials that interest the students and are appropriate to their grade level, elementary, middle or high (Roussel, 2022) (Ottenbreit-Leftwich et al., 2022).
- *Innovative Pedagogical Designs:* Applying innovative designs of learning that include problem-based learning and role play can help deliver on the objective of AI education. It can assists students in relating what they are learning in the lesson to what they already know and the world around them with ease (Ottenbreit-Leftwich et al., 2022).

Teacher Training and Professional Development

- *Teacher Readiness and Support:* The teachers in order to use AI in their classrooms require proper training, computers, and proper documentation. Inservice PD might be designed to improve teachers' coding knowledge and their acquaintance with AI instruments (Yamamoto Ravenor, 2021).
- *Collaborative Curriculum Development:* It may help to incorporate teachers into the process of the development of the curriculum, that way, the integration of AI education is realistic. There is always high likelihood of implementation and uptake if teachers are involved in the design of these curricula (Ottenbreit-Leftwich et al., 2022).

Equity and Access

- *Addressing Digital Divide:* This is because making available to all materials and processes that comprise AI differentiates the digital divide further. Therefore, measures should be taken in order to offer general and improved access in AI learning tools and informations for all students, including those from low socio-economic backgrounds (Karan & Angadi, 2023).
- *Inclusive Education Policies:* Educational institutions and governments must come up with measures and polices that will to encourage AI education to students to enhance their knowledge and full potentials of AI technologies (Karan & Angadi, 2023).

Research and Development

- *Interdisciplinary Research:* Further studies are called for to examine different aspects of the interactions in the context of the roles of AI and effects which it has on the different aspects of education. This actually entails recognizing the part of AI involving it as intervening and helping in teaching learning procedures (Xu & Ouyang, 2021).
- *Exploration of New Technologies:* The explosion of new technologies should be investigated in the context of their relevance for educational processes with the help of AI. This includes exam-

ining new databases and pedagogical practices for combining knowledge about AI into school environments.

CONCLUSION

Artificial Intelligence (AI) is transforming education by integrating cognitive science and advanced technologies to enhance teaching, learning, and administration. AI applications, such as Intelligent Tutoring Systems (ITS), personalized learning environments, and automated assessments, are reshaping traditional educational practices. These innovations bridge gaps in access, foster engagement, and improve learning outcomes, creating a modern, inclusive, and efficient educational landscape. ITS and multimedia learning provide students with context-aware, engaging, and adaptive content, while personalized learning tailors experiences to individual needs, maximizing educational effectiveness. Additionally, AI tools offer data-driven insights for educators and policymakers, improving decision-making processes and fostering a deeper understanding of student progress.

However, AI adoption in education faces significant challenges, including ethical concerns such as data privacy, algorithmic biases, and accountability in AI systems. Addressing these issues is critical to ensuring equitable and transparent implementation. Despite these challenges, AI success stories highlight its potential to enhance educator practices, increase student engagement, and improve learning outcomes. For instance, AI tools automate routine tasks for teachers, allowing them to focus on student-centered activities and professional development, while also enabling skill-building and tailored instruction for students. Policymakers benefit from AI-driven curriculum design and educational reforms.

Future directions emphasize the need for ethical frameworks, innovative AI tools, and global collaboration to overcome barriers and ensure responsible AI integration. Recommendations include equitable access to AI resources, comprehensive teacher training, and the development of innovative pedagogical approaches that harness AI's potential while mitigating its risks. This balance will shape the future of education.

REFERENCES

Ahmad, S. F., Rahmat, M. K., Mubarik, M. S., Alam, M. M., & Hyder, S. I. (2021). Artificial Intelligence and Its Role in Education. *Sustainability (Basel), 13*(22), 12902. DOI: 10.3390/su132212902

Alam, A. (2023). Harnessing the Power of AI to Create Intelligent Tutoring Systems for Enhanced Classroom Experience and Improved Learning Outcomes. In Rajakumar, G., Du, K.-L., & Rocha, Á. (Eds.), *Intelligent Communication Technologies and Virtual Mobile Networks* (Vol. 171, pp. 571–591). Springer Nature Singapore., DOI: 10.1007/978-981-99-1767-9_42

Almohesh, A. R. I. (2024). AI Application (ChATGPT) and Saudi Arabian Primary School students' autonomy in online classes: Exploring students and teachers' perceptions. *International Review of Research in Open and Distance Learning, 25*(3), 1–18. DOI: 10.19173/irrodl.v25i3.7641

Alqahtani, T., Badreldin, H. A., Alrashed, M., Alshaya, A. I., Alghamdi, S. S., Bin Saleh, K., Alowais, S. A., Alshaya, O. A., Rahman, I., Al Yami, M. S., & Albekairy, A. M. (2023). The emergent role of artificial intelligence, natural learning processing, and large language models in higher education and research. *Research in Social & Administrative Pharmacy, 19*(8), 1236–1242. DOI: 10.1016/j.sapharm.2023.05.016 PMID: 37321925

Aung, Y. Y. M., Wong, D. C. S., & Ting, D. S. W. (2021). The promise of artificial intelligence: A review of the opportunities and challenges of artificial intelligence in healthcare. *British Medical Bulletin, 139*(1), 4–15. DOI: 10.1093/bmb/ldab016 PMID: 34405854

Brown, L. E., & Kauchak, D. (2013). Educational Advances in Artificial Intelligence. *AI Magazine, 34*(4), 127–127. DOI: 10.1609/aimag.v34i4.2508

Chaipidech, P., Srisawasdi, N., Kajornmanee, T., & Chaipah, K. (2022). A personalized learning system-supported professional training model for teachers' TPACK development. *Computers and Education: Artificial Intelligence, 3*, 100064. DOI: 10.1016/j.caeai.2022.100064

Chiu, T. K. F., Meng, H., Chai, C.-S., King, I., Wong, S., & Yam, Y. (2022). Creation and Evaluation of a Pretertiary Artificial Intelligence (AI) Curriculum. *IEEE Transactions on Education, 65*(1), 30–39. DOI: 10.1109/TE.2021.3085878

Domínguez Figaredo, D. (2020). Data-driven educational algorithms pedagogical framing. *RIED.Revista Iberoamericana de Educación a Distancia, 23*(2), 65. DOI: 10.5944/ried.23.2.26470

Dorobantu, M., & Wilks, Y. (2019). MORAL ORTHOSES: A NEW APPROACH TO HUMAN AND MACHINE ETHICS: with Fraser Watts, "Mutual Enhancement between Science and Religion: In the Footsteps of the Epiphany Philosophers"; William H. Beharrell, "Transformation and the Waking Body: A Return to Truth via Our Bodies"; Marius Dorobantu and Yorick Wilks, "Moral Orthoses: A New Approach to Human and Machine Ethics"; Galen Watts, "Religion, Science, and Disenchantment in Late Modernity"; and Rowan Williams, "Epiphany Philosophers: Afterword.". *Zygon, 54*(4), 1004–1021. DOI: 10.1111/zygo.12560

Du Boulay, B. (2016). Artificial Intelligence as an Effective Classroom Assistant. *IEEE Intelligent Systems, 31*(6), 76–81. DOI: 10.1109/MIS.2016.93

Essa, S. G., Celik, T., & Human-Hendricks, N. E. (2023). Personalized Adaptive Learning Technologies Based on Machine Learning Techniques to Identify Learning Styles: A Systematic Literature Review. *IEEE Access : Practical Innovations, Open Solutions*, *11*, 48392–48409. DOI: 10.1109/ACCESS.2023.3276439

Fahd, K., Venkatraman, S., Miah, S. J., & Ahmed, K. (2022). Application of machine learning in higher education to assess student academic performance, at-risk, and attrition: A meta-analysis of literature. *Education and Information Technologies*, *27*(3), 3743–3775. DOI: 10.1007/s10639-021-10741-7

Goldsmith, J., Burton, E., Dueber, D. M., Goldstein, B., Sampson, S., & Toland, M. D. (2020). Assessing Ethical Thinking about AI. *Proceedings of the AAAI Conference on Artificial Intelligence*, *34*(09), 13525–13528. DOI: 10.1609/aaai.v34i09.7075

Good, R. (1987). Artificial intelligence and science education. *Journal of Research in Science Teaching*, *24*(4), 325–342. DOI: 10.1002/tea.3660240406

Guerin, F. (2011). Learning like a baby: A survey of artificial intelligence approaches. *The Knowledge Engineering Review*, *26*(2), 209–236. DOI: 10.1017/S0269888911000038

Guo, J., Bai, L., Yu, Z., Zhao, Z., & Wan, B. (2021). An AI-Application-Oriented In-Class Teaching Evaluation Model by Using Statistical Modeling and Ensemble Learning. *Sensors (Basel)*, *21*(1), 241. DOI: 10.3390/s21010241 PMID: 33401482

Hamal, O., El Faddouli, N.-E., Harouni, M. H. A., & Lu, J. (2022). Artificial Intelligent in Education. *Sustainability (Basel)*, *14*(5), 2862. DOI: 10.3390/su14052862

Hickman, S. E., Baxter, G. C., & Gilbert, F. J. (2021). Adoption of artificial intelligence in breast imaging: Evaluation, ethical constraints and limitations. *British Journal of Cancer*, *125*(1), 15–22. DOI: 10.1038/s41416-021-01333-w PMID: 33772149

Howard, S. K., Swist, T., Gasevic, D., Bartimote, K., Knight, S., Gulson, K., Apps, T., Peloche, J., Hutchinson, N., & Selwyn, N. (2022). Educational data journeys: Where are we going, what are we taking and making for AI? *Computers and Education: Artificial Intelligence*, *3*, 100073. DOI: 10.1016/j.caeai.2022.100073

Karan, B., & Angadi, G. R. (2023). Artificial Intelligence Integration into School Education: A Review of Indian and Foreign Perspectives. *Millennial Asia*, *09763996231158229*. Advance online publication. DOI: 10.1177/09763996231158229

Kataev, M., Bulysheva, L., & Mosiaev, A. (2022). Application of artificial intelligence methods in the school educational process. *Systems Research and Behavioral Science*, *39*(3), 531–541. DOI: 10.1002/sres.2873

Katznelson, G., & Gerke, S. (2021). The need for health AI ethics in medical school education. *Advances in Health Sciences Education : Theory and Practice*, *26*(4), 1447–1458. DOI: 10.1007/s10459-021-10040-3 PMID: 33655433

Kwong, T., Wong, E., & Yue, K. (2017). Bringing Abstract Academic Integrity and Ethical Concepts into Real-Life Situations. *Technology. Knowledge and Learning*, *22*(3), 353–368. DOI: 10.1007/s10758-017-9315-2

Lameras, P. (2022). A Vision of Teaching and Learning with AI. *2022 IEEE Global Engineering Education Conference (EDUCON)*, 1796–1803. DOI: 10.1109/EDUCON52537.2022.9766718

Lara, F. (2021). Why a Virtual Assistant for Moral Enhancement When We Could have a Socrates? *Science and Engineering Ethics*, *27*(4), 42. DOI: 10.1007/s11948-021-00318-5 PMID: 34189623

Lee, D., Huh, Y., Lin, C.-Y., & Reigeluth, C. M. (2022). Personalized Learning Practice in U.S. Learner-Centered Schools. *Contemporary Educational Technology*, *14*(4), ep385. DOI: 10.30935/cedtech/12330

Lewis, A., & Stoyanovich, J. (2022). Teaching Responsible Data Science: Charting New Pedagogical Territory. *International Journal of Artificial Intelligence in Education*, *32*(3), 783–807. DOI: 10.1007/s40593-021-00241-7 PMID: 33880114

Marks, B., & Thomas, J. (2022). Adoption of virtual reality technology in higher education: An evaluation of five teaching semesters in a purpose-designed laboratory. *Education and Information Technologies*, *27*(1), 1287–1305. DOI: 10.1007/s10639-021-10653-6 PMID: 34257511

Masters, K. (2023). Ethical use of Artificial Intelligence in Health Professions Education: AMEE Guide No. 158. *Medical Teacher*, *45*(6), 574–584. DOI: 10.1080/0142159X.2023.2186203 PMID: 36912253

McLaren, B. M., Sosnovsky, S., & Aleven, V. (2014). Preface - Emerging Technologies and Landmark Systems for Learning Mathematics and Science: Dedicated to the Memory of Erica Melis - Part 1. *International Journal of Artificial Intelligence in Education*, *24*(3), 211–215. DOI: 10.1007/s40593-014-0021-0

Minn, S. (2022). AI-assisted knowledge assessment techniques for adaptive learning environments. *Computers and Education: Artificial Intelligence*, *3*, 100050. DOI: 10.1016/j.caeai.2022.100050

Murtaza, M., Ahmed, Y., Shamsi, J. A., Sherwani, F., & Usman, M. (2022). AI-Based Personalized E-Learning Systems: Issues, Challenges, and Solutions. *IEEE Access : Practical Innovations, Open Solutions*, *10*, 81323–81342. DOI: 10.1109/ACCESS.2022.3193938

Nagao, K. (2019). Artificial Intelligence in Education. In K. Nagao, *Artificial Intelligence Accelerates Human Learning* (pp. 1–17). Springer Singapore. DOI: 10.1007/978-981-13-6175-3_1

Nye, B. D. (2016). ITS, The End of the World as We Know It: Transitioning AIED into a Service-Oriented Ecosystem. *International Journal of Artificial Intelligence in Education*, *26*(2), 756–770. DOI: 10.1007/s40593-016-0098-8

Ottenbreit-Leftwich, A., Glazewski, K., Jeon, M., Jantaraweragul, K., Hmelo-Silver, C., Scribner, A., Lee, S., Mott, B., & Lester, J. (2022). Principles for AI Education for Elementary Grades Students. *Proceedings of the 27th ACM Conference on on Innovation and Technology in Computer Science Education* Vol. 2, 627–627. DOI: 10.1145/3502717.3532143

Pardamean, B., Suparyanto, T., Cenggoro, T. W., Sudigyo, D., & Anugrahana, A. (2022). AI-Based Learning Style Prediction in Online Learning for Primary Education. *IEEE Access : Practical Innovations, Open Solutions*, *10*, 35725–35735. DOI: 10.1109/ACCESS.2022.3160177

Poon, A. I. F., & Sung, J. J. Y. (2021). Opening the black box of AI-Medicine. *Journal of Gastroenterology and Hepatology*, *36*(3), 581–584. DOI: 10.1111/jgh.15384 PMID: 33709609

Rad, H. S., Alipour, R., & Jafarpour, A. (2023). Using artificial intelligence to foster students' writing feedback literacy, engagement, and outcome: A case of Wordtune application. *Interactive Learning Environments*, *32*(9), 5020–5040. DOI: 10.1080/10494820.2023.2208170

Sanabria-Navarro, J.-R., Silveira-Pérez, Y., Pérez-Bravo, D.-D., & de-Jesús-Cortina-Núñez, M. (2023). Incidences of artificial intelligence in contemporary education. *Comunicar*, *31*(77). Advance online publication. DOI: 10.3916/C77-2023-08

Schofield, J. W., Evans-Rhodes, D., & Huber, B. R. (1990). Artificial Intelligence in the Classroom: The Impact of a Computer-Based Tutor on Teachers and Students. *Social Science Computer Review*, *8*(1), 24–41. DOI: 10.1177/089443939000800104

Seo, K., Tang, J., Roll, I., Fels, S., & Yoon, D. (2021). The impact of artificial intelligence on learner–instructor interaction in online learning. *International Journal of Educational Technology in Higher Education*, *18*(1), 54. DOI: 10.1186/s41239-021-00292-9 PMID: 34778540

Shaik, T., Tao, X., Li, Y., Dann, C., McDonald, J., Redmond, P., & Galligan, L. (2022). A Review of the Trends and Challenges in Adopting Natural Language Processing Methods for Education Feedback Analysis. *IEEE Access : Practical Innovations, Open Solutions*, *10*, 56720–56739. DOI: 10.1109/ACCESS.2022.3177752

Sharma, R., & Mohan, M. (2022). Artificial Intelligence and E-Learning: Best Practices Across the Globe. In Singh, S. (Ed.), (pp. 1–25). Advances in Marketing, Customer Relationship Management, and E-Services. IGI Global., DOI: 10.4018/978-1-7998-7959-6.ch001

Wang, X., He, X., Wei, J., Liu, J., Li, Y., & Liu, X. (2023). Application of artificial intelligence to the public health education. *Frontiers in Public Health*, *10*, 1087174. DOI: 10.3389/fpubh.2022.1087174 PMID: 36703852

White, J., & Stevens, K. (2024). Ethics of digital education. In *Edward Elgar Publishing eBooks* (pp. 252–289). DOI: 10.4337/9781803928241.00019

Woodward, J. P., & Carnine, D. W. (1988). Antecedent Knowledge and Intelligent Computer Assisted Instruction. *Journal of Learning Disabilities*, *21*(3), 131–139. DOI: 10.1177/002221948802100302 PMID: 3280714

Xu, W., & Ouyang, F. (2022). A systematic review of AI role in the educational system based on a proposed conceptual framework. *Education and Information Technologies*, *27*(3), 4195–4223. DOI: 10.1007/s10639-021-10774-y

Zafari, M., Bazargani, J. S., Sadeghi-Niaraki, A., & Choi, S.-M. (2022). Artificial Intelligence Applications in K-12 Education: A Systematic Literature Review. *IEEE Access : Practical Innovations, Open Solutions*, *10*, 61905–61921. DOI: 10.1109/ACCESS.2022.3179356

Zdravkova, K. (2023). Personalized Education for Sustainable Development. *Sustainability (Basel)*, *15*(8), 6901. DOI: 10.3390/su15086901

Zhang, J., & Tao, D. (2021). Empowering Things With Intelligence: A Survey of the Progress, Challenges, and Opportunities in Artificial Intelligence of Things. *IEEE Internet of Things Journal*, *8*(10), 7789–7817. DOI: 10.1109/JIOT.2020.3039359

Zhou, M. Y., & Lawless, W. F. (2014). An Overview of Artificial Intelligence in Education. In Khosrow-Pour, D. B. A. (Ed.), *M* (pp. 2445–2452). Advances in Information Quality and Management. IGI Global., DOI: 10.4018/978-1-4666-5888-2.ch237

Chapter 2
Educational Transformation Through Artificial Intelligence:
Implementation of AI Tools in the Teaching and Learning Process

Muh Ibnu Sholeh
https://orcid.org/0000-0003-0841-3101
STAI Kh Muhammad Ali Shodiq Tulungagung, Indonesia

ABSTRACT

The integration of artificial intelligence (AI) into educational practices holds immense promise for transforming both learning experiences and teaching methodologies. AI technologies, including machine learning and natural language processing, enable personalized learning experiences tailored to individual student needs, thereby enhancing engagement and effectiveness. Moreover, AI-driven systems automate administrative tasks such as assessment and scheduling, allowing educators to allocate more time to instructional activities. However, alongside these benefits, significant ethical considerations arise, including issues related to data privacy, algorithmic bias, and equitable access to AI tools. Addressing these challenges is crucial to ensuring that AI in education is deployed responsibly and inclusively.

INTRODUCTION

In recent years, the integration of Artificial Intelligence (AI) in the field of education has become a topic of significant interest among various stakeholders, including educators, researchers, and education practitioners. AI holds great promise for revolutionizing the teaching and learning process by offering potential solutions to enhance efficiency, effectiveness, and personalization in education. One of the most compelling aspects of AI integration in education is its ability to personalize the learning experience. AI enables customized learning tailored to the individual needs of each student by analyzing data related to their learning styles, preferences, levels of understanding, and academic progress. This allows educators

DOI: 10.4018/979-8-3693-7260-9.ch002

to design more relevant and engaging curricula for each student, ultimately improving their motivation and involvement in the learning process (Karataş dkk., 2025).

Artificial Intelligence (AI) can also automate administrative tasks in education. For example, AI systems can be used to manage classroom administration, such as tracking attendance, scheduling learning activities, and managing student records. By automating these tasks, educators gain more time and energy to focus on more important aspects of their work, such as developing curriculum and providing feedback to students(Parycek dkk., 2023). AI is also capable of offering valuable insights into student learning patterns through data analysis. By analyzing data from various sources—including exams, assignments, and online interactions—AI can identify learning trends, detect areas where students may be struggling, and suggest appropriate intervention strategies. This enables educators to provide timely and effective support to students who need it, thereby increasing their chances of academic success (Kim dkk., 2022).

It is important to remember that although AI offers great potential to enhance education, its use also brings a number of challenges and risks. Some of these include issues related to data privacy, algorithmic bias, and a lack of understanding about how AI can be effectively used in educational contexts. Therefore, it is essential for educators and other stakeholders in education to carefully consider these challenges and ensure that the use of AI in education is guided by principles of ethics and fairness (Chen dkk., 2020). In this way, the integration of artificial intelligence in education holds significant potential to revolutionize the teaching and learning process through personalization, automation, and more effective data analysis. However, to fully realize this potential, it is crucial for educators and other educational stakeholders to continuously explore various relevant AI applications while also considering the ethical implications and associated challenges of its use.

UNDERSTANDING AI IN EDUCATION

Understanding the role of Artificial Intelligence (AI) in the context of education is an important step before considering its specific applications. AI refers to the ability of machines, particularly computer systems, to simulate human intelligence processes. In education, AI plays a crucial role in analyzing data, recognizing patterns, and making data-driven decisions to improve teaching and learning outcomes. AI holds great potential to transform the educational landscape by enabling more personalized and effective learning experiences for every individual. In the field of education, AI can be used to provide customized instruction based on each student's needs, analyze data to track progress, deliver timely and accurate feedback, and develop more efficient learning strategies. Through deep data analysis, AI can identify each student's strengths, weaknesses, and learning styles, and then deliver learning materials that align with their preferences. For instance, a more visually oriented student may benefit from image- and video-based content, while students who prefer auditory learning might engage more effectively with audio materials. This kind of adaptation can significantly enhance student engagement and learning effectiveness (Jafari & Shaterzadeh-Yazdi, 2024).

AI has the ability to analyze learning data in real time and provide immediate feedback to students. AI systems can monitor student performance across various assignments and tests, then offer specific feedback on areas that need improvement. This feedback can come in the form of suggestions for further study, additional hints, or even recommendations to change learning strategies. Such an approach enables a more adaptive and interactive learning environment that evolves according to the student's needs over time (Kinshuk dkk., 2016). AI can be used to make predictions about students' learning trajectories, helping educators design more strategic and effective approaches. For example, AI can predict whether a student is at risk of falling behind based on their learning patterns and past performance. This information allows educators to take preventive actions, such as providing additional support or adjusting learning materials before the student encounters more serious difficulties (Embarak & Hawarna, 2024).

With the assistance of AI, teachers can manage administrative tasks more efficiently, allowing them to focus more on direct interaction with students and supporting their learning progress. AI can automate various tasks such as assessments, attendance tracking, and scheduling, which often consume a significant amount of time. This automation not only reduces the administrative workload for teachers but also improves the accuracy and consistency of these tasks (Aithal & Aithal, 2023). AI is also capable of recommending curriculum improvements based on data analysis. By examining learning outcomes and student feedback, AI can identify areas where the curriculum may be ineffective and suggest ways to improve it. This can help enhance the quality of education and ensure that the learning materials remain relevant. A continuously updated and student-responsive curriculum can lead to better learning outcomes and greater alignment with real-world needs (Peng dkk., 2022).

In the field of education, AI plays a vital role in analyzing data. This involves the collection and processing of relevant information about students, curricula, teaching methods, and learning environments. The data may include student progress, learning preferences, and other factors that influence the learning process. By analyzing this data, AI can identify patterns that may not be easily visible to humans, which helps educators make more informed decisions regarding teaching strategies and necessary interventions (K. Ahmad dkk., 2023). AI also contributes to recognizing patterns in educational data. Using techniques such as machine learning and deep learning, AI can learn from existing data patterns and apply this information to make predictions or provide recommendations. For instance, AI can detect patterns indicating that a student is likely to struggle in a particular subject, allowing educators to offer additional support or targeted interventions(Holmes & Luckin, 2016).

AI plays an important role in data-driven decision-making. AI algorithms can be programmed to make automatic decisions or offer recommendations based on data analysis. In adaptive learning contexts, for example, AI can use data on student progress to adjust the curriculum or provide supplementary exercises tailored to each student's needs (Zawacki-Richter dkk., 2019). By understanding the role of AI in education, educators can better recognize both the potential and limitations of this technology in enhancing teaching and learning outcomes. Moreover, a solid understanding of AI enables educators to integrate it into their teaching practices in an effective and responsible manner.

LEARNING PERSONALIZED WITH AI

Personalized learning with AI is one of the most important aspects of integrating artificial intelligence (AI) into education. This approach allows educators to tailor teaching materials and methods to meet the specific needs of each student. By using AI technology, educators can create more relevant and effective learning experiences—something that is often not possible with traditional teaching methods. The main benefit of personalized learning is its ability to provide customized learning experiences that suit each individual student. Every student has a unique learning style, pace, and set of interests. With the help of AI, educational systems can identify these differences and adjust the content and teaching strategies accordingly to meet each student's unique needs. This not only increases student engagement but also helps them achieve better learning outcomes.

AI plays a key role in analyzing student data and using that information to create personalized learning paths. AI can collect data from various sources such as test results, classroom interactions, and online learning activities. This data is then analyzed to identify learning patterns and the challenges students may face. Based on this analysis, AI can recommend additional materials, alternative teaching methods, or customized learning speeds for each student. Through this approach, AI helps create a learning environment that is adaptive and responsive to individual needs. AI is capable of thoroughly analyzing student data, which includes various aspects such as learning styles, preferences, levels of understanding, and performance across different subjects or skills. By examining this data, AI can gain a better understanding of each student's learning needs, distinguish between different learning styles and abilities, and identify areas that require additional attention (Tapalova & Zhiyenbayeva, 2022).

Based on data analysis, AI can create personalized learning pathways for each student. For example, adaptive learning platforms use AI technology to provide customized content and exercises tailored to the strengths and weaknesses of individual learners. Students who quickly master the material can be given more challenging tasks, while those who face difficulties can receive additional support or more detailed explanations. In this way, adaptive learning allows students to study at their own pace and aligns the learning process with their individual learning styles (Naseer dkk., 2024). Personalized learning with AI is a key aspect of integrating artificial intelligence into education. A concrete example of AI-driven personalized learning is the use of AI tutors. These AI tutors can offer individualized guidance, provide real-time feedback on student performance, and adjust exercises and learning materials based on students' responses. This allows each student to receive personalized attention according to their needs, thereby improving overall learning effectiveness (Rizvi, 2023).

AI tutors play an essential role in analyzing student performance data to understand their strengths and weaknesses. Based on this analysis, the AI tutor modifies the learning materials and practice activities, offering appropriate challenges to promote student progress in areas that need improvement. For instance, platforms like TutorOcean utilize AI tutors to deliver adaptive feedback and help students focus on areas where improvement is needed. AI tutors can also track students' progress over time, enabling educators to monitor individual development and adapt instruction accordingly. AI tutors provide explanations for both correct and incorrect answers, helping students gain a deeper understanding of the concepts they are learning. By offering detailed explanations, AI tutors ensure that students not only know the correct answers but also comprehend the reasoning behind them, which greatly supports their long-term understanding of the subject matter.

The use of deep AI tutors in personalized learning offers numerous benefits, including increased student engagement, improved learning outcomes, and the development of independent study skills. With customized guidance tailored to individual needs, students are better able to reach their full potential and achieve stronger academic results. Personalized learning with AI not only enhances the overall quality of education but also enables educators to more effectively support the unique needs of each student. By using AI technology wisely, education can become more inclusive, adaptive, and efficient—better preparing students to face future challenges.

INCREASE TEACHING WITH AI

Enhancing teaching with the help of Artificial Intelligence (AI) is one of the most significant advancements in modern education. AI can be applied in various aspects of teaching, from lesson planning to assessment, with the goal of increasing the efficiency, effectiveness, and overall quality of the learning process (Ahmad dkk., 2021). AI can support educators in lesson planning by providing in-depth curriculum analysis and offering suggestions on the best materials to include in each lesson. These AI systems work by analyzing student performance data—such as test results, assignments, and classroom interactions—to identify areas that require more attention. In this way, AI helps educators design more structured and relevant lessons tailored to students' needs.

AI is also capable of evaluating existing curricula and offering insights into how well students have understood the material. Based on this analysis, it can recommend adjustments to topics that are not well understood or need further reinforcement. For instance, if data shows that many students are struggling to understand a certain concept, AI may suggest allocating more time or adding supplementary materials to that topic. AI can recommend the most appropriate learning materials for each class session based on students' understanding levels and individual needs. Using machine learning algorithms, AI can adapt lesson content to make it more relevant and engaging for students. This includes recommending the use of various media types such as videos, articles, or exercises suited to each student's learning style (Tapalova & Zhiyenbayeva, 2022).

AI makes personalized learning possible by adapting content and teaching methods based on students' interaction data. These systems provide real-time feedback and adjust the difficulty level of learning materials according to each student's individual needs. As a result, every student can learn at their own pace and focus on the areas they find most challenging, ultimately increasing the overall effectiveness of the learning process (Sayed dkk., 2023). With its ability to analyze data and offer suggestions based on students' needs, AI plays a crucial role in improving lesson planning. It helps educators design more effective and relevant curricula, ensuring that each student receives materials best suited to their level of understanding and learning needs.

AI can also be used for generating learning content. Through technologies like Natural Language Generation (NLG), AI can automatically create learning materials in the form of text, images, or even videos. This technology allows educators and educational institutions to produce content more quickly and efficiently while maintaining high consistency and quality in the materials provided to students. NLG enables AI to generate informative and appropriate texts aligned with the topics being taught. AI can use existing data and information sources to write articles, summaries, or other learning materials that are easy for students to understand. For example, AI can generate explanations for complex mathematical concepts in a simpler and more structured manner, helping students grasp the material more effectively(Denny dkk., 2023).

AI can also be used to create visual learning content such as supporting images and graphics. With its ability to analyze data and generate visualizations, AI assists in producing diagrams, graphs, and illustrative representations of the concepts being taught. For instance, in science lessons, AI can generate detailed and accurate images of human anatomy or diagrams of the photosynthesis process (Alabi, 2023). AI is capable of producing educational video content. Through advanced technology, AI can create learning videos by combining relevant text, sound, and visuals. These videos may include explanations of material, practical demonstrations, or animations that make learning more engaging and interactive. This technology enables the creation of educational videos in a shorter time compared to traditional methods, while also ensuring consistent quality across all materials (Amanbekqyzy et al., 2021). By applying technologies like Natural Language Generation (NLG), AI allows for the rapid, efficient, and high-quality development of learning content. This not only supports educators in producing more engaging and easy-to-understand materials but also helps ensure that every student receives consistent and high-quality learning resources.

AI also makes a significant contribution by providing feedback to students. AI tutoring systems, for example, can deliver real-time feedback on student performance during exercises or tasks. This kind of feedback is invaluable because it allows students to immediately recognize what they are doing correctly and where they are making mistakes. With this information, students can identify their strengths and weaknesses and understand the areas in which they need improvement. This helps students to learn independently and progressively develop their skills. AI tutor systems are capable of analyzing student answers in detail and offering specific feedback. For example, in mathematics lessons, AI can detect incorrect steps in solving a problem and explain the correct method to complete it. This enables students to understand their mistakes and learn from them, which is a crucial part of the learning process (Kinshuk dkk., 2016). Real-time feedback from AI tutors allows students to correct their errors immediately. In this context, AI acts as a constant mentor, always available to provide guidance. For instance, if a student answers a question incorrectly on an online learning platform, AI can instantly give feedback and even offer similar example questions to ensure the student has fully understood the concept.

AI can also provide personalized feedback based on the ongoing analysis of student performance data. By analyzing learning patterns and assessment results, AI can offer specific and tailored advice aligned with each student's individual needs. This helps students focus on the areas that require the most improvement and develop effective learning strategies (Hooda dkk., 2022). With the application of AI technology to deliver detailed, specific, and real-time feedback, students can learn more effectively and efficiently. This enables them to continually develop their abilities and knowledge, ultimately enhancing the overall quality of education.

Beyond the classroom, AI can also assist students during their independent study time. AI chatbots, for example, can be integrated into online learning platforms to instantly answer students' questions. These chatbots are designed to understand and respond to a wide range of inquiries related to lesson materials, assignments, or concepts students find difficult to grasp. With the presence of such chatbots, students can receive additional help and explanations whenever needed, without having to wait for the availability of a teacher. This supports more independent and continuous learning outside the classroom environment (Dimitriadou & Lanitis, 2023).

AI chatbots are capable of providing instant answers to both simple and complex questions. For example, if a student needs clarification on a math concept or wants to explore a particular historical topic in more depth, AI chatbots can offer clear and informative explanations. This is particularly helpful when students are studying outside of school hours and do not have direct access to teachers (Suta dkk., 2020). AI chatbots can provide personalized assistance based on previous interactions with students. By using Natural Language Processing (NLP) technology, these chatbots can remember frequently asked questions and the common difficulties faced by specific students, offering customized explanations or learning resources tailored to their individual needs. This contributes to a more personalized and effective learning experience.

The integration of AI chatbots into online learning platforms is also enhancing accessibility to education. Students with busy schedules or those who have difficulty attending regular classes can use AI chatbots to get assistance whenever they need it. This not only supports more flexible learning but also ensures that all students have equal access to high-quality educational resources (Mageira dkk., 2022). By leveraging AI chatbots, students can continue learning independently and receive the support they need outside of regular class hours. This not only broadens learning opportunities but also ensures that students receive the educational support they require, anytime and anywhere. The use of AI in improving teaching not only brings benefits in terms of efficiency and effectiveness, but also allows educators to focus more on personal interactions with students and provide them with better support. The implementation of AI in education helps automate administrative and analytical tasks, which often consume a significant amount of educators' time. By reducing this workload, educators have more time and energy to directly engage with students, understand their individual needs, and provide more personalized guidance.

AUTOMATE TASK ADMINISTRATIVE

Automating administrative tasks through the use of artificial intelligence (AI) is an important step in increasing efficiency and effectiveness within educational environments. By freeing educators and administrators from time-consuming administrative duties, they can focus more on teaching, learning, and student development. In today's rapidly advancing digital era, the utilization of AI has become a significant breakthrough, especially in the field of education. One of the most notable benefits of AI technology is its ability to automate the student assessment process. With the help of natural language processing (NLP) and machine learning (ML) algorithms, AI systems can automatically evaluate students' responses in tests or assignments. This approach accelerates the assessment process and relieves educators from time-consuming manual grading tasks. As a result, teachers can devote more time to direct interaction with students and to developing more effective curricula.

One key area where AI can automate administrative tasks is in assessments. AI systems can be used to evaluate students' answers automatically, using NLP and machine learning algorithms to understand and assess the quality of their responses. In doing so, educators save valuable time that would otherwise be spent on manual grading, while still providing students with high-quality feedback (S. F. Ahmad dkk., 2022). Another advantage of automated evaluation through AI is its ability to deliver fast and consistent feedback to students. By deeply analyzing student responses, AI systems can identify individual strengths and weaknesses and offer specific suggestions for improvement. This not only helps students understand their current level of comprehension, but also enables them to make meaningful progress throughout the learning process.

As with any new technology, the implementation of AI in assessment also brings several challenges. One of the main challenges is ensuring accuracy and fairness in evaluation. Although AI systems can understand human language with a high level of accuracy, there is still a risk of errors or biases that must be carefully addressed. Therefore, it is essential to continuously develop and test AI systems to ensure they provide reliable and fair assessments for all students.

AI can also automate tasks such as tracking attendance and scheduling courses. AI systems can be used to automatically monitor student attendance through integrated identification systems linked with school timetables or online learning platforms. This allows educators and administrators to quickly identify absent or late students and take appropriate actions to support them (Igbokwe, 2023). AI systems can assist with course scheduling by considering various factors such as student preferences, facility availability, and curriculum requirements. By using optimization algorithms, AI can generate efficient schedules and minimize conflicts.

Automating administrative tasks with the help of artificial intelligence (AI) has a significant impact on the educational environment. In addition to helping reduce the workload of educators and administrators, this automation also improves accuracy and consistency in administrative processes. Through the use of AI technology, educational institutions can allocate their resources more efficiently, improve productivity, and place greater focus on enhancing the student learning experience(Zhai, 2023). One of the main benefits of automating administrative tasks is the substantial savings in time and effort for educators and administrators. Administrative tasks such as scheduling, attendance tracking, and assessment often consume valuable time. However, with the help of AI, these processes can be automated, allowing educators and administrators to focus on more meaningful activities, such as planning better lessons or engaging directly with students.

The use of AI in administrative tasks also improves accuracy and consistency. AI systems tend to perform tasks with a higher level of accuracy than humans, as they are not affected by emotional factors or fatigue. This helps ensure that administrative processes are carried out consistently, reducing the possibility of errors and improving operational efficiency. Automating administrative tasks allows educational institutions to allocate their resources more efficiently. By reducing the time and energy required for administrative duties, institutions can redirect more resources to critical areas such as developing innovative curricula, providing teacher training, or investing in more advanced educational technologies. Automating administrative tasks also enhances the overall student learning experience. By relieving educators from time-consuming administrative work, they can focus more on supporting the individual needs of students, providing more detailed feedback, and creating a more engaging and dynamic learning environment. Automating administrative tasks with the assistance of AI is not only about increasing the operational efficiency of educational institutions, but also about creating a better learning environment that is more responsive to student needs.

ANALYZING LEARNING DATA

One of the most significant applications of artificial intelligence (AI) in education is learning data analysis. By using AI technology, educational institutions can collect and analyze large amounts of data on student performance, enabling educators to identify trends, predict future outcomes, and gain valuable insights to support teaching decisions. AI algorithms have the ability to gather data from various relevant learning sources, including exam scores, assignments, interactions on online learning platforms, and even activity on social media. This collected data is then analyzed using machine learning and data mining techniques to identify potential patterns and trends that may not be visible to humans.

The use of AI to collect and analyze learning data opens up new opportunities to better understand the learning process and the factors that influence academic outcomes. For example, using machine learning techniques, AI can find correlations between student participation in online discussions and their academic performance. Research by Davies & Graff (2005) shows that students who actively participate in online discussions tend to achieve higher exam scores(Davies & Graff, 2005). These findings highlight the great potential of AI in uncovering hidden patterns in learning data that can help educators design more effective teaching strategies.

Data analysis carried out by AI can also help educators support the individual needs of students. By understanding students' learning patterns and preferences more deeply, educators can provide more targeted guidance and support each student's academic progress more effectively. This helps create a more inclusive learning environment that is responsive to the diverse needs of all students. The use of artificial intelligence (AI) algorithms in collecting and analyzing learning data contributes significantly to improving our understanding of the learning process and offers valuable insights for educators in designing more effective and sustainable learning experiences.

One of the key benefits of learning data analysis supported by AI is its ability to identify trends and predict students' future performance. By analyzing historical data collected from various sources—such as exam scores, participation in learning activities, and attendance levels—AI algorithms can detect patterns that are relevant to academic performance. From these patterns, AI can make predictions about students' future outcomes. For example, using machine learning techniques, AI can predict the likelihood of a student passing or failing a particular subject based on their past academic performance, attendance rate, and level of engagement in learning activities. Through in-depth analysis of this data, AI can identify factors that correlate with academic success and use this information to forecast future results.

A study conducted by Siemens and Long (2011) highlights the importance of in-depth data analysis in education and the great potential of AI to predict student learning outcomes(Luan dkk., 2020). In their article, they emphasize how analytics technology can help uncover hidden patterns in learning data and provide valuable insights for educators to support students more effectively. Through learning data analysis with the help of AI, educators can gain a deeper understanding of students' needs and potential, and take more proactive steps to support their academic progress.

AI-powered learning analytics platforms not only help in collecting and analyzing learning data but also provide valuable insights to educators. By using interactive dashboards and AI-generated reports, educators can easily view student performance data in real-time and identify students who may require additional attention. One of the main benefits of AI-powered learning analytics platforms is their ability to provide recommendations and suggestions to educators based on in-depth data analysis. For instance, AI can help identify students who are struggling to understand specific concepts. Based on the collected data, the system can recommend appropriate interventions, such as additional tutoring sessions or more in-depth learning materials.

As a concrete example, platforms like **Learning Analytics** use artificial intelligence (AI) to monitor student progress and provide accessible insights to educators and administrators. These systems have the ability to collect data from various sources, such as exam scores, participation in online discussions, and interactions with learning materials. By analyzing this data using machine learning techniques, the platform can identify at-risk students who may be falling behind, based on identified patterns. Through data analysis, the Learning Analytics platform is capable of providing deep insights into both individual student performance and overall class performance.

This approach allows educators to take proactive steps in providing additional support to students in need, such as tutoring sessions or personalized learning materials. In addition, the system can also be used to evaluate the effectiveness of teaching methods and suggest necessary adjustments to improve learning outcomes. A study conducted by Salas-Pilco dkk (2022) discusses the importance of in-depth data analysis in education and how technologies like Learning Analytics can be used to address challenges in improving the quality of teaching and learning. In his article, Ferguson elaborates on the impact of technology on learning practices and recent developments in learning analytics (Salas-Pilco dkk., 2022). Platforms like **Learning Analytics** demonstrate how the use of artificial intelligence in learning data analysis can bring tangible benefits to both educators and students in enhancing the quality of education.

Learning data analysis supported by artificial intelligence (AI) brings a variety of significant advantages to the field of education. Through this technology, educational institutions can identify trends in student performance, predict future outcomes, and provide valuable insights for educators. The use of AI in learning data analysis enables educational institutions to improve the overall quality of learning by offering timely and effective support to students. Moreover, educators can make more informed decisions in the teaching process, helping to create a more adaptive and responsive learning environment that meets individual student needs. Thus, the integration of AI into learning data analysis holds great potential to transform the educational paradigm toward a more effective and sustainable learning experience.

CONSIDERATION ETHICAL AND CHALLENGES

Although the potential benefits of artificial intelligence (AI) in education are vast, there are various ethical considerations and challenges that must be addressed to ensure that this technology is used in a responsible and inclusive manner. These considerations include issues such as data privacy, algorithmic bias, and equitable access to AI tools. One of the biggest challenges in implementing AI in the field of education is data privacy. The frequent use of AI often involves the collection and analysis of large amounts of personal student data, including academic records, behavioral information, and even biometric data. These data are highly sensitive and can be vulnerable to misuse or abuse. Therefore, it is essential to ensure that student data is protected through strict safeguards and only used for legitimate and ethical purposes.

Strong and transparent privacy policies must be implemented to protect students' personal information from unauthorized access or exploitation. This includes regulating the processes of data collection, storage, usage, and sharing in a careful and lawful manner, in accordance with applicable laws and regulations. Furthermore, educational institutions must provide transparency to students and parents regarding how their data is being used and processed by AI systems. A study by Paludi (2024) highlights the importance of ethics and privacy issues in learning analytics. In their article, they explore various ethical dilemmas associated with the use of learning analytics, including concerns over data privacy(Paludi, 2024). Their emphasis on the need to consider the ethical implications of AI in education has become increasingly relevant as the technology becomes more deeply embedded in educational environments. By adopting strong and transparent privacy policies, along with a commitment to safeguarding student data, the use of AI in education can be carried out in an ethical and responsible manner—while still leveraging the immense potential of this technology to enhance the student learning experience.

Algorithmic bias is a serious issue that can threaten the fairness and accuracy of decisions produced by artificial intelligence (AI) systems. AI algorithms are often trained using historical data, which unfortunately may reflect existing societal biases. For example, if the training data show that certain groups have historically received lower evaluations or less favorable treatment, the AI algorithm may unintentionally reinforce this bias by generating predictions or recommendations that are unfair to those groups. When AI systems rely on biased data, this can lead to unintentional discrimination or unfair outcomes for specific individuals or groups. Therefore, it is crucial to develop transparent algorithms that are free from bias. In addition, regular auditing and refinement of AI systems are essential to ensure that their decisions remain fair, inclusive, and aligned with ethical values.

A study by Chinta (2024) highlights the importance of understanding internal biases in computer systems. In their article, they explain how biases can influence decisions made by such systems and propose strategies to reduce the negative impact of these biases(Chinta dkk., 2024). By acknowledging the problem of algorithmic bias and taking appropriate steps to identify, mitigate, and address these biases during the development and implementation of AI systems, we can ensure that this technology is used in an ethical and responsible manner. This approach not only upholds fairness but also maximizes the benefits of AI for all individuals and society as a whole.

Fair access to artificial intelligence (AI) tools is a significant challenge in education. Students from economically disadvantaged backgrounds may not have the same access to AI technologies as their more financially privileged peers. This disparity can exacerbate existing educational inequalities, as access to AI tools can offer additional advantages in the learning process (Baidoo-Anu & Ansah, 2023). Therefore, it is crucial to ensure that all students—regardless of their socioeconomic background—have equal access to AI tools and technologies that can support their learning. Efforts to address this issue may include providing hardware and software devices for free or at very low cost to students in need. In addition, training should be provided to both educators and students on how to effectively utilize AI technology in the learning process. By overcoming the challenge of fair access to AI tools, we can create equal opportunities for all students to benefit from this technology in their education, while also promoting inclusivity and equity in learning environments.

When addressing the ethical and practical challenges in the use of AI in education, a thoughtful and inclusive approach is essential. Educators, policymakers, and other stakeholders must work together to develop a strong framework that ensures AI technology is used in a way that protects student privacy, eliminates algorithmic bias, and guarantees fair access for all learners. It is important to prioritize the security and privacy of student data by implementing strict and transparent privacy policies and ensuring compliance with existing regulations. Furthermore, steps must be taken to identify, mitigate, and address algorithmic bias in AI systems so that the decisions they produce are fair and accurate. It is also necessary to ensure equitable access to AI technology for all students, regardless of their economic or social conditions. This includes making hardware and software affordable and providing training to ensure the technology is used effectively in educational settings. By addressing all these aspects, we can maximize the benefits of AI technology in education while minimizing its risks and negative impacts. Through this approach, education can become more inclusive, effective, and equitable for all students, helping to build a brighter future for the next generation.

CONCLUSION

The integration of artificial intelligence (AI) in education has demonstrated great potential to revolutionize the teaching and learning process. AI has the capability to personalize learning experiences, enhance teaching practices, automate administrative tasks, and analyze learning data. However, to fully realize this potential, a number of ethical considerations and challenges must be addressed. AI refers to the simulation of human intelligence processes by machines, especially computer systems. In the educational context, AI analyzes data, recognizes patterns, and makes data-driven decisions to improve teaching methods and learning outcomes. By understanding the role of AI, educators can effectively and responsibly integrate this technology into their teaching practices.

One of the most significant benefits of AI in education is its ability to personalize the learning experience. AI algorithms can analyze student data—such as learning styles, preferences, and performance—to create personalized learning paths. Adaptive learning platforms powered by AI provide customized content and exercises based on each student's strengths and weaknesses, promoting self-paced learning and deeper engagement. AI also supports educators in various aspects of teaching, including lesson planning, content creation, and assessment. AI-powered tutoring systems can offer real-time feedback to students, allowing teachers to dedicate more time to personalized interactions. In addition, AI chatbots can assist students with their questions outside of classroom hours, encouraging continuous learning and support.

Beyond enhancing teaching and learning, AI can automate administrative tasks, enabling educators to focus more on instruction. AI-powered systems can handle tasks such as grading, attendance tracking, and course scheduling, reducing the administrative burden on teachers and school staff. Another key application of AI in education is data analysis. By collecting and analyzing large volumes of student performance data, AI can identify trends, predict outcomes, and provide insights for educators. Learning analytics platforms can help detect students at risk of falling behind and recommend interventions to support their learning needs. Despite the promising benefits of AI in education, several ethical concerns and challenges must be addressed. These include issues related to data privacy, algorithmic bias, and equitable access to AI tools. Educators and policymakers must navigate these challenges wisely to ensure that AI technology is implemented in a responsible and inclusive manner within educational environments.

The use of AI in education offers a tremendous opportunity to enhance the quality of teaching and learning. However, to unlock its full potential, it is essential to overcome the ethical and practical issues that may arise. With a thoughtful and inclusive approach, educators and policymakers can ensure that AI technology is used responsibly—protecting privacy, ensuring fairness, and providing equal access to all students. In doing so, we can maximize the benefits of AI in education and create a more effective, efficient, and inclusive learning environment.

REFERENCES

Ahmad, K., Iqbal, W., Qadir, J., Benhaddou, D., Ayyash, M., & Al-Fuqaha, A. (2023). Data-Driven Artificial Intelligence in Education: A Comprehensive Review. *IEEE Transactions on Learning Technologies*, •••, 17.

Ahmad, S. F., Alam, M. M., Rahmat, M. K., Mubarik, M. S., & Hyder, S. I. (2022). Academic and Administrative Role of Artificial Intelligence in Education. *Sustainability (Basel)*, *14*(3), 1101. DOI: 10.3390/su14031101

Ahmad, S. F., Rahmat, M. K., Mubarik, M. S., Alam, M. M., & Hyder, S. I. (2021). Artificial Intelligence and Its Role in Education. *Sustainability (Basel)*, *13*(22), 12902. DOI: 10.3390/su132212902

Aithal, P. S., & Aithal, S. (2023). Optimizing the Use of Artificial Intelligence-Powered GPTs as Teaching and Research Assistants by Professors in Higher Education Institutions: A Study on Smart Utilization. *International Journal of Management, Technology, and Social Sciences*, *8*(4), 368–401. DOI: 10.47992/IJMTS.2581.6012.0326

Alabi, M. (2023). Visual Learning: The Power of Visual Aids and Multimedia. *Technology and Visual Learning*, *9*(7).

Amanbekqyzy, A. A., Serikovna, N. A., & Erlanovna, A. A. (2021). AI-Enhanced Educational Content Creation. *Endless Light in Science*, *5*(3).

Baidoo-Anu, D., & Ansah, L. O. (2023). Education in the Era of Generative Artificial Intelligence (AI): Understanding the Potential Benefits of ChatGPT in Promoting Teaching and Learning. *Journal of AI*, *7*(1), 52–62. DOI: 10.61969/jai.1337500

Chen, L., Chen, P., & Lin, Z. (2020). Artificial Intelligence in Education: A Review. *IEEE Access : Practical Innovations, Open Solutions*, *8*, 75264–75278. DOI: 10.1109/ACCESS.2020.2988510

Chinta, S. V., Wang, Z., Yin, Z., Hoang, N., Gonzalez, M., Quy, T. L., & Zhang, W. (2024). *FairAIED: Navigating Fairness, Bias, and Ethics in Educational AI Applications* (arXiv:2407.18745). arXiv. https://doi.org//arXiv.2407.18745DOI: 10.48550

Davies, J., & Graff, M. (2005). Performance in e-learning: Online participation and student grades. *British Journal of Educational Technology*, *36*(4), 657–663. DOI: 10.1111/j.1467-8535.2005.00542.x

Denny, P., Khosravi, H., Hellas, A., Leinonen, J., & Sarsa, S. (2023). *Can We Trust AI-Generated Educational Content? Comparative Analysis of Human and AI-Generated Learning Resources* (arXiv:2306.10509). arXiv. https://doi.org//arXiv.2306.10509DOI: 10.48550

Dimitriadou, E., & Lanitis, A. (2023). A critical evaluation, challenges, and future perspectives of using artificial intelligence and emerging technologies in smart classrooms. *Smart Learning Environments*, *10*(1), 12. DOI: 10.1186/s40561-023-00231-3

Embarak, O. H., & Hawarna, S. (2024). Automated AI-driven System for Early Detection of At-risk Students. *Procedia Computer Science*, *231*, 151–160. DOI: 10.1016/j.procs.2023.12.187

Holmes, W., & Luckin, R. (2016). *Intelligence unleashed: An argument for AI in education*. Pearson : UCL Knowledge Lab.

Hooda, M., Rana, C., Dahiya, O., Rizwan, A., & Hossain, M. S. (2022). Artificial Intelligence for Assessment and Feedback to Enhance Student Success in Higher Education. *Mathematical Problems in Engineering*, *2022*, 1–19. DOI: 10.1155/2022/5215722

Igbokwe, I. C. (2023). Application of Artificial Intelligence (AI) in Educational Management. *International Journal of Scientific and Research Publications*, *13*(3). Advance online publication. DOI: 10.29322/IJSRP.13.03.2023.p13536

Jafari, D., & Shaterzadeh-Yazdi, Z. (2024). Transforming Education with AI: The Development of a Personalized Learning Algorithm for Individual Learning Styles. *Journal of Algorithms and Computation*, *56*(2).

Karataş, F., Eriçok, B., & Tanrikulu, L. (2025). Reshaping curriculum adaptation in the age of artificial intelligence: Mapping teachers' driven curriculum adaptation patterns. *British Educational Research Journal*, *51*(1), 154–180. DOI: 10.1002/berj.4068

Kim, J., Lee, H., & Cho, Y. H. (2022). Learning design to support student-AI collaboration: Perspectives of leading teachers for AI in education. *Education and Information Technologies*, *27*(5), 6069–6104. DOI: 10.1007/s10639-021-10831-6

Kinshuk, C., Chen, N.-S., Cheng, I.-L., & Chew, S. W. (2016). Evolution Is not enough: Revolutionizing Current Learning Environments to Smart Learning Environments. *International Journal of Artificial Intelligence in Education*, *26*(2), 561–581. DOI: 10.1007/s40593-016-0108-x

Luan, H., Geczy, P., Lai, H., Gobert, J., Yang, S. J. H., Ogata, H., Baltes, J., Guerra, R., Li, P., & Tsai, C.-C. (2020). Challenges and Future Directions of Big Data and Artificial Intelligence in Education. *Frontiers in Psychology*, *11*, 580820. DOI: 10.3389/fpsyg.2020.580820 PMID: 33192896

Mageira, K., Pittou, D., Papasalouros, A., Kotis, K., Zangogianni, P., & Daradoumis, A. (2022). Educational AI Chatbots for Content and Language Integrated Learning. *Applied Sciences (Basel, Switzerland)*, *12*(7), 3239. DOI: 10.3390/app12073239

Naseer, F., Khan, M. N., Tahir, M., Addas, A., & Aejaz, S. M. H. (2024). Integrating deep learning techniques for personalized learning pathways in higher education. *Heliyon*, *10*(11), e32628. DOI: 10.1016/j.heliyon.2024.e32628 PMID: 38961899

Paludi, M. (2024). Safeguarding Privacy and Data Protection Rights in AI- Enhanced Education and Learning Analytics: An Interdisciplinary Approach in Secondary High School Educational Settings. *Proceedings of the Doctoral Consortium of the 19th European Conference on Technology Enhanced Learning*, 56.

Parycek, P., Schmid, V., & Novak, A.-S. (2023). Artificial Intelligence (AI) and Automation in Administrative Procedures: Potentials, Limitations, and Framework Conditions. *Journal of the Knowledge Economy*, *15*(2), 8390–8415. DOI: 10.1007/s13132-023-01433-3

Peng, T., Luo, Y., & Liu, Y. (2022). AI-Based Equipment Optimization of the Design on Intelligent Education Curriculum System. *Wireless Communications and Mobile Computing*, *2022*, 1–13. DOI: 10.1155/2022/3614883

Rizvi, M. (2023). Investigating AI-Powered Tutoring Systems that Adapt to Individual Student Needs, Providing Personalized Guidance and Assessments. *The Eurasia Proceedings of Educational and Social Sciences*, *31*, 67–73. DOI: 10.55549/epess.1381518

Salas-Pilco, S., Xiao, K., & Hu, X. (2022). Artificial Intelligence and Learning Analytics in Teacher Education: A Systematic Review. *Education Sciences*, *12*(8), 569. DOI: 10.3390/educsci12080569

Sayed, W. S., Noeman, A. M., Abdellatif, A., Abdelrazek, M., Badawy, M. G., Hamed, A., & El-Tantawy, S. (2023). AI-based adaptive personalized content presentation and exercises navigation for an effective and engaging E-learning platform. *Multimedia Tools and Applications*, *82*(3), 3303–3333. DOI: 10.1007/s11042-022-13076-8 PMID: 35789938

Suta, P., Lan, X., Wu, B., Mongkolnam, P., & Chan, J. H. (2020). An Overview of Machine Learning in Chatbots. *International Journal of Mechanical Engineering and Robotics Research*, •••, 502–510. DOI: 10.18178/ijmerr.9.4.502-510

Tapalova, O., & Zhiyenbayeva, N. (2022). Artificial Intelligence in Education: AIEd for Personalised Learning Pathways. *Electronic Journal of e-Learning*, *20*(5), 639–653. DOI: 10.34190/ejel.20.5.2597

Zawacki-Richter, O., Marín, V. I., Bond, M., & Gouverneur, F. (2019). Systematic review of research on artificial intelligence applications in higher education – where are the educators? *International Journal of Educational Technology in Higher Education*, *16*(1), 39. DOI: 10.1186/s41239-019-0171-0

Zhai, X. (2023). ChatGPT: Artificial Intelligence for Education. *International Journal of Scientific and Research Publications*, *13*(2).

Chapter 3
AI in Professional Development for Language Teachers

Mohammad Badruddoza Talukder
https://orcid.org/0009-0008-1662-9221
International University of Business Agriculture and Technology, Bangladesh

Mst. Khadizatul Kobra
https://orcid.org/0009-0003-3130-9334
International University of Business Agriculture and Technology, Bangladesh

Sanjeev Kumar
https://orcid.org/0000-0002-7375-7341
Lovely Professional University, India

ABSTRACT

In this chapter, we looked at how AI is set to revolutionize the career growth of language teachers, particularly at tertiary institutions. As technology slowly creeps into learning institutions, AI rises as a shoo-in to heighten the skill and proficiency level of language teachers, specifically for tutors of adult learners. We discussed through previous literature that several of the programmed applications using Information technology, such as Learning platforms, paraphrasing, networks or algorithms, language processing, Quilbot Grammar checker systems, Chatbots, Language Translation services, Intelligent Tutoring Systems, Readlang, Grammarly, Learning Management Systems, Chat GPT and Teachers only needs and struggles are met. We also investigate how continuous learning is made possible through feedback mechanisms, streamlining routine processes, and implementing computer-assisted language learning and innovative teaching methods of AI's potential consequences and opportunities for teacher professionalism, lesson effectiveness, and the future of language teaching.

INTRODUCTION

In the rapidly evolving education landscape, specifically in language teaching and learning, modern technology has become an inseparable collaborator in ensuring quality education while coping with the worldwide standard. Incorporating AI into various domains has prompted considerable transformations

DOI: 10.4018/979-8-3693-7260-9.ch003

and benefits, with education being a prominent beneficiary. AI's potential to revolutionize how all the participants in the academic sector approach the teaching and learning process has garnered considerable concentration, predominantly in professional development- PD for teachers and educators. For language teachers who face unique and evolving challenges in all aspects of their teaching activities, the promise of AI-driven solutions offers stirring opportunities to enhance and improve their skills and effectiveness (Papagiannidis & Davlembayeva, 2022). The assimilation of AI into educational practices is not merely a trend following the other technology-based corporations of the modern world but a significant shift that offers unprecedented opportunities for growth and efficiency in language instruction in academia (Karanikola & Panagiotopoulos, 2023)

Language teachers and instructors tasked with the dual challenge of delivering high-quality education and adapting to diverse student needs stand to benefit immensely from AI-driven tools, i.e., every single student's capacity to perceive a topic differs from each other. These modern technological tools promise to ensure professional development by providing personalized, data-driven insights and resources if their proper application can be ensured. AI systems can analyze teaching techniques and practices, identify areas for further improvement, and make the best suggestions for targeted interventions, empowering educators to refine their skills continuously (Y. Zhang et al., 2024). Moreover, AI can ensure more time by simplifying administrative tasks, allowing teachers to focus more on pedagogical advancements and student engagement to establish quality education in language learning fields, which ultimately helps in their professional development (Mohammed Taher Qutub et al., 2023).

Professional development of language teachers is an inevitable part of ensuring high-quality education. It eradicates fossilization and helps teachers perceive and practice teaching activities from different angles, which ultimately helps the students learn the context quickly and successfully (Dhiraj & Kumar, 2023). Language teachers always play a pivotal role in fostering communication skills, cultural understanding, and critical thinking among students; they face distinct challenges, i.e., the need for continuous updates on best practices, practical strategies for diverse learner needs, and the integration of new technologies into their teaching methods (Kohnke et al., 2023). By tradition, PD has focused on enhancing teachers' instructional practices, updating their subject knowledge, improving their way of handling new generations, coping with new challenges and situations, and equipping them with new pedagogical strategies (Wilson, 2005).

However, conventional methods practiced by language teachers often face limitations, for example, one-size-fits-all approaches, insufficient personalization, and a lack of real-time feedback (Knezek & Christensen, 2014). As the education landscape evolves and develops, so must the methods and tools used for professional growth in the language teaching system. AI technologies encompass a range of technologies that mimic human cognitive functions, i.e., learning, reasoning, and problem-solving (ADEA et al., 2006). Their capacity for personalization, adaptability, and real-time analysis presents a transformative potential in addressing these new and ever-changing challenges and ultimately helping the language teachers in the PD (Soelistiono & Wahidin, 2023). In the tertiary level educational sector, AI applications include adaptive learning systems, natural language processing tools, intelligent tutoring systems, personalized learning experiences, automate administrative tasks, and offer detailed feedback on teaching practices, all of which offer innovative ways to support both learners and educators in the whole journey helping teachers refine their practices and stay current with educational trends (Dede, 2009).

The relevance of this topic is underscored by the increasing adoption of AI technologies in educational settings and the growing need for effective and adaptable professional development programs for language teachers in tertiary education (Ragas et al., 2024). As academic institutions and policymakers seek innovative solutions to enhance teaching quality and address the diverse needs of learners to ensure the best and quality education, AI offers a capable way of developing more dynamic and responsive PD programs. Understanding how AI can be leveraged effectively will be crucial in shaping the future of professional development and ensuring that language teachers are well-equipped, trained, and skilled to meet the demands of a rapidly evolving educational setting (Kabilan & Khan, 2012).

OBJECTIVES

This chapter aims to explore the integration of AI into PD for language teachers by examining its applications, benefits, and challenges. It will explore how AI technologies enhance PD and how these tools impact teachers' professional growth and instructional practices. Key objectives of this chapter include:

1. To explore how AI tools and technologies are reshaping professional development, including adaptive learning systems, intelligent feedback mechanisms, and virtual simulations.
2. To understand how AI contributes to personalized learning experiences, real-time feedback, and innovative training methods, focusing on how these benefits are particularly relevant to language teachers.
3. To discover the challenges associated with AI integration, including equity, teacher perceptions, data privacy, and ethical considerations.

LITERATURE REVIEW

This literature review examines current research and findings on how AI can enhance professional development for language teachers, focusing on its applications, benefits, challenges, and future directions. Recent advancements in AI have led to the development of sophisticated tools and platforms that impact education (Talukder et al., 2025). AI technologies, including natural language processing (NLP), machine learning, and adaptive learning systems, are increasingly integrated into educational settings (Mejeh & Rehm, 2024). These technologies offer personalized learning experiences and real-time feedback, which can particularly benefit language teaching and learning. One of the primary applications of AI in education is personalized learning, which tailors educational content to the individual needs of learners (Graesser et al., 2022). For language teachers, personalized AI tools can provide customized training modules that address specific areas of improvement, such as language proficiency or pedagogical strategies. Research by (ADEA et al., 2006) highlights the effectiveness of adaptive learning systems in creating individualized professional development pathways for educators, enabling them to progress at their own pace and focus on their unique needs. AI-driven feedback systems are another critical part of teacher professional development. These systems use algorithms to analyze teaching practices and provide actionable feedback (Alam, 2023). For language teachers, AI tools can evaluate lesson delivery, language use, and student engagement, offering insights that are difficult to obtain through traditional methods. Studies by (Hooda et al., 2022) demonstrate that real-time feedback can significantly improve teaching practices and student outcomes, underscoring the value of AI in professional growth.

Virtual simulations powered by AI offer immersive training experiences for language teachers. These simulations can replicate classroom environments, allowing teachers to practice and refine their skills in a controlled setting (Mystakidis et al., 2021). AI-driven virtual simulations can enhance teachers' pedagogical skills and classroom management strategies by providing a safe space for experimentation and reflective practice. Several case studies illustrate the successful implementation of AI in professional development for language teachers. For instance, the work of (Huang et al., 2023) explores how AI-powered platforms have been used to deliver effective professional development programs for language educators in various educational contexts. These studies reveal that AI tools can support teachers in developing new instructional strategies, improving language skills, and engaging in continuous professional learning (Dieker et al., 2014).

Despite the benefits, integrating AI into professional development presents several challenges. Issues related to data privacy, algorithmic bias, and the need for robust technological infrastructure are critical concerns (Zawacki-Richter et al., 2019). Additionally, the effective use of AI tools requires educators to possess certain levels of digital literacy and adaptability (Meace-Williams, 2024). Addressing these challenges is essential for maximizing the potential of AI in enhancing professional development. Looking ahead, research suggests several promising directions for AI in professional development. Emerging trends include the development of more sophisticated AI algorithms that better understand and support teachers' pedagogical needs (Siemens, 2013). Additionally, integrating AI with other educational technologies, such as virtual reality and gamification, holds potential for creating more engaging and effective professional development experiences (Motz et al., 2018).

AI tools have the potential to facilitate collaboration among language teachers by connecting them through online communities and networks (Meletiou-Mavrotheris & Paparistodemou, 2024). Platforms utilizing AI can analyze teachers' interests and expertise to recommend relevant professional networks and collaborative opportunities. Studies such as those by (Lai & Cheong, 2022) highlight how AI can enhance professional learning communities by fostering communication and collaboration among educators across diverse contexts. AI tools can support reflective practice by analyzing teaching sessions and providing insights that help teachers reflect on their instructional strategies (Habibi et al., 2023). Technologies like video analysis and AI-driven observation tools can highlight areas for improvement and assist in developing self-awareness among language teachers. Research by (Koehler et al., 2013) emphasizes the role of AI in enhancing reflective practice through detailed feedback and guided reflections.

Ensuring that AI-driven professional development is equitable and accessible is crucial for its effectiveness (Menabò et al., 2022). AI systems must be designed to address diverse needs and contexts, avoiding biases that could exacerbate existing educational disparities. Literature by (Canella et al., 2025) discusses strategies for creating inclusive AI tools that accommodate different learning styles and support teachers from various backgrounds. Combining AI tools with traditional professional development methods can offer a blended approach that leverages both strengths (Pham & Vu, 2024). AI can complement face-to-face workshops, coaching, and mentoring by providing additional resources and support. Research (Teräs, 2016) explores how hybrid models integrating AI with conventional professional development can enhance teacher learning outcomes. Implementing AI in professional development depends significantly on teachers' perceptions and willingness to adopt these technologies (Chien et al., 2018). Understanding teachers' attitudes towards AI and addressing their concerns is vital for fostering acceptance and practical use. Studies by (Kumar, 2024b) provide insights into factors influencing teachers' readiness to embrace AI tools and strategies for overcoming resistance.

Evaluating the long-term impact of AI on professional development is essential for understanding its effectiveness and sustainability (Kumar et al., 2019). Longitudinal studies and impact assessments can provide valuable data on how AI influences teaching practices, professional growth, and student outcomes over time. Research by Anderson & Shattuck (2012) emphasizes the need for ongoing evaluation to ensure that AI tools continue to meet educators' evolving needs. Ethical considerations are crucial when deploying AI in professional development. Data privacy, consent, and the ethical use of algorithms need to be addressed to maintain trust and ensure responsible use (Cheng et al., 2024). Literature by Shrivastava & Shrivastava (2022) discusses ethical frameworks and guidelines for implementing AI in educational settings, emphasizing the importance of transparency and accountability.

The literature indicates that AI has significant potential to ensure long-term professional development for language teachers coping with the world, i.e., through personalized learning, enhanced feedback, and virtual simulations, AI tools can support educators in improving their skills and effectiveness. However, addressing challenges related to data privacy and technology adoption is crucial for successfully implementing AI-driven professional development, as there are chances of unethical use of the technologies. Future research should continue to explore innovative applications of AI and evaluate their impact on language teaching practices to keep up the progress.

THEORETICAL FRAMEWORK

AI literacy is "a set of competencies that enables individuals to evaluate AI technologies effectively," communicate and collaborate efficiently with Artificial Intelligence; and use AI as a tool online, at home, and in the workplace" (Long & Magerko, 2020). Teachers' AI literacy can be defined by the requisite knowledge and skills, the methods for collaboratively engaging with AI, and the capacity to assess the pedagogical and ethical implications of their AI integration endeavors while teaching. To frame AI literacy in educational contexts, Ng et al. proposed a four-dimensional framework of Teacher AI Literacy consisting of:

i. Knowing and understanding AI is foundational since teachers must comprehend fundamental AI concepts with enhanced AI familiarity.
ii. Applying AI applications is critical since teachers move beyond conceptual knowledge about AI to utilizing it in teaching practices and leveraging its potential to boost teaching and learning outcomes. According to Zhang et al. (2022), this domain is dominant among the four domains of teacher AI literacy.
iii. Evaluating AI application for the teacher's pedagogical utility, efficacy, and appropriateness becomes increasingly crucial as AI's role in pedagogy continues to evolve with the change of time and need. Teachers must utilize an essential lens to look at the potential and limits of AI implementation.
iv. AI ethics involves teachers contemplating aligning AI integration in teaching with ethical standards and educational values by considering issues, i.e., AI bias, student privacy, equity and fairness, and the broader ramifications of AI technologies.

Figure 1. Four domains of teacher AI literacy

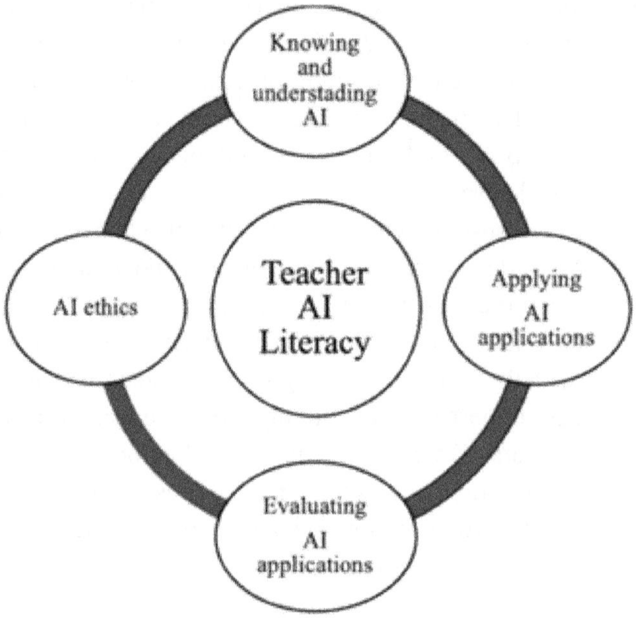

Source: Authors compiled based on (J. Zhang & Zhang, 2024)

AI in Education and Language Teaching

As with any other area of human life, the current state of foreign language education has greatly been influenced by the blessings of modern information communication technologies. (Crompton et al., 2024) define AI "as computer systems that have been designed to interact with the world through capabilities (i.e., visual perception and speech recognition) and intelligent behaviors (i.e., assessing the available information and then accepting the most sensible action to achieve aimed goal) that we would think of as essentially human." These computer systems include a variety of technologies and methods, such as machine learning, adaptive learning, natural language processing, data mining, crowd-sourcing, neural networks, algorithms, etc. In the realm of education, AI offers the potential to personalize learning experiences, enhance teaching methods, and streamline administrative tasks, i.e., Intelligent Tutoring Systems (ITS) leverage AI to provide tailored educational support, adapting to individual students' needs and improving learning outcomes (VanLEHN, 2011). These systems adapt to individual learning styles and needs, providing customized feedback and support according to the need (Tosuntaş et al., 2019), i.e., platforms like Carnegie Learning's MATHia software use AI to tailor math instruction based on a student's strengths and weaknesses (Pajares, 1992). Teachers who teach language for specific purposes can use this tool, MATHia, to speed up learning activities, which will help them become more skilled and accepted. Along with MALL, CMC, e-learning, web learning, and the application of AI-powered tools into foreign language teaching, FLT is a subset of computer-assisted language learning called CALL.

The shift from CALL to ICALL (Intelligent CALL) has been inevitable and substantially transformed student-computer interaction quality (Chinnasamy et al., 2025).

Furthermore, AI-driven tools can assist language teachers with professional development by offering data-driven actionable insights for improvement and recommendations by applying different statistical and analytical technologies for improving teaching practices based on the need and time (Wang, 2022). Tools like TeachFX use speech recognition technology to analyze classroom discussions and provide feedback on teaching effectiveness. All these help teachers reflect on their instructional methods and adapt their strategies to support student learning better.

Moreover, AI facilitates the creation of personalized learning paths for teachers, i.e., platforms like Coursera and edX use recommendation algorithms to suggest relevant courses and resources based on educators' interests and professional goals to enhance their development and keep up progress (Conklin, 2016). Additionally, AI technologies help automate administrative tasks such as grading and scheduling, keeping records, creating content, and providing them to students on time. For example, automated essay scoring systems use natural language processing techniques to evaluate and grade student essays, saving educators time and providing consistent assessments (Attali & Burstein, 2004).

AI-Powered Professional Development Tools

Language teachers need to be AI-literate to ensure effective classroom integration of AI, i.e., encompassing understanding, utilizing, monitoring, and critically reflecting on AI applications in teaching. According to a report by Education Week, 45% of teachers and language teachers feel uncomfortable with integrating AI technology because of teachers' lack of AI literacy and the practical knowledge of how AI tools can be effectively integrated into classrooms. To address PD needs, focusing on designing and providing a meaningful and content-specific teacher AI PD that enhances teachers' fundamental understanding of AI literacy as well as AI integration practices is very much essential at this moment.

Personalized Learning Platforms

Personalized learning platforms are educational technologies designed to tailor the learning experience to individual student's needs, preferences, and learning styles using data and analytics to create customized learning paths, adapt instructional content, and provide targeted feedback to optimize learning outcomes. It often employs algorithms to adjust the difficulty and type of content based on student performance and uses adaptive learning technologies to modify lessons in real-time (Walkington, 2013). Platforms like Khan Academy and Coursera allow students to follow custom-made learning paths that align with their interests and skill levels, providing a more engaging and practical learning experience (Rana et al., 2024). Insights derived from this data can help educators identify learning gaps and tailor instruction accordingly (Kumar, 2024a).

DreamBox: While Dream Box is primarily a math-focused adaptive learning platform, language teachers can leverage its principles for professional development by studying its adaptive learning technology, which personalizes instruction based on student responses (Talukder et al., 2025). This can help teachers understand how to apply adaptive learning strategies in language instruction, use data-driven insights to track and address student progress, and create engaging, interactive content inspired by DreamBox's approach. Additionally, participating in DreamBox's professional learning communities can offer valuable cross-disciplinary insights and strategies that language educators can adapt to enhance their teaching practices.

Khan Academy: Khan Academy, known for its extensive resources across various subjects, can be a valuable tool for language teachers' professional development in several ways. First, Khan Academy offers multiple instructional videos and practice exercises to help teachers explore effective teaching strategies and content delivery methods (Khan et al., 2019). Language teachers can gain insights into creating engaging and effective lessons by engaging with Khan Academy's well-structured and visually appealing materials. Additionally, Khan Academy's data analytics tools provide a model for tracking student progress and tailoring instruction to meet individual needs, which can be adapted to language teaching. Furthermore, Khan Academy's professional development resources and educator communities offer opportunities for language teachers to collaborate with peers, share best practices, and stay updated on the latest educational strategies and technologies.

Coursera: Coursera, a distance learning tool, significantly supports the PD of language teachers by offering a diverse range of high-quality online courses and specializations from top universities and institutions worldwide (Ayoub et al., 2020). Teachers can choose programs like modern language teaching methodologies, technology integration, and assessment strategies, providing flexible learning opportunities that fit their schedules (Nguyen, 2022). Courses like TESOL/TEFL certifications and specializations in Second Language Acquisition- SLA not only enhance teaching skills but also offer practical applications through assignments and peer reviews within a specific time limit (Kabilan & Khan, 2012). Additionally, Coursera facilitates networking and career advancement by connecting educators globally and providing credentials that bolster professional profiles, ultimately resulting in their Professional Development and Growth (Voudoukis & Pagiatakis, 2022).

Challenges and Considerations

- **Privacy and Data Security:** In each step of the teaching journey, a teacher must deal with sensitive information like question papers, grades and marks, and even the personal information of some needy students. Handling sensitive student data requires robust privacy measures to protect against breaches and misuse (Rubinstein & Good, 2013). Teachers must be conscientious about their ethics and rules to ensure privacy. Besides, there is a question of AI ethics that teachers must practice regularly. Otherwise, bringing professional development via AI would not be effective in the long run.
- **Equity and Access:** Ensuring all students have equal access to personalized learning technologies is crucial to preventing widening educational inequalities in a language teaching session (Gulati, 2008). Teachers frequently face this problem during distance learning in developing countries like Bangladesh, where students are not blessed with technological advancements equally due to economic issues. Consequently, the teacher must be professionally developed enough to ensure equity in teaching-learning. AI can be a way out of this problem for language teachers if they are efficient enough to apply it best.

AI-Enhanced Feedback Systems

AI-enhanced feedback systems provide real-time, automated feedback on various types of student work, from assignments and essays to projects and discussions on any topic. These systems analyze student inputs and generate personalized comments and suggestions for further improvement based on their need. Application of Intelligent Technology Enhanced Language Learning- ITELL is a blessing to academia, speeding up the process of adult learners' language learning along with the children.

- **Realtime Feedback:** AI systems can process and evaluate each student's work instantly, offering immediate personalized feedback using AI Algorithms to analyze learner responses that can help students correct mistakes and learn more effectively (Heffernan & Heffernan, 2014).
- **Consistency and Objectivity:** Unlike human graders or teachers, AI systems can provide consistent and unbiased evaluations and assessments, providing accurate and adaptive proficiency tracking, allowing for a more nuanced understanding of individual capabilities, which can help standardize feedback across diverse student groups (Chen et al., 2020).
- **Scalability:** AI feedback systems can simultaneously handle large volumes of student submissions, making them useful in large-scale educational settings (Munir et al., 2022). It helps save teacher's time and energy by providing them with more time to spend on other academic and professional activities.

Examples and Applications

- **Grammarly:** Uses AI to provide feedback on grammar, style, and readability of written text like research papers, articles, scripts, or any other discourses, saving time and maintaining the standard of education.
- **Turnitin:** Employs machine learning to assess the originality of student submissions and offer suggestions for improvement of their writing skill. Language teachers typically need to check the sign amount of writing. Turnitin helps them identify the use of Chatgpt or any other type of AI-instructed writing.

Challenges and Considerations

- **Accuracy of Feedback:** The study reveals that language teachers are using various free AI tools, i.e., Language Translator Services- LTS, Automated Writing Evaluation- AWE, Automated Error Detection- AED, Chatbots, Intelligent Tutoring System- ITS, and Web-based systems for language learning- WBS for their professional development and for making their job easy and accurate. The effectiveness of AI-generated feedback depends on the quality of the algorithms and training data. Inaccurate or overly generic feedback can hinder the learning system of any student (Giri, 2024).
- **Ethical Concerns:** The use of AI in education raises questions about the transparency and accountability of automated assessments due to systematic error and AI illiteracy of teachers.

Virtual Simulations and Training

Virtual simulations and training refer to using immersive digital environments to replicate real-world scenarios or realia for educational and training purposes. These simulations allow language teachers to practice skills, experiment with different strategies, and experience realistic situations without the risks associated with real-life practice. This virtual simulation is generally applied in Task Based Language Teaching- TBLT system to enhance the language learning procedure.

- **Immersive Learning:** Virtual simulations create a realistic learning environment where teachers can engage the learners in experiential learning. This can enhance understanding and retention of complex concepts of the learning process. It can also help the learner develop cognitive abilities, i.e., analyze context, situations, and environment, evaluate and synthesize information, and provide authentic experiences and higher engagement.
- **Safe Practice Environment:** Users can practice skills and make mistakes in a controlled setting, which is particularly valuable in high-stakes fields. Language teachers can create a situation, make learners solve it virtually, and ask them to present the whole thing via the target language. This can enhance language learning, and in this way, AI can help teachers in their PD.
- **Scalability and Flexibility:** Simulations can be scaled to accommodate large numbers of learners and can be accessed from various locations, offering flexibility in training (Aebersold & Dunbar, 2020). Webinars, instead of seminars, are becoming famous nowadays, helping professionals attend essential development training and discussions related to their field of interest via Zoom meetings, Google Meet, etc.

Challenges and Considerations

- **Cost and Complexity:** Developing high-quality virtual simulations can be expensive and technically complex, which may limit access for some institutions, especially in poor and developing countries. Besides, teachers who are going apply to the system need to be highly capable and qualified.
- **Effectiveness and Engagement:** Ensuring that simulations are engaging and educational requires careful design and ongoing evaluation, which is very important to get the ultimate result.

These elaborations illustrate a comprehensive look at personalized learning platforms, AI-enhanced feedback systems, and virtual simulations and training, offering insights into their definitions, features, applications, challenges, and constraints closely related to language teachers' professional development.

Integrating AI into Professional Development Programs

Designing AI-Infused Training Modules

AI-infused training modules weigh artificial intelligence to create dynamic and personalized professional development experiences for language teachers in different institutions. These modules integrate adaptive modern learning technologies, AI-driven material and content recommendations as per need, and intelligent feedback mechanisms to enhance training efficacy and development.

Key Components

- **Adaptive Learning Systems:** AI can tailor training modules to individual educators' needs by analyzing their performance and adjusting content accordingly. For example, platforms like Smart Sparrow and Carnegie Learning use adaptive algorithms to customize learning experiences.
- **Intelligent Content Delivery:** AI can help design content that adapts to educators' varying skill levels and learning paces. This ensures that training remains relevant and engaging.
- **Realtime Feedback and Analytics:** AI tools can provide instant feedback on educators' progress and performance during training, enabling them to make necessary adjustments and improvements.

Examples

- **Coursera for Educators:** This platform uses AI to recommend courses based on educators' interests and previous learning patterns, enhancing their professional growth.
- **Knewton:** Offers personalized learning experiences by analyzing educators' interactions and performance, helping identify areas for improvement.

Challenges

- **Complexity in Design:** Developing AI-infused training modules requires AI and instructional design expertise, which can be challenging.
- **Integration with Existing Systems:** Ensuring seamless integration with existing professional development frameworks can be complex and resource-intensive.

Professional Development Workshops and Courses

Concept: Professional development workshops and courses focused on AI provide educators with the skills and knowledge to integrate AI tools into their teaching practices. These sessions often include hands-on training, theoretical background, and practical applications.

Key Features

- **Hands-On Training:** Workshops typically include practical exercises where educators can interact with AI tools and technologies. For instance, workshops might involve using AI-driven analytics platforms or developing lesson plans with AI support.
- **Theoretical Background:** Educators receive foundational knowledge about AI technologies, including their potential applications and limitations in educational contexts.
- **Collaborative Learning:** Workshops often promote collaborative learning environments where educators can share experiences, challenges, and strategies related to AI integration.

Examples

- **AI in Education Workshops by EdTech Companies:** Companies like IBM and Google offer workshops designed to familiarize educators with AI tools and their applications in the classroom.

- **Online Courses on AI for Educators:** Platforms like edX and Coursera provide specialized courses on AI in education, including topics like AI ethics, practical implementations, and the future of AI in teaching.

Challenges

- **Keeping Up with Rapid Changes:** The rapid pace of AI development means that professional development programs must continuously update their content to stay relevant.
- **Varied Skill Levels:** Educators come with varying levels of familiarity with technology, requiring differentiated instruction within workshops.

Best Practices for AI Integration

Concept: Integrating AI into professional development programs requires adherence to best practices to ensure effectiveness and sustainability. These practices encompass designing user-friendly systems, providing ongoing support, and evaluating the impact of AI tools.

Best Practices

- **User-Centric Design:** Ensure that AI tools are designed with the end-user in mind, focusing on ease of use and alignment with educators' needs.
- **Ongoing Support and Training:** Provide continuous support and additional training opportunities to help educators adapt to new AI tools and technologies.
- **Evaluation and Feedback:** Regularly evaluate the effectiveness of AI tools and professional development programs, using feedback to make iterative improvements.

Examples

- **Iterative Design and Testing:** Regularly update AI tools based on educator feedback and emerging best practices to ensure they remain adequate and relevant.
- **Dedicated Support Teams:** Establish support teams or helpdesks to assist educators with troubleshooting and integrating AI tools into their practices.

Challenges

- **Balancing Innovation with Practicality:** Ensuring that AI tools are innovative yet practical for everyday use in educational settings.
- **Maintaining Engagement:** Keeping educators engaged with AI tools and ensuring they are used effectively in the classroom.

Facilitating Effect Assessment, Case Studies, and Success Stories

The aforementioned enabling paths and techniques were chosen for case analysis in this study to confirm their efficacy through data gathering and analysis, questionnaire surveys, and comparison experiments. The findings demonstrate that language teachers' professional quality and teaching ability have significantly improved following their training and education in AI technology. Concurrently, the AI-based teaching platform offers teachers more practical and effective teaching resources. We can consider the following factors to assess how AI empowers language teachers' PD fully; enhancement of teaching efficiency is evident when contrasting the learning outcomes and progress before and after the implementation of AI technology. AI solutions can assist educators in creating lesson plans, streamlining instruction, and swiftly modifying tactics in the classroom to enhance both the effectiveness and caliber of instruction. Improvement in the capacity for individualized instruction: AI can offer educators options for individualized instruction based on their students' needs, classroom circumstances, and the overall environmental context of learning.

The degree to which teachers' individualized teaching abilities have improved can be evaluated by comparing their instructional styles with the learning outcomes of their students before and after employment. Improvement of teachers' information literacy: As AI technology is introduced, teachers must possess a specific level of information literacy. It is feasible to assess if teachers' information literacy has improved by looking at their ability to use AI technologies, problem-solving skills, and creative thinking. Increasing the level of satisfaction among students is one of the critical metrics for assessing the impact of instruction is student satisfaction. To determine whether students have acknowledged the empowering effect, we will gather student feedback on teachers' usage of artificial intelligence instruction through questionnaire surveys, interviews, and other methods.

Case Study

A specific case study demonstrates how AI can support foreign language teachers' professional development: A college of foreign languages studies established an intelligent teaching aid system. It offers students individualized oral practice and feedback according to their speaking level and learning objectives. Foreign language instructors discovered that after utilizing the approach, the student's oral expression skills had significantly increased, and they had also gained more expertise in individualized instruction. Comparing the students' oral performance before and after employing the intelligent teaching aid system, the college discovered that the average score of the students had significantly improved in assessing the effect of empowerment. Furthermore, educators reported that implementing the system had increased their effectiveness in the classroom and made it simpler to pique students' curiosity and excitement.

This example demonstrates how using artificial intelligence technologies in foreign language instruction may significantly enhance the instruction's effectiveness and the teachers' caliber. With intelligent teaching technologies, educators can better address their students' individualized needs and improve their instruction's effectiveness and caliber, thereby realizing the empowerment of their professional development. We can observe the beneficial impact of artificial intelligence in the professional development of foreign language teachers by evaluating the effect of empowerment and conducting case analyses. In the future, artificial intelligence will present more opportunities and obstacles to the professional development of foreign language teachers due to the ongoing advancement of technology and the ongoing expansion of application scenarios.

Successful Implementations of AI in Teacher Training

AI-Driven Professional Development Platforms: AI-powered platforms like Coursera and edX have transformed teacher professional development by offering personalized learning experiences. For instance, Coursera's AI-based recommendation system suggests courses based on a teacher's previous activities and interests. According to a study by Zhang et al. (2022), AI-enhanced platforms can increase engagement and completion rates by tailoring content to individual learning needs.

Intelligent Tutoring Systems: One notable example is using intelligent tutoring systems (ITS) in teacher training. The MATHia software, developed by Carnegie Learning, is an ITS that provides real-time feedback and personalized instruction to teachers learning new pedagogical strategies.

Virtual Reality (VR) and Augmented Reality (AR): VR and AR technologies powered by AI have created immersive teacher training environments. For example, the Teach Live project uses virtual avatars to simulate classroom scenarios for teacher trainees. VR training environments can significantly enhance teachers' ability to manage classroom dynamics and implement new teaching techniques.

Teacher Testimonials and Experiences

Personalized Learning: Teachers who have used AI-based platforms for professional development often cite customized learning experiences as a critical benefit. For instance, Ms. Sarah Johnson, a high school teacher from New York, shared in a testimonial that AI-driven recommendations on platforms like Coursera helped her find courses that specifically addressed her needs for differentiated instruction.

Enhanced Feedback and Support: Dr. Alex Patel, an elementary school teacher, praised the real-time feedback provided by AI tools. According to Patel, "The immediate insights from AI tools have been invaluable in helping me adjust my teaching methods on the fly and improve student outcomes.

Practical Challenges and Adaptation: While AI tools have been beneficial, some teachers, like Ms. Emily Thompson from California, noted challenges in adapting to new technologies. Thompson mentioned that while AI tools offer great potential, learning curves, and initial resistance need to be addressed through proper training and support.

Future Directions and Considerations

Emerging Trends in AI for Education

Adaptive Learning Technologies: Adaptive learning technologies powered by AI are poised to become more prevalent. These systems adjust the difficulty of content in real-time based on student performance. For example, DreamBox Learning uses adaptive algorithms to tailor math instruction to individual students' needs.

AI-Enhanced Administrative Tools: AI also improves administrative tasks through automation and predictive analytics. For instance, AI-driven tools like TeacherMatch streamline recruitment by analyzing candidates' data to predict their suitability for specific roles.

Collaborative AI Learning Environments: The development of AI-powered collaborative learning environments is another emerging trend. Platforms like Google Classroom now incorporate AI to facilitate collaborative projects and peer assessments.

Ethical and Practical Considerations

Data Privacy and Security: As AI systems increasingly collect and analyze educational data, ensuring data privacy and security becomes crucial. Implementing robust data protection measures and compliance with regulations like GDPR and FERPA is essential.

Bias and Equity: AI systems can inadvertently perpetuate biases present in training data. Ensuring that AI tools are designed to minimize bias and promote equity is a critical concern.

Teacher Training and Support: Effective implementation of AI in education requires adequate training and support for teachers. The International Society for Technology in Education (ISTE) emphasizes the need for comprehensive professional development programs to help educators effectively integrate AI tools into their teaching practices. Technology has the potential to be a powerful catalyst for advancing gender equity in the global hotel industry. By leveraging innovative solutions and embracing digital transformation, hospitality businesses can create more inclusive and diverse work environments that benefit employees, guests, and the bottom line. However, addressing gender disparities requires a holistic and collaborative approach beyond technology alone. By working together and committing to meaningful change, the hotel industry can drive a positive and lasting impact for future generations.

The Integration of AI in FLT

Teaching foreign languages in colleges and universities has undergone radical transformation due to the advancement of artificial intelligence (AI) technology. AI can help teachers in the classroom and increase students' learning efficiency through intelligent Automatic Speech Recognition (ASR), natural language processing, and other technologies. In addition, foreign language instructors can benefit from rich educational materials and online learning environments offered by AI technology, which can help them stay current and advance their professional development. One significant development in education in recent years is the integration of AI with college-level foreign language instruction. Along with many new prospects, this integration presents several difficulties for university foreign language instruction.

First of all, the introduction of AI technology has greatly enriched foreign language teaching resources. By utilizing big data, machine learning, and other technologies, AI can analyze students' learning behaviors and habits to provide personalized learning paths and feedback for each student. This customized learning experience helps students learn a foreign language more efficiently and effectively. Second, using AI in foreign language instruction has made new teaching techniques possible. Chatbots, for instance, can mimic natural language settings, allowing students to practice oral communication while conversing with robots. Simultaneously, the intelligent tutoring system can improve the learning experience by giving students role-playing tasks to practice in an immersive setting. Nonetheless, assistance is also required to integrate AI and foreign language instruction in educational institutions.

On the one hand, teachers must adjust to the changes brought about by new technologies and acquire the skills necessary to employ AI tools in the classroom appropriately. This can necessitate that educators receive pertinent training and raise their level of information technology literacy. However, another issue that must be thoroughly discussed is balancing teachers' and AI's auxiliary teaching roles. AI can offer a wealth of knowledge and learning opportunities; however, humanistic care, motivation, and appropriate teacher recommendations are essential to teaching foreign languages. There are also ethical and societal considerations that must be taken into account when integrating AI with foreign language instruction in higher education. For instance, how to safeguard student data security and privacy to prevent AI from being abused for unfair evaluation.

In summary, there are many potential difficulties in integrating AI with college foreign language instruction. We can investigate a more successful integration method and bring fresh energy to advancing college foreign language instruction through in-depth research and practice.

A Comprehensive Review of the Current State of Foreign Language Instructors' Professional Development at Universities

A comprehensive review of the current state of foreign language instructors' professional development at universities reveals both possibilities and problems. From an opportunity standpoint, the importance and demand for foreign language education are continually rising due to the acceleration of globalization and the rapid development of information technology. This gives foreign language teachers in colleges and universities more room to grow and more opportunities for professional development. Concurrently, there has been strong policy support for foreign language teachers' professional development due to the intensifying education reform. From a challenge standpoint, professional development remains difficult for foreign language instructors at colleges and universities. Some educators lack the drive and initiative to pursue their professional growth because they do not have a strong sense of it.

The professional development of foreign language instructors has also not been given enough attention by some local colleges and universities. This underfunding results in a shortage of resources and support for teachers' professional growth. Furthermore, there is a need to enhance teachers' teaching abilities and professional quality significantly. Even though many instructors hold advanced degrees and have a wealth of teaching experience, they still require updating and upgrading their interdisciplinary knowledge, teaching strategies, and teaching tools. It is necessary to improve many teachers' capacity to embrace and implement new models and technologies, particularly in light of AI. Furthermore, there is growing competition among foreign language teachers in their field. Institutions have added top-notch foreign instructors to attract more students and offered reliable testing and certification services in tandem with the market's ongoing growth and diversification.

To meet the demands of the market and the competition, foreign language instructors at colleges and universities must constantly enhance their professional standards and methods of instruction. In summary, there are possibilities and problems for foreign language teachers in higher education regarding their professional growth. Teachers must actively seek out chances and tools for professional growth and maintain a constant state of self-improvement awareness. Schools and society should also support teachers' professional development to jointly foster the prosperity and development of foreign language education.

Artificial Intelligence-Enabled Pathways and Tactics for the Professional Development of Foreign Language Instructors

Artificial intelligence-enabled pathways and tactics for the professional development of foreign language instructors suggest the following approaches and tactics: It is essential to improve teachers' information technology training first and foremost. To flexibly use AI technology in the classroom, foreign language instructors in colleges and universities must become proficient in its core concepts, familiarize themselves with frequently used intelligent teaching tools, and grasp essential technologies such as machine learning and data analysis. Teachers can use methodical training to enhance their ability to comprehend and utilize AI technology. Second, creating an intelligent learning environment is a crucial component. Universities should use AI technologies to develop innovative environments for teaching foreign languages. For instance, adaptive learning systems give students individualized learning routes and resources, and intelligent voice technology is used to achieve real-time translation and vocal evaluation. Students' interest in learning is piqued, and their learning efficiency is enhanced in this learning environment.

Thirdly, using intelligent feedback and assessment is a practical way to raise the caliber of instruction. AI technology can measure student learning outcomes in real-time and give teachers feedback and suggestions. Teachers can better grasp the learning circumstances of their students and modify their approach to teaching in real time to enhance student outcomes using the intelligent evaluation system. Fourth, encouraging the wise use of instructional resources is another essential step toward increasing the effectiveness of foreign language instruction in colleges. AI technology can manage teaching resources intelligently and distribute and share resources appropriately. This can increase the effectiveness of resources and give teachers access to new cases and instructional materials to enhance their lesson plans. Lastly, enhancing international collaboration and exchanges is a crucial strategy for advancing foreign language instructors' career advancement. Universities can collaborate with businesses and research centers to create intelligent learning platforms and tools to support AI's full integration with foreign language instruction. Simultaneously, we ought to fortify global collaboration and exchanges, include advanced foreign intelligent teaching theories and practices, and offer additional assistance for professional growth for foreign language instructors.

In conclusion, there are a variety of avenues and approaches for the professional development of AI-enabled foreign language teachers. It is imperative, therefore, to enhance teacher preparation, create an intelligent learning environment, implement intelligent evaluation and feedback, encourage the thoughtful use of teaching resources, and foster cross-border collaboration and exchange. These steps will support innovation and growth in foreign language education while raising the professional caliber and teaching proficiency of college instructors of foreign languages.

RECOMMENDATIONS

Educational institutions in Bangladesh should strategically integrate adaptive learning technologies, AI-driven professional development tools, and AI-enhanced administrative systems to achieve academic outcomes and operational efficiency as soon as possible. By implementing adaptive learning technologies, educational institutions can offer personalized learning experiences that cater to individual student needs, improving engagement and achievement and ultimately bringing teachers professional development.

Additionally, investing in AI-powered professional development platforms, like Coursera and TeachFX, can provide language teachers with personalized learning opportunities based on their individual needs and interests and relevant feedback, ultimately refining their skills and teaching practices. Adopting AI-driven administrative tools for tasks, i.e., listing, analyzing, categorizing, grading, and scheduling, can lessen administrative burdens, allowing teachers to concentrate more on teaching and research work.

However, addressing ethical and equity concerns is imperative by ensuring robust data privacy, security, and bias minimization in AI systems to protect student data and promote fairness in the academic sector and teaching profession; Electronic Frontier Foundation. Finally, ongoing PD and support are essential to help teachers effectively incorporate these AI tools into their teaching practices, ensuring they are well-resourced to weigh modern technology's benefits while maintaining high educational standards.

CONCLUSION

This study demonstrates that applying AI technologies strongly supports language teacher's PD. Artificial intelligence has made it possible for foreign language teachers to strengthen their careers, and this development has given FLT brand new life and innovation. Foreign language teachers can effectively enhance their professional excellence and teaching abilities by conducting need-based research, establishing intelligent teaching platforms as required, and developing skill-based technical training. However, some primary constraints still need to be solved, i.e., building a strong teacher preparation program and effectively incorporating AI technology into teaching foreign languages. To begin with, applying AI technology in the classroom offers foreign language teachers a wealth of resources and personalized teaching instruments to help them better achieve students' learning objectives and enhance their teaching performance professionally and academically. Then, teachers can better determine students' learning situations, modify their pedagogical approaches as required, and provide appropriate instruction through AI's intelligent evaluation and feedback mechanism. Simultaneously, AI fosters collaboration and communication among teachers and the sharing and efficient distribution of instructional materials and teaching types of equipment.

Furthermore, language teachers actively adjust to the challenges posed by AI and continuously enhance their information literacy and technological application skills as per the update. Teachers acquired the ability to use AI tools through training, self-directed study, and hands-on experience to develop their much-needed AI literacy. The language teachers then integrated their AI skills into their regular teaching practices to create innovative lesson plans and enhance instruction in their academic field. In conclusion, AI-enabled language teacher professional development has gained popularity and is reviving the field of language education's creativity and advancement with the developing world and everything.

REFERENCES

Aebersold, M., & Dunbar, D.-M. (2020). Virtual and Augmented Realities in Nursing Education: State of the Science. *Annual Review of Nursing Research, 39*(1), 225–242. DOI: 10.1891/0739-6686.39.225 PMID: 33431644

Alam, A. (2023). Data-Driven Instructional Practices: Using Behavior Detection and Model Assignment Techniques to Inform Teaching Strategies for School Education. *2023 International Conference on Quantum Technologies, Communications, Computing, Hardware and Embedded Systems Security (iQ-CCHESS)*, 1–8. DOI: 10.1109/iQ-CCHESS56596.2023.10391777

Anderson, T., & Shattuck, J. (2012). Design-Based Research: A Decade of Progress in Education Research? *Educational Researcher, 41*(1), 16–25. DOI: 10.3102/0013189X11428813

Attali, Y., & Burstein, J. (2004). Automated Essay Scoring With E-Rater® V.2.0. *ETS Research Report Series, 2004*(2). DOI: 10.1002/j.2333-8504.2004.tb01972.x

Ayoub, A., Amin, R., & Wani, Z. A. (2020). Contribution of developed countries towards MOOCs: An exploration and assessment from a representative platform Coursera. *Asian Association of Open Universities Journal, 15*(2), 251–262. DOI: 10.1108/AAOUJ-03-2020-0016

Canella, V. B., D, M., Batista, A. G. C., & N. A., Aacute, N. A., D, U. S. T., Sousa, E., Rocha, M. L. S., & Canella, L. B. (. (2025). Necessary skills for teachers towards digital information and communication technologies in the current era. *International Journal of Education Economics and Development, 16*(1/2), 62–77. DOI: 10.1504/IJEED.2025.143605

Chen, L., Chen, P., & Lin, Z. (2020). Artificial Intelligence in Education: A Review. *IEEE Access : Practical Innovations, Open Solutions, 8*, 75264–75278. DOI: 10.1109/ACCESS.2020.2988510

Cheng, L., Han, J., & Nasirov, J. (2024). Ethical considerations related to personal data collection and reuse: Trust and transparency in language and speech technologies. *International Journal of Legal Discourse, 9*(2), 217–235. DOI: 10.1515/ijld-2024-2010

Chien, S.-P., Wu, H.-K., & Wu, P.-H. (2018). Teachers' Beliefs About, Attitudes Toward, and Intention to Use Technology-Based Assessments: A Structural Equation Modeling Approach. *Eurasia Journal of Mathematics, Science and Technology Education, 14*(10). Advance online publication. DOI: 10.29333/ejmste/93379

Chinnasamy, P., Rani, R. M., Ayyasamy, R. K., Sujithra, L. R., Mounika, T., & Cherukuvada, S. (2025). Transforming Education With AI-Driven Intelligent Tutoring Systems: In T. Murugan, K. P., & A. M. Abirami (Eds.), *Driving Quality Education Through AI and Data Science* (pp. 239–258). IGI Global. DOI: 10.4018/979-8-3693-8292-9.ch011

Crompton, H., Edmett, A., Ichaporia, N., & Burke, D. (2024). AI and English language teaching: Affordances and challenges. *British Journal of Educational Technology, 55*(6), 2503–2529. DOI: 10.1111/bjet.13460

Dede, C. (2009). Immersive Interfaces for Engagement and Learning. *Science, 323*(5910), 66–69. DOI: 10.1126/science.1167311 PMID: 19119219

Dhiraj, A., & Kumar, P. D. S. (2023). Impact of E-learning on the Higher Education Sector during the COVID-19 pandemic through Pedagogy tools: An observational Study. *Revista de Educación y Derecho, 27*(27). Advance online publication. DOI: 10.1344/REYD2023.27.40935

Dieker, L. A., & Rodriguez, J. A., Lignugaris/Kraft, B., Hynes, M. C., & Hughes, C. E. (. (2014). The Potential of Simulated Environments in Teacher Education: Current and Future Possibilities. *Teacher Education and Special Education: The Journal of the Teacher Education Division of the Council for Exceptional Children, 37*(1), 21–33. DOI: 10.1177/0888406413512683

Giri, A. (2024). Revolutionizing Student Evaluation: The Power of AI-Powered Assessment. In Moreira, F. T., & Teles, R. O. (Eds.), (pp. 333–362). Advances in Educational Technologies and Instructional Design. IGI Global., DOI: 10.4018/979-8-3693-6170-2.ch012

Graesser, A. C., Sabatini, J. P., & Li, H. (2022). Educational Psychology Is Evolving to Accommodate Technology, Multiple Disciplines, and Twenty-First-Century Skills. *Annual Review of Psychology, 73*(1), 547–574. DOI: 10.1146/annurev-psych-020821-113042 PMID: 34587781

Gulati, S. (2008). Technology-Enhanced Learning in Developing Nations: A review. *International Review of Research in Open and Distance Learning, 9*(1). Advance online publication. DOI: 10.19173/irrodl.v9i1.477

Habibi, A., Riady, Y., Samed Al-Adwan, A., & Awni Albelbisi, N. (2023). Beliefs and Knowledge for Pre-Service Teachers' Technology Integration during Teaching Practice: An Extended Theory of Planned Behavior. *Computers in the Schools, 40*(2), 107–132. DOI: 10.1080/07380569.2022.2124752

Hendricson, W. D., Andrieu, S. C., Chadwick, D. G., Chmar, J. E., Cole, J. R., George, M. C., Glickman, G. N., Glover, J. F., Goldberg, J. S., Haden, N. K., Meyerowitz, C., Neumann, L., Pyle, M., Tedesco, L. A., Valachovic, R. W., Weaver, R. G., Winder, R. L., Young, S. K., & Kalkwarf, K. L.ADEA Commission on Change and Innovation in Dental Education. (2006). Educational Strategies Associated with Development of Problem-Solving, Critical Thinking, and Self-Directed Learning. *Journal of Dental Education, 70*(9), 925–936. DOI: 10.1002/j.0022-0337.2006.70.9.tb04163.x PMID: 16954414

Hooda, M., Rana, C., Dahiya, O., Rizwan, A., & Hossain, M. S. (2022). Artificial Intelligence for Assessment and Feedback to Enhance Student Success in Higher Education. *Mathematical Problems in Engineering, 2022*, 1–19. DOI: 10.1155/2022/5215722

Huang, Y., Richter, E., Kleickmann, T., & Richter, D. (2023). Virtual Reality in Teacher Education from 2010 to 2020: A Review of Program Implementation, Intended Outcomes, and Effectiveness Measures. In Scheiter, K., & Gogolin, I. (Eds.), *Bildung für eine digitale Zukunft* (Vol. 15, pp. 399–441). Springer Fachmedien Wiesbaden., DOI: 10.1007/978-3-658-37895-0_16

Kabilan, M. K., & Khan, M. A. (2012). Assessing pre-service English language teachers' learning using e-portfolios: Benefits, challenges and competencies gained. *Computers & Education, 58*(4), 1007–1020. DOI: 10.1016/j.compedu.2011.11.011

Karanikola, Z., & Panagiotopoulos, G. (2023). Adult Education and Globally Engaged Trainers: The Case of Vocational Training Institutes. *Education Sciences, 13*(4), 362. DOI: 10.3390/educsci13040362

Khan, A., Khan, S., & Turi, S. (2019). An exploratory study focusing on teaching and learning practices at the tertiary level in Pakistan: A case study of a public sector university. *International Journal of Educational Development, 65*, 106–114. DOI: 10.1016/j.ijedudev.2017.08.008

Knezek, G. A., & Christensen, R. (2014). Tools for Analyzing Quantitative Data. In Spector, J. M., Merrill, M. D., Elen, J., & Bishop, M. J. (Eds.), *Handbook of Research on Educational Communications and Technology* (pp. 203–220). Springer New York., DOI: 10.1007/978-1-4614-3185-5_17

Koehler, M. J., Mishra, P., & Cain, W. (2013). What is Technological Pedagogical Content Knowledge (TPACK)? *Journal of Education, 193*(3), 13–19. DOI: 10.1177/002205741319300303

Kohnke, L., Moorhouse, B. L., & Zou, D. (2023). ChatGPT for language teaching and learning. *RELC Journal*, •••, 00336882231162868.

Kumar, S. (2024a). Impact of Assessment on Childhood Education Theories and Practice. In Badea, M., & Suditu, M. (Eds.), *Advances in Early Childhood and K-12 Education* (pp. 84–101). IGI Global., DOI: 10.4018/979-8-3693-0956-8.ch004

Kumar, S. (2024b). The Role of Digital Marketing on Customer Engagement in the Hospitality Industry. In Bansal, R., Ngah, A. H., Chakir, A., & Pruthi, N. (Eds.), (pp. 177–191). Advances in Business Information Systems and Analytics. IGI Global., DOI: 10.4018/979-8-3693-0815-8.ch010

Lai, J. W., & Cheong, K. H. (2022). Educational Opportunities and Challenges in Augmented Reality: Featuring Implementations in Physics Education. *IEEE Access : Practical Innovations, Open Solutions, 10*, 43143–43158. DOI: 10.1109/ACCESS.2022.3166478

Long, D., & Magerko, B. (2020). What is AI Literacy? Competencies and Design Considerations. *Proceedings of the 2020 CHI Conference on Human Factors in Computing Systems*, 1–16. DOI: 10.1145/3313831.3376727

Meace-Williams, S. (2024). *Conceptualising Welsh Secondary School Teachers' Pedagogic Use of Technology: A Case Study*. 5725652 Bytes. DOI: 10.25401/CARDIFFMET.26177323.V1

Mejeh, M., & Rehm, M. (2024). Taking adaptive learning in educational settings to the next level: Leveraging natural language processing for improved personalization. *Educational Technology Research and Development, 72*(3), 1597–1621. DOI: 10.1007/s11423-024-10345-1

Meletiou-Mavrotheris, M., & Paparistodemou, E. (2024). Sustaining Teacher Professional Learning in STEM: Lessons Learned from an 18-Year-Long Journey into TPACK-Guided Professional Development. *Education Sciences, 14*(4), 402. DOI: 10.3390/educsci14040402

Menabò, L., Skrzypiec, G., Sansavini, A., Brighi, A., & Guarini, A. (2022). Distance Education among Italian Teachers: Differences and Experiences. *Education and Information Technologies, 27*(7), 9263–9292. DOI: 10.1007/s10639-022-11008-5 PMID: 35370442

Mohammed Taher Qutub, M., Bukhari, S. S. F., Ali Fadel, S., & Sulaiman Abdulkader Aljuhan, H. (2023). The Future of English as a Foreign Language Teaching and Learning in View of the Fourth Industrial Revolution in the MENA Region. SSRN *Electronic Journal*. DOI: 10.2139/ssrn.4534567

Motz, B. A., Carvalho, P. F., De Leeuw, J. R., & Goldstone, R. L. (2018). Embedding Experiments: Staking Causal Inference in Authentic Educational Contexts. *Journal of Learning Analytics*, *5*(2). Advance online publication. DOI: 10.18608/jla.2018.52.4

Munir, H., Vogel, B., & Jacobsson, A. (2022). Artificial Intelligence and Machine Learning Approaches in Digital Education: A Systematic Revision. *Information (Basel)*, *13*(4), 203. DOI: 10.3390/info13040203

Mystakidis, S., Fragkaki, M., & Filippousis, G. (2021). Ready Teacher One: Virtual and Augmented Reality Online Professional Development for K-12 School Teachers. *Computers*, *10*(10), 134. DOI: 10.3390/computers10100134

Nguyen, L. Q. (2022). Learners' satisfaction of courses on Coursera as a massive open online course platform: A case study. *Frontiers in Education*, *7*, 1086170. DOI: 10.3389/feduc.2022.1086170

Pajares, M. F. (1992). Teachers' Beliefs and Educational Research: Cleaning Up a Messy Construct. *Review of Educational Research*, *62*(3), 307–332. DOI: 10.3102/00346543062003307

Papagiannidis, S., & Davlembayeva, D. (2022). Bringing Smart Home Technology to Peer-to-Peer Accommodation: Exploring the Drivers of Intention to Stay in Smart Accommodation. *Information Systems Frontiers*, *24*(4), 1189–1208. DOI: 10.1007/s10796-021-10227-4 PMID: 34899040

Pham, Q. H., & Vu, K. P. (2024). Leveraging lecturers' intelligence for student engagement enrichment in blended learning courses. *Cogent Education*, *11*(1), 2334930. DOI: 10.1080/2331186X.2024.2334930

Ragas, I. M., Pontillas, P. V., & Comon, J. D. (2024). Skills and Roles of Teachers in 21st Century Teaching: Basis for Professional Development Plan. *European Modern Studies Journal*, *8*(4), 344–370. DOI: 10.59573/emsj.8(4).2024.15

Rana, S., Sheshadri, T., Malhotra, N., & Mahabub Basha, S. (2024). Creating Digital Learning Environments: Tools and Technologies for Success. In Kumar, R., Ong, E. T., Anggoro, S., Toh, T. L., & Fukui, M. (Eds.), (pp. 1–21). Advances in Educational Technologies and Instructional Design. IGI Global., DOI: 10.4018/979-8-3693-8217-2.ch001

Shrivastava, S. K., & Shrivastava, C. (2022). The Impact of Digitalization in Higher Educational Institutions. [IJSCE]. *International Journal of Soft Computing and Engineering*, *11*(2), 7–11. DOI: 10.35940/ijsce.B3536.0111222

Siemens, G. (2013). Learning Analytics: The Emergence of a Discipline. *The American Behavioral Scientist*, *57*(10), 1380–1400. DOI: 10.1177/0002764213498851

Soelistiono, S. & Wahidin. (2023). Educational Technology Innovation: AI-Integrated Learning System Design in AILS-Based Education. *INFLUENCE: INTERNATIONAL JOURNAL OF SCIENCE REVIEW*, *5*(2), 470–480. DOI: 10.54783/influencejournal.v5i2.175

Talukder, M. B., Farhana, N., & Salsabil, I. T. (2025). Enhancing Tourism Through AI-Driven Professional Development of ESL Teachers in Bangladesh. In Ali, M. M., Anwar, M. N., Fazal, S., & Ayyaz, S. (Eds.), (pp. 195–222). Advances in Computational Intelligence and Robotics. IGI Global., DOI: 10.4018/979-8-3693-9077-1.ch009

Teräs, H. (2016). Collaborative online professional development for teachers in higher education. *Professional Development in Education*, *42*(2), 258–275. DOI: 10.1080/19415257.2014.961094

Tosuntaş, Ş. B., Çubukçu, Z., & İnci, T. (2019). A Holistic View to Barriers to Technology Integration in Education. *Turkish Online Journal of Qualitative Inquiry*, 349–371. DOI: 10.17569/tojqi.613969

VanLEHN, K. U. R. T.VanLEHN. (2011). The Relative Effectiveness of Human Tutoring, Intelligent Tutoring Systems, and Other Tutoring Systems. *Educational Psychologist*, *46*(4), 197–221. DOI: 10.1080/00461520.2011.611369

Voudoukis, N., & Pagiatakis, G. (2022). Massive Open Online Courses (MOOCs): Practices, Trends, and Challenges for the Higher Education. *European Journal of Education and Pedagogy*, *3*(3), 288–295. DOI: 10.24018/ejedu.2022.3.3.365

Walkington, C. A. (2013). Using adaptive learning technologies to personalize instruction to student interests: The impact of relevant contexts on performance and learning outcomes. *Journal of Educational Psychology*, *105*(4), 932–945. DOI: 10.1037/a0031882

Wang, H. (2022). An Analytical Study Based on Computer-Assisted Language Teaching. In Pei, Y., Chang, J.-W., & Hung, J. C. (Eds.), *Innovative Computing* (Vol. 935, pp. 897–902). Springer Nature Singapore., DOI: 10.1007/978-981-19-4132-0_118

Wilson, E. (2005). Powerful pedagogical strategies in initial teacher education. *Teachers and Teaching*, *11*(4), 359–378. DOI: 10.1080/13450600500137141

Zawacki-Richter, O., Marín, V. I., Bond, M., & Gouverneur, F. (2019). Systematic review of research on artificial intelligence applications in higher education – where are the educators? *International Journal of Educational Technology in Higher Education*, *16*(1), 39. DOI: 10.1186/s41239-019-0171-0

Zhang, J., & Zhang, Z. (2024). AI in teacher education: Unlocking new dimensions in teaching support, inclusive learning, and digital literacy. *Journal of Computer Assisted Learning*, *40*(4), 1871–1885. DOI: 10.1111/jcal.12988

Zhang, Y., Peng, J., & Zheng, Y. (2024). Teachers' perceptions of implementing digital multimodal composing in tertiary classrooms: Voices from Chinese EFL teachers. *International Journal of Applied Linguistics*, *34*(4), 1265–1282. DOI: 10.1111/ijal.12560

Chapter 4
AI Tools:
A Nostrum for Modern-Day Linguistic Educators and Learners

Vidhi Jalan
https://orcid.org/0009-0009-4069-0513
GLA University, Mathura, India

Akanksha Singh Fouzdar
https://orcid.org/0000-0002-2274-679X
GLA University, Mathura, India

Himani Oberai
https://orcid.org/0000-0001-8755-5030
GLA University, Mathura, India

Ankit Saxena
https://orcid.org/0000-0002-1916-2662
GLA University, Mathura, India

ABSTRACT

This chapter explores the transformative role of artificial intelligence (AI) tools in modern-day linguistic education, highlighting their impact on both educators and learners. It provides a historical overview of AI in education, from early intelligent tutoring systems to modern AI-driven platforms. The chapter examines the benefits of AI in language learning, including personalized learning, real-time feedback, and enhanced accessibility, while also addressing challenges such as contextual limitations, data privacy, and the digital divide. By analyzing popular AI tools and their applications, this chapter offers insights into the evolving landscape of linguistic education and the future of AI-assisted learning.

1. ARTIFICIAL INTELLIGENCE

In today's fast-moving and dynamic world, the hand of Artificial Intelligence (AI) is invariably present in our lives. From the very moment we are awake; AI-powered simulated assistants such as Alexa and Siri answer to our queries, monitor our schedules, and even regulate our smart home devices.

DOI: 10.4018/979-8-3693-7260-9.ch004

It is an emerging branch of computer science that primarily pays heed to developing systems capable of executing tasks that classically need human wisdom (Zhang, Zhu, & Su, 2023). It is essentially characterized by its ability to imitate human cognitive roles such as learning, analyzing, rationalizing, problem-solving, opinion formulation, and comprehending language. There are multifarious ways to explain it but in the most generic terms it can be understood as a technology that is powered enough to dissect critical problems and perform tasks to attain a specific predefined goal without explicit human support (Chiu, & et al., 2023).

1.1 Relevance of Artificial Intelligence in Different Domains

In the twenty-first century, AI has become a ubiquitous force that is predominantly influencing various facets of contemporary life. The seamless incorporation of AI into everyday routines has altered humans' approach to living, working, and relating to the world. It has undoubtedly made human lives easier, swifter, and smoother in multiple ways. The various sectors, starting from healthcare, finance, and transportation to education, have transformed immensely because of AI.

One of the most promising areas of AI application is education. Intelligent Tutoring Systems (ITS) are revolutionizing personalized learning by adapting to a learner's proficiency and needs. For example, tools like Carnegie Learning and DreamBox provide tailored learning experiences that consider a student's learning trajectory and offer instant feedback. AI also powers platforms like Duolingo and Rosetta Stone, which provide language learning opportunities through gamification, speech recognition, and adaptive content. These systems are not only making education more accessible but also enhancing engagement and retention rates among learners.

In healthcare, early diagnosis with uncanny exactness and minimally invasive procedures became a reality with AI-powered tools such as the Da Vinci Surgical System and IBM Watson Health. In transportation, AI plays a significant role in navigation and real-time driving decisions. In finance, it has become handy for traders to analyze the market with precision; automated transactions have simplified lives, and virtual assistants offer bespoke services to bank users. In the entertainment industry, AI-powered software provides tailored recommendations based on an individual's search history and preferences. For instance, Amazon Prime recently announced plans to revamp its features by integrating generative AI (Gen-AI) for customized recommendations. E-commerce platforms such as Myntra, Ajio, and Amazon rely on AI for customer satisfaction, risk anticipation, supply chain optimization, and studying consumer expectations (Flavián & Casaló, 2021).

The intersection of AI and utility sectors has undeniably amplified human potential and convenience. It has become an integral part of human lives, paving the way for a more ingenious and interconnected future.

1.2 Artificial Intelligence: Historical Overview

The inception of the concept of AI goes back to 1950s when Alan Turning in his pivotal paper "Computing Machinery and Intelligence" incubated the thought of machines that could mimic human intellect. But the term "Artificial Intelligence" (AI) was coined in 1956 at the Dartmouth Conference marking it as a separate field of study. In the beginning, AI powered programs, primarily, worked upon rudimentary problem-solving tasks such as acting chess player, etc.

In the 1960s, serious endeavours were made to allow computers comprehend, interact, and produce human's language. For it, Natural Language Processing (NLP) technology was found that abled computers understand, infer, manipulate, and comprehend human language. ELIZA, a basic chatbot is considered as one of the first NLP program developed by Joseph Weizenbaum at the MIT Artificial Intelligence Laboratory (Lu, 2019). It aimed to simulate human discussion by deploying pattern matching and replacement methodologies. Subsequently in the 1970s, Rule-Based Systems were evolved that imitated human's decisive skills. It drew conclusions and gave decisions based on the data entered. It is, although, a remarkable attempt to make machines automated but had its limitations like lack of scalability and flexibility. Notably, these initial developments paved a solid path for heralding AI in its full form. The domain witnessed significant advancements with the arrival of technologies like, machine learning, data-driven approaches, and neural networks (Gupta, Liao, Choudhary, & Agrawal, 2023).

1.2.1 Intelligent Tutoring System (ITS)

Subsequently, an amalgamation of AI and education came into forefront. Many serious efforts were made to integrate the two and as a result Intelligent Tutoring System (ITS) was developed. ITS was a technology meant to give personalized instructions, spontaneous feedbacks to learners; characteristically, without any human interference. The AI-driven program acted as a human mentor to a learner. The early examples of ITSs are Programmed Logic for Automatic Teaching Operations (PLATO) System and SCHOLAR.

1.2.2 PLATO and SCHOLAR

In 1960s, PLATO became one of the first machine-based learning programs developed at the University of Illinois. It was a pioneering attempt that aimed to offer interactive educational content to its learners. It encompassed interactive feedbacks, evaluation exercises with impromptu feedback, and many more. It nurtured the concept of interactive digital learning with the features like chat rooms and message boards. It undoubtedly acted as a precursor to today's e-learning concept as many features of it are still significant today. Despite many benefits, it had its own challenges like limited technology and high cost which made the technology accessible majorly to affluent class (Stephan & Klima, 2021).

SCHOLAR is another major product of Intelligent Tutoring System designed by Jaime Carbonell in the beginning of 1970s. It was explicitly developed for teaching Geography based on mixed-initiative interaction. It allowed an interaction between machine and learner. It gave an opportunity to a learner to have interaction similar to human interaction. It stimulated an active involvement of the learner as the question was followed by an answer and then another question from the SCHOLAR. For instance, if a learner asks "What is the capital of Italy?" then SCHOLAR would respond "Rome is the capital of Italy. Do you want to know its position on the map or its population size?" SCHOLAR's ability to imitate human tutoring carved the base for more advance ITS and AI driven educational tools.

1.2.3 CALL (Computer Assisted Language Learning)

SCHOLAR and PLATO acted as precursors to CALL which is another major achievement in the amalgamation of technology and education, specifically language learning. It involved the use of technology to expedite the efficiency of learning and teaching language. Initially, CALL programs were primarily based on repetitive exercises and practice sessions. These repetitive drills eased out the process of memorization of vocabulary, jargons, specific expressions and grammatical constructions. The programs offered spontaneous feedback which helped the learner in multiple ways and played a significant role in the learning process (Shadiev & Yu, 2024).

In the 1980s, there was a remarkable shift as CALL programs became more interactive rather than just a drill. The various programs began to integrate multimedia features—audio and video lessons to offer more interesting and authentic experience. In 1999, language learning software-Rosetta Stone came into being. It works on Dynamic Immersion model that allows one to unravel their innate skills to learn a language.

In present time, one can learn twenty-five different languages through it. Its Dynamic Immersion model emulates the process of acquiring the first language (L1). It offers wide exposure to new language (L2) through visual and conceptual clues so as one interprets the meaning associated to it rather than simply translating or memorizing it. It uses scientific proven methods to build a more profound and permanent understanding of the language to be acquired (L2).

It does not focus much on grammar or translation rather focuses on giving more interactive experience to a learner. It became significant in the field of language learning because of the employment of fascinating approach and innovative technology. It proved as a good source for acquiring proficiency in English; especially for the beginners.

1.2.4 CALL after 1990s

With the advent of internet in the late 1990s, a breakthrough came in CALL programs as it opened multiple avenues for effective learning. It allowed the learners to interact with varied native speakers of the language one wanted to learn and permitted the learners to join the language communities available on the internet. In this era, numerous websites offering language-based lessons, exercises, and resources came into existence (An, Chai, Li, Zhou, & Yang, 2023).

After the enormous expansion in the use of smartphones and tablets, a new era of language learning dawned upon. Learners were able to access language learning mobile applications such as Babbel, Mesmerise, and Duolingo at their convenience. It ultimately led to the increased flexibility and accessibility in language learning.

Subsequently, in the 21st century, an integration of AI and CALL turned into a reality. It changed the face of language learning forever. AI driven language learning tools adjust according to the proficiency level of the student and give personalized feedback. A remarkable shift led to a more bespoke and adaptive teaching-learning experiences (Shadiev & Yu, 2024).

1.2.5 AI-IDLE

It heralded the novel learning concept of AI-mediated informal digital learning of English (AI-IDLE). It stands at the juncture of CALL and English language learning outside the classroom. AI-IDLE has lately gained impetus because it offers an all-inclusive understanding of how language learner involves in "self-directed, informal English learning using a range of different digital devices (e.g., smartphones, desktop computers) and resources (e.g., web apps, social media) independent of formal context". AI-IDLE activities, beyond linguistic benefits, offer a huge range of benefits to a learner such as improved self-awareness about language proficiency, enriched vocabulary size, augmented intercultural understanding capability, better communication readiness, assuaged linguistic anxiety, and increased sense of gratification. These extensive studies have validated that AI-IDLE has turned out to be an essential element of English language (L2) learning. It allows learners to access content at his/her convenience as reins of learning are in the hands of the learner completely (Liu, Darvin, & Ma, 2024).

With time, CALL underwent a transition and from basic drill and practice tool it became an advance AI driven language learning program. It has developed immensely since its foundation, incorporating multitude of tools, applications, and approaches precisely designed to accelerate language acquisition experience. It has become an essential tool for learning language, transforming the language acquisition process more intensive yet flexible for the user.

2. THEORETICAL SUPPOSITION AND LITERATURE REVIEW

Artificial intelligence has increasingly become a revolutionary force in different spheres, including education. The latest integration of AI with linguistic education represents one of the major fields of interest. AI-enabled tools have been proven to enhance language learning by providing an adaptive learning path, immediate feedback, and flexibility in educational experience. It has been a blessing to introduce AI in this sector, making education more accessible while recasting traditional modalities of teaching to newer, flexible, and adaptive pathways to learning (Chiu, & et al., 2023).

NLP technology is another fundamental evolution in this regard. NLP refers to the science of enabling a machine to understand human language, interpret it, and then respond accordingly; these tools have played a crucial role in applications that apply to language learning. The arrival of ITS and AI-based apps like Duolingo and Grammarly have changed the way new language-learning curves are curried on-the-fly, providing corrections and hints instantly according to one's proficiency in that language (Chiu, & et al., 2023). They posture themselves as potential bridges over the lacunas created by the sedentary process of traditional language learning techniques, mainly lack of one-on-one instructions and lagging human educators' feedback. AI provides an environment that is more interactive and responsive by allowing immediate feedback and self-paced learning (Zhang, Zhu, & Su, 2023).

But much is lost, however, in the implementation of AI in language education. The issue is that an AI system can hardly capture all the richness of human language. As language is heavily rooted in cultural and social contexts, it presents challenges for the understanding of AI systems. They include idiomatic expressions, the humor sense, and subtlety of emotions. While AI programs went a long way toward identifying patterns and improving grammaticality, they still fall behind on issues related to the more complex, humanistic elements of language use. This gap therefore offers further potential for research into the refinement of AI so that understanding and integration of culture and emotional factors can further be included in language learning procedures (Flavián, & Casaló, 2021).

Another very important area being advanced by AI is personalized learning. In traditional language classrooms, most follow a 'one size fits all' model, which means that even if learners come from different socio-cultural backgrounds, differ in their aims, needs, or learning styles, they all follow the same curriculum and are all expected to learn in exactly the same way. AI can create customized learning experiences based on a student's progress, his strengths, and his weaknesses. These tools can customize learning content according to the pace at which a student learns for a very personalized experience. However, while personalization is one significant advantage, there also lies the challenge of ensuring that AI can adapt itself to varied learning styles and modalities. This implies that an AI system should be developed in such a way that it serves the various types of learners who would vary with their cognitive abilities, emotional intelligence, and motivation and is highly dependent on the sophistication of the understanding of human psychology and learning theories (Lu, 2019).

Another application area of potential for AI in linguistic education is gamification. The application of gamification is done by making use of the elements of games such as rewards, points, and track of progress to cause high levels of motivation among the learners by making the learning process engaging. Usually, AI tools utilize strategies of gamification to keep learners interested and motivated enough to practice constantly. While there are pros of gamification in that it increases motivation and, therefore, better learning outcomes, gamification also has its shortcomings. There is potential for the learner to spend more time trying to get rewards rather than mastering the language. Furthermore, over-reliance on gamification causes very surface-level learning wherein students may be memorizing things without an in-depth understanding of how the language works. In this way, the challenge for AI is trying to balance gamification with meaningful educational content that promotes a deeper, more intrinsic understanding of language (Zhan, Tong, Lan, & Zhong, 2024).

AI's real-time potential for assessment and feedback is disrupting language education in powerful ways. Classrooms often have delayed feedback, and assessments may involve standardized testing that can't get at the many nuances of a speaker's language ability. AI can immediately offer quick and highly individualized feedback based on learner performance. This makes it possible to let learners correct their mistakes in a continuous and active learning process (Lu, 2019). But much remains to be developed concerning AI and the assessment of more complex language skills, which can include creativity in communication, critical thinking, and meaningful conversation. Traditional AI systems tend to focus on grammar, vocabulary, and syntax; the future of AI in language education will most likely be concerned with the development of holistic assessment devices that not only evaluate such higher-order linguistic skills but also take into consideration other elements in coming up with an all-around assessment for language learning (Lin, Huang, & Lu, 2023).

But along with this aspect of AI is that of ethics in education. Because AI tools are most of the time gathering loads of data in making a tailored learning experience, concerns about data privacy and security have surfaced to be at the forefront. Learners give these systems sensitive personal information, including learning preferences, performance data, and communication patterns. These are critical data for AI to create personalized learning experiences, but they raise a problem of how secure this information is kept and used. There is therefore an upsurge need for transparent AI systems protecting the user's privacy but maintaining quality in education (Liang, Hwang, Chen, & Darmawansah, 2023).

The most important challenge to the massive adoption of AI in language learning comes from the digital divide, apart from the level of private concerns. Although the resources made possible by AI could democratize education and bring high-quality resources to most users around the world, many learners have limited access due to weak infrastructure and limited resources in developing regions. The elimination of the digital divide will be very important for all learners to gain access to the benefits of AI, especially the ones who possess varying economic, social statuses, and also a different kind of geographical locality (Celik, 2023).

In a nutshell, AI has the potential to revolutionize how language is taught because it allows customized, flexible, and scalable learning solutions. However, what the full potential of AI will actually look like, time will only tell. With fine-tuning of AI to solve the most challenging issues of language learning, such as understanding nuances in second languages, balancing gamification with meaningful content, privacy of data, and overcoming the accessibility barrier, AI will dramatically make language education more inclusive, efficient, and effective.

3. ROLE OF ARTIFICIAL INTELLIGENCE IN EDUCATION (AIEd)

AIEd has undeniably revolutionized the entire teaching and learning process. It has and will bring transformative changes in the way personalization, approachability, and competence function in the landscape of education (Zhang, Zhu, & Su, 2023).

One of the most remarkable contributions of AI in education is providing personalized learning experiences. Empowering AIEd tools can dive deep into students' learning behavior and can trace key strengths and weaknesses of learners. E-study material would consequently be recommended based on these aspects, adapting to create an individualized learning process so as to one can learn and progress at his/ her comfortable pace (Fosso Wamba, Guthrie, Queiroz, & Minner, 2024).

Furthermore, AI augments the convenience and productivity of the mentors. The automated AIEd tools asses' assignments promptly and give disinterested feedbacks, making teaching more effective and student targeted. AIEd managerial tools turn time-taking tasks, such as, class preparation, evaluation, and relevant resource identification, among many others easier and efficient (Lu, 2019).

AI has a significant role in globalizing education. AIEd tools that work on Natural Language Processing (NLP) and Machine Learning (ML) aid in content translation. The herculean task of translation of content into different leading languages is done within a few minutes through AIEd resulting in greater accessibility of it worldwide. Besides, AI powered products like speech recognition of speech or text-to-voice software, facilitate equal learning opportunities for differently abled learners; ultimately making education all inclusive (Stephan & Klima, 2021).

Certainly, amalgamation of AI and education comes with its own set of challenges like data privacy, tech-friendliness as a prerequisite, absence of human touch but the power of AI to transform education sector cannot be overlooked. With the passage of time, AI driven technologies are surely to construct more engaging, more justifiable, and more productive teaching-learning environment. Taking it in consideration, the **current chapter** focuses primarily on the role and importance of AI in education specifically English language teaching and learning.

3.1 English as a Lingua Franca: Straddling as a Global Medium for Communication

In the globalized world, English has become a first *lingua franca*; it means that it serves as a common medium of communication among people from very diverse linguistic backgrounds. It allows people to exchange thoughts and ideas with one another and eventually work and grow together. In the past, British Empire had ruled over maximum parts of the world and in the current times, the United States has become a global leader; these altogether became a reason for making English as a global language of communication (Mauranen, 2023).

English functions as a cornerstone for exploring widespread growth and development opportunities. Without the proper knowledge of English, one may miss on many global opportunities from studying to job to business. To study in global leading universities like Harvard University or Yale University one must have good command over English. To access the pool of e-knowledge in the form of journals, e-books, blogs, and videos, one must again have good understanding of English. In international job market, fluency in English is largely viewed as a precondition for career advancement. MNCs prefer people who are fluent in English so that there is no scope for any communication gap. For industrialists, English is vital for building international relations and scaling their businesses at the global level. In all, the evolution of global trade, travel, and learning opportunities has created a swelling need for a common language. In this regard, English is considered as the most favored language that is largely used in corporate businesses, diplomacy, academia, etc. It has gained the status of primary or working language of communication and to grasp ample of the enticing opportunities present across the globe one has to be conversant in it.

3.2 Teaching and Learning Language: Traditional or AI Methodology

The indispensable need of English language has created a huge demand for teaching and learning English. But at the same time, a question arises that which method of teaching conventional or AI-driven is more effective? Conventional methods of teaching and learning English language, although foundational, are full of challenges and largely incomplete, taking in consideration, today's progressive and interconnected world (Liang, Hwang, Chen, & Darmawansah, 2023). There are numerous challenges involved in traditional teaching and learning methodology making it limited and inadequate. On the other hand, AI-driven tools offer a solution to these limitations but also come with its own set of challenges.

3.2.1 Dearth of Personalization

First and foremost, challenge in conventional style of language learning and teaching is that it lacks personalization. In a traditional classroom setup, a teacher unwittingly adopts one-size-fits-all attitude; overlooking the individual learner's needs and grasping pace. In a huge class, a mentor may not get ample of time to understand and resolve individual's shortcomings like difficulty in correct pronunciation or misunderstanding of the grammatical concepts; encumbering their overall language learning endeavours.

The paucity of individualization often leads to disengagement and dissatisfaction among advance as well as slow learners. An advance learner may not find any challenge whereas a slow learner may not catch up the pace and may feel too challenged. In both the cases, the main motive of learning gets defeated and students' potential remains unexplored (Zhai, & et al., 2021).

3.2.2 Limited Interaction With the Mentor

Another major challenge in conventional teaching and learning English language is restricted interaction and one to one practice opportunities. It has often been observed that in old-styled language classes the major focus lies on correct grammar and vocabulary enrichment through either rote learning or worksheets. There is almost no or limited chances for life-like interaction resulting in less proficiency in speaking skills. The traditional style may be feasible for creating a sound understanding of the theoretical aspects but lacks in developing confidence of a learner as they often undervalue speaking and listening activities which are essentially important for language acquisition. A wide gap between theoretical knowledge and practical application leads to inefficiency in language acquisition. A learner might outshine in written exams but may feel apprehensive and under confident when having a conversation in a real world, especially with the native speakers.

3.2.3 Mentor-Driven Setup

Next, significant drawback of traditional linguistic classrooms is that it runs on teacher-driven-approach. An instructor is observed as a sage on the stage rather than guide on the side. Unknowingly, in such setups', impassive learning environment is created where learners act as inactive receivers rather than active participants.

This approach may throttle ingenuity, analytical thinking, and active participation as learners may rely completely on mentor, making least efforts on his/her end to internalize language actively (Celik, 2023).

3.2.4 Obsolete Evaluation System

Next, critical limitation of traditional language classroom is outdated evaluation techniques. Classical examination may not prove to be a valid yardstick to judge a learner's language adeptness or communicative skills. The intent of a learner gradually shifts from truly acquiring and internalizing the language to just scoring the marks (Mauranen, 2023).

3.2.5 Delay in Feedback

Moreover, in conventional language teaching and learning method feedbacks are not instantaneous. The evaluation technique in this format is written examination or assignments in which feedback is delayed, largely generic, and do not provide productive and specific insights. In this method, there is more emphasis on written proficiency rather than speaking resulting in minimal feedback on pronunciation, clarity, etc.

As student-to-teacher ratio is often high in such formats so it stifles students from getting personalized feedback which is essential to overcome individual language acquisition challenges (Zhai, & et al., 2021).

3.2.6 Enthusiasm and Motivation Often Fizzle Out

Furthermore, in traditional language classrooms as teaching pedagogy is monotonous and tedious and students are more of passive learners; there are high chances of learners' disengagement and low enthusiasm. The lack of real-life application and more of bookish knowledge may not do the complete justice to learners (Mauranen, 2023).

Thus, it can be observed that conventional language teaching and learning methods may be good to acquaint the students with the basic concepts and ideas of grammar, sentence structure, etc., but there is no or very little scope for practicing especially speaking, getting productive feedbacks, etc. It fails to address the varied requirements of the current times. The absence of individualization, restricted one on one interaction, and teacher-driven methodology, amid other drawbacks; underscore the need for more novel approach that intermingles technology and active learning methods (Lin, Huang, & Lu, 2023). For giving more efficient, comprehensive, and holistic linguistic acquisition experience; fusion of AI and traditional methods is inevitable. AI powered teaching and learning strategies will undoubtedly make the process of language acquisition more effectual. An intellectual, flexible, and adaptive English learning setup where learners can actively practice, identify weaker areas; engage in formative assessment, and get instantaneous feedbacks can possibly become a reality with the fusion of the two (Cope and Kalantzis, 2016).

4. POPULAR AI TOOLS FOR ACADEMIC WRITING

Some of the most popular AI tools in language learning have managed to change things for better, providing personalized learning in adaptive, interactive platforms that are obviously giving instant feedback and assessing students in a real-time progress manner. All these are instant responses, self-paced, without the delay associated with traditional education. Plus, some have gamification integrated into them, while others just happen around real-time conversation and multimedia resources. AI tools make learning any language for anyone way more engaging, efficient, and attuned to the individual's need by providing self-directed learning and improvements in accessibility (Casal & Kessler, 2023).

4.1 Duolingo

Currently the most popular language learning app which uses AI to drive gamification in language learning, Duolingo is a pretty attractive tool for any English Language Learner. This app adjusts lessons to the learners according to their proficiency levels via algorithms for adaptive learning. Indeed, Duolingo offers generous practice in any language with its vocabulary building exercises, grammar, reading comprehension, and listening skill. Its gamification through reward points, badges, and levels encourages the learner to practice at a higher frequency. The app also makes use of speech recognition technology so learners receive real-time correction of their pronunciation. These turns learning into more of a game than an intimidating activity that one used to dread. Additionally, community features allow learners to exercise alongside peers from other parts of the globe. Together, these features have made Duolingo a strong and engaging method that ELLs can apply to improve their English language.

4.2 Grammarly

Grammarly is an AI writing assistant that helps ELLs a lot in refinement of their writing skills. It gives live feedback regarding grammar, punctuation, spelling, and style. Thus, Grammarly would be a wonderful aid for both academic and professional use of communication. Grammarly's advanced AI operates contextual analysis and gives tips on vocabulary and sentence structure so that the improvement needs of the ELLs are catered to specifically. The explanation of correction also goes with the platform so that users will understand their mistakes and learn from them. It enhances writing accuracy while teaching users about grammar rules and language nuances. What's more, adaptation to a wide range of writing platforms, such as email and social media to word processors ensures consistent support for the learner in all writing contexts. It also ensures originality in academic writing with its feature on plagiarism detection. In a nutshell, Grammarly is an efficient tool for ELLs to develop and refine their writing skills in the English language.

4.3 Elsa Speak

Elsa Speak is an AI application, designed to enhance the English pronunciation skills of ELLs. The advanced speech recognition technology utilizes audio patterns one speaks, and the immediate, nuanced feedback one gets is in terms of pronunciation accuracy and intonation as well as fluency. Its learning paths are based on proficiency levels, making it possible for learners to work towards areas that require improvement. Another feature of Elsa Speak is interactive exercises simulating real-life conversations, and it gives users much more confidence to speak in English. The AI present in the app keeps track of the users' progress continuously and gives them targeted exercises, based on their pace of learning, towards areas where they tend to pronounce English words incorrectly. Since Elsa Speak gives instant feedback, ELLs can be modified on the spot, which helps them improve even more quickly. It is very easy to navigate and offers engaging learning activities that make it accessible to all kinds of learners. Elsa Speak is an indispensable tool for ELLs who want to enhance their spoken English and be able to pronounce more clearly and realistically.

4.4 Babbel

Babbel is a full-scale learning application that uses AI to organize structured, interactive, and personalized learning for ELLs. The content of the curriculum is framed by linguistic experts on vocabularies, grammar, reading, listening, and speaking. Babbel makes use of AI to personalize lessons to the user's level and learning goals, enabling the content to stay relevant and challenging. The app features speech exercises involving dialogue that simulates the way conversations take place in reality for learners to effectively communicate in real life. Babbel gives the complete feature of speech recognition wherein users can practice their speaking by listening to feedback produced in real-time to improve on pronunciation. The interactive style is supported by a spaced repetition technique to make vocabulary stronger and easier to understand grammatical structures. Since Babbel focuses on conversational language and cultural context, it is very useful to ELLs who wish to use English for everyday purposes. In general, Babbel provides a comprehensive, engaging platform for mastering the language.

4.5 Rosetta Stone

Of course, Rosetta Stone proved to be one of the best well-known language learning applications while using its proprietary dynamic immersion method for teaching ELLs the English language. The app simulates contextual learning through images, text, and sound that mirror the natural process of learning the language. This method allows learners to think in the language rather than translating from their first language. The Rosetta Stone app makes use of artificial intelligence to adjust the lessons learned to match the student's pace and level of proficiency. All the important language skills in terms of vocabulary, grammar, pronunciation, and listening are engaged while building speech confidence. It uses speech recognition technology that provides instant feedback on pronunciation, letting the learner focus on the same and fine-tune their spoken English. Rosetta Stone's mobile app just provides yet another avenue through which users can learn on the go while still permitting them to practice at will. The approach by Rosetta Stone as immersive, user-centered makes it a very powerful tool in the hands of ELLs trying to strive for fluency in English.

4.6 ReadTheory

ReadTheory is an AI-based learning platform specifically designed for improving the reading comprehension of ELLs. In addition to presenting reading activities based on levels, from beginner to advanced, the adaptive learning technology will determine where a learner is reading at and focus on the level of difficulty for the texts and questions that are presented to them. ReadTheory gives immediate feedback on comprehension questions, helping the learners understand their mistakes and can improve reading strategies. It tracks the progress of users over time, creating a chance to watch improvement and identify areas that need more development in both the learners and the educators. ReadTheory exposes the ELLs to varied reading materials, which help expand vocabulary while reinforcing understanding of grammatical structures in context. The exercises will keep learners interactive, making reading more enjoyable and effective. ReadTheory is hence an improved resource for ELLs who want to read better.

4.7 Mango Languages

Mango Languages is also artificial intelligence: it's a high end-platform of practical, conversation-based teaching of the English language to Language Learners, which appears to be highly feasible because it provides the learner with interactive lessons emphasizing real-life communication skills. It is very easy for learners who aim to apply what they learn in everyday situations. Mango has a very intuitive interface, guiding the learners through vocabulary, grammar, pronunciation, and cultural insights in a holistic way. It applies AI technology in adjusting with the pace of learning and preference of the student, adapting the information to the direction of the learner's goals.

The speech recognition feature helps in practicing pronunciation and thereby refining them with instant feedback. Finally, Mango Languages employs spaced repetition in their vocabulary retention for long-term learning. In providing actual, practical use of a language and cultural understanding, the resource will be particularly effective for ELLs who wish to feel confident using or understanding English in everyday situations.

4.8 Quillbot

Quillbot is an AI-powered writing assistant aimed at supporting the creation of new writing techniques for ELLs. For example, some features it provides include paraphrasing and grammar checking in order to allow the user to perfect his or her writing style and precision. With advanced AI algorithms in Quillbot, sentences can be transformed keeping the original meaning intact while helping ELLs learn alternative ways to express something. The tool also provides synonyms and alternative word choices; thus, it widens the vocabulary of the user, and it provides a variety that keeps them from sticking to repetition. Suggestions of grammar and spelling ensure that the written content does not carry any errors and enhances the expression and professionalism of the text written. Quillbot may integrate several writing tools, including Google Docs and Microsoft Word. Quillbot allows the development of a student's ability to write and communicate effectively in the English language by providing live feedback and suggestions for ELLs.

4.9 Speechify

Speechify is an application of text-to-speech, AI-powered, designed to enhance listening skills and comprehension of ELLs. The platform will transform written text into spoken words so that users will listen to articles, books, or any written content. The voices of speechify are of very high quality and natural sounding, making the listening experience more engrossing and effective. The feature of customizable playback speed of the application allows learners to regulate their own speed depending on the capacity to understand, thus enhancing learning. The option to Speechifying supports different text formats in such a way that it adapts well to the type of material for learning. ELLs can enhance pronunciations, intonation, and fluency besides getting accustomed to various accents and speech in listening to text. This would make speechifying significantly useable in most contexts as it could integrate with reading and writing tools. As a tool for ELLs who would like to improve their listening and comprehension skills in English, it is very useful.

4.10 Replika

Replika is an AI chatbot aimed toward a unique, conversational setting for ELLs to practice. Building on the use of natural language processing algorithms, the chatbot lets users engage in interactive text-based conversations that mirror real life and assist individuals in improving their speaking and writing skills. A non-judgmental space for learning can be offered to any learner anxious about speaking to other people. Replika might be adjusted according to the user's level of proficiency in language competency; thus, it provides a learning experience that is tailored to a user. The AI also gives corrections and suggestions that are helpful in the process of improving the grammar, vocabulary, and sentence structure for learners. In addition, the conversational style of Replika compels users to think in English and aids in cognitive language development. Friendly, interactive, and an easily accessible means of effective practice and improvement of conversational English for ELLs, Replika makes room for a relaxed and supportive environment of interaction.

5. BENEFITS

In the contemporary educational landscape, learning has become increasingly dynamic, with Artificial Intelligence (AI) rapidly evolving and revolutionizing various aspects of education and knowledge acquisition. Among the myriad AI-powered educational tools, Intelligent Tutoring Systems (ITS) stand out as particularly impactful. These systems leverage sophisticated AI algorithms to enhance users' learning experiences significantly. By fostering interactive and immersive learning environments through virtual and augmented reality technologies, ITS and similar AI tools are transforming the educational paradigm (Kannan & Munday, 2018).

The growing preference for AI-powered language learning tools among students can be attributed to several key benefits:

Personalized Learning Trajectories: AI-enabled language learning tools excel in creating individualized learning pathways tailored to each student's unique needs. Unlike traditional classroom settings, which often lack personalized approaches, these AI systems meticulously monitor learners' progress, strengths, preferred learning styles, and competencies. This data is then utilized to develop customized learning materials that align with the learner's capabilities, thereby enhancing engagement and overall learning efficacy (Kessler, 2018). For instance, if a student struggles with basic English sentence construction, the AI system can generate targeted exercises to address this specific challenge.

Increased Involvement & Motivation: ITS and similar AI-based learning tools incorporate gamification elements such as challenges, reward systems, and quizzes. This gamified approach transforms the learning process into an exciting and motivating experience, encouraging learners to actively pursue their educational goals. The integration of natural language processing (NLP) and interactive agents further enables real-time conversations, significantly enriching the learning experience and maintaining high levels of engagement.

Prompt Review and Assessment: Traditional classroom settings often face constraints in providing timely, individualized feedback. AI-powered learning tools address this limitation by offering instant assessment of learners' responses and immediate, personalized feedback. This rapid feedback mechanism allows learners to quickly identify and rectify their mistakes, facilitating prompt improvement (Porter & Grippa, 2020).

Exposure to Multifaceted Learning Resources: Recognizing the diverse proficiency levels and learning preferences among students, AI-based learning tools offer a comprehensive range of resources. These include written materials, audio tracks, visual tutorials for practical activities, and virtual dialogues. ITS, in particular, excels in tailoring these resources to individual learner requirements. To provide exposure to real-world language use, these systems often incorporate authentic materials such as podcasts and videos, further enhancing the learning experience.

Multilingual Learning Opportunities: AI-based language learning tools offer learners the opportunity to expand their linguistic repertoire by facilitating simultaneous learning of multiple languages. This feature caters to individuals with personal interests in polyglotism or those seeking to enhance their professional qualifications through multilingual proficiency.

Enhanced Accessibility and Flexibility: Unlike traditional classroom settings constrained by specific schedules and locations, AI-powered language learning tools offer unparalleled accessibility. These platforms, accessible via any internet-connected device, provide a broad audience with the freedom to engage in learning at their convenience. This flexibility particularly benefits adult learners and professionals who previously found it challenging to attend conventional classes due to other commitments. The removal of temporal and spatial barriers enables learners to capitalize on opportunities for personal development.

Promotion of Self-Directed Learning: AI-based learning tools empower learners to take control of their educational journey. Through continuous updates on assessments, feedback, and suggested corrective measures, these platforms foster a sense of responsibility and discipline in learners. The ability to monitor personalized progress cultivates a self-driven learning experience, as learners gain a clear picture of their performance trajectory.

Real-Time Conversational Practice: Language acquisition necessitates continuous practice, a requirement often unmet in traditional learning systems due to limited real-time practice opportunities. AI-powered tools such as chatbots provide an excellent solution, allowing learners to engage in continuous speaking, listening, and writing practice.

Data-Driven Insights for Educators: While AI tools offer immediate feedback to learners on their performance and proficiency levels, the data collected is also invaluable for educators. This information enables teachers to refine their pedagogical approaches and better understand learner differences. Consequently, educators can identify areas where additional support may be required, ultimately enhancing the overall learning experience (Almurtadha, 2019).

Scalability and Cost-Effectiveness: AI-based language tools offer a scalable solution to address the needs of a large learner base. Many of these tools are either free or available at a low cost, contrasting with traditional education systems that often require significant resources such as infrastructure and textbooks. While conventional systems may struggle to accommodate large numbers of learners, AI-powered systems can efficiently serve a vast user base without compromising on quality.

Continuous Improvement of AI Tools: AI-based language tools are continuously evolving based on the data they gather. For instance, Intelligent Tutoring Systems continuously incorporate user feedback to enhance learner interactions and experiences. This ongoing refinement ensures that AI tools remain current with the latest educational practices and learner needs.

In conclusion, AI tools in language learning offer a comprehensive solution to modern educational challenges, from personalized learning experiences and immediate feedback to real-time language practice and data-driven insights. As AI technology continues to advance, its potential to revolutionize language education will only grow, equipping educators and learners with powerful tools to achieve their linguistic goals.

6. CHALLENGES & LIMITATIONS

Intelligent Tutoring Systems (ITS) and other AI-enabled language learning tools have significantly revolutionized and advanced the educational landscape (Crompton, Jones, & Burke, 2024). However, they present several challenges:

Contextual and Semantic Limitations: Despite their sophistication, these systems still struggle to achieve human-like comprehension based on context and cultural references. ITS tools often fail to grasp nuances such as sarcasm, humor, or subtle expressions, leading to misinterpretation and errors in understanding.

Data-Driven Limitations and Biases: AI-based learning tools rely heavily on large datasets. If the quality, diversity, or representativeness of these datasets is compromised, it can result in ineffective learning experiences. Inadequate or biased datasets may lead to misleading feedback for learners.

Speech Processing Constraints: Despite considerable advancements, language-based AI tools still face challenges in accurately processing speech. Issues such as varying accents, pronunciation discrepancies, and background noise poses interference. In language learning, precision in these areas is crucial for providing accurate feedback to learners. Errors in speech processing can lead to frustration and negatively impact the learning experience.

Limited Human-Emulative Interactions: AI-based learning tools cannot fully replicate the dynamic and empathetic nature of human interaction. Language learning encompasses more than mastering accent, pronunciation, and grammar; it involves developing an understanding of cultural context and social cues. The lack of genuine human interaction can limit the scope of learning (Khanzode & Sarode, 2020). While some tools offer conversation practice with live language tutors, the majority of the learning systems are based on self-learning.

Over-Reliance on Gamification: While elements such as quizzes, badges, and leaderboards can enhance learner engagement, an excessive dependence on these features for motivation raises concerns about their long-term effectiveness and impact on genuine language acquisition.

Limited Customization for Diverse Learning Needs: Although Intelligent Tutoring Systems and other AI-based language tools attempt to cater to individual learning styles, they often fall short in accommodating learners with various disabilities. This limitation compromises the inclusivity and overall efficiency of these systems.

Lack of Transparency: AI-enabled language learning tools frequently operate as "black boxes," with opaque decision-making processes. This lack of clarity can foster mistrust among users, particularly when learners or educators receive feedback that appears genuinely incorrect or inconsistent.

Data Privacy and Security Vulnerabilities: To personalize the learning experience, AI-enabled tools collect substantial personal information, including sensitive data such as voice recordings and behavioural patterns. Inadequate security measures may lead to data breaches or unauthorized access to learners' information, making data privacy and security a significant concern in the use of AI-based tools.

Cost-Intensive Development and Maintenance: The development and implementation of AI-based language learning tools require substantial financial investment in technology, research, and development. This high cost often limits access to these advanced tools in resource-constrained educational settings. Additionally, the need for constant updates and ongoing maintenance presents a significant long-term financial burden.

Over-Reliance on Gamification: Using quizzes, badges, leaderboards, etc keep learners engaged, but over reliance on them for motivating learners is doubtful.

Narrow Customization for Learning Modalities: Intelligent Tutoring Systems or other AI based language tools focus on the learning style of the learner and offer the solution. However, these tools may not be able to offer much effective solutions to the learners with different disabilities, thereby, limiting the inclusivity and efficiency of these systems.

Lack of Transparency: AI enabled language learning tools often operate as "Black Boxes". Their decision-making process lacks transparency. Such lack of clarity among the users be it learners or educators can develop mistrust among them particularly in scenarios where they receive seemingly incorrect feedback from the system.

Vulnerabilities in Data Privacy & Security: In order to personalize the learning experience, the AI-enabled learning tools collect lot of personal information of the learner. Particularly language learning tools deals with lot of sensitive information in the form of learner's voice recordings, behavioral pattern, etc. Inadequate data security measures by the providers may lead to data breach or unauthorized access to learners' information. Thus, data privacy and security is a major concern while using AI based tools.

Cost Intensive Development: Developing and implementing AI based language learning tools involves huge cost. Lot of investment needs to be done in creating technology, research and development. This limits the access of these high-tech tools to the low resource based educational set ups. Also, these systems require constant updating and involves high maintenance. This again is a huge burden over the long term.

Digital Divide & Accessibility Issues: The efficacy of AI-based learning tools is significantly impacted by access to reliable internet services. In regions and communities where many people lack basic amenities, the prospect of utilizing such impactful learning tools remains distant. This digital divide clearly exacerbates existing inequalities, limiting access to quality education for all.

Alignment with Traditional Education Practices: Traditional education systems often appear resistant to AI-enabled learning tools. This reluctance may stem from educators' preconceptions, reluctance to leave their comfort zones established by traditional teaching pedagogies, or lack of access to training in these new technologies. Integrating AI-based education with traditional systems requires careful and strategic planning, along with proper coordination.

Infrastructure Deficiencies in Developing Nations: Developing nations face significant infrastructural challenges. Additionally, these countries often lack comprehensive policies and regulations governing the use of AI in education. These deficiencies present a substantial obstacle to implementing such user-friendly systems.

Hence, while AI-based language learning tools present numerous challenges and limitations, this should not deter us from exploring their potential benefits. Instead, we should strive to improve these tools and address the aforementioned deficiencies, ensuring that the advantages of AI in education can be more equitably distributed and effectively implemented.

7. CONCLUSION

But at the least, recent years have marked the emerging area of AI combined with education-the potential of which will allow new aspects to address language acquisition as fundamentally strengthened learning experience. AI tools, once built within the holy sanctum of world matters of computer science and data processing, have now reached the stage of enjoying a more crucial place in helping educators and learners navigate the complexities of modern linguistic education. From intelligent tutoring systems (ITS) to the latest modern AI-driven platforms for language learning, AI promises to revolutionize how languages are taught and learned. Like anything transformative, however, this introduction of AI to education presents significant promises and challenges.

Perhaps one of the greatest advantages that AI tools bring to linguistic education is the capability of personalization they bring. Traditional classroom settings usually tend to have the focus skewed toward general needs for all students at the expense of providing individual needs based on constraints in time, resources, and human capacity. AI-driven platforms like Duolingo, Grammarly, and Replika help fill this gap with learning experiences custom-fit to the learner's pace, strengths, and weaknesses. With these, instant feedbacks can be given off, which would necessarily cut off the lag between the effort of students and instructional correction-the long-recognized disadvantage that has been plaguing traditional learning. Such timely feedback would result in a much more lively dynamic learning environment, keeping learners engaged and motivated to continue improving.

Scalability and cost-effectiveness in education have been pushed to unprecedented levels by the utilization of AI. This can reach the child from all walks of life, even in resource-poor regions, while human mentoring can be limited by geography and economic barriers. AI tools tend to be user-friendly; hence, it provides opportunities toward multilingual education, making it feasible in a world where English has been recognized as the lingua franca. These abilities, to learn and practice languages in real-time interact with virtual assistants, and engage in gamified learning processes, all become stimulating and enriched.

Despite the above advantages, many challenges and limitations are present, even above the benefits. It is obvious that the AI tools have reached an extremely high level of sophistication but lack contextual and semantic interpretability. Even cultural references, idioms, and emotional tones are generally problematic to AI's adequate interpretation. This may sometimes lead to inaccurate or very vague responses instead of helping the learning procedure hinder it. In addition, a focus on gamification can trivialize the depth of language learning and automatically favor superficial mastery over profound understanding even if motivating up to a point.

Data privacy and security is another issue. Of their nature, AI tools scoop up huge amounts of personal data in their pursuit of enhanced algorithms and learning models. Even though this ability to amass immense amounts of data is what helps improve AI algorithms and models, the danger of misusing this data remains an impactful ethical issue, more so, since the digital façade seems to be under a constant threat of invasion. Moreover, access to AI-driven tools in learning regions of developing countries is still largely hindered due to inadequate infrastructure.

Therefore, it cannot be said that AI is the magic bullet for linguistic education, despite its potential to become a transformative force in the modern linguistic education system. It will depend on the proper balance between innovation and responsibility in the future. Educators and developers must work together to develop these tools, make them inclusive and transparent, and provide them with the potential to offer quality education to any learner. AI won't replace human teachers, but rather can be a superpower in complementing teaching. It will complement teaching to allow the educator to focus on higher-order tasks that demand critical thinking, creativity, and interpersonal communication. Proper guidance will make AI an important ally in achieving a more accessible, personalized, and effective learning experience for linguistic educators and learners worldwide.

8. FUTURE SCOPE OF RESEARCH

The potential of research in this AI-linguistic education context is enormous, not to mention scope for un-transformation of the process of language learning and teaching. Some areas that could be developed in the immediate future relate to improving algorithms for natural language processing in order to better handle the complexities of human language - idiomatic expressions, cultural nuances, and emotional undertones. Better interpretability and response of the AI tool to these subtleties will further bring this ability of an AI tool regarding more accurate and contextually relevant feedbacks to the learners.

Another area that holds tremendous promise for further research is personalization. Currently AI tools are providing very personalized learning experiences, yet there remains the possibility of creating more complex adaptive learning systems where not only a learner's proficiency will be considered but also the learner's long-term goals as well as their preferred learning styles. The potential to merge both psychological and educational theories with AI may yield more sophisticated models capable of adapting in real-time to individual learning trajectories in generating more effective learning environments.

Huge research will also be needed in the ethical considerations involving data privacy and security since AI tools rely increasingly on vast amounts of personal data, and the concern over the ethical use of this data is crucial. How can AI models be made transparent and secure so that the learner's privacy remains in check but the impact is still potent?

Future research could address questions of whether AI will be used to encourage multilingualism and cross-cultural learning. AI can facilitate totally immersive environments for multilingualism that teach new languages while giving in-depth insights into the culture through virtual exchanges and simulations. Its ability to assess and make evaluations on higher-order linguistic skills, like critical thinking and nuanced communication, would make it stronger in education.

The other important area for further study is the digital divide. Low-resource AI tools can be developed to be cost-effective, which may aid in democratization of education and help reach those students from underrepresented groups. Further research may also involve the harmonious blend of the traditional method of teaching with AI to optimize a hybrid approach wherein human-driven and AI-driven learning acquires its best form.

REFERENCES

Almurtadha, Y. (2019). LABEEB: Intelligent Conversational Agent Approach to Enhance Course Teaching and Allied Learning Outcomes Attainment. *Journal of Applied Computer Science & Mathematics*, *13*(27), 9–12. DOI: 10.4316/JACSM.201901001

An, X., Chai, C. S., Li, Y., Zhou, Y., & Yang, B. (2023). Modeling students' perceptions of artificial intelligence assisted language learning. *Computer Assisted Language Learning*, •••, 1–22. DOI: 10.1080/09588221.2023.2246519

Casal, J. E., & Kessler, M. (2023). Can linguists distinguish between ChatGPT/AI and human writing?: A study of research ethics and academic publishing. *Research Methods in Applied Linguistics*, *2*(3), 100068. DOI: 10.1016/j.rmal.2023.100068

Celik, I. (2023). Towards Intelligent-TPACK: An empirical study on teachers' professional knowledge to ethically integrate artificial intelligence (AI)-based tools into education. *Computers in Human Behavior*, *138*, 107468. DOI: 10.1016/j.chb.2022.107468

Chiu, T. K., Xia, Q., Zhou, X., Chai, C. S., & Cheng, M. (2023). Systematic literature review on opportunities, challenges, and future research recommendations of artificial intelligence in education. *Computers and Education: Artificial Intelligence*, *4*, 100118. DOI: 10.1016/j.caeai.2022.100118

Crompton, H., Jones, M. V., & Burke, D. (2024). Affordances and challenges of artificial intelligence in K-12 education: A systematic review. *Journal of Research on Technology in Education*, *56*(3), 248–268. DOI: 10.1080/15391523.2022.2121344

Flavián, C., & Casaló, L. V. (2021). Artificial intelligence in services: Current trends, benefits and challenges. *Service Industries Journal*, *41*(13-14), 853–859. DOI: 10.1080/02642069.2021.1989177

Fosso Wamba, S., Guthrie, C., Queiroz, M. M., & Minner, S. (2024). ChatGPT and generative artificial intelligence: An exploratory study of key benefits and challenges in operations and supply chain management. *International Journal of Production Research*, *62*(16), 5676–5696. DOI: 10.1080/00207543.2023.2294116

Gupta, V., Liao, W. K., Choudhary, A., & Agrawal, A. (2023). Evolution of artificial intelligence for application in contemporary materials science. *MRS Communications*, *13*(5), 754–763. DOI: 10.1557/s43579-023-00433-3

Kannan, J., & Munday, P. (2018). New trends in second language learning and teaching through the lens of ICT, networked learning, and artificial intelligence.

Kessler, G. (2018). Technology and the future of language teaching. *Foreign Language Annals*, *51*(1), 205–218. DOI: 10.1111/flan.12318

Khanzode, K. C. A., & Sarode, R. D. (2020). Advantages and disadvantages of artificial intelligence and machine learning: A literature review. [IJLIS]. *International Journal of Library and Information Science*, *9*(1), 3.

Liang, J. C., Hwang, G. J., Chen, M. R. A., & Darmawansah, D. (2023). Roles and research foci of artificial intelligence in language education: An integrated bibliographic analysis and systematic review approach. *Interactive Learning Environments*, *31*(7), 4270–4296. DOI: 10.1080/10494820.2021.1958348

Lin, C. C., Huang, A. Y., & Lu, O. H. (2023). Artificial intelligence in intelligent tutoring systems toward sustainable education: A systematic review. *Smart Learning Environments*, *10*(1), 41. DOI: 10.1186/s40561-023-00260-y

Liu, G. L., Darvin, R., & Ma, C. (2024). Exploring AI-mediated informal digital learning of English (AI-IDLE): A mixed-method investigation of Chinese EFL learners' AI adoption and experiences. *Computer Assisted Language Learning*, •••, 1–29. DOI: 10.1080/09588221.2024.2310288

Lu, Y. (2019). Artificial intelligence: A survey on evolution, models, applications and future trends. *Journal of Management Analytics*, *6*(1), 1–29. DOI: 10.1080/23270012.2019.1570365

Mauranen, A. (2023). *Reflexively speaking: Metadiscourse in English as a lingua Franca* (p. 236). de Gruyter.

Porter, B., & Grippa, F. (2020). A platform for AI-enabled real-time feedback to promote digital collaboration. *Sustainability (Basel)*, *12*(24), 10243. DOI: 10.3390/su122410243

Shadiev, R., & Yu, J. (2024). Review of research on computer-assisted language learning with a focus on intercultural education. *Computer Assisted Language Learning*, *37*(4), 841–871. DOI: 10.1080/09588221.2022.2056616

Stephan, K. D., & Klima, G. (2021). Artificial intelligence and its natural limits. *AI & Society*, *36*(1), 9–18. DOI: 10.1007/s00146-020-00995-z

Zhai, X., Chu, X., Chai, C. S., Jong, M. S. Y., Istenic, A., Spector, M., Liu, J.-B., Yuan, J., & Li, Y. (2021). A Review of Artificial Intelligence (AI) in Education from 2010 to 2020. *Complexity*, *2021*(1), 8812542. DOI: 10.1155/2021/8812542

Zhan, Z., Tong, Y., Lan, X., & Zhong, B. (2024). A systematic literature review of game-based learning in Artificial Intelligence education. *Interactive Learning Environments*, *32*(3), 1137–1158. DOI: 10.1080/10494820.2022.2115077

Zhang, B., Zhu, J., & Su, H. (2023). Toward the third generation artificial intelligence. *Science China. Information Sciences*, *66*(2), 121101. DOI: 10.1007/s11432-021-3449-x

Chapter 5
Benefits and Challenges of Integrating AI Tools in Language Education

Mansour Amini
https://orcid.org/0000-0003-2149-4604
Universiti Sains Malaysia, Malaysia

Ali Zahabi
King Mongkut's University of Technology, Thonburi, Thailand

Malini Ganapathy
Universiti Sains Malaysia, Malaysia

ABSTRACT

The integration of AI tools in language education offers a range of benefits and poses several challenges that must be examined to ensure ethical, responsible, and effective use. AI tools can enhance personalized learning, provide targeted practice exercises, deliver real-time feedback, and increase accessibility for students. However, AI tools can reinforce existing biases in training data. Privacy and data security are also critical issues, necessitating measures to ensure transparency regarding data usage. Furthermore, the "black box" nature of AI tools can obscure decision-making processes, underscoring the need for clear explanations and accountability mechanisms. Over-reliance on AI may reduce essential human interactions and critical thinking opportunities in language learning, while the digital divide could exacerbate educational inequalities. To harness the benefits of AI in language education effectively, educators must navigate these challenges thoughtfully ensuring AI tools complement rather than replace the human elements crucial to language acquisition.

INTRODUCTION

The integration of artificial intelligence (AI) tools in language education, as highlighted in various studies (e.g., Cohen et al., 2024; Umar, 2024; İnci Kavak et al., 2024; Stavytska et al., 2024; Luo & Qiu, 2024), signifies a transformative shift with the potential to greatly enhance learning experiences. These

DOI: 10.4018/979-8-3693-7260-9.ch005

AI tools provide personalized feedback, tailored lesson plans, and individualized learning experiences, which ultimately lead to improved language proficiency and increased student engagement. AI-powered language learning platforms can analyze a student's performance in real-time, identifying areas of weakness and providing targeted exercises to address these gaps. This personalized approach ensures that each student receives the support they need, making the learning process more efficient and effective. Additionally, AI tools can adapt to the pace of the learner, offering more challenging material as the student's skills improve, thus maintaining their interest and motivation (Cohen et al., 2024; Umar, 2024).

Despite these significant benefits, several challenges must be carefully addressed to ensure the ethical, responsible, and effective application of AI in language education. One major concern is the potential for misinformation, where AI tools might provide incorrect information or explanations. In this regard, ensuring the accuracy and reliability of AI-generated content is crucial (Luo & Qiu, 2024). For example, a challenge is the loss of human connection, as over-reliance on AI tools might reduce face-to-face interactions between teachers and students, which are essential for developing communication skills and emotional intelligence (Stavytska et al., 2024). Ethical concerns, such as ensuring fairness and avoiding algorithmic bias, are also paramount. AI systems must be designed to treat all students equitably, regardless of their background (İnci Kavak et al., 2024). Another challenge could be data privacy issues as protecting students' personal information and ensuring that data collected by AI tools is used responsibly is essential for maintaining trust (Umar, 2024). Addressing these challenges requires a collaborative effort among educators, policymakers, researchers, and technology developers to ensure the responsible and equitable integration of AI in language education. This collaborative approach will help create dynamic, inclusive, and effective language learning environments that empower learners to thrive in today's interconnected world. By working together, stakeholders can develop guidelines and best practices that maximize the benefits of AI while mitigating its risks, ultimately transforming language education for the better (Cohen et al., 2024; Umar, 2024; İnci Kavak et al., 2024; Stavytska et al., 2024; Luo & Qiu, 2024).

BENEFITS OF INTEGRATING AI TOOLS IN LANGUAGE EDUCATION

Artificial intelligence offers numerous advantages in language education, improving learning outcomes through personalized learning, real-time feedback, and adaptive content delivery. AI-driven learning platforms analyze student performance and adapt instructional materials accordingly, ensuring that learners progress at an optimal pace (Smith & Johnson, 2023). These platforms use sophisticated algorithms to tailor exercises based on students' strengths and weaknesses, increasing engagement and retention rates.

Moreover, AI tools enhance accessibility by providing language support for students with disabilities. For example, speech-to-text applications assist hearing-impaired students by transcribing lectures in real-time, while AI-generated subtitles help non-native learners follow video content more effectively (Brown, 2022). These tools reduce language barriers and create inclusive learning environments. Another significant benefit of AI is its ability to provide instant, data-driven feedback. Unlike traditional classroom settings where students must wait for instructors to review their work, AI-powered writing assistants analyze essays in real-time, offering detailed grammatical corrections and stylistic recommendations (Jones & Lee, 2024). Studies indicate that such tools improve writing proficiency by 30% in ESL learners compared to conventional peer review methods.

Furthermore, AI chatbots and virtual tutors facilitate conversational practice, allowing students to engage in interactive, real-world language use without the fear of judgment (Garcia, 2023). These AI-driven conversational agents mimic human interactions, helping students build confidence and fluency through contextually relevant dialogues. Research by Wang (2023) highlights that learners using AI chatbots demonstrate a 25% improvement in spontaneous speech production compared to those in traditional oral practice settings. Despite these benefits, it is crucial to address ethical considerations and ensure that AI implementation aligns with pedagogical best practices. Institutions must integrate AI tools thoughtfully, balancing technological advancements with human-centered teaching strategies.

STUDENTS' PERSONALIZED LEARNING EXPERIENCES

One of the most significant advantages of AI tools in language education is their ability to provide personalized learning experiences. AI systems are designed to adapt to each student's unique needs, learning style, and proficiency level. This personalization is achieved through the analysis of student performance data, which allows AI tools to tailor instructional materials and learning activities accordingly. By addressing individual strengths and weaknesses, AI tools provide customized support, adjusting to individual learning needs dynamically., fostering greater engagement and autonomy. This tailored approach not only boosts motivation but also accelerates language acquisition, as students receive targeted support that aligns with their specific learning requirements. AI tools dynamically adapt to student progress, ensuring personalized learning paths that foster engagement, motivation, and efficient knowledge retention (Creely, 2024; Umar, 2024).

AI tools have a profound potential to revolutionize educational experiences by providing highly customized learning paths for each student. Utilizing advanced data analytics, these tools can identify individual weaknesses and deliver targeted practice exercises tailored to specific needs, thereby enhancing the overall learning journey (Cota-Rivera et al., 2024; Onesi-Ozigagun et al., 2024; Sandhu et al., 2024; Umar, 2024). Through meticulous analysis of student performance data, AI-driven adaptive systems are able to create personalized learning pathways. This ensures that educational content is presented in a manner that aligns with the student's pace and comprehension level. The result is a learning experience that is not only more engaging but also more effective in boosting academic performance (Onesi-Ozigagun et al., 2024).

AI-powered systems are designed to adjust their teaching strategies based on real-time data about student progress. This adaptability allows AI tutors to provide personalized support that can address the unique challenges faced by each student, thus making the educational experience more individualized (Cota-Rivera et al., 2024). Educators gain deeper insights into each student's learning style and needs, facilitating the creation of a more inclusive and effective educational environment. This personalized approach helps to cater to diverse learning preferences, thereby improving overall student engagement and satisfaction with the learning process (Onesi-Ozigagun et al., 2024). Students can progress at their own pace while receiving targeted support where needed.

By integrating AI into educational practices, there is potential for creating a more engaging and student-centered learning environment. The ability of AI tools to adapt to individual learning needs and provide tailored support enhances the effectiveness of educational interventions, ultimately leading to improved learning outcomes (Cota-Rivera et al., 2024; Onesi-Ozigagun et al., 2024; Sandhu et al., 2024).

The automation of routine tasks further allows educators to concentrate on developing critical thinking skills and nurturing a deeper understanding of the subject matter among students.

These tools also incorporate adaptive learning technologies that customize the educational content to match the learner's individual needs and pace. This personalized approach ensures that students are neither overwhelmed nor under-challenged, thereby maintaining their interest and motivation to learn (Al-Shallakh, 2024).

The integration of learning analytics (LA) into educational settings, as discussed by Khor and Muthulakshmi (2023), further underscores the challenges associated with personalized learning. Learning analytics involves the collection and analysis of data to enhance educational outcomes, offering insights that can help tailor learning experiences to individual needs. While this can lead to more effective and personalized education, it also presents challenges related to accuracy, opportunity costs, and privacy concerns. For instance, the accuracy of learning analytics depends on the quality and completeness of the data collected. If the data is inaccurate or incomplete, the insights derived may be misleading or incorrect, potentially impacting the effectiveness of personalized learning interventions. By adopting a thoughtful and ethical approach to AI integration, educators can create a more engaging, effective, and equitable educational environment that supports the development of critical thinking skills and prepares students for success in an increasingly AI-driven world (Cota-Rivera et al., 2024; Onesi-Ozigagun et al., 2024; Sandhu et al., 2024).

This personalization helps maintain student engagement and motivation, as they are presented with challenges and materials that are neither too easy nor too difficult. For instance, AI-powered chatbots can simulate real-life conversations, providing interactive practice opportunities for students to improve their speaking and listening skills. Moreover, educators must provide ongoing training and support to stakeholders, including teachers, students, and parents, to ensure they understand the capabilities and limitations of AI tools.

GAMIFICATION AND CONTENT CURATION

The incorporation of AI-powered gamification and content curation further enhances the language learning experience. Gamification elements, such as interactive quizzes, challenges, and rewards, make learning more engaging and enjoyable. These elements also foster a sense of competition and achievement, which can motivate students to practice more frequently and persistently. Additionally, AI tools that curate content based on individual interests and proficiency levels ensure that students are exposed to relevant and stimulating materials. This personalized content helps deepen comprehension and encourages a passion for language learning, as students are more likely to engage with content that resonates with their interests and learning goals (Ali et al., 2024). AI tools such as ChatGPT, Grammarly, and Duolingo play pivotal roles in enhancing various aspects of language learning. ChatGPT, for example, offers conversational practice and interactive language use, allowing students to improve their speaking and writing skills in a dynamic setting. Grammarly provides advanced writing assistance, including grammar and style corrections, which helps students develop more polished and coherent writing. Duolingo combines gamified lessons with adaptive learning algorithms to deliver engaging and effective language instruction. Speech recognition technologies also contribute significantly to language education by assessing pronunciation and providing corrective feedback. Real-time translation tools further aid comprehension by facilitating understanding of foreign language texts and conversations. Collectively, these AI tools contribute to a more comprehensive and effective language learning experience (Stavytska et al., 2024). Therefore, AI-driven platforms that include gamified elements make the learning process more engaging. By turning language exercises into interactive games, students are more likely to remain engaged and retain information better. This gamification not only makes learning fun but also reinforces strategic thinking and problem-solving skills (Sadji Evenddy, 2024).

ENHANCING COMMUNICATIVE ABILITIES

The implementation of AI in language education also improves communicative abilities and the way students and AI interact in learning environments, influencing engagement and collaboration within educational settings. AI tools create dynamic and inclusive learning environments that support diverse learning needs and styles. By providing tailored resources and support, these tools help students develop the skills necessary to excel in a globalized and interconnected world. Interaction dynamics refer to how AI-driven tools facilitate student engagement, fostering interactive learning through real-time feedback, conversational AI, and peer collaboration. The ability to engage with AI-powered platforms fosters greater adaptability and competence in navigating various linguistic and cultural contexts (Ali et al., 2024; Umar, 2024). This a comprehensive method that integrates AI-driven learning with human instruction to improve overall language proficiency. ensures that both students and teachers benefit from the integration of AI in education, leading to a more efficient and effective learning process (Golub et al., 2024; Stavytska et al., 2024).

Real-Time Feedback

AI in language education, exemplified by tools like ChatGPT and Elsa Speak, offers valuable immediate feedback mechanisms that greatly benefit students by providing real-time corrections and enhancing the learning process (Al-Shallakh, 2024; İnci Kavak et al., 2024; Kim, 2024; Sadji Evenddy, 2024). Traditional language learning methods often involve waiting for feedback from teachers, which can create delays and anxiety for students. AI-powered tools, such as language learning apps and writing assistants, provide real-time feedback on exercises, assignments, and language use. The reduction in performance-related anxiety is another advantage, as students can focus on improving their skills without the pressure of waiting for evaluations from their instructors (Golub et al., 2024). AI tools employ Natural Language Processing (NLP) and Machine Learning (ML) to deliver customized feedback on grammar, vocabulary, and pronunciation. This allows students to promptly address errors and continuously refine their language skills. Research highlights that this instant feedback mechanism boosts engagement, strategic thinking, and self-motivation for learning. It particularly enhances communication abilities, which is especially beneficial for introverted students who might be less inclined to participate in traditional classroom settings (Kim, 2024). Additionally, AI grammar checkers play a crucial role in swiftly identifying and correcting writing errors, further supporting the development of language proficiency in educational contexts (İnci Kavak et al., 2024).

Furthermore, the impact of AI on student motivation and confidence is also noteworthy. AI tools that provide immediate feedback and recognize achievements can play a crucial role in building self-efficacy among students. Instant feedback helps students understand their progress and areas for improvement, reinforcing a positive attitude towards learning. This immediate responsiveness supports the development of a growth mindset, where students view challenges as opportunities for growth rather than as obstacles (Cota-Rivera et al., 2024). By encouraging a mindset focused on continuous improvement, AI tools contribute to fostering resilience and a proactive approach to learning.

Leveraging AI for immediate feedback in language education enables educators to create more effective and engaging learning experiences tailored to individual student needs. This approach promotes continuous improvement and helps students achieve higher levels of language proficiency (Al-Shallakh, 2024). The combination of real-time feedback, adaptive learning, and gamification not only enhances language skills but also cultivates a love for learning, setting students on a path to lifelong success in communication and beyond (Kim, 2024; Sadji Evenddy, 2024).

Streamlining Administrative Tasks for Educators

In addition to enhancing the learning experience, AI tools significantly streamline administrative tasks for educators. Tasks such as grading assignments, tracking attendance, and managing administrative records can be automated, which enables teachers to allocate more time to direct student interaction and the development of critical thinking skills. This reduction in administrative burden allows educators to focus on creating meaningful and engaging learning experiences that foster a deeper understanding of the subject matter (Cota-Rivera et al., 2024; Sandhu et al., 2024). By reducing the administrative burden, AI allows teachers to dedicate more time to fostering critical thinking and creativity in their students (İnci Kavak et al., 2024). The efficiency gained from automating routine tasks translates into more opportunities for educators to engage with students on a personal level and address their individual needs.

Increased Accessibility

AI tools have profoundly transformed language education by making it more accessible and inclusive, particularly for students with disabilities. The use of AI technologies not only enhances learning outcomes and improves teacher efficiency but also ensures that a broader range of students, including those with disabilities, can benefit from educational opportunities that were previously inaccessible. By providing adaptive learning tools and fostering greater engagement and autonomy, AI supports the development of language skills across diverse student populations (Kishore et al., 2024). The integration of AI-driven technologies, such as speech-to-text systems, has been instrumental in this regard. These technologies provide critical support for students with learning difficulties, enabling them to engage more fully in educational activities and participate more actively in classroom discussions. For instance, speech-to-text systems facilitate the transcription of spoken words into written text, which can be especially beneficial for students with dyslexia or other learning challenges that affect their reading and writing abilities (Kishore et al., 2024). This technological support not only helps students complete assignments more independently but also fosters greater autonomy in their learning processes.

Furthermore, AI-driven technologies have made substantial contributions to language education by offering tools that enhance accessibility and inclusivity. The ability of AI to support students with disabilities represents a major step forward in educational equity. However, it is essential to remain vigilant about ethical considerations, including data privacy and algorithmic fairness, to ensure that the deployment of AI tools in education achieves its intended benefits without compromising the integrity of the educational process. By addressing these concerns and leveraging the strengths of AI, educators can create more effective and equitable learning environments that cater to the needs of all students.

While the advantages of AI in education are substantial, its implementation is not without challenges. As institutions adopt AI-driven tools, they must consider ethical concerns, potential biases in AI systems, and disparities in access to technology. AI can enhance learning experiences, but if not carefully managed, it may inadvertently widen the gap between privileged and underserved students (Chen & Patel, 2024). Therefore, a balanced approachthat integrates AI while addressing its limitations—is essential for ensuring equitable education outcomes.

CHALLENGES OF INTEGRATING AI TOOLS IN LANGUAGE EDUCATION

The integration of AI tools into language education presents numerous challenges, with bias and fairness emerging as significant concerns. Issues such as over-reliance on AI, data privacy concerns, and the digital divide must be addressed to ensure that AI tools are used ethically and effectively.

Bias and Fairness

While AI tools hold great promise for enhancing language education, they also present significant challenges related to bias and fairness. Bias in AI can lead to unfair or discriminatory outcomes, making it essential to implement strategies for identifying and mitigating such biases. Similarly, addressing algorithmic bias is crucial to ensure that AI systems do not perpetuate or exacerbate existing inequalities.

Addressing these challenges requires a multifaceted approach that includes diverse datasets, technical solutions, ethical guidelines, and ongoing monitoring. Likewise, research highlights the importance of confronting biases to prevent the reinforcement of existing disparities (e.g., Barnes & Hutson, 2024). In educational contexts, the presence of bias is not merely a technical glitch but a reflection of deeper systemic issues that can influence outcomes in ways that disadvantage certain groups of students. One prominent concern is the potential for AI systems to disadvantage non-native speakers and those using various dialects. Many AI systems, including those used for language learning, are trained predominantly on data from native speakers. This can lead to a skewed representation that may not account for the linguistic nuances and challenges faced by non-native speakers (Shuford, 2024). For instance, language models trained on texts from native speakers may struggle to accurately understand or generate text from non-native speakers, leading to unfair outcomes in educational assessments. This issue is compounded when dialectical variations are not adequately represented in the training data, further disadvantaging students who use less common dialects or regional variations.

To mitigate these biases, it is crucial to employ diverse datasets that represent a wide array of linguistic backgrounds. A diverse dataset ensures that the AI system can better understand and cater to the needs of all users, regardless of their linguistic or cultural backgrounds (Barnes & Hutson, 2024). Technical solutions also play a role in addressing bias. These include the development of algorithms that can detect and correct biased outputs, as well as the implementation of fairness-aware machine learning techniques.

Adhering to ethical guidelines and ensuring transparency in AI development are also essential to create fair and unbiased systems. Research has shown that gender disparities and biases can significantly impact scoring outcomes, underscoring the importance of balanced training data to ensure fairness and inclusivity in educational assessments (Latif et al., 2023). For example, if an AI scoring system is trained on data that reflects gender biases present in traditional assessments, it may perpetuate those biases in its evaluations. Ensuring that training data is representative and free from bias is therefore crucial for achieving equitable outcomes in AI-assisted educational assessments.

Therefore, addressing bias in AI also requires embracing transparency and accountability throughout the AI development process. Transparency allows stakeholders to understand how AI systems make decisions and to identify potential sources of bias. Accountability ensures that developers and institutions are responsible for the impacts of their AI systems and are committed to addressing any issues that arise. Moreover, continuous monitoring and evaluation of AI systems are necessary to identify and rectify biases that may emerge over time. As language use and educational practices evolve, AI systems must be updated to reflect these changes and to address any new forms of bias that may arise. This ongoing process requires collaboration between educators, technologists, and policymakers to create and maintain AI systems that are fair, inclusive, and effective in supporting language education.

Ethical Implications

Ethical concerns in AI-based education include biases in content recommendations, the potential for AI-generated misinformation, and the risks of unauthorized student data usage. For example, AI writing assistants may inadvertently reinforce dominant linguistic norms, disadvantaging non-native speakers. Furthermore, the improper storage or sharing of AI-collected student data could lead to privacy violations.

Educators must also be prepared to address issues related to data privacy, algorithmic bias, and error handling, establishing clear guidelines and accountability mechanisms to manage these concerns effectively (du Preez et al., 2024; Sayyadnejad et al., 2024).The transparency and accountability of AI systems are critical to building trust among educators and students. Transparency is essential for ensuring that AI tools are used responsibly and that their outputs can be critically evaluated by users (Hassija et al., 2023; Sayyadnejad et al., 2024).

One critical consideration is the establishment of clear policies and guidelines aligned with ethical principles. Educators must ensure that the use of AI in their classrooms adheres to standards of privacy, data protection, and non-discrimination (Paschal & Melly, 2023). Regular audits should be conducted to identify potential biases or unintended consequences in AI algorithms and content. Clear accountability frameworks can help ensure that ethical standards are maintained and that any issues arising from AI tool usage are addressed in a timely and effective manner (du Preez et al., 2024; Sayyadnejad et al., 2024).

Privacy and Data Security

Data privacy concerns are paramount, as AI systems often handle sensitive information that must be protected from unauthorized access and misuse. The complex landscape of data privacy in educational settings can be understood through several key perspectives and models. Students' perceptions of privacy are crucial in addressing these concerns. The Student Personal Information Privacy Perception (SPIPP) model, as highlighted by Maguraushe et al. (2024), provides a framework for understanding how students perceive their privacy in the context of data collection and utilization. This model emphasizes the importance of considering privacy awareness and expectations when implementing data privacy principles. According to the SPIPP model, students' understanding of and attitudes towards privacy significantly influence their comfort levels with the use of their personal information. This awareness can be influenced by various factors, including the transparency of data practices and the perceived security of data storage methods.

Privacy concerns are another significant challenge in the context of learning analytics. The collection of detailed student data raises questions about how this information is stored, used, and shared. The potential for data breaches or unauthorized access to personal information necessitates robust security measures and privacy safeguards. As Khor and Mutthulakshmi (2023) suggest, addressing these concerns requires a comprehensive approach that includes implementing strong data protection policies and ensuring transparency about data practices. Diverse students' perspectives on privacy and technology integration add another layer of complexity to this issue. Kumi-Yeboah (2023) explores how different students perceive privacy in the context of technology use and data collection. The study reveals that students from diverse backgrounds may have varying levels of comfort and trust regarding data practices. For some, there may be a heightened sense of fear and anxiety about data encroachment, driven by concerns about how their personal information is being used and who has access to it. This variability in perceptions highlights the importance of considering diverse viewpoints when developing and implementing privacy policies in educational settings.

Moreover, error handling mechanisms must be in place to address any inaccuracies or malfunctions in AI systems. This includes procedures for identifying, reporting, and correcting errors to prevent adverse impacts on users and ensure the reliability of AI tools. Accountability mechanisms are also vital for holding AI developers and users responsible for the impacts of their AI systems.

Educational awareness is crucial in addressing these concerns. As Kumi-Yeboah (2023) suggests, increasing students' understanding of data privacy practices and the measures in place to protect their information can help alleviate some of the fears and anxieties associated with data collection. By fostering an environment of transparency and trust, educational institutions can better address students' privacy concerns and build confidence in their data handling practices. The study by Belligoni et al. (2023) on smartphone location data concerns among college students provides further insights into privacy issues. The research indicates that college students have significant concerns about the privacy implications of location data collection. These concerns highlight the importance of trust in the handling of personal information and underscore the need for clear policies and guidelines regarding data use. Paschal and Melly (2023) emphasize the importance of trust and policy recommendations for secure data handling. Their work suggests that to address privacy concerns effectively, educational institutions must establish and communicate robust policies that govern data collection, storage, and use. These policies should be designed to protect students' personal information from unauthorized access and ensure that data practices are transparent and ethical.

In addition, the collection and utilization of student data for personalized learning present a complex interplay of benefits and challenges. The SPIPP model (Maguraushe et al., 2024) highlights the importance of understanding students' privacy perceptions, while Khor and Mutthulakshmi (2023) emphasize the challenges related to accuracy, opportunity costs, and privacy concerns in learning analytics. Kumi-Yeboah (2023) underscores the need to consider diverse students' perspectives on privacy and technology, while Belligoni et al. (2023) and Paschal and Melly (2023) highlight the importance of trust and policy recommendations for secure data handling. Addressing these concerns requires a multifaceted approach that balances the benefits of personalized learning with robust privacy protections and transparency.

The Digital Divide

The digital divide significantly hinders equitable access to AI tools in education, particularly for students in underserved regions who often lack the necessary technology or reliable internet, worsening educational disparities (Afzal et al., 2023; Bentley et al., 2024; Lahiri, 2024). This issue is most pronounced in rural areas and among lower-income families, where access to essential digital resources is limited. Gender disparities also contribute, with girls in certain regions having less access to technology than boys (Afzal et al., 2023). Addressing this divide requires not just providing technology but also understanding and overcoming the unique challenges faced by students from diverse backgrounds. Public-private partnerships are suggested as a strategy to supply technological resources to disadvantaged schools, ensuring all students can benefit from AI advancements. Furthermore, the the high costs of learning analytics software, hardware, and training, which can limit accessibility in low-resource regions. should be considered to maintain accessibility, ultimately aiming to make education more inclusive and effective for every student (Afzal et al., 2023).

Transparency and Accountability

AI tools, despite their potential to revolutionize various fields, often operate as "black boxes," presenting significant challenges in understanding how decisions are made. This lack of transparency can obscure the rationale behind AI-generated outcomes and recommendations, making it difficult for users to trust and effectively utilize these tools (Li et al., 2024). To address these challenges, it is crucial for both educators and students to have access to clear, understandable explanations of how AI tools function and produce their recommendations. Ensuring that AI systems are interpretable and that their decision-making processes are transparent is not just a technical necessity but a fundamental requirement for fostering trust and effective use of AI technologies (Xu, 2024). One promising approach to mitigating the "black box" problem is the development and application of Explainable Artificial Intelligence (XAI). XAI is an emerging field dedicated to making AI systems more transparent and interpretable. It focuses on creating methods and techniques that can elucidate the inner workings and decision-making processes of AI models. By enhancing the ability to explain how AI systems arrive at their conclusions, XAI aims to build greater trust and understanding among users (Hassija et al., 2023; Sayyadnejad et al., 2024).

Natural Language Processing (NLP) models, such as Generative Pre-trained Transformers (GPT), represent a significant advancement in this area. These models can be employed to generate explanations for specific AI models based on their inputs and outputs. Such explanations can provide valuable insights into the reasoning behind AI-generated decisions, thereby helping users to grasp how AI models operate and make recommendations. For instance, a GPT model can describe the factors influencing an AI's decision-making process and clarify how different inputs affect the outcomes. This transparency can enhance user comprehension and trust, making AI tools more accessible and manageable (Hassija et al., 2023).

Nevertheless, the effectiveness of explanations generated by NLP models like GPT depends heavily on the quality and accuracy of the training data used to develop these models. If the training data is flawed or biased, the explanations provided may also be inaccurate or misleading. Furthermore, the complexity of the AI model being explained can impact the clarity and usefulness of these explanations. To ensure that the explanations are reliable and robust, it is essential to integrate them with other techniques, such as model-agnostic methods and model-specific interpretability techniques. Model-agnostic methods, which are designed to be applicable to a wide range of AI models, and model-specific techniques, which are tailored to the nuances of individual models, can collectively enhance the overall interpretability and transparency of AI systems (Hassija et al., 2023). By focusing on transparency and interpretability through techniques such as XAI and NLP-based explanations, we can enhance users' understanding and trust in AI tools. Additionally, implementing robust guidelines and accountability mechanisms will help address ethical concerns and ensure the responsible use of AI technologies.

Less Human Interaction

Another important aspect to consider is the balance between AI-powered learning and traditional teaching methods. While AI can enhance and complement traditional instruction, it should not replace the human element in language education. Educators must maintain their role as facilitators, mentors, and guides, providing emotional support, and cultural context that AI tools may not be able to replicate. Despite the significant advancements in AI tools and technologies, they cannot fully replicate or replace the profound value that human interaction brings to these domains. This value is evident through its impact on the evolution of language, the development of user-centered software, and the creation of effective communication tools for specific communities.

The iterated learning framework, a key method in the study of language evolution, underscores this significance. This framework involves transmitting linguistic information across multiple generations of learners, highlighting how language evolves through repeated cycles of interaction (Helander, 2014; Rogalska-Chodecka, 2019). The process of iterated learning allows languages to adapt and refine themselves based on the interactions of each new generation. This cyclical transmission process is not just a method of teaching but a driving force behind the evolution of language itself. Each generation of learners modifies and refines language structures based on their interactions, demonstrating that human interaction is a fundamental component in the progression and development of language.

For example, the principles of Human-Computer Interaction (HCI) are crucial throughout the entire software development process. By incorporating HCI principles, developers can create software that is not only functional but also user-friendly and high-quality. This approach emphasizes the importance of considering human factors, such as behavioral, cognitive, and perceptual elements, during the design and development stages (Calp & Akçayol, 2015). When developers prioritize user experience and interaction, they can produce software that meets users' needs and expectations, ensuring a more intuitive and accessible experience. This user-centered approach is particularly vital in today's fast-paced technological landscape, where the success of a software product often depends on its usability and the quality of interaction it provides. For example, designing technology that supports natural and intuitive interactions for people with hearing or speech impairments can bridge communication gaps and enhance user experience (Rogalska-Chodecka, 2019). Therefore, by integrating human interaction thoughtfully and effectively, we can enhance the quality of outcomes across various domains and ensure that technology continues to support and enrich human experiences.

The (Negative) Impact on Students' Critical Thinking

The integration of AI in educational settings has sparked debates regarding the potential risks of students becoming overly dependent on AI-generated solutions, which could impair their critical thinking and problem-solving abilities (Pahuja et al., 2024). Although AI tools are designed to enhance collaboration and deepen students' understanding, there is concern that their misuse might lead to decreased motivation and self-confidence in learners.While AI tools offer numerous benefits, it is crucial to ensure that their implementation does not inadvertently lead to a reliance that undermines students' critical thinking abilities. Excessive dependence on AI-generated solutions could potentially diminish students' motivation to engage actively with the material and develop independent problem-solving skills (Darvishi et al., 2024; Pahuja et al., 2024). Therefore, it is essential for educators to strike a balance between leveraging AI's capabilities and fostering critical thinking and problem-solving skills among students. Educators should be mindful of promoting independence among students, ensuring that AI tools complement rather than replace traditional learning methods.

Several studies have shown that students are more inclined to rely on AI for assistance rather than actively engaging with the material, which highlights the risk of excessive dependence on AI in education (**Darvishi et al., 2024**). To mitigate this issue, it is essential to adopt a balanced approach. This involves educators playing a pivotal role in moderating discussions, offering guidance, and encouraging practices that foster critical thinking alongside the use of AI tools. Such a strategy would help ensure that students not only benefit from AI but also develop the crucial skills needed to thrive in an increasingly AI-driven world (Lodge et al., 2024).

The reliance on AI-generated solutions can create a scenario where students merely accept the information provided without questioning or critically evaluating it, which is a vital part of the learning process (Pahuja et al., 2024). This dependency could lead to a decline in students' ability to think independently and solve problems creatively, as they might begin to see AI as a crutch rather than a tool to enhance their learning (Darvishi et al., 2024).

Moreover, the misuse of AI tools can have a detrimental impact on students' motivation and self-efficacy. When students rely too heavily on AI, they may lose the confidence to tackle challenging tasks on their own. This can result in a decrease in intrinsic motivation, as students might feel less capable of achieving success without AI assistance. Over time, this can undermine their sense of self-efficacy, which is crucial for long-term academic and personal development. To address these challenges, it is imperative to strike a balance between leveraging AI's capabilities and fostering students' independent thinking and problem-solving skills. Educators play a key role in this process by facilitating discussions that encourage students to engage with the material critically, rather than passively accepting AI-generated content. By providing guidance and promoting an environment where questioning and exploration are encouraged, teachers can help students develop the skills needed to navigate complex problems and think critically (**Lodge et al., 2024**).

Educators must empower students to critically scrutinize AI-generated information and content. By fostering critical thinking skills and media literacy, students can learn to discern the accuracy, reliability, and potential biases in AI-produced language materials. This approach helps students develop independence and discernment in their intellectual pursuits within technology-rich learning environments (Moustaghfir & Brigui, 2024). By adopting a balanced approach that integrates AI with traditional teaching methods and emphasizes critical thinking, educators can help students develop the essential skills required to succeed in an AI-driven world (Lodge et al., 2024; Sako, 2024).

CONCLUSION

The advent of AI in education marks a significant transformation in the way learning and teaching are conceptualized and delivered. Across various domains, AI's influence is reshaping educational practices, offering new tools and methods that promise to enhance learning outcomes. However, as explored throughout this paper, the integration of AI in education is a complex process that requires careful consideration of various factors to ensure its effective and ethical implementation.

AI's potential to revolutionize language education is particularly noteworthy. By providing personalized learning experiences, dynamic content, and real-time feedback, AI can significantly enhance language acquisition and literacy. These tools allow educators to cater to the diverse needs of learners, offering tailored instructional materials that align with individual proficiency levels and learning styles. AI's capability to analyze student performance and adjust content delivery accordingly helps maintain engagement and motivation, ensuring that students are neither overwhelmed nor under-challenged. In this way, AI tools can create more inclusive and responsive learning environments, where each student has the opportunity to succeed. Moreover, AI's role in generating dynamic content is a valuable asset in language education. For instance, AI-powered chatbots can simulate real-life conversations and text-to-speech tools can produce engaging audio content, supporting learners in improving their pronunciation and comprehension. These tools help bring language to life, making the learning process more engaging and effective.

However, the integration of AI into educational settings is not without its challenges. A significant concern is the potential for over-reliance on AI, which could undermine students' critical thinking and problem-solving abilities. As AI becomes more prevalent, there is a risk that students may become passive recipients of information, relying on AI-generated answers and feedback without engaging critically with the material. This dependency could erode students' confidence in their own abilities, diminishing their motivation to tackle challenging tasks independently. To counteract this, educators must play an active role in fostering critical thinking alongside the use of AI tools. It is essential to strike a balance between leveraging AI's capabilities and encouraging students to think independently. Educators can do this by moderating discussions, guiding students in their use of AI tools, and creating learning environments that promote questioning, exploration, and critical evaluation. By doing so, they can ensure that students develop the necessary skills to navigate an increasingly AI-driven world while maintaining their ability to think creatively and solve problems effectively.

The ethical considerations surrounding AI integration are another critical aspect that educators must address. As AI tools become more embedded in educational practices, there is a pressing need to establish clear guidelines and accountability mechanisms to manage potential issues such as data privacy, algorithmic bias, and error handling. Transparency in AI systems is crucial to building trust among educators and students. XAI offers a promising solution by making AI systems more transparent and interpretable. Through techniques that explain the inner workings and decision-making processes of AI models, XAI can help educators and students understand how AI-generated recommendations are made, allowing them to use these tools more effectively and responsibly.

Furthermore, the issue of the digital divide must be considered when integrating AI into education. The benefits of AI are not universally accessible, particularly for students in underserved regions who may lack the necessary technology and internet connectivity. This digital divide exacerbates existing disparities in education, creating significant barriers for students who are already at a disadvantage. Ensuring equitable access to AI tools is essential to prevent further widening of the gap between different demographics. Strategies such as establishing technology resource centers in schools and forming public-private partnerships can help bridge this divide, providing students with the resources they need to fully participate in the digital aspects of their education.

In addition to technical solutions, there is a need for ongoing training and support for educators, students, and parents. As AI tools become more prevalent, it is vital that all stakeholders understand their capabilities and limitations. Training should cover responsible AI use, interpretation of AI-generated feedback, and critical evaluation of AI-produced content. This knowledge will empower educators to use AI tools effectively and help students develop a critical perspective towards the information and recommendations provided by AI systems. Another important consideration is the role of human interaction in education. While AI offers numerous advantages, it cannot replace the inherent value of human interaction in the learning process. Human interaction is fundamental to language learning, where communication and cultural context are essential. Educators must continue to play a central role in providing emotional support, cultural insights, and nuanced feedback that AI tools cannot replicate. The integration of AI should complement, not replace, the human element in education, ensuring that students receive a well-rounded learning experience.

The integration of AI in education is not merely a technological shift but a pedagogical one that requires a thoughtful and balanced approach. AI has the potential to enhance educational practices by providing personalized learning experiences, generating dynamic content, and offering immediate feedback. However, its implementation must be guided by ethical principles, ongoing training, and a commitment to maintaining the human element in education. By adopting a balanced approach, educators can harness the benefits of AI while addressing its potential drawbacks. This approach involves promoting critical thinking, ensuring transparency and accountability in AI systems, bridging the digital divide, and preserving the value of human interaction. In doing so, educators can create equitable and effective learning environments that prepare students for success in an increasingly AI-driven world.

Therefore, the successful integration of AI in education hinges on a holistic strategy that prioritizes ethical considerations, fosters critical thinking, and ensures equitable access to technology. By embracing AI's potential while remaining mindful of its challenges, educators can transform educational practices in a way that benefits all students, helping them develop the skills and knowledge needed to thrive in the digital age.

REFERENCES

Afzal, A. M., Khan, S. A., Daud, S., Ahmad, Z., & Butt, A. (2023). Addressing the digital divide: Access and use of technology in education. *Journal of Social Sciences Review*, *3*(2), 883–895. DOI: 10.54183/jssr.v3i2.326

Al-Shallakh, M. A. I. (2024). Embedding artificial intelligent applications in higher educational institutions to improve students' pronunciation performance. *Theory and Practice in Language Studies*, *14*(6), 1897–1906. DOI: 10.17507/tpls.1406.31

Ali, Y. K., Mammadova, M., Geyis, A. J., & Mehdiyeva, G. B. (2024). Enhancing esl education with ai: Innovations in teaching methods and au-thentic materials. *International Journal of Membrane Science and Technology*, *11*(1), 497–505. DOI: 10.15379/ijmst.v11i1.3687

Barnes, E., & Hutson, J. (2024). Navigating the ethical terrain of ai in higher education: Strategies for mitigating bias and promoting fairness. *Forum for Education Studies*, *2*(2), 1229. DOI: 10.59400/fes.v2i2.1229

Belligoni, S., Stevens, K. A., Hasan, S., & Yu, H. (2023). Privacy and security concerns with passively collected location data for digital contact tracing among US college students. *PLoS One*, *18*(11), e0294419. DOI: 10.1371/journal.pone.0294419 PMID: 37992048

Bentley, S. V., Naughtin, C. K., McGrath, M. J., Irons, J. L., & Cooper, P. S. (2024). The digital divide in action: How experiences of digital technology shape future relationships with artificial intelligence. *AI and Ethics*, *2024*(4), 901–915. Advance online publication. DOI: 10.1007/s43681-024-00452-3

Calp, M. H., & Akcayol, M. A. (2015). The importance of human-computer interaction in the development process of software projects. *Global Journal of Information Technology: Emerging Technologies*, *5*(1), 48–54. DOI: 10.18844/gjit.v0i0.114

Cohen, S., Mompelat, L., Mann, A., & Connors, L. (2024). The linguistic leap: Understanding, evaluating, and integrating ai in language education. *Tydskrif vir Taalonderrig*, *4*(2), 23–31. DOI: 10.54475/jlt.2024.012

Cota-Rivera, E. I., González Correa, M. E., Bernal Marín, L. A., Marquez Montenegro, M. Y., Herrera, A. M., & Martinez Martinez, M. A. (2024). Transforming Education With the Power of Artificial Intelligence: Case Studies. In Demir, Ş., & Demir, M. (Eds.), *Enhancing Higher Education and Research With OpenAI Models* (pp. 113–140). IGI Global Scientific Publishing., DOI: 10.4018/979-8-3693-1666-5.ch006

Creely, E. (2024). Exploring the role of generative ai in enhancing language learning: opportunities and challenges. *International Journal of Changes in Education*, 1-10. DOI: 10.47852/bonviewIJCE42022495

Darvishi, A., Khosravi, H., Sadiq, S., Gašević, D., & Siemens, G. (2024). Impact of ai assistance on student agency. *Computers & Education*, *210*, 104967. DOI: 10.1016/j.compedu.2023.104967

du Preez, V., Bennet, S., Byrne, M., Couloumy, A., Das, A., Dessain, J., Galbraith, R., King, P., Mutanga, V., Schiller, F., Zaaiman, S., Moehrke, P., & van Heerden, L. (2024). From bias to black boxes: Understanding and managing the risks of ai – an actuarial perspective. *British Actuarial Journal*, *29*, e6. Advance online publication. DOI: 10.1017/S1357321724000060

Golub, T. P., Kovalenko, O. O., Zhygzhytova, L. M., & Kotkovets, A. L. (2024). Ai-powered pedagogy: foreign language study in higher education. *Академічні Студії. Серія «педагогіка», 4*, 50-56. DOI: 10.52726/as.pedagogy/2023.4.7

Hassija, V., Chamola, V., Mahapatra, A., Singal, A., Goel, D., Huang, K., Scardapane, S., Spinelli, I., Mahmud, M., & Hussain, A. (2023). Interpreting black-box models: A review on explainable artificial intelligence. *Cognitive Computation, 16*(1), 45–74. DOI: 10.1007/s12559-023-10179-8

Helander, M. G. (Ed.). (2014). *Handbook of human-computer interaction*. Elsevier.

İnci Kavak, V., Evis, D., & Ekinci, A. (2024). *The use of chatgpt in language education*. Experimental and Applied Medical Science., DOI: 10.46871/eams.1461578

Khor, E. T., & Mutthulakshmi, M. (2023). A systematic review of the role of learning analytics in supporting personalized learning. *Education Sciences, 14*(1), 51. DOI: 10.3390/educsci14010051

Kim, E. (2024). A study on using ai learning for elementary school students struggling with english. The Korea Association of Primary English Education, 30(2), 81-104. DOI: 10.25231/pee.2024.30.2.81

Kishore, H. S., Solomon Paul Raj, D., & Senthilkumar, K. R. (2024). AI for Accessibility: A Case Study of Enhancing Library Services for Users With Disabilities. In Senthilkumar, K., & Jagajeevan, R. (Eds.), *Improving Library Systems with AI: Applications, Approaches, and Bibliometric Insights* (pp. 214–225). IGI Global Scientific Publishing. DOI: 10.4018/979-8-3693-5593-0.ch015

Kumi-Yeboah, A., Kim, Y., Yankson, B., Aikins, S., & Dadson, Y. A. (2023). Diverse students' perspectives on privacy and technology integration in higher education. *British Journal of Educational Technology, 54*(6), 1671–1692. DOI: 10.1111/bjet.13386

Lahiri, A. (2024). Sociological implications of the digital divide: Exploring access to information and social inequality in the age of artificial intelligence and automation. RESEARCH REVIEW. *International Journal of Multidisciplinary, 9*(1), 156–167. DOI: 10.31305/rrijm.2024.v09.n01.019

Latif. E., Zhai. X., Liu, L.. (2023). AI Gender Bias, Disparities, and Fairness: Does Training Data Matter?. arXiv.org, abs/2312.10833 DOI: 10.48550/arxiv.2312.10833

Li, Z., Dhruv, A., & Jain, V. (2024). Ethical considerations in the use of ai for higher education: a comprehensive guide. In *2024 IEEE 18th International Conference on Semantic Computing (ICSC)*. DOI: 10.1109/ICSC59802.2024.00041

Lodge, J. M., De Barba, P., & Broadbent, J. (2024). Learning with generative artificial intelligence within a network of co-regulation. *Journal of University Teaching & Learning Practice, 20*(7). Advance online publication. DOI: 10.53761/1.20.7.02

Luo, J., & Qiu, L. (2024). Review of artificial intelligence-based tools in EFL classroom. *Arts. Culture and Language, 1*(7), 1–5. DOI: 10.61173/s266nr95

Maguraushe, K., da Veiga, A., & Martins, N. (2024). A personal information privacy perceptions model for university students. *Information Security Journal: A Global Perspective*, 33(4), 394-424. DOI: 10.1080/19393555.2024.2329554

Moustaghfir, S., & Brigui, H. (2024). Navigating critical thinking in the digital era: An informative exploration. *International Journal of Linguistics. Literature and Translation*, *7*(1), 137–143. DOI: 10.32996/ijllt.2024.7.1.11x

Onesi-Ozigagun, O., Ololade, Y. J., Eyo-Udo, N. L., & Ogundipe, D. L. (2024). Revolutionizing education through ai: A comprehensive review of enhancing learning experiences. *International Journal of Applied Research in Social Sciences*, *6*(4), 589–607. DOI: 10.51594/ijarss.v6i4.1011

Pahuja, A., Kaur, S., Budhraja, K., & Kathuria, S. (2024). Examining the Impact of AI on Education: Ethical, Psychological, and Pedagogical Perspectives. In Saluja, S., Nayyar, V., Rojhe, K., & Sharma, S. (Eds.), *Ethical AI and Data Management Strategies in Marketing* (pp. 208–225). IGI Global Scientific Publishing., DOI: 10.4018/979-8-3693-6660-8.ch015

Paschal, M. J., & Melly, I. K. (2023). Ethical Guidelines on the Use of AI in Education. In Keengwe, J. (Ed.), *Creative AI Tools and Ethical Implications in Teaching and Learning* (pp. 230–245). IGI Global Scientific Publishing., DOI: 10.4018/979-8-3693-0205-7.ch013

Rogalska-Chodecka, K. (2019). The Role of Interaction in Language Evolution. Evidence from Two Iterated Learning Experiments with Human Participants. *Theoria et Historia Scientiarum*, *16*, 115. DOI: 10.12775/ths.2019.007

Sadji Evenddy, S. (2024). Investigating AI's automated feedback in english language learning. *FLIP Foreign Language Instruction Probe*, *3*(1), 76–87. DOI: 10.54213/flip.v3i1.401

Sako, T. (2024). Enhancing critical thinking through ai-assisted collaborative task-based learning: A case study of prospective teachers in Japan. *Journal of English Language Teaching and Linguistics*, *9*(2), 157. DOI: 10.21462/jeltl.v9i2.1319

Sandhu, R., Channi, H. K., Ghai, D., Cheema, G. S., & Kaur, M. (2024). An Introduction to Generative AI Tools for Education 2030. In Doshi, R., Dadhich, M., Poddar, S., & Hiran, K. (Eds.), *Integrating Generative AI in Education to Achieve Sustainable Development Goals* (pp. 1–28). IGI Global Scientific Publishing. DOI: 10.4018/979-8-3693-2440-0.ch001

Sayyadnejad, M. M., Asgari, A., Sami, A., & Tahyori, H. (2024). Exploring the black box: analyzing explainable ai challenges and best practices through stack exchange discussions. 23 April 2024, PREPRINT (Version 1) available at Research Square DOI: 10.21203/rs.3.rs-4304124/v1

Shuford, J. (2024). Examining ethical aspects of ai: Addressing bias and equity in the discipline. [JAIGS]. *Journal of Artificial Intelligence General Science*, *3*(1), 262–280. DOI: 10.60087/jaigs.v3i1.119

Stavytska, I., Shalova, N., & Korbut, O. (2024). Exploring the impacts and techniques of teaching with artificial intelligence tools. *Перспективи Та Інновації Науки*, *6*(40), 40–48. DOI: 10.52058/2786-4952-2023-16(34)

Umar, U. (2024). Advancements in English language teaching: Harnessing the power of artificial intelligence. *FLIP Foreign Language Instruction Probe*, *3*(1), 29–42. DOI: 10.54213/flip.v3i1.402

Chapter 6

Bridging Gaps: AI-Driven Accessibility in Language Education

Andi Asrifan
https://orcid.org/0000-0002-9934-6129
Universitas Negeri Makassar, Indonesia

Arsad Bahri
https://orcid.org/0000-0002-2693-6662
Universitas Negeri Makassar, Indonesia

Shafa Shafa
UIN Sultan Aji Muhammad Idris Samarinda, Indonesia

Sri Rahmadhani Siregar
https://orcid.org/0009-0008-7943-2864
UIN Syekh Ali Hasan Ahmad Addary Padangsidimpuan, Indonesia

Widya Rizky Pratiwi
https://orcid.org/0000-0003-0738-752X
Universitas Terbuka, Indonesia

Sajed S. Ingilan
https://orcid.org/0000-0002-4466-2028
University of Southeastern Philippines, Philippines

ABSTRACT

Language education accessibility, especially for visually and hearing-impaired pupils, depends on AI. Advanced automated language teaching systems for the disabled are limited despite broad language technology developments. Manual input makes present solutions challenging for limb-impaired people and increases remote help. AI, especially NLP, offers unique solutions for diverse demands and talents, ensuring language learning equality. AI frameworks rarely consider visually impaired users. The chapter suggests using AI and NLP to personalize language learning. These technologies can give audio descriptions, text-to-speech, and interactive platforms for inclusive learning that maximizes student potential. AI-driven solutions can empower handicapped learners and improve their communication, independence, and social integration by including beneficiaries, instructors, and families and cooperating across stakeholders.

DOI: 10.4018/979-8-3693-7260-9.ch006

1. INTRODUCTION

In recent years, language instruction has experienced a transformational shift due to the integration of artificial intelligence (AI). Nonetheless, the utilization of AI technology to assist individuals with visual and auditory disabilities remains insufficiently investigated and inadequately advanced. Notwithstanding significant progress in natural language processing (NLP) and assistive technology, current solutions frequently depend on traditional input-output mechanisms, such as keyboards or visual indicators, thereby marginalizing several learners with physical and sensory limitations. The issues are exacerbated by reliance on human facilitators and the absence of scalable, adaptive solutions that address varied student requirements.

This chapter examines how AI-powered accessibility solutions can close the educational gap and offer equal chances in language acquisition. This study investigates the contributions of NLP, intelligent tutoring systems, and multimodal AI interfaces in improving access, customisation, and engagement for learners with impairments. The discourse highlights the necessity of transcending a uniform approach and adopting inclusive solutions that actively engage learners with disabilities in the design and execution of educational technologies. This chapter underscores the significance of inclusive design and stakeholder engagement in the development of effective educational technologies through a critical study of existing research, new technologies, and case studies. Integrating user-centered AI technologies into the educational framework can empower disenfranchised learners and establish accessibility as a fundamental tenet in the future of language education.

Language education applications, especially those designed for visually challenged or deaf individuals, are still in the early stages of development (Csizér & Kontra, 2020; Fan et al., 2020; Aljedaani et al., 2021; Papastratos et al., 2021). Despite significant advancements in research in general language technologies, robust automated language instruction tools remain limited for individuals with impairments such as vision, hearing, sensory, speech, and arm movement. The current solutions for language teaching and learning typically necessitate using a keyboard or stylus-based device, allowing students to input answers or manipulate objects. However, this poses a significant limitation for individuals with limb impairments. Furthermore, the dependence on on-site or remote helpers who can read or sign instructional content and provide feedback on student input further exacerbates these challenges (Starks & Reich, 2023; Alzahrani, 2020). Consequently, the entire language education process becomes exceptionally time-consuming and ultimately unsustainable for individuals with impairments. Thus, there is an urgent need for innovative and inclusive language education applications that cater specifically to the diverse needs and abilities of visually challenged or deaf individuals, ensuring equal access and opportunities for language learning and development.

AI-driven technologies, particularly natural language processing (NLP), promise to overcome these challenges by offering innovative solutions that cater to individuals with disabilities (Neha et al., 2024; Chopra et al., 2024). Many researchers have proposed groundbreaking NLP-based frameworks to address various types of disabilities. However, it is crucial to note that the focus of these frameworks tends to revolve around computer science, domain-specific content enrichment, or the education process, neglecting the needs of end-users, particularly visually impaired individuals. To bridge this gap, it is imperative to integrate technology seamlessly into the real education ecosystem and embrace the principles of open education philosophy (Alam & Mohanty, 2024; Bandyopadhyay et al., 2021; Ghosh, 2024). This ensures that language teaching and learning for the impaired can thrive and benefit from the transformative potential of AI-driven technologies. By fostering a holistic approach, which considers the voices and perspectives of beneficiaries, teachers, and families, we can create an inclusive environment that maximizes the potential of every learner (Beninghof, 2020; Lai et al., 2022; Li & Li, 2022). This approach requires collaboration and coordination among various stakeholders in the education system. The education sector can unlock remarkable opportunities for visually impaired individuals by integrating AI and NLP. These cutting-edge technologies can facilitate personalized and adaptive learning experiences, revolutionizing how language is taught and learned. By harnessing the power of AI-driven tools, we can empower visually impaired learners to develop strong linguistic skills, enhancing their communication abilities and paving the way for increased independence and integration within society (Zdravkova, 2022; Chopra et al., 2024; Mitra et al., 2023; Almufareh et al., 2024). Moreover, integrating AI and NLP in language teaching for the impaired ensures that accessibility barriers are systematically addressed. By leveraging the advancements in these technologies, educators can provide tailored resources, such as audio descriptions, text-to-speech capabilities, and interactive learning platforms, that cater specifically to the needs of visually impaired learners (Parashar et al., 2023; Chopra et al., 2024; Almufareh et al., 2024). This comprehensive approach enables equal access to educational materials and fosters a sense of empowerment and inclusivity among learners, boosting their confidence and overall educational outcomes. The seamless integration of AI-driven technologies, particularly NLP, within the education ecosystem holds great promise for revolutionizing language teaching and learning for visually impaired individuals (Zdravkova, 2022; Chen, 2024; Alqahtani et al., 2023). By prioritizing the inclusion of end-users and stakeholders, we can develop comprehensive frameworks that cater to this community's unique needs and challenges. Through AI, we can unlock new horizons of accessibility, independence, and educational growth, propelling visually impaired individuals toward success in both academic and personal spheres.

1.1. Background and Rationale

Artificial intelligence (AI) is no longer an element of a science-fiction novel (Hudson et al., 2023; Osawa et al., 2022; Ajeesh & Rukmini, 2023). With the digital explosion of the fourth industrial revolution, AI's influence on professional and everyday life is undeniable, whether we know it or not. From smartphones to social media platforms, web search engines to educational technologies, the average digital native heavily relies, one way or another, on the immense power of AI to function effectively and efficiently in the vast online world (Hassani et al., 2021; Gill et al., 2022; Srinivasa et al., 2022). We are, without a doubt, far from creating AI that surpasses human cognition and moral reasoning and dives into the realm of science fiction. Nevertheless, contemporary AI has been successfully developed with cognitive tasks replicating various human functions, such as intelligent problem-solving through advanced reasoning capabilities and even making morally complex decisions. Furthermore, with the proper algorithm and the vast wealth of Big Data, AI can transcend human capabilities by effectively organizing and skillfully interpreting an immense amount of information and knowledge, surpassing what would be humanly possible. AI's tremendous potential and growth continue to reshape and redefine various industries and aspects of our lives, and its ongoing development and advancements are poised to have an even greater impact in the future (Ahmad et al., 2021; Feijóo et al., 2020).

Large and comprehensive algorithms capable of identifying rules and patterns in human language (Natural Language Processing algorithms) and transforming non-structured data into structured ones (called machine learning algorithms) made several AI-driven technologies in Natural Language Processing possible (Khurana et al., 2023; Li et al., 2021). In Natural Language Processing, large and comprehensive algorithms capable of identifying rules and patterns in human language and transforming non-structured data into structured data have been made possible by several AI-driven technologies. From virtual assistants that help you operate home devices through voice commands to online fraud-detection virtual agents to the recommendations to improve speech and text effectiveness for non-native speakers, AI has been promoting a major change in daily living (Feijóo et al., 2020; Rahman et al., 2020).

2. THE ROLE OF AI IN LANGUAGE EDUCATION

AI technologies can also evaluate user input to operate as a non-judgmental tutor that delivers instantaneous feedback, inspires introspection, digs into minutiae, and encourages rapid iteration, akin to a human instructor. Unlike traditional tutoring, where each input response cycle takes time, AI systems may scale learning by giving each learner a unique experience and creating the need for new private, secure, and calibrated interactivity.

AI-driven language education tools develop organically from the requirement for insights and feedback in learning processes and the potential of popular AI technologies when enough relevant data is available. Language education has used AI for speech recognition, word prediction, generation, translation, sentiment analysis, conversational bots, and more (Zhai & Wibowo, 2023; Allouch et al., 2021). AI tools have helped language learners in several ways. They aid speech, grammar, and vocabulary. Speech recognition transcribes non-native speakers and evaluates pronunciation. Teachers can assess students' spoken language skills and give constructive criticism using the technology. Students may effortlessly produce literature and improve their vocabulary with word prediction and generation. These tools propose words and phrases to help students form sentences and express themselves. (Kuddus, 2022; Deng & Yu, 2022; Lee, 2023). Translation AI models help foreign language learners (Kuddus, 2022; Deng & Yu, 2022; Lee, 2023). These models help students understand and study multilingual materials by translating sentences and phrases. AI-driven technologies automatically grade assignments, assuring fairness and efficiency (Naseer et al., 2024; Darvishi, 2022).

Language teaching uses AI for sentiment analysis, too. This technology analyzes pupils' writing emotions to interpret it. Understanding the sentiment underlying the words can help instructors comprehend students' thoughts and feelings and highlight areas where they may need more support (Blewitt et al., 2021; Gkonou & Miller, 2021; Li et al., 2024). Conversational agents interact with students and personalize language learning at different levels (Belda-Medina & Calvo-Ferrer, 2022; Dokukina & Gumanova, 2020). These AI assistants provide assistance, answer questions, and facilitate practice sessions via text or speech. In a relaxed, engaging setting, learners can practice speaking and listening by replicating real-life conversations. AI can also identify learners' emotions and decipher non-literal language. This ability helps students who struggle with metaphorical terms or non-literal language obtain proper instruction and support. Summarization, coreference resolution, and other AI models apply to natural language processing. Language teachers can use these methods to assist pupils in understanding complicated texts. In language teaching, AI-driven tools have transformed student learning. Language learners can improve their abilities, overcome language hurdles, and receive individualized feedback using speech recognition, translation, sentiment analysis, conversational agents, and other AI technologies. AI technology has great potential to improve language instruction and empower learners worldwide.

2.1. Overview of AI Technologies

Advances in representation learning, in which linguistic units are embedded into agnostic activations with representations of their constituents, have filled the linguistic gap, connecting the deep learning era of NLP to its rich resource-filled past (Sciolette et al., 2023). Knowledge transfer methods exist to address the data shortages that impede these technologically complex capabilities of AI-empowered language education, making these models trainable for specific tasks even when task-corresponding data is scarce. Recent progress in methods advances the project to package these AI capabilities into easily configurable models with automated labeling, making these advances practically applicable to a wide variety of language educational contexts for learners, teachers, and learners who are educators (Mageira et al., 2022; Alharbi, 2023; Bhutoria, 2022). These groundbreaking capabilities can impact large-scale second language educational testing with a few policy and design shifts.

Deep neural networks, especially with representation techniques, have shown great potential in performing many natural language processing tasks, including text classification, semantic analysis, grammar checking, question answering, and machine translation (Alshemali & Kalita, 2020; Sorin et al., 2020). Hidden Markov models (HMMs) and maximum entropy classifiers (MaxEnts) remain popular tools in statistical learning. Unsupervised learning, primarily involving dimensionality reduction techniques and language models, such as word phrases and latent variable conditional models, has also been productively explored (Li et al., 2021; Behrens et al., 2022). Before the deep learning era, syntactic parsing was an important mediating technology that directly provided the semantic composition of linguistic expression through interval-based semantic labeling methods. Many quality resources to assess AI technologies, such as gold-labeled syntactic-semantic parses, and a wide variety of language applications, such as question answering, have historically employed syntactic parses to map questions to answers.

2.2. Applications in Language Learning

Melanie Mitchell, in "Artificial Intelligence Hits the Barrier of Meaning," provided that after several years of great innovations and limitations of deep learning, it has become increasingly obvious that one approach to solving these mistakes is to mimic human learning using tools and methodologies that linguists have been developing for over a century (Mitchell, 2023; Mitchell, 2021). This article summarizes some of these claims to give educators easier access to these concerns.

Alex described his AI-driven software, 'OpenAI,' as one that addresses the problem of bridging digital learning divides, especially in remote learning, because so many kids worldwide do not have high-speed, reliable internet (Faturoti, 2024; Machusky & Herbert-Berger, 2022). The software is designed to provide an equitable, much cheaper way to educate 800 million children to meet higher learning standards called for by the experts. However, there has been very little public outcry against the increase in litigation of the private for-profit communities, both in the USA and other post-industrial societies (High, 2022). There has been very little knowledge of or protests against their destructive uses of the 'lives-structures' for grossly unfair advantage, discrimination, and profiteering rather than contributing to mission-oriented educators preparing better-educated citizens with language skills and knowledge to handle a rapidly changing world. It is not too late to bridge the chasms in language learning pointed out in the article by properly understanding and granting linguistics and AI the help for universal language understanding as we encounter the need to build new tools.

3. CHALLENGES AND OPPORTUNITIES IN AI-DRIVEN ACCESSIBILITY

Reviewing and responding to diverse case studies of AI-driven accessibility also highly motivates and energizes readers to actively pose thought-provoking and crucial questions for future work that delves deeper into this vital field of study (Alharbi, 2023) (Song & Song, 2023; Dai et al., 2023). It is our utmost encouragement for NLP, machine learning, and HCI researchers and students alike to contemplate a comprehensive spectrum of significant questions deeply and strategically align themselves more closely with experienced practitioners and dedicated educators from the language education and pedagogy realm. Many substantial and prominent challenges still exist that demand immediate attention and resolution in the ambitious pursuit of AI-driven accessibility. However, with the knowledge and insights imparted through the collective contributions presented within this esteemed collection of papers, we find ourselves at a pivotal milestone where transformative progress becomes not only conceivable but exceptionally attainable (Haddad et al., 2022; Sannino, 2024; Kohl et al., 2022).

3.1. Barriers to Inclusive Language Education

Despite breakthroughs in digital education, language learning remains difficult (Okoye et al., 2023; Alakrash & Abdul Razak, 2021). We divide these into time, resources, and teachers. As mentioned, underprivileged students need resources and are at a learning disadvantage. Quality digital resources help second language learners fill learning gaps and lack language exposure outside the classroom. Many valuable but unused resource innovations exist. While disregarded, incorporating student data, such as learning behaviors or speech patterns, with AI to better English language instruction is gaining popularity (Gayed et al., 2022; Sun, 2021; Zhao, 2021). Educational access is multidimensional and requires more than digital tools. Academic contexts create resource shortages beyond digital product access. Working within development institutions and technology businesses to prioritize resource generation is easy.

However, education best empowers underprivileged people. Learning best builds understanding-based global bridges (Hofstetter et al., 2021; Ferguson-Patrick, 2020; Mansilla & Wilson, 2020). So, the biggest need is still direct, live, one-on-one teacher instruction. This most personal zone can provide our best contributions. Effective AI tutors and interpreters can reach marginalized communities from fragmented, underfunded educational systems (Prasse-Freeman, 2023). In making these skills available, this final frontier contains our most important lessons in academic accountability and ethical duty. A prevalent social fallacy is that digital tools reduce inequality. Educational technology can boost learning, but it is asking the incorrect question. We know intelligence, education, and information spread widely, and no intellectual monopoly exists.

3.2. Potential Solutions and Innovations

While some forward steps have been independently taken in open-source datasets for pronunciation error detection and feedback from promising adults, none focus on beginners or identifying AWE efficacy's unique demands (Qin et al., 2023; Brena et al., 2021). These dangers are largely unaddressed in the peer-reviewed press, given that relatively little ESL/EFL AI work has examined beginner L2 learners in general, and a relative handful of pursuits is further narrowed in terms of learning platforms and machine learning approaches. For reasons related to pedagogical inflexibility, classroom studies radically outnumber robust corpus investigations, particularly concerning computer-encouraged L2 oral speech.

At the same time, deep learning has been seen as computationally demanding, and almost all available open datasets are premised on other machine learning approaches like support vector machines.

Though research on AI-based accessibility in this area remains scarce, some potential solutions can be inferred from existing work on oral fluency assessment and recent industry efforts (Privitera et al., 2024; Kharbat et al., 2021). Unfortunately, the classic NLP pipeline - in which speech recognition, pronunciation assessment, and feedback generation tools are typically developed separately and in serial order - remedies none of these concerns. As of this writing, commercially developed AI tools still primarily involve proprietary versions of these three components, often optimizing the process with an additional segmentation tool. Although some open-source resources are now available, most licensing agreements are complex and opaque, their system design principles are rarely described to end users, and many products feature significant privacy risks, in which student manipulation, error, and exploitation are possible at every stage of scores' transmission (Chan, 2023).

4. CASE STUDIES AND BEST PRACTICES

The following section introduces simple language data analyzers, including instant data response tools. The collection aims to reach teachers interested in providing hands-on data literacy lessons who might want to keep their initial AI experiences easy to manage. These tools naturally include promising pitfalls, as even simple language analyzers might create many AI ethics issues.

In an age of data mining, language educators need to be highly proficient in data literacy and utilize consumer tools wisely to navigate the vast amount of information available effectively (Burk & Miner, 2020; Ifenthaler et al., 2021). While educators are not expected to possess expert knowledge in Artificial Intelligence (AI), they need to assume the roles of both educators and researchers within their specific contexts. By doing so, they can shed light on the immense potential benefits and effectively navigate any potential challenges associated with AI (Xu et al., 2021; Bermudez-Contreras et al., 2020). To provide comprehensive guidance on harnessing the potential benefits and mitigating potential issues, this chapter presents user-friendly data mining tools that are accessible and easy to use (Kuppuswamy et al., 2024; Plotnikova et al., 2022). By incorporating these language data analyzers into their teaching activities, educators will be equipped with practical and valuable resources to enrich their classroom experiences greatly. These tools offer unique perspectives that dismantle potential problems, transforming them into promising practices with positive outcomes. Overall, this work serves as a meaningful realization of the recent call for responsible integration of AI in education. It emphasizes ethics and privacy considerations and the need for educators to develop a strong foundation in data literacy. By adopting this approach, language educators will be empowered to shape a future where AI and education harmoniously coexist, facilitating the growth and development of students while safeguarding their privacy and ensuring ethical practices.

4.1. Successful Implementations

In primary, secondary, and tertiary education and beyond, technology-influenced and AI-assisted learning is not a thing of the future (Umali, 2024; Harmsen, 2024). We are already there. Despite ongoing strides forward, there is more to be done. Inclusive education systems can only fulfill their purpose when they offer all learning, skills development, and knowledge acquisition opportunities. This goes beyond just attending or sitting in a classroom. It requires much more from the learning system so that every person can develop cognitive, affective, psycho-motor skills, literacy, and numeracy to the levels where they can perform their desired role in society. Supporting facts show that strategic and useful AI-driven educational improvements can support learners by creating programs that cater to individual strengths and weaknesses, provide content in imaginative, inclusive ways, and develop resources that maximize student learning through AI sophistication. (Wei, 2023)

This report identifies how AI can be leveraged effectively in education to offer services for all, notably those with wide-ranging and unique needs requiring personalized support. AI has been proven to improve education outcomes across the board. It identifies promising AI use cases, individual need considerations, and effective cooperation between actors across the ecosystem, concluding with policy considerations for AI in education (Bozkurt et al., 2021; Chen et al., 2023; Wang et al., 2023). There are clear opportunities to effectively leverage AI as a cross-cutting technology to ensure equity in modern schooling and lifelong learning.

4.2. Lessons Learned

Nowadays, models are quite large and slow to train, and their practical deployment requires large amounts of data, which is not always available, especially for the less commonly spoken languages (Raiaan et al., 2024). Thus, a practical approach when training on low-resource language data is to first train on a language with overlapping vocabulary and grammar and then further train (or fine-tune) the model on the low-resource language data (Khanna et al., 2021; Ngo et al., 2022). Recently, Google has shown how training data from multiple very low-resource languages can extract language-independent multilingual audio representations. Aside from multilingual downstream applications, this sort of multilingual model can help low-resource languages that do not have enough task-specific in-language data and also grow the number of languages supported by existing technology to aid students learning in their native or target language (Escamilla et al., 2021).

However, improvements in language learning technologies do not always come from simply training bigger and better models (Zhang & Zou, 2022; Rogerson-Revell, 2021). While we have already discussed how natural automatic speech recognition technologies have contributed to keeping students practicing and engaged when learning a foreign language, it is only fair that the learning environment also provides individualized feedback to steer them toward the goal. It may be crucial to understand the sentiment and the meaning the user displays in interaction and consider it in the designed response. That is not a simple task, especially across multiple language modalities. However, suppose we want AI-driven accessibility in language education (Borger et al., 2023; Yuen and Schlote2024). In that case, we will have to work on understanding the language the user speaks, particularly the meaning the users display, not just the one they play.

5. ETHICAL CONSIDERATIONS IN AI-DRIVEN ACCESSIBILITY

Reflection on the use of AI in setting industry standards within the field of education is equally important (Abulibdeh et al., 2024; Renz & Hilbig, 2020). When diverse voices are excluded from these processes, those trained on the data begin to cater to a certain norm, failing to communicate effectively with other readers and learners based on culture or language. PR and participatory design processes show that engagement with wider community stakeholders before the application and creation of learning resources can play an important role in ensuring that a diversity of linguistic backgrounds is included in language resource development (Heckert et al., 2020). At the same time, effective democratic engagement in capitalizing on education's potential should also be pushed in broader access to technology and computational thinking education. As the Agency for Fundamental Rights has highlighted, societal literacy lessens the capacity for malign actors to use AI malfeasantly to disrupt democratic processes.

The observed benefits of AI-driven remodeling of learning materials are valuable. Still, it is equally important to consider potential societal and ethical implications, especially when deploying educational technology (Hopster, 2021; Nguyen et al., 2023). The OECD Principles on AI emphasize respecting human rights, democratic values, and diversity, preventing harm, and fostering equally shared benefits. Based on this, AI capabilities should be developed and deployed in line with these principles, ensuring that developments address inclusivity gaps and foster support across different socioeconomic and cultural stances rather than exacerbating divides and injecting content that reinforces any particular denominator (Cachat-Rosset & Klarsfeld, 2023; Díaz-Rodríguez et al., 2023).

5.1. Privacy and Data Security

Dignity, non-discrimination, and data-driven recommender systems present memorable challenges for keeping user trust and promoting user well-being (Zardiashvili & Fosch-Villaronga, 2020). For instance, AI recommendations may influence the identity of media users assume and the narratives users find worth sharing. Social media content often revolves around views perceived as being ignored or suppressed by dominant platforms, suggesting that certain users are ineligible to participate in conversations. The systems should be designed in such a way as to reduce the formation of echo chambers and expose people to diverse stories and perspectives that could certify social commonness and increase comprehension (Dai et al., 2023; Niemi, 2021).

Given the sensitive nature of the language education domain, privacy considerations are key to the trustworthiness of future AI-driven accessibility tools (Fedele et al., 2024; Williamson & Prybutok, 2024). The sensitive nature of the language education domain means that personal data is of particular concern. The ultimate proprietor of personal data should be the individual to whom it relates. The strength of data protection regulations plays a vital part in the levels of trust. Greater clarity of purpose and greater data protection accountability to individuals and the society served could also provide clear accountability and control over data usage (Klimova et al., 2023; Alzubaidi et al., 2023).

5.2. Bias and Fairness

Bias and fairness are probably the most widely discussed problems within the AI community (Varona & Suárez, 2022; Ferrara, 2023; Fletcher et al., 2021). Unfortunate as it may be, the challenges presented by these two issues in reality are truly overwhelming. As is widely known and acknowledged, the training data can inherently possess biases, leading to the subsequent production of biased predictions by the model. For instance, various products existing in the real world might exhibit biases against different minority groups. Thus, if a model is trained on such biased inputs, it inevitably produces inherently biased predictions against these very target groups. Similarly, if the training dataset contains a majority of misinformation, it will inevitably yield an unequal and fundamentally unfair model (Deepak, 2020).

Quantifying the bias in the training data and during the model's prediction is important. Moreover, various methods have been proposed to address this problem for various NLP tasks (Raza et al., 2024; Anoop et al., 2022). For example, we can use adversarial learning to remove the bias in the training data. We can quantify fairness during prediction time using different fair metrics, e.g., Calibration, DPPL, etc. To remedy the bias in the training data, we can either design adversarial loss terms for bias reduction or use re-sampling, re-weighting, and so on. Furthermore, we can measure and regularize the stereotypes in text classification to make the predictions as fair as possible.

6. FUTURE DIRECTIONS AND EMERGING TRENDS

Language education has come a long way since basic technological aids were first developed half a century ago (Pregowska et al., 2021). The authors of "The Computer and the Language Teacher" (Ducks, 1968), a volume that laid the groundwork for technological applications in language education, remarked: "We shall not be satisfied with present achievements, but shall resolutely continue to deny the potential of the machine and to seek that application of its as-yet untapped powers that will bring interaction with it much closer to what our intuitions of ideal instruction suggest as relevant, effective and efficient." There is still much potential in the field that has yet to be realized. Inspiration can be found in the emerging artificial intelligence-driven language technologies that many industries and international organizations are developing and piloting to benefit consumers worldwide (Trattner et al., 2022; De et al., 2023; Kulkov et al., 2024). This essay has attempted to describe the major, most inspiring trends towards AI-driven accessibility and to prompt language educators and the AI industry to work together to develop technologies that make language learning and assessment experiences available to all.

To discuss emerging trends in AI-driven accessibility in language education, consider young Talia (Yuan et al., 2024; Famaye et al., 2024). This four-year-old already has a firm grasp of basic concepts common to most visual object recognition and description systems, including bereft reference and the capacities these systems have for understanding, describing, and recognizing objects from visual inputs. Moreover, as is typical for children her age, she has also acquired a significant vocabulary in one or more languages (Leona et al., 2021). Young Talia, the brightest friend of many members of the AI industry, is also blind. She lives in a world that relies on visual perception for many of its most common spoken languages called community interaction functionalities. AI-driven applications that significantly transformed accessibility in a physical context have not yet developed language and cognition capabilities that enable blind children to take advantage of what everyone is discussing (Mehta et al., 2023).

6.1. Advancements in AI Technologies

AI technology has consistently evolved through its application phase in question-answering, student feedback, tutorial coaching, and intelligent tutoring. In today's trend toward assisting languages, tools have varied, underscoring that AI-based eLearning chatbots with advanced reasoning capabilities supported by other tools, including automatic speech recognition and various shared-enabled techniques such as multimodal merging, necessitate the integration of multiple perceptions (Chang et al., 2023; Stracqualursi & Agati, 2024). Throughout the past decades, basic AI research has evolved from knowledge representation to propositional and predicate reasoning for logical reasoning analysis, which refers to a particular physical skill set. Following initial fundamental studies in spoken language understanding, progress has been driven by making the software contextually rich, informationally complete, and meaningfully representable—this is especially true for users whose cognitive capabilities remain at lower levels (e.g., people with sight-related visual impairment) (Dai et al., 2023).

AI-driven education is feasible based on ongoing and future advancements (Williamson & Eynon; Bhutoria, 2022). The advancement of AI in education, historical major AI technology, followed by the most recent transformational technological progress and enabling techniques through AI-based interpretability proposed by recent advancements. The role of educational AI should be emphasized, considering outstanding issues (Hwang et al., 2020; Khosravi et al., 2022).

Technology presents a crucial tool in light of the rapid advancements in AI-based solutions (Sarker, 2022; Sharma et al., 2022). Documenting cutting-edge research findings, this paper surveys the current applications and explores how AI contributes to accessible language and translates education. Major AI techniques include Natural Language Processing, Computer Vision, Genetic Algorithms, and Deep Learning. Neural networks embody another major direction in AI, and innovations in that direction have generated new solutions for deep learning.

6.2. Impact on Educational Systems

Grabe underlines the importance of establishing criteria determining the difference between learning experience and effectiveness in an educational system (Gul et al., 2023; Shah et al., 2020). He also notes the need to familiarize teachers with these techniques and, again, to use them as a support tool for their knowledge due to the lack of validity and innovative implementation of these technologies in the educational context (Strohm et al., 2020; Karaca et al., 2021). In this model, digital literacy is a necessity that educational systems need to counteract. Finally, it is also important to create standardizations for these technologies within existing protocols, direct them to a specific cultural context, evaluate their shortcomings, and establish guidelines for implementation in contexts that are different from those for which they were modeled (Wei, 2023).

Recently, Dauch of Google AI suggested five guidelines for practitioners to responsibly design technology for well-being, which should be a useful backbone to make the powerful educational impact positive (Jędrejko et al., 2023; Andersen et al., 2023). At the level of educational systems, it is important to promote the idea that teachers should be the shapers, not the subject, of material to be used in the classroom context. In this way, edTech can support greater integration and real personalized education. In this way, the drawbacks of machine learning, i.e., interpretability of results and ethical implications, can be integrated with the added value of those technologies and balanced.

7. CONCLUSION AND RECOMMENDATIONS

7.1 Conclusion

This chapter highlights the transformative potential of AI-driven technology to improve language education accessibility for visually and hearing-impaired people. NLP and AI can overcome these learners' traditional hurdles and provide personalized and adaptive learning experiences. Using AI, educators can provide audio descriptions, text-to-speech, and interactive platforms to create an inclusive learning environment. AI's seamless integration into the education ecosystem will transform language learning, ensuring equal access and empowering disabled students. However, achieving these benefits entails overcoming various obstacles. AI-driven educational technologies must address ethical issues, including data privacy and AI model bias, to ensure trust and fairness. To meet the needs of disabled learners, comprehensive frameworks that prioritize end-users and stakeholders are essential.

7.2 Recommendations

a. Effective adoption of AI-driven accessibility solutions requires collaboration between educators, technology developers, policymakers, and end-users. The solutions developed through this collaborative method are comprehensive, user-friendly, and tailored to disabled learners.
b. Data privacy and prejudice require strong ethical foundations. AI tools' transparency, security, and fairness will help users trust them and maximize their benefits.
c. User-Centric Design: Involving visually and hearing-impaired people in AI-driven educational tool design and testing will ensure that the products are useful and address their needs.
d. Continuous Training and assistance: Training educators on AI tools and providing technical assistance can help integrate these technologies into the classroom.
e. Policy and Standardization: Establishing AI rules and standards for education can structure implementation and ensure consistency and quality across educational contexts.

REFERENCES

Abulibdeh, A., Zaidan, E., & Abulibdeh, R. (2024). Navigating the confluence of artificial intelligence and education for sustainable development in the era of industry 4.0: Challenges, opportunities, and ethical.... *Journal of Cleaner Production*, *437*, 140527. Advance online publication. DOI: 10.1016/j.jclepro.2023.140527

Ahmad, Z., Rahim, S., Zubair, M., & Abdul-Ghafar, J. (2021). Artificial intelligence (AI) in medicine, current applications and future role with special emphasis on its potential and promise in pathology: Present and future impact.... *Diagnostic Pathology*, *16*(1), 24. Advance online publication. DOI: 10.1186/s13000-021-01085-4 PMID: 33731170

Ajeesh, A. K., & Rukmini, S. (2023). Posthuman perception of artificial intelligence in science fiction: An exploration of Kazuo Ishiguro's Klara and the Sun. *AI & Society*, *38*(2), 853–860. Advance online publication. DOI: 10.1007/s00146-022-01533-9

Alakrash, H. M., & Abdul Razak, N. (2021). Technology-based language learning: Investigation of digital technology and digital literacy. *Sustainability (Basel)*, *13*(21), 12304. Advance online publication. DOI: 10.3390/su132112304

Alam, A., & Mohanty, A. (2024). Integrated constructive robotics in education (ICRE) model: A paradigmatic framework for transformative learning in educational ecosystem. *Cogent Education*, *11*(1), 2324487. Advance online publication. DOI: 10.1080/2331186X.2024.2324487

Alharbi, W. (2023). AI in the foreign language classroom: A pedagogical overview of automated writing assistance tools. *Education Research International*, *2023*, 1–15. Advance online publication. DOI: 10.1155/2023/4253331

Aljedaani, W., Aljedaani, M., AlOmar, E. A., Mkaouer, M. W., Ludi, S., & Khalaf, Y. B. (2021). I cannot see you—the perspectives of deaf students to online learning during covid-19 pandemic: Saudi arabia case study. *Education Sciences*, *11*(11), 712. DOI: 10.3390/educsci11110712

Allouch, M., Azaria, A., & Azoulay, R. (2021). Conversational agents: Goals, technologies, vision and challenges. *Sensors (Basel)*, *21*(24), 8448. Advance online publication. DOI: 10.3390/s21248448 PMID: 34960538

Almufareh, M. F., Kausar, S., Humayun, M., & Tehsin, S. (2024). A conceptual model for inclusive technology: Advancing disability inclusion through artificial intelligence. *Journal of Disability Research*, *3*(1), 20230060. DOI: 10.57197/JDR-2023-0060

Alqahtani, T., Badreldin, H. A., Alrashed, M., Alshaya, A. I., Alghamdi, S. S., bin Saleh, K., Alowais, S. A., Alshaya, O. A., Rahman, I., Al Yami, M. S., & Albekairy, A. M. (2023). The emergent role of artificial intelligence, natural learning processing, and large language models in higher education and research. *Research in Social & Administrative Pharmacy*, *19*(8), 1236–1242. DOI: 10.1016/j.sapharm.2023.05.016 PMID: 37321925

Alshemali, B., & Kalita, J. (2020). Improving the reliability of deep neural networks in NLP: A review. *Knowledge-Based Systems*, *191*, 105210. Advance online publication. DOI: 10.1016/j.knosys.2019.105210

Alzahrani, N. M. (2020). Augmented reality: A systematic review of its benefits and challenges in e-learning contexts. *Applied Sciences (Basel, Switzerland), 10*(16), 5660. Advance online publication. DOI: 10.3390/app10165660

Alzubaidi, L., Al-Sabaawi, A., Bai, J., Dukhan, A., Alkenani, A. H., Al-Asadi, A., Alwzwazy, H. A., Manoufali, M., Fadhel, M. A., Albahri, A. S., Moreira, C., Ouyang, C., Zhang, J., Santamaría, J., Salhi, A., Hollman, F., Gupta, A., Duan, Y., Rabczuk, T., & Gu, Y. (2023). Towards Risk-Free Trustworthy Artificial Intelligence: Significance and Requirements. *International Journal of Intelligent Systems, 2023*(1), 4459198. DOI: 10.1155/2023/4459198

Andersen, C., Jacobsen, S., Uvebrant, K., Griffin, J. F.IV, Vonk, L. A., Walters, M., Berg, L. C., Lundgren-Åkerlund, E., & Lindegaard, C. (2023). Integrin α10β1-selected mesenchymal stem cells reduce pain and cartilage degradation and increase immunomodulation in an equine osteoarthritis model. *Cartilage, 19476035231209402*, 19476035231209402. Advance online publication. DOI: 10.1177/19476035231209402 PMID: 37990503

Anoop, K., Gangan, M. P., Deepak, P., & Lajish, V. L. (2022). Towards an enhanced understanding of bias in pre-trained neural language models: A survey with special emphasis on affective bias. In Responsible Data Science: Select Proceedings of ICDSE 2021 (pp. 13-45). Singapore: Springer Nature Singapore. [PDF] DOI: 10.1007/978-981-19-4453-6_2

Bandyopadhyay, S., Bardhan, A., Dey, P., Bhattacharyya, S., Bandyopadhyay, S., Bardhan, A., ... & Bhattacharyya, S. (2021). Education Ecosystem: A Chronological Perspective. Bridging the Education Divide Using Social Technologies: Explorations in Rural India, 43-75. https://doi.org/DOI: 10.1007/978-981-33-6738-8_3

Belda-Medina, J. & Calvo-Ferrer, J. R. (2022). Using chatbots as AI conversational partners in language learning. Applied Sciences. mdpi.com

Beninghof, A. M. (2020). Co-teaching that works: Structures and strategies for maximizing student learning. tesl-ej.org

Bermudez-Contreras, E., Clark, B. J., & Wilber, A. (2020). The neuroscience of spatial navigation and the relationship to artificial intelligence. [frontiersin.org]. *Frontiers in Computational Neuroscience, 14*, 523744. DOI: 10.3389/fncom.2020.00063 PMID: 32848684

Bhutoria, A. (2022). Personalized education and artificial intelligence in the United States, China, and India: A systematic review using a human-in-the-loop model. Computers and Education: Artificial Intelligence. sciencedirect.com

Blewitt, C., O'connor, A., Morris, H., Nolan, A., Mousa, A., Green, R., Ifanti, A., Jackson, K., & Skouteris, H. (2021). "It's embedded in what we do for every child": A qualitative exploration of early childhood educators' perspectives on supporting Children's social and emotional learning. [mdpi.com]. *International Journal of Environmental Research and Public Health, 18*(4), 1530. DOI: 10.3390/ijerph18041530 PMID: 33562768

Borger, J. G., Ng, A. P., Anderton, H., Ashdown, G. W., Auld, M., Blewitt, M. E., Brown, D. V., Call, M. J., Collins, P., Freytag, S., Harrison, L. C., Hesping, E., Hoysted, J., Johnston, A., McInneny, A., Tang, P., Whitehead, L., Jex, A., & Naik, S. H. (2023). Artificial intelligence takes center stage: Exploring the capabilities and implications of ChatGPT and other AI-assisted technologies in scientific research and education. [wiley.com]. *Immunology and Cell Biology*, *101*(10), 923–935. DOI: 10.1111/imcb.12689 PMID: 37721869

Bozkurt, A., Karadeniz, A., Baneres, D., Guerrero-Roldán, A. E., & Rodríguez, M. E. (2021). Artificial intelligence and reflections from educational landscape: A review of AI Studies in half a century. [mdpi.com]. *Sustainability (Basel)*, *13*(2), 800. DOI: 10.3390/su13020800

Brena, R. F., Zuvirie, E., Preciado, A., Valdiviezo, A., Gonzalez-Mendoza, M., & Zozaya-Gorostiza, C. (2021). Automated evaluation of foreign language speaking performance with machine learning. [IJIDeM]. *International Journal on Interactive Design and Manufacturing*, *15*(2), 317–331. DOI: 10.1007/s12008-021-00759-z

Burk, S., & Miner, G. D. (2020). *It's All Analytics!: The Foundations of AI*. Big Data and Data Science Landscape for Professionals in Healthcare, Business, and Government. [HTML] DOI: 10.4324/9780429343988

Cachat-Rosset, G. & Klarsfeld, A. (2023). Diversity, equity, and inclusion in artificial intelligence: an evaluation of guidelines. Applied Artificial Intelligence. tandfonline.com

Chan, C. K. Y. (2023). A comprehensive AI policy education framework for university teaching and learning. [springer.com]. *International Journal of Educational Technology in Higher Education*, *20*(1), 38. DOI: 10.1186/s41239-023-00408-3

Chang, D. H., Lin, M. P. C., Hajian, S., & Wang, Q. Q. (2023). Educational design principles of using AI chatbot that supports self-regulated learning in education: Goal setting, feedback, and personalization. Sustainability. mdpi.com

Chen, Y. (2024, May). Enhancing Language Acquisition: The Role of AI in Facilitating Effective Language Learning. In 2024 3rd International Conference on Humanities, Wisdom Education and Service Management (HWESM 2024) (pp. 593-600). Atlantis Press. atlantis-press.com

Chen, Y., Jensen, S., Albert, L. J., Gupta, S., & Lee, T. (2023). Artificial intelligence (AI) student assistants in the classroom: Designing chatbots to support student success. [HTML]. *Information Systems Frontiers*, *25*(1), 161–182. DOI: 10.1007/s10796-022-10291-4

Chopra, A., Patel, H., Rajput, D. S., & Bansal, N. (2024). Empowering Inclusive Education: Leveraging AI-ML and Innovative Tech Stacks to Support Students with Learning Disabilities in Higher Education. In Applied Assistive Technologies and Informatics for Students with Disabilities (pp. 255-275). Singapore: Springer Nature Singapore. [HTML]

Csizér, K. & Kontra, E. H. (2020). Foreign language learning characteristics of deaf and severely hard-of-hearing students. The Modern Language Journal. wiley.com

Dai, Y., Liu, A., & Lim, C. P. (2023). Reconceptualizing ChatGPT and generative AI as a student-driven innovation in higher education. Procedia CIRP. sciencedirect.com

Darvishi, A., Khosravi, H., Sadiq, S., & Gašević, D. (2022). Incorporating AI and learning analytics to build trustworthy peer assessment systems. [wiley.com]. *British Journal of Educational Technology, 53*(4), 844–875. DOI: 10.1111/bjet.13233

De Angelis, L., Baglivo, F., Arzilli, G., Privitera, G. P., Ferragina, P., Tozzi, A. E., & Rizzo, C. (2023). ChatGPT and the rise of large language models: The new AI-driven infodemic threat in public health. [frontiersin.org]. *Frontiers in Public Health, 11*, 1166120. DOI: 10.3389/fpubh.2023.1166120 PMID: 37181697

Deepak, P. (2020). Ethical considerations in data-driven fake news detection. Journal: Data Science for Fake News The Information Retrieval Series, 205-232. [HTML]

Deng, X. & Yu, Z. (2022). A systematic review of machine-translation-assisted language learning for sustainable education. Sustainability. mdpi.com

Díaz-Rodríguez, N., Del Ser, J., Coeckelbergh, M., de Prado, M. L., Herrera-Viedma, E., & Herrera, F. (2023). Connecting the dots in trustworthy Artificial Intelligence: From AI principles, ethics, and key requirements to responsible AI systems and regulation. [sciencedirect.com]. *Information Fusion, 99*, 101896. DOI: 10.1016/j.inffus.2023.101896

Dokukina, I. & Gumanova, J. (2020). The rise of chatbots–new personal assistants in foreign language learning. Procedia Computer Science. sciencedirect.com

Escamilla, K., Hopewell, S., & Slavick, J. (2021). Teaching (bi) multilingual learners: Connecting languages. [HTML]. *The Reading Teacher, 75*(3), 363–371. DOI: 10.1002/trtr.2044

Famaye, T., Irgens, G. A., & Adisa, I. (2024). Shifting roles and slow research: Children's roles in participatory co-design of critical machine learning activities and technologies. [clemson.edu]. *Behaviour & Information Technology*, •••, 1–22.

Fan, M., Antle, A. N., & Warren, J. L. (2020). Augmented reality for early language learning: A systematic review of augmented reality application design, instructional strategies, and evaluation outcomes. [HTML]. *Journal of Educational Computing Research, 58*(6), 1059–1100. DOI: 10.1177/0735633120927489

Faturoti, B. (). Online learning during COVID19 and beyond: A human right based approach to internet access in Africa. International Review of Law. tandfonline.com

Fedele, A., Punzi, C., & Tramacere, S. (2024). The ALTAI checklist as a tool to assess ethical and legal implications for a trustworthy AI development in education. Computer Law & Security Review. sciencedirect.com

Feijóo, C., Kwon, Y., Bauer, J. M., Bohlin, E., Howell, B., Jain, R., Potgieter, P., Vu, K., Whalley, J., & Xia, J. (2020). Harnessing artificial intelligence (AI) to increase wellbeing for all: The case for a new technology diplomacy. [sciencedirect.com]. *Telecommunications Policy, 44*(6), 101988. DOI: 10.1016/j.telpol.2020.101988 PMID: 32377031

Ferguson-Patrick, K. (2020). Cooperative learning in Swedish classrooms: Engagement and relationships as a focus for culturally diverse students. Education Sciences. mdpi.com

Ferrara, E. (2023). Fairness and bias in artificial intelligence: A brief survey of sources, impacts, and mitigation strategies. Sci. mdpi.com

Fletcher, R. R., Nakeshimana, A., & Olubeko, O. (2021). Addressing fairness, bias, and appropriate use of artificial intelligence and machine learning in global health. [frontiersin.org]. *Frontiers in Artificial Intelligence*, *3*, 561802. DOI: 10.3389/frai.2020.561802 PMID: 33981989

Gayed, J. M., Carlon, M. K. J., Oriola, A. M., & Cross, J. S. (2022). Exploring an AI-based writing Assistant's impact on English language learners. [sciencedirect.com]. *Computers and Education: Artificial Intelligence*, *3*, 100055. DOI: 10.1016/j.caeai.2022.100055

Ghosh, S. S. (2024). Nurturing Sustainable and Inclusive Learning Ecosystems: A Glimpse Into the Future of Indian Education. In Preparing Students for the Future Educational Paradigm (pp. 256-277). IGI Global. [HTML] DOI: 10.4018/979-8-3693-1536-1.ch011

Gill, S. S., Xu, M., Ottaviani, C., Patros, P., Bahsoon, R., Shaghaghi, A., Golec, M., Stankovski, V., Wu, H., Abraham, A., Singh, M., Mehta, H., Ghosh, S. K., Baker, T., Parlikad, A. K., Lutfiyya, H., Kanhere, S. S., Sakellariou, R., Dustdar, S., & Uhlig, S. (2022). AI for next generation computing: Emerging trends and future directions. [PDF]. *Internet of Things : Engineering Cyber Physical Human Systems*, *19*, 100514. DOI: 10.1016/j.iot.2022.100514

Gkonou, C. & Miller, E. R. (2021). An exploration of language teacher reflection, emotion labor, and emotional capital. Tesol Quarterly. wiley.com

Gul, M. I., Khan, I. A., Shah, S., & El-Affendi, M. (2023). Can Nonliterates Interact as Easily as Literates with a Virtual Reality System? A Usability Evaluation of VR Interaction Modalities. Systems. mdpi.com

Haddad, C. R., Nakić, V., Bergek, A., & Hellsmark, H. (2022). Transformative innovation policy: A systematic review. [sciencedirect.com]. *Environmental Innovation and Societal Transitions*, *43*, 14–40. DOI: 10.1016/j.eist.2022.03.002

Harmsen, E. (2024). A Future Perspective on the Digitalised Work Environment: Understanding the Role of Artificial Intelligence and Social Robots in Future Work Environments. diva-portal.org

Hassani, H., Huang, X., & Silva, E. (2021). The human digitalisation journey: Technology first at the expense of humans?. Information. mdpi.com

Heckert, A., Forsythe, L. P., Carman, K. L., Frank, L., Hemphill, R., Elstad, E. A., Esmail, L., & Lesch, J. K. (2020). Researchers, patients, and other stakeholders' perspectives on challenges to and strategies for engagement. [springer.com]. *Research Involvement and Engagement*, *6*(1), 1–18. DOI: 10.1186/s40900-020-00227-0 PMID: 33042576

High, S. (2022). A fruitless exercise? The political struggle to compel corporations to justify factory closures in Canada. [HTML]. *Labor History*, *63*(3), 297–315. DOI: 10.1080/0023656X.2022.2098261

Hofstetter, J. S., De Marchi, V., Sarkis, J., Govindan, K., Klassen, R., Ometto, A. R., Spraul, K. S., Bocken, N., Ashton, W. S., Sharma, S., Jaeger-Erben, M., Jensen, C., Dewick, P., Schröder, P., Sinkovics, N., Ibrahim, S. E., Fiske, L., Goerzen, A., & Vazquez-Brust, D. (2021). From sustainable global value chains to circular economy—Different silos, different perspectives, but many opportunities to build bridges. [springer.com]. *Circular Economy and Sustainability*, *1*(1), 21–47. DOI: 10.1007/s43615-021-00015-2 PMID: 34888550

Hopster, J. (2021). What are socially disruptive technologies?. Technology in Society. sciencedirect.com

Hudson, A. D., Finn, E., & Wylie, R. (2023). What can science fiction tell us about the future of artificial intelligence policy?. AI & SOCIETY. springer.com

Hwang, G. J., Xie, H., Wah, B. W., & Gašević, D. (2020). Vision, challenges, roles and research issues of Artificial Intelligence in Education. [sciencedirect.com]. *Computers and Education: Artificial Intelligence*, *1*, 100001. DOI: 10.1016/j.caeai.2020.100001

Ifenthaler, D., Gibson, D., Prasse, D., Shimada, A., & Yamada, M. (2021). Putting learning back into learning analytics: Actions for policy makers, researchers, and practitioners. [springer.com]. *Educational Technology Research and Development*, *69*(4), 2131–2150. DOI: 10.1007/s11423-020-09909-8

Jędrejko, K., Lazarev, A., Jędrejko, M., & Muszyńska, B. (2023). Ergogenic properties, safety evaluation and regulations of selected ingredients in testosterone booster dietary supplements. [tandfonline.com]. *Food Reviews International*, •••, 1–29.

Karaca, O., Çalışkan, S. A., & Demir, K. (2021). Medical artificial intelligence readiness scale for medical students (MAIRS-MS)–development, validity and reliability study. BMC medical education. springer.com

Khanna, T., Washington, J. N., Tyers, F. M., Bayatlı, S., Swanson, D. G., Pirinen, T. A., Tang, I., & Alos i Font, H. (2021). Recent advances in Apertium, a free/open-source rule-based machine translation platform for low-resource languages. [springer.com]. *Machine Translation*, *35*(4), 475–502. DOI: 10.1007/s10590-021-09260-6

Kharbat, F. F., Alshawabkeh, A., & Woolsey, M. L. (2021). Identifying gaps in using artificial intelligence to support students with intellectual disabilities from education and health perspectives. [HTML]. *Aslib Journal of Information Management*, *73*(1), 101–128. DOI: 10.1108/AJIM-02-2020-0054

Khosravi, H., Shum, S. B., Chen, G., Conati, C., Tsai, Y. S., Kay, J., & Gašević, D. (2022). Explainable artificial intelligence in education. [sciencedirect.com]. *Computers and Education: Artificial Intelligence*, *3*, 100074.

Khurana, D., Koli, A., Khatter, K., & Singh, S. (2023). Natural language processing: state of the art, current trends and challenges. Multimedia tools and applications. springer.com

Klimova, B., Pikhart, M., & Kacetl, J. (2023). Ethical issues of the use of AI-driven mobile apps for education. Frontiers in Public Health. frontiersin.org

Kohl, K., Hopkins, C., Barth, M., Michelsen, G., Dlouhá, J., Razak, D. A., Abidin Bin Sanusi, Z., & Toman, I. (2022). A whole-institution approach towards sustainability: A crucial aspect of higher education's individual and collective engagement with the SDGs and beyond. [emerald.com]. *International Journal of Sustainability in Higher Education, 23*(2), 218–236. DOI: 10.1108/IJSHE-10-2020-0398

Kuddus, K. (2022). *Artificial intelligence in language learning: Practices and prospects.* Advanced Analytics and Deep Learning Models. [HTML]

Kulkov, I., Kulkova, J., Rohrbeck, R., Menvielle, L., Kaartemo, V., & Makkonen, H. (2024). Artificial intelligence-driven sustainable development: Examining organizational, technical, and processing approaches to achieving global goals. [wiley.com]. *Sustainable Development (Bradford), 32*(3), 2253–2267. DOI: 10.1002/sd.2773

Kuppuswamy, P., Ansari, M. D., Mohan, M., & Al Khalidi, S. Q. (2024). Data Mining for Predictive Analytics. Intelligent Techniques for Predictive Data Analytics, 1-24. [HTML]

Lai, Y., Saab, N., & Admiraal, W. (2022). Learning strategies in self-directed language learning using mobile technology in higher education: A systematic scoping review. Education and Information Technologies. springer.com

Lee, S. M. (2023). The effectiveness of machine translation in foreign language education: A systematic review and meta-analysis. [HTML]. *Computer Assisted Language Learning, 36*(1-2), 103–125. DOI: 10.1080/09588221.2021.1901745

Leona, N. L., van Koert, M. J., van der Molen, M. W., Rispens, J. E., Tijms, J., & Snellings, P. (2021). Explaining individual differences in young English language learners' vocabulary knowledge: The role of Extramural English Exposure and motivation. [sciencedirect.com]. *System, 96*, 102402. DOI: 10.1016/j.system.2020.102402

Li, G., Liu, F., Sharma, A., Khalaf, O. I., Alotaibi, Y., Alsufyani, A., & Alghamdi, S. (2021). Research on the natural language recognition method based on cluster analysis using neural network. [wiley.com]. *Mathematical Problems in Engineering, 2021*(1), 9982305. DOI: 10.1155/2021/9982305

Li, L., Gow, A. D. I., & Zhou, J. (). The role of positive emotions in education: A neuroscience perspective. Mind. [HTML]

Li, Z. & Li, J. (2022). Using the flipped classroom to promote learner engagement for the sustainable development of language skills: A mixed-methods study. Sustainability. mdpi.com

Machusky, J. A., & Herbert-Berger, K. G. (2022). Understanding online learning infrastructure in US K-12 schools: A review of challenges and emerging trends. [HTML]. *International Journal of Educational Research, 114*, 101993. DOI: 10.1016/j.ijer.2022.101993

Mageira, K., Pittou, D., Papasalouros, A., Kotis, K., Zangogianni, P., & Daradoumis, A. (2022). Educational AI chatbots for content and language integrated learning. [mdpi.com]. *Applied Sciences (Basel, Switzerland), 12*(7), 3239. DOI: 10.3390/app12073239

Mansilla, V. B., & Wilson, D. (2020). What is global competence, and what might it look like in Chinese schools? [sagepub.com]. *Journal of Research in International Education, 19*(1), 3–22. DOI: 10.1177/1475240920914089

Mehta, P., Chillarge, G. R., Sapkal, S. D., Shinde, G. R., & Kshirsagar, P. S. (2023). Inclusion of Children With Special Needs in the Educational System, Artificial Intelligence (AI). In AI-Assisted Special Education for Students With Exceptional Needs (pp. 156-185). IGI Global. [HTML]

Mitchell, M. (2021). Abstraction and analogy-making in artificial intelligence. [PDF]. *Annals of the New York Academy of Sciences, 1505*(1), 79–101. DOI: 10.1111/nyas.14619 PMID: 34173249

Mitchell, M. (2023). Abstraction and analogy in AI. [HTML]. *Annals of the New York Academy of Sciences, 1524*(1), 17–21. DOI: 10.1111/nyas.14995 PMID: 37014085

Mitra, S., Lakshmi, D., & Govindaraj, V. (2023). Data analysis and machine learning in AI-assisted special education for students with exceptional needs. In *AI-Assisted Special Education for Students With Exceptional Needs* (pp. 67–109). IGI Global. [HTML] DOI: 10.4018/979-8-3693-0378-8.ch004

Naseer, F., Khalid, M. U., Ayub, N., Rasool, A., Abbas, T., & Afzal, M. W. (2024). Automated Assessment and Feedback in Higher Education Using Generative AI. In Transforming Education With Generative AI: Prompt Engineering and Synthetic Content Creation (pp. 433-461). IGI Global. [HTML] DOI: 10.4018/979-8-3693-1351-0.ch021

Neha, K., Kumar, R., & Sankat, M. (2024). AI Wizards: Pioneering Assistive Technologies for Higher Education Inclusion of Students with Learning Disabilities. In Applied Assistive Technologies and Informatics for Students with Disabilities (pp. 59-70). Singapore: Springer Nature Singapore. [HTML]

Ngo, T. V., Nguyen, P. T., Nguyen, V. V., Ha, T. L., & Nguyen, L. M. (2022). An Efficient Method for Generating Synthetic Data for Low-Resource Machine Translation: An empirical study of Chinese, Japanese to Vietnamese Neural Machine Translation. [tandfonline.com]. *Applied Artificial Intelligence, 36*(1), 2101755. DOI: 10.1080/08839514.2022.2101755

Nguyen, A., Ngo, H. N., Hong, Y., Dang, B., & Nguyen, B. P. T. (2023). Ethical principles for artificial intelligence in education. [springer.com]. *Education and Information Technologies, 28*(4), 4221–4241. DOI: 10.1007/s10639-022-11316-w PMID: 36254344

Niemi, H. (2021). AI in learning: Preparing grounds for future learning. Journal of Pacific Rim Psychology. sagepub.com

Okoye, K., Hussein, H., Arrona-Palacios, A., Quintero, H. N., Ortega, L. O. P., Sanchez, A. L., Ortiz, E. A., Escamilla, J., & Hosseini, S. (2023). Impact of digital technologies upon teaching and learning in higher education in Latin America: An outlook on the reach, barriers, and bottlenecks. [springer.com]. *Education and Information Technologies, 28*(2), 2291–2360. DOI: 10.1007/s10639-022-11214-1 PMID: 35992366

Osawa, H., Miyamoto, D., Hase, S., Saijo, R., Fukuchi, K., & Miyake, Y. (2022). Visions of Artificial Intelligence and Robots in Science Fiction: A computational analysis. [springer.com]. *International Journal of Social Robotics, 14*(10), 2123–2133. DOI: 10.1007/s12369-022-00876-z PMID: 35874175

Papastratis, I., Chatzikonstantinou, C., Konstantinidis, D., Dimitropoulos, K., & Daras, P. (2021). Artificial intelligence technologies for sign language. [mdpi.com]. *Sensors (Basel), 21*(17), 5843. DOI: 10.3390/s21175843 PMID: 34502733

Parashar, B., Sharma, R., Parashar, V., Rana, G., Nayyar, A., & Harish, V. (2023). An Overview of the Accessibility and Need of AI Animation Tools for Specially Abled Students. AI-Assisted Special Education for Students With Exceptional Needs, 1-22. [HTML]

Plotnikova, V., Dumas, M., & Milani, F. P. (2022). Applying the CRISP-DM data mining process in the financial services industry: Elicitation of adaptation requirements. [HTML]. *Data & Knowledge Engineering, 139*, 102013. DOI: 10.1016/j.datak.2022.102013

Prasse-Freeman, E. (2023). Reassessing reification: ethnicity amidst "failed" governmentality in Burma and India. Comparative Studies in Society and History. cambridge.org

Pregowska, A., Masztalerz, K., Garlińska, M., & Osial, M. (2021). A worldwide journey through distance education—from the post office to virtual, augmented and mixed realities, and education during the COVID-19 pandemic. Education Sciences. mdpi.com

Privitera, A. J., Ng, S. H. S., Kong, A. P. H., & Weekes, B. S. (2024). AI and Aphasia in the Digital Age: A Critical Review. Brain Sciences. mdpi.com

Qin, Y., Luo, Y., & Zhai, Y. (2023). French error type annotation for dictation: A platform with automatic error type annotation for French dictation exercises. Frontiers in Psychology. frontiersin.org

Rahman, S., Irfan, M., Raza, M., Moyeezullah Ghori, K., Yaqoob, S., & Awais, M. (2020). Performance analysis of boosting classifiers in recognizing activities of daily living. [mdpi.com]. *International Journal of Environmental Research and Public Health, 17*(3), 1082. DOI: 10.3390/ijerph17031082 PMID: 32046302

Raiaan, M. A. K., Mukta, M. S. H., Fatema, K., Fahad, N. M., Sakib, S., Mim, M. M. J., ... & Azam, S. (2024). A review on large Language Models: Architectures, applications, taxonomies, open issues and challenges. IEEE Access. ieee.org

Raza, S., Garg, M., Reji, D. J., Bashir, S. R., & Ding, C. (2024). Nbias: A natural language processing framework for BIAS identification in text. [PDF]. *Expert Systems with Applications, 237*, 121542. DOI: 10.1016/j.eswa.2023.121542

Renz, A., & Hilbig, R. (2020). Prerequisites for artificial intelligence in further education: Identification of drivers, barriers, and business models of educational technology companies. [springer.com]. *International Journal of Educational Technology in Higher Education, 17*(1), 14. DOI: 10.1186/s41239-020-00193-3

Rogerson-Revell, P. M. (2021). Computer-assisted pronunciation training (CAPT): Current issues and future directions. Relc Journal. sagepub.com

Sannino, A. (). Transformative agency as warping: How collectives accomplish change amidst uncertainty. Pedagogy. tandfonline.com

Sarker, I. H. (2022). AI-based modeling: techniques, applications and research issues towards automation, intelligent and smart systems. SN Computer Science. springer.com

Sciolette, F., Giovannetti, E., & Marchi, S. (2023). LexicO: an Italian Computational Lexicon derived from Parole-Simple-Clips. Umanistica Digitale. unibo.it

Shah, A. A., Gong, Z., Pal, I., Sun, R., Ullah, W., & Wani, G. F. (2020). Disaster risk management insight on school emergency preparedness–a case study of Khyber Pakhtunkhwa, Pakistan. [HTML]. *International Journal of Disaster Risk Reduction*, *51*, 101805. DOI: 10.1016/j.ijdrr.2020.101805

Sharma, A., Sharma, V., Jaiswal, M., Wang, H. C., Jayakody, D. N. K., Basnayaka, C. M. W., & Muthanna, A. (2022). Recent trends in AI-based intelligent sensing. [mdpi.com]. *Electronics (Basel)*, *11*(10), 1661. DOI: 10.3390/electronics11101661

Song, C. & Song, Y. (2023). Enhancing academic writing skills and motivation: assessing the efficacy of ChatGPT in AI-assisted language learning for EFL students. Frontiers in Psychology. frontiersin.org

Sorin, V., Barash, Y., Konen, E., & Klang, E. (2020). Deep learning for natural language processing in radiology—Fundamentals and a systematic review. [HTML]. *Journal of the American College of Radiology*, *17*(5), 639–648. DOI: 10.1016/j.jacr.2019.12.026 PMID: 32004480

Srinivasa, K. G., Kurni, M., & Saritha, K. (2022). Harnessing the Power of AI to Education. In *Learning, teaching, and assessment methods for contemporary learners: pedagogy for the digital generation* (pp. 311–342). Springer Nature Singapore. [HTML] DOI: 10.1007/978-981-19-6734-4_13

Starks, A. C., & Reich, S. M. (2023). "What about special ed?": Barriers and enablers for teaching with technology in special education. Computers & Education. sciencedirect.com

Stracqualursi, L. & Agati, P. (2024). Twitter users perceptions of AI-based e-learning technologies. Scientific Reports. nature.com

Strohm, L., Hehakaya, C., Ranschaert, E. R., Boon, W. P., & Moors, E. H. (2020). Implementation of artificial intelligence (AI) applications in radiology: Hindering and facilitating factors. [springer.com]. *European Radiology*, *30*(10), 5525–5532. DOI: 10.1007/s00330-020-06946-y PMID: 32458173

Sun, Z., Anbarasan, M., & Praveen Kumar, D. J. C. I. (2021). Design of online intelligent English teaching platform based on artificial intelligence techniques. [HTML]. *Computational Intelligence*, *37*(3), 1166–1180. DOI: 10.1111/coin.12351

Trattner, C., Jannach, D., Motta, E., Costera Meijer, I., Diakopoulos, N., Elahi, M., Opdahl, A. L., Tessem, B., Borch, N., Fjeld, M., Øvrelid, L., De Smedt, K., & Moe, H. (2022). Responsible media technology and AI: Challenges and research directions. [springer.com]. *AI and Ethics*, *2*(4), 585–594. DOI: 10.1007/s43681-021-00126-4

Umali, J. N. D. (2024). Artificial Intelligence Technology Management of Teachers, Learners Motivation and Challenges Encountered. Educational Research (IJMCER). ijmcer.com

Varona, D. & Suárez, J. L. (2022). Discrimination, bias, fairness, and trustworthy AI. Applied Sciences. mdpi.com

Wang, T., Lund, B. D., Marengo, A., Pagano, A., Mannuru, N. R., Teel, Z. A., & Pange, J. (2023). Exploring the potential impact of artificial intelligence (AI) on international students in higher education: Generative AI, chatbots, analytics, and international student success. [mdpi.com]. *Applied Sciences (Basel, Switzerland), 13*(11), 6716. DOI: 10.3390/app13116716

Wei, L. (2023). Artificial intelligence in language instruction: impact on English learning achievement, L2 motivation, and self-regulated learning. Frontiers in Psychology. frontiersin.org

Williamson, B. & Eynon, R. (). Historical threads, missing links, and future directions in AI in education. Learning. tandfonline.com

Williamson, S. M. & Prybutok, V. (2024). Balancing privacy and progress: a review of privacy challenges, systemic oversight, and patient perceptions in AI-driven healthcare. Applied Sciences. mdpi.com

Xu, Y., Liu, X., Cao, X., Huang, C., Liu, E., Qian, S., ... & Zhang, J. (2021). Artificial intelligence: A powerful paradigm for scientific research. The Innovation, 2(4). cell.com

Yuan, Y., Li, H., & Sawaengdist, A. (2024). The impact of ChatGPT on learners in English academic writing: Opportunities and challenges in education. *Language Learning in Higher Education, 14*(1), 41–56. DOI: 10.1515/cercles-2023-0006

Yuen, C. L., & Schlote, N. (2024). Learner Experiences of Mobile Apps and Artificial Intelligence to Support Additional Language Learning in Education. [sagepub.com]. *Journal of Educational Technology Systems, 52*(4), 00472395241238693. DOI: 10.1177/00472395241238693

Zardiashvili, L. & Fosch-Villaronga, E. (2020). "Oh, dignity too?" said the robot: human dignity as the basis for the governance of robotics. Minds and Machines. springer.com

Zdravkova, K. (2022). The potential of artificial intelligence for assistive technology in education. In Handbook on Intelligent Techniques in the Educational Process: Vol 1 Recent Advances and Case Studies (pp. 61-85). Cham: Springer International Publishing. [HTML] DOI: 10.1007/978-3-031-04662-9_4

Zhai, C. & Wibowo, S. (2023). A systematic review on artificial intelligence dialogue systems for enhancing English as foreign language students' interactional competence in the university. Computers and Education: Artificial Intelligence. sciencedirect.com

Zhai, X., Chu, X., Chai, C. S., Jong, M. S. Y., Istenic, A., Spector, M., Liu, J.-B., Yuan, J., & Li, Y. (2021). A Review of Artificial Intelligence (AI) in Education from 2010 to 2020. [wiley.com]. *Complexity, 2021*(1), 8812542. DOI: 10.1155/2021/8812542

Zhang, R., & Zou, D. (2022). Types, purposes, and effectiveness of state-of-the-art technologies for second and foreign language learning. *Computer Assisted Language Learning, 35*(4), 696–742. DOI: 10.1080/09588221.2020.1744666

Chapter 7
Leveraging AI Tools for Language Learning Activities

Kelly M. Torres
https://orcid.org/0000-0003-4374-6366
The Chicago School, USA

Aubrey Statti
The Chicago School, USA

ABSTRACT

The integration of artificial intelligence (AI) in education is revolutionizing traditional language learning methodologies by enabling personalized, efficient, and dynamic learning experiences. AI-driven tools have enhanced second language acquisition by providing individualized learning paths, real-time feedback, and tailored interventions, thus significantly improving learner outcomes across various educational. These tools can analyze extensive data to support students' unique learning needs, adapting content and offering contextually relevant language practice. However, the integration of AI in language education faces challenges related to equitable access, data privacy, and the need for ongoing teacher training. As AI technologies evolve, educators must ensure they are implemented responsibly to uphold academic integrity and foster inclusive learning. This paper explores the benefits, challenges, and future directions of AI integration in language learning, drawing on current research in the field.

INTRODUCTION

The integration of artificial intelligence (AI) in education is transforming traditional teaching methods, especially in the domain of language learning (Huang et al., 2023; Woo & Choi, 2021; Xia et al., 2024; Yu-Ching & Lin, 2024). The field of second language acquisition continues to progress with an emphasis on individualized learning, which can often be accomplished through the integration of innovative AI tools (Panagiotis et al., 2023; Parmaxi, 2020; Shadiev & Yu, 2022; Woo & Choi, 2021; Zhang & Zou, 2020). These AI-driven technologies offer educators unprecedented opportunities to create engaging, personalized, and effective learning activities in relatively short timeframes, thereby revolutionizing the educational landscape. As Simms (2024) explained, "generative artificial intelligence such as ChatGPT

DOI: 10.4018/979-8-3693-7260-9.ch007

represent the next evolution in technological innovation, offering interactive learning experiences that can be personalized for each student" (p. 158).

Advancements in AI have resulted in technology-driven language learning contexts, which previously experienced challenges with technological integration in improving language outcomes for learners at varying levels of proficiency (Huang et al. 2023; Mageira et al., 2022; Sun et al., 2021; Yu-Ching & Lin, 2024). Particularly, the advent of AI tools presents a significant shift in how language learning is approached in K-12 classrooms, higher education, as well as online and in-person settings. Unlike traditional methods, AI-driven technology can analyze vast amounts of data to offer personalized learning paths, identify specific areas where students may struggle, and deliver targeted interventions in real-time. This capability allows educators to design and implement activities that are not only interactive but also profoundly align with each student's unique learning profile. For example, AI can facilitate personalized practice sessions, provide instant feedback on language use, and even adapt content to suit the learner's current proficiency level and learning pace (Alharbi, 2023; Rusmiyanto et al., 2023; Wang et al., 2024). AI tools can also be employed to assist learners in identifying errors, monitoring their progress and abilities, and in receiving prompt feedback. Thus, initial research indicates success in developing language learning abilities and progress (Baha et al., 2023; Chen et al., 2022; Woo & Choi, 2021; Zhang & Zou, 2022).

Moreover, AI tools enable the creation of dynamic learning environments where students can engage in immersive and contextualized language practice. AI-based platforms utilize "sophisticated algorithms to detect subtle linguistic nuances and cultural cues, enabling them to offer more contextually relevant and culturally sensitive learning materials" (Xia et al., 2024, p. 3). Further, Jeon (2022) discovered that tools such as conversational agents and language simulation platforms allow learners to practice real-life interactions in a virtual setting, thus enhancing their language acquisition through practical application. This technology also supports diverse learning styles and needs (e.g., text-to-speech, tutoring support, graphic simulation) further amplifying the learning experience (Zhai et al., 2021). However, the integration of AI in language learning is not without its challenges. Ensuring that these tools are accessible to all students, regardless of their technological resources, remains a critical concern for educational institutions. Therefore, educators must address issues related to equitable access and data privacy while also maintaining the authenticity and integrity of the learning process. Educators must further be sufficiently trained in utilizing these tools in their classrooms (Mouta et al., 2023; Woo & Choi, 2021). As AI technology becomes increasingly more sophisticated, there is a need for ongoing evaluation and adaptation to address biases, ensure data security, and uphold academic integrity.

BACKGROUND

Language learning is a complex process that requires understanding the target language through the development of input and output skills. Traditional language instructional methods often fall short in providing personalized feedback and interactive practice, which are considered crucial for mastering a new language. AI tools, such as ChatGPT, Pi.ai, Claude 3, or Google Gemini, can address these gaps by offering tailored learning experiences that adapt to the needs of individual students. Song and Song (2023) shared that the integration of these types of platforms allow language learners to have immediate access to resources that offer interactive and personalized experiences resulting in increases of student motivation, engagement, and levels of language proficiency.

Language Classrooms

Second language acquisition and foreign language learning in the classroom requires a unique approach to teaching and knowledge acquisition. Learners must be intentional when developing language knowledge and skills. This process includes a focus on primary language components link grammar, vocabulary, and pronunciation as well as an attention to macro skills, such as reading, writing, listening, and speaking (Woo & Choi, 2021). Additionally, Xia et al. (2024) posited that "the evolving global communication landscape demands proficiency in multiple languages, facilitated increasingly through digital platforms" (p. 1). Thus, language learning is continuing to increase in significance and educators must also be intentional when developing curriculum and lesson plans. Complex factors must be taken into account in language learning classrooms, particularly with the integration of innovative technologies like AI, as they offer educators a dynamic set of tools to create engaging and effective curricula.

AI Tools

AI platforms are capable of generating human-like text based on the input it receives. Specifically, with recent innovations, technologies have evolved beyond simply broadcasting or displaying messages to actively generating messages themselves. For example, AI systems are "designed to perform human cognitive functions, such as learning, problem solving, and pattern recognition" (Singer et al., 2023, p. 294). They can engage in conversations, answer questions, provide explanations, and even create original content. Within the realm of education, Chan and Hu (2023) found that students generally have positive attitudes toward AI and recognize the benefits these tools offer toward acquiring new content. For example, AI is considered an invaluable resource for language learning since it can simulate real-life conversations, offer instant feedback, and generate diverse and contextually relevant language practice activities (Pokrivcakova, 2019; Wang et al., 2023). Interacting with simulations allows students to practice practical real-world tasks such as giving directions in a virtual city simulation. The AI tool evaluates learners target language use and then offers contextual vocabulary suggestions. This dynamic interaction not only enhances language proficiency but also fosters confidence in applying language skills in real-world scenarios.

REVIEW OF THEORETICAL FRAMEWORKS AND AI INTEGRATION

In a review of recently published literature on the topic, studies frequently evaluated the integration of AI in educational settings through the theoretical lens of Vygotsky's (1978) zone of proximal development theory (ZPD) (Ghimire et al., 2024; El Naggar, 2024; Ferguson et al., 2022; Simms, 2024). ZPD postulates that optimal learning occurs when the space between what a learner does with guidance and what they can do without guidance is at a minimum. According to the ZPD framework, tasks that require too little from the learner lead to cognitive underload and the lack of challenge for the learner leads to a significant lack of learning. In contrast, tasks that are too complex for students to complete without learning create cognitive overload and thus also create a lack of learning (Vygotsky, 1978).

The importance of scaffolding to facilitate higher-order learning and skill development is in the forefront of the ZPD framework (Vygotsky, 1978). Additionally, in order to provide appropriate difficulty levels for diverse learners as prescribed for optimal learning by ZPD, AI tools are effective (Ferugson et al., 2022). Thus, "AI tools provide instant feedback, support language diversity, and guide students in the writing process, and educators can enhance student writing proficiency within their ZPD" (Ghirmire et al., 2024, p. 38). AI tools therefore allow for students to receive personalized assistance and support that is gradually removed as the student's skills develop and competence is displayed (Simms, 2024). Further, ZPD provides guidance for not only young learners, but also for professional development and improvements to professional practice.

Further, cognitive load theory (CLT) indicates the importance of cognitive load considerations in learning (Sweller, 1988; Sweller et al., 2011; Sweller, 2016), specifically when using AI with students (Ferguson et al., 2022). According to the premise of CLT, there are three different types of cognitive load: intrinsic, extraneous, and germane. Intrinsic cognitive load is associated with the complexity of the learning task. Extraneous cognitive load is related to task presentation. Lastly, germane cognitive load is created by processing and constructing schemas for learning new skills through processing new information (Sweller et al., 2011). According to CLT, there must be an appropriate level of cognitive load in order for effective learning to occur. As such, both ZPD and CLT indicate that the value of attending to cognitive needs, learning ability levels, and learning needs for students when integrating AI into educational applications, including the use of appropriate challenges, personalized experiences, and real-time feedback (Ferguson et al., 2022).

Moreover, the use of AI is supported by constructivist learning theories, which focus on constructing knowledge through experience and reflections (Simms, 2024). One concern with the integration of AI into learning environments is the lack of social interactions and the reliance on bot interactions. Therefore, collaborative learning and the importance of social interactions in the learning process are crucial when considering the use of generative AI in education (El Naggar et al., 2024). With thoughtful integration of AI into language learning classrooms, students can collaborate to enhance engagement and learning. For example, students may have conversations on global topics inspired through AI tools in the language they are learning. These conversations can simulate real-world interactions, allowing students to practice vocabulary, grammar, and cultural nuances in context. AI tools can provide immediate feedback on pronunciation, sentence structure, and word choice targeted to a particular country allowing for learners to refine their skills in real time. Essentially, AI tools allow for students learning new languages to engage in active learning through the "dynamic exchange of ideas and...deeper understanding through social engagement" (Simms, 2024, p. 159).

Further, in addition to learning theory, current research focused on the use of AI in language acquisition also often include an emphasis on various technology integration and instructional design models (Xia et al., 2024; Yu-Ching & Lin, 2024), such as the Technology Acceptance Model (TAM) (Davis, 1989); the ADDIE model (Aldoobie, 2015), and the Technological Pedagogical Content Knowledge (TPACK) (Koehler & Mishra, 2008). These various instructional design and technology integration frameworks are also important when considering the inclusion of AI into language learning. Following the guidelines of a framework encourages educators to be intentional and thoughtful in the integration of these tools into the classroom. For example, in the ADDIE model (Aldoobie, 2015), learning needs are first analyzed, followed by the design and development of the curriculum. The new technology is then implemented into the curriculum and most importantly, evaluated for its effectiveness. The ADDIE model can be repeated as revisions are needed and the effectiveness of the new AI tools clarified. The consideration of the TPACK (Koehler & Mishra, 2008) model is also important because it stresses the value of teacher knowledge when utilizing new tools, a factor noted throughout the research on language learning and AI use. Instructors following the TPACK model demonstrate the value of utilizing appropriate pedagogical strategies and therefore enhance the student's individual learning experience (Yu-Ching & Lin, 2024). Lastly, the TAM (Davis, 1989) denotes the "usability and perceived usefulness of AI-driven systems strongly influence learner acceptance and sustained use" (p. 1), critical factors when integrating in new technology, specifically cutting-edge technology such as AI.

PRACTICAL APPLICATIONS

One of the most significant challenges in language learning is finding opportunities for conversational practice particularly with individuals who possess advanced or native-like proficiencies. Moreover, language learning is considered to be anxiety provoking for many students resulting in learners feeling self-conscious producing language output. Wang et al. (2023) proposed that in order to solve these challenges, chatbots can serve as a conversational partner, allowing students to practice speaking and listening in a safe and controlled environment. Moreover, Huang et al. (2021) indicated that newer versions of AI allow for the contextualization of language to focus on location-based dialects. For instance, AI chatbots implemented into language classrooms to simulate various scenarios could include ordering food at a restaurant, asking for directions, or discussing hobbies and use terms and slang that are commonplace to a particular target language location. Ultimately, AI offers numerous practical applications in language learning classes resulting in students experiencing an enhanced learning experience (Ji et al., 2023).

One primary benefit of using AI is its focus on creating personalized learning environments, where AI algorithms assess individual student performance and tailor content to meet their specific learning goals. Precisely, through the inclusion of AI-powered learning technologies, educators scaffold student learning toward targeted outcomes (Darvishi et al., 2024). This approach ensures that each student receives targeted instruction, fostering more efficient and effective learning. Additionally, AI-powered language learning apps, such as Duolingo and Babbel, utilize adaptive learning techniques to provide interactive and engaging exercises that reinforce vocabulary, grammar, and pronunciation skills. Regarding pronunciation skills, AI powered language apps (e.g., ELSA Speak) analyze pronunciation and give immediate feedback. While in class or as an at home learning activity, learners can complete lessons on pronunciation, students can practice speaking phrases aloud into an app and receive a score and suggestions for improvement. Unlike typical classroom language experiences in which the educator has limited time to practice one-on-one pronunciation skills with students, AI language apps allow for repeated attempts ensuring repetition of targeted practice. Another practical application is the use of AI-driven chatbots and virtual assistants, which provide students with instant feedback and conversational practice. These tools simulate real-life conversations, helping learners improve their speaking and listening skills in a low-pressure environment.

In a study conducted by Yuan (2023), participants responded positively to AI chatbots resulting in the finding that these bots provide personalized error corrections and user-centric features allowing for more immersive language learning. For instance, student tasks might include interacting with a chatbot simulating a restaurant server, ordering food, and asking questions. The chatbot responds naturally, reinforcing sentence structures and vocabulary further promoting authentic conversations. AI tools also analyze speech for fluency, clarity, and grammar during student presentations. This type of tool is valuable for student presentations since they can receive an AI-generated report identifying their strengths and areas for improvement (e.g., sentence coherence). Another practical application is for students to watch a video in the target language with AI-generated subtitles. They are then tasked with answering comprehension questions, using the AI's transcript to verify their answers. Qiao and Zhoa (2023) further discovered that student engagement with AI tools fostered self-regulatory processes and greater improvement in target language speaking skills.

Writing in a new language can likewise be a daunting task due to the nuances of grammar and writing styles. AI provides writing assistance to students by offering instant feedback on their written work. For example, Song and Song (2023) found AI useful in suggesting corrections and sentence restructuring, which are both vital in improving students' writing skills over time. Additionally, AI platforms can generate writing prompts and provide model essays to guide students in their writing practice. AI tools can also provide personalized grammar instruction by identifying common errors in students' work and explaining the underlying rules. Based on this information, the platform can then generate grammar exercises and quizzes to reinforce learning to ensure that students grasp the fundamental structures of the target language. For example, tools such as Quizlet or Memrise use algorithms to adapt to student's learning paces and helps them practice new skills. Providing students grammar quizzes through these tools related to a particular course topic ensures they receive personalized and immediate feedback on their progress and suggested areas for continual study. Marzuki et al. (2023) stated that "the evolution of teaching writing in the current age of technological proliferation cannot be dissociated from the rapid advancement of digital tools" (para 6) underscoring the idea that these technologies are becoming increasingly intertwined within our instructional approaches.

Alharbi (2023) identified AI-powered writing assistance tools as being characterized into four groups: 1) automated writing evaluation tools, 2) corrective feedback automated writing tools, 3) AI-powered machine translators, and 4) GPT automatic text generators. Given advancements in AI automated writing systems, Alharbi (2023) further recommended that educators should embrace these tools since students will most likely continue to employ them to complete their coursework. Therefore, including AI tools, such as GPT-4, could be helpful in assisting students in brainstorming ideas and drafting and revising text. Learners can guide these types of chatbots to generate content that is tailored to match the tone and style required for specific language writing tasks (e.g., academic writing, business communication, creative storytelling). For instance, AI-powered platforms like Google Docs use machine learning algorithms to facilitate real-time collaboration by suggesting edits and improvements as multiple users work on a document simultaneously. This type of collaboration ensures consistency and coherence in group writing projects, making the process more efficient and productive, and provides a platform for peer learning and interaction in the target language. Including AI writing tools (e.g., Grammarly, ProWritingAid, ChatGPT) allows for real-time corrections, style suggestions, and explanation for writing improvement. One practical application of using AI tools for writing skill development is to require learners to write short essays or dialogues for submission to an AI platform. The AI platform will highlight grammar errors, suggest synonyms, and identify repetitive structures. Educators can then pair this activity with peer review for collaborative learning experiences. In fact, Seufer et al. (2021) discovered that instructor and peer feedback coupled with AI-assisted language support significantly impacted student performance.

For personalized learning, AI-based platforms can analyze a student's strengths and weaknesses over time, offering customized exercises and feedback to improve specific skills in the foreign language. This data makes the learning process more focused and effective resulting in higher learner outcomes. For example, research has demonstrated notable reading gains for students who use AI technology for literacy activities (Srinivasan & Murthy, 2021; Sumakul et al., 2022). To enhance reading skills, AI-generated reading passages are tailored to learners' proficiency levels and interests. Likewise, these tools can create comprehension questions that challenge students to think critically about the text. Educators can then utilize AI to analyze students' responses to receive detailed feedback and suggestions for further reading materials that match students' literacy levels. Another fundamental aspect of language learning is vocabulary acquisition. AI platforms such as ChatGPT, Univerbal, Zaplingo, and Talkpal can develop interactive vocabulary exercises (e.g., fill-in-the-blank sentences, matching activities) to reinforce students' understanding and usage of words in context.

BENEFITS OF AI TOOLS

Huang et al. (2023) conveyed that prior AI tools have lacked the ability to tailor content to students' differing language proficiency levels resulting in challenges associated with students not receiving similar learning outcomes. However, with the recent advancements and sophistication of newer AI tools, language activities are easily tailored to all learners. In a classroom with diverse learning levels, educators can wield AI tools for personalized learning targeted on students' competence levels and readiness to move forward, consequently creating a more inclusive learning environment for all students (Ghimire et al., 2024).

As discovered by Wang et al. (2022), this personalization ensures that each student is appropriately challenged and supported within their coursework which ultimately leads to more effective learning gains. Additionally, AI's ability to provide instant feedback is vital in students identifying and correcting errors in real-time, reinforcing correct language usage, and accelerating their learning processes. Using generative AI or AI "can promote personalized learning by adapting resources to each student's learning pace and style, potentially improvement outcomes in writing skills and learning engagement" (Ghimire et al., 2024, p. 38). Additionally, unlike human tutors or instructors, AI tools are available to students 24 hours a day, seven days a week, making enhanced and personalized instruction more accessible. Essentially, interactive AI tools can make language learning more available, successful, engaging, and enjoyable. Gamification elements of AI apps further create fun, competitive learning environments promoting students to achieve higher proficiency levels. Platforms such as Kahoot! and Gimkit provide real-time feedback through competitive language games fostering learner motivation and engagement.

By simulating real-life scenarios and providing diverse activities, students' interests and motivation are maintained throughout their language courses (Song & Song, 2023; Wang et al., 2022). Additionally, AI tools can be accessed anytime and anywhere resulting in the language learning process becoming more flexible and accommodating for students with varying schedules and learning preferences. Educators also benefit from the integration of AI into their classrooms since it provides options for automating repetitive tasks (e.g., grading) and generating lessons. As a result, educators have more time to focus more on personalized instruction and student support. Incorporating AI in language learning classes also enables the analysis of large datasets to identify common learning obstacles and trends, allowing educators to adjust their teaching strategies and schedules accordingly. Basically, through the use of AI tools, classroom teachers can further focus on streamlining their administrative tasks and improving teaching quality and strategies, thus being able to provide more personalized student support to diverse learners (Ghimire et al., 2024).

Further, Ghimire et al. (2024) concluded through their research the positive impacts of AI tools on English language teaching efficiency in international contexts, specifically in the nation of Nepal. Their findings indicated that tools such as ChatGPT, Gemini, Grammarly, and Duolingo increase student engagement, personalized learning, and student writing skills. Additionally, much of the current research is focused on the use of ChatGPT specifically with language learners. For example, Yu-Ching and Lin (2024) noted that GPT-3.5 can assist students with time management in the writing process when learning a new language by providing guidance for structuring their thoughts and writing in a logical manner. Their research stressed the potential for utilizing interactive AI elements in language learning to create pioneering learning experiences for language learners and an emergence of thoughtful student expression through writing.

ADDRESSING ETHICAL CONCERNS AND OVERCOMING CHALLENGES

Despite the benefits evident in Ghirmire et al.'s (2024) findings, ethical issues and concerns were also present in their research as well as other recent related studies (Darvishi et al. 2024; Dwivedi et al., 2023, Owan et al., 2023). Tang and Su (2024) concluded five primary ethical concerns with AI use in the classroom. Their findings revealed that educators should be cognizant of algorithmic bias and discrimination, data privacy leakage, lack of transparency, decreased autonomy, and academic misconduct. Singer et al. (2023) also urged caution when implementing AI technologies, noting, "the technology is simply a tool to improve our efficiency and effectiveness, not a cure-all for practice or education issues" (p. 300). Yu-Ching and Lin (2024) also stressed the need for caution in its utilization, noting the concerns for limited contextual understanding and a lack of empathy.

Dignum (2023) indicated that AI "has the potential to impact our lives and our world as no other technology has done before" (p. 195). However, like other educational contexts, the integration of AI language learning tools presents both opportunities and challenges. An additional concern of these tools is the importance of ensuring that they are accessible to a diverse range of students and varying learning needs. Owan et al. (2023) conveyed that accessibility of AI tools is a major obstacle that educators face when implementing these platforms into their courses. As a result, ensuring that AI-powered platforms and applications are accessible to all students, regardless of their technical skills, learning abilities, or access to resources, is crucial. To overcome this challenge, Darvishi et al. (2024) recommended educators scaffold AI technology use allowing for student agency through receipt of personalized nudges in the learning process. Additionally, selecting user-friendly and widely supported AI tools can minimize technical issues and barriers and allow access to readily available resources focused on overcoming identified challenges. Further, offering ongoing technical support throughout the course can help address any issues that arise, preventing minor problems from becoming major obstacles. Another key consideration is the selection of AI tools themselves. Educators should prioritize platforms that are known for their stability and ease of use.

Regular feedback from students is also essential in refining the use of AI tools in the classroom (Darvishi et al., 2024). By soliciting student input on their experiences with technology, educators can identify common issues and adjust their approach as needed. Unfortunately, student input on classroom technology is often neglected in the feedback cycle of the curriculum design process (Dawson et al., 2023). Still, this imperative feedback loop helps to improve the immediate learning environment and informs the selection and implementation of AI tools in future courses. In addition to addressing technical concerns, educators should also consider the pedagogical implications of using AI in language learning. AI tools have the potential to personalize learning experiences, providing students with tailored feedback and adaptive learning paths that foster autonomy (Kuddus, 2022). However, this personalization must be balanced with the need to foster a collaborative and interactive classroom environment. Indeed, Su and Zou (2020) warned that educators should integrate AI tools in a way that complements traditional teaching methods and encourages students to engage with both the technology and each other. Ultimately, by focusing on accessibility, reliability, and student support, educators can harness the full potential of AI in language learning. This approach not only ensures that all students have the opportunity to succeed but also enriches the overall learning experience, making it more interactive, dynamic, and effective in helping students achieve their language learning goals.

Loss of Critical Thinking Skills

Another primary concern is students being passive learners and relying on technology, rather than critical thinking skills to solve problems (Ghimire et al., 2024). Indeed, Furguson et al. (2022) noted that "using a self-directed learning approach means learners may not discover important learning materials due to a lack of knowledge of tasks and challenges that need to be solved" (pp. 1-2). When students become too reliant on AI to produce outcomes, such as a writing sample, learning ceases and the AI tool is no longer beneficial to the learning environment or the learner. However, when used correctly and supported by evidence-based practices, AI tools can enhance creating thinking skills in a variety of learning environments (Simms, 2024), including language learning classrooms. To avoid the lack of critical thinking in the learning process, students should be instructed to use AI platforms as a tool, not solely as a text generator for academic work (Singer et al., 2023). Yu-Ching and Lin (2024) posited that "as students engage with AI, they under a dynamic partnership… [and that] this collaboration with OpenAI's GPT-3.5 fosters critical thinking and empowers students to develop a distinctive writing voice" (p. 78). Their research denotes the potential for a dynamic learning experience, robust of critical thinking, when the tools are used correctly.

Accuracy and Bias

AI tools, while advanced, are not infallible and can sometimes provide incorrect suggestions or exhibit biases, particularly in language nuances and cultural contexts. Tang and Su (2024) found that algorithmic bias is a primary concern in current research on the topic. While new AI algorithms continue to evolve over time (Dwivedi et al., 2023), when utilizing and applying AI information, it is important to note that generative AI is "only as inclusive and equitable as the information informing them. If only certain works inform a generative AI tool (e.g., English-language works only, U.S. centric works, or works from one specific demographic), the output ...receive[d] from that tool will also be both limited to and influenced by the voices or works it has been trained on" (Cornell University, 2024, para. 6). Indeed, Simms (2024) indicated that validating the accuracy of AI can be challenging and that AI may produce incorrect, or misleading information students may choose to rely on or believe, without appropriate evidence. These inaccuracies can arise from the data on which the AI is trained, which may not fully represent the diversity of language usage. In fact, Vall and Araya (2023) indicated that AI algorithms amplify exiting biases found in language learning materials and practices. Further, Gupta et al. (2022) expressed concerns that AI-based recommendations could be conditioned from society's implicit biases. Specifically, Singer et al. (2023) noted that "ChatGPT is trained on a dataset that reflects the biases and limitations of the data on which it has been trained. It is important to be aware of these limitations and address any potential biases and discriminatory effects in the use of ChatGPT" (p. 299). In addition to the concern of biases, is the reality that ChatGPT, as well as other generative AI, may misunderstand a prompt or the data it is provided and thus produce an inaccurate response.

To address these areas, educators should encourage students to critically evaluate AI-generated feedback and cross-reference with reliable language resources (e.g., dictionaries, grammar guides, native speakers). Moreover, regular updates and improvements to AI algorithms by developers are essential to reduce biases and enhance accuracy. Educators can advocate for and participate in the development and testing of AI tools to ensure they meet the specific needs of language learners. Gupta et al. (2022) shared that researchers are proposing ways to address algorithmic learning objectives to address AI generated biases. As a result, providing feedback to developers about common errors and cultural nuances can help significantly improve the tools performance. Additionally, educators can create a balanced approach by combining AI feedback with human insights, ensuring that students receive well-rounded and accurate guidance. Often, AI systems learn from large datasets that may not comprehensively represent the diversity of language use across different regions, dialects, or socio-cultural settings. For instance, an AI language model trained primarily on English as used in the United States might not accurately interpret idiomatic expressions or slang from other English-speaking countries (e.g., United Kingdom, Australia). In the context of language learning, such discrepancies can lead to misunderstandings or reinforce incorrect language usage. For example, an AI tool might incorrectly suggest a word or phrase that is technically correct in one dialect but inappropriate or nonsensical in another.

A balanced approach that combines AI-generated feedback with human insights is essential for providing students with well-rounded and accurate guidance. While AI can efficiently handle repetitive tasks and provide immediate feedback, Kim et al. (2022) stressed that human educators bring an irreplaceable depth of understanding, particularly in interpreting cultural and contextual subtleties. Examples include that educators can offer personalized explanations, clarify confusing AI suggestions, and provide context that AI might miss or provide incorrectly. This combination of AI efficiency and human expertise creates a more effective and comprehensive learning environment. For instance, after a student uses an AI tool to practice language skills, a teacher could review the AI's feedback, identify any inaccuracies or biases, and offer additional explanations or alternative phrases. This approach not only corrects potential errors but also helps students understand why the AI tool might have made a particular suggestion, deepening their linguistic and cultural knowledge. Essentially, AI should be viewed as a learning agent and not as replacing the role of the educator (Kim et al., 2022; Sumakul et al., 2022).

Academic Integrity

The integration of AI in language learning, particularly in writing tasks, brings with it the challenge of maintaining academic integrity. Unfortunately, the convenience and efficiency of AI tools, such as grammar checkers and content generators, can sometimes lead students to rely too heavily on these technologies. Interestingly, Dwivedi et al. (2023) posited that the academic sector will likely experience the most disruptive effects of AI tools, such as ChatGPT. Research conducted by Darvishi et al. (2024) highlighted the negative influence of student reliance on AI tools impacting their ability to learn from AI assistance. These sentiments were further expressed by Marzuki et al. (2023) who indicated educators have continually expressed concerns that students may become too reliant on these tools. Additionally, Tang and Su (2024) noted that the topics of decreased autonomy and academic misconduct are understudied in current literature focused on AI use in the classroom. Thus, while an immediate concern for educators, the academic integrity of AI use is underexplored and in need of additional investigation in order to support educators and learners when applying AI use in the classroom.

Basically, in language learning contexts, where the goal is to build proficiency in vocabulary and grammar the macro skills reading, writing, speaking, and listening, AI tools should be seen as aids rather than crutches. Specifically, when students use AI to generate entire essays or complete tasks with minimal effort, they fail to benefit from the valuable process of grappling with language, organizing their thoughts, and expressing their ideas authentically. This potential outcome not only hampers their learning but also raises concerns about the authenticity and originality of their work. Educators may also be unable to recognize AI generated content and student generated content, thus creating additional challenges for educators to address potential academic misconduct (Dwivedi et al., 2023).

To address these concerns, educators must establish clear guidelines and ethical use policies regarding AI in the classroom. These guidelines should explicitly state the role of AI tools as support mechanisms that are designed to enhance the writing process rather than replace the student's own individual efforts. Ultimately, the goal of writing tasks is to develop learners with the proficiency to effectively articulate their ideas (Song & Song, 2023). When addressing how to ethically use AI within class assignments, educators can suggest employing these tools to only focus on improvements in sentence structure or grammar. As Gayed et al. (2022) cited, AI focused writing tools are effective in providing support in low-level writing tasks, which should be the focus of their implementation into academic settings.

One effective strategy to ensure academic integrity in language learning is to design assignments that inherently require critical thinking and personal reflection. Lin and Mubarok (2021) pointed out students need to be encouraged to form opinions, make judgments, or predictions, and engage in various learning activities. These types of assignment focuses are more challenging for AI to handle autonomously, as they demand a deep engagement with the material, nuanced understanding of the content, and personal insights that only the student can provide. Classroom examples of these types of assignments include students reflecting on their own language learning journey, analyzing a piece of literature from their cultural perspective, or discussing how language shapes their identity. These types of original tasks make it difficult for students to rely solely on AI, as the unique, personal element is essential and would be missing from AI generated content. In addition to designing assignments that promote original thinking, educators should emphasize the importance of proper citation practices and the ethical use of AI tools.

Teaching students how to correctly attribute sources and ideas, even when aided by AI, reinforces the value of academic honesty. This valuable lesson is essential given that students who feel overwhelmed with their assignments may feel tempted to use AI platforms (Gayed et al., 2022). As a result, this instruction should cover the responsible use of AI, guiding students on how to use these tools for proofreading, brainstorming, or enhancing their work, rather than as shortcuts for generating assignment content. Likewise, educators can incorporate lessons on digital literacy and critical thinking to help students understand the limitations of AI. For instance, students should be made aware that while AI can provide useful suggestions, it may also introduce errors or biases, especially in nuanced language tasks. By critically evaluating AI-generated content and cross-referencing with reliable sources, students can learn to navigate AI tools as part of a broader, more thoughtful approach to language learning. Indeed, Markauskaite et al. (2022) asserted that AI produces bias and generates output that should be critically analyzed and that the development of skills focused on human knowledge is a vital component of being critical consumers of these tools.

Another approach to fostering academic integrity is through collaborative learning activities that involve AI tools. For example, students could work in groups to peer-review each other's work with the help of AI, discussing the AI's suggestions and collectively deciding on the best ways to improve the text. This interaction not only promotes critical engagement with AI tools but also builds a community of learners who value originality and support each other's learning. Ultimately, AI within this assignment example is perceived as a mediating tool to support collaborative learning experiences. In an effort to develop collaborative learning activities, Woo and Choi (2021) also recommended the use of NAO, a programmable robot, that can be used for group conversations in language learning classrooms. NAO has speech recognition and dialogue abilities in 20 languages and also has cameras and microphones to speak and interact with humans and to recognize shapes and objects. Students learning a new language can enjoy conversation with the interactive and moving robot throughout the classroom (https://www.aldebaran.com/en/nao).

Using AI-supported language learning as a mediating tool is integral in language learning pedagogical design (Yang & Kyun, 2022). By setting clear expectations, designing thoughtful assignments, and teaching responsible AI use, educators help students maintain academic integrity while still benefiting from the advancements that AI offers to language learning. Through this balanced approach, students develop language skills and also the ethical and critical thinking skills necessary for success in academic and professional settings.

Balancing Automation and Human Interaction

While AI can automate many aspects of writing and feedback, it cannot replace the nuanced understanding and encouragement provided by human instructors. The personal touch that teachers bring to the classroom, including their ability to understand individual student needs and provide tailored support, is irreplaceable. To balance automation and human interaction, AI tools should be used to complement, not replace, teacher instruction and feedback. This balanced approach could include AI-generated insights in identifying common errors and trends in student writing. Specifically, AI tools are adept at identifying patterns, correcting grammar, and providing standardized feedback across a wide range of student submissions. For example, AI can quickly pinpoint common errors in verb conjugation, sentence structure, or word choice across a class of students. This capability allows for immediate correction and helps students recognize and avoid recurring mistakes. However, the human touch is vital in addressing the subtleties of language learning that AI might overlook, such as understanding the cultural context of language use, interpreting tone, or offering encouragement tailored to a student's progress. Further, educators can discern the emotional and cognitive aspects of language learning, such as when a student struggles with confidence or motivation and provide support that is both empathetic and pedagogically sound. Hence, allowing educators to focus their efforts on providing more personalized and in-depth feedback is still an essential aspect of foreign and second language classrooms.

To create an effective balance, educators can also use AI-generated insights as a preliminary review tool (Chen et al., 2022; Chiu, 2021; Seo et al., 2021). For instance, after students submit their essays or language exercises, AI can be employed to conduct an initial analysis, highlighting areas that need improvement, such as consistent grammatical errors or issues with clarity. This preliminary feedback allows educators to save time on routine corrections, enabling them to focus on providing more in-depth and personalized feedback during one-on-one interactions. For example, if an AI tool identifies that a student consistently misuses certain grammatical structures, the teacher can use this information to tailor their feedback, perhaps by explaining the rule in a way that relates to the student's native language or by providing additional practice exercises that target this specific issue. This targeted approach ensures that the student not only understands the error but also learns how to avoid it in the future, thus enhancing their overall language proficiency.

Furthermore, AI can assist teachers in identifying trends within a group of students, such as a common difficulty with certain language constructs or vocabulary usage. This data can inform educators in their curriculum design decisions that address these shared challenges, fostering a collaborative learning environment where students learn from AI insights and their instructor and peers. Incorporating AI in this fashion allows for a more dynamic and responsive teaching approach. Educators can also deliver a richer learning experience by combining the efficiency of AI with the depth of human understanding. For instance, after AI has flagged specific issues, teachers can engage in meaningful discussions with students about their writing, exploring not just what needs to be corrected, but also why those errors occur and how they relate to broader language concepts. These discussions can lead to deeper insights into the language, helping students correct their mistakes and develop a more profound understanding of language mechanics and usage. Moreover, the personalized feedback provided by teachers, informed by AI but deeply rooted in the teacher's expertise and understanding of the student, can help foster critical thinking and creativity. Instructors can guide students to think beyond the immediate corrections and to consider the broader implications of their language choices, encouraging them to express their ideas more effectively and with greater confidence.

Data Privacy and Security

An immediate concern with the use of AI in language learning classrooms is the lack of sufficient privacy for student and instructor use of these tools (Woo & Choi, 2021). For example, ChatGPT interactions are frequently reviewed by OpenAI trainers in order to "improve their system or to ensure compliance with their policy and safety requirements" (Singer et al., 2023, p. 299). Transparency about data usage is essential when integrating AI tools. Educators should inform students about what data is being collected, how it will be used, and the measures in place to protect it. Additionally, educators should regularly review the data practices of the AI tools they use and stay updated on any changes to ensure ongoing compliance with privacy standards.

By prioritizing data privacy and security, educators can build trust and ensure that AI tools are used responsibly. Within the context of language learning, where AI tools might collect data on student performance, language preferences, and even speech patterns, it is crucial that these tools have robust security measures in place. This process involves selecting AI platforms that have been rigorously tested for security vulnerabilities and that provide clear and comprehensive privacy policies. These policies should outline the types of data collected, the purposes for which the data will be used, and the safeguards implemented to protect this information from unauthorized access or breaches. Chiefly, transparency is key to building trust between educators and students. Educators should clearly communicate how AI tools handle data, explaining what is collected, why it is necessary for the learning process, and how it will be utilized to enhance the educational experience. For instance, in language learning, data might be used to track progress, tailor exercises to individual needs, or provide insights into areas where a student might be struggling. By understanding these uses, students can better appreciate the value of the data being collected while remaining aware of their rights and protections.

AI education policy is considered a widely debated topic (Chan, 2023) resulting in educational institutions taking strong stances in its use. Therefore, educators need to stay informed about any updates or changes to the AI tool's privacy policy, understand how these changes might affect student data, and adjust the use of these tools if needed. For example, if an AI language learning app introduces a new feature that involves sharing data with third parties, educators must assess the implications of this change and determine whether it aligns with the privacy expectations of students and the school. In addition to regulatory compliance, educators can further protect student privacy by implementing best practices such as minimizing data collection to only what is necessary for the educational process, anonymizing data where possible, and ensuring that data is securely stored and transmitted. These practices help to mitigate the risks associated with data breaches and unauthorized access. Perhaps, in a language learning environment where students might use AI-powered apps to practice speaking or receive feedback on their writing, educators could ensure that any recorded audio or written data is encrypted and stored securely. By anonymizing student identities in these datasets, the impact of any potential data breach can be minimized.

Fostering Student Confidence and Engagement

Some students may feel intimidated or skeptical about using AI tools, fearing they might hinder their learning or make their efforts redundant. To foster confidence and engagement, educators can highlight the benefits of AI, such as personalized learning and instant feedback, and integrate AI tools in a way that supports and enhances students' skill development. Demonstrating how AI can be a valuable aid rather than a replacement can help alleviate these concerns. Encouraging a growth mindset and emphasizing that mistakes are part of the learning process can also help students feel more comfortable experimenting with AI tools. According to Zeeb et al. (2020), growth mindset is malleable through the classroom activities that students engage in daily. As a result, integrating AI tools into language learning can be transformative in providing mindset interventions that positivity affects learners' academic motivation.

Since personalized instruction and instant feedback significantly enhances the learning experience (Alamri et al., 2020; Owan et al., 2023; Yang & Ogata, 2022; Zheng et al., 2022), students' exposure to AI-enhanced language learning can positively impact their growth mindset in this area. Although most students embrace AI and have general positive attitudes toward it (Chan & Hu, 2023; Schiavo et al., 2024), some students may initially feel intimidated or skeptical about using these tools, fearing that they might either undermine their learning efforts or render their contributions redundant. To address these concerns and foster a positive learning environment, educators must strategically introduce AI tools in ways that emphasize their supportive role rather than viewing them as replacements. For example, sharing academic success stories of students who have effectively used AI tools can significantly boost learners' confidence and enthusiasm. Educators can present examples of how AI has positively impacted other students' language learning journeys, such as improving their writing clarity, expanding their vocabulary, or increasing their overall proficiency. These real-world examples can serve as powerful motivators, showing students that AI tools can be a valuable part of their educational toolkit.

Fostering a classroom environment where students feel safe to experiment and make mistakes is essential. Torralba et al. (2020) described psychological safety as being a top priority since it leads to learners becoming high performers. Encourage students to view AI tools as part of a supportive network designed to help them succeed. Creating a classroom culture that values effort, learning, and improvement allows educators to more fully assist students in feeling higher levels of comfort integrating AI tools into their language learning practices. Addressing students' concerns about AI tools in language learning involves highlighting the benefits, sharing success stories, integrating tools gradually, encouraging a growth mindset, providing training, and creating a supportive environment. Chiu et al. (2022) stressed the role of teacher support impacting student motivation and autonomy in interacting with chatbots further underscoring the role of pedagogical and considerations of AI application. Through taking these steps, educators support students in building their confidence in using AI tools, ultimately enhancing their language learning experience and fostering a more engaged and motivated student body.

Equitable Access

Ensuring equitable access to AI tools is another important consideration. Not all students have the same access to technology and resources, which can create disparities in learning opportunities. Familoni and Onyebuchi (2024) shared that lack of access can further exacerbate digital divides located within educational settings. Additionally, AI tools should be selected based on their accessibility considerations. For example, tools that offer features like text-to-speech, speech-to-text, and customizable interfaces can make learning more accessible to all students. Schneiderman (2020) postulated that AI technologies offer great promises in removing access barriers, resulting in more accessible learning conditions. Prioritizing equity in the selection and implementation of AI tools guarantees that all students benefit from the technology. Specifically, disparities in technology access create significant gaps in educational opportunities negatively impacting students' abilities to benefit from AI-enhanced language learning tools. Addressing these disparities requires a multifaceted approach to ensure that all students, regardless of their circumstances, have the resources and support needed to take full advantage of AI in their educational journeys.

Research has further continuously demonstrated the power of AI in enhancing students' academic performance (Luckin et al., 2022; VanLehn et al., 2020). Tools that provide contextualized vocabulary and grammar explanations can support students as they develop their language skills. Still, AI tools should be sensitive to and inclusive of the cultural and linguistic diversity of learners. This level of inclusivity is vital as more students are exposed to AI learning environments (Mohammed & Watson, 2019). Tools offering multilingual support and recognizing different cultural contexts ensure that students from various backgrounds find the technology relevant and helpful. Incorporating AI tools into curriculum materials that reflect diverse perspectives and language uses can make the technology more relevant and engaging for students from various backgrounds. Regularly assessing the effectiveness of strategies aimed at improving access to AI tools is also essential. Collecting feedback from students and educators can help identify any ongoing barriers or gaps in access, allowing for refinement of approaches to ensure that all students can fully participate in and benefit from AI-enhanced language learning. Essentially, Kim (2023) stressed the need for educators to be considered AI ready to optimize and embrace its benefits. Readily available access to professional development training on the implementation of AI into their curriculum and strategies for supporting students' utilization of these tools is critical (Familoni & Onyebunchi, 2024). Training can include introductory workshops or tutorials that explain the features and benefits of the tools, along with support to address any technical issues students may encounter.

CONCLUDING THOUGHTS

The successful implementation of AI in language learning requires careful planning, training, and evaluation. Singer et al. (2023) noted that "the effectiveness of this tool depends on our ability to think creatively, ethically, and divergently, and how well we integrate it into our thinking" (p. 300). Educators must be equipped with the necessary skills and knowledge to effectively integrate AI tools into their teaching practices. Nazaretshy et al. (2022) stressed the need for professional development programs and ongoing support to assist teachers in their navigation of the complexities of AI technology in order to leverage its full potential. Fortunately, AI tools can often be explored and experimented with often for a low cost and without a long-period commitment (Woo & Choi, 2021). Educators can investigate potential tools for their classroom, both in person and online settings, to determine which platforms will be most effective for their specific student needs and learning levels. As described by Luckin et al. (2022) ensuring that educators are AI ready empowers them to understand the full potential of this tool within their professional setting. Particularly, through these types of trainings, educators can realize that AI tools can strengthen their teaching approaches and dispel their concerns that these technologies will eventually replace them in the classroom (Ghamrawi et al., 2023; Nazaretsky et al., 2022).

Additionally, as AI platforms continue to develop and improve, future research is needed in order to assess the use of AI tools in specific areas of language learning, such as writing instruction (Yu-Ching & Lin, 2024), grammar, and pronunciation. Additional research is needed to understand how to best address issues of accessibility and AI use as well as concerns of academic dishonesty and AI use. Continuous evaluation and feedback from both students and teachers are also essential to ensure that AI tools remain effective and relevant. Regular assessments and adjustments based on this feedback will help refine the use of AI in the language classroom, addressing any challenges and maximizing its benefits. AI platforms can adjust the difficulty level of assessments based on the learner's responses, ensuring that they are neither too easy nor too complex.

A practical application of adjusting learning complexity occurs via platforms like EdTech adaptive assessments in which students take a quiz on a topic such as verb conjugations. The AI app increases the difficulty level as students answer correctly or provides simpler questions if they struggle thus giving target feedback at the learner's proficiency level. Furthermore, Celik et al. (2022) emphasized that educators play a significant role in the development of AI technology by acting as models for training algorithms and checking for the accuracy of automated output. The integration of AI tools in language learning classrooms represents a significant advancement in educational technology and enhancement of the learning environment (Woo & Choi, 2021). Through personalized, engaging, and flexible learning experiences, AI enhances the effectiveness of language instruction and supports students in achieving their language learning goals. However, educator content knowledge is essential in crafting classroom activities through AI tools (Kim et al., 2022) With careful planning, training, and evaluation, the potential of AI in education can be fully realized benefiting both students and educators alike.

REFERENCES

Alamri, H., Lowell, V., Watson, W., & Watson, S. L. (2020). Using personalized learning as an instructional approach to motivate learners in online higher education: Learner self-determination and intrinsic motivation. *Journal of Research on Technology in Education*, *52*(3), 322–352. DOI: 10.1080/15391523.2020.1728449

Aldebaran. (n.d.). *NAO*. https://www.aldebaran.com/en/nao

Aldoobie, N. (2015). ADDIE Model. *American International Journal of Contemporary Research*, *5*(6), 68–72.

Alharbi, W. (2023). AI in the foreign language classroom: A pedagogical overview of automated writing assistance tools. *Education Research International*, *2023*, 1–15. Advance online publication. DOI: 10.1155/2023/4253331

Baha, T. A., Hajji, M. E., Es-Saady, Y., & Fadili, H. (2023). The impact of educational chatbot on student learning experience. *Education and Information Technologies*, *29*(8), 10153–10176. DOI: 10.1007/s10639-023-12166-w

Celik, I., Dindar, M., Muukkonen, H., & Jarvela, S. (2022). The promises and challenges of artificial intelligence for teachers: A systematic review of research. *TechTrends*, *66*(4), 616–630. DOI: 10.1007/s11528-022-00715-y

Chan, K. Y. C. (2023). A comprehensive AI policy education framework for university teaching and learning. *International Journal of Educational Technology in Higher Education*, *20*(38), 38. Advance online publication. DOI: 10.1186/s41239-023-00408-3

Chan, K. Y. C., & Hu, W. (2023). Students' voices on generative AI: Perceptions, benefits, and challenges in higher education. *International Journal of Educational Technology in Higher Education*, *20*(43), 43. Advance online publication. DOI: 10.1186/s41239-023-00411-8

Chen, X., Zou, D., Xie, H., Cheng, G., & Liu, C. (2022). Two decades of artificial intelligence in education. *Journal of Educational Technology & Society*, *25*(1), 28–47. https://www.jstor.org/stable/48647028

Chen, Y., Jensen, S., Albert, L. J., Gupta, S., & Lee, T. (2023). Artificial intelligence (AI) student assistants in the classroom: Designing chatbots to support student success. *Information Systems Frontiers*, *25*(1), 161–182. DOI: 10.1007/s10796-022-10291-4

Chiu, T. K. F. (2021). A holistic approach to the design of artificial intelligence (AI) education for K-12 schools. *TechTrends*, *65*(5), 796–807. DOI: 10.1007/s11528-021-00637-1

Chiu, T. K. F., Moorhouse, B. L., Chai, C. S., & Ismailov, M. (2022). Teacher support and student motivation to learn with artificial intelligence (AI) based chatbot. *Interactive Learning Environments*, •••, 1–17. DOI: 10.1080/10494820.2022.2129392

Cornell University Center for Teaching Innovation. (2024). Ethical AI for teaching and learning. https://teaching.cornell.edu/generative-artificial-intelligence/ethical-ai-teaching-and-learning

Darvishi, A., Khosravi, H., Sadiq, S., Gasevic, D., & Siemens, G. (2024). Impact of AI assistance on student agency. *Computers & Education, 210*, 104967. Advance online publication. DOI: 10.1016/j.compedu.2023.104967

Davis, F. D. (1989). Perceived usefulness, perceived ease of use, and user acceptance of Information Technology. *Management Information Systems Quarterly, 13*(3), 319. DOI: 10.2307/249008

Dawson, P., Henderson, M., Ryan, T., Mahoney, P., Boud, D., Phillips, M., & Molloy, E. (2023). Technology and feedback design. In J. M. Spector, B.B., Lockee, & M. D. Childress (Eds), *Learning, design, and technology,* (pp. 695-739). Springer. DOI: 10.1007/978-3-319-17461-7_124

Dignum, V. (2023). Responsible artificial intelligence: recommendations and lessons learned. In Eke, D. O., Wakunuma, K., & Akintoye, S. (Eds.), *Responsible AI in Africa: Challenges and opportunities* (pp. 195–214). Springer.

Dwivedi, Y. K., ... (2203). Opinion Paper: "So what if ChatGPT wrote it?" Multidisciplinary perspectives on opportunities, challenges and implications of generative conversational AI for research, practice and policy. *International Journal of Information Management, 71*, https://doi.org/DOI: 10.1007/978-3-031-08215-3_9

El Naggar, A., Gaad, E., & Inocencio, S. A. M. (2024). Enhancing inclusive education in the UAE: Integrating AI for diverse learning needs. *Research in Developmental Disabilities, 147*, 104685–104685. DOI: 10.1016/j.ridd.2024.104685 PMID: 38330845

Familoni, B. T., & Onyebuchi, N.Babajide Tolulope FamiloniNneamaka Chisom Onyebuchi. (2024). Advancements and challenges in AI integration for technical literacy: A systematic review. *Engineering Science & Technology Journal, 5*(4), 1415–1430. Advance online publication. DOI: 10.51594/estj.v5i4.1042

Ferguson, C., van den Broek, E. L., & van Oostendorp, H. (2022). AI-Induced guidance: Preserving the optimal Zone of Proximal Development. *Computers and Education. Artificial Intelligence, 3*, 100089-. DOI: 10.1016/j.caeai.2022.100089

Gayed, J. M., Carlon, M. K. J., Oriola, A. M., & Cross, J. S. (2022). Exploring an AI-based writing assistant's impact on English language learners. *Computers & Education, 3*, 100055. Advance online publication. DOI: 10.1016/j.caeai.2022.100055

Ghamrawi, N., Shal, T., & Ghamrawi, N. A. R. (2023). Exploring the impact of AI on teacher leadership: Regressing or expanding? *Education and Information Technologies, 29*(7), 8415–8433. DOI: 10.1007/s10639-023-12174-w

Ghimire, P. R., Neupane, B. P., & Dahal, N. (2024). Generative AI and AI Tools in English Language Teaching and Learning. *An Exploratory Research, 9*(1-2), 30–40. DOI: 10.3126/eltp.v9i1-2.68716

Gupta, M., Parra, C. M., & Dennehy, D. (2021). Questing racial and gender bias in AI-based recommendations: Do espoused national cultural values matter? *Information Systems Frontiers, 24,* 1465.1481. https://link.springer.com/article/10.1007/s10796-021-10156-2

Huang, X., Zhou, D., Cheng, G., Chen, X., & Xie, H. (2023). Trends, research issues, and applications of artificial intelligence in language education. *Journal of Educational Technology & Society*, *26*(1), 112–131. https://www.jstor.org/stable/4870797

Jeon, J. (2024). Exploring AI chatbot affordances in the EFL classroom: Young learners' experiences and perspectives. *Computer Assisted Language Learning*, *37*(1), 1–26. DOI: 10.1080/09588221.2021.2021241

Ji, H., Han, I., & Ko, Y. (2023). A systematic review of conversational AI in language education: Focusing on the collaboration with human teachers. *Journal of Research on Technology in Education*, *55*(1), 48–63. DOI: 10.1080/15391523.2022.2142873

Kim, J. (2023). Leading teachers' perspective on teacher-AI collaboration in education. *Education and Information Technologies*, *29*(7), 8693–8724. DOI: 10.1007/s10639-023-12109-5

Kim, J., Lee, H., & Cho, Y. H. (2022). Learning design to support student-AI collaboration: Perspectives of leading teachers for AI in education. *Education and Information Technologies*, *27*(5), 6069–6104. DOI: 10.1007/s10639-021-10831-6

Koehler, M. J., & Mishra, P. (2008). Introducing TPCK. In AACTE Committee on Innovation and Technology (Ed.), *Handbook of technological pedagogical content knowledge (TPCK) for educators* (pp. 3–29). Routledge.

Lin, C. J., & Mubarok, H. (2021). Learning analytics for investigating the mind map-guided AI chatbot approach in an EFL flipped speaking classroom. *Journal of Educational Technology & Society*, *24*(4), 16–35. https://www.jstor.org/stable/48629242

Luckin, R., Cukurova, M., Kent, C., & du Boulay, B. (2022). Empowering educators to be AI-ready. *Computers and Education: Artificial Intelligence*, *3*, 100076. Advance online publication. DOI: 10.1016/j.caeai.2022.100076

Mageira, K., Pittou, D., Papasalouros, A., Kotis, K., Zangogianni, P., & Daradoumis, A. (2022). Educational AI chatbots for content and language integrated learning. *Applied Sciences (Basel, Switzerland)*, *12*(7), 3239. DOI: 10.3390/app12073239

Markauskaite, L., Marrone, R., Poquet, O., Knight, S., Martinez-Maldonado, R., Howard, S., Tondeur, J., De Laat, M., Shum, S. B., Basevic, D., & Siemens, G. Rethinking the entwinement between artificial intelligence and human learning: What capabilities do learners need for a world with AI? *Computers and Education: Artificial Intelligence, 3.*https://doi.org/DOI: 10.1016/j.caeai.2022.100056

Marzuki, U., Rusdin, D., & Indrawati, I. (2023). The impact of AI writing tools on the content and organization of students' writing: EFL teachers' perspective. *Cogent Education*, *10*(2), 2236469. Advance online publication. DOI: 10.1080/2331186X.2023.2236469

Mohammed, P. S., & Watson, E. (2019). Towards inclusive education in the age of artificial intelligence: Perspectives, challenges, and opportunities. In J. Knox, Y. Wang, & M. Gallagher, M. (Eds) A*rtificial intelligence and inclusive education. perspectives on rethinking and reforming education*. Springer. https://doi.org/DOI: 10.1007/978-981-13-8161-4_2

Mouta, A., Torrecilla-Sánchez, E. M., & Pinto-Llorente, A. M. (2023). Design of a future scenarios toolkit for an ethical implementation of artificial intelligence in education. *Education and Information Technologies*, *29*(9), 10473–10498. DOI: 10.1007/s10639-023-12229-y

Nazaretsky, T., Ariely, M., Cukurova, M., & Alexandron, G. (2022). Teachers' trust in AI-powered educational technology and a professional development program to improve it. *British Journal of Educational Technology*, *53*(4), 914–931. DOI: 10.1111/bjet.13232

Owan, V. J., Abang, K. B., Idika, D. O., Etta, E. O., & Bassey, B. A. (2023). Exploring the potential of artificial intelligence tools in educational measurement and assessment. *Eurasia Journal of Mathematics, Science and Technology Education*, *19*(3), em2307. Advance online publication. DOI: 10.29333/ejmste/13428

Panagiotis, P., Krystalli, P., & Arvanitis, P. (2023). Technology as a motivational factor in foreign language learning. *European Journal of Education*, *6*(1), 69–84. https://revistia.org/files/articles/ejed_v6_i1_23/Panagiotidis.pdf. DOI: 10.2478/ejed-2023-0007

Parmaxi, A. (2020). Virtual reality in language learning: A systematic review and implications for research and practice. *Interactive Learning Environments*, *31*(1), 172–184. DOI: 10.1080/10494820.2020.1765392

Pokrivcakova, S. (2019). Preparing teachers for the application of AI-powered technologies in foreign language education. *Sciendo*, *7*(3), 135–153. DOI: 10.2478/jolace-2019-0025

Qiao, H., & Zhao, A. (2023). Artificial intelligence-based learning: Illuminating the impact of speaking skills and self-regulation in Chinese EFL context. *Frontiers in Psychology*.https://www.ncbi.nlm.nih.gov/pmc/articles/PMC10652775/

Rusmiyanto, R., Huriati, N., Fitriani, N., Tyas, N. K., Rofi'I, A., & Sari, M. N. (2023). The role of artificial intelligence (AI) in developing English language learner's communication skills. *Journal of Education*, *6*(1), 750–757. Advance online publication. DOI: 10.31004/joe.v6i1.2990

Schiavo, G., Businaro, S., & Zancanaro, M. (2024). Comprehension, apprehension, and acceptance: Understanding the influence of literacy and anxiety on acceptance of artificial intelligence. *Technology in Society*, *77*, 102537. Advance online publication. DOI: 10.1016/j.techsoc.2024.102537

Schneiderman, B. (2020). Bridging the gap between ethics and practice: Guidelines for reliable, safe, and trustworthy human-centered AI systems. *ACM Transactions on Interactive Intelligent Systems*, *10*(4), 1–31. DOI: 10.1145/3419764

Seo, K., Tang, J., Roll, I., Fels, S., & Yoon, D. (2021). The impact of artificial intelligence on learner-instructor interaction in online learning. *International Journal of Educational Technology in Higher Education*, *18*(54), 54. Advance online publication. DOI: 10.1186/s41239-021-00292-9 PMID: 34778540

Shadiev, R., & Yu, J. (2022). Review of research on computer-assisted language learning with a focus on intercultural education. *Computer Assisted Language Learning*, *37*(4), 841–871. DOI: 10.1080/09588221.2022.2056616

Simms, R. C. (2024). Work with ChatGPT, not against: 3 teaching strategies that harness the power of artificial intelligence. *Nurse Educator*, *49*(3), 158-. DOI: 10.1097/NNE.0000000000001634

Singer, J. B., Báez, J. C., & Rios, J. A. (2023). AI creates the message: Integrating ai language learning models into social work education and practice. *Journal of Social Work Education, 59*(2), 294–302. DOI: 10.1080/10437797.2023.2189878

Song, C., & Song, Y. (2023). Enhancing academic writing skills and motivation: Assessing the efficacy of ChatGPT in AI-assisted language learning for EFL learners. *Frontiers in Psychology, 14*, 1260843. Advance online publication. DOI: 10.3389/fpsyg.2023.1260843 PMID: 38162975

Srinivasan, V., & Murthy, H. (2021). Improving reading and comprehension in K-12: Evidence from a large-scale AI technology intervention in India. *Computers and Education: Artificial Intelligence, 2*, 100019. Advance online publication. DOI: 10.1016/j.caeai.2021.100019

Su, F., & Zou, D. (2020). Technology-enhanced collaborative language learning: Theoretical foundations, technologies, and implications. *Computer Assisted Language Learning, 35*(8), 1754–1788. DOI: 10.1080/09588221.2020.1831545

Sumakul, D. T., Hamied, F. A., & Sukyadi, D. (2022). Artificial intelligence in EFL classrooms: Friend or foe. *LEARN Journal, 15*(1), 232-256. https://so04.tci-thaijo.org/index.php/LEARN/article/view/256723

Sun, Z., Anbarasan, M., & Kumar, D. P. (2021). Design of online intelligent English teaching platform based on artificial intelligence techniques. *Computational Intelligence, 37*(3), 1166–1180. DOI: 10.1111/coin.12351

Sweller, J. (1988). Cognitive load during problem solving: Effects on learning. *Cognitive Science, 12*(2), 257–285. DOI: 10.1207/s15516709cog1202_4

Sweller, J. (2016). Cognitive Load Theory, Evolutionary Educational Psychology, and Instructional Design. In Geary, D., & Berch, D. (Eds.), *Evolutionary Perspectives on Child Development and Education. Evolutionary Psychology*. Springer., DOI: 10.1007/978-3-319-29986-0_12

Sweller, J., Ayres, P., & Kalyuga, S. (2011). Cognitive load theory in perspective. In *Cognitive load theory* (pp. 237–242). Springer., DOI: 10.1007/978-1-4419-8126-4_18

Tang, L., & Su, Y. (2024). Ethical implications and principles using artifical intelligence models in the classroom: A systemic literature review. *International Journal of Interactive Multimedia and Artificial Intelligence, 8*(5), 25–36. DOI: 10.9781/ijimai.2024.02.010

Torralba, K. D., Jose, D., & Byrne, J. (2020). Psychological safety, the hidden curriculum, and ambiguity in medicine. *Clinical Rheumatology, 39*(3), 667–671. DOI: 10.1007/s10067-019-04889-4 PMID: 31902031

Vall, R. R., & Araya, F. G. (2023). Exploring the benefits and challenges of AI-language learning tools. *International Journal of Social Science and Humanities Invention, 10*(1), 7569–7576. https://valleyinternational.net/index.php/theijsshi. DOI: 10.18535/ijsshi/v10i01.02

VanLehn, C., Banerjee, F. M., & Wetzel, M. J. (2020). Teaching algebraic model construction: A tutoring system, lessons learned and an evaluation. *International Journal of Artificial Intelligence in Education, 30*(3), 459–480. DOI: 10.1007/s40593-020-00205-3

Vygotsky, L. S. (1978). *Mind in society: The development of higher psychological processes*. Harvard University Press.

Wang, X., Liu, Q., Pang, H., Tan, S. C., Lei, J., Wallace, M. P., & Li, L. (2023). What matters in AI-supported learning: A study of human-AI interactions in language learning using cluster analysis and epistemic network analysis. *Computers & Education, 194*, 104703. Advance online publication. DOI: 10.1016/j.compedu.2022.104703

Wang, X., Pang, H., Wallace, M. P., Wang, Q., & Chen, W. (2022). Learners' perceived AI presences in AI-supported language learning: A study of AI as a humanized agent from community of inquiry. *Computer Assisted Language Learning*. Advance online publication. DOI: 10.1080/09588221.2022.2056203

Wang, X., Pang, H., Wallace, M. P., Wang, Q., & Chen, W. (2024). Learners' perceived AI presences in AI-supported language learning: A study of AI as a humanized agent from community of inquiry. *Computer Assisted Language Learning*, *37*(4), 814–840. DOI: 10.1080/09588221.2022.2056203

Woo, J. H., & Choi, H. (2021). Systematic Review for AI-based Language Learning Tools. *Diji'teol Ke-ontencheu Haghoe Nonmunji/Dijiteol Kontencheu Hakoe Nonmunji, 22*(11), 1783–1792. DOI: 10.9728/dcs.2021.22.11.1783

Xia, Y., Shin, S.-Y., & Kim, J.-C. (2024). Cross-Cultural Intelligent Language Learning System (CILS): Leveraging AI to facilitate language learning strategies in cross-cultural communication. *Applied Sciences, 14*(13), 5651-. DOI: 10.3390/app14135651

Yang, C. C. Y., & Ogata, H. (2023). Personalized learning analytics intervention approach for enhancing student learning achievement and behavior engagement in blended learning. *Education and Information Technologies*, *28*(3), 2509–2528. DOI: 10.1007/s10639-022-11291-2

Yang, H., & Kyun, S. (2022). The current research trend of artificial intelligence in language learning: A systematic empirical literature review from an active theory perspective. *Australasian Journal of Educational Technology*, *38*(5), 180–210. DOI: 10.14742/ajet.7492

Yu-Ching, T., & Lin, Y. (2024). Enhancing English as a foreign language (EFL) learners' writing with ChatGPT: A university-level course design: EJEL. *Electronic Journal of e-Learning*, *22*(2), 78–97. DOI: 10.34190/ejel.21.5.3329

Zhai, X., Chu, X., Chai, C. S., Jong, M. S., Istenic, A., Spector, M., Liu, J. B., & Li, Y. (2021). A review of artificial intelligence (AI) in education from 2010 to 2020. *Complexity*, *2021*(1), 8812542. Advance online publication. DOI: 10.1155/2021/8812542

Zhang, R., & Zou, D. (2020). Types, purposes, and effectiveness of state-of-the-art technologies for second and foreign language learning. *Computer Assisted Language Learning*, *35*(4), 696–742. DOI: 10.1080/09588221.2020.1744666

Zhang, R., & Zou, D. (2022). Self-regulated second language learning: A review of types of benefits of strategies, modes of teacher support, and pedagogical implications. *Computer Assisted Language Learning*, *37*(4), 720–765. DOI: 10.1080/09588221.2022.2055081

Zheng, L., Long, M., Zhong, L., & Gyasi, J. F. (2022). The effectiveness of technology-facilitated personalized learning on learning achievements and learning perceptions: A meta-analysis. *Education and Information Technologies*, *27*(8), 11807–11830. DOI: 10.1007/s10639-022-11092-7

Chapter 8
Language Teaching in the Age of AI:
Potential, Challenges, and Future Prospects

Ilham Chniet
https://orcid.org/0000-0003-1126-3028
Mohamed First University, Morocco

Mehdi Kaddouri
https://orcid.org/0000-0001-7696-0276
Mohammed First University, Morocco

Khalid Mhamdi
https://orcid.org/0009-0007-3994-7743
Mohammed First University, Morocco

Meriem Marhraoui
https://orcid.org/0009-0004-5994-5794
Mohammed First University, Morocco

Mohamed Khaldi
https://orcid.org/0000-0002-1593-1073
Abdelmalek Essadi University, Morocco

ABSTRACT

The use of artificial intelligence (AI) in language learning is a rapidly expanding field that has been gaining increasing interest since the 2000s. Despite its numerous advantages, its integration also poses challenges. This chapter explores these issues and emerging trends in language teaching, structured into three distinct sections. The first highlights the potential of AI to develop language skills. The second section examines how AI-based tools enhance the learning experience in terms of motivation, engagement, autonomy, and interactions, while addressing the main pedagogical, technological, and ethical challenges. The final section provides an overview of current research in this innovative field, presenting recent advances in AI-assisted language teaching/learning.

DOI: 10.4018/979-8-3693-7260-9.ch008

1. INTRODUCTION

The use of digital technologies for language learning dates back to the 1960s (Davis, 2011). One of the most recent technological developments that has garnered increasing interest in this context is artificial intelligence (AI). While numerous definitions of AI exist, a common semantic denominator appears to emerge. Artificial intelligence refers to computer systems capable of simulating human cognitive processes such as learning and decision-making. According to the Organisation for Economic Co-operation and Development (OECD, 2019), AI is defined as a "machine-based system that, given a defined set of human-defined objectives, can make predictions, recommendations, or decisions that influence real or virtual environments."

Currently, artificial intelligence is attracting considerable attention across various fields, including education, due to the numerous possibilities it offers (Xu & Ouyang, 2022). The United States recorded the highest number of publications from 2000 to 2019, while the United Kingdom and China rank second and third, respectively (Huang et al., 2023). Renowned for its many advantages (Alhalangy & AbdAlgane, 2023), AI has continued to generate growing scientific interest since 2016 (Huang et al., 2023). The evolution of artificial intelligence has traversed four distinct phases. The first phase (2000-2004) focused on the development of intelligent robots, computers, and virtual reality (VR). Between 2005 and 2009, AI made significant advancements with intelligent tutoring systems and educational computing. The development of networks then facilitated progress in automatic image recognition and speech recognition during the third phase (2010-2014). Finally, AI truly permeated the field of education during the fourth phase (2014-2018) with the proliferation of distance learning (Song & Wang, 2020).

Since 2005, artificial intelligence (AI) has experienced a growing trend in language education (Huang et al., 2023). However, it is particularly since the launch of ChatGPT in November 2022 that generative AIs (GenAI) have garnered global interest due to their ability to produce coherent and grammatically correct texts (Generative Pre-trained Transformer). This advancement has brought new perspectives to the field and altered traditional methods where teachers played a central role in the acquisition of language skills (Law, 2024).

Several recent studies focus on the potential of leveraging artificial intelligence (AI) to enhance learners' communication skills across various dimensions: speaking, listening, reading, and writing (notably: Liu, 2023; Mohamed et al., 2024; Rusmiyanto et al., 2023; Yang, 2024). However, the integration of AI in language teaching presents various challenges for both teachers and students, as well as for the implementation of AI technologies themselves. The challenges related to teachers include a lack of familiarity and confidence with AI tools for their integration into language teaching. Many teachers do not possess the technical skills necessary to use these tools effectively (Kohnke et al., 2023). Often left without sufficient support in the face of the rapid rise of AI technologies, some teachers fear that AI will replace their role, leading to reluctance in adopting these technologies. The additional workload and time required to understand and apply AI in their teaching practices are also significant obstacles (Kohnke et al., 2023).

On the student side, AI could encourage dependency and laziness (Makeleni et al., 2023). The proliferation of automated cheating through AI-based writing tools also poses a problem of academic dishonesty (Makeleni et al., 2023). The use of these technologies also raises concerns about the protection of students' privacy, particularly regarding the collection and analysis of personal data (Yang, 2024). In addition, there are other concerns about the reliability of AI in teaching and the accuracy of automated writing assessment and speech recognition (Huang et al., 2023). Many AI tools are primarily developed for widely spoken languages, creating an imbalance in access to technologies for speakers of languages from the Global South. The digital divide and educational inequalities are likely to be exacerbated in developing countries, where the infrastructure and funding needed to adopt these technologies are lacking (Huang et al., 2023; Makeleni et al., 2023). This chapter is part of this exploration. The questions that this chapter seeks to address are as follows:

- How can AI transform pedagogical practices and the acquisition of language skills in the language classroom?
- How can AI enhance the overall language learning experience?
- What future perspectives does AI offer for language education?

This chapter will focus on three main axes: firstly, it will examine how AI can transform pedagogical practices and the acquisition of language skills in the classroom. Next, it will analyze how AI can enhance the overall language learning experience. Lastly, it will explore the future perspectives that AI offers for language education.

2. THE PEDAGOGICAL POTENTIAL OF AI IN LANGUAGE CLASSROOMS

Artificial intelligence (AI) continues to demonstrate its transformative potential in language learning by offering innovative methods for developing linguistic, writing, oral, and comprehension skills. This section will first examine the historical evolution of computer systems in grammar instruction. Subsequently, the focus will shift to AI tools that enhance the quality of academic writing, oral performance, and reading skills, while also addressing the associated challenges. These reflections will illuminate not only the opportunities presented by AI but also the issues that require careful attention to ensure ethical and effective use in the field of language education.

2.1. AI and Language Skills Development

The idea of using computer systems for grammar learning dates back several decades. Pijls et al. (1987) highlighted the limitations of traditional grammar and spelling instruction, where rule analysis predominates over productive practice, rendering feedback irrelevant and exercises monotonous. To address these shortcomings, a computer-assisted learning system was developed, integrating a linguistic expert system that comprises subcomponents such as a phrase generator and a syntactic parser using a more formalized notation; a pedagogical module to diagnose students' knowledge through a catalog of common errors; a tutoring module to determine what knowledge to convey and how; and a user interface—the key component—a graphical syntax tree editor that allows students to visualize and modify the trees generated by syntactic analysis. This system marked a notable advancement, paving the way for a new era of grammar learning.

Today, in the age of artificial intelligence, researchers are exploring new approaches, such as the application of universal grammar hypotheses to AI systems like mBERT and GPT-4, which utilize presumed universal linguistic rules to process and generate natural language (Roberts et al., 2023). These advancements have demonstrated a generally positive impact, with users expressing high confidence in the suggestions of tools like Grammarly and QuillBot, which significantly enhance the quality of academic writing (Syifa'a Awalin et al., 2023; Syahnaz & Fithriani, 2023). Additionally, chatbots for grammar learning offer the potential for dynamic interaction. Lestari & Wicaksono (2023) identified three distinct methods for using ChatGPT to accomplish grammatical tasks: automated translation, response personalization, and phrase revision, contributing to a reduction in language learning anxiety (Chen & Lin, 2023).

Despite notable progress in grammar learning and vocabulary acquisition (Resy Oktadela et al., 2023), these tools are not without limitations. Current grammar-checking approaches primarily rely on predefined rules, linguistic data, or a hybrid combination, each having its strengths and weaknesses depending on the languages processed (Bhirud, 2017). Concerns persist regarding the unintentional alteration of meaning by automated suggestions (Alotaibi, 2023) and the limited detection of errors in less represented languages (Fitria, 2023). Linguistic diversity remains a significant challenge, and the future of these technologies lies in their ability to integrate the specificities of each language while drawing on theories like universal grammar to develop truly multilingual systems (Hockly, 2023).

2.2. AI and Writing Skills

2.2.1. Potential of AI for Writing Skills

The integration of artificial intelligence in academic writing is generally perceived positively, particularly for its impact on grammatical accuracy and textual structure. Tools such as ChatGPT, Grammarly, and Wordtune are recognized for enhancing lexical choices and the coherence of sentences. Grammarly aids in identifying and correcting grammatical errors while providing explanations that facilitate mastery of linguistic rules (Alotaibi, 2023). Wordtune, on the other hand, refines vocabulary usage and ensures greater precision in linguistic choices (Al Mahmud, 2023). ChatGPT stands out for its performance in grammatical and stylistic checking, proving particularly useful for academic writing (Feng et al., 2024). Generative AI systems also provide substantial support by offering tailored corrections, thereby increasing the quality of written outputs (Liu et al., 2024).

2.2.2. Challenges and Issues of Integrating AI Into the Development of Writing Skills

Several challenges are associated with the use of AI technologies in the learning process. One of the primary concerns is the excessive reliance on these tools, which may diminish learners' ability to autonomously learn and apply grammatical rules (Alotaibi, 2023). Furthermore, the quality and accuracy of suggestions provided by tools like Grammarly or ChatGPT are not always reliable and require human revision to avoid semantic errors or inappropriate modifications (Feng et al., 2024). Data privacy issues and concerns regarding how user text information is stored and processed by AI platforms represent another major challenge (Khalifa & Albadawy, 2024). Additionally, it is important to develop strategies to optimize the writing process while preserving learners' creativity and critical thinking (Malik et al., 2023), and to evaluate the impact of writing assistance tools on learners' writing performance (Syahnaz & Fithriani, 2023). These challenges underscore the necessity of establishing ethical and academic standards to ensure the responsible use of these technologies. Moreover, further studies are needed to assess the impact of AI-based paraphrasing tools, particularly their influence on learners' writing performance (Syahnaz & Fithriani, 2023).

2.3. The Role of Artificial Intelligence in the Development of Oral Performance

2.3.1. Optimize Oral Performance Through Speech Recognition and Instant Feedback

Artificial intelligence (AI) is revolutionizing language learning in the classroom, particularly in the development of oral skills. Applications like Orai integrate voice recognition technology, allowing learners to practice speaking while receiving instant feedback on their pronunciation and fluency (Yang, 2007; Li et al., 2020). These tools also facilitate vocabulary acquisition and grammatical accuracy, significantly enhancing oral performance (Chen et al., 2018; Makhlouf, 2021; Junaidi, 2020). Divekar et al. (2022) demonstrated that by combining AI with augmented reality, it is possible to create simulations of authentic conversations that enrich not only conversational skills but also learners' comprehension.

2.3.2. The Integration of AI in Developing Listening Skills in Language Learning

The use of artificial intelligence (AI) is also relevant for the development of listening skills in language learning. Speech recognition technology powered by AI allows learners to practice their pronunciation and oral skills. It analyzes their speech and provides feedback on accuracy, fluency, and intonation (Aspers & Corte, 2019). Games incorporating speech recognition techniques allow learners to interact with non-playable characters (NPCs) to practice listening and speaking (Huang et al., 2023).

Intelligent tutoring systems (ITS) also integrate speech recognition to offer personalized advice on pronunciation and simulate conversations (Yang, 2024). Similarly, AI-based assessment systems can automatically evaluate and provide feedback on students' listening abilities. These systems can offer more comprehensive evaluation results than traditional scores (Yang, 2024).

However, instructors have emphasized that some AI tools applicable to teaching English, including those that could improve listening and pronunciation skills, are too expensive (Kohnke et al., 2023). Indeed, considerations such as cost and the complementary role of the teacher remain important.

2.3.3. Reduced Anxiety and Increased Learner Engagement

AI, when used as a conversation partner, can help decrease anxiety related to speaking (Hsu et al., 2021). Learners feel more comfortable practising speaking, which boosts their confidence and willingness to communicate (Yang et al., 2022; Yuan, 2023). Voice chatbots offer dynamic interactions that increase the engagement of beginner learners and contribute to the development of basic communication skills (Kang, 2022).

2.3.4. Limitations and Prospects for Improving AI For the Development of Oral Skills

Despite these benefits, challenges remain. Exchanges with chatbots remain less rich and varied than those with native speakers, which limits their effectiveness for advanced learners (Hill et al., 2015). In addition, while AI can improve pronunciation and fluency, it does not fully replace human interaction, which is essential for capturing cultural and contextual nuances (Annamalai et al., 2023). To maximize the effectiveness of AI, it is therefore necessary to integrate these tools in a complementary way to traditional pedagogical practices, while continuing to explore their potential in more immersive and interactive learning environments.

2.4. AI and Reading Skills

Artificial intelligence also significantly influences the development of reading skills. It is now widely utilized in this area, optimally integrated through personalized approaches that address the specific needs of learners (Chea & Xiao, 2024; Sri et al., 2022). The use of ChatGPT has enabled 80% of learners to achieve high reading results (Muhammad Yusuf Salam et al., 2023). Similarly, platforms such as Paraphraser.io and Quillbot are recommended for activities during reading sessions, while Storywiz.io is suggested for post-reading activities (Rahman & Nor, 2024). Haggag (2021) advocates for the integration of AI tools in preparation for standardized exams like the TOEFL to enhance reading and writing skills. Specific tools like Reading Progress (RP) have also demonstrated effectiveness in improving learners' reading competencies (AbdRoof Asmail & Dahassi, 2024). Beyond technical aspects, AI also helps motivate learners to read by making the learning process more accessible, engaging, and effective across various educational contexts (Chea & Xiao, 2024).

2.5. AI and Translation: New Perspectives for Language Learning

2.5.1. Machine Translation: A Field in Continuous Evolution

Although Bar-Hillel (1960) asserted that "high-quality fully automatic translation is not an achievable goal" (p. 27) in the short term, advancements in artificial intelligence, particularly through neural networks and deep learning, have profoundly transformed the landscape of machine translation. Tools such as Google Translate and OpenAI's models have enhanced the accuracy and fluency of translations, making them useful in various contexts. Nevertheless, despite these advancements, these systems continue to face limitations when dealing with complex contexts, cultural references, idiomatic expressions, or specialized content.

Early research in machine translation dates back to the 1940s and 1950s, with pioneers like Warren Weaver conceptualizing translation as a decoding problem. In the 1960s, translation systems primarily relied on rule-based linguistic correspondences, utilizing dictionaries and grammatical rules (Allen, 2003). These approaches required significant efforts to encode lexical data. The emergence of translation memories and parallel corpora in the 1980s marked a significant advancement. The 1990s saw the rise of statistical systems, supported by increased computing power and the growing accessibility of online textual resources facilitated by the expansion of the Internet (Śmigielska, 2023). In 2013, Michael Cronin introduced the notion of "objectile" to describe the transformation of the original text into an object capable of multiple variants, promoting a more creative and flexible approach. The real turning point occurred in 2016 with the introduction of neural models, which revolutionized the field. Neural machine translation (NMT) relies on deep neural networks to analyze vast bilingual corpora, continuously adjusting their parameters to improve translation quality (Rubino, 2011).

2.5.2. Artificial Intelligence: A Revolution in the Field of Translation

Digital tools have profoundly influenced translation studies. They have facilitated the comparative analysis of monolingual corpora and provided insights into the specific characteristics of translated texts (Baker, 1993). Access to corpora from various temporal and geographical contexts has enhanced the understanding of how translated texts are received (Zanettin, 2014). The increase in computing power and the proliferation of digital textual resources have opened new avenues for analysis and research in translation (Koehn, 2020).

Today, university learners widely utilize machine translation systems such as Google Translate, DeepL, and Reverso in their academic activities. Approximately 91% of participants consider these tools to be "fairly reliable" after taking a dedicated course, which has bolstered their confidence in these technologies. While these tools enhance speed and productivity, excessive use can hinder the development of learners' linguistic and analytical skills (Molino, 2023). Machine translation systems and digital tools have also transformed the translation process by enabling a more in-depth analysis of texts. Advanced models, such as GPT, can disambiguate words by focusing on specific contexts, thereby enriching the understanding of translation variations.

2.5.3. Ethical and Professional Issues of AI Translation

The challenges of integrating machine translation technologies are numerous and complex, particularly concerning the management of cultural and contextual nuances, which can lead to errors and misunderstandings (Kanglang, 2021). Despite advancements in disambiguation, humans remain superior due to their ability to interpret complex contexts. Furthermore, the ongoing improvement of translation systems could reduce the demand for human translators, threatening the linguistic and cultural expertise they provide (Akgun & Greenhow, 2022). It is also essential to reevaluate translator training to leverage new opportunities while considering the limitations of these tools. Developing new approaches for compensating contributions, such as crowdsourcing, is crucial for protecting translators' intellectual property (Palumbo, 2019). The future of translation may thus involve enhanced collaboration between humans and machines rather than direct competition (Kosowicz, 2024).

In conclusion, while machine translation has made significant strides, it remains imperfect, and the challenges related to understanding the cognitive processes of communication and language continue to be central to research in artificial intelligence (Poibeau, 2016). As an analytical tool in digital humanities, machine translation offers possibilities for interaction with texts but also raises ethical and legal questions, particularly regarding the status of translators. Rather than viewing AI as a competitor, it is vital to see it as an ally that enriches and supports human work while acknowledging the inherent limitations of both parties. The integration of artificial intelligence in language learning opens new perspectives for the development of linguistic, writing, and oral skills. Although these tools offer significant advantages, they also present ethical and practical challenges that require thorough reflection. By balancing technology and pedagogy, it is possible to optimize the learning experience while preserving the essence of human communication.

3. AI FOR IMPROVING THE LEARNING EXPERIENCE IN THE LANGUAGE CLASSROOM

Artificial intelligence is transforming the learning experience in the language classroom by offering innovative tools that improve learner engagement. The perception and acceptance of these technologies by learners and teachers is essential to maximizing their potential. This section explores how AI facilitates autonomy, enriches educational interactions, and personalizes language learning.

3.1. AI Perception and Acceptance: Keys to Language Learner Engagement

Acceptance of technology, influenced by factors such as ease of use and perceived usefulness, is a key factor that can enhance the learning experience. It positively influences learners' attitudes toward its use (Boštjan Šumak et al., 2011), stimulates their intrinsic motivation and engagement, makes them more receptive and open to using it (Pan, 2020), and promotes self-regulated learning (An et al., 2023). The perception and acceptance of artificial intelligence (AI) also play a crucial role in learners' motivation and engagement. This motivation depends not only on the intrinsic characteristics of AI tools and the design of courses but also on the pedagogical skills of teachers (Sumakul & Hamied, 2023). Alenizi et al. (2023) and Annamalai et al. (2023) observed that learners generally display moderately positive attitudes toward the use of AI, despite some reservations. This positive perception of AI facilitates active engagement among learners, which can enhance their perseverance in language learning (Ghafouri, 2024). Furthermore, AI has a significant impact on learners' emotions, reinforcing their engagement and motivation (Wang, 2024). For instance, learners who used QuillBot to improve their paraphrasing skills expressed positive feelings and enthusiasm (Mohammad et al., 2023). This constructive interaction with AI seems to encourage a proactive attitude toward learning.

However, the acceptance of AI does not solely depend on learners. Performance expectations, social influence, and knowledge of AI are determining factors in teachers' behavioral intentions to adopt these technologies. Teachers who view AI as an effective tool for improving learning outcomes and who receive support from their peers and institution are more likely to integrate it into their courses (An et al., 2023). This fosters a coherent learning environment in which AI not only supports learners but also enriches the overall pedagogical experience. Thus, the perception and acceptance of AI technologies represent a significant challenge for their integration and the optimal exploitation of their potential, both by learners and educators. Lin et al. (2017) found that a lack of experience with AI technologies is often correlated with a negative perception, which can lead to resistance to their adoption (Pokrivcakova, 2019). This observation underscores the importance of training in such technologies and support throughout the integration process.

In summary, the acceptance of AI by both learners and teachers is a key factor for its successful integration into language education. An approach that considers learners' emotions, teachers' expectations, and the need for training can foster a richer and more effective learning environment.

3.2. AI: A Catalyst for Autonomy and Engagement in the Language Classroom

By facilitating access to a variety of resources and offering individualized feedback, AI technologies support independent practice (Rusmiyanto et al., 2023). These tools, designed to create learning experiences tailored to learners' needs, promote learner autonomy. Interactive platforms and AI chatbots, which provide real-time feedback and opportunities for language practice such as conversation, writing or listening comprehension, play a critical role in learner engagement (Rusmiyanto et al., 2023). According to Chen, Chen, and Lin (2020), these technologies have a positive impact on academic engagement and outcomes in a variety of educational contexts. In addition, adaptive assessments and personalized feedback contribute significantly to learners' progress, stimulating their involvement in their learning (Qiao & Zhao, 2023).

The integration of artificial intelligence (AI) into language learning represents a major opportunity for the development of language skills. Yang (2007) emphasizes that these technologies offer simplified access to varied and efficient tools, facilitating the understanding of content, the accomplishment of academic tasks and participation in class discussions. Learners recognize the user-friendliness of these devices and show a growing willingness to adopt them, considering AI to be more challenging and engaging than traditional learning methods (Chea & Xiao, 2024).

Furthermore, AI significantly contributes to the accessibility of educational resources, particularly in the field of writing. Interfaces such as Grammarly stand out for their ease of use and automated assessments, tailored to all skill levels (Alotaibi, 2023). Recent innovations, such as Automated Writing Evaluation (AWE) and Automated Error Correction (AWCF), provide flexible solutions that enrich writing programs. They promote a collaborative and interactive approach, encouraging exchanges among learners while improving the structure, clarity, and linguistic precision of texts, addressing vocabulary, morphology, syntax, and semantics (Keezhatta & Muhammed Salim, 2019; Pandarova et al., 2019). Thus, these technological advancements enhance the learning experience and effectively support the development of language skills (Koltovskaia, 2020).

3.3. An Interactive Environment Enabled by AI

AI-powered language learning systems have the capability to facilitate collaborative and interactive learning, allowing students to work together to solve problems and engage in meaningful exchanges (Ouyang & Jiao, 2021). The use of chatbots in these learning environments fosters increased social presence, enhancing learners' motivation to practice oral expression and improve their academic outcomes (Huang, 2022; Zou et al., 2023). Moreover, they provide opportunities for interaction beyond time and location constraints, thereby expanding access to educational resources and diverse language exchanges, which is a significant asset for language learning in an increasingly connected world (Yang, 2007).

Although AI can offer powerful tools for the development of language skills, it should not replace human interactions, which are fundamental for learners' learning and socio-emotional development. It is essential to strike a balance between the potential benefits of artificial intelligence (AI) and the importance of human guidance and social interaction in AI-assisted learning environments (Rusmiyanto et al., 2023). The use of AI in language learning also faces limitations regarding cultural sensitivity. De la Vall et al. (2023) report that current AI systems struggle to grasp the nuances of idiomatic expressions, regional accents, and sociocultural contexts, which can lead to misunderstandings or communication errors. This insensitivity to linguistic subtleties diminishes learners' ability to develop authentic and creative language use and may deprive them of a deeper understanding of the nuances of the target language.

3.4. AI for Personalizing Language Learning

AI tools open new perspectives for the personalization of language learning, addressing the inherent challenges posed by the diversity of learner profiles. For instance, Chen and his collaborators developed a location-based language learning system that optimizes English learning according to the learner's location (Chen et al., 2019). This capability results in continuous access to educational resources and more contextualized learning. Large Language Models (LLMs) can generate texts tailored to the lexical and syntactic levels of learners, thus easing the task for teachers in finding appropriate materials. These texts can be used to create comprehension exercises or questions based on the generated content (Mavropoulou, 2023). By leveraging learning data analytics, these tools enable the adaptation of activities and educational content to the specific needs of each individual, thus facilitating a smooth progression in their language acquisition (Rusmiyanto et al., 2023; Shadiev & Yang, 2020). However, this reliance on large data sets can pose challenges. If the data used to train these models is not representative or of high quality, the effectiveness and relevance of the recommendations or responses provided by the AI may be compromised (De la Vall et al., 2023).

3.5. The Impact of AI on the Assessment of Language Skills

The integration of artificial intelligence (AI) in the assessment of language skills also represents a significant advancement in the field of language learning. Researchers are actively exploring new models to address traditional challenges associated with language assessment. The model developed by Yang and his colleagues (2023) has demonstrated its effectiveness in analyzing arguments and evaluating the content of argumentative essays, thus providing valuable support for automatic grading systems. Furthermore, learners' interactions with informative corrective feedback on errors, such as that offered by Pigai, can not only improve writing quality but also reduce the anxiety associated with this activity and decrease error rates (Yang et al., 2023). Automated Writing Evaluation (AWE) systems have also become indispensable tools for teachers, helping to reduce their workload and providing valuable support to learners in the writing and revision processes (Huang et al., 2023). Chatbot-Assisted Dynamic Assessment (CA-DA) has been identified as a particularly effective method for vocabulary learning, even providing valuable insights into each learner's learning strategies (Jeon, 2023).

In summary, the integration of AI in language teaching offers unique opportunities to enhance the learning experience. By considering learners' perceptions, the accessibility of tools, and the personalization of content, AI can become a valuable ally for teachers. However, maintaining a balance with human interactions remains crucial for holistic and effective learning.

4. PERSPECTIVES OF AI FOR LANGUAGE TEACHING

Artificial intelligence (AI) offers promising prospects for language teaching, transforming the way learning and assessment are conducted. Current research trends reveal a growing interest in adaptive and immersive systems, although technical and ethical challenges persist. This section examines the advances of AI in language learning and offers recommendations for the successful integration of these technologies.

4.1. AI and Language Learning Research Trends

It is challenging to pinpoint current research trends in the field of language learning in the era of AI due to the rapid technological advancements, the diversity of research approaches, and the lack of standardization in methodologies, which complicate the comparison of results. The diversity of expertise areas and the contextual differences of studies make the observed trends difficult to generalize. However, AI systems used for writing assessment (AWE) appear to be garnering increasing interest, having accounted for 17.02% of the topics addressed in 516 studies published between 2000 and 2019, as indicated by a recent meta-analysis conducted by Huang et al. (2023).

Adaptive learning systems have also been a primary focus of study for several researchers, according to multiple meta-analyses, highlighting their potential to provide tailored learning experiences (Andika, 2024; Bhatti et al., 2024; Huang et al., 2023; Sbardella & Pakula, 2024). Meanwhile, more advanced personalized learning algorithms that adapt to the needs, styles, and objectives of learners in real-time continue to develop (Bhatti et al., 2024). Profiling and prediction domains are generating increasing interest among researchers (Chen et al., 2020a; Zawacki-Richter et al., 2019). AI technologies such as user modeling, natural language processing (NLP), natural language generation, speech recognition (ASR), and machine translation remain the most frequently used in language learning systems (Gamper & Knapp, 2002). Intelligent tutoring systems for reading and writing (ITS-RW) represent 13.01% of the studies, according to Huang et al. (2023), highlighting the growing need to develop effective educational tools to enhance reading and writing skills among learners.

Another theme that ranks third (11.31%) in the meta-analysis by Huang et al. (2023) and seems poised to secure its place in the future of AI for language learning is the integration of Virtual/Augmented Reality (VR/AR) with AI. This powerful combination is a current trend in research due to its potential to make experiences more immersive by simulating real-world scenarios in which learners can practice their language skills in a more realistic environment (Mirzaei et al., 2018; De la Vall et al., 2023).

On the other hand, the increased integration of AI with other educational technologies, such as Learning Management Systems (LMS) and adaptive learning platforms, indicates that this field requires further investigation (Villegas-Ch & Palacios-Pacheco, 2020). This exploration is essential for analyzing data on learner performance, identifying their strengths and weaknesses, and providing specific recommendations to enhance their experience. Such integration would leverage the respective advantages of each technology and foster innovation in the field of language learning.

4.2. Major Technical and Ethical Challenges of AI for Language Teaching

The integration of artificial intelligence (AI) in language learning faces various inherent technical limitations. Crompton et al. (2024) revealed that recurring issues such as technical malfunctions and connectivity difficulties persist, hindering the effectiveness of AI devices in educational contexts. The responses provided by AI systems are sometimes contextually inappropriate or lack grammatical and syntactic coherence (Haristiani, 2019). Huang et al. (2022) also identify additional obstacles, such as the monotonous voice of voice assistants, the high cognitive load induced by these technologies, and a novelty effect that may diminish learners' long-term engagement. Moreover, learners often perceive the interactions offered by these technologies as artificial and lacking genuine emotion, which could limit their engagement and the authenticity of exchanges (Thompson et al., 2018).

The ethical implications of using AI in language learning also raise serious concerns, particularly regarding algorithmic bias and its impact on fairness and inclusivity (Luan et al., 2020; Buolamwini & Gebru, 2018). The question of the confidentiality of personal data is another source of worry for learners, generating anxiety about the unexplored and potentially intrusive nature of these tools (Crompton et al., 2024). Protecting learners' privacy and the need for informed consent are also major issues, especially since the use of these technologies involves the collection and exploitation of personal data (Rusmiyanto et al., 2023; Xu & Yuan, 2021). Furthermore, the question of intellectual property regarding AI-generated works raises debates about authorship attribution and the authenticity of creative productions (Eshraghian, 2020; Nah et al., 2023). Additionally, the use of AI in language learning carries the risk of standardizing linguistic practices and disseminating dominant ideologies, thereby restricting cultural and linguistic diversity (Crompton et al., 2024).

In light of these challenges, efforts must be made to develop an ethical framework specifically tailored to artificial intelligence in education. Integrating principles of transparency, data protection, and equity becomes crucial (Hwang et al., 2020; Zhang & Aslan, 2021). Supporting teachers in adopting these technologies, as well as developing digital competencies among learners, is essential for responsible and balanced use of AI in classrooms (Pavelieva, 2024; Kucuk, 2023).

To address the identified challenges, it is imperative to develop a robust ethical framework and clear guidelines governing the integration of AI in language learning. This includes adopting data privacy and security policies that ensure the protection of learners' personal information and respect for their informed consent (Rusmiyanto et al., 2023). Ongoing training for teachers on AI tools is essential to maximize the pedagogical effectiveness of these technologies and minimize the risks of inequalities in access or excessive dependence (Pavelieva, 2024). Furthermore, developers must strive to reduce algorithmic biases to ensure equitable access to educational resources and assessments for all learner groups, regardless of their background or socio-economic status (Buolamwini & Gebru, 2018; Rusmiyanto et al., 2023). An ethical framework dedicated to AI in education would thus guide the use of AI technologies while an inclusive and responsible approach to language teaching.

4.3. Global Recommendations for the Successful Integration of AI in Language Teaching

Successfully integrating artificial intelligence (AI) in language classrooms requires providing practical recommendations to educators, developers, and learners: Offering tailored ongoing training programs for teachers that consider the effective integration of AI technologies into their pedagogical practices is essential for language educators (Hennessy et al., 2021). Involving various stakeholders in selecting AI tools based on clear criteria—such as relevance, effectiveness, and usability—is crucial; these tools should complement, rather than replace, human interaction and feedback in language learning, serving as support rather than a substitute for human presence. Strengthening partnerships between educators, AI tool developers, and researchers is necessary to ensure that technologies meet pedagogical needs and classroom realities. To ensure that learners' personal expression and critical thinking are not compromised while leveraging the advantages offered by AI technologies, it is important to maintain a balance between the use of AI and human critical reflection, preserving human control and creativity in the writing process (Malik et al., 2023). A gradual approach to integrating AI into the language curriculum should be proposed, starting with simple activities before progressing to more complex applications. Finally, future research must address ethical issues such as data privacy protection and algorithmic bias (Touboula, 2023). These efforts are essential for ensuring ethical and effective application of AI in the field of language learning.

In conclusion, the integration of AI in language teaching represents a significant opportunity, but it must be approached with caution. By considering technical and ethical challenges, as well as recommendations for thoughtful implementation, it is possible to create an enriched and inclusive learning environment. A collective commitment from educators, developers, and researchers is essential to maximize the benefits of AI while preserving the fundamental human values of education.

5. CONCLUSION

The integration of artificial intelligence (AI) in language learning represents a significant evolution of the contemporary educational landscape, as it allows for more personalized, interactive, and effective learning experiences. While the potential benefits are undeniable (Kucuk, 2023), this transformation also raises a range of pedagogical, technical, and ethical challenges. Language learning, traditionally viewed as an inherently human activity, involves not only linguistic competencies but also an understanding of cultural and social subtleties. In this regard, the fundamentally social aspect of language acquisition warrants particular attention. Authentic interactions between individuals, grounded in mutual recognition as dialogical subjects, play a crucial role in the learning process. Therefore, it is essential to question the true capacity of AI to replicate this relational dimension: can it truly replace the richness of human exchange without risking the dehumanization of educational practices through the automation of learning? This inquiry calls for a careful balance, in which AI serves as a guiding tool for learning without ever replacing the essential human presence at the heart of any language learning process.

This chapter highlights both the transformative potential and the structural limitations of AI in the development of linguistic skills—particularly in writing, speaking, and comprehension. Grammar-checking tools, for instance, reveal varying performance depending on the languages involved, raising concerns about the unintended alteration of meaning caused by automated suggestions, as well as the limited detection of errors in less-represented languages.

In terms of speaking skills, while AI can enhance pronunciation and fluency, the richness and variety of interactions remain insufficient for advanced learners, and fail to fully account for cultural and contextual nuances. In the field of translation, despite significant technical advancements, automatic systems still struggle to handle complex contexts, idiomatic expressions, and specific cultural references. Moreover, excessive use of these tools, while boosting productivity, may hinder the development of learners' linguistic and analytical skills. On a technical level, malfunctions, connectivity issues, and responses that are sometimes incoherent or contextually inappropriate limit the effectiveness of AI tools in educational settings. From an ethical standpoint, several major issues remain: algorithmic bias affecting equity and inclusion, protection of personal data, intellectual property rights, and the risk of linguistic standardization at the expense of cultural diversity. The acceptance of AI by both teachers and learners is also identified as a critical factor in ensuring its effective and meaningful integration into pedagogical practices.

These findings call for further research in several areas: the development of systems that better integrate linguistic and cultural specifics; the enrichment of interactions with conversational agents; the improvement of translation system accuracy in complex contexts; as well as the optimization of connectivity and the functionality of voice-assistant tools. It is also essential to develop a rigorous ethical framework, including clear policies on data protection, reducing algorithmic bias, and clarifying intellectual property rights. Finally, the impact of teacher training and support on their ability to effectively integrate AI in a critical and informed manner must be given particular attention to ensure the harmonious pedagogical adoption of these emerging technologies.

REFERENCES

Aeni, N., Khang, A., Al Yakin, A., Yunus, M., & Cardoso, L. (2024). Revolutionized teaching by incorporating artificial intelligence chatbot for higher education ecosystem. In *AI-Centric Modeling and Analytics* (pp. 43–76). CRC Press.

Al Mahmud, F. (2023). Investigating EFL students' writing skills through artificial intelligence: Wordtune application as a tool. *Journal of Language Teaching and Research, 14*(5), 1395–1404. DOI: 10.17507/jltr.1405.28

Alenizi, M. A. K., Mohamed, A. M., & Shaaban, T. S. (2023). Revolutionizing EFL special education: How ChatGPT is transforming the way teachers approach language learning. Innoeduca. *International Journal of Technology and Educational Innovation, 9*(2), 5–23. DOI: 10.24310/innoeduca.2023.v9i2.16774

Alhalangy, A., & AbdAlgane, M. (2023). Exploring the impact of AI on the EFL context: A case study of Saudi universities. *Journal of Intercultural Communication, 23*(2), 41–49. DOI: 10.36923/jicc.v23i2.125

Ali, Z. (2020, February). Artificial intelligence (AI): A review of its uses in language teaching and learning. [). IOP Publishing.]. *IOP Conference Series. Materials Science and Engineering, 769*(1), 012043. DOI: 10.1088/1757-899X/769/1/012043

Alotaibi, E. (2023). The Impact Of AI-Powered Grammarly on Enhancing Grammar Proficiency Among Saudi EFL Students. Remittances Review, 8(4). https://remittancesreview.com/menu-script/index.php/remittances/article/view/1105

Alshriedeh, A. (2021). The Effect of an Artificial Intelligence Program on EFL Students on Reading Skill. *Ilkogretim Online, 20*(5), 1727. DOI: 10.17051/ilkonline.2021.05.190

Amelia, R., & Irham, M. (2021). Exploring Teachers' and Students' Perceptions on Using Grammarly as a Tool for Enhancing Students' Writing Quality. *Journal of English Language Teaching and Linguistics, 6*(1), 1–15. DOI: 10.21462/jeltl.v6i1.286

An, F., Xi, L., & Yu, J. (2023). The relationship between technology acceptance and self-regulated learning: The mediation roles of intrinsic motivation and learning engagement. *Education and Information Technologies, 29*(3), 2605–2623. DOI: 10.1007/s10639-023-11959-3 PMID: 37361728

An, X., Chai, C. S., Li, Y., Zhou, Y., Shen, X., Zheng, C., & Chen, M. (2023). Modeling English teachers' behavioral intention to use artificial intelligence in middle schools. *Education and Information Technologies, 28*(5), 5187–5208. DOI: 10.1007/s10639-022-11286-z

Annamalai, N., Ab Rashid, R., Hashmi, U. M., Mohamed, M., Alqaryouti, M. H., & Sadeq, A. E. (2023). Using chatbots for English language learning in higher education. *Computers and Education: Artificial Intelligence, 5*, 100153. DOI: 10.1016/j.caeai.2023.100153

Arifin, M. N., Heriyanto, E., Kurniadi, D., & Arvianti, I. (2024). Analyzing grammar errors among HelloTalk users and proposing effective correction strategies. *English Learning Innovation, 5*(1), 26–37. DOI: 10.22219/englie.v5i1.31569

Asmail, A. (2024). The impact of employing the "Reading Progress" tool based on artificial intelligence analyzes via the Microsoft Teams platform on developing reading skills among primary school students. *Artificial Intelligence Information Security*, *2*(3), 79–167.

Aspers, P., & Corte, U. (2019). What is Qualitative in Qualitative Research. *Qualitative Sociology*, *42*(2), 139–160. DOI: 10.1007/s11133-019-9413-7 PMID: 31105362

Ayedoun, E., Hayashi, Y., & Seta, K. (2019). Adding communicative and affective strategies to an embodied conversational agent to enhance second language learners' willingness to communicate. *International Journal of Artificial Intelligence in Education*, *29*(1), 29–57. DOI: 10.1007/s40593-018-0171-6

Barrot, J. S. (2023). Using ChatGPT for second language writing: Pitfalls and potentials. *Assessing Writing*, *57*, 100745. DOI: 10.1016/j.asw.2023.100745

Beuls, K., & Van Eecke, P. (2023). Construction Grammar and Artificial Intelligence. arXiv. https://arxiv.org/pdf/2309.00135

Bhatti, I., Mohi-U-din, S. F., Hayat, Y., & Tariq, M. (2024). Artificial intelligence applications for students with learning disabilities: A systematic review. European Journal of Science. *Innovation and Technology*, *4*(2), 40–56.

Bhirud, N. S. (2017). Grammar checkers for natural languages: a review. International Journal on Natural Language Computing (IJNLC), 6.

Cano, P., Mayne, J., Catiggay, L., Michael, J., Florida, M., Mathew, J., Pua, R., Jane, M., & Samonte, C.Paulo Miguel A. Cano. (2024). Natural Language Processing of Grammar Checker Tools for Academic Writing: A Systematic Literature Review. *Journal of Electrical Systems*, *20*(7), 1151–1156. https://media.proquest.com/media/hms/PFT/1/uizFZ. DOI: 10.52783/jes.3611

Chen, B., Bao, L., Zhang, R., Zhang, J., Liu, F., Wang, S., & Li, M. (2024). A multi-strategy computer-assisted EFL writing learning system with deep learning incorporated and its effects on learning: A writing feedback perspective. *Journal of Educational Computing Research*, *61*(8), 60–102. DOI: 10.1177/07356331231189294

Chen, C. M., & Huang, Y. M., & Kinshuk. (2018). Effects of an intelligent tutoring system on students' learning outcomes and attitudes in the context of English as a foreign language. *Journal of Computer Assisted Learning*, *34*(4), 376–393.

Chen, L. C., & Chang, K. H. A novel frequency-range analysis (FRA) method for determining critical words among English high-stakes tests. Journal of Intelligent & Fuzzy Systems, (Preprint), 1-16.

Chen, M. P., Wang, L. C., Zou, D., Lin, S. Y., & Xie, H. (2019). Effects of caption and gender on junior high students' EFL learning from iMap-enhanced contextualized learning. *Computers & Education*, *140*, 103602. DOI: 10.1016/j.compedu.2019.103602

Chen, M.-R. A., & Lin, Y.-H. (2023). AI Chatbot-Supported Grammar Tense Learning on EFL Students Learning Effectiveness. INTED Proceedings. DOI: 10.21125/inted.2023.0353

Chen, X., Zou, D., Xie, H., & Cheng, G. (2021). Twenty years of personalized language learning. *Journal of Educational Technology & Society*, *24*(1), 205–222.

Chomphooyod, P., Suchato, A., Tuaycharoen, N., & Punyabukkana, P. (2023). English grammar multiple-choice question generation using Text-to-Text Transfer Transformer. *Computers and Education Artificial Intelligence, 5*, 100158. DOI: 10.1016/j.caeai.2023.100158

Crawford, J., Cowling, M., & Allen, K. A. (2023). Leadership is needed for ethical ChatGPT: Character, assessment, and learning using artificial intelligence (AI). Journal of University Teaching & Learning Practice, 20(3), 02.

Crompton, H., Edmett, A., Ichaporia, N., & Burke, D. (2024). AI and English language teaching: Affordances and challenges. *British Journal of Educational Technology, 55*(6), 2503–2529. DOI: 10.1111/bjet.13460

Darwin, R., Rusdin, D., Mukminatien, N., Suryati, N., Laksmi, E. D., & Marzuki, . (2024). Critical thinking in the AI era: An exploration of EFL students' perceptions, benefits, and limitations. *Cogent Education, 11*(1), 2290342. DOI: 10.1080/2331186X.2023.2290342

El Shazly, R. (2021). Effects of artificial intelligence on English speaking anxiety and speaking performance: A case study. *Expert Systems: International Journal of Knowledge Engineering and Neural Networks, 38*(3), e12667. DOI: 10.1111/exsy.12667

Feng, Y., Han, J., & Lan, X. (2024). After one year of ChatGPT's launch: Reflections on artificial intelligence in scientific writing. *European Journal of Nuclear Medicine and Molecular Imaging, 51*(5), 1203–1204. DOI: 10.1007/s00259-023-06579-5 PMID: 38236428

Fu, Y., & Lee, J. (2023). The role of AI in language learning: Perspectives from EFL teachers. *Journal of Educational Technology Development and Exchange, 16*(3), 205–221.

Geng, H., & Li, Y. (2023). The impact of AI on vocabulary acquisition in EFL contexts. *Language Learning & Technology, 27*(2), 89–105.

Ghasemi, E., & Karami, H. (2024). Evaluating AI-driven adaptive learning systems for EFL learners. *Journal of Computer Assisted Learning, 40*(1), 123–140.

Gupta, R., & Singh, P. (2023). AI-based language learning tools: Benefits and challenges in EFL education. *International Journal of Emerging Technologies in Learning, 18*(5), 45–60.

Haider, M. Z., & Yasmin, S. (2023). AI in EFL learning: A study on ChatGPT's impact on students' writing performance. *Journal of Educational Technology & Society, 26*(3), 312–327.

Hamidi, H., & Hatami, J. (2023). Analyzing the use of AI in language learning: Insights from Iranian EFL learners. *Interactive Learning Environments, 31*(5), 615–630.

Hamuddin, B., Julita, K., Rahman, F., & Derin, T. (2020). Artificial Intelligence in EFL Context: Rising Students' Speaking Performance with Lyra Virtual Assistance. *International Journal of Advanced Science and Technology, 29*(5), 6735–6741. https://repository.unilak.ac.id/1512/1/Artificial%20Intelligence%20in%20EFL%20Context-%20Rising%20Students%E2%80%99%20Speaking%20Performance%20with%20Lyra%20Virtual%20Assistance2.pdf

Haristiani, N., Danuwijaya, A. A., Rifai, M. M., & Sarila, H. (2019). Gengobot: A chatbot-based grammar application on mobile instant messaging as language learning medium. *Journal of Engineering Science and Technology*, *14*(6), 3158–3173.

He, Y., & Zhu, H. (2024). AI-powered feedback and its effects on EFL learners' writing skills. *Language Learning Journal*, *52*(1), 12–29.

Hill, J., Ford, W. R., & Farreras, I. G. (2015). Real conversations with artificial intelligence: A comparison between human–human online conversations and human–chatbot conversations. *Computers in Human Behavior*, *49*, 245–250. DOI: 10.1016/j.chb.2015.02.026

Hossain, M. A., & Rahman, M. (2023). AI in EFL contexts: Enhancing reading comprehension through technology. *Journal of Language and Linguistic Studies*, *19*(2), 132–150.

Hu, Z., & Zhang, W. (2024). The impact of AI-based pronunciation tools on EFL learners. *Journal of Second Language Pronunciation*, *10*(2), 115–130.

Huang, C., & Wang, J. (2023). Integrating AI in EFL classrooms: Teacher perceptions and challenges. *Journal of Computer Assisted Learning*, *39*(1), 76–90.

Huang, X., Zou, D., Cheng, G., Chen, X., & Xie, H. (2023). Trends, Research Issues and Applications of Artificial Intelligence in Language Education. *Educational Technology & Society*, *26*(1), 112–131. JSTOR. https://doi.org/DOI: 10.2307/48707971

Iqbal, S., & Anwar, N. (2024). AI-enhanced EFL learning: Student engagement and motivation. *International Journal of Educational Technology in Higher Education*, *21*(1), 203–222.

Jafari, K., & Chalak, A. (2023). The effectiveness of AI chatbots in improving EFL learners' speaking abilities. *Journal of Language Teaching and Research*, *14*(1), 110–125.

Junaidi, J. (2020). Artificial intelligence in EFL context: Rising students' speaking performance with Lyra virtual assistance. *International Journal of Advanced Science and Technology*, *29*(5), 6735–6741.

Kang, H. (2022). Effects of artificial intelligence and native speaker interlocutors on ESL learners' speaking ability and affective aspects. *Multimedia-Assisted Language Learning*, *25*, 9–43. DOI: 10.15702/mall.2022.25

Kassem, M. A., & Al-Awadhi, A. (2024). AI in language learning: A review of current applications and future trends. *Educational Technology Review*, *52*(1), 87–105.

Kessler, M. (2023). Supplementing mobile-assisted language learning with reflective journal writing: A case study of Duolingo users' metacognitive awareness. *Computer Assisted Language Learning*, *36*(5-6), 1040–1063. DOI: 10.1080/09588221.2021.1968914

Khalifa, M., & Albadawy, M. (2024). Using Artificial Intelligence in Academic Writing and Research: An Essential Productivity Tool. *Computer Methods and Programs in Biomedicine Update*, *5*, 100145. DOI: 10.1016/j.cmpbup.2024.100145

Kim, N.-Y. (2019). A Study on the Use of Artificial Intelligence Chatbots for Improving English Grammar Skills. *Journal of Digital Convergence*, *17*(8), 37–46. DOI: 10.14400/jdc.2019.17.8.037

Kim, S., & Park, J. (2023). AI-driven personalized learning in EFL education: A case study in South Korea. *Journal of Educational Computing Research, 59*(5), 1111–1128.

Kohnke, L., Moorhouse, B. L., & Zou, D. (2023). Exploring generative artificial intelligence preparedness among university language instructors: A case study. *Computers and Education Artificial Intelligence, 5*, 100156–100156. DOI: 10.1016/j.caeai.2023.100156

Koltovskaia, S. (2020). Student engagement with automated written corrective feedback (AWCF): An exploratory study. *Journal of Language and Linguistic Studies, 16*(2), 468–479.

Kukulska-Hulme, A., & Lee, H. (2020). Intelligent assistants in language learning: analysis of features and limitations. CALL for widening participation: short papers from EUROCALL 2020, 1(1), 172-176.

Le, T. M., & Duc, N. H. (2024). The impact of AI-based tools on EFL learners' writing performance and motivation. *Language Learning & Technology, 28*(2), 123–144.

Li, X., & Xie, H. (2023). Investigating the effectiveness of AI-based feedback on EFL learners' writing. *Journal of Language Teaching and Research, 14*(4), 859–874.

Liu, Y., & Chen, H. (2024). A study on the effect of AI-assisted vocabulary learning on EFL learners. *International Journal of Emerging Technologies in Learning, 19*(7), 124–138.

Makeleni, S., Mutongoza, B. H., & Linake, M. A. (2023). Language Education and Artificial Intelligence: An Exploration of Challenges Confronting Academics in Global South Universities. *Journal of Culture and Values in Education, 6*(2), 158–171. DOI: 10.46303/jcve.2023.14

Ming, Y., & Yang, Y. (2024). The role of AI in language learning: A systematic review. *Journal of Computer Assisted Learning, 40*(2), 222–234.

Nader, N., & Khedri, S. (2024). The role of artificial intelligence in promoting EFL learning outcomes: A systematic review. *International Journal of Educational Research, 103*, 101682.

Navarro, D., & Henshaw, J. (2024). ChatGPT as a tool for teaching English writing: Exploring its potential and limitations. *Journal of English for Academic Purposes, 64*, 101123.

Nguyen, T. H., & Tran, T. H. (2023). AI-powered learning and EFL: Implications for teaching and learning. *Computer Applications in Engineering Education, 31*(2), 345–356.

Orji, R. U. (2023). Artificial intelligence and EFL learning: Opportunities and challenges for learners. *Educational Technology Research and Development, 71*(4), 1229–1247.

Ozdilek, Z. (2024). ChatGPT in EFL classrooms: Impacts on students' reading comprehension and motivation. *Journal of Computer Assisted Learning, 40*(2), 102–116.

Pablos, P. O., & Parra, D. C. (2023). ChatGPT and English teaching: Perceptions of teachers and students. *International Journal of Educational Research, 122*, 102335.

Pan, X. (2020). Technology Acceptance, Technological Self-Efficacy, and Attitude Toward Technology-Based Self-Directed Learning: Learning Motivation as a Mediator. *Frontiers in Psychology, 11*, 564294. Advance online publication. DOI: 10.3389/fpsyg.2020.564294 PMID: 33192838

Pavelieva, T. Y. (2024). Platforms for teaching grammar with the help of artificial intelligence: Prospects and problems. International Journal of Advanced Studies in Education and Sociology, 7(1), 13–17. http://sic-publ.press/index.php/es/article/view/194

Pijls, F., Daelemans, W., & Kempen, G. (1987). Artificial intelligence tools for grammar and spelling instruction. *Instructional Science, 16*(4), 319–336. DOI: 10.1007/BF00117750

Qiu, Z., & Zhang, J. (2023). Exploring the integration of AI in English language education: Benefits and barriers. *Journal of Computer Assisted Learning, 39*(2), 208–225.

Reimann, P., & Niegemann, H. M. (2023). The influence of adaptive learning systems on EFL vocabulary retention. *Language Teaching Research, 27*(2), 273–290.

Renandya, W. A., & Widodo, H. P. (2024). AI for English language learning: Teachers' beliefs and practices in Asian contexts. *RELC Journal, 55*(1), 3–21.

Sari, N. E., & Megawati, F. (2020). Grammarly as an alternative assessment tool for EFL writing: Students' perceptions. *Journal of English Language Teaching and Linguistics, 5*(2), 219–229. DOI: 10.21462/jeltl.v5i2.403

Shin, Y., & Kang, H. (2023). AI chatbots in language learning: A study on user satisfaction and learning outcomes. *Language Learning & Technology, 27*(1), 101–118.

Su, L., & Wu, X. (2024). A study on the effects of AI-based listening tools on EFL learners. *Journal of English Language Teaching and Linguistics, 9*(1), 35–52.

Šumak, B., Heričko, M., & Pušnik, M. (2011). A meta-analysis of e-learning technology acceptance: The role of user types and e-learning technology types. *Computers in Human Behavior, 27*(6), 2067–2077. DOI: 10.1016/j.chb.2011.08.005

Sun, Y., & Zhao, Z. (2024). AI-based translation tools in EFL writing: Enhancing accuracy and coherence. *Journal of Second Language Writing, 35*, 100939.

Taher, B., & Chaaban, Y. (2023). AI-enhanced grammar learning: A case study of Syrian EFL learners. *TESOL Quarterly, 57*(2), 333–354.

Vafadar, D., & Qomi, H. (2023). AI in EFL assessment: A review of tools and techniques. *Language Assessment Quarterly, 20*(2), 187–204.

Wang, L., & Zhang, Q. (2024). AI-based tools for EFL learning: An exploration of teachers' perspectives. *Journal of Language Teaching and Research, 15*(1), 22–35.

Xia, L., & Wang, Y. (2023). AI-supported collaborative learning in EFL contexts: Teacher and student perspectives. *Educational Technology Research and Development, 71*(3), 1123–1139.

Yang, A. (2024). Challenges and Opportunities for Foreign Language Teachers in the Era of Artificial Intelligence. *International Journal of Education and Humanities, 4*(1), 39–50. DOI: 10.58557/(ijeh).v4i1.202

Yang, Z., & Li, L. (2023). AI-powered language learning platforms: An empirical study on student engagement. *Computers & Education, 182*, 104455.

Zhang, B., & Liu, J. (2024). AI-based speaking practice for EFL learners: A comparative study. *Journal of English for Academic Purposes*, *57*, 101140.

Zhao, Y., & Huang, X. (2024). The impact of AI tools on EFL learners' reading skills and motivation. *Journal of Language Teaching and Research*, *15*(3), 305–318.

Chapter 9
Students' Perspectives on the Grammarly Application in English Writing Classes

Phan Thi Ngoc Le
https://orcid.org/0000-0002-2337-9135
VNU University of Languages and International Studies, Vietnam National University, Hanoi, Vietnam

ABSTRACT

This chapter shed light on the students' perspectives on both pros and cons of the Grammarly application in English writing classes. To accomplish the research purpose, the chapter author used a closed-ended questionnaire and semi-structured in-depth interviews, with 120 participants from four English classes that the author directly taught. The findings show that students had a positive attitude towards the Grammarly tool, which might enhance the quality of their English writing in grammar knowledge and language style, and increase their motivation and confidence in writing. Besides the undeniable benefits, the Grammarly tool also caused students some difficulties in detecting tenses in sentences, accessing to premium features of Grammarly, and depending on the Internet connection stability. Despite these limitations, the growing popularity of AI-powered automated written feedback tools is indisputable. Thus, students should carefully consider incorporating Grammarly into their writing process to maximize the benefits that this tool can bring to learning English writing.

INTRODUCTION

Writing is one of the four key components of learning a foreign language. People can communicate their thoughts, feelings, and opinions to others through written language (Amelia, 2022). According to Munawwaroh (2017), writing skill requires extensive practice and habituation. Not only must learners be able to put words together into a phrase, but they also need to understand context, syntax, prepositions, and other elements; thus, enhancing grammar proficiency is one way to improve writing skills (Munawwaroh, 2017). At the university level, writing necessitates a formal tone, style, and quality in both its content and organization (Benaiche, 2023). To master writing skill, students must routinely practice and grasp the necessary content, as well as have a wide vocabulary, a thorough understanding of gram-

DOI: 10.4018/979-8-3693-7260-9.ch009

mar, and the capacity to connect sentences and main ideas (Tran & Bui, 2023). According to Karyuatry (2018), to develop writing ideas, students should be aware of a wide range of grammatical rules, ranging from sentence construction and forms to the usage of articles. Due to its complexity, writing in a second language presents a number of challenges for students learning a foreign language in general and English in particular. Because writing requires higher-order thinking skills, most EFL students believe that it is a difficult skill to learn. Given that writing is the most challenging language skill, students lose interest in learning to write as a result of the challenges associated with the writing process (Vitalis et al., 2021).

To evaluate the writing quality, elements of language such as word frequency, lexical diversity, and acceptable language can be used to assess a written text at standard quality (McNamara et al., 2010). Developing writing methods and critical thinking skills is essential for improving writing quality, as it is one of the needs for sophisticated language use. According to Fowler (2007), a writer's ability to see and explore their own world through language can have a significant impact on the quality of their writing. To produce a quality piece of writing, the writer must take into account many processes, like as brainstorming, outlining, drafting, revising, and editing. It is clear that while the first two phases of outlining and brainstorming can be completed orally, the next two stages (revising and editing) would require the assistance of peers or teachers to be implemented. In the past, learners frequently had to identify their own errors or ask tutors to proofread and edit their work. Lecturers are responsible for guiding learners and play an important role in providing feedback, especially on grammar so that students can promptly detect and correct errors. Giving students corrective feedback is an essential part of the learning process when it comes to L2 writing (Sabarun, 2019). Corrective feedback from teachers can help improve students' writing skills (Daneshvar & Rahimi, 2013; Kinasto, 2016). Specifically, teachers' constructive feedback can reduce grammatical errors, improve writing skills, and facilitate composition writing for students (Fitria et al., 2022).

Nowadays, technology plays a significant role in our everyday life. Technology has evolved and provided new avenues for making learning and teaching more engaging and simple (Dewi, 2019). Students who are learning English as a second language require technology as a tool to help them recognize typos and other linguistic faults in their work. Furthermore, to support teachers in correcting students' papers, especially in large writing classes, it is necessary to have automatic text correction software capable of evaluating learners' writing. Therefore, a grammar checker is a very useful tool for writers to use when finding typos and other linguistic issues in their work. The creation of online grammar checkers is now thought to be the answer to this issue (Perdana & Farida, 2019). With the support of online grammar checking tools, students can self-check and correct errors they make in their writing. These technologies provide feedback on spelling and grammar mistakes and analyze the writing using artificial intelligence and deep learning (Nazari et al., 2021). According to Perdana and Farida (2019), these tools are in line with the ideas of technological education, which emphasized the use of technology to advance learning and boost academic results. Grammar checkers, such Paper Rater, Language Tool, Pro Writing Aid, Grammarly, and others, are widely available to help detect faults and other language issues in written work (Amelia, 2022). Among the automated feedback tools, Grammarly is highly appreciated by many language experts and English learners because of its ability to detect errors and provide the most effective and reputable error correction suggestions (Perdana & Farida, 2019). Besides, through the use of Grammarly, learners may quickly correct typos, punctuation errors, and other errors such as missing apostrophes or commas. According to Dewi (2019), a further benefit of the application is that not only does it offer additional robust capabilities like plagiarism detection and vocabulary improvement in the premium edition, but it also assists in improving the writing style of the learners.

Numerous research conducted worldwide have assessed Grammarly's efficacy in enhancing writing abilities and emphasized that this is an effective tool that students can use to identify mistakes in their work (Zinkevich & Ledeneva, 2021; Fitria et al., 2022; Astuti et al., 2023; Benaiche, 2023) while some studies focused on Grammarly's drawbacks (Ardhy et al., 2023; Anggita at el., 2023). In Vietnam, some studies have also mentioned the undeniable benefits of Grammarly applications (Vo & Nguyen, 2021; Tran & Bui, 2023), while also pointing out the shortcomings that this application brings in the classroom (Ha, 2023; Nguyen & Hoang, 2023). At Vietnam National University (VNU), where I am teaching, Grammarly has been widely applied in teaching English skills, especially writing skills, because it is a useful tool that can assist students in identifying linguistic errors in their work while editing EFL writing. However, there has not been any research on the specific advantages and disadvantages of this application from the perspectives of students, who are the ones directly using the application in their learning process. Therefore, this study was conducted to clarify students' perceptions about the benefits and drawbacks of using Grammarly in English writing classes. I hope that the research can provide learners with an overview of the effectiveness of Grammarly so that they can maximize the advantages of this application in their English learning process.

LITERATURE REVIEW

Academic Writing

Writing is regarded as a crucial language skill that requires students to arrange their thoughts coherently and in accordance with the required format. When learning a language, writing serves as a means for authors to communicate with readers in addition to recording information. Writing is challenging since it requires students to possess a broad vocabulary, strong grammar skills, and the capacity for logical thought in order to produce precise and appealing writing (Le & Ngo, 2024). The most reliable and thorough method of determining a learner's level of language proficiency is through the use of writing abilities, especially through academic writing skills at the university level.

Academic writing is one of the important skills in the language learning process, helping learners to develop strategies in writing, while expanding and improving their knowledge in different topics (Graham & Perin, 2007). According to Irvin (2010), academic writing is always a form of assessment that requires learners to demonstrate knowledge and proficiency with specific skills of thinking, interpreting, and presenting. Although academic writing is an interesting skill, it is also challenging for students, especially non-major students who have just entered university. Le (2020) stated that this skill not only requires learners to have language skills (vocabulary, grammar) and knowledge about different areas of social life, but also other skills such as analysis, synthesis, argumentation to express their views in writing. These features of academic writing were also reported in other studies. In earlier study of Taylor (2009), academic writing is never just about "writing", but it has a serious, objective, formal style, and vocabulary that is often abstract and difficult to understand. Therefore, in academic writing, it is important to consider the writer's position, the topic, the intended audience, and the style of the language (Taylor, 2009). Besides, according to Le and Ngo (2024), academic writers must provide evidence to support their claims and use easy-to-understand academic language to provide all the material. More specifically, academic writing skills are the ability to express ideas, knowledge, and messages accurately, logically, and clearly in an academic setting (Le & Ngo, 2024).

From these above studies, it can be seen that academic writing is of great significance to university students, researchers, and those working in research and education. However, this is still one of the skills that cause difficulties for both teachers and students in the teaching and learning process (Vo, 2015), especially in the ability to select vocabulary and sentence structures to build a framework and convey their ideas in a logical and consistent manner. Therefore, teaching academic writing is a big challenge for foreign language teachers in general and English teachers in particular. It requires teachers to have measures to provide the most thorough corrective feedback so that learners can improve their writing skills.

Overview of Automated Writing Feedback

Written corrective feedback means providing thorough and comprehensive review to second language learners with grammatical errors in their writing (Loewen, 2012). It can be classified into three main types, namely direct error correction, indirect error correction, and synthetic error correction (Tran & Bui, 2023). With direct error correction, learners are given the precise steps to take to fix their mistakes. In indirect error correction, learners see mistakes but are still required to fix them on their own. Synthetic error correction involves classifying or identifying faults according to their type, then using annotations to provide a quick explanation of the error, either with or without examples. Since Truscott (1996) brought up the topic of text mistake correction efficacy, there has been a heated discussion about it for the past twenty years. Shintani et al. (2014) then talked on whether or not text mistake correction increases second language learners' writing productivity and whether or not this effect is affected by different feedback formats, different types of errors, individual differences, and the timing of error correction.

Around the beginning of the 21st century, automatic writing error correction systems appeared. The widespread use of technology has made it easier for educators and students to access trustworthy checkers like Grammarly, Prowriting Aid, Ginger, Spellcheck Plus, and Grammar Check. With the help of these tools, students can receive fast, automated feedback on their spelling, punctuation, and capitalization in addition to grammar. Teachers are also using automated writing feedback more frequently as an additional form of feedback to help students write in their second language (L2) (Koltovskaia, 2022). As regards definitions of automated writing feedback, according to Tran and Bui (2023), the automatic text correction feature allows users to use information provided by the automatic text review tool to detect grammatical errors in their writing. Essentially, automatic text error correction is the same as regular text error correction because both can be provided through direct, indirect, and synthetic error correction methods (Tran & Bui, 2023). Therefore, automated writing feedback software has been widely utilized to support L2 students' writing development. These technologies offer automatic feedback to help foreign language learners write more accurately.

The majority of previous studies have focused on the consistency between the automated writing feedback system and human raters to examine the accuracy of automated feedback. Domeji and Knutsson (2002) found that learners who used a Swedish checker tool to identify errors were accurate and efficient in doing so. The participants were given a text with 37 grammatical errors, and they were split into two groups: one that used the program to correct errors, and the other that did not. According to the findings, the tool-using group discovered 85% of the faults while the tool-less group only discovered 60% of them. Their results confirmed the encouraging effect that grammar checkers can have on increasing writing accuracy. Due to its quick, individualized feedback that includes explanations of grammar, spelling, sentence structure, and word usage, automated writing feedback helps students write better and increases their sense of autonomy (Wang et al., 2013). Besides, Kim (2014) claimed that by using the technologies, instructors' workloads might be reduced and learners' autonomy would be encouraged by receiving immediate feedback. The development of grammar checkers over time has demonstrated their benefits and attracted the curiosity of more scholars. Moreover, according to Frankenberg-Garcia (2020), automated writing feedback tools can offer real-time feedback to L2 students and predictive text suggestions.

However, the automated writing feedback tool has several features that distinguish it from teacher correction. First, text error correction allows students additional time to edit their work by automatically identifying a number of errors, providing thorough real-time information, and quickly correcting these errors in a matter of seconds. By providing specific and direct correction suggestions for errors found, it can draw the writer's attention to these errors and correct them more effectively (Lee, 2017). Second, automatic text correction provides comprehensive, consistent, and accurate explanations instantly; explanations that teachers have difficulty implementing because of lack of time or resources (Tran & Bui, 2023). Finally, according to Ranalli (2018), automatic error correction is also neutral. That means error correction suggestions do not depend on the teacher's current mood or mental state, such as exhaustion from checking papers and attitude toward students. However, the disadvantages of using automatic error correction are that it lacks pedagogical capabilities, overcorrects errors, and does not take into account individual differences (Ranalli, 2018).

Grammarly Tool

Grammarly is an application that helps check spelling and grammar errors in sentences. The application was launched in 2009 by Alex Shevchenko and Max Lytvyn. Grammarly is headquartered in San Francisco and has become a popular tool globally, including Vietnam. Millions of users use Grammarly, an online proofreading tool, every day to ensure that their messages, documents, and social media posts are impactful, clear, and free of errors. Grammarly can be used to scan documents and automatically detect potential grammar, spelling, punctuation, word choice, and style mistakes in writing (Grammarly, 2019). Grammarly was developed to make it simpler for us to review spelling and punctuation, check grammar, and detect plagiarism (Grammarly, 2020). Besides, being able to install Grammarly into the extension of any web browser such as Chrome or Safari can help users feel secure in writing grammatically correctly on almost any website because Grammarly will check directly and accurately detect errors for users when we are typing text online. Additionally, Grammarly's web interface is easy to use and adaptable to a range of platforms and devices, providing users with convenience (Dembsey, 2017).

Many authors around the world have given different views on Grammarly's features. According to Read (2010), Grammarly also assesses a learner's vocabulary based on how they use language. As a result, it was effective in locating and fixing the important problems that were present. Lu (2012) claimed that Grammarly was used to find synonyms for nouns, verbs, and modifiers as well as to suggest uncommon and unusual terms. Besides, the study of Daniels ad Leslie (2013) revealed that along with identifying potential misspellings of the term and offering multiple alternatives, Grammarly would also add the proper word. It can offer recommendations for the verb's form and there are suggested alterations and explanations given (Daniels & Leslie, 2013). Grammarly was also utilized in the study of Qassemzadeh and Soleimani (2016) to aid students in learning passive structures. Besides, Grammarly alerts students to their grammatical mistakes in writing, encouraging them to proofread their work. Stated differently, they possess greater writing experience (Yulianti & Reni, 2018). Moreover, Grammarly has the ability to sort errors into six categories: contextual spelling, grammar, punctuation, sentence structure, style, and vocabulary enhancement (O'Neill & Russell, 2019). However, O'Neill & Russell (2019) noted that Grammarly has a flaw in that some of the feedback is inaccurate. This issue can arise because the user is not using a premium subscription and is instead utilizing free access. According to Bailey and Andrea (2020), Grammarly offers statistics on the many kinds of errors, syntactic difficulty, and overall writing grade. It suggests synonyms to help in paraphrasing in written work. Grammarly provides automated corrections for serious errors (Bailey & Andrea, 2020). According to Fitria (2021), Grammarly is an English grammar checker that makes the claim to be a simple tool for academics and students to use to write better. It is frequently used to proofread theses for grammatical errors. It offers thorough feedback, corrects spelling, grammar, and punctuation mistakes, and makes corrective suggestions to make work understandable, precise, effective, error-free, and memorable (Fitria, 2021). Thus, it is evident from the aforementioned research that Grammarly is among the top applications for checking grammar errors.

There are two types of Grammarly: paid and free, differentiated based on payment per month or year, which will allow users to take advantage of all of its capabilities. In terms of the free version of Grammarly, users must first use their email address to check in to the app.grammarly.com website in order to access this free plan. After uploading the text, the user is presented with two primary sections. First, there is the overall score, which is a percentage based on Grammarly's judgment of the text's accuracy. The second item is the total number of problems the program identified and the suggested remedies (all suggestions). Currently, people can access and utilize the free version whenever, anywhere they write, through desktop software, mobile apps, or web browser extensions. It offers numerous useful features, which is an automated proofreading system that can identify errors related to 150 grammar rules from basic to advanced along with suggestions for users about spelling, punctuation, and word choice (Barrot, 2022). Therefore, it is appropriate for reviewing emails and writing on the Internet as well (Fitria, 2021; Nova, 2018). As regards the paid version, Grammarly Premium is even better with the ability to check more than 400 grammar rules along with unique functions such as suggesting better word usage or checking for plagiarism. Its improvements include recommendations for improving vocabulary, identifying plagiarism (Lazic et al., 2020), and suggesting citations (Nova, 2018; Wardatin et al., 2022). In line with the findings of Lazicet et al. (2020), Eyong's (2022) study revealed that Grammarly plagiarism detectors are highly successful in reducing plagiarism in graduate students' research processes. In his study, Eyong (2022) also asserted that all students should use the Grammarly application when conducting their research in order to identify and fix issues with their work and to reduce the possibility of plagiarism. Besides, Grammarly Premium, according to Wardani (2022), evaluates his work to see whether he regularly uses the same terms, provides helpful suggestions for vocabulary adjustments, and suggests suitable synonyms for specific phrases. Another benefit of Grammarly Premium that students in Wardani's (2022) study observed was the ability to assess the originality of the information in their writing. Grammarly users can use the free version with limited features or the premium version that offers advanced utilities such as more accurate error correction suggestions, along with a plagiarism check feature (O'Neill & Russell, 2019).

Concerning the process to use Grammarly, Tran and Bui (2023) noted that before scanning text, users need to set four goals: readers, formality, field, and intent. After selecting the target, Grammarly users can upload the text to the Internet or use the offline application to check text errors. Koltovskaia (2020) mentioned three steps in the process of uploading the written texts to the website of Grammarly. In the first step - uploading, users upload the texts to the website. In the second step – correction, the website will then automatically scan the paper and display the results of any potential errors. With only a single click on the green suggestion button, writers can easily fix any mistake in this part by using the website's ideas for each underlined word. According to Tran and Bui (2023), Grammarly has a number of features to correct errors: 1) grammar error checking feature: allows users to check the use of tenses in accordance with the context and the agreement between subject and verb; 2) spelling and punctuation checking feature: allows users to check for misspelled words and misused punctuation, and give suggestions to make simple, complex, and compound sentence structures clearer; 3) vocabulary check feature: helps users avoid using alliteration and suggests other advanced vocabulary; 4) writing style check feature: helps the text have a clear, articulate, and logical style that meets the needs of the target audience the writer is aiming for; 5) Plagiarism feature: allows users to scan files for instances of plagiarism, especially in academic writing. In the last step – downloading, once the correction phase is complete, the writer can simply download the paper from the website, making no changes other than to the corrected words.

Review of Studies on Students' Perspectives on the Grammarly Application in Writing in the World

There are several studies worldwide on the benefits of Grammarly application in writing. According to Zinkevich and Ledeneva (2021), Grammarly has a lot more features than other built-in spell and grammar checks, and its contextual awareness (style, tone, vocabulary) accomplishes the same goal. In the study of Fitria et al. (2022), students responded favorably to using Grammarly to help them review their thesis writing. The results demonstrated that the Grammarly app has a number of advantages, including time saving for students when checking their grammar, and clear and simple feedback to grasp (Fitria et al., 2022). Wardatin et al. (2022) also emphasized that integrating Grammarly into self-study is essential to raising the quality of the final writing version and enhancing learners' autonomy in achieving their learning objectives. Astuti et al. (2023) categorized six main advantages of Grammarly in checking correctness, clarity, engagement, delivery, plagiarism, and convenience. Besides, Ardhy et al. (2023) implied that by helping students correct grammatical and stylistic errors, Grammarly is a helpful app to increase the quality of students' English writing. In addition, according to Benaiche (2023), Grammarly provides automated correction input on grammar, spelling, punctuation, conciseness, and conventions in its free version. Not only does the program point out the flaws, but it also offers several recommendations for fixing the mistakes that have been made (Benaiche, 2023). Similarly, the study of Prasetya and Raharjo (2023) showed that the use of Grammarly improved the overall writing quality, vocabulary use, and grammatical accuracy of English language learners due to its user-friendliness and personalized feedback.

However, besides the undeniable benefits mentioned above, the review also acknowledges the limitations of the Grammarly application in writing. Grammarly's drawbacks include the inability to identify the tenses that students have used, the inability for students to obtain feedback in the form of a file, and the cost of accessing all of Grammarly's premium capabilities (Fitria et al., 2022). Moreover, Wardatin et al. (2022) also added that the two primary concerns about using Grammarly were related to technical difficulties and the use of certain features. According to Astuti et al. (2023), the shortcomings of Grammarly included its inability to function without an Internet connection, its requirement for both stability in electricity and Internet connectivity, as well as its inability to function effectively on other connected platforms; its incompleteness as a free version necessitated paying for access to the premium version; and its inability to recognize certain proper nouns. In addition, Ardhy et al. (2023) pointed certain restrictions on this application, like the need for reliable Internet access and enough storage. Moreover, the Grammarly software still has many shortcomings that affect its overall reliability during the writing process. Benaiche (2023) revealed limitations of Grammarly when it comes to resolving more complex writing errors, like sentence structure and the order, relevancy, and flow of ideas; solving problems related to critical thinking and in-depth knowledge of the subject. Similarly, according to Anggita at el. (2023), Grammarly might not offer thorough feedback on higher-order writing issues like content organization, coherence, and clarity because this tool mostly concentrated on minor grammar problems. Besides, users are also required to use premium versions to access more features (Anggita at el., 2023).

Review of Studies on Students' Perspectives on the Grammarly Application in Writing in Vietnam

In Vietnam, in recent years, the Grammarly application has begun to be widely used in English classes and brought many benefits to learners as revealed in a numerous studies. According to Vo and Nguyen (2021), Grammarly brings many psychological benefits to students such as more confidence due to prompt and reliable feedback, more comfort than receiving teachers' feedback. The results of Ha's (2023) study showed that ESL students' grammatical accuracy increased dramatically when they used Grammarly for writing or editing, especially in verb forms, singular and plural nouns, spelling, articles, verb omission, and prepositions. Additionally, students had a positive impression of Grammarly due to its simple usage for editing their work, which gave them more confidence while writing (Ha, 2023). Similarly, students felt that AI-powered tools like Grammarly offered helpful feedback on their sentence structure, grammar, and word choice (Nguyen & Hoang, 2023). Tran and Bui (2023) also revealed that Grammarly brings foreign language learners many benefits, including improving the ability to detect errors in spelling, grammar, sentence structure, word usage, style errors, and provide error correction suggestions.

Since this is a mechanical tool, there will always be drawbacks. To begin with, not every mistake that Grammarly identified is accurate; for instance, it was unable to recognize certain proper nouns (Vo & Nguyen, 2021). Furthermore, Vo and Nguyen (2021) also claimed that if students rely too much on the technology, they may become lazy since they think it will help them correct later. Similarly, Ha (2023) demonstrated that, depending on Grammarly made students unable to identify and fix their own grammatical mistakes when writing on their own. There are also some limitations of this tool in correcting capitalization mistakes, run-on sentences, pronoun possession, fragments, and verb tense issues (Ha, 2023). Besides, according to Nguyen and Hoang (2023), AI-powered tools like Grammarly were less effective in providing examples and explanations. Another obstacle mentioned in Tran and Bui's (2023) study is that users must register for premium version of Grammarly to use advanced features in checking plagiarism and providing advanced error correction suggestions. Furthermore, these suggestions of Grammarly are not always accurate, which can change the sentence meaning and relying too much on this tool can make it difficult for students to recognize writing errors on their own (Tran & Bui, 2023).

RESEARCH GAP

As we can see from the review of the literature, Grammarly application in writing has been researched by many scholars around the world with both benefits and limitations. In Vietnam, this issue has attracted moderate attention from researchers. Those studies have provided the conceptual framework for this study. However, it can be seen that at VNU there has not been any studies on the application of Grammarly in English classes. In a learning environment where academic writing is focused like VNU, considering both the advantages and disadvantages of Grammarly from learners' perspectives is necessary to make appropriate adjustments in the process of using this tool in the future. These objectives can be achieved through the following two research questions:

1. What benefits did Grammarly application bring to students in English writing classes?
2. What challenges did students encounter when using Grammarly in English writing classes?

METHODOLOGY

Research Study Design

Background

Purposive sampling was employed in this study to choose participants. The study included 120 participants from four English classes at VNU that I directly teach. The English course lasts for 15 weeks, in which the Grammarly was applied in writing lessons, specifically as follows. The first step involved showing the students how to use Grammarly online or how to install it on browsers such as Chrome, Firefox, and Microsoft Word. For the convenience of all students in the class, the free version of Grammarly was recommended to use. I guided students on basic ways to use Grammarly to identify spelling and grammar mistakes. Then, in each writing lesson, students were required to write a paragraph or an essay about a topic corresponding to the lesson content, but at this time, students were asked not to use Grammarly. Students must write and save the original draft, then submit this draft to the teacher by email. In the next step, after I confirmed receiving the submission, students started using Grammarly to edit the draft based on error correction suggestions from Grammarly. Students then submitted their completed writing to the teacher.

Ethical Considerations for the Study

This study took ethical considerations very seriously. First, from the very first class of the semester, every student from four English classes was made aware of the Grammarly application in English writing lessons. I explained the purpose and methods of the study to them, and I also showed them how to utilize Grammarly when writing. I also explained how the data from interviews and questionnaires would be combined and utilized in the study. They asked me a few clarification questions regarding Grammarly usage, and then they all agreed to help me with this study by an informed-consent form. I also promised them that I would be the only one to access and make use of the information obtained from the interviews and surveys. Pseudonyms were also assigned to each participant so that their anonymity and data confidentiality could be guaranteed.

Data Collection

In this study, I used a combination of quantitative and qualitative methods, including a closed-ended questionnaire and semi-structured in-depth interviews to find the answers for the two research questions.

Questionnaire

According to Mazikana (2023), questionnaires are effective and affordable at gathering a sizable amount of data on subjects related to basic education; therefore, questionnaires were chosen as the main research method to collect data in this study. There are two parts in the questionnaire corresponding to the two research questions. The questionnaire items were adapted from the questionnaire exploring learners' attitudes toward Grammarly in academic writing classes of Khan et al. (2024).

Part 1 has 14 statements related to the benefits of Grammarly application, which are divided into 2 groups namely language acquisition and language attitudes related benefits. Part 2 includes 10 statements about challenges of Grammarly application, which are divided into 3 groups concerning tools, language acquisition, and language attitude aspects. For all 24 items, a 5-point Likert scale (strongly disagree, disagree, neutral, agree, strongly agree) was adopted because Bouranta et al. (2009) suggested that the use of 5-point Likert scales would result in higher response rates and less confusion among participants.

The question form is one page long and can be completed in 10 minutes. Besides, the survey was designed in simple English for the convenience of students of different language majors. The knowledge utilized in the questionnaire was easy to understand because students already understood the theoretical framework and a general summary of the study issue. Before releasing the questionnaires to the entire participant group, I piloted them with five students to assess and make any revisions to ensure they were in line with the objectives. In order to prevent any confusion or misunderstandings, I then made some changes to the questionnaire's design and the wording of a few questions. Since I am the participant group's instructor, I distributed the questionnaire in class so that students could finish it during the break time. To prevent participants from misinterpreting technical words, explanations were provided. Because of the advantages that questionnaires offer, time can be saved by both participants and researchers while still obtaining the intended outcomes. These qualities allow for the quick and simple completion of data collecting.

Interviews

To investigate more information emerged from the issues in the questionnaire, I used semi-structured in-depth interviews with 20 students from four classes (5 students per class). Semi-structured interviews use a series of open-ended questions related to the research topic area, allowing the researcher to gain more by developing open-ended topics (Harvey-Jordan & Long, 2001). Besides, Merriam (2009) asserted that because semi-structured interviews follow a prearranged set of questions and issues to be covered, they are the most efficient technique for gathering data. However, neither the questions' exact wording nor their sequence are predetermined.

The interview form includes 10 questions based on the two research questions and the issues emerged from the questionnaire. Before the interview, an outline of the study and an explanation of key concepts were provided. Every in-person interview was conducted in both Vietnamese and English to triangulate the data gathered from surveys and to learn more about students' beliefs and expectations. Students were invited to participate in an interview at the university cafeteria during breaks in an effort to make responders feel at ease and secure and to encourage them to be more open in their comments.

Before starting any interview, I requested consent from each participant to record the conversation. Additionally, they were informed that they were under no obligation to register their names. Questioning and answering then proceeded in the order listed on the interview schedule. To follow the speaker and record any further questions that arose throughout the interview, I also took notes in addition to recording the conversation. The average length of each interview was fifteen to twenty minutes.

Data Analysis

Questionnaire

In terms of the questionnaire, following the data collection procedure, the survey questionnaire's contents were organized to answer the study questions. The work was made easier because the researcher had already carefully planned the questionnaire and interview questions to match the study subjects. Data obtained from the Likert questionnaire were described through mean scores and standard deviation. Then, the data was synthesized and displayed in the form of charts and tables using statistical methods. Following that, comments were made in regard to pertinent knowledge addressed in the Literature Review.

To ensure data reliability, the reliability coefficient was verified using a split-half approach based on the Spearman-Brown formula. With Rsb = 0.94 for part 1 and Rsb = 0.73 for part 2, the Spearman-Brown reliability (Rsb) in this case is high, above the criterion of 0.7. Thus, it can be concluded that the collected data is trustworthy.

Interviews

As regards interviews, all of the interviews were transcribed. Subsequently, transcripts were combined and arranged based on the study questions. In each set of responses, the researcher made comparisons and contrasts to gain a deeper and more comprehensive knowledge of the data that was gathered from the respondents.

When additional background for the subject was required, all of the participant notes from the interviews were compiled and supplied as quotations. This allowed the researcher to identify new trends or subgroups in the responses from the respondents. In order for the researchers to refer to the transcripts as needed, they were attached together with the quotations' page numbers.

RESEARCH RESULTS AND DISCUSSIONS

Research Question 1: What Benefits Did Grammarly Application Bring to Students in English Writing Classes?

To learn about students' perspectives on the benefits of Grammarly application, I relied on data obtained from a survey combined with interviews. Data on benefits of Grammarly from the survey are presented in Table 1 below.

Table 1. Benefits of Grammarly application

Benefits of Grammarly Application		
Statements	**Mean**	**Standard Deviation**
Language Acquisition related Benefits		
1. Grammarly assists learners in checking tense errors.	3.76	0.71
2. Grammarly provides learners with correct punctuation.	4.61	0.50
3. Grammarly offers suggestions for appropriate sentence structures.	4.58	0.50
4. Grammarly helps learners to detect improper usage of articles.	4.56	0.51
5. Grammarly helps learners to check correct spelling in their writing.	4.54	0.53
6. Grammarly assists learners in correcting wrong word forms.	4.28	0.47
7. Grammarly helps learners with word choice for academic writing.	3.85	0.78
8. Grammarly assists learners in organizing their ideas in their writing.	3.88	0.78
9. Grammarly helps learners with appropriate use of linking words in writing.	4.28	0.51
Language Attitude related Benefits		
10. Grammarly increases inspiration in checking writing with user-friendly interface.	3.90	0.78
11. Grammarly provides more diverse activities during writing lessons.	3.90	0.78
12. Grammarly makes learners motivated with rewriting after feedback.	4.46	0.47
13. Grammarly enhances learners' confidence in writing.	4.67	0.55
14. Grammarly encourages learners to be more responsibly involved in writing process.	4.08	0.70

Table 1 shows that students had good perceptions of the benefits of Grammarly application in both language acquisition and language attitudes with the mean scores ranging from 3.76-4.67. Every factor also displayed a low standard deviation (SD< 0.8), which suggests that the data were closely distributed around the mean.

In terms of language acquisition related benefits, the aspect gaining the highest means scores is that Grammarly can provide learners with correct punctuation (M= 4.61). In the interviews, students also admitted that their most common punctuation mistakes are incorrect use or absence of commas in the right places. One student shared that:

> *In sentences, I often make punctuation errors when joining two independent clauses. They are joined by a semicolon and a conjunctive adverb (as a result, however, therefore, thus...), followed by a comma. But I often use two commas instead of semicolon. Using Grammarly helps me identify these errors.* (S1)

Grammarly's punctuation correction function was clearly reported in the study of Benaiche (2023). The author stated that Grammarly helps users to employ proper punctuation, like commas, semicolons, and periods, to accurately represent the intended meaning in their writing. According to Baron (2001), the main goal of punctuation is to improve understanding and clarity while also helping the reader separate a text for a subsequent verbal presentation. Therefore, the beneficial function in correcting punctuation of Grammarly can assist learners in distinguishing between words, phrases, and complicated sentences, which helps them correctly understand the links and structure of the text.

The next three benefits with small margin of mean scores ranging (M= 4.54-4.58) that Grammarly can help learners improve the quality of their writing belong to sentence structures, articles, and spelling. One student said, "*Grammarly helps me identify some wordy, long, and complex sentences that can prevent the text readability*" (S2). When asked specifically about what types of sentence structures are often corrected by Grammarly, a few students shared about overuse of subordinate clauses and passive voice. This result is consistent with the findings of Zinkevich and Ledeneva (2021), who stated that 15% of writing errors that Grammarly can assist students in fixing are related to the excessive or improper use of the passive voice. Furthermore, as indicated by the notable improvement in the participants' grammar test scores, Fitria (2021) provided evidence in favor of the claim that utilizing Grammarly improved the participants' writing's grammatical accuracy. In agreement, Grammarly can be a helpful tool for enhancing the grammatical accuracy of written documents, according to research cited by O'Neill and Russell (2019).

Besides, in the interviews, students also emphasized that spelling words correctly is important because it guarantees clarity in the thoughts and messages that are conveyed. One student said, "*Most of my errors were in my spelling. Grammarly makes it easier for me to spell check and I do not need to use a dictionary*" (S3). Accordingly, Altamimi and Rashid (2019) asserted that precise word spelling is essential for conveying the exact significance of the subject matter because misspellings can change the reader's comprehension and the writer's intentions, which can lead to ambiguity and confusion. Grammarly's spelling correction function is also mentioned by many foreign and Vietnamese scholars such as Prasetya and Raharjo (2023), Ha (2023), Tran and Bui (2023). In addition, the interviews also confirmed the helpfulness of Grammarly in checking article misuse. One student shared, "*I think Grammarly is a reliable tool for correcting article errors in my writing. I often cannot distinguish when to use a definite article and an indefinite article*" (S4). Zinkevich and Ledeneva (2021) also reported that the incorrect use of articles is the second most common error (20%) detected by Grammarly from students. Thus, this error needs to be regularly checked because it even shows up in the writing of advanced-level students.

Two aspects in language acquisition gaining the same mean scores (M= 4.28) are correcting wrong word forms and appropriate use of linking words in writing. This was also confirmed in the interview when students highlighted Grammarly's ability to detect the wrong use of word forms and provide more precise and varied linking word suggestions. In the study of Zinkevich and Ledeneva (2021), some specific wrong linking words beginning a sentence pointed by Grammarly include "*And, But, In order to, In addition, To begin with*". Moreover, O'Neill and Russell's (2019) study discovered that Grammarly can also successfully enhance English language learners' vocabulary usage in their writing. When compared to the control group that got conventional writing instruction, the participants who utilized Grammarly saw a considerable improvement in their vocabulary scores. Grammarly has been proposed by Hakiki (2021) as a useful tool for improving non-native English speakers' vocabulary. From these results, it can be seen that Grammalry can enable students to improve the coherence, diversity, and avoidance of repetitive terms in their writing, all of which will raise the standard of academic writing.

As regards language attitudes related benefits of Grammarly, all students agreed that Grammarly's feedback increased their confidence in writing with the highest mean score (M= 4.67), followed by the motivation in rewriting the drafts (M= 4.46). In the interviews, students explained more about these issues. One student said, "*The prompt and reliable feedback of Grammarly has made this fact possible. As a result, we are conscious of our errors and promptly fix them*" (S5). Another student compared the feedback of Grammarly with that of the teacher, "*Being corrected by Grammarly is more comfortable for students than receiving corrections from teachers because we do not need to reveal our weaknesses to our classmates*" (S6). Moreover, according to S7, students gained more confidence when their assignments were carefully corrected by Grammarly before being turned in to the teacher. This result is consistent with the study of Vo and Nguyen (2021), which indicated that this tool was practical because it assisted students in raising their level of grammar awareness while they completed their work, which leads to the improvement of their confidence. Sharing the same opinion, Ha (2023) stated that Grammarly was easy to use for revising their work, which increased their confidence when writing.

From the data obtained from Table 1 and interviews, students had good perspectives on the undeniable benefits of Grammarly in terms of both language acquisition and language attitude. However, it can be seen that some mentioned benefits still received mean scores that are not too high (M < 4). This implies that there are still aspects where Grammarly is not yet able to best serve students in improving their writing. The following section goes into further detail about those challenges.

Research Question 2: What Challenges Did Students Encounter When Using Grammarly in English Writing Classes?

In part 2 of the questionnaire, the challenges of Grammarly are divided into 3 main groups related to tools, language acquisition, and language attitudes. The findings obtained from part 2 are shown in table 2 below.

Table 2. Challenges of Grammarly application

Challenges of Grammarly Application		
Statements	**Mean**	**Standard Deviation**
Tools Challenges		
1. Grammarly's single-page websites can be boring for users.	3.93	0.56
2. Grammarly has limited correction suggestions for the free version.	4.26	0.49
3. Grammarly requires a stable Internet connection.	4.35	0.51
Language Acquisition Challenges		
4. Grammarly cannot identify the tenses to use in some parts of writing.	4.30	0.60
5. Grammarly cannot recognize some proper nouns.	4.09	0.67
6. Grammarly's suggestions can make sentences change meaning.	3.85	0.77
7. Grammarly's feedback and explanations may be confusing.	3.08	0.56
Language Attitude Challenges		
8. Grammarly may hinder learners' own correcting ability.	2.72	0.69
9. Grammarly's suggestions may cause uncertainty to determine its usefulness.	2.68	0.71
10. Grammarly may make learners feel lazy and dependent on writing assistance tools.	2.38	0.55

Table 2 shows that students mainly had difficulty with aspects related to Grammarly tool and language acquisition (M= 3.08-4.35). Additionally, all the factors showed a low standard deviation (SD< 0.8), indicating that the data were probably distributed tightly around the mean.

In terms of tools related challenges, all students agreed that Grammarly requires a stable Internet connection (M= 4.35) and it has limited correction suggestions for the free version (M= 4.26). One student explained these obstacles in the interviews, "*Slow internet connections might make it difficult to use Grammarly, leading to data loss and performance delays. It may also result in performance lags and slow responses. Moreover, slow Internet can make users feel uncomfortable and reduce productiv-*

ity" (S8). This finding was in line with the study of Astuti et al. (2023), who claimed that Grammarly could not work without an Internet connection, and it needed stability in both electricity and internet connectivity. Another student was not satisfied with the suggestions of the free Grammarly version and said, "*The free Grammarly only helps users check some grammar errors like article, punctuation, spelling, and so on. If you want to have suggestions on more complex errors or check plagiarism, you have to pay for the premium version*" (S9). Sharing the same findings, Tran and Bui (2023) also revealed that to use Grammarly's advanced capabilities, which include plagiarism detection and advanced error correction recommendations, users must sign up for the premium edition of the app. In agreement, Grammarly's free edition, according to Cavaleri and Dianati (2016), is good at spotting minor mistakes such as misplaced commas and improper use of articles. Fitria et al. (2022) mentioned that students might get disappointed with the free Grammarly' performance because the premium version has many more outstanding features including contextual spelling, vocabulary enrichment recommendations, plagiarism detection, and a thorough explanation of every grammar mistake. Besides, most students in the questionnaire agreed that Grammarly's single-page websites can be boring for users (M= 3.93). In the interview, this point was also confirmed by students. One student expressed his opinion, "*I think the single-input form of Grammarly website might be repetitive and uninteresting*" (S10). In agreement, participants in the study of Khan et al. (2024) claimed that Grammarly's features are not user-friendly and that the app is not designed with particular devices in mind.

As regards language acquisition related challenges, the statement gaining the highest mean scores (M= 4.30) is that Grammarly cannot identify the tenses to use in some parts of writing. It was followed by another weakness of Grammarly (M= 4.09) in recognizing some proper nouns. In the interview, these obstacles were confirmed by students. One student admitted, "*Grammarly is unable to determine which tenses, such as simple past or simple present, I need to use in specific sections of my work. Grammarly can only identify errors related to punctuation, subject-verb agreement, and spelling*" (S11). Another student said, "*Not every mistake that Grammarly found was accurate. For instance, it was unable to recognize certain proper nouns. Because of this, students will make more errors when they use it subconsciously*" (S12). It can be seen that verb tenses and proper nouns are the most common grammatical aspects that the free version of Grammarly has not really had the correct suggestions according to some studies like Vo and Nguyen (2021), Fitria et al. (2022), Ha (2023). Specifically, two students in Ha's (2023) study complained that Grammarly occasionally indicated proper names as errors and suggested using alternative words in their place because it had trouble identifying them. This result is also consistent with Yang's (2018) discussion, which proposed that Grammarly's narrow scope of error detection accounts for the students' average degree of trustworthiness toward this tool. Regarding the prevalence of Grammarly's free version, the data seems to corroborate the survey's conclusions. The free version of Grammarly might not recognize sentence structure and might recommend confusing terms, as was previously highlighted. Calma et al. (2022), Ebadi et al. (2022), and Nguyen et al. (2021) are all in agreement with this outcome. Moreover, Ha (2023) found that the free version of Grammarly was effective in helping students with errors pertaining to verb form, plural/singular nouns, spelling, articles, verb omission, and prepositions. However, it was unable to recognize and fix errors realted to verb tenses, run-ons, possessive pronouns, fragments, and capitalization (Ha, 2023). The fact that the free version can only check 150 grammatical rules as opposed to the premium version's 250 is one of its drawbacks. Thus, using the premium version would be preferable in order to assist students with run-ons, verb tense mistakes, and fragments. Besides, Dodigovic and Tovmasyan (2021) discovered that Grammarly Premium primarily gave accurate comments on problems identified in verb tense, sentence structure, and subject-verb agreement when comparing the findings produced by Grammarly with those of human raters.

One interesting finding is that Grammarly did not cause many difficulties for students in language attitudes (M< 3). This result is reasonable with what was obtained about the benefits related to language attitudes in Table 1 with high mean scores (M> 3.9). During interviews, students also reaffirmed these aspects. One student shared:

> *Grammarly is a useful tool for my writing skills. But I only consider it a tool to support suggestions, not completely dependent on this application. Besides suggestions from Grammarly, I still consider feedback from friends, and especially from teachers, to best improve my writing.* (S13)

This finding is contrasting with that of some studies. According to Ha (2023), students could get dependent on Grammarly and lose interest in correcting their own errors. It was observed that extended usage of Grammarly can lead to students becoming lazy and paying less attention to their assignments (Ha, 2023). Sharing the same views, students may find it challenging to identify writing errors on their own if they depend too heavily on this technology (Tran & Bui, 2023). Similarly, Khan et al. (2024) also concluded that over-reliance on Grammarly can hinder students' ability to learn how to edit and proofread their own work. This different result in my study was explained in more detail in the interview. One student expressed her opinion:

> *The reason we do not depend too much on Grammarly is that we were carefully guided to use this tool during writing class activities. We have to independently write the original draft and submit it to teacher; we will then follow the teacher's instructions to use this tool to improve the draft.* (S14)

From the above sharing, it is clear that teachers play an important role in guiding, coordinating and organizing writing practice activities with Grammarly for students. This result is in line with students' opinions in the study of Wardatin et al. (2022). They all agreed that Grammarly can automatically improve writing, but teachers also have a big part to play in helping students understand why certain essay faults occur. They believed that writing instructors were essential in enhancing their general knowledge in order to provide insightful clarification and explanation in an understandable manner (Wardatin et al., 2022). In addition, students also stated that in addition to using the Grammarly tool, there were still a variety of peer checking activities during writing class to receive comments from other students, and importantly, receive final feedback from the teacher. Therefore, Grammarly is considered a useful tool by students, acting as an interesting supplementary activity during writing lessons, increasing students' interest and motivation, not as a barrier to learners' own correcting ability or make them feel lazy and dependent on writing assistance tools. This finding is also different from the study of Tambunan et al. (2022) which noted that different students in class have different learning preferences, styles, and motivation which may affect how successful Grammarly is for them. In addition, although Grammarly can be a useful tool for spotting and fixing grammatical mistakes, some students might prefer more conventional teaching strategies such exercises and activities that take place in a classroom, not technology-based activities related to AI tools like Grammarly (Gain et al., 2019). This is a very satisfying outcome in this study since with students' awareness and understanding of this tool, teachers can make reasonable adjustments and specific instructions to help students use this tool effectively.

CONCLUSION

Major Findings

This study was conducted to investigate the perspectives of 120 students about the Grammarly application in English writing classes. With the combination of quantitative and qualitative methods, the findings of this study confirm the effectiveness of Grammarly in identifying errors and improving the quality of students' writing. It was revealed that students regarded Grammarly as a useful tool for enhancing several aspects of their writing such as punctuation, sentence structures, articles, and spelling. Besides, Grammarly application also had a positive impact on learners' language attitudes as the feedback of this tool could increase their confidence and motivation in writing.

However, this application requires a stable Internet connection and it has limited correction suggestions for the free version. Besides, it seems that the tool has trouble recognizing and correcting mistakes related to proper nouns, verb tenses, sentence meaning and so on. Despite these shortcomings, the research results also show a positive point that using Grammarly does not prevent learners' ability to write independently and self-correct errors due to the appropriate application process and the teacher's close supervision during writing lessons. This emphasizes the teacher's role in applying this tool appropriately and guiding students carefully during class time so that students might not become over-reliant on writing assistance tools.

Implications

First, this research offers a number of theoretical insights. Despite the increasing popularity of digital tools and software devoted to academic research, there is a dearth of scientific literature on the use of Grammarly, particularly in English writing classes at VNU. Furthermore, by examining the positive and negative effects of Grammarly on the writing learning process, this study advances the body of knowledge of this subject. In this sense, this study considers the viewpoint of students, who were the direct users of Grammarly but were not previously explored, rather than teachers, who have already been extensively studied in the literature.

Moreover, this study has several practical implications for both teachers and students. First, the substantial increase in students' writing grammatical accuracy when using Grammarly and their positive perceptions of the tool highlight the pedagogical value of incorporating AI-powered automated written feedback tools into English teaching curricula. Second, the research identifies particular typical writing errors produced by students as well as the kinds of problems that Grammarly Free Version can and cannot correctly identify. From there, this can spread knowledge of this tool among educators and students, enabling them to take full use of its benefits and minimize its drawbacks to produce high quality writing that satisfies academic requirements.

Besides, it is advised that English teachers, particularly those who teach writing-based subjects like writing or translation, introduce their students to this tool because of its beneficial features. Nonetheless, educators must make sure that students possess sufficient grammatical understanding to identify and utilize Grammarly's feedback efficiently. Moreover, prior to incorporating the Grammarly program into the educational process, both teachers and students should have sufficient language teaching and software operation instructions. To fully benefit from Grammarly, teachers and students should also balance their use of the program, as excessive use of technology might have unfavorable effects. Additionally, by moving around the classroom, teachers are motivated to help students who are struggling with the software.

Limitations and Suggestions for Further Research

Applying the Grammarly tool to teach writing for students has partly achieved initial positive results along with inspiration from students to use new tools in learning. However, there is still a need for further research to discover and further improve the effectiveness of applying new AI-powered automated written feedback tools in teaching and learning English writing. More participants should be included in the experiment for the results to be more reliable and useful. In addition, a comparison between Grammarly and teachers' feedback should be done using different student groups and learning environments. At the same time, during the implementation process, it is necessary to base on the teaching content, curriculum content, learners, and local characteristics to build a detailed, flexible, and appropriate teaching plan to bring the highest efficiency in applying AI-powered tools in English education.

REFERENCES

Altamimi, D., & Ab Rashid, R. (2019). Spelling Problems and Causes among Saudi English Language Undergraduates. *Arab World English Journal, 10*(3), 178–191. DOI: 10.24093/awej/vol10no3.12

Amelia, M. D. (2022). *The effectiveness of Grammarly application on students' accuracy in writing.* Education Thesis. Pendidikan Bahasa Inggris, STKIP PGRI Bangkalan.

Anggita, D., Sumarni, S., Darmahusni, D., & Sulistyaningrum, S. D. (2023). A systematic review of online grammar checker for EFL learners: Potential and limitations for English self-directed learning. *Proceedings of EEIC, 3*, 30–39.

Ardhy, A. A. S., Waris, A. M., & Kryati, L. (2023). Students' Perception of The Use of The Grammarly Application in Their Writing. *ETERNAL (English, Teaching, Learning, and Research Journal), 9*(02), 221-243. DOI: 10.24252/Eternal.V92.2023.A4

Astuti, D., Darmahusni, D., Sumarni, S., & Suseno, M. (2023, June). The use of Grammarly in the academic writing of undergraduate students: Advantages, weaknesses, and challenges (systematic review). In English Language and Literature International Conference (ELLiC). *Proceedings, 6*, 593–607.

Bailey, D., & Lee, A. R. (2020). An Exploratory Study of Grammarly in the Language Learning Context: An Analysis of Test-Based, Textbook-Based and Facebook Corpora. *TESOL International Journal, 15*(2), 4–27. https://files.eric.ed.gov/fulltext/EJ1268470.pdf

Baron, N. S. (2001). Commas and canaries: The role of punctuation in speech and writing. *Language Sciences, 23*(1), 15–67. DOI: 10.1016/S0388-0001(00)00027-9

Barrot, J. S. (2022). Integrating technology into ESL/EFL writing through Grammarly. *RELC Journal, 53*(3), 764–768. DOI: 10.1177/0033688220966632

Benaiche, M. (2023). *The Effectiveness of Using Grammarly in the Writing Process.* Master Thesis in Language and Culture, Department of Letters and English Language, University of 8 Mai 1945 Guelma. http://dspace.univguelma.dz/jspui/handle/ 123456789/15398

Bouranta, N., Chitiris, L., & Paravantis, J. (2009). The relationship between internal and external service quality. *International Journal of Contemporary Hospitality Management, 21*(3), 275–293. DOI: 10.1108/09596110910948297

Calma, A., Cotronei-Baird, V., & Chia, A. (2022). Grammarly: An instructional intervention for writing enhancement in management education. *International Journal of Management Education, 20*(3), 36–75. DOI: 10.1016/j.ijme.2022.100704

Cavaleri, M. R., & Dianati, S. (2016). You want me to check your grammar again? The usefulness of an online grammar checker as perceived by students. *Journal of Academic Language and Learning, 10*(1), A223–A236. https://journal.aall.org.au/index.php/jall/article/view/393

Daneshvar, E., & Rahimi, A. (2013). Written Corrective Feedback and Teaching Grammar. *Procedia: Social and Behavioral Sciences*, •••, 136.

Daniels, P., & Leslie, D. (2013). Grammar software ready for EFL writers. *OnCue Journal, 9*(4), 391-401. https://jaltcue.org/files/OnCUE/OCJ9.4/OCJ9.4_pp391_401_AC_Daniels_Leslie.pdf

Dembsey, J. (2017). Closing the Grammarly® gaps: A study of claims and feedback from an online grammar program. *Writing Center Journal, 36*(1), 63–100. https://www.jstor.org/stable/44252638. DOI: 10.7771/2832-9414.1815

Dewi, N. A. (2019). *The Effectiveness of Grammarly Checker towards Students' Writing Quality of the Fourth Semester of English Department at IAIN Tulungagung*. IAIN Tulungagung. http://repo.uinsatu.ac.id/12020/

Dodigovic, M., & Tovmasyan, A. (2021). Automated Writing Evaluation: The Accuracy of Grammarly's Feedback on Form. *International Journal of TESOL Studies, 3*(2), 71–88. https://www.tesolunion.org/journal/details/info/8MTEw3LjM3/Automated-Writing-Evaluation:-The-Accuracy-of-Grammarly's-Feedback-on-Form

Domeij, R., Knutsson, O., & Eklundh, K. S. (2002). Different ways of evaluating a Swedish grammar checker. *Paper presented at Association for Computational Linguistics, 3*(1), 262-267.

Ebadi, S., Gholami, M., & Vakili, S. (2022). Investigating the effects of using Grammarly in EFL writing of articles. *Interdisciplinary Journal of Practice. Theory and Applied Research, 40*(1), 85–105. DOI: 10.1080/07380569.2022.2150067

Eyong, E. I. (2022). Grammarly Plagiarism Checker in Promoting Quality. *Journal of Research in Multidisciplinary Methods and Applications, 1*(4), 01220104003. http://www.satursonpublishing.com/jrmma/article/view/a01220104003

Fitria, R. A. (2021). *Students' perceptions of the use of grammarly in undergraduate thesis writing at iain Palangka Raya*. IAIN Palangka Raya.

Fitria, R. A., Sabarun, S., & Miftah, M. Z. (2022). Students' perception of the use of grammarly in undergraduate thesis writing. PROJECT (Professional Journal of English Education), 5(2), 366-371.

Fowler, J. (2007). Thinking and Writing at Masters Level: A Reflective Passage. *British Journal of Nursing (Mark Allen Publishing), 16*(14), 887–890. DOI: 10.12968/bjon.2007.16.14.24332 PMID: 17851352

Frankenberg-Garcia, A. (2020). Combining user needs, lexicographic data and digital writing environments. *Language Teaching, 53*(1), 29–43. DOI: 10.1017/S0261444818000277

Gain, A., Rao, M., & Bhat, S. K. (2019). Usage of grammarly–online grammar and spelling checker tool at the health sciences Library, Manipal Academy of Higher Education, Manipal: A study. *Library Philosophy and Practice, 26*(10), 1–13.

Graham, S., & Perin, D. (2007). A Meta-analysis of writing instruction for adolescent students. *Journal of Educational Psychology, 99*(3), 445–476. DOI: 10.1037/0022-0663.99.3.445

Grammarly. (2019). *Grammarly.Edu.* Available at: https://www.grammarly.com

Grammarly. (2020). *Grammarly: free online writing assistant*. Available at: https://www.grammarly.com/

Ha, T. T. A. (2023). *Exploring the impact of Grammarly on grammatical accuracy in second language writing of fifth-grade students in Vietnam: A mixed- methods case study*. Bachelor in TESOL, University of Techonology and Education, Ho Chi Minh, Vietnam.

Hakiki, G. N. R. (2021). Perception of EFL students on the use Grammarly application in writing class. *Eduvelop: Journal of English Education and Development*, *4*(2), 99–106. DOI: 10.31605/eduvelop.v4i2.891

Harvey-Jordan, S., & Long, S. (2001). The process and the pitfalls of semi-structured interviews. *Community Practitioner*, *74*(6), 219.

Irvin, L. L. (2010). What Is "Academic" Writing? *Writing spaces. Reading and Writing*, •••, 3–17. https://wac.colostate.edu/docs/books/writingspaces1/irvin--what-is-academic-writing.pdf

Karyuatry, L. (2018). Grammarly as a tool to improve students' writing quality: Free online-proofreader across the boundaries. [Jurnal Sains Sosial Dan Humaniora]. *JSSH*, *2*(1), 83–89. DOI: 10.30595/jssh.v2i1.2297

Khan, M. O., Nazim, M., & Alzubi, A. A. F. (2024). Exploring Arab EFL Learners' Attitudes: Is Grammarly a Game -Changer in Academic Writing Classes? *Educational Administration: Theory And Practice*, *30*(4), 1365–1371. DOI: 10.53555/kuey.v30i4.1612

Kim, J. (2014). The effectiveness of automated essay scoring in an EFL college classroom. *Multimedia-Assisted Language Learning*, *17*(3), 11–36. DOI: 10.15702/mall.2014.17.3.11

Kisnanto, Y. (2016). The Effect of Written Corrective Feedback on Higher Education Students' Writing Accuracy. *Jurnal Pendidikan dan Bahasa, 16*(2). Retrieved from DOI: 10.17509/bs_jpbsv.vl6i2.4476

Koltovskaia, S. (2020). Student engagement with automated written corrective feedback (AWCF) provided by Grammarly: A multiple case study. *Assessing Writing*, *44*(3), 100450. DOI: 10.1016/j.asw.2020.100450

Koltovskaia, S. (2022). Postsecondary L2 writing teachers' use and perceptions of Grammarly as a complement to their feedback. *ReCALL (Cambridge, England),* 1-15. DOI: 10.1017/S0958344022000179

Lazic, D., Thompson, A., Pritchard, T., & Tsuji, S. (2020). Student preferences: using Grammarly to help EFL writers with paraphrasing, summarizing, and synthesizing. In *CALL for widening participation: short papers from EUROCALL 2020* (pp. 183-189). Research-publishing.net. DOI: 10.14705/rpnet.2020.48.1186

Le, T. B. N., & Ngo, V. G. (2024). Difficulties of first-year students of English Language at Hanoi University when writing paragraphs in academic English. *Journal of Education*, *24*(11), 47–52. https://tcgd.tapchigiaoduc.edu.vn/index.php/tapchi/article/view/1908

Le, T. T. H. (2020). English non-major students' difficulties in writing academic essays and some suggested solutions. *Vietnam Journal of Educational Science*, *30*, 42–48. http://lib.yhn.edu.vn/bitstream/YHN/5131/1/N385.pdf

Lee, K. (2017). Rethinking the accessibility of online higher education: A historical review. *The Internet and Higher Education*, *33*, 15–23. DOI: 10.1016/j.iheduc.2017.01.001

Loewen, S. (2012). The role of feedback. In Gass, S., & Mackey, A. (Eds.), *The Routledge handbook of second language acquisition* (pp. 24–41). Routledge.

Lu, X. (2012). The relationship of lexical richness to the quality of ESL learners' oral narratives. *Modern Language Journal, 96*(2), 190–208. DOI: 10.1111/j.1540-4781.2011.01232_1.x

Mazikana, A. T. (2023). *The Good Part of Using a Questionnaire: Advantages and Disadvantages.* Available at *SSRN*: DOI: 10.2139/ssrn.4386399

McNamara, D. S., Crossley, S. A., & McCarthy, P. M. (2010). Linguistic Features of Writing Quality. *Written Communication, 27*(1), 57–86. DOI: 10.1177/0741088309351547

Merriam, S. B. (2009). Qualitative research. A guide to design and implementation, (2nd e.d.). San Francisco, CA: Jossey-Bass.

Munawwaroh, K. (2017). Using Mind Mapping to Improve Students' Skill in Descriptive Writing at Semester Two of Batanghari. *Jurnal Ilmiah Dikdaya, 7*(1), 26–33. DOI: 10.33087/dikdaya.v7i1.27

Nazari, N., Shabbir, M. S., & Setiawan, R. (2021). Application of Artificial Intelligence powered digital writing assistant in higher education: Randomized controlled trial. *Heliyon, 7*(5), 1–9. DOI: 10.1016/j.heliyon.2021.e07014 PMID: 34027198

Nguyen, T. T. H., Do, T. T. Y., & Vu, V. P. (2021). The effects of web-based technology Quizizz on EFL students' vocabulary achievement. *Journal of Inquiry into Languages and Cultures, 5*(3), 245–254.

Nguyen, T. T. H., & Hoang, T. T. H. (2023). Exploring the use of adaptive learning technology in higher education writing classes: Students' perspectives. *VNU Journal of Foreign Studies, 39*(4), 16-38. https://jfs.ulis.vnu.edu.vn/index.php/fs/article/view/5082/4460

Nova, M. (2018). Utilizing Grammarly in evaluating academic writing: A narrative research on EFL students' experience. *Premise: Journal of English Education and Applied Linguistics, 7*(1), 80–96. DOI: 10.24127/pj.v7i1.1332

ONeill, R., & Russell, A.ONeill. (2019). Stop! Grammar time: University students' perceptions of the automated feedback program Grammarly. *Australasian Journal of Educational Technology, 35*(1). Advance online publication. DOI: 10.14742/ajet.3795

Perdana, I., & Farida, M. (2019). Online grammar checkers and their use for EFL writing. *Journal of English Teaching* [JETALL]. *Applied Linguistics and Literatures*, 2(2), 67–76. DOI: 10.20527/jetall.v2i2.7332

Prasetya, R. E., & Raharjo, D. H. (2023). Enhancing English Language Writing Skills: An Evaluation of the Efficacy of Grammarly Application. *Journal of English Language & Studies, 8*(2), 320–338. DOI: 10.30870/jels.v8i2.19294

Qassemzadeh, A., & Soleimani, H. (2016). The impact of feedback provision by Grammarly software and teachers on learning passive structures by Iranian EFL learners. *Theory and Practice in Language Studies, 6*(9), 1884–1894. DOI: 10.17507/tpls.0609.23

Ranalli, J. (2018). Automated written corrective feedback: How well can students make use of it? *Computer Assisted Language Learning, 31*(7), 653–674. DOI: 10.1080/09588221.2018.1428994

Read, J. (2010). The place of vocabulary in language assessment. In *Assessing Vocabulary*. Cambridge University Press., DOI: 10.1017/CBO9780511732942.002

Sabarun, S. (2019). The influence of different types of feedbacks on learners' writing performance at higher education. *Proceedings of International Conference on English Language Teaching (INACELT), 3*(1), 205–226.

Shintani, N., Ellis, R., & Suzuki, W. (2014). Effects of written feedback and revision on learners' accuracy in using two English grammatical structures. *Language Learning, 64*(1), 103–131. DOI: 10.1111/lang.12029

Tambunan, A. R. S., Andayani, W., Sari, W. S., & Lubis, F. K. (2022). Investigating EFL students' linguistic problems using Grammarly as automated writing evaluation feedback. *Indonesian Journal of Applied Linguistics, 12*(1), 16–27. https://ejournal.upi.edu/index.php/IJAL/article/view/46428. DOI: 10.17509/ijal.v12i1.46428

Taylor, G. (2009). *A student's writing guide: How to plan and write successful essays*. Cambridge University Press. DOI: 10.1017/CBO9780511609749

Tran, T. T. L., & Bui, T. O. (2023). The effectiveness of using Grammarly software to improve foreign language learners' writing skills. *Journal of educational equipment. Applied Research, 1*(302), 37–39. https://vjol.info.vn/index.php/tctbgd/article/view/92218/78055

Truscott, J. (1996). The case against grammar correction in L2 writing classes. *Language Learning, 46*(2), 327–369. DOI: 10.1111/j.1467-1770.1996.tb01238.x

Vitalis, T., Antonius, K., & Arnoldus, H. (2021). Students' Perception Towards the Application of Grammarly: The Automatic Grammar Checker In Writing Narrative Text In The Third Semester At Stkip Ypup Makassar. [Jurnal Inovasi Pendidikan Dasar]. *JIPD, 5*(2), 123–133. DOI: 10.36928/jipd.v5i2.858

Vo, H. K. N., & Nguyen, T. Q. (2021). Applying Grammarly as an Online Grammar Checker Tool to Enhance Writing Skills for English-Major Students. *Proceedings of The 9th OpenTESOL International Conference 2021, Language Education in Challenging Times: Designing Digital Transformations*, 454-467, Publishing House of Economics, Ho Chi Minh City.

Vo, T. K. A. (2015). Using E-Learning as a tool to support writing skill development at the Faculty of English, Danang University of Foreign Languages. *Journal of Science and Technology, Danang University, 4*(89), 1-5. https://jst-ud.vn/jst-ud/article/view/2386

Wang, Y.-J., Shang, H.-F., & Briody, P. (2013). Exploring the impact of using automated writing evaluation in English as a foreign language university students' writing. *Computer Assisted Language Learning, 26*(3), 234–257. DOI: 10.1080/09588221.2012.655300

Wardatin, F. N., Setiawan, S., Mustofa, A., & Nugroho, H. A. (2022). Integrating self-directed learning in facilitating writers engagement through Grammarly: Exploring the perceptions of premium users. *EnJourMe (English Journal of Merdeka). Culture, Language, and Teaching of English, 7*(1), 32–46. DOI: 10.26905/enjourme.v7i1.6580

Wardatin, N. K. (2022). *Investigating EFL students' perception of Grammarly Premium as an automatic writing evaluation in the aspects of writing: A narrative inquiry*. Degree of Sarjana in English language education, Islamic University of Malang.

Yang, H. (2018). The efficiency of online grammar checker in English writing performance and students' perceptions. *Korean Journal of English Language, 18*(3), 328–348. DOI: 10.20527/jetall.v2i2.7332

Yulianti, E. (2018). Utilizing Grammarly in Teaching Writing Recount Text Through Genre Based Approach. *International Journal of Science. Technology in Society, 6*(1), 1–5. DOI: 10.11648/j.ijsts.20180601.11

Zinkevich, N. A., & Ledeneva, T. V. (2021). Using Grammarly to Enhance Students' Academic Writing Skills. *Professional Discourse & Communication, 3*(4), 51–63. DOI: 10.24833/2687-0126-2021-3-4-51-63

ADDITIONAL READING

Anastasia, W., Murtisari, E., & Isharyanti, N. (2024). Lower-proficiency EFL students' use of Grammarly in writing: Behavior, cognition, and affect. *The JALT CALL Journal, 20*(1), 1–25. DOI: 10.29140/jaltcall.v20n1.1089

Driane, L. A., Roza, V., Melani, M., & Reflinda, R. (2024). EFL Students' Perceptions on Using Grammarly in Thesis Writing at English Education Department Students. *Continuous Education: Journal of Science and Research, 5*(1), 40-61. DOI: 10.51178/ce.v5i1.1785

Jomaa, N., & Jibroo, H. (2024). Corrective Feedback of Grammarly in Enhancing L2 Writing by EFL Kurdish Students. [BAES]. *Bulletin of Advanced English Studies, 9*(1), 1–15. DOI: 10.31559/BAES2024.9.1.1

Qub'a, A. A., Guba, M. N. A., & Fareh, S. (2024). Exploring the use of grammarly in assessing English academic writing. *Heliyon, 10*(15), 1–13. DOI: 10.1016/j.heliyon.2024.e34893 PMID: 39157336

Rababah, L. M., & Talafha, D. K. (2024). Unlocking Writing Potential: Assessing the Impact of Grammarly on Jordanian EFL Students' Writing Proficiency. *Theory and Practice in Language Studies, 14*(5), 1486–1492. DOI: 10.17507/tpls.1405.21

Suryanto, S., Habiburrahim, H., Akmal, S., Zainuddin, Z., Safrul, M., & Hanani, F. (2024). Scrutinizing the Impacts of Grammarly Application on Students' Writing Performance and Perception. *Jurnal Ilmiah Peuradeun, 12*(2), 465–490. DOI: 10.26811/peuradeun.v12i2.1235

Wahyu, T., & Zur, S. (2024). EFL Students' Perceptions on Grammarly Use in Proofreading Essay Tasks. *AL LUGHAWIYAAT, 4*(2), 104–119. DOI: 10.31332/alg.v4i2.8046

Wulandari, S., Laeli, A., & Astutik, I. (2024). Using Grammarly Software to Check the Problems in Essay Writing: EFL Pre-service Teachers' Perceptions. *New Language Dimensions*, *5*(1), 12–22. DOI: 10.26740/nld.v5n1.p12-22

KEY TERMS AND DEFINITIONS

AI: Artificial intelligence (AI) is a field of computer science that deals with cognitive problems typically associated with human intelligence, such as learning, creativity, and image recognition. The goal of AI is to create self-learning systems that can figure out what data means. AI then applies the knowledge it gains to solve new problems in a human-like way.

AI Written Feedback Tools: Artificial intelligence (AI) written feedback tools are technological developments intended to help writers with different parts of the writing process. These tools give writers feedback and assistance by using machine learning and natural language processing techniques.

Grammarly: It is an AI tool, which helps writers by providing real-time editing suggestions for spelling, grammar, and writing style. It can even recommend changes according to the kind of writing, including technical, business, creative, and academic writing.

Students' Perspectives: The views and experiences of students in diverse educational environments are referred to as the "student perspective." It entails learning about their ideas, viewpoints, and perceptions on several subjects.

Writing: Writing is a communication tool that can be used to share experiences or sentiments in written form. Writing requires sophisticated thought that incorporates all aspects of writing, including word choice, organization, audience, purpose, clarity, coherence, sequencing, and transcribing.

Writing Quality: The characteristics of a piece of writing that elevate it to a high degree are referred to as writing quality. It includes many elements, including structure, clarity, coherence, and cohesiveness.

Writing Evaluation: It is the field of study that encompasses the theories and methods used to determine how well a writer performs or has potential when given a writing assignment.

English Writing Courses: Writing courses teach you how to create essays, reports, and creative pieces as well as how to use writing approaches for successful and clear communication. Sharing your work will be encouraged so that others may provide feedback, which can help you improve your writing skills.

Chapter 10
An Exploratory Study of the ChatGPT Use of Vietnamese Graduate Students in a Research Writing Course

Vu Phi Ho Pham
https://orcid.org/0000-0001-7459-8509
Industrial University of Ho Chi Minh City, Vietnam

Nhung Hong Nguyen
Lam Son Secondary School, Vietnam

ABSTRACT

This exploratory qualitative study aims to explore the ChatGPT use of Van-Lang-University graduate students in a research writing course and the cognitive levels of their reactions to its responses. The data was collected from observations and interviews with twelve Vietnamese graduate students studying in a research writing class at this university. According to the findings, the participants opted for ChatGPT as a help-seeking strategy during their course due to several reasons including its convenience, instant feedback, and multifunction. Additionally, they had critical reactions to ChatGPT's feedback and advocated that ChatGPT could not replace lecturers' roles in future language classrooms. To develop the growth of critical ChatGPT use for research writing in Master's programs in English Language Studies at Van Lang University, actions from relevant stakeholders is required, including policymakers, lecturers teaching research writing, and MA students.

1. INTRODUCTION

The use of Artificial Intelligence (AI) tools in learning academic writing has brought many profound but controversial impacts due to their pros and cons. Many students advocate this use in their classrooms because it can assist them in content generation, translation, and automated proofreading and editing. According to Golan et al. (2023), it can help to increase output and content by streamlining the writing and creative processes. Besides, it is useful for groups with little expertise to spark creativity

DOI: 10.4018/979-8-3693-7260-9.ch010

in a particular area of interest and point out gaps in the literature. Ozfidan et al. (2024) report that AI tools such as Google Translate, Grammarly, and ChatGPT are commonly used. This approval shows how flexible and helpful these tools are for managing many stages of the writing process, from editing to conception. The students appreciated how the AI tools helped them to save time and improve their writing in general and the areas of grammar and vocabulary in particular, which are crucial for academic writing. They also show that some individuals were concerned about the potential for plagiarism and an excessive dependence on these tools. Instructors must face considerable worry that an over-reliance on AI may cause learners to miss out on important learning opportunities and critical writing skills. This highlights the need of assisting students in developing critical AI literacy so that they can use AI technology responsibly, preserve their writing voice, and develop critical writing abilities.

ChatGPT (Generative Pre-train Transformer) is worth mentioning among recent AI tools. It was developed by OpenAI and released in November 2022. It operates under the principle that "big data + big computing power + algorithm = intelligent model", enabling its users to extract meaningful information from vast amounts of trained text data and produce increasingly sophisticated and humanized text responses. This also allows for the recognition of multi-round human-computer dialogue using natural language (Cheng et al., 2023). Bai et al. (2023) reveal five functions of ChatGPT including conversation, language translation, educational aid, coding, and creative content generation. Concerning educational support, ChatGPT can be a valuable tool for improving writing in higher education. Specifically, it can generate texts, summarize information, and create outlines, all of which can save writing time and improve the output quality. Additionally, it can identify stylistic and grammatical errors, improving the readability of written material (Atlas, 2023). In addition, it can help students develop their research skills by giving them access to resources and information on a particular subject, pointing out previously undiscovered aspects, and introducing them to new research areas, all of which can help them better understand and assess the subject (Kasneci et al., 2023). Moreover, with features like educational resources, study aids, memory enhancement, research support, skill development, and facilitation of language acquisition, ChatGPT's various abilities underscore its value as a potent educational resource, especially in the areas of learning and memory (Bai et al., 2023).

ChatGPT 3.5 and ChatGPT 4.0 are two prominent versions of ChatGPT introduced by OpenAI. The GPT-3.5 model can bring many beneficial effects on students' learning, including quickly retrieving information on a variety of topics, better conceptual understanding of complex topics, and developing students' problem-solving skills, writing and communication skills, storytelling skills, or critical thinking skills according to OpenAI (2023). Students can also leverage ChatGPT's potential for tailored learning and non-judgmental emotional support. With an astounding estimated 1 trillion parameters, GPT-4 was made publicly available on March 14, 2023, marking a significant turning point in its development as one of the most sophisticated conversational chatbot models ever. GPT-3.5 and GPT-4.0 saw a number of improvements over the rest of 2023, such as the addition of speech recognition, picture production, PDF reading capabilities, sophisticated data analysis, plugin integration, and the ability for users to create custom ChatGPT-powered chatbots. According to Espejel et al. (2023), while GPT-4 has demonstrated notable advancements over previous ChatGPT models, it still has some of the same drawbacks. These constraints include the inability to draw lessons from experience, the creation of misleading information, the giving of damaging advise, and the limited context window. Moreover, OpenAI (2023) informs that to log into ChatGPT 4.0, its users have to pay $20 per month at that time. This leads to some inconveniences for underprivileged learners; therefore, the researcher opted for surveying the English-majored MA students' use of ChatGPT 3.5 (free version).

The use of ChatGPT in research writing courses has a controversial influence. On the one hand, language instructors and students in higher education have shown favorable attitudes towards using ChatGPT due to it advantages. Sabzalieva and Valentini (2023) study that it can assist groups in researching and solving problems together. Additionally, Keyue (2023) reports that it can help learners collect reference resources for their research papers or essays, allowing them to work more efficiently and dedicate more attention and time to creative projects. Besides, Song and Song (2023) reveal that the EFL students using ChatGPT show improved writing production in several areas, including structure, coherence, grammar, and vocabulary. In addition, it can produce a less stressful learning environment for students to practice and improve their academic writing abilities and motivation because of its interactive features and quick feedback can make the writing process more interesting and pleasurable. Pham (2024) also studies that it is a great tool for project development and ideation since it can enhance self-confidence, comprehension, and participation in language classes. Furthermore, Pham and Le (2024) believe that it is a useful tool for language learning, demonstrated in four ways. First, it can help students absorb material faster by providing timely answers to their questions. Second, it can facilitate the creation of topics for group discussion among students, which the lecturers may ask their students for deeper explanations. Third, it can improve students' reading ability by assisting in memorizing new information for long-term learning. Last, but not least, using this tool in the learning activities contributes to a less stressful classroom atmosphere, making it a more enjoyable place to study. This can result in promoting active engagement and relaxed the learning environment.

On the other hand, there have been several concerns about using ChatGPT in language teaching and learning expressed by language teachers and learners in higher education. Specifically, the potential for plagiarism is one issue with utilizing the GPT-3 for assessments in higher education. Essay-writing AI systems are made to produce essays in response to prompts or given specifications. Thus, it is possible that students will utilize these systems to submit writings that are not their own, thereby cheating on their assignments (Dehouche, 2021). Supportively, Cotton et al. (2024) report that ChatGPT can enable cheating because it is challenging to differentiate between writing produced by a computer and that produced by a person. In order to guarantee that these technologies are employed in an ethical and responsible manner, universities need to carefully weigh the benefits and dangers of this use. To prevent and identify academic dishonesty, this may entail providing proper guidance and offering teachers and students assistance and training. In addition, Nguyen (2023) studies that EFL teachers at Van Lang University also determine several possible issues with this chatbot, including the concern about students' excessive dependency on ChatGPT because of inappropriate use. Moreover, Pham and Le (2024) report that users of ChatGPT could become disinterested in live lectures. Students using ChatGPT excessively may find it difficult to think critically and creatively, leading to work distractions.

Although many researchers have investigated the attitudes of lecturers and students at universities towards the benefits and challenges of ChatGPT use, few have explored how English-majored postgraduate students use this tool. As a result, this motivated the researchers to conduct the current study, entitled *"An Exploratory Study of the ChatGPT Use of Vietnamese graduate Students in a Research Writing Course at Van Lang University"*.

2. LITERATURE REVIEW

2.1 Critical Thinking and Bloom's Cognitive Taxonomy

Critical thinking (CT) was differently defined throughout the period. Paul and Elder (1992) defined it as the intellectually disciplined process of actively and skillfully conceptualizing, applying, analyzing, synthesizing, and/or evaluating information gathered from, or generated by, observation, experience, reflection, reasoning, or communication as a rubric to belief and action. Bloom et al. (1956) first introduced a cognitive taxonomy, providing well-developed definitions of six primary categories of cognitive domains. They were six nouns including knowledge, comprehension, application, analysis, synthesis, and evaluation (Krathwohl, 2002). The goal of this hierarchical model of is to categorize the anticipated behavior of students, including how people are expected to behave, think, or feel after engaging in a particular instructional unit (Bloom et al., 1956). Recently, it is known as the six levels of verbal learning goals. The top three categories including analysis, synthesis, and evaluation were seen to reflect CT skills, whereas the three bottom categories were thought to indicate fundamental abilities that a thinker possesses. According to Assaly and Smadi (2015), it is classified into two levels of thinking skills which are lower-order thinking skills (remember, understand, and apply) and higher-order thinking skills (analyze, evaluate, and create).

To be more specific, Omar et al. (2012) summarize and report each level's definition. Additionally, Newton et al. (2020) investigated to ascertain whether Bloom's Taxonomy presentation guidelines are widely accepted in UK higher education. A collection of 47 publicly accessible verb lists was gathered from 35 universities and textbooks.

Table 1. Summary of categories in Bloom's Taxonomy

Cognitive levels	Definitions	Sample action verbs
Remember	extract factual responses, assessing the ability to remember and identify certain information	recall, tell, list, state, name, define, label, and repeat
Understand	comprehend what the information means	arrange, explain, classify, translate, distinguish, demonstrate, paraphrase, discuss, report, locate, generalize, and summarize
Apply	apply information to real-world circumstances (fresh and tangible)	modify, apply, operate, prepare, illustrate, operate, use, solve, produce, and choose
Analyze	(1) disintegrate into components or shapes. (2) establish a connection with the presumptions, categorize, and differentiate	distinguish, examine, identify, categorize, analyze, question, differentiate, experiment, test, categorize, calculate, contrast, outline, infer, discriminate, and compare
Evaluate	(1) rearrange the individual concepts to form a new whole. (2) create a structural pattern using a variety of components.	create, combine, develop, rewrite, compile, compose, argue, design, plan, support, revise, and formulate
Create	make comparisons and use certain criteria to differentiate the value	appraise, critique, decide, evaluate, judge, rate, assess, and justify

Note. Adapted from Omar et al. (2012) and Newton et al. (2020)

2.2 Task-Based Language Teaching (TBLT)

Willis (1996) advocated that tasks should be activities where learners use the target language to communicate a goal. He developed the original TBLT model into a model having six steps. His model included pre-task (input, meaning-focused), task, assessment task, planning, task presentation, and post-task language emphasis. Additionally, Oxford (2006) listed several types of tasks, including reasoning-gap, question-and-answer, structured and semi-structured dialogues, puzzles and games, interviews, debates, sharing personal experiences, attitudes, and feelings, problem-solving, decision-making, opinion-gap or opinion exchange, information-gap, comprehension-based, and basic cognitive processes (like comparing listing and ordering/sorting).

According to Tuyen et al. (2024), ChatGPT can help both teachers and learners in the task-based approach. Teachers can utilize ChatGPT to fulfill their objectives for each phase. Additionally, it offers particular exercises and demonstrations that assist them in improving their teaching strategies. It is also an excellent platform for students who want immersive and practical learning. This allows students to ask ChatGPT questions like they do with their instructors. The ChatGPT model can also aid in the development of analytical and creative problem-solving abilities by producing thorough explanations and responses to a given issue. More interestingly, students can argue with ChatGPT about the arguments, answers, and other concepts that are offered. Consequently, ChatGPT provides interactive assistance to students at any time and from any location. In addition, it is a useful resource and guidance for students conducting a project to investigate their subject or topic (Liang and Luo, 2024). It aids each student by attending to their specific learning demands in the classroom. Additionally, it offers personalized comments on the written work of the students who participated in their study. They also admitted that its ability to respond instantly and hold follow-up conversations was helpful.

2.3 Self-Regulated Learning (SRL)

According to Schunk and Zimmerman (2007), SRL involves the ability to monitor and control one's own cognitive processes, behavior, and emotions while pursuing a goal. Panadero (2017) introduced SRL as a key conceptual framework for understanding the cognitive, motivational, and emotional elements of learning. Research on SRL also tended to conceptualize it as an individual activity, focusing on the cognitive processes within individuals that contribute to supposedly independent and autonomous learning (Bransen and Govaerts, 2020).

Self-regulated learning plays a certain role in language learning, which students may take an active role in the learning process with SRL strategies including self-motivation, planning, organizing, repeating, self-monitoring, and self-evaluation (Artino and Stephens, 2009). In addition, Roohani and Asiabani (2015) report EFL learning is significantly impacted by the use of SRL techniques as goal-setting, self-efficacy, asking for help, organizing, practicing, time management, feedback, and self-evaluation.

In terms of characteristics of self-regulated learners, Richards and Rodgers (2001) studied that possible task roles for learners were group member, monitor, risk-taker, strategy-user, goal-setter, self-evaluator, and more. Zimmerman (2002) claimed that self-regulated learners actively participated in their education and made informed choices about what, where, and how they studied, which planning, monitoring, time management, and asking for assistance are some of the tasks involved. Perry et al. (2017) showed that SRL was associated with students developing into flexible, lifelong learners who can work and study both independently and cooperatively. They were also critical and creative thinkers, problem solvers, and thinkers. Moreover, Jansen et al. (2022) reviewed that self-regulated learners took an active role in their education and chose carefully what, where, and how to study. It entailed tasks like organizing, keeping an eye on things, managing their time, and asking for assistance.

ChatGPT can support self-regulated learners in many ways. According to Wu et al. (2023), it can help them feel more motivated, which supports the SRL process throughout the planning stage. They may utilize ChatGPT to get fresh perspectives and ideas for their learning activities whenever they need them throughout the performance phase (i.e., when they experience learning obstacles). Throughout the self-reflection stage, they can ask ChatGPT for feedback on their learning and suggestions for improvement. In general, ChatGPT can offer detailed explanations, step-by-step guidance, and personalized, interactive educational learning. Additionally, Chiu (2024) shows that the three stages of SRL including forethought, performance, and self-reflection can be supported by ChatGPT-based learning exercises. During the planning stage, learning exercises might offer more detailed explanations and illustrations to help clarify the issue as well as other ideas for teaching methods. During the performance phase, students can practice and get more original problem-solving ideas, as well as prepare to apply what they have learned and practiced by using ChatGPT. In addition, they can make quick, personalized, and infinite requests. Teachers believe that by offering feedback, allowing students to practice self-reflection approaches, and offering further suggestions for development, this AI tool can assist them in their self-reflection process in the final phase. These suggest that ChatGPT may provide a creative, interesting, and interactive student-centered setting that is oriented on their requirements. Moreover, this setting, which promotes "think pair and share" thinking, helps high-ability children realize their full potential while developing the SRL skills of low-ability pupils (Xia et al., 2023).

2.4 Ethical Concerns

There have been several concerns about using ChatGPT in language teaching and learning expressed by language teachers and learners in higher education. Specifically, Nguyen (2023) investigated the opinions of EFL teachers on the use of ChatGPT in writing classes at Van Lang University using a mixed-methods case study employing a purposive sampling technique. Her study used interviews and an online Google Forms-based questionnaire to gather data from twenty experienced EFL instructors. The purpose of this study was to find out how Van Lang University instructors evaluate using ChatGPT during writing sessions. It also aimed to provide important insights into their recommendations for using ChatGPT effectively in writing classes. According to her findings, despite these positive perceptions, they also determined several possible issues with this chatbot, including the concern about students' excessive dependency on ChatGPT as a result of incorrect use.

Using ChatGPT in EFL classrooms requires careful consideration of ethical concerns including respect for privacy, cheating, fairness, and teachers' roles (Mhlanga, 2023 and Zeb et al., 2024). Rerading personal privacy, when learners use ChatGPT, the information that they provide may be leaked since ChatGPT is trained using vast amounts of data gathered from the internet. Hence, Mhlanga (2023) reveals that it is crucial to ensure that students' personal information is protected and not misused by others. Before implementing ChatGPT in the classroom, teachers should obtain their permission and explain how their data is collected, processed, and stored. For cheating, Zeb et al. (2024) report that ChatGPT users can commit plagiarism and academic dishonesty because it may facilitate cheating, and it can be difficult to tell the difference between human and machine-generated work. Additionally, it is required of academic writing to properly recognize the original authors and confirm the study by acknowledging their effort using citations and references. However, ChatGPT and other AI language models cannot provide adequate citations as they do not have access to pertinent sources or the appropriate citation style. About fairness, undesirable assumptions, biases, and prejudices can be reinforced and propagated by language models such as ChatGPT. Therefore, a thorough investigation of these systems is necessary, taking into account the potential for prejudice and discrimination before deploying AI systems like ChatGPT in educational settings (Mhlanga, 2023). With regards to human role, Kim (2020) supports that one of the most important aspects of education is the bond that forms between a teacher and their students. By building relationships with their students, teachers may learn about their unique needs as well as their talents and limitations. ChatGPT lacks the emotional intelligence, empathy, and interpersonal abilities of human teachers due to the AI language model's characteristics. As a result, ChatGPT finds it challenging to understand each learners' particular needs, provide tailored support, and a supportive and stimulating learning environment. Concerning teachers' roles in the classrooms, ChatGPT cannot provide experience learning or hands-on training which are the best ways to learn for many students. Hence, it is the responsibility of educators to offer these opportunities, and they can accomplish this through practical projects, laboratory experiments, or field excursions (Jacobs, 2020). Suportively, Mhlanga (2023) studies that the teachers should critically understand ChatGPT's limitation to ensure that the platform is used in ways of enhancing rather than replacing the function of human educators.

2.5 Related Studies

ChatGPT can help English-majored students in different ways. Stokel-Walker (2022) disclosed that it was proficient at producing a wide range of written texts, including research articles and assignments. According to Curtis (2023), it could speed up the writing and editing process. Additionally, Su and Yang (2023) conducted an exploratory study to identify ChatGPT's advantages for education including developing virtual tutors, responding to student inquiries, and offering individualized learning experiences. Besides, Nguyen (2023) showed that Van-Lang-university EFL instructors saw ChatGPT as a helpful tutor in writing classes since it could respond to constant queries, suggest books that would help students generate ideas, and provide feedback on students' work to improve language skills and inspire them to write more. In addition, Kohnke et al. (2023) revealed that it could provide linguistic input, stimulate learners' interest, and real-time assistance, allowing them to practice their language skills anytime and anywhere. It could also adjust the level of difficulty, offer personalized learning materials, and facilitate an authentic language-learning environment. The authors also discussed its capabilities in supporting language learning tasks including correcting language mistakes. According to Xiao and Zhi (2023), ChatGPT might be a useful tool for learning and could help students with language-related tasks. They outlined three main advantages of using this tool. Firstly, it was similar to a personal instructor or students' learning partner by providing them with a customized, immediately available, and adaptable feedback system. Secondly, applying critical thinking skills to tasks like changing prompts, training the model, and confirming and accepting its outputs helped them improve language proficiency. It could help them become critical learners by double-checking and evaluating the data produced by this chatbot and accepting information after careful consideration. It implied that the students assessed the accuracy, relevance, and specificity of the information provided by ChatGPT rather than accepting it at face value. They could also modify prompts to train this tool, which could lead to their learning outcomes' improvement.

English-majored students in tertiary education use ChatGPT differently. Bok and Cho (2023) revealed that students anticipated that lecturers would provide easily available, understandable explanations of ChatGPT-generated feedback. Apart from further explanations of its comments, several students said that they wanted to have their professors confirm the correctness and dependability of the system. Overall, the participants in their study made the case that instructors should have a crucial role in offering personalized, culturally aware, and nuanced feedback, which challenged ChatGPT. In addition, Šedlbauer et al. (2024) revealed that college students had two primary strategies for entering queries into ChatGPT. The first technique was verifying the validity of its answers and the other involved carefully making the query and eventually refining it. After receiving ChatGPT's responses, they rated the quality of the output. Furthermore, Dong (2024) showed that students often consulted individuals whom they were trustworthy for the right advice and help (their professors) when their need arose, especially throughout the focus group discussion.

ChatGPT's roles in academic writing courses are differently perceived by English-majored students at universities and colleges. Chen (2023) highlighted the significance of human agency or the dominant and controlling role of humans, which ChatGPT was perceived as a machine proofreader and quick search engine. Thorp (2023) and Chen (2023) argued that ChatGPT was not an author and that human authors must use this AI tool carefully. Both authors emphasized the significance of human agency in using ChatGPT and the necessity for more research into how authors would perceive this use. As a result, the expert highlighted the significance of human agency in writing training. This included having clear guidelines, analyzing ChatGPT feedback critically, and ongoing observations to uphold human roles in students' learning to write with ChatGPT. In addition, Phan and Nguy n (2023) studied that ChatGPT could be a valuable tool for lecturers, students, and managers, but it should not replace human expertise and critical thinking. Moreover, Šedlbauer et al. (2024) revealed that college students had two primary strategies for entering queries into ChatGPT. The first technique was verifying the validity of its answers and the other involved carefully making the query and eventually refining it. After receiving ChatGPT's responses, they rated the quality of the output.

In previous study, the ChatGPT use of EFL students were investigated based on four theories including self-determination theory, constructivist language learning theory, technology acceptance model (TAM), and social learning theory. From the self-determination theory perspective, Du and Alm (2024) reported that ChatGPT, which offered rapid feedback and adaptable, customized learning experiences, could help students feel more competent and autonomous in their language learning. Besdies, Solak (2024) used three theories for his study which were constructivist language learning theory, technology acceptance model and social learning theory. Constructivist approach might be aided by AI, particularly ChatGPT, which offer dynamic and interactive language learning environments. Students would have meaningful conversations, got quick feedback, and modified their comprehension of the material in response to their interactions with the AI in real time. For the technology acceptance model, teachers and students had positive attitudes and agreed that ChatGPT wass a useful tool for removing language barriers, personalizing instruction, fostering language acquisition, offering real resources, and enhancing the educational process. About social learning theory, when learners used ChatGPT, they witnessed the good experiences of others. They also supported that positivity about ChatGPT's future role, particularly when combined with other technologies, sets an example for prospective users and influences their expectations and choices.

2.6 Research Gaps

Many previous authors have studied undergraduates' ChatGPT use relied on learning theories including SRL, but few have introduced the conceptual framework of this use as a support tool for English-majored graduate students in research writing courses with the task-based teaching approach. Particularly, how graduate students employ ChatGPT for different learning tasks such as group discussions, case studies, reading comprehension, peer feedback, and projects receive little attention. Moreover, few studies have evaluated their reactions to its feedback according to Bloom's Cognitive Taxonomy.

2.7 Research Objectives

Upon examining pertinent literature, the interaction between humans and AI is unavoidable. This requires more research to find strategies for using ChatGPT critically and properly involving ethical concerns. Therefore, the current study aims to fill these research gaps. Specifically, it explores the ChatGPT use of English-majored graduate students at VLU during their research writing course and the cognitive levels of their reactions to its responses.

2.8 Research Questions

To achieve these research objectives, this research addresses two research questions:

1. To what extent do graduate students use ChatGPT to assist their study in a research writing course?
2. What cognitive levels do graduate students' reactions to ChatGPT's feedback relate to?

3. METHODS

3.1 Pedagogical Setting and Participants

Research writing was a compulsory subject and accounted for three credits in the curriculum of Master of Art in English Language Studies at Van Lang University. In this course, the students had twelve meetings with their lecturer and learned with a task-based approach. More specifically, the teaching techniques used in this course were lectures, discussions, presentations, Q&A, modeling, task-solving, reading comprehension, peer feedback, teacher feedback, group work, and individual work.

This research was conducted between September 2023 and October 2023 in a research writing course at Van Lang University. Among a population of fifty-three English-majored MA students, the authors carried out this survey with twelve of them who belonged to the academic year 2023-2025 and studied in an intake class of main author.

Table 2. Demographic information of participants

<table>
<tr><th rowspan="2">Participants</th><th rowspan="2" colspan="2">Information</th><th colspan="2">N = 12</th></tr>
<tr><th>No. of respondents</th><th>Percent</th></tr>
<tr><td rowspan="8">English-majored MA students</td><td rowspan="2">Biological Gender</td><td>Male</td><td>3</td><td>25%</td></tr>
<tr><td>Female</td><td>9</td><td>75%</td></tr>
<tr><td rowspan="4">Age Range</td><td>From 23 to 32 years old</td><td>10</td><td>83.3%</td></tr>
<tr><td>From 33 to 42 years old</td><td>2</td><td>16.7%</td></tr>
<tr><td>From 43 to 52 years old</td><td>0</td><td>0%</td></tr>
<tr><td>53 years old and above</td><td>0</td><td>0%</td></tr>
<tr><td rowspan="2">Educational Institution</td><td>Van Lang University</td><td>12</td><td>100%</td></tr>
<tr><td>Other universities</td><td>0</td><td>0%</td></tr>
</table>

Table 2 reveals demographic information of recruited English-majored MA students. There were twelve participants in this study, nine of them were female students (75%) while the other five were male students (25%). A majority of them were aged between 23 and 32 years old (83%) and there were two participants aged from 33 to 42 years old (16.7%).

Table 3. Controlled variables in the current study

<table>
<tr><th rowspan="2">Participants</th><th rowspan="2" colspan="2">Information</th><th colspan="2">N = 12</th></tr>
<tr><th>No. of respondents</th><th>Percent</th></tr>
<tr><td rowspan="13">English-majored MA students</td><td rowspan="3">ChatGPT's version use</td><td>ChatGPT version 3.5</td><td>12</td><td>100%</td></tr>
<tr><td>ChatGPT version 4.0</td><td>0</td><td>0%</td></tr>
<tr><td>Other versions</td><td>0</td><td>0%</td></tr>
<tr><td rowspan="4">Time of practice using ChatGPT</td><td>Less than a month</td><td>3</td><td>25%</td></tr>
<tr><td>From a month to less than two months</td><td>5</td><td>41.7%</td></tr>
<tr><td>From two months to less than three months</td><td>0</td><td>0%</td></tr>
<tr><td>Three months and more</td><td>4</td><td>33.3%</td></tr>
<tr><td rowspan="4">Time of using ChatGPT for learning research writing</td><td>Less than four hours a week</td><td>6</td><td>50%</td></tr>
<tr><td>From four hours to less than seven hours a week</td><td>6</td><td>50%</td></tr>
<tr><td>From seven hours to less than fourteen hours a week</td><td>0</td><td>0%</td></tr>
<tr><td>Fourteen hours a week and more</td><td>0</td><td>0%</td></tr>
<tr><td rowspan="2">Formal training in using ChatGPT that they attended before studying in the research writing</td><td>Yes</td><td>0</td><td>0%</td></tr>
<tr><td>Not yet</td><td>12</td><td>100%</td></tr>
</table>

Table 3 illustrates variables that were controlled in the current study including ChatGPT's version use, time of practice using ChatGPT, time of using ChatGPT for learning, and specific training in using ChatGPT that they attended. As can be seen from Table 3, all participants used ChatGPT 3.5 (free version) because of its cost-efficiency and convenience. Additionally, 47.1% of participants had a two-month experience practicing using ChatGPT, followed by those having three-month experiences (33.3%), and less-than-a-month experiences (25%). While six participants spent less than four hours a week using this chatbot for learning research writing (50%), the others were inclined to spend more time on this educational purpose (50%). In addition, 100% did not take part in any specific formal training for employing ChatGPT. These data can be interpreted that although participants have practiced using ChatGPT for a long time, they have not had the opportunity to participate in professional training sessions to be guided in using it properly. Moreover, they have been hesitant to use ChatGPT version 4.0 due to its monthly maintenance costs. These findings indicate that the ChatGPT use of English-majored MA students for studying research writing is spontaneous and have not undergone formal training before attending this course. Hence, this group of graduate students is worth investigating to use ChatGPT as a support tool for learning research writing.

3.2 Design of the Study

This qualitative research is a case study, in which the data for analysis was gathered through observations and interviews. In this study, the researchers used a convenient sampling technique by selecting all research writing learners who were conveniently accessible and readily available in a postgraduate course at VLU. Besides, all references to ChatGPT in the following are to ChatGPT 3.5.

3.3 Data Collection and Analysis

First of all, the authors asked for the class lecturer's and students' permission for the current survey. Naturalistic observations were conducted during the course. Firstly, the researchers planned the observations by reviewing ethical considerations, choosing unobstructed observations as an observation method, and selecting an observation sheet as the main tool for data collection. Recordings were not allowed in this class. To conduct observations, they gained familiarity with the environment, did note-taking, and remained unobstructed. For data analysis, they categorized the observed behaviors of the English-majored MA students, analyzed the data to identify themes, and determined relationships and connections between them. Finally, they developed interview questions, sought advice from an expert in the field of CALL in teaching research writing to modify them, and carried out the interviews. The semi-structured interviews were conducted after the course had finished and its items were designed in Vietnamese so that the interviewees could clearly express their experiences on ChatGPT use throughout this course. Then, the qualitative collected information was divided into themes, transcribed, and analyzed.

To ensure validity, the current survey was built upon SRL theory, in which participants' personal experiences were discovered to support their self-study. The survey was also piloted by ten English-majored MA students in another research writing class at VLU. Before the launch of the interviews, the researchers carried out observations. They also consulted with the expert three times and considered his valuable comments for improving the interview questions. Furthermore, one of the authors was the lecturer who could alleviate them immediately during the research process.

Figure 1. Training procedure in a meeting in the research writing course and its learning tasks

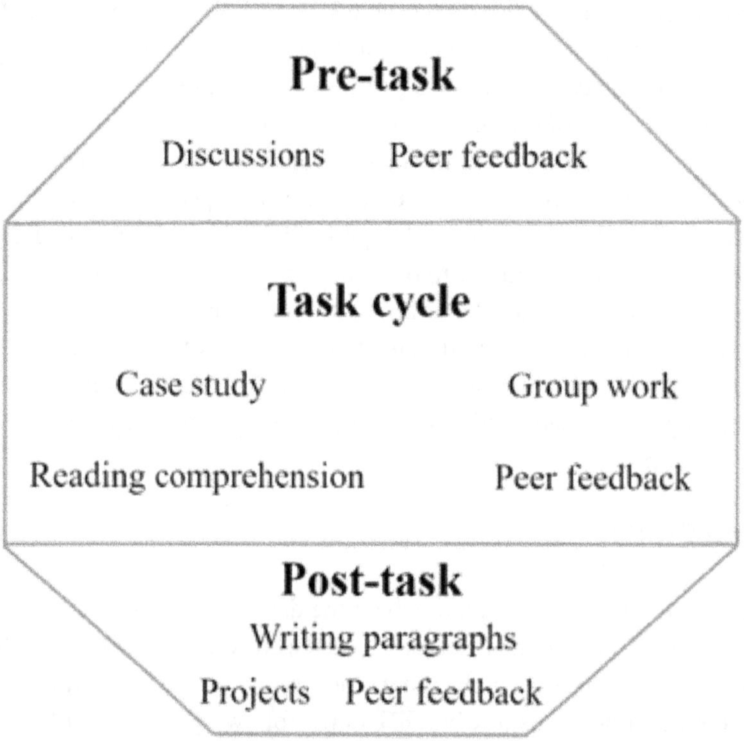

Note. The training procedure shows the progress and learning tasks that students have to carry out during a meeting

Figure 1 indicates how English-majored MA students were trained within a particular meeting in the research writing course surveyed. In this course, every meeting has three phases including pre-task, task cycle, and post-task. In the pre-task stage, these MA students often had group discussions to answer their instructor's queries. The task cycle involved evaluating case studies, working in groups, and reading for comprehension with follow-up questions, followed by writing paragraphs and projects in the post-task phase. Peer feedback took place in every phrase.

3.4 Ethical Issues

The researchers carried out the current survey with the class lecturer's and students' permission. In addition, they ensured that all participants were fully informed about the purpose, procedures, risks, and benefits of the research. Besides, the participants were provided voluntary consent to participate, which meant that they were willing to participate in this investigation. Their identities were strictly confidential, even from their instructor to ensure that they were not influenced by subjective psychological factors such as anxiety, embarrassment, and so forth when being observed and answering questions in interviews.

4. FINDINGS

Research Question 1: To What Extent do Graduate Students Use ChatGPT to Assist Their Study in a Research Writing Course?

Reasons for Choosing ChatGPT as a Support Tool

All twelve participants preferred using ChatGPT for learning research writing because it was convenient and speedy. When compared to using other AI chatbots such as Google Bard, Poe, and so forth, one disclosed that it was easier to get access to ChatGPT by Gmail (8.3%). In addition, they showed that it could provide quick results and immediate help to alleviate their learning problems (100%).

> **S5:** When compared to other AI chatbots such as Microsoft Bing AI, Google Bard, and Poe, I saw that ChatGPT was more popular. Additionally, it is easier to get access to ChatGPT than to Bard which requires Microsoft emails.
>
> **S10:** ChatGPT can provide immediate answers for many fields I do not have much knowledge about.

English-majored MA students at VLU were keen on using ChatGPT due to its multifunctional characteristics. For instance, they explained that it could help them search for information, plan questions, write content, synthesize, deliver feedback on their classmates' writing assignments, narrow the scope of the research, outline, translate, generalize information, and solidify knowledge.

> **S6:** I use ChatGPT to suggest errors in grammar, spelling, language use, cohesion, coherence, and ideas of my classmates' paragraphs when giving peer feedback.
>
> **S7:** I use ChatGPT to search for definitions of specialized phrases and synthesize information. Moreover, I use ChatGPT to help condense knowledge and focus on exercises.
>
> **S11:** ChatGPT can help to write the content that you need very quickly, brainstorm ideas, and make outlines.

These findings could be interpreted that when English-majored MA students at Van Lang University dealt with difficulties, they were inclined to use ChatGPT due to its practical characteristics. This indicated that it was believed to be a helpful tool for learning research writing by the participants.

Characteristics of Queries/Prompts Given to ChatGPT

Once the researchers had observed the participants's use of ChatGPT to assist them in hadling given learning tasks, they identified several themes of questions' characteristics that they gave to ChatGPT based on the categories of those tasks. In other words, the recruited participants asked ChatGPT different kinds of questions when they handled different learning tasks such as discussions, case studies, reading comprehension, peer feedback, and projects. The characteristics of questions that they gave to ChatGPT involved concept-checking questions, reasoning questions, detailed questions, imperatives, definition-determining questions, information-seeking questions, example-discovering questions, application questions, and connective questions. Notably, imperatives, concept-checking, reasoning, and applications questions contributed to four main kinds of questions that they asked ChatGPT more frequently, when compared to the others. For discussions, case studies, and reading comprehension, they often sought help from ChatGPT's responses for checking concepts, determining definitions, and seeking information and applications while they often asked ChatGPT to relate concepts or situations and suggest applications for particular topics.

S1: Give feedback on …
S2: How many...?
S3: Why…? / Give me reasons for … / Several studies have explored [fact]?
S4: Infinitives at the beginning of sentences
S6: What is/are...?
S7: How to …?
S8: [statement]?
S9: How do/does A affect B?
S10: How can…?
S12: How do/does A relate to B?

These findings could be interpreted that the participants could ask different types of detailed questions to ChatGPT to help them solve different learning tasks, even though they had never joined formal training workshops on using it. This indicated that they would use ChatGPT more effectively to support their study in the research writing course with the lecturer's guidances on its appropriate use.

Reactions to ChatGPT's Feedback

From the findings of interviews, English-majored MA students at Van Lang University reacted to the content supplied by ChatGPT in different ways. To be more precise, all participants requested ChatGPT to offer more references and details and then verified the information supplied by cross-referencing it with other academic sources, including Google Scholar, and their own opinions. This meant that they had background knowledge of this subject and desired to explore it more. They also paraphrased, edited, and used ChatGPT to make outlines, but did not copy their content.

S1: I usually ask ChatGPT to examine the information given more carefully to see if this information is accurate and reasonable or not.
S3: I compare with my personal views or views of a certain article author.
S4: I usually reread and filter which ideas I think are appropriate and then find more documents from different research channels to verify.
S6: I usually verify the information and select appropriately
S9: I usually review and check the accuracy of the information and then write in my own words.
S10: I often analyze phrases and structures of ChatGPT's responses to pick up synonyms and paraphrases.

Overview, owing to the recognition of ChatGPT's responses' limitations, English-majored MA students at VLU did not totally copy its feedback. These findings could be interpreted that they had critical reactions to the content of ChatGPT such as understanding, applying, analyzing, synthesizing, and evaluating, in the early stages that they used this AI tool to support learning to write research. For the indications of these findings, appropriate guidance on ChatGPT use for learning to write research of their instructor through different kinds of tasks could help them use this tool more critically.

Research Question 2: What Cognitive Levels do Graduate Students' Reactions to ChatGPT's Feedback Relate to?

Emotional Reactions

Overall, from the findings of observations and interviews, English-majored Master's students who participated in the survey disclosed favorable attitudes although they had several concerns about using ChatGPT to assist them in learning research writing. To be more precise, while they preferred its convenience, instant help, and usefulness, they doubted its accuracy and artificial learning environment. Most participants claimed that it took time to double-check the information that ChatGPT offered (66.7%). In addition, their assignments would be readily interpreted as written by artificial intelligence if they did not completely comprehend what ChatGPT offers to paraphrase, which reduced their comfort (8.3%). Furthermore, they discussed if ChatGPT played a predominant role in research writing courses, the self-learning environment would be insufficient and negative when compared to that having human teachers' guidance and supervision (16.7%).

S1: I don't feel much comfortable. ChatGPT sometimes provides wrong information and double-checking is time-consuming. Additionally, if I do not fully understand what ChatGPT suggests to paraphrase, the article will easily be thought of as using AI to write. In general, it will cause a loss of comfort during my study. Therefore, I will need human teachers' guidance and supervision.
S5: Sometimes the environment of self-learning with ChatGPT is not as sufficient as learning in traditional classrooms.
S9: ChatGPT is a convenient and fast tool but requires users to have certain qualifications to verify the information.
S10: Using ChatGPT is convenient but not completely reliable and accurate.
By comparison, all participants preferred its convenient and speedy features and usefulness (100%).
S3: Using ChatGPT can help to find the information I need very quickly.
S6: Using ChatGPT is quite convenient and can help me come up with many good ideas

In other words, these findings could be interpreted that although English-majored MA students at VLU enjoyed using ChatGPT to support their learning to write research, they were concerned about the accuracy and reliability of ChatGPT's feedback, insufficient learning environment, and the cost of time for double-checking. This could indicate that they did not completely believe and rely on the content of ChatGPT, which could result in their need to receive their instructor's support and feedback.

Perceptions of Future ChatGPT Uses

According to the findings of interviews, although English-majored MA students believed that the role of human lecturers is irreplaceable in foreign language classes, they could not guarantee this scenario would not happen in the future because of human usage. A participant argued that while ChatGPT might give users adequate knowledge, it was unable to identify ideological and personality variations and those in acquisition speed even amongst students in the same class and training period, especially when teaching a large group of students (8.3%). As a consequence, AI-powered instruction was like instructing a fish to climb a tree if it was unable to recognize the distinctions between students, which might lead to a decline in their engagement. Additionally, eight participants argued that teachers' roles were irreplaceable which resulted from ChatGPT's lack of practical experience, emotional intelligence, and cultural aspects (66.7%).

> **S7:** Instructors convey practical experience and knowledge based on theory. Hence, it is easier to absorb knowledge and apply it in life.
> **S8**: Impossible because AI is just AI, maybe it will provide enough information for users but it cannot recognize differences in ideology and personality, which there is often a difference in acquisition speed even though they are in the same class and training time, especially teaching with a large group of students. If AI cannot acknowledge differences among learners, teaching is like teaching a fish to climb a tree, which can result in the reduction of learner engagement.
> **S9:** Humans create ChatGPT and AI, so AI can never replace humans. If humans do not program it, it cannot have certain knowledge, including human emotions. This proves that humans do not program machines, so no matter how much science develops, without humans, it is nothing more or less than a machine.
> **S10:** ChatGPT cannot replace the lecturer's position because there are in-depth questions and cultural aspects that cannot be queried by ChatGPT and the information provided to students is for reference only and cannot impart valuable experience and information from lecturers.
> **S12:** Its data is still inaccurate, not up-to-date, and in-depth.

By comparisons, a participant was uncertain about the future of ChatGPT in foreign language classrooms because it depended on how people would use this chatbot (8.3%).

> **S6:** It is impossible to say in advance because it depends on how people use ChatGPT.

In other words, these findings could be interpreted that ChatGPT could not replace human lecturers' positions soon, but its replacement is unpredictable in the more distant future. This could indicate that more current research needs to investigate the use of ChatGPT for learning, particularly for learning writing research to make reasonable recommendations for this use. As a result, the abuse of ChatGPT by lacking-awareness individual English-majored MA students and the replacement of ChatGPT would be prevented from the early stage.

5. DISCUSSIONS

According to the findings in this study, the graduate students preferred using ChatGPT because it could assist them in writing content and delivering feedback, which mirrors the results of Stokel-Walker (2022), Su and Yang (2023), Nguyen (2023), and Xiao and Zhi (2023). For their reactions to ChatGPT's feedback, the results of this survey demonstrated that they evaluated and verified the information supplied by cross-referencing it with their own thoughts, their instructors' lectures, and other scholarly sources, such as Google Scholar. This was similar to the findings of Bok and Cho (2023), Šedlbauer et al. (2024), and Dong (2024). These findings were also consistent with the properties of four theories introduced by Solak (2024), and Du and Alm (2024), including self-determination theory, constructivist language learning theory, technology acceptance model (TAM), and social learning theory.

The present study reported several research findings that were not found in the literature review that English-majored MA students asked ChatGPT different categories of questions when they used it as a tool to help with group discussions, case study resolution, reading comprehension, peer feedback, and final project management. Their questions involved concept-checking questions, reasoning questions, detailed questions, imperatives, definition-determining questions, information-seeking questions, example-discovering questions, application questions, and connective questions. Additionally, their reactions to ChatGPT's responses belonged to five levels of understand, apply, analyze, evaluate, and create in Bloom's cognitive taxonomy such as finding more in-depth information, verifying, outlining, and comparing with different information sources and personal views. From the findings, recruited English-majored MA students were believed to use ChatGPT as a support tool for learning research writing with critical thinking. These reactions' characteristics matched with those revealed by Bloom et al. (1956) and Paul and Elder (1992). In addition, the findings that the participants used ChatGPT critically were similar to those of Xiao and Zhi (2023). Furthermore, the findings that they used the technique of verifying the validity of ChatGPT's responses also advocated those in the study of Šedlbauer et al. (2024). However, the participants in this investigation did not rate the quality of ChatGPT's feedback.

The graduate students at Van Lang University were considered to be self-regulated learners because they had characteristics of self-regulated learners studied by Richards and Rodgers (2001), Zimmerman (2002), Perry et al. (2017), and Jansen et al. (2022). Additionally, ChatGPT supported their learning in different ways during the stages of SRL, which complimented Chiu's (2024) results. Moreover, the findings reported that they opted for using ChatGPT as an assistant tool for studying research writing due to its practical functions such as convenient and speedy information search, content synthesis, outline development, and feedback delivery, which were similar to those of Kohnke et al. (2023) and Su and Yang (2023).

The participants believed that ChatGPT's replacement for the role of human instructors in foreign language classes, especially research writing, would not take place, which advocates the findings of Phan and Nguy n (2023) and Dong (2024). To be more precise, the participants emphasized humans' roles in proofreading and feedbacking within the human-ChatGPT interactions, which correlated with Chen (2023), Thorp (2023), and Dong (2024). Additionally, they promoted the idea that teachers should play a major role in providing students with individualized, nuanced, and culturally sensitive feedback in the classrooms where learners could use ChatGPT to support their studies, which was similar to the findings of Bok and Cho (2023).

The ChatGPT Use of Vietnamese English-Majored Master's Students at Van Lang University addresses ethical concerns involving privacy, cheating, fairness, and teachers' roles. The investigation's findings highlight the role of the instructor in the classroom and ChatGPT is a support tool for the participants. This alleviates the ethical concerns raised by Mhlanga (2023). Besides, these students used ChatGPT critically and avoided violating scientific ethics such as cheating and plagiarism that were reported by (Zeb et al., 2024). Furthermore, other ethical issues reported by Mhlanga (2023) were also carefully considered by examining ChatGPT's responses.

6. CONCLUSION

6.1 Main Findings of the Current Research

The main findings indicated that using ChatGPT as an assistant tool could be considered to be a help-seeking strategy for several reasons such as being convenient, speedy, and multifunctional. Additionally, the prompts that they asked ChatGPT were diverse such as concept-checking questions, reasoning questions, detailed questions, imperatives, definition-determining questions, information-seeking questions, example-discovering questions, application questions, and connective questions. Among them, imperatives, concept-checking, reasoning, and application questions were four dominant categories. In addition, they had different reactions to ChatGPT's responses to take advantage of its content for supporting their learning tasks throughout the twelve-meeting period mentioned. For instance, they used its content to find more in-depth information for their lessons, edit, analyze its sentence components, verify, compare with different research sources, and so forth. Additionally, the majority of them verified the appropriateness of ChatGPT's responses with reliable academic sources. Hence, their reactions to these responses belonged to five levels of understand, apply, analyze, evaluate, and create in Bloom's cognitive taxonomy. They did not entirely believe in ChatGPT and revealed that human instructors' support and feedback were essential. Subsequently, they advocated that ChatGPT could not replace lecturers' roles in future language classrooms for several reasons such as its lack of hands-on experience, pedagogical skills, emotional intelligence, and cultural aspects. Moreover, they avoid being involved in ethical concerns when using ChatGPT to support their study in the research writing course at Van Lang University.

Figure 2. Conceptual framework of the ChatGPT use of Vietnamese postgraduate students in a research writing course at Van Lang University

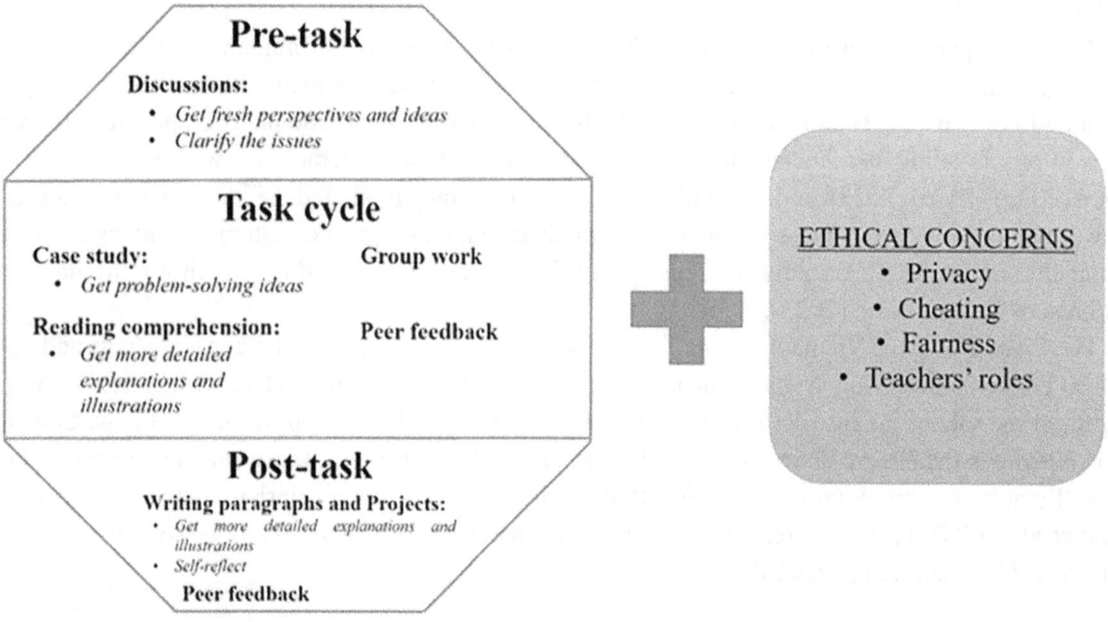

Note. Adapted from Willis (1996), Artino and Stephens (2009), Roohani and Asiabani (2015), Mhlanga (2023), and Zeb et al. (2024)

Figure 2 was adapted from Willis (1996), Artino and Stephens (2009), Roohani and Asiabani (2015), Mhlanga (2023), and Zeb et al. (2024) and introduced as a conceptual framework for the ChatGPT Use of Vietnamese postgraduate students in a research writing course at Van Lang University based on the findings in this research. When the students discussed before doing the tasks, they used ChatGPT to brainstorm different viewpoints and ideas and clarify problems. While they performed tasks such as case study, group work, and reading comprehension, this tool provided them with detailed explanations and illustrations. This helped them to come up with ideas to alleviate their issues. For composing paragraphs and conducting projects post-task, they received thorough explanations from ChatGPT and then self-reflected. ChatGPT also assisted them in giving feedback to their classmates. While handling those learning tasks, they used ChatGPT to support their research and took ethical considerations into account.

6.2 Pedagogical Implications

The study has shown useful information about English-majored MA students' use of ChatGPT as a support tool for learning research writing. The results imply that ChatGPT can be critically used to help Van-Lang-University English-majored MA students study research writing. To promote the development of critical use of ChatGPT for research writing in Master's programs in English Language Studies, relevant stakeholders need to take action.

In terms of English-majored MA students at VLU, they should be critical when using ChatGPT to support their learning in the research writing courses. To achieve this aim, they should strictly follow their instructors' guidance on the critical use of ChatGPT through learning tasks such as discussions, case studies, reading comprehension, peer feedback, and final projects. When receiving ChatGPT's responses, they should understand, apply, analyze, synthesize, and evaluate their accuracy and appropriateness. During this process, they should employ other AI tools, learn from their peers, and seek help and support from human experts, including their instructors. Furthermore, to help the following generations of English-majored MA students at VLU use ChatGPT more critically, they should work with their teachers to make recommendations and develop guidelines about using ChatGPT in research writing courses.

With regards to lecturers teaching research writing for English-majored students in postgraduate programs at VLU, they should be careful when enabling their students to use ChatGPT to assist in learning writing research. To accomplish this objective, they should design their lessons carefully with the implementation of scaffolded experimental activities that allow their English-majored graduate students to practice using ChatGPT and verify its content. Additionally, while their English-majored MA students are using ChatGPT in lectures, they should closely monitor how they use it and give them feedback. Moreover, they should regularly conduct investigation research on how to use ChatGPT to support the research writing learning of their English-majored MA students to control the employment of this AI tool as a learning assistance so that it will develop positively and reasonably, avoiding the bad scenario that they will depend on this chatbot.

Concerning policymakers at VLU, they should develop more plagiarism-detecting softwares which have text recognition features created by ChatGPT to help lecturers control the honesty and effort of their English-majored MA students when they carry out their projects, which helps them offer objective and fair assessments. This will indirectly prevent lazy students from being overreliant on this chatbot.

6.3 Limitations

The current research is not free from limitations, which four main limitations were found. Firstly, a small number of participants prevented the researcher from making generalizations of the findings. Secondly, these research results may change if the participants use other versions of ChatGPT, including ChatGPT 4.0, which is believed to provide more specific information with references. Thirdly, it is an exploratory study, which only explores the ways of using ChatGPT as an assistant tool for English-majored MA students to learn writing research. Finaally, if this research investigates English-majored postgraduate courses with different lecturers using different teaching methods or at other educational institutions, the results may be different.

6.4 Recommendations for Further Research

From the above limitations, the current study focuses on the Master's students at VLU. It may be great if future studies are expanded to investigate undergraduate students at the same university to make the final results more convincing. Additionally, research in the future should gather data from larger groups of English-majored MA students so that the researchers can generalize their findings. In addition, they can encourage their participants to use other versions of ChatGPT to examine whether their findings are different or similar to those in the current research. Future research should also determine English-majored MA students' use of ChatGPT for learning in other kinds of postgraduate courses such as Second Language Acquisition, IT in Foreign Language Teaching, Pragmatics, and so forth to evaluate the differences among research findings. Besides, to further advance this research area, future studies can measure ChatGPT's impacts on English-majored graduate students' learning outcomes in this research writing course and others. Moreover, the use of ChatGPT for research assistance is controversial in other academic settings, and the use of ChatGPT by English-majored MA students needs to be monitored across multiple courses, so longitudinal studies should be undertaken to determine the social changes.

REFERENCES

Alharbi, M. A. (2020). Exploring the potential of Google Doc in facilitating innovative teaching and learning practices in an EFL writing course. *Innovation in Language Learning and Teaching, 14*(3), 227–242. DOI: 10.1080/17501229.2019.1572157

Artino, A. R.Jr, & Stephens, J. M. (2009). Academic motivation and self-regulation: A comparative analysis of undergraduate and graduate students learning online. *The Internet and Higher Education, 12*(3), 146–151. DOI: 10.1016/j.iheduc.2009.02.001

Assaly, I. R., & Smadi, O. M. (2015). Using Bloom's Taxonomy to Evaluate the Cognitive Levels of Master Class Textbook's Questions. *English Language Teaching, 8*(5), 100–110. DOI: 10.5539/elt.v8n5p100

Atlas, S. (2023). *ChatGPT for higher education and professional development: A guide to conversational AI.* The University of Rhode Island. Retrieved from https://digitalcommons.uri.edu/cba_facpubs/548

Bahri, H., & Mahadi, T. S. T. (2016). Google translate as a supplementary tool for learning Malay: A case study at Universiti Sains Malaysia. *Advances in Language and Literary Studies, 7*(3), 161–167. https://files.eric.ed.gov/fulltext/EJ1127217.pdf

Bai, L., Liu, X., & Su, J. (2023). ChatGPT: The cognitive effects on learning and memory. *Brain-X, 1*(3), 1–9. DOI: 10.1002/brx2.30

Bloom, B. S., Englehart, M. D., Furst, E. J., Hill, W. H., & Krathwohl, D. R. (1956). *Taxonomy of Educational Objectives. The Classification of Educational Goals.* Longmans, Green and Co Ltd., Retrieved from https://web.archive.org/web/20201212072520id_/https://www.uky.edu/~rsand1/china2018/texts/Bloom%20et%20al%20-Taxonomy%20of%20Educational%20Objectives.pdf

Bok, E., & Cho, Y. (2023). Examining Korean EFL college students' experiences and perceptions of using ChatGPT as a writing revision tool. *Journal of English Teaching through Movies and Media, 24*(4), 15-27. DOI: https://doi.org/DOI: 10.16875/stem.2023.24.4.15

Bransen, D., & Govaerts, M. J. (2020). How to conceptualise self-regulated learning: Implications for measurement. *Medical Education, 54*(8), 684–686. DOI: 10.1111/medu.14183 PMID: 32311141

Chen, T. J. (2023). ChatGPT and other artificial intelligence applications speed up scientific writing. *Journal of the Chinese Medical Association, 10*(4), 1097. DOI: 10.1097/JCMA.0000000000000900 PMID: 36791246

Cheng, K., He, Y., Li, C., Xie, R., Lu, Y., Gu, S., & Wu, H. (2023). Talk with ChatGPT about the outbreak of Mpox in 2022: Reflections and suggestions from AI dimensions. *Annals of Biomedical Engineering, 51*(5), 870–874. DOI: 10.1007/s10439-023-03196-z PMID: 37031289

Chiu, T. K. (2024). A classification tool to foster self-regulated learning with generative artificial intelligence by applying self-determination theory: A case of ChatGPT. *Educational Technology Research and Development, 72*(4), 1–16. DOI: 10.1007/s11423-024-10366-w

Cotton, D. R., Cotton, P. A., & Shipway, J. R. (2024). Chatting and cheating: Ensuring academic integrity in the era of ChatGPT. *Innovations in Education and Teaching International, 61*(2), 228–239. DOI: 10.1080/14703297.2023.2190148

Curtis, N. (2023). To ChatGPT or not to ChatGPT? The impact of artificial intelligence on academic publishing. *The Pediatric Infectious Disease Journal, 42*(4), 275. DOI: 10.1097/INF.0000000000003852 PMID: 36757192

Dang, T. H. N. (2024). EFL Students' Perceptions of Peer Feedback in Writing Classes at a University in HCM City. *International Journal of Language Instruction, 3*(2), 18–28. DOI: 10.54855/ijli.24322

Dehouche, N. (2021). Plagiarism in the age of massive generative pre-trained transformers (GPT-3). *Ethics in Science and Environmental Politics, 2*, 17–23. DOI: 10.3354/esep00195

Dinh, A. D., & Pham, N. M. C. (2024). A Qualitative Study into How Non-English Major Students Emotionally Respond to Teacher-Written Feedback. *International Journal of TESOL & Education, 4*(3), 62–77. DOI: 10.54855/ijte.24434

Dong, L. (2024). "Brave New World" or not?: A mixed-methods study of the relationship between second language writing learners' perceptions of ChatGPT, behaviors of using ChatGPT, and writing proficiency. *Current Psychology (New Brunswick, N.J.), 43*(21), 1–15. DOI: 10.1007/s12144-024-05728-9

Du, J., & Alm, A. (2024). The Impact of ChatGPT on English for Academic Purposes (EAP) Students' Language Learning Experience: A Self-Determination Theory Perspective. *Education Sciences, 14*(7), 1–17. DOI: 10.3390/educsci14070726

Espejel, J. L., Ettifouri, E. H., Alassan, M. S. Y., Chouham, E. M., & Dahhane, W. (2023). GPT-3.5, GPT-4, or BARD? Evaluating LLMs reasoning ability in zero-shot setting and performance boosting through prompts. *Natural Language Processing Journal, 5*, 100032. DOI: 10.1016/j.nlp.2023.100032

Golan, R., Reddy, R., Muthigi, A., & Ramasamy, R. (2023). Artificial intelligence in academic writing: A paradigm-shifting technological advance. *Nature Reviews. Urology, 20*(6), 327–328. DOI: 10.1038/s41585-023-00746-x PMID: 36829078

Ho, P. X. P. (2024). Using ChatGPT in English Language Learning: A Study on I.T. Students' Attitudes, Habits, and Perceptions. *International Journal of TESOL & Education, 4*(1), 55–68. DOI: 10.54855/ijte.24414

Ho, T. L. U. (2024). Problems with Academic Writing Encountered by EFL Postgraduate Students at a University in the Mekong Delta. *International Journal of Language Instruction, 3*(1), 1–16. DOI: 10.54855/ijli.24311

Jansen, R. S., van Leeuwen, A., Janssen, J., & Kester, L. (2022). Exploring the link between self-regulated learning and learner behaviour in a massive open online course. *Journal of Computer Assisted Learning, 38*(4), 993–1004. DOI: 10.1111/jcal.12675

Kasneci, E., Seßler, K., Küchemann, S., Bannert, M., Dementieva, D., Fischer, F., Gasser, U., Groh, G., Günnemann, S., Hüllermeier, E., Krusche, S., Kutyniok, G., Michaeli, T., Nerdel, C., Pfeffer, J., Poquet, O., Sailer, M., Schmidt, A., Seidel, T., & Kasneci, G. (2023). ChatGPT for good? On opportunities and challenges of large language models for education. *Learning and Individual Differences*, *103*, 102274. Advance online publication. DOI: 10.1016/j.lindif.2023.102274

Keyue, X. (2023). Papers Concealing Usage of ChatGPT to be Rejected or Withdrawn. *Global Times*. Retrieved from https://www.globaltimes.cn/page/202302/1285398.shtml

Kim, J. (2020). Learning and teaching online during Covid-19: Experiences of student teachers in an early childhood education practicum. *International Journal of Early Childhood*, *52*(2), 145–158. DOI: 10.1007/s13158-020-00272-6 PMID: 32836369

Kohnke, L., Moorhouse, B. L., & Zou, D. (2023). ChatGPT for Language Teaching and Learning. *RELC Journal*, *54*(2), 537–550. DOI: 10.1177/00336882231162868

Krathwohl, D. R. (2002). A revision of Bloom's taxonomy: An overview. *Theory into Practice*, *41*(4), 212–218. DOI: 10.1207/s15430421tip4104_2

Liang, X., & Luo, J. (2024). Integration of ChatGPT into Project-based Learning: A Course Design Framework. *International Journal of Chinese Language Teaching*, *5*(1). Advance online publication. DOI: 10.46451/ijclt.20240104

Mhlanga, D. (2023). Open AI in education, the responsible and ethical use of ChatGPT towards lifelong learning. In *FinTech and artificial intelligence for sustainable development: The role of smart technologies in achieving development goals* (pp. 387–409). Springer Nature Switzerland., DOI: 10.1007/978-3-031-37776-1_17

Newton, P. M., Da Silva, A., & Peters, L. G. (2020). A pragmatic master list of action verbs for Bloom's taxonomy. *Frontiers in Education*, *5*, 1–6. DOI: 10.3389/feduc.2020.00107

Nguyen, T. T. H. (2023). EFL Teachers' Perspectives toward the Use of ChatGPT in Writing Classes: A Case Study at Van Lang University. *International Journal of Language Instruction*, *2*(3), 1–47. DOI: 10.54855/ijli.23231

Nurmayanti, N., & Suryadi, S. (2023). The Effectiveness of Using Quillbot in Improving Writing For Students Of English Education Study Program. *Jurnal Teknologi Pendidikan: Jurnal Penelitian dan Pengembangan Pembelajaran,* *8*(1), 32-40. DOI: https://doi.org/DOI: 10.33394/jtp.v8i1.6392

Omar, N., Haris, S. S., Hassan, R., Arshad, H., Rahmat, M., Zainal, N. F. A., & Zulkifli, R. (2012). Automated analysis of exam questions according to Bloom's taxonomy. *Procedia: Social and Behavioral Sciences*, *59*(7), 297–303. https://reader.elsevier.com/reader/sd/pii/S1877042812037263?token=6B2AC3430535A2B0AD0FBE49E8D873D4AC811B8638C4B9174025393B65885F9F213F4AE64D2D1D4482B682CCABEC4D66&originRegion=eu-west-1&originCreation=20230520140845. DOI: 10.1016/j.sbspro.2012.09.278

Open, A. I. (2023). What learning benefits can ChatGPT provide to students? What are the risks of using ChatGPT in academic environment? Retrieved from https://chat.openai.com/

Oxford, R. L. (2006). Task-based language teaching and learning: An overview. *Asian EFL journal, 8*(3), 94-121. ISSN 1738-1460

Ozfidan, B., El-Dakhs, D. A. S., & Alsalim, L. A. (2024). The use of AI tools in English academic writing by Saudi undergraduates. *Contemporary Educational Technology, 16*(4), ep527. DOI: 10.30935/cedtech/15013

Panadero, E. (2017). A review of self-regulated learning: Six models and four directions for research. *Frontiers in Psychology, 8*, 422. DOI: 10.3389/fpsyg.2017.00422 PMID: 28503157

Paul, R., & Elder, L. (1992). Critical thinking: What, why, and how. *New Directions for Community Colleges, 77*(2), 3–24. https://web.iitd.ac.in/~nkurur/2014-15/IIsem/cyl565/CriticalThinking.pdf. DOI: 10.1002/cc.36819927703

Perry, N. E., Yee, N., Mazabel, S., Lisaingo, S., & Maatta, E. (2017). Using self-regulated learning for creating inclusive classrooms for ethnically and linguistically diverse in Canada. In Cabrera, N. J., & Leyendecker, B. (Eds.), *Handbook of positive development of minority and youth* (pp. 361–385). Springer. DOI: 10.1007/978-3-319-43645-6_22

Pham, V. P. H. (2024). Vietnamese Graduate Students' Perspectives on the Use of ChatGPT. In Bui, H. P., Namaziandost, E. (eds) *Innovations in Technologies for Language Teaching and Learning.* Studies in Computational Intelligence, vol 1159. Springer, Cham. DOI: https://doi.org/DOI: 10.1007/978-3-031-63447-5_9

Pham, V. P. H., & Le, A. Q. (2024). ChatGPT in Language Learning: Perspectives from Vietnamese Students in Vietnam and the USA. *International Journal of Language Instruction, 3*(2), 59–72. DOI: 10.54855/ijli.24325

Phan, T., & Nguy n, V. (2023). Application of ChatGPT in Teaching, Research, and Management at the University Level. *Scientific Journal of Tan Trao University, 9*(3), 170–182. DOI: 10.51453/2354-1431/2023/974

Roohani, A., & Asiabani, S. (2015). Effects of self-regulated strategy development on EFL learners' reading comprehension and metacognition. *GEMA Online Journal of Language Studies, 15*(3), 31–49. ISSN 1675-8021.

Sabzalieva, E., & Valentini, A. (2023). *ChatGPT and artificial intelligence in higher education: quick start guide.* United Nations Educational, Scientific and Cultural Organization. Retrieved from https://eduq.info/xmlui/handle/11515/38828

Sari, A. N. (2024). Exploring the Potential of Using AI Language Models in Democratising Global Language Test Preparation. *International Journal of TESOL & Education, 4*(4), 111–126. DOI: 10.54855/ijte.24447

Schunk, D. H., & Zimmerman, B. J. (2007). Influencing children's self-efficacy and self-regulation of reading and writing through modeling. *Reading & Writing Quarterly, 23*(1), 7–25. DOI: 10.1080/10573560600837578

Šedlbauer, J., Činčera, J., Slavík, M., & Hartlová, A. (2024). Students' reflections on their experience with ChatGPT. *Journal of Computer Assisted Learning*, *40*(2), 1–9. DOI: 10.1111/jcal.12967

Shofiah, N., Putera, Z. F., & Solichah, N. (2023). Challenges and opportunities in the use of artificial intelligence in education for academic writing: A scoping review. In *Conference Psychology and Flourishing Humanity (PFH 2023)* (pp. 174-193). Atlantis Press. DOI: https://doi.org/DOI: 10.2991/978-2-38476-188-3_20

Solak, E. (2024). Revolutionizing language learning: How ChatGPT and AI are changing the way we learn languages. [IJTE]. *International Journal of Technology in Education*, *7*(2), 353–372. DOI: 10.46328/ijte.732

Song, C., & Song, Y. (2023). Enhancing academic writing skills and motivation: Assessing the efficacy of ChatGPT in AI-assisted language learning for EFL students. *Frontiers in Psychology*, *14*, 1–14. DOI: 10.3389/fpsyg.2023.1260843 PMID: 38162975

Stokel-Walker, C. (2022). AI bot ChatGPT writes smart essays-should academics worry? *Nature*, *12*. Advance online publication. DOI: 10.1038/d41586-022-04397-7 PMID: 36494443

Su, A. A. T., & Tran, T. H. N. (2024). The Benefits and Weaknesses of ChatGPT on Students' Learning Writing. *International Journal of AI in Language Education*, *1*(1), 20–28. DOI: 10.54855/ijaile.24112

Su ( ), J., & Yang ( ), W. (2023). Unlocking the Power of ChatGPT: A Framework for Applying Generative AI in Education. *ECNU Review of Education*, *6*(3), 355-366. https://doi.org/DOI: 10.1177/20965311231168423

Thorp, H. H. (2023). ChatGPT is fun, but not an author. *Science*, *379*(6630), 313. DOI: 10.1126/science.adg7879 PMID: 36701446

Tuyen, T., Ha, N. D. N., & Loc, N. (2024). Exploring The Relationship Between ChatGPT and Task-based Approach: Opportunities and Challenges. In *20th International Conference of the Asia Association of Computer-Assisted Language Learning (AsiaCALL 2023)* (pp. 22-36). Atlantis Press. DOI: https://doi.org/DOI: 10.2991/978-94-6463-396-2_3

Willis, J. (1996). *A framework for task-based learning*. Addison Wesley.

Wu, T. T., Lee, H. Y., Li, P. H., Huang, C. N., & Huang, Y. M. (2024). Promoting Self-Regulation Progress and Knowledge Construction in Blended Learning via ChatGPT-Based Learning Aid. *Journal of Educational Computing Research*, *61*(8), 3–31. DOI: 10.1177/07356331231191125

Xia, Q., Chiu, T. K. F., Chai, C. S., & Xie, K. (2023). The mediating effects of needs satisfaction on the relationships between prior knowledge and self-regulated learning through artificial intelligence chatbot. *British Journal of Educational Technology*, *54*(4), 967–986. DOI: 10.1111/bjet.13305

Xiao, Y., & Zhi, Y. (2023). An exploratory study of EFL learners' use of ChatGPT for language learning tasks: Experience and perceptions. *Languages (Basel, Switzerland)*, *8*(3), 212–224. DOI: 10.3390/languages8030212

Yetkin, R., & Özer-Altınkaya, Z. (2024). AI in the language classroom: Insights from pre-service English teachers. *E-Learning and Digital Media*, *0*(0), 20427530241267011. Advance online publication. DOI: 10.1177/20427530241267011

Zeb, A., Ullah, R., & Karim, R. (2024). Exploring the role of ChatGPT in higher education: Opportunities, challenges and ethical considerations. *The International Journal of Information and Learning Technology*, *41*(1), 99–111. DOI: 10.1108/IJILT-04-2023-0046

Zimmerman, B. J. (2002). Becoming a self-regulated learner: An overview. *Theory into Practice*, *41*(2), 64–70. DOI: 10.1207/s15430421tip4102_2

Chapter 11
Can Poe Help Us With Lexical Collocations?

Chieu Hoang Xuan Nguyen
Ho Chi Minh City University of Technology and Education, Vietnam

ABSTRACT

This primary research investigates the use of Poe AI, an AI-powered chatbot, in assisting Vietnamese EFL learners and teachers in learning and teaching lexical collocations. The study involved four teachers and twelve students in Ho Chi Minh City. The students were required to use Poe AI to complete a questionnaire consisting of a cloze task, a translation task, and a writing brainstorming task. The teachers were required to use Poe AI to prepare for a section of teaching lexical input to students. Open-ended questions about their perceptions regarding the use of Poe AI were included at the end of the questionnaires. The findings indicate that both learners and teachers were positive about the use of Poe AI in learning about lexical collocations and preparing materials for lexical input. It is suggested that Poe AI be introduced to learners to assist their collocation learning, while teachers should develop related skills to benefit from this tool. Simultaneously, more scientific research concerning their own teaching context should be carried out.

INTRODUCTION

Artificial intelligence has made headlines for the past decade. This technology has enabled the creation of many robots that can communicate with users, which are also known as chatbots. After the ground-breaking advent of ChatGPT, a lot of other chatbots have been created or trained to carry out specific tasks, and for distinct purposes. One of those newly developed chatbots is Poe AI, which was released in 2023.

According to Smutny and Schreiberova (2020), chatbots have gained increasing popularity as tools that are interactive and provide information when requested. Not only can they play the role of question answerers, they are also believed to have positive impacts on language learners around the world. Xu, Hong, Zhang, Jiang, and Liu (2023) pointed out that chatbots can replicate environments in which conversations are made, allowing students to practice different skills, especially communication ones. Besides, these chatbots are able to provide personalized interactions, which can greatly improve learners' language learning experience (Xu et al., 2023). Lodge, Thompson, and Corrin (2023) suggested

DOI: 10.4018/979-8-3693-7260-9.ch011

that language learning experiences can be customized with the use of AI-powered tools. This may also mean that language learners can benefit from the personalized interactions with these chatbots, which are trained in multiple languages including English, to enhance not only their communication skills but also other language aspects such as grammar and vocabulary. Speficially, the learning of lexical collocations which are chunks of words that are arbitrarily used together is expected to be assisted by the use of AI-powered chatbots. In addition to being a potentially useful AI-powered tool for learners to acquire lexical collocations, Poe AI is also expected to provide teachers with assistance during the process of teaching lexical collocations.

Although the merits of AI-powered chatbots such as Poe AI are recognized in many parts of the world, there have been controversies and concerns related to the challenges these chatbots pose to different stakeholders in educational settings. These concerns include academic integrity (Barrett & Pack, 2023), and over-reliance (Neji, Boughattas, & Ziadi, 2023). This begs serious discussions upon institutional adjustments for the use of AI-powered tools, especially amidst the situation lacking consensus on the best way to apply them in education (Barrett & Pack, 2023).

Moreover, the use of AI-powered chatbots and tools is not widely seen in the context of Vietnam, especially in the field of language teaching and learning, as little has been done to investigate this at different educational levels in Vietnam. Although there have been a number of studies on the use of ChatGPT and similar tools in tertiary level in Vietnam (e.g., Duong & Le, 2024; Nguyen & Pham, 2024; Pham & Le, 2024), there has been extremely little research focusing on secondary students. This highlights the gap of literature and the present study can contribute to narrowing the gap by providing insights into whether learners of secondary and tertiary levels in Vietnam can learn lexical collocations through the use of Poe AI.

LITERATURE REVIEW

The Merits of AI-Powered Chatbots in Language Learning and Teaching

The uses of chatbots playing the roles of information deliverers and question answerers have not been uncommon (Smutny & Schreiberova, 2020) since the advent of the very first chatbot, ELIZA, developed by Joseph Weizenbaum (1966) almost 60 years ago. These days, educational contexts have witnessed the increasing popularity of chatbots in motivating learners on their scientific learning journey, assisting first-year university students with their new environment (Carayannopoulos, 2018) and helping educators and teachers around the world conduct and facilitate in-class learning activities with even large class sizes (Schmulian & Coetzee, 2019). Chatbots are believed to be not only an instant respondent to students' inquiry or request for help (Xu, Wang, Collins, Lee, & Warschauer, 2021), but they are also providers of authentic, natural language, which is extremely useful for students to conduct daily conversation practice (Fryer, Ainley, Thompson, Gibson, & Sherlock, 2017). Another impressive role that these chatbots can play is providing thorough feedback, supporting procedures of assessment (Jia, Chen, Ding, & Ruan, 2012), which usually accounts for a large part in teachers' workload.

Not only do chatbots serve common pedagogical purposes in a language classroom, but they are also believed to provide aid in classes in which English translation may be useful. According to Stapleton and Kin (2019), an AI-driven translator can provide the translations with a higher level of accuracy. Furthermore, these researchers also found that AI-driven tools can provide learners with excellent assistance in terms of vocabulary and grammar, especially when it comes to composition writing. These tools are also said to help learners, especially university students, to correct their writing, improve their lexical range and grammatical range. In the study conducted by Fithriani (2023), students showed positive attitude towards the use of QuillBot in an EFL academic writing course as this tool helped them improve their arguments, correct their grammatical errors and suggest better language use.

Besides all of the aforementioned uses of AI-powered chatbots in assisting learners and teachers in in-class activities, as long as electronic devices and internet connection are available, they are believed to become amazing companions for learners and teachers outside the classroom. For learners, these bots are going to enhance their autonomy and allow them to practice and study at their own pace and convenience, while for teachers, their workload, especially when including repetitive and tedious tasks, can be greatly reduced, which benefit teachers psychologically. With such amazing abilities, chatbots are considered to be great supporters in constructing an interactive and authentic language environment which encourages students to actively learn and make progress, achieving learning outcomes more effectively (Wang, Petrina, & Feng, 2017). According to previous researchers, a chatbot that can serve in a language learning context needs to have a number of common features.

Firstly, a useful chatbot for educational purposes should offer easy availablity, which means that students are able to have access to it at anytime during the week. They can practice their language skills, inquire about a language project or learn additional vocabulary at their own pace and whenever they are ready to. This feature sets them apart because students' partners or peers may not offer the same availability and flexibility (Haristiani, 2019; Winkler & Soellner, 2018). One more thing to add is that their peers may not have the capibility of providing them with extra language knowledge, which has to have a high level of accuracy and suitability (Fryer, Nakao, & Thompson, 2019), because a chatbot is programmed with the use of natural language, which is the target language of all students.

Secondly, it is obvious that a useful, educational chatbot needs to have the ability to provide information of a broad range of topics such as idiomatic language, pronunciation explanation and even suggested ideas for writing tasks. This allows the students to inquire freely until they are satisfied with the amount of information they receive, which can help them complete a certain academic task or simply for extensive learning activities. Last but not least, these chatbots should be supporters and assistants that never fall prey to fatigue, irritation and stress so that they can help students, and even teachers to escape work that has a high level of repetition (Fryer et al., 2019; Kim, 2018). Teachers may feel obliged to answer frequently-asked questions from students about language or a random topic, or students may feel the urge to ask about things they cannot memorize well or they still have not managed to comprehend, and these chatbots can become helpful assistants, providing answers instantly without feeling exhausted or challenged. In order to effectively investigate the use of AI-powered tools in educational contexts, it is important to have a framework.

According to Huang, Hew and Fryer (2022), there are two primary aspects to investigate: usability and utility. Usability is the ability of a system or tool to allow its users to achieve particular goals and complete certain tasks with efficiency and satisfaction (Kirschner, Strijbos, Kreijns, & Beers, 2004). Meanwhile, utility is the functionality of that specific tool or system as it offers necessary elements, materials or functions to meet the needs of the users. Combined, these can help determine whether a system or tool is sufficiently useful for users (Kirschner et al., 2004). According to Kirschner et al. (2004), while usability deals with technological affordances, utility can be defined by the pedagogical or educational affordances and social affordances (see Figure 1). These refer to the ability of a chatbot to serve pedgogical and social purposes such as providing knowledge and responding to a learner during a conversation practice.

Regarding specifically the technological uses, an AI-driven chatbot should offer users timely responses while interacting. The interaction with chatbots can help enhance learners' autonomy because of their heightened satisfaction with their own self-learning space. Moreover, not only are chatbots required to instantly respond to a question of request of the user, but it is supposed to allow users to access it at their own convenience, which means that learners can definitely practice their language skills with the chatbots anywhere and anytime. Besides timeliness, chatbots are equipped with corpus data of the natural language, which is English to EFL learners, so the environment that these chatbots provide is authentic and native-like. Next, a chatbot should be easy to use, or user-friendly. The interface should make it easy for users to navigate, while the availability of the chatbot should be provided in different forms, from a web-page to a mobile application, so that learners can conveniently access on any device. Finally, the chabot should be able to provide users with personalized experience, which means that different learners may have different approaches or registers, but require similar responses.

Figure 1. Affordance perspective

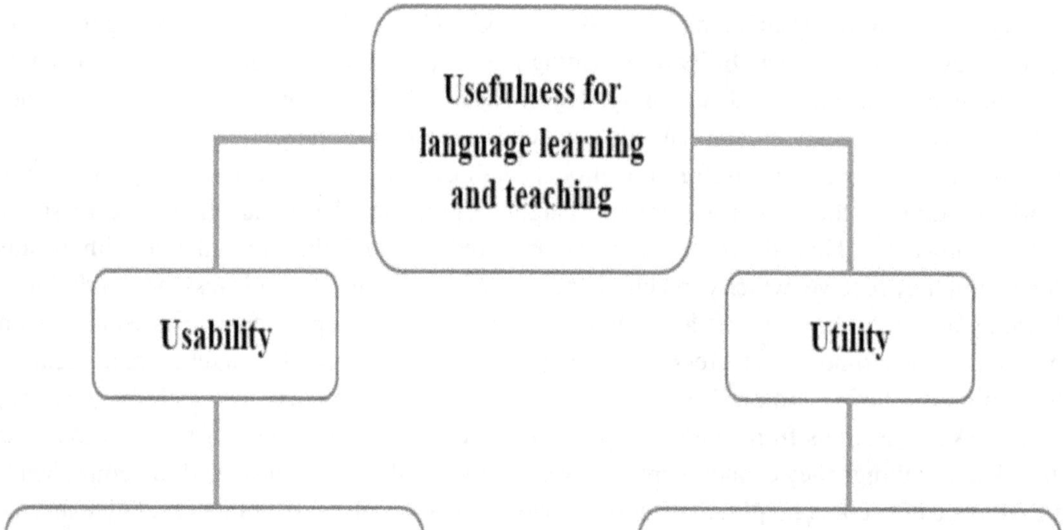

(Huang et al, 2022, adapted from Kirschner et al., 2004)

Concerning pedagogical uses, Huang et al. (2022) investigate the particular ways that chatbots have been utilized in to assist learners with their language learning, along with the impact of such on their behavioral and cognitive outcomes. Huang et al. (2022)'s exhaustive review of the literature demonstrates that chatbots have been used in five main pedagogical ways. Firstly, they have been used as interlocutor to help learners practice their language skills. Learners ask and receive responses for their input. For example, in Ayeoun et al.'s (2019) and Kim's (2016) studies, learners interacted with chatbots to practice making discursive speeches about daily topics such as daily routines, travelling … Besides, chatbots were implemented to assist students' learning of four language skills. The learning topics are related to vocabulary, grammar, academic pragmatics, and meaning negotiation strategies. For instance, in Jia and Ruan's (2008) study, learners used chatbots to help them with grammar through a series of fill-in-the-banks tasks. Most interestingly, Tegos, Demetriadis and Tsiatsos (2014) find that chatbots can help facilitate a group discussion by providing prompts for learners after determining which student may need more help than the others. Secondly, chatbots can provide ideal simulation for a number of fun in-class activities such as role-play (Ayedoun et al., 2019) in which they act as a character to elicit answers and responses from the students. Thirdly, chatbots are found to play a crucial role in the process of knowledge transmission as they can become teacher assistant to deliver certain instructional materials (Tegos et al., 2014). Fourthly, chatbots are similar to a helpline thanks to which learners can get the answers to any of their language problems (Wang et al., 2017). Lastly, chatbots can determine suitable materials and recommendations for learners according to their proficiency level (Willis, 2019).

Overall, AI-powered chatbots have been found to provide not only information, but also assistance to different stakeholders due to their access to huge datasets during their procedures of training with Large Language Models (LLMs), Custom Language Models (CLMs), Natural Language Processing (NLP) and Machine Learning (ML). These chatbots are believed to hold fascinating potential in the field of language learning and teaching.

The Demerits of AI-Powered Chatbots in Language Learning and Teaching

Despite chatbots' fascinating uses in educational contexts, that they still have a number of weaknesses is inevitable. With regards to their features, chief of these is how fleeting a chatbot can maintain students' excitement while using. The effect of its novelty may not be long-lasting after the students have exhaustively experienced all of the features (Fryer et al., 2019; Ayedoun, Hayashi, & Seta, 2019). Similarly, chatbots' low emotional connection and depth of conversation may hinder learners from being engaged in the learning process. This highlights that their development has to be continuous (Nguyen & Pham, 2023). Another drawback related to the developers of chatbot is that it is relatively challenging to keep updating and upgrading the language of chatbots in conversations to maintain the quality and interactivity (Brandtzaeg & Følstad, 2018). About the reliability of the information they offer, although they can replicate dialogues, their responses could include minor mistakes or false information, which causes it to fail to support students' learning (Ghafar, 2023; Rudolph et al., 2023).

In addition to issues related to the chatbots' programmed features, Barrett and Pack (2023) pointed out that the use of chatbots has been banned by many institutions due to the concern about academic integrity. With the ability of instantly responding to a prompt or request, AI-powered chatbots have become useful tools for learners to carry out tasks and have assignments done, which raises a serious question about ethics. Besides, over-reliance on these tools is seen as a problem (Neji et al., 2023). This begs serious discussions upon institutional adjustments for the use of AI-powered tools, especially amidst the situation lacking consensus on the best way to apply them in education (Barrett & Pack, 2023).

According to Le et al. (2022), in the context of Vietnam, the integration of such chatbots into Vietnamese classrooms has not been advanced due to concerns about infrastructure and cost. Rudoph et al. (2023) further emphasize that to successfully apply AI-powered chatbots in Vietnamese classroom, an awareness of how these work should be adjusted appropriately to the context of Vietnam.

Application of AI-Powered Tools in Language Education in Asian Contexts

According to Hong's (2023), foreign language learning and teaching may be significantly revolutionized by the application of chatbots such as ChatGPT, especially in China. It is in the area of customized learning experiences that ChatGPT is able to offer various research prospects, such as how AI-driven tools can impact learners' language acquisition, which is also a guiding question of the present study.

The study conducted by Japoshvili-Ghvinashvili and Suleman (2023) in Pakistan discovers that the use of an AI-powered chatbot in classroom activities contributes to learners' improvement of language skills through the provision of individualized feedback. This has postitively motivated the learners, resulting in better engagement in the classroom. Moreover, official guidelines on how to comprehensively integrate this technology in the classroom is necessary to minimize the risks involved. Similarly, a study conducted by Rakhmonov and Kurbonova (2023) in Uzbekistan reveals that learners were greatly encouraged to interact with peers and teachers in the classroom more, thanks to the use of AI technologies.

Pham and Le (2024) conducted a study about Vietnamese and American university learners' perceptions of the use of ChatGPT for their language acquisition. The findings reveal that learners have positive attitude towards ChatGPT's ability of providing instant answers to their queries, ideas for group discussions and aiding explanation of topics by their teachers. However, there is no consensus about whether ChatGPT offers useful assistance in reinforcing recently acquired knowledge. Also, in comparison with their instructors, ChatGPT is not rated better, with a high level of consensus. Although most learners agree that ChatGPT provides them with an empowering and encouraging environment, as well as sources for checking the authenticity of the information, their perspectives differ on whether ChatGPT can effectively lower their anxiety in the classroom and engage them in learning activities outside the classroom.

In a study conducted in a university in Vietnam, Nguyen (2023) finds that most of the English teachers agreed that the use of an AI-driven chatbot can help their students improve their productive skills. They were also positive about the potential application of that chatbot in their writing classes. Nguyen (2023) also emphasizes the need for professional training for instructors in order to raise their awareness of the shortcomings and challenges associated with AI technologies. As a result, guidelines for appropriate chatbot use can be proposed. Furthermore, it is necessary to realize that little has been done to explore the use of AI-powered chatbots by Vietnamese learners at all educational levels, especially secondary levels. The current study aims to explore how Vietnamese EFL high school students can learn lexical collocations, as well as how teachers prepare for their lessons on collocations through the use of Poe AI.

Poe AI: A Newly Developed AI Product

Poe AI (Platform for Open Exploration) is an AI product developed by Quora. It is a platform that allow users to inquire and receive prompt answers, and have conversations with different AI-powered chatbots. Currently, Poe AI is available on different operating systems such as iOS, Android and Windows, and web.

Poe AI is a combination of different models of AI bots trained by different companies to conduct different tasks, as the AI ecosystem is growing. One of the most important features for an AI model to become useful for public use is its speed and a user-friendly interface, which are not an easy task even for big technology companies. However, Poe AI is believed to fill this gap and reach a large audience of online users.

According to a blog article by GenApe AI (2024), although the process of using Poe AI is relatively similar to that of ChatGPT, Poe AI provides users with multiple models, catering different contexts and user needs, which means that users can select any AI model that suits their needs before starting to inquire. This also indicates that it is completely possible for users to create a custom bot to serve a specific purpose. Another plus point of Poe AI is that it requires no registration, subscription or login. It is convenient because users can visit Poe official website, log in directly and easily with a Google account and start using it. When compared with ChatGPT, Poe AI can gain more popularity for its convenience of allowing users to access different AI models from one single website, and its sensitivity to the topics mentioned in the answers, which enables it to offer follow-up questions and a comprehensive experience.

What is a Collocation?

Why can *curiosity* be *aroused*, but *attention* cannot? Instead, we can *draw* or *catch* somebody's *attention*. These are considered the typical combinations of words, which are naturally understood and utilized by native speakers. According to Lewis (1997), collocations are the backbone of his Lexical Approach, which stresses the notion of *chunking* and that *ready-made chunks* are said to be more easily retrieved by students as they are stored in their long-term memory.

Benson et al. (1986) uses combinations with the noun *murder* to explain what a free combination and an idiom are like. Regarding free combinations, *to condemn a murder* and *to discuss a murder* are two of many acceptable combinations of this noun. Meanwhile, *to scream blue murder* is an idiom including this node noun, and the meaning of this whole expression (to scream loudly) does not reflect the meaning of each constituent part in the expression, making it a frozen one. Existing between the two ends of this spectrum are loosely fixed combinations, or also known as collocations whose (1) meanings reflect the meaning of each component in the combination. This characteristic sets it apart from idioms. Other points worth noting are that collocations are (2) frequently used combinations and (3) psychologically salient, or in other words, spring up to one's mind immediately, which sets collocations apart from free combinations. By and large, Benson et al. (1986) concludes that fixed combinations, recurrent combinations or collocations are fixed, identifiable, and non-idiomatic phrases and chunks.

Two major approaches to determining whether a combination is considered a collocation are phraseological approach and statistical approach. While the former identifies a collocation using its restricted suitability, the latter identifies a collocation based on statistical measures, such as the frequency of a word combination's co-occurrence in a corpus. According to phraseologists, a collocation is a word combination possessing a particular grammatical pattern in the first place (Cowie, 1994; Nesselhauf,

2005), in which a base is always present. Meanwhile, the statistical approach indicates that collocations can be identified by determining the co-occurrence of words with a level of frequency (Durrant, 2009; Sinclair, 1991). Statistical measures such as Mutual Information (MI) score, t-score, Log Dice … have been adopted in a number of previous studies to determine the strength of a certain word combination and the likelihood of it co-occurring rather than by chance.

Regarding the classification of collocations, there are two categories: grammatical collocations and lexical collocations. In this study, I focused on lexical collocations because these seem to be more challenging than their grammatical counterparts for the following reasons. First, while grammatical collocations may follow a number of syntactic riles, lexical collocations can vary. Second, the way two or more content words are combined can solely be attributed to arbitrariness, which means that it is not easy to explain why this node word must go with this collocating word, instead of others. Third, cultural nuances can be a blockage to one learner's understanding and acquisition of a certain collocation, especially the one whose equivalent in the learner's first language does not exist. According to Benson et al. (1997), there are six sub-types of lexical collocations; however, the seventh sub-type, *noun 1 of noun 2* was then added (Hausmann, 1999). Hence, there are seven sub-types of lexical collocations:

1. adjective + noun (e.g., clear sky)
2. verb + noun (e.g., conduct a study)
3. noun + noun (e.g., success story)
4. adverb + adjective (e.g., physically disabled)
5. verb + adverb, or adverb + verb (e.g., run quickly)
6. noun (subject) + verb (action) (e.g., bomb explodes)
7. noun 1 of noun 2 (e.g., a colony of ants)

Collocation Learning and Teaching in Vietnam

Teaching collocations is undoubtedly necessary. In Bahns and Eldaw's (1993) study, the findings suggested that the learners found it difficult to paraphrase the target collocations, although they succeeded in their translation task. Moreover, although the learners may seem to comprehend the sentences containing collocations, they may not be able to produce the same collocations in the context where they need those, indicating a gap between their receptive and productive lexical knowledge. All of the results led to a conclusion that EFL learners' knowledge of vocabulary and knowledge of collocations are not parallel, which means that even when a learner may manage to use single lexical items, it does not mean that the learner may produce semantically and grammatically correct collocations.

The explanation to this is that learners do not pay attention to the collocations because they are not taught explicitly. This can be witnessed in the Vietnamese context because the emphasis of English learning and teaching in the Asia-Pacific area and Vietnam specifically is still put on reading skills and grammar learning (Nunan, 2003). Therefore, Bahns and Eldaw (1993) concluded that it is crucial that collocations be taught explicitly so that learners can remember and produce collocations that do not have a paraphrase, or collocations that do not have a degree of equivalence between their mother tongue and the target language. Furthermore, to successfully acquire a lexical item, besides focusing on the link between the form and the meaning of a word as most Vietnamese EFL teachers are, more emphasis should be placed on collocations.

Regarding approaches to teaching collocations, Lewis (1997) confirms that teachers should not attempt to break a collocation into smaller pieces to figure out the meaning, and looking at the collocation as a whole is highly recommended, while learners should be encouraged to think of using collocations in their expressions. Various techniques to teach vocabulary such as songs, storytelling (Nguyen, 2016) and translation have been adopted by Vietnamese EFL teachers. Besides, Vietnamese EFL learners are found to acquire vocabulary mostly from extensive reading (Vu & Peters, 2021, 2022), audiovisual input (Nguyen & Boers, 2018) and input-based, as well as output-based tasks (Duong, Perez, Desmet, & Peters, 2020). Interestingly, computer-assisted learning has been found to be employed to teach and learn vocabulary (Bui, Boers, & Coxhead, 2019). Above all, explicit instruction still plays a major role (Le-Thi, Rodgers, & Pelicer-Sánchez, 2018).

Lewis (1997) suggested particular approaches and types of practice exercises to teach collocations in classrooms. Firstly, teachers should pay attention to the most optimal way to help learners build lexicons by analyzing their needs and situtations. The second suggestion is that teachers should comprehend the arbitrariness of collocations, which is seen in many collocations, as learners may raise questions about this. Another suggestion is that the act of noticing and recording collocations or expressions should be done in groups, rather than individually. More importantly, a notebook for collocations and expressions is encouraged as students can easily re-access those and the use of dictionaries is advised. Lewis (1997) also advised that useful collocations containing the new word should be taught along with the new lexical item to enlarge their vocabulary repertoire. Then, learners are required to practise the chunk orally before writing it down into their lexical notebook. Last but not least, a variety of exercise types should be designed and provided for the students to help with their revision of the target collocations, such as cloze passages, collocation grids, matching exercises, and collocation maps.

Besides, there are a number of materials that can facilitate and enhance EFL learners; acquisition of lexical collocations. The use of dictionaries (Alhaisoni, 2016; Cao, 2018; Lew & Doroszewska, 2009; Rahimi & Mohemi, 2012) and games (Rasti-Behbahani, 2021; Trinh, Nguyen, & Tran, 2022) to assist learners' vocabulary processing and acquisition has been investigated in previous studies. The use of dictionaries, especially electronic dictionaries, has been proven to exert positive impacts on learners' retention of lexical items in general, which facilitates EFL learners' acquisition of vocabulary in general. According to Trinh, Tran, Vo, and Huynh (2021), electronic dictionaries, or online dictionaries can contribute to the vocabulary learning process, especially the acquisition of collocations (Cao, 2018), because of their flexibility and interactivity. Learners are able to access the online dictionaries as long as internet connection is available. Moreover, learners' exposure to concordances further improves their understanding of the meaning of a collocation and the context in which the collocation can be used. With regards to digital games, Trinh et al. (2022) found that when learning vocabulary, learners can be greatly assisted if games are provided both in and outside the classroom. This agrees with the findings in Rasti-Behbahani's (2021) study on the effectiveness of games on learners' ability to recall the form and the meaning of lexical items thanks to the visual aids and audio files embedded in the games. Overall, the use of supporting materials and tools to teach collocations has been proven to positively influence learners' vocabulary learning process in general, and collocation learning specifically.

METHODOLOGY

This study adopted the mixed-methods approach to investigate the use of AI-powered chatbot Poe AI in assisting EFL learners in learning lexical collocations. In this study, questionnaires for Vietnamese EFL learners and Vietnamese EFL teachers were developed and distributed, and a number of open-ended questions at the end of the questionnaires aimed to collect learners' and teachers' perceptions of Poe AI.

Research Questions

This study was conducted with a view to investigating whether Poe AI chatbot is useful in helping EFL learners learn lexical collocations and teachers prepare lexical materials for vocabulary sections in their lessons. The perceptions of both learners and teachers were then explored. The research questions of this study are as follows:

1. How effectively does Poe AI help learners learn lexical collocations?
2. How effectively does Poe AI help teachers prepare lexical input materials to teach lexical collocations?
3. What are the perceptions of learners and teachers about Poe AI, in terms of technological affordances and pedagogical affordances?

Research Design and Instruments

In order to determine whether Poe AI is an effective tool to provide EFL learners with assistance while learning collocations, this study adopted the explanatory mixed-methods approach, collecting both quantitative data and qualitative data.

Two online questionnaires were utilized to collect both quantitative and qualitative data. In the questionnaire for learners, there are four main parts. The first part is a cloze-text task, which requires the learners to use Poe AI to find the missing collocating word of the word in bold. The most important thing to note is that the missing collocating word is the same in three sentences in one set. An example of a set of sentences in Part 1 of the questionnaire is shown below (see Figure 2).

Figure 2. Example of a question in Part 1 of the questionnaire

1. The child's impressive ____ **ability** to solve complex math problems at a young age surprised her teachers.

2. Regularly challenging oneself with puzzles and brain teasers can help maintain and improve ____ **skills** as we age.

3. Proper nutrition, nurturing relationships, and engaging activities are all important factors in a child's ____ **development** during the early years.

In this example, the missing collocating word in the adjective *cognitive* because *cognitive* collocates with all three nouns *ability, skills* and *development.* Also, *cognitive* fits all the blanks contextually.

All the collocations investigated in this first section were taken from the Academic Collocation List by Ackermann and Chen (2013). First, the researcher visited the site https://www.eapfoundation.com/vocab/academic/acl/ where the Academic Collocation List is provided for free public access. The most important advantage of accessing this list on this site is that the list of the collocations can be sorted either by headword, by collocation type (as presented in Figure 3) or by frequency.

Figure 3. Collocation types in the Academic Collocation List

- adjective + noun (1773 in total)
- adverb + adjective (124 collocations)
- adverb + verb (17)
- adverb + past particle (124)
- noun + noun (62)
- verb + adjective (30)
- verb + adverb (29)
- verb + noun (310)

(Ackermann & Chen, 2013)

This allows the researcher to conveniently find different collocations of one collocating word. For this step, the researcher decided to look up the collocations by headword so that a broader picture of all collocating words of one node word can be provided. Headwords that collocate with a number of different words of parts of speech were looked up. For example, the headword *academic* appears in 19 adjective-noun collocations. However, to diversify the types of lexical collocations in the sentences, for headwords that are adjective, adverb and noun, the researcher also attempted to look up collocations of different types containing those headwords. For instance, an adjective can not only collocate with a noun, but it can also collocate with an adverb. A noun can not only collocate with a verb in a verb-noun collocation, but it can also collocate with an adjective in an adjective-noun collocation. Similarly, an adverb can be paired with a verb and an adjective. This is to ensure that learners are exposed to all types of lexical collocations and instill in them the awareness that a collocating word can collocate with different words of different parts of speech, creating many collocations. Another point to consider is that all inflectional morphological errors are disregarded because this research study only investigates whether learners can effectively learn about collocations, not whether they can produce the collocations without grammatical errors. All of the sentences presented in this part were suggested by Poe AI. The reason for the choice of a cloze task is because this was one of the most important instruments to investigate learners' knowledge of collocations, as used in Bahns and Eldaw's (1993) study. Bahns and Eldaw (1993) examined the extent to which verb-noun collocations were correctly produced in cloze and translation tests. They investigated the extent to which the freedom of the translation task would allow the learners to express meaning of the collocational phrases (verb-noun collocations) in correct English even if the collocation is not known to them, compared with the cloze task.

The second part is a translation task, which requires the learners to use Poe AI to translate a short text in Vietnamese into English, before extracting the English collocations that match the highlighted Vietnamese collocations in the given text. An example of a question in Part 2 of the questionnaire is demonstrated below (see Figure 4).

Figure 4. Example of a question in Part 2 of the questionnaire

Ông Nhật Chiêu không chỉ dịch và giới thiệu các bài thơ, tác giả lồng ghép những phân tích sâu sắc về lịch sử, văn hóa, cảm thức thiên nhiên, triết lý, lý tưởng thẩm mỹ của người Nhật, giúp độc giả hiểu về ngữ cảnh và ý nghĩa của từng bài.

The English translation of the text in Figure 4 provided by Poe AI is as follows:

"Mr. Nhat Chieu not only translates and introduces poems and authors, but he also incorporates in-depth analyses of the history, culture, sense of nature, philosophy, and aesthetic ideals of the Japanese people, helping readers understand the context and meaning of each piece."

The English collocations that match the highlighted Vietnamese collocations are *in-depth analyses* (phân tích sâu s c), *sense of nature* (c m th c thiên nhiên) and *aesthetic ideals* (lý tư ng th m m). All of the texts in Part 2 were taken from newspaper articles retrieved from www.vnexpress.net. Before choosing a certain extract for this section, the researcher decided to choose a number of news articles, especially descriptive ones, as they are closely related to the genre of reading passages in the IELTS, which may be familiar to all of the participants. Moreover, the researcher had to read through different articles to ensure that the level of difficulty of such extracts should range from B1 to C1, according to the

Common European Framework of Reference for Languages (CEFR). In order to do this, the researcher input a chosen extract from the aforementioned online news source into Poe AI and retrieve the English translation. Then, Cathoven tool was utilized (www.cathoven.com) to check for the difficulty level of the English translation. The general difficulty level should range from B1-C1, while the clause level and the sentence level should range from B1-B2 so that it does not cause too much trouble for the participants while reading. Next, the vocabulary level should be *Native* to ensure that the language provided by Poe AI is authentic and in the most natural and native-like form. The use of this AI-driven tool assisted the researcher to carry out such task with ease and in a time-saving manner.

The third part is a writing brainstorm task, which requires the learners to use Poe AI to research for information and ideas for an IELTS Writing Task 2 question. The learners were required to extract the collocations from the information provided by Poe AI. The reason underlying the choice of this task is that Lexical Range is one of the four criteria in scoring an IELTS essay, according to the IELTS Writing Band Descriptors for public access. Finally, the fourth part is a section of four open-ended questions preliminarily investigating learners' perceptions of the tool Poe AI in learning collocations. This section is followed by an invitation to participate in a semi-structured interview, and only participants that confirm their willingness to participate in the interview were contacted after the questionnaire was completed.

In the online questionnaire for teachers, there are two parts. The first part requires the teachers to pick a lesson unit from the textbook they currently use and use Poe AI to research for collocations related to the lexical items introduced in that lesson, as well as example sentences for the collocations. The second part includes five open-ended questions investigating the teachers' perceptions of Poe AI in assisting them to prepare to teach collocations.

Conceptual Framework

To explore learners' and teachers' perceptions, the researcher adapted the conceptual framework developed by Kirschner et al. (2004). In this study, social affordances are not an aspect to investigate because learning collocations in this study involves no social interactions among learners or between learners and the chatbot, or Poe AI, and the learner participants and teacher participants in this study used Poe AI only to obtain information, rather than to conduct conversations for practice. Although communicative elements such as asking and answering questions, or clarifying a statement were needed, they are only the vehicles to help the users receive the information they wanted. Therefore, only technological affordances and pedagogical affordances are explored, thanks to which it is possible to determine whether Poe AI is useful and effective in helping learners learn collocations and teachers teach collocation or not (see Figure 5).

Figure 5. The conceptual framework of the present study

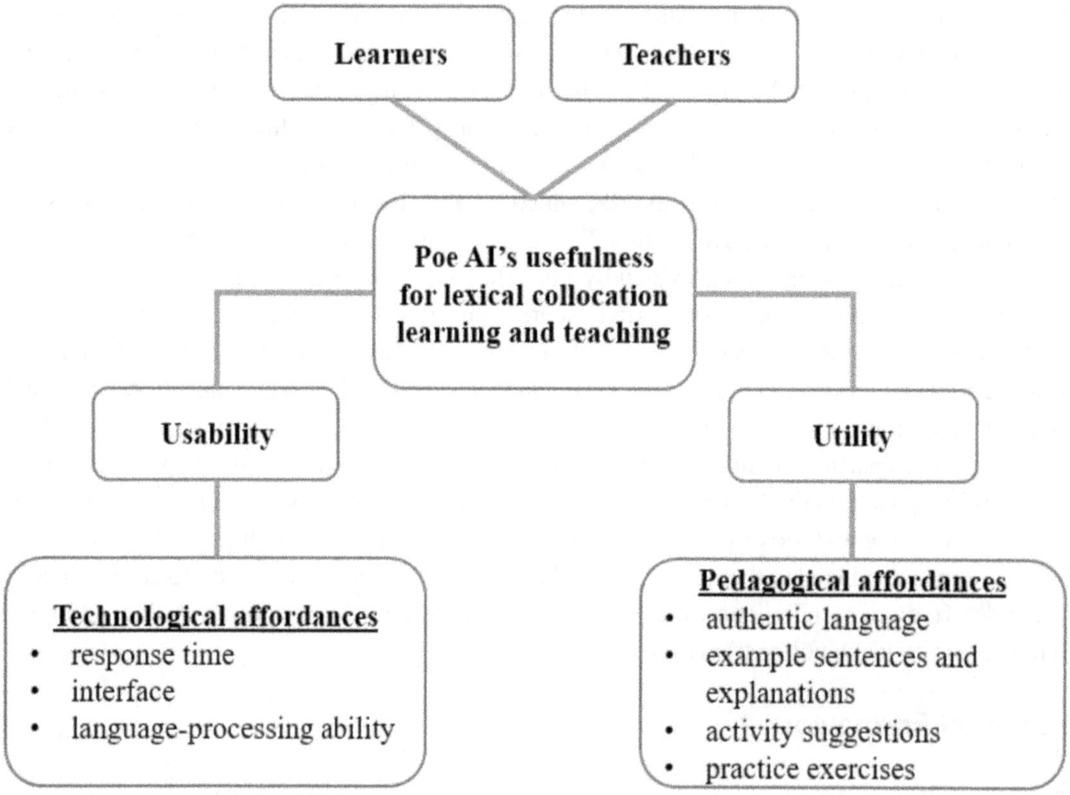

Participants

There are twelve EFL learners and four teachers participating in answering the questionnnaire. Among the twelve EFL learners, there are two college non-majored students coming from two different universities in Ho Chi Minh City. The other eight students are high school students from Ho Chi Minh City as well. The majority of the learner participants have been exposed to the English language for more than eight years (see Table 1).

Figure 6. Demographic information of learner participants

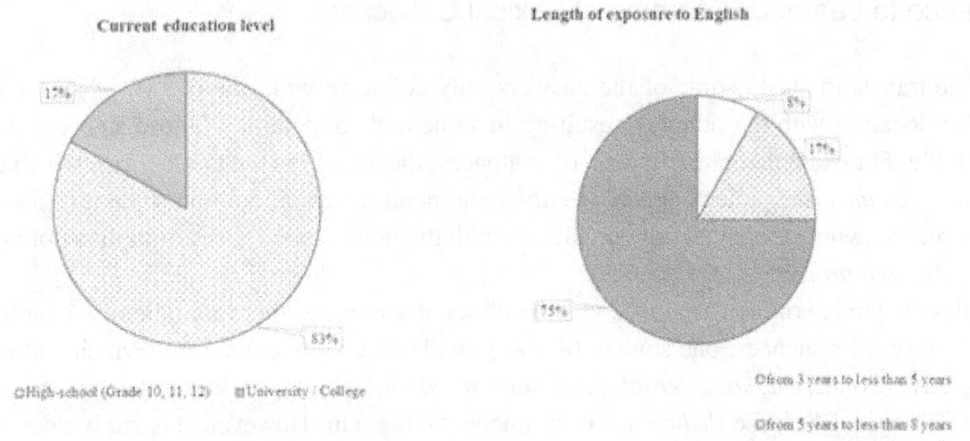

Concerning the teacher participants, three out of four teachers hold the Master's degree in TESOL. All four teachers currently conduct General English courses and half of the teacher participants carry out IELTS preparation courses to high school students and university students (see Table 1).

Table 1. Demographic information of teacher participants

	Years of experience	Students' proficiency level	Conducts courses in
Teacher 1	3 years, with Master's degree in TESOL)	Beginner Pre-intermediate	General English Cambridge KET - PET
Teacher 2	5 years, with Master's degree in TESOL	Intermediate Upper-intermediate	General English Cambridge KET – PET IELTS
Teacher 3	3 years, with Bachelor's degree in TESOL	Beginner Pre-intermediate	General English Cambridge KET - PET
Teacher 4	5 years, with Master's degree in TESOL	Intermediate Upper-intermediate	General English Cambridge KET – PET IELTS

FINDINGS

Perceived Merits of Poe AI

Assistance to Learners' Learning of Lexical Collocation

For the translation task, some of the answers only collocate with one or two of the given words, without collocating with the other(s), resulting in some odd collocations. Those answers are ruled as unacceptable. For example, in the first set of sentences, the answer is the noun *effort*, which collocates with adjective *concerted*, adjective *considerable*, and noun *research*, but one student (8.3%) provided the noun *project*, while this noun only collocates with the noun *research*, resulting in a noun-noun collocation *research project*.

Besides the predetermined answer keys for each set of sentences, there are other acceptable answers. For the first set of sentences, one student (8.3%) provided the noun *dedication*, which collocates with both adjectives *concerted*, *considerable*, and noun *research*, although it does not grammatically fit the blank in Sentence 1 because *dedication* is an uncountable noun. However, this study does not regard grammatical errors, so that can be overlooked. In the end, there are three acceptable answers to the first set of sentences (see Table 2). Overall, learner participants' correct answers to four sets of sentences in the fill-in-the-blank task accounted for more than 60%.

Table 2. Answers to the fill-in-the-blank items

Items	Correct answer	Students' attempts
1. The city government, local businesses, and community organizations made a **concerted** _____ to clean up and revitalize the downtown area. 2. Completing the home renovation project required **considerable** _____ from the homeowners, who spent several months carefully planning carrying out the various tasks involved. 3. The team of scientists has devoted a significant **research** _____ over the past two years to studying the effects of climate change on the local ecosystem.	effort	Acceptable: *dedication, collaboration* Unacceptable: *project*
4. It is a _____ **assumption** that all teenagers are rebellious and irresponsible, but in reality, the majority are hardworking and respectful young adults. 5. While unicorns are considered mythical creatures, sightings of unusual white deer are **fairly** _____ in certain rural areas. 6. Despite their diverse backgrounds and perspectives, the community members were able to unite around the _____ **goal** of improving the local school system.	common	Unacceptable: *widespread, big*
7. The candidate's polished speaking style and confident demeanor may _____ **the impression** that she was well-prepared and qualified for the position. 8. The market research study _____ valuable **insight** into the target audience's buying behaviors and preferences, which will help the company develop more effective marketing strategies. 9. The committee members agreed to _____ careful **consideration** to all the proposals submitted before making their final decision.	give	Unacceptable: *convey, reinforce*

continued on following page

Table 2. Continued

Items	Correct answer	Students' attempts
10. The political views and voting patterns of young adults are **heavily** _____ by the opinions and behaviors of their peers. 11. The traditional art and music of the indigenous community has had a significant **cultural** _____ on the broader regional identity and creative expression. 12. The CEO's personal beliefs and values **strongly** _____ the company's overall culture and the decisions made by the leadership team.	impact	Unacceptable: *emphasize, do*
13. The new government policy on immigration has been _____ **controversial**, sparking heated debates and protests from both supporters and critics. 14. Given the current weather forecasts, it is _____ **likely** that the hurricane will make landfall in the region within the next 24 hours. 15. The new manufacturing process implemented by the company has proven to be _____ **efficient**, increasing production output by 30%.	highly	Acceptable: *extremely* Unacceptable: *more*

In the translation task, common collocations in the five extracts, such as *tăng huy t áp* (*high blood pressure*) and *b nh tim m ch* (*cardiovascular disease*), are identical in both the researcher's attempts and the students' attempts. There are other identical English collocations suggested by Poe AI in both the reseacher's attempt and students' attempts (see Table 3).

Table 3. Identical collocations in the attempts of the researcher and the students

Highlighted Vietnamese phrases	English collocations
tăng huy t áp	high blood pressure
b nh tim m ch	cardiovascular disease
ban t ch c	organizing committee
có huy chương	won medals
s ki n th thao	sporting event
cu c chi n giá	price war
chu i cà phê	coffee chains
gi m phát kéo dài	prolonged inflation
n n văn minh nhân lo i	human civilization
d li u quan sát	observational data
mô hình khí h u	climate models
tăng đáng k	increased significantly

Besides the identical ones, there are Vietnamese phrases that have been translated into different collocations which carry the same meaning. For example, Poe AI suggested two phrases that have the same meaning for *v n đ s c kh e nghiêm tr ng: serious health problems* and *serious health issues*. Both *health problem* and *health issue* are common collocations, and learners can also notice that adjective *serious* collocates with both nouns *issue* and *problem*. There are other different collocations suggested by Poe AI in the researcher's attempt and the students' attempts that can be useful for enhancing learners' repertoire of collocations, such as *reduced/diminished quality of life*.

Regarding the types of lexical collocations, Poe AI demonstrated the ability of suggesting collocations of different categories for one same translation. For instance, for the Vietnamese phrase *vai trò c a nó trong tương lai* in the fifth extract, Poe AI suggested two phrases that have the same meaning, but one is a noun-noun collocation, while the other includes an adverbial phrase: *its future role* and *its role in the future*. Similarly, for the phrase *đ dài m t ngày*, a noun-noun collocation and a noun1-of-noun2 collocation were suggested: *day length* and *length of a day*. Another interesting example is the collocations suggested by Poe AI for *thi u chu đáo* in the second extract. Poe AI suggested an adverb-adjective collocation and a verb-noun collocation: *(not) sufficiently considerate* and *lack diligence* (see Table 4).

Table 4. Poe AI translations for five extracts

No.	Researcher's attempt	Student's attempt
1	Sleep apnea, if left untreated, can lead to ***serious health problems*** such as high blood pressure, cardiovascular disease, stroke, and diabetes. Patients with sleep apnea often feel fatigued during the day, have difficulty concentrating, and are at increased risk of accidents, leading to a ***reduced quality of life***.	Sleep apnea can lead to ***serious health issues*** if left untreated, such as high blood pressure, cardiovascular disease, stroke, and diabetes. Patients often experience daytime fatigue, poor concentration, and are at increased risk of accidents, resulting in a ***diminished quality of life***.
2	The organizing committee was not ***sufficiently considerate*** in their treatment of the newly independent East African nation that gained independence in 2011. The country has not won any medals in the two most recent Olympic Games and has never participated in any ***team sports events*** at the world's biggest sporting event.	The organizing committee ***lacked diligence*** in their treatment of the newly independent East African nation that has not won any medals in the two most recent Olympic Games and has never participated in any ***team competition*** at the biggest sporting event on the planet.
3	The price war between coffee chains in China is occurring against the backdrop of prolonged deflation. The ***situation is exacerbated*** by weak ***consumer sentiment***, as the economy and ***wages have declined***.	The appearance of a price war between the coffee chains in China is taking place against the backdrop of prolonged deflation. The ***situation has become more serious*** due to the weak ***consumer psychology***, as the economy and ***incomes have declined***.
4	Supposing that humans were to disappear, the world would gradually become a paradise for wild animals and weeds, with only a few ***dilapidated structures*** left as remnants of human civilization.	Hypothetically, if humans were to disappear, the world would gradually become a paradise for wild animals and weeds, with only a few ***crumbling ruins*** remaining as reminders of human civilization.
5	An international group of scientists examined the 200-year period from 1900 to 2100, using observational data and climate models to understand how climate change has impacted the length of a day in the past and to predict ***its future role***. They found that the impact of climate change on ***day length*** has increased significantly.	An international team of scientists examined the 200-year period from 1900 to 2100, using observational data and climate models to understand how climate change has impacted the length of a day in the past and predict ***its role in the future***. They found that the impact of climate change on the ***length of a day*** has increased significantly.

A difference between the researcher's attempt for the third extract and the students' attempts that is worth considering is the English noun for *ti n lương*, as Poe AI suggested both *wages* and *incomes*. However, according to Cambridge Learners' Dictionary, *wage* and *income* are not equivalents, because while *wage* means an amount of money paid to an employee weekly, *income* is the total amount of money earned from work or investments. This can be attributed to the fact that the context of the Vietnamese text does not specifically point out this difference. Besides *wages* and *incomes*, *salaries* would also be an appropriate alternative.

In the writing brainstorming task, for the question about international travel, learners asked Poe AI to suggest the benefits and the drawbacks of increased tourism. The collocations suggested by Poe AI for this question task are presented below (see Table 5).

Table 5. Collocations related to the topic of increased tourism

Advantages of increased tourism	Disadvantages of increased tourism	Suggestions
o economic benefits o cultural exchange o preservation of heritage o improved transportation and services o job creation o revenue for local businesses o tax income for the government o cultural understanding o preservation of natural attractions o improved infrastructure and service o break down barriers and stereotypes o greater awareness and appreciation o historical/architectural sites o put significant strain on o environmental degradation o a diminished quality of life o heritage sites o diminish their authenticity o increased travel emissions o fragile ecosystems o vulnerable communities o unequal distribution of tourism's economic benefits o multinational corporations	o overcrowding and infrastructure strain o commodification of culture o environmental degradation o displacement of local populations o increased cost of living o exploitation of local communities o vulnerability to market fluctuations o inflated prices and cost of living o spread of infectious diseases o pose public health risks	o carefully balance the potential upsides and downsides o promote sustainable, responsible tourism models o maximize the benefits o mitigate the drawbacks o upgrade transportation networks o long-term sustainability

The collocations suggested by Poe AI for the task about looking for life on other planets are demonstrated below (see Table 6).

Table 6. Collocations related to the topic of space exploration

Viewpoint 1	Viewpoint 2
o technological advancements o national prestige o potential scientific breakthroughs commercially viable innovations o long-term survival o habitable exoplanets o extraterrestrial life o scientific curosity o understanding of the universe o broaden the boundaries of human knowledge o national prestige o maintain competitiveness o technological leadership o drive innovation o immediate needs	o pressing issues on Earth o resource allocation o questionable outcomes o speculative endeavors o a high degree of uncertainty and risk o lack of direct and tangible benefits o lack of direct relevance to people's daily lives

It can be seen that Poe AI suggested collocations of different categories, from adjective-noun collocations, verb-noun collocations to noun1-of-noun2 collocations. This can help learners enhance their lexical range for their receptive and productive skills.

Assistance to Teachers' Preparation of Lexical Collocation Lessons

When asked to use Poe AI to prepare activities for a lesson about lexical collocations of one certain topic, the first teacher (Teacher #1) planned to conduct a lesson on leisure activities for her pre-intermediate learners. Besides activities such as going shopping, playing badminton, … introduced in the vocabulary section, Teacher #1 used Poe AI to look up for more collocations with verbs *go*, *play* and *do*. Teacher #1 intended to provide learners with a game of matching (see Figure 7). After this activity, Teacher #1 planned to explain why certain activities go with a certain verb (*go*, *play*, *do*) and give learners a number of example sentences generated by Poe AI. They are as follows:

a. I love to **do photography** during my travels to capture the beauty of different landscapes.
b. On weekends, I enjoy **going sightseeing** to explore new places and learn about their history.
c. In the evenings, we often gather with friends to **play cards** and share stories.

Figure 7. Collocations with verbs go, play and do

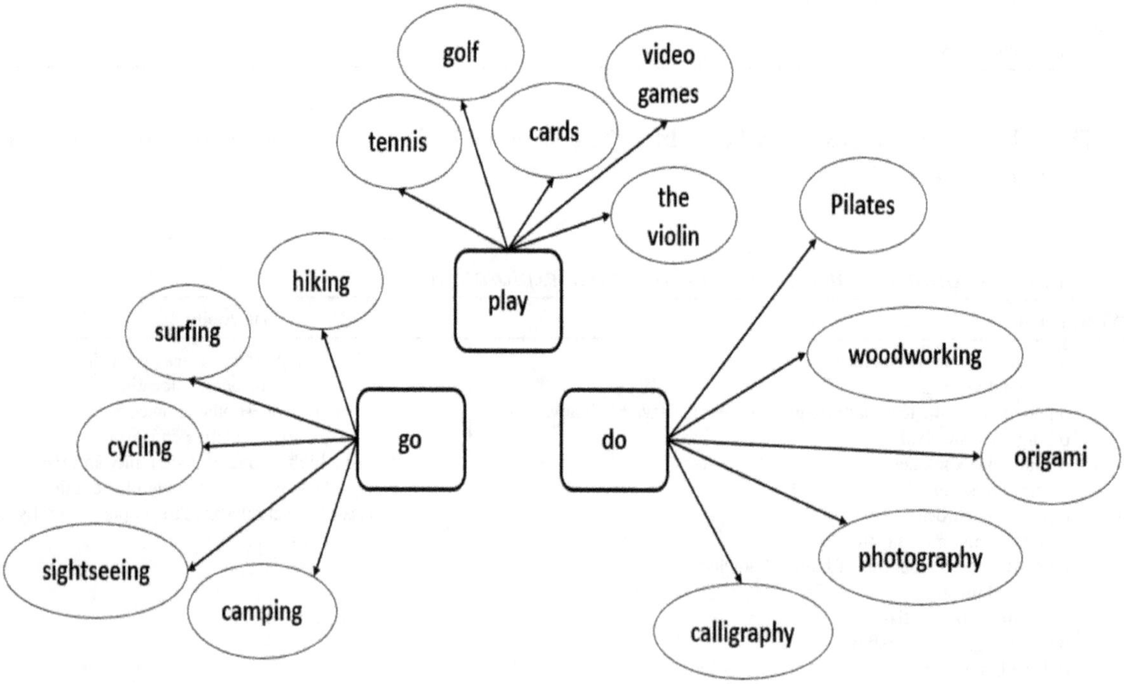

The second teacher (Teacher #2) planned to conduct a lesson on describing people's personalities for her intermediate learners. Key words that need introducing are *extroverted introverted*, *creative*, *responsible* and *integrity*. Teacher #2 used Poe AI to look up for example sentences for each key word, and relevant collocations (see Table 7).

Table 7. Collocations about personalities

Key words	Example sentences	Relevant collocations
extroverted (adj)	Sarah is very *extroverted* and loves being the center of attention at parties.	extroverted personality extroverted individual extroverted behavior highly extroverted
introverted (adj)	Jane is an *introverted* person who prefers to spend time alone rather than in large social. gatherings.	socially introverted introverted tendencies inherently introverted
responsible (adj)	Parents are *responsible* for taking care of their children.	responsible behavior responsible decision responsible person
creative (adj)	My friend is *creative* and enjoys making DIY crafts in her free time.	creative thinking creative process creative ideas
integrity (n)	Keeping your word and being reliable are signs of *integrity*.	strong integrity uncompromising integrity

The third teacher (Teacher #3) planned to conduct a lesson on describing emotions for her upper-intermediate learners. Teacher #3 used Poe AI to create a vocabulary matching exercise (see Figure 8).

Figure 8. Matching exercise about emotions

1. pour your heart out	a. to make yourself eager to do something
2. burst out laughing	b. to suddenly start laughing
3. pluck up the courage	c. to make yourself brave enough to do something
4. bottle up your feelings	d. to still think that something good might be true
5. burst into tears	e. to not tell anyone about your emotions
6. go to pieces	f. to suddenly start laughing
7. work up the enthusiasm	g. to tell someone all your problems and feelings
8. hold out hope	h. to be so upset that you cannot deal with life

Afterwards, teacher #3 used Poe AI to look up for example sentences for each key collocation, and relevant collocations so that learners can use to paraphrase their own words. The relevant collocations include ones that express the opposite emotion or situation (see Table 8).

Table 8. Collocations about emotions

Key collocation	Example sentences	Relevant collocations
pour my heart out	After a long day, I just needed to pour my heart out to my best friend.	share your feelings express yourself keep it to yourself shut down emotionally
burst out laughing	When she told the joke, everyone in the room burst out laughing.	laugh uncontrollably suddenly chuckle become serious stifle laughter
pluck up the courage	He finally plucked up the courage to ask her out on a date.	summon the bravery gather the courage lose confidence shrink away in fear
bottle up my feelings	It's not healthy to bottle up your feelings; you should talk about them.	suppress your emotions keep feelings inside express your emotions let your feelings out
burst into tears	She couldn't hold it together and suddenly burst into tears at the pressure of the moment.	suddenly cry start weeping hold back tears remain composed
go to pieces	When he heard the bad news, he just went to pieces and couldn't think straight.	break down fall apart stay calm maintain composure
work up the enthusiasm	I really need to work up the enthusiasm to start my new exercise routine.	build excitement generate motivation lose interest become apathetic
hold out hope	Even after the setback, she continued to hold out hope for a better outcome.	maintain optimism keep faith give up hope lose faith

The fourth teacher (Teacher #4) planned to conduct a lesson on teaching vocabulary in the pre-reading stage. The words include *vegetarian*, *carbon footprint*, *alternatives*, *emissions*, and *renewable*. Teacher #4 used Poe AI to collect example sentences, IPA transcripts and relevant collocations for the vocabulary. She also requested Poe AI to create a simple fill-in-the-blank practice task for the learners (see Figure 9).

Figure 9. Fill-in-the-blank exercise for the pre-reading stage

Fill in the Blanks

1. A _______ diet can help reduce the overall _______ of an individual by decreasing the demand for meat products.
2. Many people are seeking _______ to traditional meat-based meals to support their health and the environment.
3. Reducing _______ is crucial for addressing climate change and promoting a sustainable future.
4. Investing in _______ energy sources, such as solar and wind, can significantly lower our overall _______.

The example sentences, IPA transcripts and relevant collocations suggested by Poe AI are shown below (see Table 9).

Table 9. Collocations about environment

Key words & IPA transcripts	Example sentences	Relevant collocations
vegetarian (adj) /ˌvɛdʒ.ɪˈtɛr.i.ən/	The vegetarian meal was filled with fresh vegetables and flavorful grains.	vegetarian diet vegetarian dishes vegetarian restaurant
emissions (n) /ɪˈmɪʃ.ənz/	The government is implementing new policies to reduce greenhouse gas emissions.	carbon emissions industrial emissions emissions reduction
renewable (adj) /rɪˈnjuː.ə.bəl/	The company is investing heavily in renewable energy sources.	renewable energy renewable power renewable technology
carbon footprint (n) /ˈkɑːr.bən ˈfʊt.prɪnt/	Reducing our carbon footprint is essential for mitigating the effects of climate change.	carbon footprint tracking reduce carbon footprint carbon footprint assessment
alternative (n) /ɔːlˈtɜːrnətɪv/	We need to find an alternative to plastic that is more environmentally friendly.	effective alternative cost-effective alternative renewable alternative

Students' and Teachers' Positive Attitudes Towards Poe AI

When asked about their experience using Poe AI to complete the questionnaire, all learners believed that Poe AI's speed of responding to a question is remarkably fast, which makes the process of exploring knowledge easier and more convenient. The majority of the learners agreed that the information provided by Poe AI is both accurate and diverse, which means that for a one single question or request, Poe AI can gather a lot of information and supply all at once. Besides, the learners agreed that Poe AI is a highly interactive AI-driven tool and proves to respond as naturally as a human-being. This is also believed to be an advantage that can surpass the interactivity between teachers and learners, as Learner #5 shared, "*Poe AI seems to be more patient when answering my questions*". As a bot, Poe AI does not show signs of impatience, fatigue or stress when responding to different types of questions and providing answers or knowledge of various topics. Interestingly, Learner #6 also praised Poe AI's ability to process languages well by responding naturally to questions in both Vietnamese and English, which positively fosters effective translanguaging in language learning. Learner #12 also commented, "*Poe AI seems to be useful for vocabulary learning because I feel like it suggested more academic and complex collocations than ChatGPT*." This may prompt that Poe AI can be more suitable as a vocabulary learning buddy for learners than ChatGPT.

All four teachers agreed Poe AI's responding speed is very fast, which helps teachers save a lot time while preparing for their lessons. They also believed that the amount of information provided by Poe AI is useful and diverse, giving them a lot of amazing ideas to include in their own lessons. Moreover, they felt comfortable when interacting with Poe AI, as this chatbot proved to be friendly and willing to help (see Table 10).

Table 10. Poe AI's merits perceived by Ss and Ts

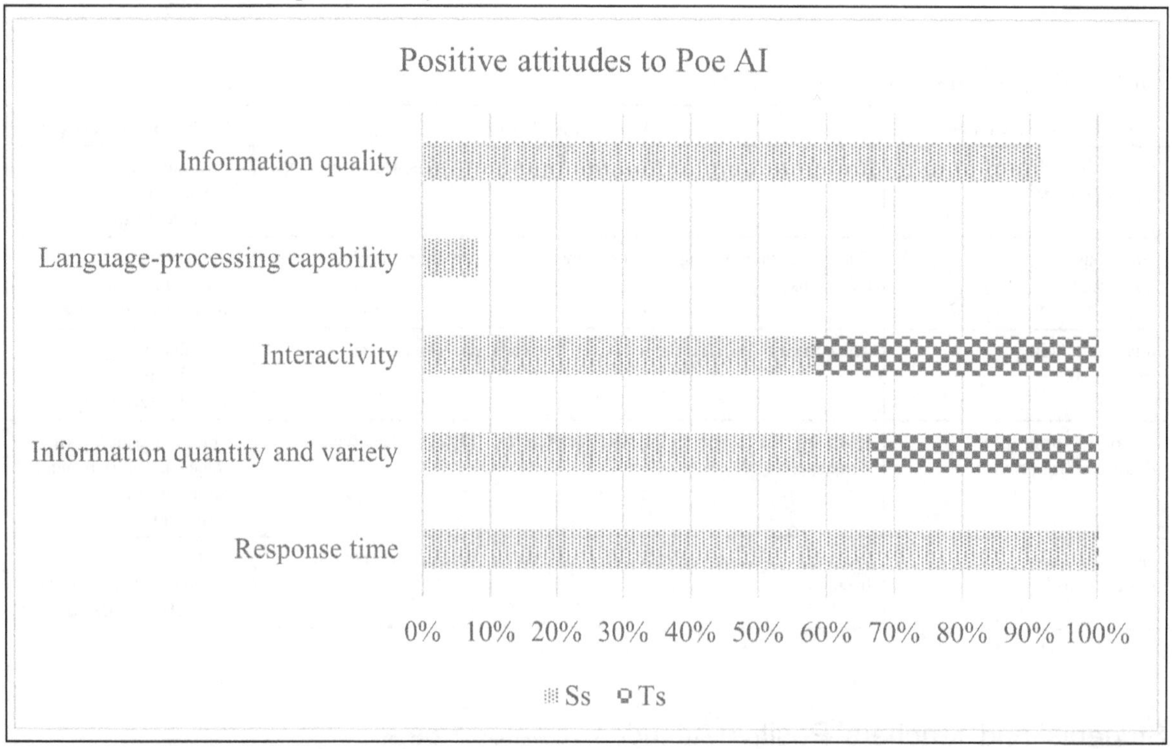

When asked about the possiblity of using other AI-driven tools or bots for learning English in the future, eleven out of twelve learners agreed that these tools and bots hold considerable potential, especially in terms of language learning (see Table 11).

Table 11. Quotes about Poe AI's merits perceived by students and teachers

Questions	Positive answer
1. What do you think about Poe AI's features (response time, interactivity …)?	"very easy to use" (Learner #1) "super-fast, almost immediately after I posted a question […] and a lot of information is provided" (Learner #2) "smart, and feels like a human" (Learner #4) "what Poe AI gives me is easy to understand, very good explanations" (Learner #9) "Poe AI processes both Vietnamese and English naturally" (Learner #12) "very speedy" (Teacher #1) "Poe AI is very interactive; I feel like Poe AI is a friend" (Teacher #2) "Poe AI can quickly meet my demands, even with very specific information, such as my students' proficiency levels" (Teacher #4) "Poe AI gives me alternatives when I'm not satisfied yet; Poe AI can also self-correct by giving me the adjustments" (Teacher #3)
2. Do you think using Poe AI helps you learn lexical collocations?	"definitely, Poe AI gives me a list of collocations that I can use" (Learner #3) "yes, there are example sentences also" (Learner #7) "very easy to use and example sentences are interesting, contextually appropriate" (Teacher #2) "effective assistance" (Teacher #4)
3.* Do you have any challenges while using Poe AI to prepare for the lesson?	"not really, as long as the class context, students' proficiency levels and age groups are provided" (Teacher #1)
4. In the future, would you consider using other AI-driven bots or tools to learn collocations?	"yes, as this would save a lot of time and I can look up collocations of different topics" (Learner #6) "using AI-driven tools in teaching is extremely useful" (Teacher #1) "Poe AI, or other bots can help create simple, yet effective practice tasks" (Teacher #3)

Note. Question 3 is only present in teacher participants' questionnaire.

Regarding the possibility of using other AI-driven tools or bots in the future, all four teachers agreed that they will continue updating new technologies to improve their language teaching. They believed that these tools and bots can save a lot of time, and provide interesting ideas. Moreover, the process of making practice exercise and tasks can become less labor-intensive and time-consuming, as these bots, such as Poe AI, are able to efficiently manage that.

Limitations of Poe AI

Despite the aforementioned merits, Learner #12 believed that not all of the information provided by Poe AI was accurately responding to the input question, which may raise an interesting question about whether there should be a set of questions or requests specifically formed for the use of AI-driven chatbots such as Poe AI. Otherwise, users may not efficiently obtain what they need on the first attempt. This agrees with Learner #1's sharing about Poe AI's ability to instantly provide answers, but the degree of accuracy of those may not be highly reliable. Learner #1 noted, "*Poe AI is fast, but it does not always provide accurate answers.*"

Meanwhile, Learner #6 also shared that specifically for the third task of the questionnaire, in which learners are required to use Poe AI to find information and ideas for one writing task question and collect the collocations, the amount of information presented by Poe AI was arranged in a non-linear manner, not in a way that supports linear thinking. In other words, Poe AI can gather and provide information abundance, but without presenting it in a form of arguments. Last but not least, Learner #1 believed that Poe AI sometimes fails to translate a Vietnamese text into English effectively and accurately, and commented "*there are some parts Poe AI could not provide the English translation*" (see Table 12).

Table 12. Poe AI's limitations perceived by Ss and Ts

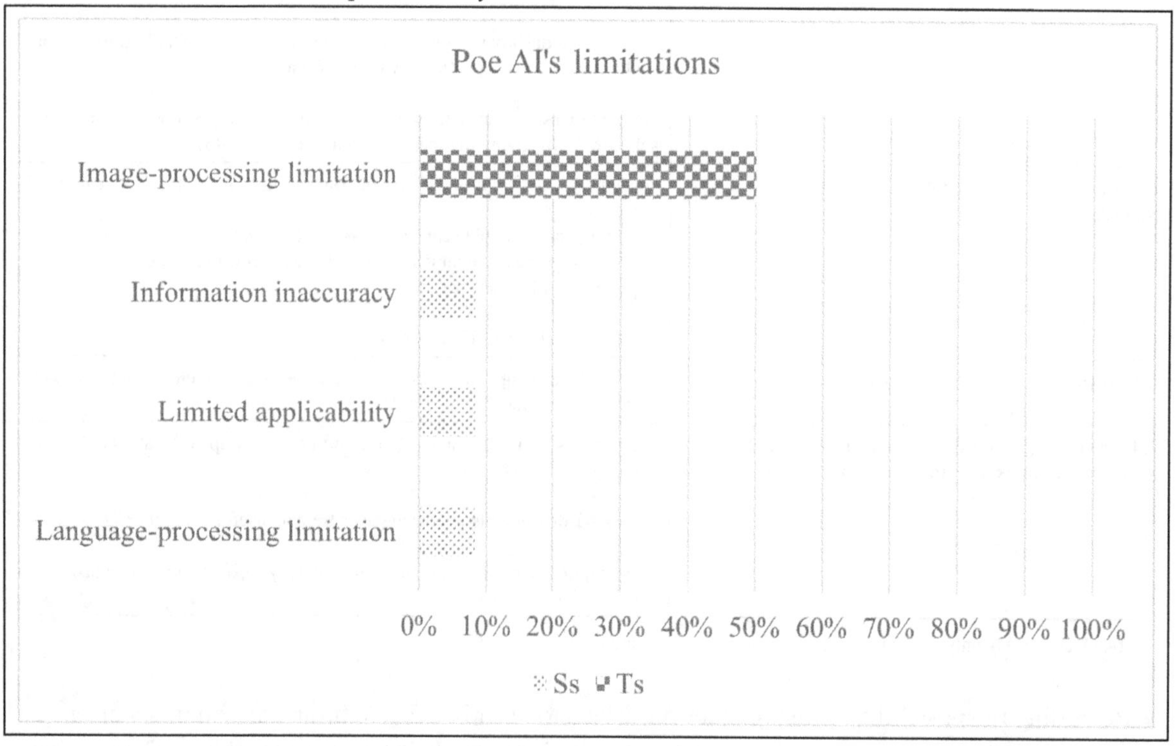

For the teachers, the inability to process screenshots, which are not saved as files, is said to be a shortcoming of Poe AI. Teacher #3 argued that the screenshot-processing ability, or stronger Optical Character Recognition (OCR) technology, would make Poe AI become even more popular and helpful (see Table 13).

Table 13. Quotes about Poe AI's limitations perceived by students and teachers

Questions	Areas for improvement
1. What do you think about Poe AI's features (response time, interactivity ...)?	"Poe AI does not process screenshots, which I took directly from the screen without saving as files" (Learner #9) "the information was not presented in a linear way, so Poe AI is not very suitable for constructing arguments" (Learner #6) "I have a lot of screenshots, but Poe AI does not process those, so it is quite inconvenient" (Teacher #3)
2. Do you think using Poe AI helps you teach lexical collocations?	"although Poe AI gives me useful collocations, there are so many that I may not memorize and use all" (Learner #1)
3. In the future, would you consider using other AI-driven bots or tools to learn collocations?	"AI tools seem promising, but sometimes I feel I do not put all my trust in them" (Learner #12)

DISCUSSION

Although AI-driven chatbots have become increasingly popular in educational contexts around the world, in terms of boosting learners' motivation and assisting teachers in facilitating classroom activities (Carayannopoulos, 2018; Schmulian & Coetzee, 2019), these bots have not been commonly utilized or adopted for language learning and teaching, especially in the Vietnamese context. This study was conducted in order to explore the use of Poe AI, a newly developed chatbot, in the process of teaching and learning English, focusing on lexical collocations, in the context of Vietnam. From the findings reported in the previous section, there are a number of critical points to take into consideration.

Poe AI is considered a useful tool for learners to learn English collocations and for teachers to prepare vocabulary lessons with an addition of collocations. The majority of learners and teachers in this study believed that Poe AI provides abundant, relevant information at a great speed, with a high level of interactivity. This resonates with findings of previous studies in which chatbots, in general, are discovered to be instant respondents to requests (Xu et al., 2021), and providers of authentic language for practice (Fryer et al., 2017). Furthermore, Poe AI can greatly assist learners as an English translator providing accurate translations, providing opportunities for them to learn vocabulary and even grammar, and enhancing their experience with composition writing. This point agrees with Stapleton and Kin's (2019) findings, which reveal that an AI-powered tool can provide highly accurate translations. Concerning specifically the use of Poe AI in composition writing, learners showed a general positive attitude towards the assistance provided by Poe AI in suggesting ideas and suitable collocations for a writing task question. This positive attitude towards the use of an AI-driven bot has been seen in Fithriani's (2023) study, in which learners' arguments are properly improved by QuillBot and grammatical errors are also pinpointed, as well as corrected.

About learning collocations, Poe AI not only provides example sentences, but it also supplies learners with similar phrases and detailed explanations. In other words, Poe AI plays the role of an online dictionary with accurate information and examples to ensure learners' understanding of the meaning and the use of a lexical item. Poe AI are able to do similar things, with great speed and conciseness. Instead of "looking up" the dictionaries, learners can conveniently ask for the particular piece of information to be given. More interestingly, the learners in this study thought that Poe AI was patient and friendly while giving answers to their questions and requests, because chatbots are assistants that may not be susceptiable to fatigue or stress when dealing with repetitive and tedious work. This agrees with the findings of studies by Fryer et al. (2019) and Kim (2018). However, this is against the shortcomings identified by Nguyen and Pham (2023) and also Fryer et al. (2019), which indicate that AI-powered chatbots' low emotional sensitivity may hinder learners' engagement after the initial excitement for this novelty fades. Although the learner participants in the present study demonstrated positive attitudes to the use of Poe AI, it can be understood that the time they spent learning collocations with Poe AI has not been significant enough to determine whether the enthusiasm while using an AI-powered chatbot would disappear, obstructing their learning process.

Regarding the teachers, they hold high hopes for the application of Poe AI in the preparation stage because Poe AI can help create simple, yet effective, practice exercise in the classroom. Moreover, for a vocabulary lesson, or a vocabulary section in a skill lesson, Poe AI can provide interesting example sentences that contain the specific context, enhancing learners' understanding of the meaning and the use of a particular lexical item. Besides, Poe AI can suggest relevant collocations of one lexical item, which helps make the vocabulary lesson more thorough and ambitious, ensuring that learners are better-equipped with the authentic language for communicative purposes. Not only can Poe AI give information about the meaning, the use and relevant collocations of a lexical item, but it can also provide the IPA transcript of that item, reminding learners of the pronunciation. This echoes a finding in a study by Fryer et al. (2019), in which chatbots are said to have the ability to provide extra language knowledge with accuracy and suitability, fostering learners' autonomy.

Gamification is believed to bring great benefits to a language classroom, especially during vocabulary lessons (Rasti-Behbahani, 2021; Trinh et al., 2022). In addition to the ability of creating simple, effective vocabulary practice exercises, Poe AI can suggest interesting ideas for quick in-class games in order to bring excitement to the classroom and facilitate learners' acquisition of lexical items and collocations better. For example, a teacher plans to have a game activity as a drill for learners to memorize and be able to use collocations about doing household chores, such as *do the washing-up*, *have breakfast*, *mop the floor*, *take out the garbage* and *dust the furniture*. Poe AI would suggest a game called Collocation Relay, supported by the objective, a list of materials, instructions for setup and rules and steps to conduct. Figure 10 shows how this game activity can be conducted in a classroom of intermediate learners.

Figure 10. Steps to conduct the game activity Collocation Relay

How to Play:

1. **Explain the Rules**:
   - Each team will take turns sending one member to the card area.
   - The student must pick a card, read the collocation aloud, and then use it in a new sentence.
   - If they use it correctly, they bring the card back to their team. If not, they put it back and the next team member goes.

2. **Starting the Relay**:
   - Set a timer for a certain amount of time (e.g., 10 minutes).
   - Teams take turns sending one member at a time to the card area.

3. **Scoring**:
   - Each correct collocation used in a sentence earns the team a point.
   - Bonus points can be awarded for creativity or using the collocation in a complex sentence.

4. **Wrap-Up**:
   - After the time is up, tally the points.
   - Discuss the collocations and their meanings as a class.
   - Optionally, provide small rewards for the winning team.

Although Poe AI is useful, there are a number of limitations and reminders. Poe AI can be highly interactive, processing the question and request instantly and providing the answers immediately, but it may require a request with details or specific contexts, so that it can provide the most satisfactory answer. For example, when requesting Poe AI to create a vocabulary practice exercise, it is advised that teachers should include information such as learners' proficiency levels, age, learners' areas of interest … so that Poe AI can narrow down the pool of data it has got before responding. This indicates that teachers should be provided with training sessions on how to apply Poe AI in their language teaching, which echoes Barrett and Pack's (2023), Nguyen's (2023), and Rudoph et al.'s (2023) suggestions for systematic guidelines, as well as professional training to raise teachers' awareness about the use of AI-driven chatbots and other tools in education. Moreover, only by doing this can teachers become fully aware of the potential AI-powered chatbots offer, and more importantly, the risks they pose to both learning and teaching. Fully aware of the risks related to academic integrity, and over-reliance on these tools, teachers can approach their teaching with more confidence.

For learners, especially those with limited experience with AI technologies, it is slightly unfamiliar initially for them to pose questions or make requests for a chatbot because they may not know how to interact with a non-human bot. For specifically lower-proficiency learners, interacting with Poe AI, or chatbots in general, in the target language may be a challenge, but asking questions and receiving the information in their L1 may not ideally assist their language learning journey.

Last but not least, considering the context of Vietnam, it is the issue of cost and infrastructure that the application of Poe AI in language teaching and learning may be delayed (Le et al., 2022). It requires systematic efforts from authorities to make this possible, along with guidelines and timely training on strategies to maximize the benefits of Poe AI.

RECOMMENDATIONS & CONCLUSION

This study has found that learners and teachers have positive attitude towards the use of Poe AI in the process of learning and teaching collocations. It has been discovered that Poe AI can effectively suggest a number of collocations that are useful for a particular writing task, finding collocating words of common collocations and providing the English translations of collocations. This means that learners can use Poe AI to actively look up a collocation that they wish to acquire, obtain example sentences, other collocations that have a similar meaning, or find an English collocation they wish to use from a Vietnamese phrase. Poe AI can be of great assistance for teachers, providing simple and interesting information and ideas for the stage of lesson preparation, in-class activities, and vocabulary practice exercises. Poe AI not only provides the meaning, the use, example sentences and the IPA transcript of a lexical item, but it can also provide relevant collocations so that teachers can introduce to learners so as to enhance their receptive and productive skills. The additional collocations suggested by Poe AI can help learners learn new words, recognizing these words in a reading or a listening task, while memorizing and acquiring these can be useful for them in a writing or speaking task. To maximize the use of Poe AI in learning and teaching collocations, there are a number of recommendations for different stakeholders.

For teachers, Poe AI can be used for both the preparation stage and in-class teaching time. Teachers can consider doing more research about the application of AI-driven chatbots such as Poe AI in their own language teaching contexts. Besides, it is important to gradually introduce the application of AI-driven tools and bots into the general educational context where teachers work so that colleagues can form discussion groups and explore new technologies that assist and facilitate the process of language teaching and learning. Most importantly, ethical issues related to AI technologies should be discussed and consulted with the administrators so that the risks of AI-related problems can be minimized.

To ensure that learners can benefit from AI technologies in general, and AI-driven chatbots such as Poe AI specifically, it is advised that teachers should first introduce them to the classroom and the application should be under supervision. Collaboration with the department of Information Technology (IT) and Computer Science is highly recommended so that knowledge about AI technologies is properly obtained and shared, with caution and meaningful instructions. Overuse of AI technologies such as Poe AI chatbot should be warned ahead and relevant regulations should be imposed so that learners do not have excessive reliance on an AI chatbot, or violate regulations on academic integrity to complete their studies. In other words, ethics should be conveyed to learners before a task or project allowing the use of AI-driven bots is assigned.

In order to assist both learners and in-service teachers with the application of AI-powered chatbots and tools to enhance the process of teaching and learning English in general, it is important that administrators pay more attention to the great potential of AI technologies in language learning and teaching. Not only can administrators allow the use of such AI technologies in language teaching and learning with moderation and certain regulations, but they can also encourage more scientific research and professional development in this particular field.

Although this study was conducted with care and ethics, there are inevitable limitations. The sample size is not large enough for a reliable generalization of the findings. A larger sample of Vietnamese EFL learners and teachers can result in a more detailed picture of the phenomenon. Moreover, to better explore Poe AI's effectiveness in helping these stakeholders with language learning and teaching, experimental designs and the data collection procedure that spans for a longer time can gather more interesting data, which can result in more thorough and practical recommendations. For further research concerning this phenomenon, it is suggested that the use of AI-powered chatbots in facilitating learners' spoken communicative skills and how these bots can actually help in the classroom within the deliberate teaching time and during post-stages of the lessons be investigated. These ideas can further enhance the existing body of literature concerning AI-powered chatbots in language learning and teaching.

All learner and teacher participants in this study showed a positive attitude towards the use of Poe AI and a positive outlook for the future use of further AI technologies in language learning and teaching. It would be an immeasurable benefit for learners and teachers in the Vietnamese context of language learning and teaching to have access to AI-driven tools and bots to enhance not only the process of teaching and learning the target language, but also learners' autonomy and teachers' lesson preparation stage.

REFERENCES

Ackermann, K., & Chen, Y. H. (2013). Developing the Academic Collocation List (ACL) - A corpus-driven and expert-judged approach. *Journal of English for Academic Purposes, 12*(4), 235–247. DOI: 10.1016/j.jeap.2013.08.002

Alhaisoni, E. (2016). EFL teachers' and students' perceptions of dictionary use and preferences. *International Journal of Linguistics, 8*(6), 31. DOI: 10.5296/ijl.v8i6.10267

Ayedoun, E., Hayashi, Y., & Seta, K. (2019). Adding communicative and affective strategies to an embodied conversational agent to enhance second language learners' willingness to communicate. *International Journal of Artificial Intelligence in Education, 29*(1), 29–57. DOI: 10.1007/s40593-018-0171-6

Bahns, J., & Eldaw, M. (1993). Should we teach EFL students collocations? *System, 21*(1), 101–114. DOI: 10.1016/0346-251X(93)90010-E

Barrett, A., & Pack, A. (2023). Not quite eye to A.I.: Student and teacher perspectives on the use of generative artificial intelligence in the writing process. *International Journal of Educational Technology in Higher Education, 61*(20), 59. DOI: 10.1186/s41239-023-00427-0

Benson, M., Benson, E., & Elson, R. (1997). *The BBI dictionary of English word combinations*. John Benjamins. DOI: 10.1075/z.bbi1(2nd)

Benson, M., Benson, E., & Ilson, R. F. (1986). *The BBI Combinatory Dictionary of English: A guide to word combinations*. John Benjamins Publishing Company. DOI: 10.1075/z.bbi1(1st)

Brandtzaeg, P. B., & Følstad, A. (2018). Chatbots: Changing user needs and motivations. *Interactions (New York, N.Y.), 25*(5), 38–43. DOI: 10.1145/3236669

Bui, T., Boers, F., & Coxhead, A. (2020). Extracting multiword expressions from texts with the aid of online resources. *ITL International Journal of Applied Linguistics, 171*(2), 221–252. DOI: 10.1075/itl.18033.bui

Cao, D. T. P. (2018). *The effect of an online collocation dictionary on advanced learners' use of collocations in L2 writing* [Doctoral dissertation, University of Leeds]. https://etheses.whiterose.ac.uk/22829/

Carayannopoulos, S. (2018). Using chatbots to aid transition. *The International Journal of Information and Learning Technology, 35*(2), 118–129. DOI: 10.1108/IJILT-10-2017-0097

Duong, P. T., Perez, M. M., Desmet, P., & Peters, E. (2021). Differential effects of input based and output-based tasks on L2 vocabulary learning. *Canadian Journal of Applied Linguistics, 24*(3), 120–144. DOI: 10.37213/cjal.2021.31183

Duong, T. K. H., & Le, T. T. H. (2024). Utilizing artificial intelligence in writing feedback: Benefits and challenges forfFirst-year students at Hanoi University of Industry. *Proceedings of the AsiaCALL International Conference, 6*, 238-249. DOI: DOI: 10.54855/paic.24617

Durrant, P. (2009). Investigating the viability of a collocation list for students of English for academic purposes. *English for Specific Purposes, 28*(3), 157–169. DOI: 10.1016/j.esp.2009.02.002

Fithriani, R. (2023). Utilizing artificial intelligence-based paraphrasing tool in EFL writing class: A focus on Indonesian university students' perceptions. *Scope: Journal of English Language Teaching, 7*(2), 210–218. DOI: 10.30998/scope.v7i2.14882

Fryer, L. K., Ainley, M., Thompson, A., Gibson, A., & Sherlock, Z. (2017). Stimulating and sustaining interest in a language course: An experimental comparison of Chatbot and Human task partners. *Computers in Human Behavior, 75*, 461–468. DOI: 10.1016/j.chb.2017.05.045

Fryer, L. K., Nakao, K., & Thompson, A. (2019). Chatbot learning partners: Connecting learning experiences, interest and competence. *Computers in Human Behavior, 93*, 279–289. DOI: 10.1016/j.chb.2018.12.023

GenApe AI. (2024, June 19). *What are the differences between Poe and ChatGPT? –GenApe AI.* https://www.genape.ai/blogs/poe-chatbot/

Haristiani, N. (2019). Artificial intelligence (AI) chatbot as language learning medium: An inquiry. *Journal of Physics: Conference Series, 1387*(1), 2020. DOI: 10.1088/1742-6596/1387/1/012020

Hausmann, F. J. (1989). Le dictionnaire de collocations. In Hausmann, F. J., Reichmann, O., Wiegand, H. E., & Zgusta, L. (Eds.), *Wörterbücher: ein internationales Handbuch zur Lexikographie. Dictionaries. Dictionnaires* (pp. 1010–1019). Mouton De Gruyter. DOI: 10.1515/9783110095852.1.7.1010

Hong, W. C. H. (2023). The impact of ChatGPT on foreign language teaching and learning: Opportunities in education and research. *Journal of Educational Technology and Innovation, 5*(1). Advance online publication. DOI: 10.61414/jeti.v5i1.103

Huang, W., Hew, K. F., & Fryer, L. K. (2022). Chatbots for language learning—Are they really useful? A systematic review of chatbot-supported language learning. *Journal of Computer Assisted Learning.* John Wiley and Sons Inc. DOI: 10.1111/jcal.12610

Japoshvili-Ghvinashvili, M., & Suleman, N. (2023). Assisting ELT teachers: Designing activities for the use of ChatGPT in teaching and learning. *Pakistan Journal of Multidisciplinary Innovation, 2*(1), 24–35. DOI: 10.59075/pjmi.v2i1.219

Jia, J., Chen, Y., Ding, Z., & Ruan, M. (2012). Effects of a vocabulary acquisition and assessment system on students' performance in a blended learning class for English subject. *Computers & Education, 58*(1), 63–76. DOI: 10.1016/j.compedu.2011.08.002

Jia, J., & Ruan, M. (2008). Use chatbot CSIEC to facilitate the individual learning in English instruction: A case study. In *Lecture Notes in Computer Science (including* subseries Lecture Notes in Artificial Intelligence and Lecture Notes in *Bioinformatics)* (Vol. 5091 LNCS, pp. 706–708). Springer Verlag. DOI: 10.1007/978-3-540-69132-7_84

John Benjamins. Nguyen, C. D. (2016). Creating spaces for constructing practice and identity: Innovations of teachers of English language to young learners in Vietnam. *Research Papers in Education, 32*(1), 56–70. DOI: 10.1080/02671522.2015.1129644

Kim, N.-Y. (2016). Effects of voice chat on EFL learners' speaking ability according to proficiency levels. *Multimedia-Assisted Language Learning, 19*(4), 63–88.

Kim, N.-Y. (2018). A study on chatbots for developing Korean college students' English listening and reading skills. *Journal of Digital Convergence*, *16*(8), 19–26.

Kirschner, P., Strijbos, J.-W., Kreijns, K., & Beers, P. J. (2004). Designing electronic collaborative learning environments. *Educational Technology Research and Development*, *52*(3), 47–66. DOI: 10.1007/BF02504675

Le-Thi, D., Rodgers, M., & Pellicer-Sánchez, A. (2018). Teaching formulaic sequences in an English-language class: The effects of explicit instruction versus coursebook instruction. *TESL Canada Journal*, *34*(3), 111–139. DOI: 10.18806/tesl.v34i3.1276

Lew, R., & Doroszewska, J. (2009). Electronic dictionary entries with animated pictures: Lookup preferences and word retention. *International Journal of Lexicography*, *22*(3), 239–257. DOI: 10.1093/ijl/ecp022

Lewis, M. (1997). *Implementing the Lexical Approach: Putting theory into practice*. http://ci.nii.ac.jp/ncid/BA35070833

Lodge, J. M., Thompson, K., & Corrin, L. (2023). Mapping out a research agenda for generative artificial intelligence in tertiary education. *Australasian Journal of Educational Technology*, *39*(1), 1–8. DOI: 10.14742/ajet.8695

Neji, W., Boughattas, N., & Ziadi, F. (2023). Exploring new AI-based technologies to enhance students' motivation. *Issues in Informing Science & Information Technology*, *20*, 95–110. DOI: 10.28945/5149

Nesselhauf, N. (2003). The use of collocations by advanced learners of English and some implications for teaching. *Applied Linguistics*, *24*(2), 223–242. DOI: 10.1093/applin/24.2.223

Nesselhauf, N. (2005). *Collocations in a learner corpus*.

Nguyen, C., & Boers, F. (2018). The effect of content retelling on vocabulary uptake from a TED talk. *TESOL Quarterly*, *53*(1), 5–29. DOI: 10.1002/tesq.441

Nguyen, T. T. H. (2023). EFL Teachers' perspectives toward the use of ChatGPT in writing classes: A case study at Van Lang university. *International Journal of Language Instruction*, *2*(3), 1–47. DOI: 10.54855/ijli.23231

Nunan, D. (2003). The impact of English as a global language on educational policies and practices in the Asia-Pacific region. *TESOL Quarterly*, *37*(4), 589. DOI: 10.2307/3588214

Pham, V. P. H., & Le, A. Q. (2024). ChatGPT in language learning: Perspectives from Vietnamese students in Vietnam and the USA. *International Journal of Language Instruction*, *3*(2), 59–72. DOI: 10.54855/ijli.24325

Pham, V. P. H., & Nguyen, M. T. (2024). ChatGPT va hoat đong giang day: Cac thach thuc moi cua giang vien. *Tap Chi Khoa hoc va Cong nghe Dai hoc Cong nghe Dong Nai*, No. 01-2024, 115-123. Retrieved from https://vjol.info.vn/index.php/dntu/article/view/91869

Rahimi, M., & Momeni, G. (2012). The effect of teaching collocations on English language proficiency. *Procedia: Social and Behavioral Sciences*, *31*, 37–42. DOI: 10.1016/j.sbspro.2011.12.013

Rakhmonov, I. U., & Kurbonova, R. S. (2023). The pedagogical principles and effectiveness of utilizing ChatGPT for language learning. *Research in Education, 2*(9), 226–243. https://researchedu.org/index.php/re/article/view/4899

Rasti-Behbahani, A. (2021). Why digital games can be advantageous in vocabulary learning. *Theory and Practice in Language Studies, 11*(2), 111–118. DOI: 10.17507/tpls.1102.01

Rudolph, J., Tan, S., & Tan, S. (2023). ChatGPT: Bullshit Spewer or the End of Traditional Assessments in Higher Education? *Journal of Applied Learning and Teaching, 6*(1), 9–18. DOI: 10.37074/j

Schmulian, A., & Coetzee, S. A. (2019). The development of messenger bots for teaching and learning and accounting students' experience of the use thereof. *British Journal of Educational Technology, 50*(5), 2751–2777. DOI: 10.1111/bjet.12723

Sinclair, J. M. (1991). *Corpus, concordance, collocation*. Oxford University Press.

Smutny, P., & Schreiberova, P. (2020). Chatbots for learning: A review of educational chatbots for the Facebook Messenger. *Computers & Education, 151*, 103862. Advance online publication. DOI: 10.1016/j.compedu.2020.103862

Stapleton, P., & Kin, B. L. K. (2019). Assessing the accuracy and teachers' impressions of Google Translate: A study of primary L2 writers in Hong Kong. *English for Specific Purposes, 56*, 18–34. DOI: 10.1016/j.esp.2019.07.001

Tegos, S., Demetriadis, S., & Tsiatsos, T. (2014). A configurable conversational agent to trigger students' productive dialogue: A pilot study in the CALL domain. *International Journal of Artificial Intelligence in Education, 24*(1), 62–91. DOI: 10.1007/s40593-013-0007-3

Trinh, T. H., Nguyen, M. N., & Tran, T. T. H. (2022). Teachers and students' perceptions of using digital games in improving vocabulary at non-English-majored class. *AsiaCALL Online Journal, 13*(5), 112–131. DOI: 10.54855/acoj.221358

Trinh, T. L. A., Tran, T. K. N., Vo, T. B. N., & Huynh, T. T. S. (2021). The difference effects of paper dictionaries vs. online dictionaries. *AsiaCALL Online Journal, 12*(3), 28–38.

Vu, D. V., & Peters, E. (2021). Incidental learning of collocations from meaning input: A longitudinal study into three reading modes and factors that affect learning. *Studies in Second Language Acquisition, 44*(3), 685–707. DOI: 10.1017/S0272263121000462

Vu, D. V., & Peters, E. (2022). Learning vocabulary from reading-only, reading-while listening, and reading with textual input enhancement: Insights from Vietnamese EFL learners. *RELC Journal, 53*(1), 85–100. DOI: 10.1177/0033688220911485

Wang, Y. F., Petrina, S., & Feng, F. (2017). VILLAGE—Virtual immersive language learning and gaming environment: Immersion and presence. *British Journal of Educational Technology, 48*(2), 431–450. DOI: 10.1111/bjet.12388

Winkler, R., & Soellner, M. (2018). Unleashing the Potential of Chatbots in Education: A State-Of-The-Art Analysis. *Proceedings - Academy of Management, 2018*(1), 15903. DOI: 10.5465/AMBPP.2018.15903abstract

Xu, X., Hong, W. C. H., Zhang, Y., Jiang, H., & Liu, J. (2023). Learning paths design in personal learning environments: The impact on postgraduates' cognitive achievements and satisfaction. *Innovations in Education and Teaching International*. Advance online publication. DOI: 10.1080/14703297.2023.2189603

Xu, Y., Wang, D., Collins, P., Lee, H., & Warschauer, M. (2021). Same benefits, different communication patterns: Comparing children's reading with a conversational agent vs. a human partner. *Computers & Education*, *161*, 4059. DOI: 10.1016/j.compedu.2020.104059

Chapter 12

Language Course Writing Task and AI-Generated Writing Detection:
An Ethical Concern

Yoke Lian Lau
https://orcid.org/0000-0002-7949-7683
Universiti Malaysia Sabah, Malaysia

Anna Lynn Abu Bakar
https://orcid.org/0000-0002-2540-3637
Universiti Malaysia Sabah, Malaysia

Shi Kien Chau
https://orcid.org/0009-0006-0783-2960
Mun Yee Chinese Primary School, Malaysia

Ruoh Yih Sik
SK St. Thomas, Malaysia

Jenny Tze Kie Yap
https://orcid.org/0000-0003-1247-8450
Universiti Teknologi MARA, Malaysia

Hui Wen Yong
University Malaysia Sabah, Malaysia

Jee Chin Tan
https://orcid.org/0009-0001-3932-0955
University Malaysia Sabah, Malaysia

Alagesan Ambikapathy
Uma Publications Sdn BhdD, Malaysia

ABSTRACT

This research made use of an AI detector known as GPTZero to determine the proportion of each assignment that was written by humans and by AI. Based on the findings, it can be observed that the assignment receives higher marks when the percentage of the AI writing score is larger. One of the limitations of the research is that the use of ChatGPT for proofreading will also be identified as AI. There is a possibility that fairness will be a problem in the field of applying AI in education. The establishment of control mechanisms is necessary prior to the complete implementation of AI in educational settings to prevent AI from destroying human talents. The research aims to examine the frequency of student utilization of AI in writing tasks and to investigate students' attitudes towards AI tools in Mandarin writing. The research questions are: I) How to identify the ethnicity of an individual utilising AI ii) What measures should responsible AI use in the event of damage resulting from following AI recommendations and responses?

DOI: 10.4018/979-8-3693-7260-9.ch012

INTRODUCTION

AI-Giarism

ChatGPT, an Artificial Intelligence chatbot, was introduced to the public in November 2022. The academic sphere is facing a new challenge, shifting from conventional plagiarism to AI-generated plagiarism. Plagiarism is characterised as a form of cheating (Devlin, 2005); hence, the newly termed phenomenon of AI-giarism is also classified as cheating. AI-giarism is a modern term derived from plagiarism, primarily referring to the act of appropriating content generated by AI algorithms (Khalaf; 2024a,2024b).AI-giarism is a fusion of the concepts of AI and plagiarism, referring to AI-assisted plagiarism. The topic of AI-generated plagiarism raises significant ethical concerns within academia. Numerous experts investigate this subject and provide a comprehensive elucidation, revealing the nature of AI-giarism (Hern, 2022).

'Hallucinations' is a principal idea about AI that necessitates clarification, particularly in relation to AI-generated writing. When AI produces wrong information, it is termed a "AI hallucination," which elucidates how systems generate or interpret data in unforeseen and often erroneous manners. This is beneficial for deep learning, image and speech recognition, and generative models (Maleki et al., 2024; Salvagno et al., 2023; Sun et al., 2024). Tang (2023, 2024) contends that ChatGPT may lead to 'hallucinations' and the propagation of inaccurate information. Biassed content may be produced if ChatGPT is directed to utilise these materials. Additionally, some researchers believe that 'hallucinations' are a byproduct of ChatGPT and analogous AI writing tools.

ChatGPT has the capability to retain user information in order to enhance future responses. Even though, AI is capable of learning in a manner that is similar to that of humans; however, it is unable to evaluate and reprocess knowledge during conversations, as it is dependent on the complexity of the language and symbols used (Salvagno et al., 2023). Excessive reliance on AI may be detrimental to the user. For instance, this will restrict users to producing similar work, diminish user critical thinking abilities, and users would forfeit the opportunity to examine data independently (Janet, 2024).

AI Writing in Academic

Some scholars examine the application of AI in academic writing. For example, Amirjalili et al. (2024) examined the capacity of AI to adhere to academic writing standards while preserving the distinct identities of human authors. The evaluation emphasizes assertiveness, self-identification, and authorial presence. Nguyen (2023) on the other hand, elucidates research indicating that participants are amenable to the progression of AI applications in education. Most participants are cognizant of the applications' limitations. Anson (2022) asserts that the imminent primary challenge for writing educators is the recent advancements in natural language, exemplified by text that emulates human writing. Neural networks and other deep learning methodologies employ sophisticated predictive machine analysis to generate new content from billions of human-written texts. Khalifa and Albadawy (2024) delineated six primary fields wherein AI enhance academic writing and research. Maphoto et al. (2024) examine the potential of generative AI to improve the academic writing abilities of a significant group of students at a distant learning institution.

Aside from that, researchers like Imran and Almusharraf (2023) investigate the role of ChatGPT as a writing assistant in academic contexts. The data obtained indicates that AI is an essential component in the continuous advancement of education, with the recent addition of the ChatGPT chatbot. Hadi Mogavi et al. (2024) seeks to investigate the user experience and perspectives of initial users of ChatGPT across diverse educational domains. Zirar (2023) aims to investigate the influence of language models on student learning and evaluation in higher education.

Hung and Chen (2023) examined the benefits and drawbacks of Chinese students employing ChatGPT for academic endeavors. They emphasize the difficulties of reconciling AI's prospective advantages with the necessity of maintaining academic integrity. Kim et al. (2024) interviewed 20 Chinese higher education students about their experiences with GenAI-assisted academic writing after using a ChatGPT4-integrated writing system created by the research team. Students expected that AI will improve their writing processes and performance in multiple ways, including serving as a digital peer, virtual tutor, and multitasking writing assistant, as revealed by the survey.

Hutson (2024) analyses the impact of AI on communication, critical thinking, research and writing pedagogy, as well as the alleviation of social and digital disparities. It advocates for the modification of the curriculum to address the transformative influence of AI on higher education. Malon et al. (2024) sought to examine the merits and drawbacks of AI paraphrase tools for students' writing skills. The results revealed that employing AI-integrated paraphrasing tools has risks and drawbacks, including the possibility of plagiarism, reliance on automated recommendations, and the erosion of context and original significance. Livberber & Ayvaz (2023) investigate the influence of ChatGPT.

AI-Generated Writing in Malaysia

Selvanathan and Narayanan (2024) examine the impact of ChatGPT on higher education in Malaysia. They examine the possible advantages and disadvantages of ChatGPT for students, educators, and organizations. The study suggests that ChatGPT may undermine the quality of education, notwithstanding its advantages.

According to Wan Ismail et al. (2024), AI tools possess the capacity to transform the teaching and learning processes in higher education. The lack of instructional integration constrains the capabilities of these technologies. Ng (2024) examines the influence of AI technology on the academic writing skills of Malaysian undergraduate students and the effects of hedonic motivation, usage frequency, feedback mechanisms, and personalized learning on academic writing proficiency. Osman et al. (2023) examine the intricate relationship among the implementation of AI in academia, perceived behavioral control, trust, intention, and attitude.

Abdul Rahman et al. (2023) investigate the efficacy of Automated Writing Evaluation (AWE) software in detecting grammatical faults and enhancing the writing skills of students at Malaysian public universities and analyses their perceptions of the software. Shahbudin (2024) investigates the impact of AI on Malaysian book writing. Tumiran et al. (2024) assert that the integration of AI in fostering a fairer academic writing environment can be enhanced by examining its potential to encourage inclusive and diverse viewpoints in scholarly writing. Ismail (2024) does a survey of Malaysian undergraduates utilizing AI technology to produce academic papers in English as a second language.

What are Students' Opinions on AI-Generated Writing?

Chan (2023, 2024) examines the perspectives of 393 undergraduate and graduate students across many disciplines on AI-generated plagiarism scenarios. The findings indicate that users have mixed opinions about less advanced AI applications, however, display a strong aversion to AI-generated material. Malik et al. (2023) performed a case study examining students' perceptions of AI in academic essay writing. 245 undergraduate students from 25 postsecondary institutions in Eastern and Central Indonesia participated in a Google form to articulate their views on AI-assisted academic writing.

Regie et al. (2024) examine the academic writing experiences of Filipino students with generative AI. In academic writing, perceptions of AI are neutral, although attitudes and usage demonstrate a positive association. Grammarly, Quillbot, and Google Docs are recommended for content creation, collaboration, and grammatical checking. Črček & Patekar (2023) investigated the frequency of university students' usage of ChatGPT for academic writing, analyzed the way students employ the technology, and assessed students' perspectives on the ethical implications of its use.

Tossell et al. (2024) examined the practical ramifications of incorporating ChatGPT into essay writing assignments in an undergraduate engineering curriculum. Their findings underscore how ChatGPT transformed students' conceptions of AI from a tool for cheating to a collaborative resource, revealing its instructional potential. Johnson et al. (2024) delineate a library training initiative developed by a consortium of academic librarians. Zou and Huang (2023) examined doctoral students' thoughts of the impact of ChatGPT on L2 writing and their expected responses through reflection papers and focus group interviews.

Dong (2024) examines the interrelationship between second or foreign language (L2) writing learners' perceptions of ChatGPT, their usage patterns, and their L2 writing competencies, including complexity, accuracy, and fluency. Yan (2023) attempted to utilize ChatGPT's text creation capabilities during a one-week L2 writing practicum. Šedlbauer et al. (2024) conduct a study investigating undergraduate students' interactions using ChatGPT, revealing challenges associated with the substantial use of AI.

Malik et al. (2024) investigated the influence of the ChatGPT on the creativity of academic and research writing, as well as on the management of plagiarism. Yeliena et al. (2024) examine the advantages and disadvantages of utilizing ChatGPT in higher education. It also analyses the experiences of university students in producing academic projects that adhere to academic integrity requirements utilizing AI.

What are Educators' Opinions on AI-Generated Writing?

ElSayary (2023) investigates educators' perceptions regarding the use of ChatGPT as a digital resource to improve teaching and learning processes. Aljuaid (2024) analyzed the merits and drawbacks of replacing academic writing teaching with AI technologies. AI enhances grammar and style; yet its influence on critical thinking and creativity is uncertain.

The Research Objectives

i) To examine the frequency of student utilization of AI in writing tasks
ii) To investigate students' attitudes towards AI tools in Mandarin writing

The Research Questions

i) How to identify the ethnicity of an individual utilising AI?
ii) What measures should responsible AI use in the event of damage resulting from following AI recommendations and responses?

A Limitation of the Study

The unavailability of reliable tools capable of accurately detecting subtle variations in AI-generated content that emulate human writing styles is the limitation of the study. If students utilize ChatGPT for proofreading, the webservice will also detect the text as having been authored by AI.

LITERATURE REVIEW

The Ethical Implications of AI Writing Are a Significant Worry

Lucía (2023) delineates challenges presented by AI technology to legal academia: Is the utilisation of autonomous essay writing software considered plagiarism? Is it ethically permissible to employ this method if the initial response is adverse? Is plagiarism commonly committed by essay-generating software? Duplicating previous work without appropriate attribution is plagiarism, irrespective of AI models' capacity to produce novel content from it. Barrot (2023) asserts that ChatGPT enables users to partake in genuine and realistic interaction experiences. ChatGPT can function as an effective educator and language resource. Nonetheless, some researchers voice apprehensions over its influence on writing instruction and the preservation of academic integrity. Kayaalp et al. (2023) assert that AI technologies, including ChatGPT, can offer advantageous support for academic writing when employed judiciously and with a nuanced understanding of their capabilities and limitations. Garrote Jurado et al. (2023) urge educational institutions to proactively include digital technologies and deepen comprehension of AI developments.

Dehouche (2021) provides instances of author-generated content utilising GPT-3 and emphasises critical enquiries regarding intellectual property and GPT-3's ability to facilitate reproduction via these instances. Miao et al. (2023) assert that academic nephrology institutions must collaborate to promote ethical AI use and uphold academic integrity in the face of swift technological advancement. Researchers ought to undertake substantial enquiries into the enduring impacts of AI on academic integrity, plagiarism detection mechanisms, and scholarly publications. Sioux (2024) contends that a major issue in higher education is the utilisation of "cut-and-paste" and paraphrase technologies by students to falsely attribute others' work as their own. It argues that the moral indignation linked to plagiarism complicates the resolution of inadequate enforcement and punishing mechanisms.

Thanh (2024) conducted a literature study to identify, select, evaluate, elucidate, and synthesise studies on artificial intelligence in education and learning, as well as associated issues. Ethical standards are crucial for the advancement and incorporation of AI technologies in educational environments to ensure their judicious use and regulation. An AI-enhanced personalised learning environment is highly advantageous for students. Zachia Raiza (2024) examines the capacity of AI to automate grammar verification, plagiarism identification, and citation formatting, thereby allowing scholars to focus on conceptual tasks. Concerns regarding authorship and the ethics of intellectual property emerge when AI substantially influences writing. Halbert et al. (2024) present a model of optimal methods for employing AI to enhance the identification and resolution of plagiarism among students. Younger institutions lacking a policy can recognise the importance of addressing this issue directly. The notion is to safeguard the institution's integrity and the interests of all stakeholders.

Jarrah et al. (2023) examine the literature regarding ChatGPT in academic writing and its ramifications for plagiarism. Scopus, Google Scholar, ScienceDirect, and ProQuest were utilised to examine terms related to ChatGPT in academia, research, higher education, publishing, and ethics. Authors can leverage ChatGPT's functionalities while upholding ethical conduct by conforming to recognised citation protocols. Marzuki et al. (2023) evaluate the influence of AI writing tools on student writing by examining content and organisation as rated by EFL instructors and demonstrates that granting EFL students access to AI writing tools can improve their writing skills. Brian and ChatGPT? (2023) were concern with several issues such as is a human presence required for authorship? What does it imply about the present condition of scholarship when ChatGPT seems academically coherent, despite its lack of comprehension regarding the reality associated with the language it utilises?

Eaton (2023) examines post plagiarism, an era in human civilisation and society marked by the advancement of innovative technologies including AI, neurotechnology, and brain-computer connections. In anticipation of the extensive integration of artificial intelligence and neurotechnology in education, it is essential to prioritise global ethics. Ricardo et al. (2023) emphasise the importance of defining clear rules and criteria for the utilisation of language models in academic writing within their discourse on authorship ethics. Preventing academic fraud and copyright infringement is crucial, as is ensuring that publications generated by language models receive appropriate and transparent attribution.

Bick et al. (2023) examine the ethical ramifications, utility, and advantages of AI tools in academic writing, focussing specifically on thesis composition from a student's viewpoint. The students underscored the importance of assessing sources, utilising suitable language, and preserving coherence in LLM arguments. John et al. (2024) supports the findings by Bick et. Al as he assert that academic and research institutions must adopt generative AI tools in academic writing, as banning their use is untenable.

University Statement Regarding the Clarification of AI Usage in Academia

The SDSU University Library (2024) offers directives for referencing AI tools. They offer guidance on the appropriate attribution of AI tools. It also acknowledged the 10 leading AI-based writing detection technologies. Madonna University (2023) states that Generative AI is advantageous for various writing tasks, including producing emails and draughting research papers.

CMI (2024) meets its quality and monitoring standards, as well as those of regulatory bodies, by upholding consistent criteria. Plagiarism is the act of appropriating another author's ideas, work, segments, or excerpts without appropriate citation. Students are required to demonstrate originality in their work in accordance with the BTEC (2024) standards. They must identify instances of direct plagiarism from AI-generated responses and understand that clearance will not be granted until they can independently exhibit adherence to the grading criteria.

As per SOAS (2024), students may utilise AI as a primary resource for an essay topic, aiding in reflection, identification of key aspects, improvement of understanding regarding the subject, and clarification of complex concepts. BSSS (2023) points out that measures may be enacted in response to violations of assessment protocol. The University of Liverpool (2024) has implemented a policy regarding the use of

AI in academic environments. To uphold academic integrity, students must ethically present findings, conclusions, and data, cooperate when suitable, appropriately attribute credit, and generate original work.

Hampton University (2024) recommend the incorporation of generative AI language into the Student Code of Conduct to tackle plagiarism. The Open University (2024) introduced an online course on generative AI and plagiarism. It mentions that the use of AI-generated solutions in an assignment, without due acknowledgement, constitutes academic dishonesty, regardless of whether it infringes on any individual's intellectual property rights, particularly when such responses are difficult to distinguish from one's original work.

The SEAMEO Secretariat Malaysia (2021) aims to execute the Digitisation Enhancement Program to enhance educators' proficiency and capacity to integrate digital tools into the educational framework, thereby delivering quality education services in Malaysia. GenAI technology is normally allowed to enhance advantages, according to UMPSA (2024). Students, professors, and non-academic staff are urged to participate in GAI training and professional development to guarantee the effective and ethical application of GAI, according to Universiti Teknologi Malaysia (2024).

Development and Enhancement of a Robust AI Writing Detector

Price and D. Sakellarios (2023) analyse the efficacy of readily accessible AI detection tools in identifying AI-generated content and the consequent effects on grading methodologies employed by educators. ComonLit and Quill (2024) investigate the function of AI, ChatGPT, and AIWritingCheck.org within educational contexts. The progression of advanced AI writing has resulted in the development of several AI writing detection systems as online services. For instance, SCISPACE (2024) and Turnitin (2024).

Lori et al. (2024) assert that no detection technique can consistently identify text created by AI. Due to their analogous nature, some individuals may conflate Turnitin's AI detector with plagiarism detection. Turnitin's AI detector generates a summary score and a flag report, like its plagiarism detection system. Similarly, Baron (2024) discovered that detecting plagiarism and AI-generated content may become progressively difficult, despite advancements in algorithms by Turnitin and other systems.

Lanke et al. (2022) on the other hand assert that concerns regarding academic plagiarism have led to the development of sophisticated plagiarism detection technologies. The "Smart Assignment Plagiarism Detector" allows educators to efficiently evaluate plagiarism by uploading a folder with a single click. Nwohiri et al. (2021) developed a system utilising forensic linguistics and natural language processing to efficiently detect plagiarism, whereas Elkhatat et al. (2023) assessed the efficacy of AI content recognition algorithms in differentiating between human-generated and AI-generated text and evaluates the effectiveness of several AI content recognition algorithms in differentiating between AI-generated content and human-generated content.

Scott et al. (2024) perform a comparative analysis of original manuscripts and transcriptions. Similarly, Parker et al. (2024) investigates the use of AI in undergraduate assessments, focussing on the proficiency of graduate teaching assistants (GTAs) in identifying AI-generated evaluations and the efficacy of ChatGPT, an AI model, in producing high-quality outputs. PapersOwl (2024) offered an extensive overview of the AI writing detector.

Steponenaite and Barakat (2023) employ written assignments in computer science and biology produced by ChatGPT to identify plagiarism inside an AI-driven framework. Xiao et al. (2022) investigate the capacity of AI technologies to commit plagiarism and present their initial findings using contemporary plagiarism detection algorithms. These AI-driven methodologies possess the capability to focus on widely used academic plagiarism detection software.

RESEARCH METHODOLOGY

Theoretical Framework

AI users anticipate potential benefits, although it seems that AI may completely replace the user's employment. Conversely, AI may undertake human tasks and obligations, eliciting concern among individuals. Both AI and the internet are products of human ingenuity; nevertheless, regrettably, humanity has developed an addiction to both. In the digital age, individuals exhibit addiction to and misuse of the internet. Humanity has entered an era of dependency on AI, routinely seeking solutions from AI before to commencing any work. Kardefelt-Winther (2014) introduces the concept of compensating internet usage. He argues that the theoretical progress of internet addiction research has been impeded by methodological deficiencies and conceptual obstacles.

Internet consumers recognise the advantages of online engagement; with the extensive availability of mobile phones, the compensating internet use theory is transitioning into compensatory mobile phone use. The world is entering a phase of compensatory measures for AI employment. Individuals often seek validation from AI, such as ChatGPT, to check the veracity of a solution they already possess. If the reaction corresponds with our cognitive expectations, individuals will regard AI as remarkable. Should the AI's solution diverge from our own logic, we shall prioritise the AI's response.

In order to prevent the misuse of AI technologies, the development of an extra supervision mechanism has become essential. Before the extensive implementation of AI, a management system was established to manage the duration of children's smartphone usage, thereby curbing excessive play. Upon reaching the time limit, the device will be locked and unable to connect to the internet. Unfortunately, it is becoming increasingly apparent that addiction to smartphones affects not just children but even adults. A similar situation is already transpiring; to deter students from becoming dependent on AI for all assignments, AI writing detectors have been created. Nonetheless, it is not exclusively students that utilise these tools; adults, including professors and lecturers, are also employing AI.

The AI writing detection tool serves as a regulatory mechanism to maintain equilibrium between usage and addiction avoidance. To augment AI capabilities, it is essential to implement control mechanisms that prevent mankind from becoming subservient to AI, thereby guaranteeing that individuals maintain their capacity for critical thought and do not become complacent. Nandhini and David (2024) propose that the adaptive AI system may surpass its human counterpart if the human-AI collaboration is assessed using an external success criterion.

Chow et al. (2023) examine how expectations regarding the operational efficiency of AI technology influence adoption intentions by employing a novel assessment of AI intelligence grounded in task performance. They propose a four-tier system for the approval or rejection of AI services, including compensating acceptance as one of the levels. Their conceptual model of AI includes three mediating constructs: perceived AI intelligence, performance expectancy, and effort expectancy, in addition to cybersecurity and anthropomorphism. Social compensation theory posits that individuals who struggle with face-to-face interactions are more likely to feel at ease in online environments (Weidman et al.,

2012). They investigated whether individuals with elevated social anxiety have improved well-being when using the internet as a coping strategy.

The OECD (2019) contends that public policy matters and initiatives are essential for the development of human-centred, reliable AI. AI, particularly certain forms of machine learning, introduces novel ethical and societal challenges. The two essential democratic principles are the dangers of embedding analogue biases into the digital domain and the safeguarding of human rights. The decisions made by advanced AI systems may appear enigmatic. It is imperative to ensure that AI systems are transparent and accountable for their results. AI systems must operate securely and accurately. National governments must promote responsible AI research and development to construct dependable AI systems.

The Scientific Foresight Unit (2020) analyses human-robot interactions and human-human collaborations. It promotes the idea of cooperation between humans and artificial intelligence. Vellinga (2024) posed a significant inquiry. Can a compensation fund adequately reconcile the recompense for damages caused by AI systems with the progression of AI technology and its economic development? Kardefelt-Winther (2017) analyses the propensity to see Internet consumption concerns via the perspective of addiction. An addiction viewpoint, based on our comprehension of substance use disorders, is asserted to have not much enhanced the knowledge of the origins and antecedents of Internet use disorders.

Hassanipour et al. (2024) conducted an analysis of the permissible limits for plagiarism in paraphrased chatbot content. Although ChatGPT effectively mitigates text plagiarism, the practice persists extensively. Researchers must use caution when employing this chatbot.

Research Location

At the Centre for the Promotion of Knowledge and Language Learning at Universiti Malaysia Sabah, a lecturer is required to provide a total of twelve hours of instruction weekly. The foreign language course consists of four sessions weekly, each lasting three hours.

A Mandarin instructor provided the research data, comprising individual assignments from the first semester of 2023/2024. Mandarin classes at level 2 were where the assignments were acquired. The assignment was evaluated individually and accounted for ten percent of the total grade.

Students are required to electronically submit their individual assignments by using the link that has been supplied for Google Drive. People who are unable to upload a soft copy have the option of requesting that a hard copy be directly delivered to them whenever it is convenient for them. To guarantee a passing mark in the Mandarin class, it is imperative that the assignment be finished and turned in successfully.

The Efficacy of GPT-Zero as an AI Writing Detection Tool

GPTZero was created by Edward Tian and Alex Cui in 2022 to detect text generated by ChatGPT (Paullet et al., 2024). The developer instituted a preventive measure since students were utilizing the technology for academic dishonesty. Abburi et al. (2023) demonstrated that their suggested model surpassed the most advanced baselines across many benchmark datasets. They executed multiple enhancements. Utilizing the available LLMs, our model proficiently categorized English essays authored by non-native English speakers, exceeding current text identification methodologies. Hareesh (2024) conducted a comparative analysis of ZeroGPT and GPTZero. enumerated the pros and disadvantages of these two AI plagiarism detection technologies. *Table 1* presents a comparison between GPTZero and ZeroGPT.

Table 1. Comparison between GPTZero and ZeroGPT

Specifications	GPTZero	ZeroGPT
Free Plan	Offers 10,100 words per month	Unlimited words, but 2,000 words per check
User Dashboard	Document history	Only guest user
Additional Features	Check for AI vocabulary and plagiarism	AI humanizer and summarizer tools
Compatibility	Classrooms and workspaces	Only Chrome extension and WhatsApp compatibility
Integrations	Easy integrations with third-party tools	Only Chrome Extension
AI Model Detection	Detects any AI model, including ChatGPT/GPT-4, Claude 3.0 sonnet, Google Gemini, Meta Llama, and Microsoft Copilot	Works with any large language model
Premium Plan Features	DeepScan with sentence highlighter	Everything in free
Sentence Highlighting	Only in a premium plan	Sentences with AI-generated content are highlighted by default
Report Download	Download generated reports via PDFs	N/A
API Integration	Anyone can add its API to their workspace	N/A
Login		

Habibzade (2023) concludes that GPTZero was evaluated with thirty text excerpts from medical sources and twenty generated by ChatGPT in response to arbitrary medical enquiries. GPTZero exhibits a significant false-negative rate and a negligible false-positive rate.

GPTZero, as the world's first AI-generated text detection tool, holds significant importance. After conducting many comparisons using the same job to evaluate the other tools, GPTZero remains the most effective and significant tool for this research. Our team utilized the complete AI writing work, the 50% AI writing task, and the 100% human writing task to evaluate these techniques and determined that GPTZero is the most effective and accurate tool for detecting AI-generated plagiarism.

Assignment Selection

Only students who were officially registered and actively engaged in the Mandarin class were chosen for this study. The research findings were solely obtained from electronically submitted assignments. The Mandarin instructor at UMS provided a name list which showed that there are 30 students in Group 1 and 28 students in Group 2 for the two portions of level 2. Level 2 Mandarin is achieved by choosing 15 assignments from group 1 and 15 assignments from group 2. The process of random selection is employed to mitigate any potential bias. *Table 2* shows the details of the Mandarin classes that were included in the research.

Table 2. The details of the Mandarin classes were included in the research

	Level and Group	Quata of a class	Registered Students	Assignment hand in soft copy	Assignment hand in hard copy	Selected for the research
1	Mandarin 2, Group 1(M2G1)	30	30	28	2	15
2	Mandarin 2, Group 2(M2G2)	30	28	27	1	15

Coding

Coding was performed on all selected assignments; for M2G1, the coding numbers were 1–15, and for M2G2, they were 16–30.

ANALYSIS AND RESULTS

Students had to submit a translation in either English or Malay for their Mandarin text writing assignments, but only the text written in Mandarin use for the study. *Table 3* displays the results from detecting AI-generated writing using the web service as below.

Table 3. Results of AI writing detection for M2G1

Code	Total words	Human Writing %	AI writing %	Lecturer Given Mark
1	276	64.80	35.20	6
2	313	73.99	26.01	1
3	275	70.48	29.52	6
4	398	0.08	99.92	10
5	392	7.88	91.12	5
6	390	11.95	88.05	6
7	310	0.08	99.92	9
8	251	99.25	0.75	10
9	298	76.03	23.97	9
10	257	99.20	0.80	9
11	516	0.08	99.92	10
12	195	74.98	25.02	7
13	216	0.08	99.92	10
14	175	42.15	57.85	9
15	200	61.55	38.45	9

Table 4 shows the M2G2 AI-generated writing using the GPTZero. The outcomes are expressed as percentages for human-generated versus AI-generated text.

Table 4. Results of AI writing detection for M2G2

Code	Total words	Human Writing %	AI writing %	Lecturer Given Mark
16	474	21.62	78.38	8
17	178	70.85	29.15	9
18	228	93.02	6.98	9
19	205	27.65	72.35	9
20	234	71.18	28.82	3
21	244	61.98	38.02	9
22	142	77.73	22.27	7
23	176	51.74	48.26	8
24	198	68.06	31.94	9
25	196	59.69	40.31	6
26	247	45.92	54.08	7
27	137	0.08	99.92	8
28	266	31.12	68.88	6
29	175	16.12	83.88	5
30	119	0.08	99.92	8

Table 5 displays the overall amount of AI writing across several categories. Nearly all the selected tasks incorporate segments generated by AI writing

Table 5. The total of AI writing in several categories for M2G1 and M2G2

AI writing					
Group	0-10.99%	11-59.99%	60-79.99%	80-89.99%	90-100%
M2G1	2	7	0	1	5
M2G2	1	8	2	1	2

For M2G1, two assignments indicated that over 90% of the content was written by humans, whereas in one assignment for M2G1, over 90% of the content was human writing. Most of the AI writing projects were scored between 11% to 60%. Most students will still write their assignments independently, but they will use ChatGPT as an assistant. Seven items from M2G1 and eight items from M2G2. Over 90% of the AI writing assignments consisted of five from M2G1 and 2 from M2G2.

Table 6 displays the scores for M2G1 and M2G2. A concise dataset is presented in a table format, displaying the scores out of ten for each category as below.

Table 6. Scores for M2G1 and M2G2

Group	AI writing 80-100%	Score 5-7	Score 8-9	Score 10
M2G1	6	2	1	3
M2G2	3	1	2	0
	Human writing 80-100%			
M2G1	2	0	1	1
M2G2	1	0	1	0

Assignments with a higher AI writing percentage were graded more favorably than those with a higher score in human writing percentage. Only one person scored ten marks in the human writing percentage for M2G1, but no one from M2G2 achieved this number. Three students scored full grades in AI writing from M2G1, but none scored full marks from M2G2.

Results of Short Survey

The brief survey encompasses approximately 100 UMS Mandarin learners. *Table 7* presents the survey findings.

Table 7. Results of the brief survey

		A		B		C		D	
1	Have you ever utilized AI programs to accomplish your Mandarin writing assignments?	Yes	6	No	58	Prefer not to disclose	36		
2	Are you confident in your ability to accomplish the work independently, without the use of AI tools?	Confident	17	Not confident	52	Prefer not to disclose	31		
3	Rationale for not utilizing AI techniques in the Mandarin writing assignment.	My Mandarin instructor will undoubtedly recognize if I utilize AI tools to compose it.	36	I lack proficiency in utilizing AI tools.	15	It is excessively lazy for me to utilize AI tools.	16	I can complete the assignment independently.	33
4	Do you believe AI tools are powerful?	Yes	63	No	2	Don't know what AI is	0	Prefer not to disclose	35
5	Are you aware that numerous web services exist to detect AI-generated writing? For instance, GPT-Zero?	Yes, I am aware	11	No, I am not aware	46	Prefer not to disclose	43		

DISCUSSION AND FINDING

I) To Examine the Frequency of Student Utilisation of AI in Writing Tasks

Pie 1 illustrates the total percentage of AI writing for Mandarin Level 2 Group 1 (M2G1).

Figure 1. Total of AI writing percentage M2G1

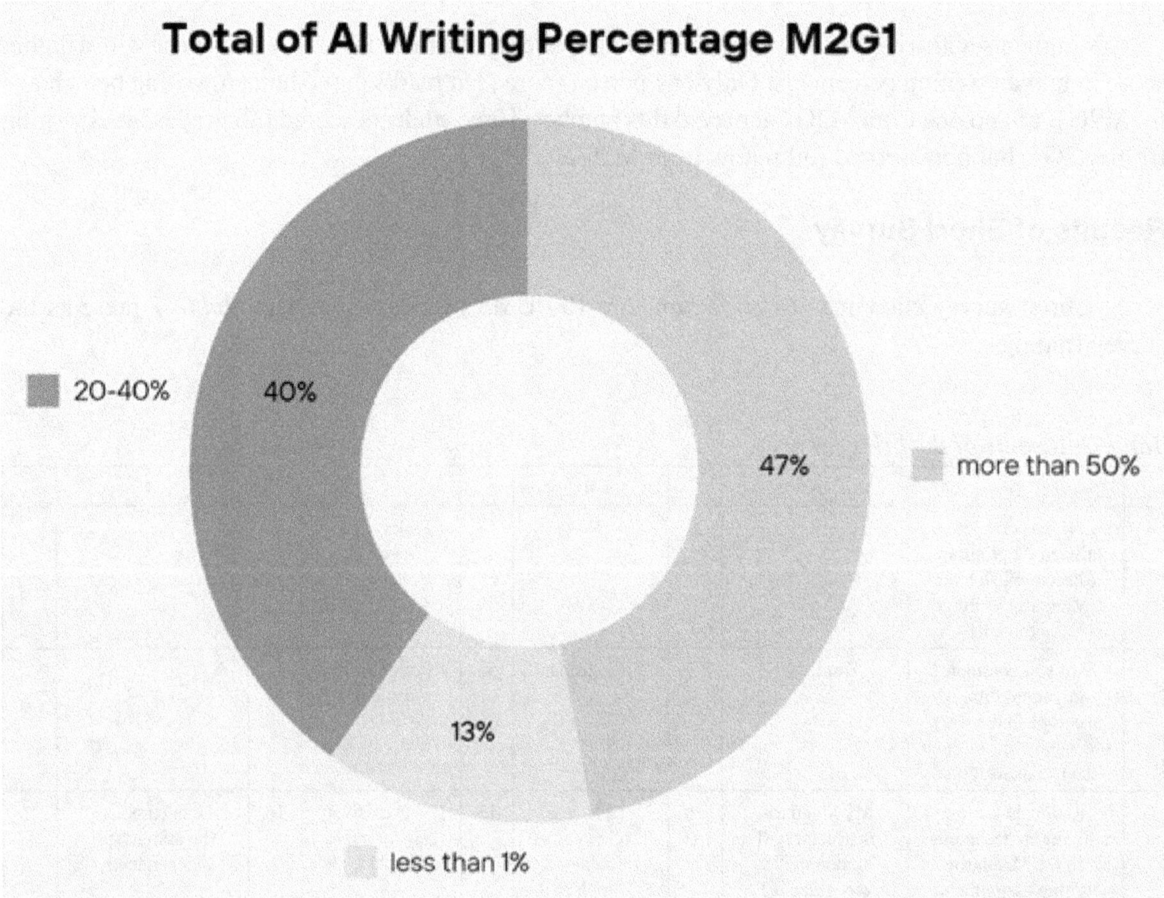

Our research team discovered that the utilization of AI in writing tasks was prevalent and frequent among UMS undergraduate students enrolled in the Mandarin course. Pie chart 1 illustrates the overall percentage of AI-generated writing for M2G1. 47% of the assignments contained over 50% AI-generated content, 13% contained less than 1% AI-generated content, and 40% contained AI-generated content ranging from 20% to 40%. The AI-generated report did not influence the lecturer's assessment. Notwithstanding their elevated AI writing percentage, the students continued to attain superior grades.

Pie 2 shows the total number of AI writing percentages of Mandarin Level 2 Group 2(M2G2).

Figure 2. Total of AI writing percentage of M2G2

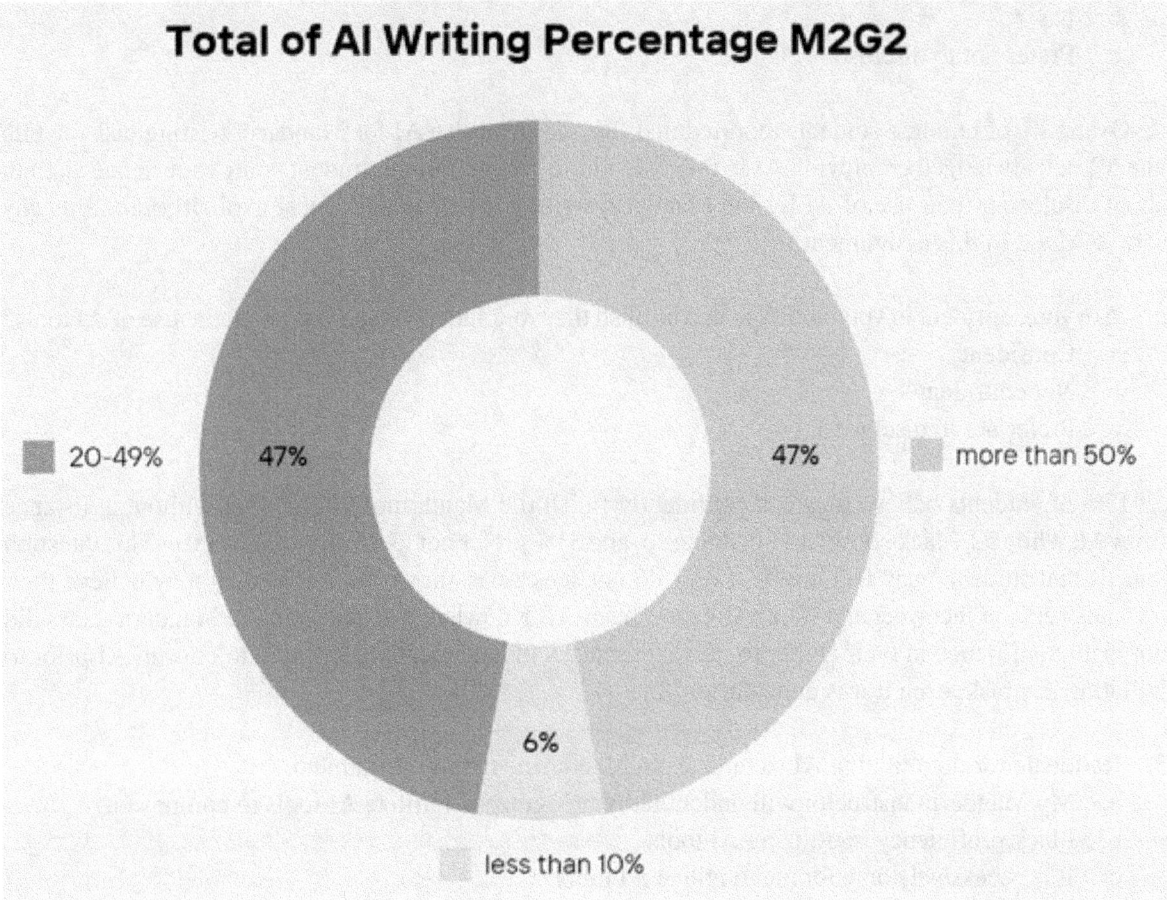

Seven of the fifteen projects displayed over 50% AI-generated text, one assignment contained less than 10% AI writing, and seven assignments featured AI writing between 20% and 49%. Five assignments scored nine marks, four assignments scored eight marks, two assignments scored seven marks, two assignments scored six marks, one assignment scored five marks, and one assignment scored three marks.

The Mandarin Course guidelines unambiguously exclude students from using AI tools—including Google Translate and ChatGPT—for writing tasks; however, students continue to use AI tools for these projects. Since many students will probably seek help from AI algorithms, this tendency will challenge the acquisition of totally original writing assignments from future students. To investigate how students in Mandarin composition view artificial intelligence technology.

II) To Investigate Students' Attitudes Towards AI Tools in Mandarin Writing

The brief survey conducted among students revealed that the majority harbour a favourable attitude towards the presence of AI and acknowledge its potential integration into their lives in the foreseeable future. The survey posed to the learners are as follows:

1. Have you ever utilized AI programs to accomplish your Mandarin writing assignments?
   a. Yes
   b. No
   c. Prefer not to disclose

Over 58% of hundred students reported that they never utilise AI for Mandarin writing tasks, while just 6% acknowledged employing AI in their Mandarin writing. Some students may experience anxiety about disclosing their use of AI for the Mandarin writing work, as the course explicitly prohibits any sort of AI aid in this assignment.

2. Are you confident in your ability to accomplish the work independently, without the use of AI tools?
   a. Confident
   b. Not confident
   c. Prefer not to disclose

17% of students believe they can confidently finish the Mandarin writing work without assistance from AI, while 52% lack confidence in doing so, and 31% prefer not to divulge their stance. This question reveals that students may feel unsafe if they do not seek assistance from AI, as they may believe their own answers are incorrect and want validation from AI. Knowledge acquired in the Mandarin class did not instil confidence in their ability to do writing tasks independently; they tend to consult AI prior to initiating any task, even if it is quite basic.

3. Rationale for not utilizing AI techniques in Mandarin writing assignment.
   a. My Mandarin instructor will undoubtedly recognize if I utilize AI tools to compose it.
   b. I lack proficiency in utilizing AI tools.
   c. It is excessively lazy for me to utilize AI tools.
   d. I can complete the assignment independently.

When asked why they avoided utilising AI in writing activities, 36% of students stated that they anticipated their Mandarin instructor would eventually find its use. Only 15% said they were ignorant of how to use AI to help with writing assignments. Furthermore, 32% feel they can compose it independently. 16% of them ascribed their performance to a reluctance to use AI, suggesting disinterest in the grades received for their writing work.

Do you believe AI tools are powerful?

a. Yes
b. No
c. Don't know what AI is
d. Prefer not to disclose

All students assert their understanding of AI, with 63% acknowledging its potency, while only two individuals regard AI as inconsequential. This indicates that students are aware that AI could influence their future and be applicable across all sectors of their lives.

4. Are you aware that numerous web services exist to detect AI-generated writing? For instance, GPT-Zero?
   a. Yes, I am aware
   b. No, I am not aware
   c. Prefer not to disclose

11% of the students are cognisant of the existence of various AI writing detecting methods. Moreover, 46% were uninformed about it, and 43% preferred not to disclose it. Many UMS Mandarin students continue to receive support from AI.

i) How to Identify the Ethnicity of an Individual Utilising AI

Our team found ourselves in a paradoxical situation; we compel students to learn AI, mandate that our personnel be proficient in AI, and encourage its use among government officials and lecturers, yet we prohibit students from utilising AI for their coursework. We believe that the judicious use of AI may significantly enhance students' learning experiences, particularly in language acquisition. Instructors utilise AI for their research while mistreating students and prohibiting them from employing it in writing assignments.

ii) Relevant Bias in AI

We believe that the process for determining an individual's ethnicity through AI requires further clarification. AI can be employed by anyone impartially; however, the techniques and contexts of its application, together with the way of its utilisation, must be evaluated to prevent allegations of AI plagiarism from educators when students request assistance from AI for their tasks as it demonstrate equity and improved impartiality in the field of artificial intelligence.

iii) What Measures Should Responsible AI Use in the Event of Damage Resulting From Following AI Recommendations and Responses?

Another pertinent problem is the responsibility of AI in the event of any harm or damage caused by its actions, particularly when users act based on AI suggestions and responses. What is the status of artificial intelligence? Are we part of a team, utilising tools, or are we subservient in some manner? All these problems should be addressed soon, as the development of AI is progressing rapidly. Before we relinquish control of AI, we must consider the laws and regulations governing responsible AI. If individuals are accountable for their speech, then AI should be equally accountable.

AI is increasingly favoured by students at UMS for the completion of their writing assignments. Out of thirty distinct assignments, only three were entirely composed by humans. Despite the prohibition of AI technologies for written assignments, students in the Mandarin foreign language course nevertheless favour utilising ChatGPT for their writing projects.

To mitigate grading bias, educators ought to consistently evaluate all student contributions utilising the GPT-Zero online tool.

This will help eliminate instances where AI-generated projects are preferred over human creations. A controversy may emerge when certain students claim that ChatGPT is employed exclusively for proof-reading and grammar correction, even though the assignments are entirely centred on those objectives. The version modified by ChatGPT and approved by the GPT-Zero online platform will continue to be classified as AI-generated material. To avert any inequitable punishment of youth, it is imperative to handle this additional concern.

The teachers assert that these tasks fulfil the rigorous standards and criteria necessary for attaining a high grade. They received guidelines and were mandated to write an assignment utilising solely the vocabulary present in the textbooks. Through pedagogical experience, instructors may readily discern when students compose sentences that diverge from the conventional style of Malaysian Mandarin. The Malaysian populace demonstrates diversity in diction, customs, and Mandarin language and writing conventions.

The lecturers assert that those students employ ChatGPT to edit their assignments. Refrain from utilising ChatGPT for assignment completion. Furthermore, numerous AI tools available online can obscure the identify of information generated by ChatGPT. These tools possess the ability to convert AI-generated content into prose that resembles human writing. Students may utilise these strategies to evade detection by the AI writing system.

The intricacy of instruction has been progressively escalating. Historically, educators were tasked with instruction, while learners were accountable for practice. During instruction, an AI is employed, and the students request the AI to compose text. An AI detector must be utilised by the instructor to ascertain work produced by AI. To evade detection by the AI detector, students must modify their work to exhibit human-like characteristics. Two examples of human literary works have been preserved to the present day.

Conversely, it is conceivable that, in the future, human writing endeavours may become obsolete and exceedingly rare in the realm of teaching.

Academics are wasting their valuable time deliberating on the raised issues. The enhancement of learning quality, academic content, or pedagogical approaches is not the principal emphasis of their endeavours. They are dedicated to acknowledging writing generated by AI, while students focus on evading detection by AI detectors in their written assignments.

The field of education is currently experimenting to ascertain the optimal implementation of AI technology, notwithstanding its incomplete integration into educational institutions.

AI must surmount various racial and ethnic obstacles before it can effectively supplant human educators in the domain of education, especially in language acquisition and instruction. To avert AI from dominating humans or inflicting harm, it is imperative to implement preventative measures prior to the potential overwhelming influence of AI.

RECOMMENDATIONS AND SUGGESTIONS

The Office of Educational Technology (2023) raises concerns regarding the neutrality of algorithmic principles. Educators often encounter anxiety. To alleviate AI-related risks in educational technology, educators must leverage beneficial aspects to further educational goals. as well as participate in a debate about the topic. To what degree do the suggestions of AI models correspond with educational goals? Students must employ AI technology and systems securely and efficiently. They must safeguard data privacy, mitigate algorithmic bias, furnish warnings and explanations, and facilitate user interaction with humans. Although it may hinder the adoption process, those most affected by AI in education must participate in the development of the model, system, or tool.

Our research team determined that we must establish a guideline about AI's accountability for its contributions in the event of any damage. If AI functions as a human collaborator. Our team believes that GPTZero is an effective tool for detecting student writing tasks generated by AI; however, we concur with Habibzade (2023) that the performance metrics of GPTZero and similar technologies require further investigation across various scientific disciplines and larger sample sizes.

Sabzalieva and Valentini (2023) examined critical facets concerning the use of ChatGPT. The *Flow Chart 1* developed by Aleksandr Tiulkanov, an AI and Data Policy Lawyer, in January 2023, is presented below to ascertain the prerequisites for the safe use of ChatGPT.

Figure 3. When is it safe to use ChatGPT

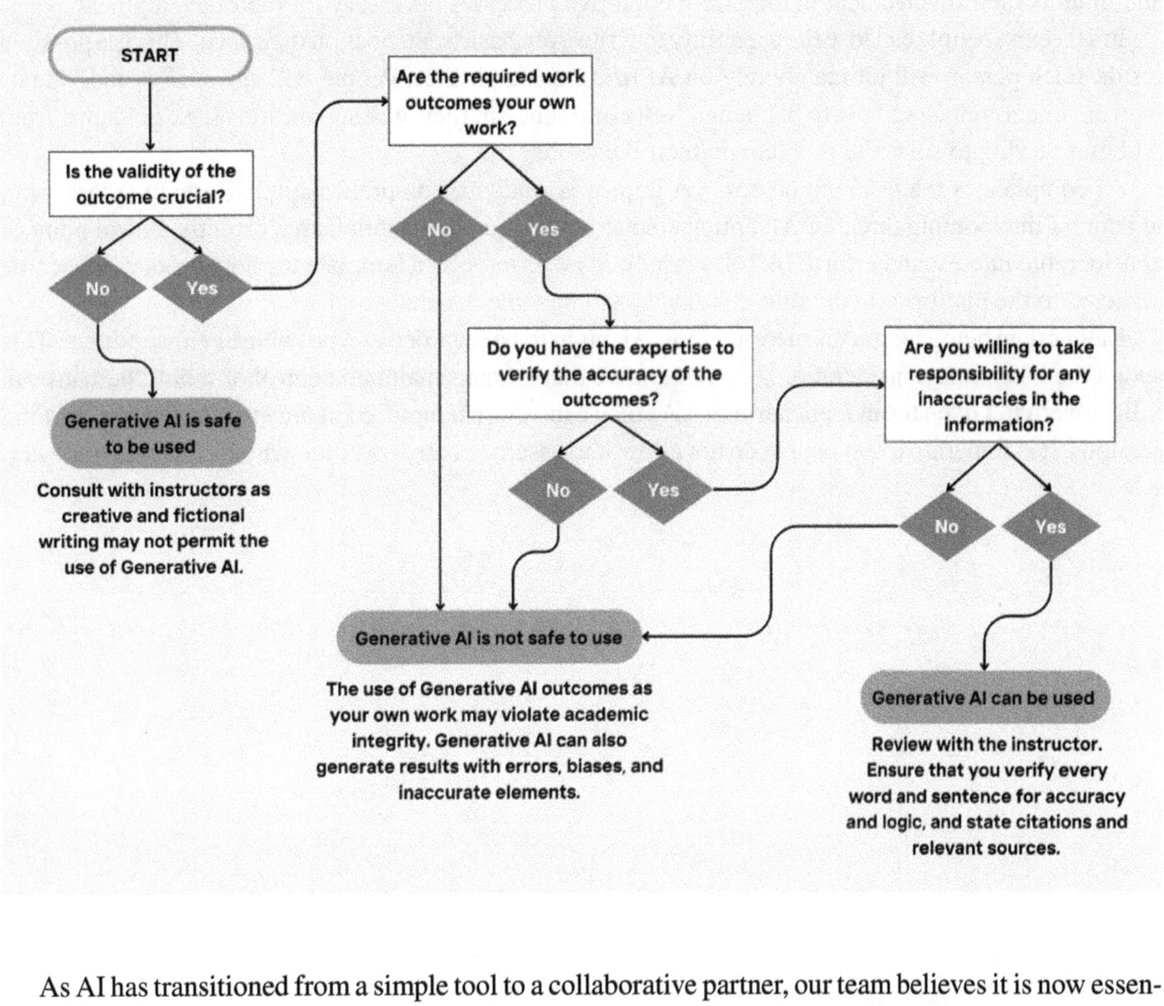

As AI has transitioned from a simple tool to a collaborative partner, our team believes it is now essential to consider the tasks of AI in this role. In the event of project failure as indicated by AI, what form of recompense might we seek from the AI or the entities responsible for its creation or ownership? We must formulate a comprehensive guideline before entirely depending on AI and risking the repercussions of its outputs. Therefore, we advise evaluating the usefulness of AI, specifying its tasks, and outlining the compensation for any losses caused by AI. This is the imperative task we must execute at this time.

CONCLUSION

AI-generated work is deemed plagiarism in this study. Since the work is not created by the students themselves but is instead generated by AI.

People are neglecting the development of their metacognitive skills despite being interested in learning how to use AI. Some of the assignments in this study show that even without reading the AI-generated material carefully, several errors are evident that suggest it was created by AI. Excessively prioritizing AI in the educational system is not beneficial. AI is rendering the need for highly skilled instruction at educational institutions unnecessary. This hinders young individuals from developing writing abilities and inhibits their involvement in important cognitive processes necessary for their development.

In 10 years, people can lose the capability to write even basic sentences on their own. This is a possible result. Each person will ultimately rely on AI to compose phrases. People will see a lot of individuals who are uncertain about how to begin and lack confidence in their writing abilities seek guidance from AI before trying to solve the problem on their own soon.

AI complicates the teaching process yet improves students' comprehension. Efforts to devise ways to address the looming threat of AI, anticipated to be the most substantial, are currently a focal point of considerable interest and effort. TikTok's brief clips will serve as a template for how users will become addicted to the platform. In the future, humans will become dependent on AI as well.

Rather than being viewed as merely a tool, AI ought to be regarded as a possible enemy or threat. This should be taken into consideration. It is imperative that humans maintain control of it until humans can fully govern it. Given the evident harm that AI may cause, as exemplified in only two Mandarin learning sessions, it is imperative that people do not allow it to assume control over the whole education industry.

ACKNOWLEDGEMENT

Ethical standards

The manuscript does not contain clinical studies or patient data.

Conceptualization: Yoke Lian Lau, Anna Lynn Abu Bakar, Jenny Tze Kie Yap; **Methodology:** Shi Kien Chau, Ruoh Yih Sik, Yoke Lian Lau; **Formal analysis and investigation:** Yoke Lian Lau, Hui Wen Yong, Jee Chin Tan, Alagesan Ambikapathy, Jenny Tze Kie Yap; **Writing - original draft preparation:** Yoke Lian Lau; **Writing - review and editing:** Anna Lynn Abu Bakar; **Funding acquisition:** Yoke Lian Lau; **Resources:** Yoke Lian Lau, Hui Wen Yong, Jee Chin Tan; **Supervision:** Anna Lynn Abu Bakar.

Conflict of interest

The authors declare that they have no conflict of interest.

Grant:

The research is supported by UMS Internal Grant DKP0004

REFERENCES

Abburi, H., Roy, K., Suesserman, M., Pudota, N., Veeramani, B., Bowen, E., & Bhattacharya, S. (2023). *A Simple yet Efficient Ensemble Approach for AI-generated Text Detection* [Conference session]. roceedings of the Third Workshop on Natural Language Generation, Evaluation, and Metrics (GEM).

Abdul Rahman, N. A., Zulkornain, L. H., Che Mat, A., & Kustati, M. (2023). Assessing writing abilities using AI-powered writing evaluations. *Journal of ASIAN Behavioural Studies*, *8*(24), 1–17. DOI: 10.21834/jabs.v8i24.420

Aljuaid, H. (2024). The impact of artificial intelligence tools on academic writing instruction in higher education: A systematic review. *Arab World English Journal*, *1*(1), 26–55. DOI: 10.24093/awej/ChatGPT.2

Amirjalili, F., Neysani, M., & Nikbakht, A. (2024). Exploring the boundaries of authorship: A comparative analysis of AI-generated text and human academic writing in English literature. *Frontiers in Education*, *9*, 1347421. Advance online publication. DOI: 10.3389/feduc.2024.1347421

Anson, C. M. (2022). AI-Based Text Generation and the Social Construction of "Fraudulent Authorship": A Revisitation. *Composition Studies*, *50*(1), 37–46. https://eric.ed.gov/?id=EJ1361686

Baron, P. (2024). Are AI detection and plagiarism similarity scores worthwhile in the age of ChatGPT and other generative AI? *Scholarship of Teaching and Learning in the South*, *8*(2), 151–179. DOI: 10.36615/sotls.v8i2.411

Barrot, J. S. (2023). Using ChatGPT for second language writing: Pitfalls and potentials. *Assessing Writing*, *57*, 100745. DOI: 10.1016/j.asw.2023.100745

Bick, M., Breaugh, J., Dong, C. W., Pina, G., & Waldner, C. (2023). *AI and the future of academic writing: Insights from the ESCP Business School Prompt-o-thon workshop in Berlin*. ESCP Business School, Berlin Campus.

Brian, L. F., & ChatGPT. (2023). Should Using an AI Text Generator to Produce Academic Writing Be Plagiarism? *FORDHAM INTELL. PROP. MEDIA & ENT. L.J, XXIII*(947-969).

BSSS. (2023). *Student Guide: AI and Academic Integrity*. chrome-extension://efaidnbmnnnibpcajpcglclefindmkaj/https://www.bsss.act.edu.au/__data/assets/pdf_file/0005/571721/BSSS_Student_Guide_AI_and_Academic_Integrity.pdf

BTEC. (2024). *BTEC Centre Guide to Plagiarism 2024 - 2025*. chrome-extension://efaidnbmnnnibpcajpcglclefindmkaj/https://qualifications.pearson.com/content/dam/pdf/Support/Quality%20Assurance/btec-centre-guide-to-plagiarism.pdf

Chan, C. K. (2023). Is AI Changing the Rules of Academic Misconduct? An In-depth Look at Students' Perceptions of 'AI-giarism'. *Computers and Society*, 1-19. https://doi.org//arXiv.2306.03358DOI: 10.48550

Chan, C. K. (2024). Students' perceptions of 'AI-giarism': Investigating changes in understandings of academic misconduct. *Education and Information Technologies*. Advance online publication. DOI: 10.1007/s10639-024-13151-7

Chow, C. S., Zhan, G., Wang, H. F., & He, M. (2023). Artificial Intelligence (AI) Adoption: An Extended Compensatory Level of Acceptance. *Journal of Electronic Commerce Research, 2*(1).

CMI. (2024). *CMI Plagiarism, Collusion and Artificial Intelligence (AI) Statement*. chrome-extension://efaidnbmnnnibpcajpcglclefindmkaj/https://www.managers.org.uk/wp-content/uploads/2023/12/cmi-plagiarism-collusion-and-ai-misuse-statement.pdf

ComonLit, & Quill. (2024). *A Toolkit for Addressing AI Plagiarism in the Classroom*. chrome-extension://efaidnbmnnnibpcajpcglclefindmkaj/https://s3.amazonaws.com/quill-image-uploads/uploads/files/A_Toolkit_for_Addressing_AI_Plagiarism_in_the_Classroom_2747.pdf

Črček, N., & Patekar, J. (2023). Writing with AI: University students' use of ChatGPT. *Journal of Language and Education, 9*(4), 128–138. DOI: 10.17323/jle.2023.17379

Dehouche, N. (2021). Plagiarism in the age of massive generative pre-trained transformers (GPT-3). *Ethics in Science and Environmental Politics, 21*, 17–23. DOI: 10.3354/esep00195

Devlin, M. (2005). *Higher Education Avoiding plagiarism and cheating A guide for students at Swinburne University of Technology*. Swinburne University of Technology.

Dong, L. (2024). "Brave new world" or not?: A mixed-methods study of the relationship between second language writing learners' perceptions of ChatGPT, behaviors of using ChatGPT, and writing proficiency. *Current Psychology (New Brunswick, N.J.), 43*(21), 19481–19495. DOI: 10.1007/s12144-024-05728-9

Eaton, S. E. (2023). Postplagiarism: Transdisciplinary ethics and integrity in the age of artificial intelligence and neurotechnology. *International Journal for Educational Integrity, 19*(1), 23. Advance online publication. DOI: 10.1007/s40979-023-00144-1

Elkhatat, A. M., Elsaid, K., & Almeer, S. (2023). Evaluating the efficacy of AI content detection tools in differentiating between human and AI-generated text. *International Journal for Educational Integrity, 19*(1), 17. Advance online publication. DOI: 10.1007/s40979-023-00140-5

ElSayary, A. (2023). An investigation of teachers' perceptions of using ChatGPT as a supporting tool for teaching and learning in the Digital Era. *Journal of Computer Assisted Learning*, *40*(3), 931–945. DOI: 10.1111/jcal.12926

Garrote Jurado, R., Pettersson, T., & Zwierewicz, M. (2023). Students' attitudes to the use of artificial intelligence. *ICERI Proceedings, 1*, 514-519. https://doi.org/DOI: 10.21125/iceri.2023.0191

Habibzadeh, F. (2023). GPTZero performance in identifying artificial intelligence-generated medical texts: A preliminary study. *Journal of Korean Medical Science*, *38*(38), e319. Advance online publication. DOI: 10.3346/jkms.2023.38.e319 PMID: 37750374

Hadi Mogavi, R., Deng, C., Juho Kim, J., Zhou, P., & Kwon, D., Y., Hosny Saleh Metwally, A., Tlili, A., Bassanelli, S., Bucchiarone, A., Gujar, S., Nacke, L. E., & Hui, P. (. (2024). ChatGPT in education: A blessing or a curse? A qualitative study exploring early adopters' utilization and perceptions. *Computers in Human Behavior: Artificial Humans*, *2*(1), 100027. DOI: 10.1016/j.chbah.2023.100027

Halbert, J. D., DiMatteo-Gibson, D., Cabrera, M., Mazurowski, T., & Ingram, M. (2024). Artificial intelligence's role in student plagiarism: A graduate University's model of best practices. *Journal of Leadership, Accountability and Ethics*, *21*(3). Advance online publication. DOI: 10.33423/jlae.v21i3.7208

Hampton University. (2024). *Directing The Ethical Landscape: Challenges In Addressing The Ethical Usage Of Generative Artificial Intelligence (Ai) And Academic Dishonesty* [PPT].

Hareesh, P. (2024, August 23). *Battle of the AI content detectors: ZeroGPT vs GPTZero*. ZeroGPT - Free ChatGPT Detector (AI Plagiarism Checker). https://zerogpt.tools/zerogpt-vs-gptzero

Hassanipour, S., Nayak, S., Bozorgi, A., Keivanlou, M., Dave, T., Alotaibi, A., Joukar, F., Mellatdoust, P., Bakhshi, A., Kuriyakose, D., Polisetty, L. D., Chimpiri, M., & Amini-Salehi, E. (2024). The ability of ChatGPT in paraphrasing texts and reducing plagiarism: A descriptive analysis. *JMIR Medical Education*, *10*, e53308–e53308. DOI: 10.2196/53308 PMID: 38989841

Hern, A. (2022, December 31). *AI-assisted plagiarism? ChatGPT bot says it has an answer for that*. the Guardian. https://www.theguardian.com/technology/2022/dec/31/ai-assisted-plagiarism-chatgpt-bot-says-it-has-an-answer-for-that

Hung, J., & Chen, J. (2023). The benefits, risks and regulation of using ChatGPT in Chinese academia: A content analysis. *Social Sciences (Basel, Switzerland)*, *12*(7), 380. DOI: 10.3390/socsci12070380

Hutson, J. (2024). Rethinking plagiarism in the era of generative AI. *Journal of International Communication*, *4*(1). Advance online publication. DOI: 10.54963/jic.v4i1.220

Imran, M., & Almusharraf, N. (2023). Analyzing the role of ChatGPT as a writing assistant at higher education level: A systematic review of the literature. *Contemporary Educational Technology*, *15*(4), ep464. DOI: 10.30935/cedtech/13605

Ismail, A. A. (2024). *Over-Reliance Of AI Tools In Academic Writing Tasks: The Malaysian Tertiary Level Context*. In *E-Prosiding Persidangan Antarabangsa Sains Sosial & Kemanusiaan kali ke-9 (PASAK9 2024)* (pp. 218-224). PASAK 9.

Janet, T. (2024, May 15). *5 reasons to avoid using AI for academic writing*. LinkedIn. https://www.linkedin.com/pulse/5-reasons-avoid-using-ai-academic-writing-janet-tumulty-k2mye

Jarrah, A. M., Wardat, Y., & Fidalgo, P. (2023). Using ChatGPT in academic writing is (not) a form of plagiarism: What does the literature say? *Online Journal of Communication and Media Technologies, 13*(4), e202346. DOI: 10.30935/ojcmt/13572

John, K. S., Hussin, S. N., Mohd Yusoff, R., Mohd Rocky, N. A., Mohd Nawi, M. N., Syed Hussain, S. S., & Mohd Mutalip, S. S. (2024). Mini review on the ethical use of AI bots in academic writing. *International. The Journal of Learning in Higher Education, 19*(2), 65–72. DOI: 10.24191/ijelhe.v19n2.1924

Johnson, S., Owens, E., Menendez, H., & Kim, D. (2024). Using chatgpt-generated essays in library instruction. *Journal of Academic Librarianship, 50*(2), 102863. DOI: 10.1016/j.acalib.2024.102863

Kardefelt-Winther, D. (2014). A conceptual and methodological critique of internet addiction research: Towards a model of compensatory internet use. *Computers in Human Behavior, 31*, 351–354. DOI: 10.1016/j.chb.2013.10.059

Kardefelt-Winther, D. (2017). Conceptualizing Internet use disorders: Addiction or coping process? *Psychiatry and Clinical Neurosciences, 71*(7), 459–466. DOI: 10.1111/pcn.12413 PMID: 27278653

Kayaalp, M. E., Ollivier, M., Winkler, P. W., Dahmen, J., Musahl, V., Hirschmann, M. T., & Karlsson, J. (2023). Embrace responsible ChatGPT usage to overcome language barriers in academic writing. *Knee Surgery, Sports Traumatology, Arthroscopy : Official Journal of the ESSKA, 32*(1), 5–9. DOI: 10.1002/ksa.12014 PMID: 38226673

Khalaf, M. A. (2024a). Aigiarism: The New Form of Plagiarism in the Era of ArtificialIntelligence. *Short Communication*, 1.

Khalaf, M. A. (2024b). Does attitude towards plagiarism predict aigiarism using ChatGPT? *AI and Ethics*. Advance online publication. DOI: 10.1007/s43681-024-00426-5

Khalifa, M., & Albadawy, M. (2024). Using artificial intelligence in academic writing and research: An essential productivity tool. *Computer Methods and Programs in Biomedicine Update, 5*, 100145. DOI: 10.1016/j.cmpbup.2024.100145

Kim, J., Yu, S., Detrick, R., & Li, N. (2024). Exploring students' perspectives on generative AI-assisted academic writing. *Education and Information Technologies*. Advance online publication. DOI: 10.1007/s10639-024-12878-7

Lanke, M. M., Porwal, M. A., Sarolkar, M. S., Palaskar, M. G., & Kakad, S. (2022). AI based student's assignments plagiarism detector. *International Journal for Research in Applied Science and Engineering Technology, 10*(12), 991–999. DOI: 10.22214/ijraset.2022.48080

Livberber, T., & Ayvaz, S. (2023). The impact of artificial intelligence in academia: Views of Turkish academics on ChatGPT. *Heliyon, 9*(9), e19688. DOI: 10.1016/j.heliyon.2023.e19688 PMID: 37809772

Lori, S., Stephanie, F., & Benjamin, B. (2024). *Evaluating the Effectiveness of Turnitin's AI Writing Indicator Model.* chrome-extension://efaidnbmnnnibpcajpcglclefindmkaj/https://teaching.temple.edu/sites/teaching/files/media/document/Evaluating%20the%20Effectiveness%20of%20Turnitin%E2%80%99s%20AI%20Writing%20Indicator%20Model_0.pdf

Lucía, R. (2023, November 20). *2023: An intelligent learning Odyssey*. International Bar Association | International Bar Association. https://www.ibanet.org/2023-an-intelligent-learning-odyssey

Madonna University. (2023). *Generative AI and Academic Writing Tasks What.* chrome-extension://efaidnbmnnnibpcajpcglclefindmkaj/https://madonna.edu/resources/writing-center/online-tutoring/ChatGPTandAcademicWritingTasksRevised.pdf

Maleki, N., Padmanabhan, B., & Dutta, K. (2024). AI hallucinations: A misnomer worth clarifying. *2024 IEEE Conference on Artificial Intelligence (CAI)*. https://doi.org/DOI: 10.1109/CAI59869.2024.00033

Malik, A. R., Pratiwi, Y., Andajani, K., Numertayasa, I. W., Suharti, S., Darwis, A., & Marzuki, . (2023). Exploring artificial intelligence in academic essay: Higher education student's perspective. *International Journal of Educational Research Open*, *5*, 100296. DOI: 10.1016/j.ijedro.2023.100296

Malik, M. A., Amjad, A. I., Aslam, S., & Fakhrou, A. (2024). Global insights: ChatGPT's influence on academic and research writing, creativity, and plagiarism policies. *Frontiers in Research Metrics and Analytics*, *9*, 1486832. Advance online publication. DOI: 10.3389/frma.2024.1486832 PMID: 39583913

Malon, J. C., Virtudazo, J., Vallente, W., Ayop, L., & Malon, M. F. (2024). Expressing ideas: AI-integrated paraphrasing to students' writing skills. *International Journal of Educational Methodology, volume-10-2024*(volume-10-issue-4-november-2024), 531-542. https://doi.org/DOI: 10.12973/ijem.10.4.531

Maphoto, K. B., Sevnarayan, K., Mohale, N. E., Suliman, Z., Ntsopi, T. J., & Mokoena, D. (2024). Advancing students' academic excellence in distance education: Exploring the potential of generative AI integration to improve academic writing skills. *Open Praxis*, *16*(2), 142–159. DOI: 10.55982/openpraxis.16.2.649

Marzuki, W., Widiati, U., Rusdin, D., Darwin, , & Indrawati, I. (2023). The impact of AI writing tools on the content and organization of students' writing: EFL teachers' perspective. *Cogent Education*, *10*(2), 2236469. Advance online publication. DOI: 10.1080/2331186X.2023.2236469

Miao, J., Thongprayoon, C., Suppadungsuk, S., Garcia Valencia, O. A., Qureshi, F., & Cheungpasitporn, W. (2023). Ethical dilemmas in using AI for academic writing and an example framework for peer review in nephrology academia: A narrative review. *Clinics and Practice*, *14*(1), 89–105. DOI: 10.3390/clinpract14010008 PMID: 38248432

Nandhini, S., & David, D. (2024). AI, Pluralism, and (Social) Compensation. *arXiv*, 1-10. https://doi.org//arXiv.2404.19256DOI: 10.48550

Ng, S. Z. (2024). *The Effects Of Ai Tools On Undergraduates' Academic Writing Proficiency In Malaysia* [Unpublished doctoral dissertation]. Universiti Tunku Abdul Rahman.

Nguyen, Q. H. (2023). *AI and Plagiarism: Opinion from Teachers, Administrators and Policymakers*. In *Proceedings of the AsiaCALL International Conference*. PAIC. https://doi.org/DOI: 10.54855/paic.2346

Nwohiri, A., JODA, O., & Ajayi, O. (2021). AI-powered plagiarism detection: Leveraging forensic linguistics and natural language processing. *Fudma Journal Of Sciences, 5*(3), 207-218. https://doi.org/ DOI: 10.33003/fjs-2021-0503-700

OECD. (2019). *Artificial Intelligence in Society*. https://www.oecd.org/en/publications/2019/06/artificial-intelligence-in-society_c0054fa1.html

Office of Educational Technology. (2023). *Artificial Intelligence and the Future of Teaching and Learning Insights and Recommendations*. chrome-extension://efaidnbmnnnibpcajpcglclefindmkaj/https://www.ed.gov/sites/ed/files/documents/ai-report/ai-report.pdf

Osman, Z., Ahmad Khan, B. N., Ismail, M. N., Yusoff, Y., Alwi, N. H., & Mohamad Jodi, K. H. (2023). Artificial intelligence usage in higher education: Academicians' perspective. *International Journal of Academic Research in Accounting. Finance and Management Sciences, 13*(4). Advance online publication. DOI: 10.6007/IJARAFMS/v13-i4/19391

PapersOwl. (2024). *Free plagiarism checker online for students - PapersOwl*. Write My Essay For Me | Essay Writing Service by PapersOwl.com. https://papersowl.com/free-plagiarism-checker

Parker, L., Carter, C., Karakas, A., Loper, A. J., & Sokkar, A. (2024). Graduate instructors navigating the AI frontier: The role of ChatGPT in higher education. *Computers and Education Open, 6*, 100166. DOI: 10.1016/j.caeo.2024.100166

Paullet, K., Pinchot, J., Kinney, E., & Stewart, T. (2024). Can gptzero detect if students are using artificial intelligence to create assignments? *Issues in Information Systems, 25*(3), 165–174. DOI: 10.48009/3_iis_2024_113

Price, G., & Sakellarios, D., M. (. (2023). The effectiveness of free software for detecting AI-generated writing. *International Journal of Teaching. Learning and Education, 2*(6), 31–38. DOI: 10.22161/ijtle.2.6.4

Regie, B. B., Janet, C. R., Leah, C. S., Leo, J. M., Norlie, G. A., & Marjorie, C. A. (2024). Perceptions and Extent of Utilization of Generative Artificial Intelligence (AI) among Filipino Students. *International Journal of Education and Research, 12*(7), 107–126.

Ricardo, P., Ingrid, W. R., Vania, R. U., & Neri, D. S. (2023). *SEMEAD 2023*.

Sabzalieva, E., & Valentini, A. (2023). *ChatGPT and Artificial Intelligence in higher education: Quick start guide*. United Nations Educational, Scientific and Cultural Organization.

Salvagno, M., Taccone, F. S., & Gerli, A. G. (2023). Artifcial intelligence hallucinations. *Critical Care, 27*(180), 1–2. DOI: 10.1186/s13054-023-04473-y PMID: 37165401

Scientific Foresight Unit. (2020). *The ethics of artificial intelligence: Issues and initiatives*. EPRS European Parliamentary Research Service.

SCISPACE. (2024). *Academic AI Detector*. AI Chat for scientific PDFs | SciSpace. https://typeset.io/

Scott, C., Yu, T., Choi, J. S., Langdon, H., & Wesley, M. (2024). *Plagiarism Detection Using Keystroke Logs*. In *Proceedings of EDM2024*.

SDSU. University Library. (2024, December 9). *Research by subject: AI at SDSU: AI citation and plagiarism*. Research by Subject at San Diego State University. https://libguides.sdsu.edu/AI4Students/citation

Secretariat Malaysia, S. E. A. M. E. O. (2021). *Education In Malaysia In The AI and Digital Era*. https://chrome-extension://efaidnbmnnnibpcajpcglclefindmkaj/www.internship.seameo.org/images/Library/GBM/RETRAC/2023/Educational%20Forum/Malaysia.pdf

Šedlbauer, J., Činčera, J., Slavík, M., & Hartlová, A. (2024). Students' reflections on their experience with ChatGPT. *Journal of Computer Assisted Learning*, *40*(4), 1526–1534. DOI: 10.1111/jcal.12967

Selvanathan, B., & Narayanan, S. (2024). Chatgpt in higher education Malaysia: An opportunity or threat to the education system? *International Journal of Academic Research in Progressive Education and Development*, *13*(3). Advance online publication. DOI: 10.6007/IJARPED/v13-i3/21455

Shahbudin, M. H. (2024). The Role And Influence Of Artificial Intelligence (Ai) In Novel Writing In Malaysia. *American Journal of Humanities and Social Sciences Research*, *8*(7), 100–105.

Sioux, M. (2024). A Closer Look at Plagiarism within the Context of Student Academic Writing in an Era of Generative Artificial Intelligence. *Briefly Speaking Council on Higher Education*, 1-10.

SOAS. (2024). *Recommendations for students on use of Generative AI (e.g., Open AI's 'Chat GPT')*. chrome-extension://efaidnbmnnnibpcajpcglclefindmkaj/https://www.soas.ac.uk/sites/default/files/2023-07/ChatGPT%20and%20generative%20AI%20%E2%80%93%20a%20guide%20for%20students.pdf

Steponenaite, A., & Barakat, B. (2023). Plagiarism in AI Empowered World. In Antona, M., & Stephanidis, C. (Eds.), Lecture Notes in Computer Science: Vol. 14021. *Universal Access in Human-Computer Interaction. HCII 2023*. Springer., DOI: 10.1007/978-3-031-35897-5_31

Sun, Y., Sheng, D., Zhou, Z., & Wu, Y. (2024). AI hallucination: Towards a comprehensive classification of distorted information in artificial intelligence-generated content. *Humanities & Social Sciences Communications*, *11*(1), 1278. Advance online publication. DOI: 10.1057/s41599-024-03811-x

Tang, B. L. (2024). AIgiarism is plagiarism: Artificial intelligence can (be perceived to) plagiarize and can also be plagiarized. *Science Editing*. Advance online publication. DOI: 10.6087/kcse.346

Thanh, T. D. (2024). AI's Impact on Academic Writing and Mitigating Challenges in the Digital Era. *International Academic Journal of Education & Literature*, *5*(1), 1–7. DOI: 10.47310/iajel.2023.v05i01.002

The Open University. (2024). *Generative AI and plagiarism*. Distance Learning Courses and Adult Education - The Open University. https://www.open.ac.uk/libraryservices/beingdigital/activity/XK1383#page1

Tiulkanov, A. (2023). AI and Data Policy Lawyer.

Tossell, C. C., Tenhundfeld, N. L., Momen, A., Cooley, K., & De Visser, E. J. (2024). Student perceptions of ChatGPT use in a college essay assignment: Implications for learning, grading, and trust in artificial intelligence. *IEEE Transactions on Learning Technologies*, *17*, 1069–1081. DOI: 10.1109/TLT.2024.3355015

Tumiran, M. A., Mohammad, N., & Bahri, S. (2024). Implications of leveraging AI in students' academic writing: A review analysis. [MJSSH]. *Malaysian Journal of Social Sciences and Humanities, 9*(8), e002954. DOI: 10.47405/mjssh.v9i8.2954

Turnitin. (2024). *AI writing detection in the classic report view*. https://guides.turnitin.com/hc/en-us/articles/28457596598925-AI-writing-detection-in-the-classic-report-view

UMPSA. (2024). *Guidelines For Using Generative Artificial Intelligence At Universiti Malaysia Pahang Al-Sultan Abdullah*. chrome-extension://efaidnbmnnnibpcajpcglclefindmkaj/https://caic.umpsa.edu.my/media/attachments/2024/05/21/ai-bi-garis-panduan-kecerdasan-buatan-generatif_translation-bi.pdf

Universiti Teknologi Malaysia. (2024). *Guidelines for the Use of Generative Artificial Intelligence in Teaching and Learning Universiti Teknologi Malaysia*. chrome-extension://efaidnbmnnnibpcajpcglclefindmkaj/https://fke.utm.my/wp-content/uploads/2024/11/Guidelines-for-the-Use-of-Generative-Artificial-Intelligence-in-Teaching-and-Learning-UTM-1.pdf

University of Liverpool. (2024). *CODE OF PRACTICE ON ASSESSMENT APPENDIX L Academic Integrity Policy 2024-25 Applicable to all cohorts*. chrome-extension://efaidnbmnnnibpcajpcglclefindmkaj/https://www.liverpool.ac.uk/media/livacuk/tqsd/code-of-practice-on-assessment/appendix_L_cop_assess.pdf

Vellinga, N. E. (2024). Rethinking compensation in light of the development of AI. *International Review of Law Computers & Technology, 38*(3), 391–412. DOI: 10.1080/13600869.2024.2324554

Wan Ismail, W. S., Awang, N. A., & Mohd Pauzi, N. (2024). An overview of the use of artificial intelligence (AI) tools in higher education. *International. The Journal of Learning in Higher Education, 19*(3), 27–40. DOI: 10.24191/ijelhe.v19n3.1932

Weidman, A. C., Fernandez, K. C., Levinson, C. A., Augustine, A. A., Larsen, R. J., & Rodebaugh, T. L. (2012). Compensatory internet use among individuals higher in social anxiety and its implications for well-being. *Personality and Individual Differences, 53*(3), 191–195. DOI: 10.1016/j.paid.2012.03.003 PMID: 22791928

Xiao, Y., Chatterjee, S., & Gehringer, E. (2022). A new era of plagiarism the danger of cheating using AI. *2022 20th International Conference on Information Technology Based Higher Education and Training (ITHET)*, 1-6. https://doi.org/DOI: 10.1109/ITHET56107.2022.10031827

Yan, D. (2023). How ChatGPT's automatic text generation impact on learners in a L2 writing practicum: An exploratory investigation. https://doi.org/DOI: 10.35542/osf.io/s4nfz

Yeliena, P., Rashmi, G., & Hayri, U. (2024). The Use of AI Chatbots In Higher Education: The Problem of Plagiarism. *Review of Artificial Intelligence in Education, 5*, 1–8. DOI: 10.37497/rev.artif.intell.educ.v5i00.31

Zachia Raiza, J. B. (2024). Integrating Artificial Intelligence in Academic Writing. *International Multidisciplinary Journal of Research for Innovation, Sustainability and Excellence, 1*(8), 280-293. https://risejournals.org/index.php/imjrise/article/view/637#:~:text=AI%20can%20automate%20routine%20tasks,for%20over%2Dreliance%20on%20AI

Zirar, A. (2023). Exploring the impact of language models, such as ChatGPT, on student learning and assessment. *Review of Education*, *11*(3), e3433. Advance online publication. DOI: 10.1002/rev3.3433

Zou, M., & Huang, L. (2023). The impact of ChatGPT on L2 writing and expected responses: Voice from doctoral students. *Education and Information Technologies*, *29*(11), 13201–13219. DOI: 10.1007/s10639-023-12397-x

Chapter 13
Enhanced Handwritten Text Recognition With Spell Checking by Building a Small Language Model (SLM) With Jaro-Winkler Algorithm

Lavanya Kandasamy
Vellore Institute of Technology, India

Anshi Bajaj
Vellore Institute of Technology, India

Gagandeep Singh Dhindsa
https://orcid.org/0009-0005-5185-377X
Vellore Institute of Technology, India

Atharwa Tagalpallewar
Vellore Institute of Technology, India

ABSTRACT

In today's digital era, the ability to efficiently process handwritten text has remained a significant challenge with the increasing demand for digitized historical records, forms, and handwritten notes. The Jaro-Winkler algorithm and big data analytics are used in this research to create an innovative approach to handwritten text recognition and spell check. Handwriting recognition, a challenging task due to its inherent variability, is achieved through the application of advanced machine learning techniques to vast datasets of text samples. We present the implementation of Optical Character Recognition along with the integration of the Jaro-Winkler algorithm for spell checking, demonstrating its effectiveness in rectifying errors. In comparison with existing methods, the experimental results demonstrate the performance of the system in both handwritten text recognition and spell check. Furthermore, this research explores the practical applications of our system across various domains, emphasizing its potential to revolutionize the way handwritten documents are processed and archived.

DOI: 10.4018/979-8-3693-7260-9.ch013

1. INTRODUCTION

Optical Character Recognition (OCR) has witnessed significant advancements in recent years. Traditional and recent OCR methods often struggle with the variability in handwriting and complex document layouts, lack of robustness, dictionary limitations resulting in suboptimal accuracy. However, modern OCR technologies, driven by deep learning models such as convolutional neural networks (CNNs) and recurrent neural networks (RNNs), have addressed these limitations. The disadvantages of OCR systems, particularly in handling handwritten text and complex formats, have been mitigated by the development of end-to-end OCR models. These models can directly convert images to text without explicit segmentation, and they are capable of recognizing multilingual text, accommodating a wide range of scripts and languages. In addition to handwriting recognition, the system incorporates the Jaro-Winkler algorithm a well-established technique in the realm of string similarity and spell checking. The landscape of spell checking has undergone a transformative shift, propelled by the Jaro-Winkler algorithm as a groundbreaking alternative to traditional methods. Conventional spell checkers, rooted in static dictionaries, have historically grappled with issues related to contextual understanding and the relevance of suggestions. Recent spell checkers also suffer with limited contextual understanding, rigid dictionaries, difficulty with homophones, inflexibility, false positives and negatives and inability to detect contextual errors. These limitations have resulted in suggestions that often fail to capture the intended word in context.

In contrast, the Jaro-Winkler algorithm introduces a paradigm shift in spell checking. The J-W algorithm is a variation of Damerau-Levenshtein. It leverages a dynamic approach to string similarity and spell checking, utilizing a combination of character matching and a prefix scaling factor. This unique approach brings a heightened level of contextual awareness, thereby minimizing false positives and elevating the quality of spelling suggestions. One of the key advantages of the Jaro-Winkler algorithm lies in its ability to consider not only individual words but also their contextual placement within sentences or documents. The integration of big data analytics tools ensures that our system can handle large volumes of handwritten text data, making it suitable for applications in various domains, including digitization, archives, and accessibility enhancement.

In a variety of fields, such as education, healthcare, and historical record preservation, handwriting recognition is essential for digitising handwritten documents, automating data entry, and facilitating accessibility. However, because of differences in handwriting styles, cursive writing, and linguistic complexity, standard OCR systems have trouble processing handwritten text. By combining sophisticated preprocessing methods, adaptive spell-checking, and deep learning-based recognition, this study overcomes the shortcomings of current OCR models and improves accuracy, particularly in multilingual settings. Key obstacles still exist despite OCR technology developments, such as script misclassification, problems with diacritical identification, and segmentation mistakes in languages without clear word boundaries. These difficulties impair the accuracy of spell-checking and prevent its widespread use in practical applications. By creating a strong OCR-based spell-checking system with intelligent preprocessing, context-aware correction, and accessibility-focused design, the proposed study seeks to close these gaps and guarantee a smooth transition into educational institutions with inadequate infrastructure. This paper includes the implementation of optical character recognition (OCR) and augmentation of Jaro Winkler algorithm. Furthermore, we present experimental results that underscore the system's superior performance in both handwriting recognition and spell checking when compared to existing methods. Finally, we discuss the practical applications of our system, showcasing its potential to transform handwritten document processing and archival practices.

2. LITERATURE REVIEW

The focus on Optical Character Recognition (OCR) and presentation of technique to rectify text errors. These errors typically arise due to subpar scanned document quality or limitations in OCR software. The method proposed facilitates OCR in error correction by employing an enhanced hill climbing algorithm to navigate its surroundings. These correction suggestions are drawn from the actual text, rather than relying solely on OCR data. The assessment of correction candidates is carried out using a defined set of weights, determined through rigorous testing (Nguyen et al., 2023). This article introduces a tool known as Image Text Extraction (ITE) that leverages deep learning to integrate text detection and data generation. The objective is to handle texts of varying languages and sizes in a unified process. The system is assessed using real passports and medical receipt documents to gauge its performance. The outcomes demonstrate its effectiveness and efficiency (Ye et al., 2018). A statistical and rule-based spelling and grammar checker for Indonesian text: This article introduces helpful tools for improving grammar and spelling in Indonesian writing. It combines coding techniques with statistical methods. In the Rules section, there are 38 rules to assist in checking and enhancing spelling, word choice, and punctuation. The spell checker examines each word for spelling mistakes and offers corrections using a method called Damerau Levenshtein distance. Additionally, there's a feature to support custom text. The tool employs an effective method, the pair/joint interaction hidden Markov model, to choose the best correction. It utilizes a three-part language structure to spot sentences with grammatical issues. The Rule-Based Checker, this part of the tool has 38 rules to find and fix common mistakes in grammar, spelling, and word choice. It also helps explain what's wrong. Spelling Checker: It goes through every word to find typos. Think of it like a super smart spell-check. It also suggests better words when it finds a mistake(Fahda et al., 2017).

The Smith-Waterman algorithm is particularly adept at finding matching sections within long strings. This capability is especially valued in fields like genomics, where researchers are on the lookout for similarities in lengthy DNA sequences. On the other hand, the Jaro-Winkler algorithm is highly effective when it comes to comparing shorter elements, like names or codes. This method is commonly employed when there's a need to ensure unique or distinct identifiers, without any confusion or repetition. The choice between these algorithms depends on the specific task and the nature of the data being worked with. Both serve their purposes effectively(Agbehadji et al., 2018). Active Verb Spell Checking in Indonesian Language Using the Jaro-Winkler Distance Algorithm: This study employs the Jaro-Winkler distance algorithm to enhance the accuracy of spelling analysis for Indonesian active verbs. Essentially, this algorithm aids in determining whether a word is spelled correctly. In this specific case, the focus is on a specific linguistic category: active verbs. By applying this technique, the aim is to encourage precise instruction writing. This is crucial for ensuring the text's meaning is correctly conveyed. The primary objective of this article is to guarantee the accurate spelling of frequently used verbs in Indonesian. This, in turn, enhances comprehension in writing and communication. The paper discusses the utilization of Jaro-Winkler distance algorithm for analysis the spelling of Indonesia active verbs. Purpose: The primary objective is to ensure that frequently used verbs are accurately written in Indonesian. Method: They employ the Jaro-Winkler distance algorithm to assess the similarity between pairs of words. Significance: This system proves highly beneficial for identifying and rectifying spelling errors in Indonesian, particularly those related to common verbs. Advantages: It simplifies the process of verifying the correct spelling of frequently used verbs in Indonesian writing. Ensure accurate spelling of frequently used verbs in Indonesian. Utilizes the Jaro-Winkler distance algorithm, specifically effective for comparing short sentences like verbs. Special Feature: Assists in verifying the accuracy of common verbs beginning with "Mem-" and "P". Crucial for clear and effective communication, as it relies on accurate writing (Anggoro et al., 2022).

Two-stage frameworks, which can be broadly categorised as top-down and bottom-up approaches, have historically been used to handle multi-person pose estimation. Top-down methods estimate people's poses after first detecting them with a person detector. Although this approach frequently produces excellent accuracy, it is computationally costly and prone to failure in complex settings involving obstruction and crowding because its success is highly dependent on the person detector's dependability. Conversely, bottom-up approaches identify key points independently of instance before classifying them into distinct postures. Despite avoiding the need for a person detector, these approaches are laborious, add a lot of hyperparameters, and frequently result in mistakes and inefficiencies due to their reliance on heuristic-based grouping algorithms. PETR, a fully end-to-end system that redefines pose estimation as a hierarchical set prediction challenge by utilising transformers, represents a significant advancement in this discipline. The problem of feature misalignment, which has long dogged conventional approaches, is resolved by PETR's dynamic emphasis on pertinent characteristics through the employment of attention mechanisms. In contrast to previous methods, PETR is a more efficient and successful solution since it does not require manually designed modules like ROI cropping and non-maximum suppression (NMS). PETR has been thoroughly tested on benchmark datasets including MS COCO and CrowdPose, and the findings show that it performs better than current single-stage and bottom-up methods while simultaneously attaining competitive accuracy with top-down approaches (Schick et al., 2020).The paper compares the Carp Rabin algorithm and Jaro-Winkler Distance for assessing the equality of Sunda languages. Jaro-Winkler, known for accurate short string matching, is employed in duplicate detection, especially for names. In contrast, the Rabin Karp algorithm, utilizing hashing for effective string matching with multiple patterns, has applications in plagiarism detection. With a time complexity of O(n) for texts of length n and patterns of length m, the paper aims to analyze the processing time and similarity values of both algorithms within a text similarity detection system.(Manaf et al., 2019) The study extensively examined existing research on the application of spelling checker technology across multiple languages. Out of 202 reviewed articles, 23 were chosen for this investigation, covering diverse languages such as African, Arabic, Chinese, English, Indian, and Indonesian. The research systematically categorized and presented the solutions employed in each language, presenting the findings in it. Article selection was based on inclusion criteria focusing on title, abstract, language, and country keywords (Zukarnain et al., 2019).

3. MOTIVATION

Building a Small Language Model (SLM) with the Jaro-Winkler algorithm to improve and enhance spelling errors can be a valuable project for several reasons Language Improvement directly addresses the issue of spelling errors, which can significantly impact the clarity and professionalism of written communication. Personal Growth it offers a chance to expand your programming and natural language processing skills, providing hands-on experience with algorithms and machine learning. Practical Application spell-checker with enhanced algorithms like Jaro-Winkler can be used in various applications, from word processors to chat applications, contributing to more accurate and efficient communication. Project with strong motivations is developing a Small Language Model (SLM) with the Jaro-Winkler algorithm to improve spelling accuracy. First of all, it tackles a widespread problem head-on: typos. This effort is intrinsically valuable because these mistakes can significantly impair the professionalism and clarity of written communication. Beyond the obvious benefits, taking on this project presents a special chance for personal development. Enhancing programming and natural language processing abilities is made possible by it, as it offers practical exposure to algorithms and machine learning. Word processors, chat programs, and other tools are included in this useful application, which promotes more precise and effective communication. Furthermore, the project contributes to education by expanding knowledge of string similarity metrics, such as Jaro-Winkler, which are useful for a variety of text processing applications. Increased spelling accuracy has the potential to have a wide range of effects, including helping dyslexics and language learners comprehend more easily. A more specialized and useful tool for users is provided by customization capabilities, which enable tailoring to particular domains or industries. Adding this project to the larger open-source community also encourages originality and imaginative problem-solving. Such a project, which demonstrates technical proficiency and a dedication to the advancement of language processing, can greatly benefit a person's career and resume.

4. METHODOLOGY

In the methodology section, we detail the implementation of Optical Character Recognition (OCR) technologies, specifically leveraging available Application Programming Interfaces (APIs). These modern OCR models address enduring challenges in handling variability in handwriting and complex document layouts, offering improved accuracy over traditional methods. Additionally, our system incorporates the Jaro-Winkler algorithm, a technique in string similarity and spell checking. Our experimental results showcase the system's performance in both handwriting recognition and spell checking, highlighting its potential to transform handwritten document processing and archival practices. The following figure describes the overall working of the system. This figure is an acute representation of the framework incorporated in this project. Based on this framework we are able to construct a system capable of recognizing handwritten text and then carrying out spell checking on it. The quality of handwriting has a significant impact on OCR performance; irregular or cursive scripts result in recognition problems. Preprocessing methods that improve input quality, such as noise reduction and image enhancement, make text easier for OCR engines to understand. Better segmentation is ensured by skew correction, which aligns misoriented text, while binarization enhances contrast. By defining character boundaries, morphological procedures lower the likelihood of misunderstandings. Advanced pre-processing improves readability and removes distortions to improve OCR performance. Adaptive thresholding separates text from non-text areas, while noise reduction eliminates background artefacts. Character outlines are sharpened via edge detection, and low-visibility text is enhanced by contrast correction. Even with intricate handwriting styles, these improvements lead to increased recognition accuracy.

OCR is faster and more effective than hand transcribing or conventional recognition techniques. With automated processing, human participation is reduced and large-scale data extraction is handled with few errors. OCR is a more dependable and scalable option for digitisation, data input, and document analysis when pre-processing optimisations is used to increase accuracy. The Levenshtein Distance method is helpful for correcting errors but ineffective for extracting vast amounts of text since it determines the smallest number of modifications (insertions, deletions, and substitutions) needed to match two strings. In a similar vein, complicated handwritten or printed text cannot be recognised using the computationally demanding Smith-Waterman technique, which was created for local sequence alignment. OCR extracts and processes text directly without the need for laborious character-by-character comparisons when combined with binarization, edge detection, and adaptive thresholding. Compared to conventional text-matching algorithms like Smith-Waterman and Levenshtein Distance, OCR with sophisticated pre-processing techniques offers more efficiency and accuracy. These methods are computationally costly and less successful for real-time large-scale text recognition since they rely on character-level comparison and sequence alignment. On the other hand, OCR greatly increases speed and accuracy by processing whole photos, applying image enhancement, noise reduction, and segmentation, and extracting text in a structured manner. The main benefit of OCR is that, in contrast to Smith-Waterman and Levenshtein, which have trouble with non-uniform inputs, it can dynamically accommodate differences in handwriting, fonts, and distortions. Deep learning-based models enable OCR to recognise patterns beyond simple string matching, adjust to various scripts, and increase accuracy through preprocessing optimisations. Because of this, OCR is not only quicker but also more scalable, dependable, and useful for real-world uses including automation, large-scale data processing, and document digitisation. Languages that use accent marks, like Arabic, Vietnamese, or French, frequently have problems with accent and diacritical recognition. These markings could be missed by OCR or misinterpreted, leading to misspelt words with different meanings. Furthermore, erroneous tokenisation can result from Word Segmentation Errors in languages like Chinese, Japanese, or Thai that lack clear spaces, which can impact the accuracy of spell-checking and identification. Furthermore, when OCR misinterprets homographs—words that have the same appearance but distinct meanings in various languages—contextual spelling and grammar issues occur (e.g., “Polish” in English vs. “polish” as a verb). Without strong language detection and context-aware correction, traditional spell-checkers—which are made for monolingual text—might not be able to adequately fix such mistakes. Language model integration, adaptive dictionaries, and AI-driven contextual analysis are necessary to overcome these obstacles and enhance the accuracy of multilingual OCR and spell-checking dependability

Figure 1. System framework diagram

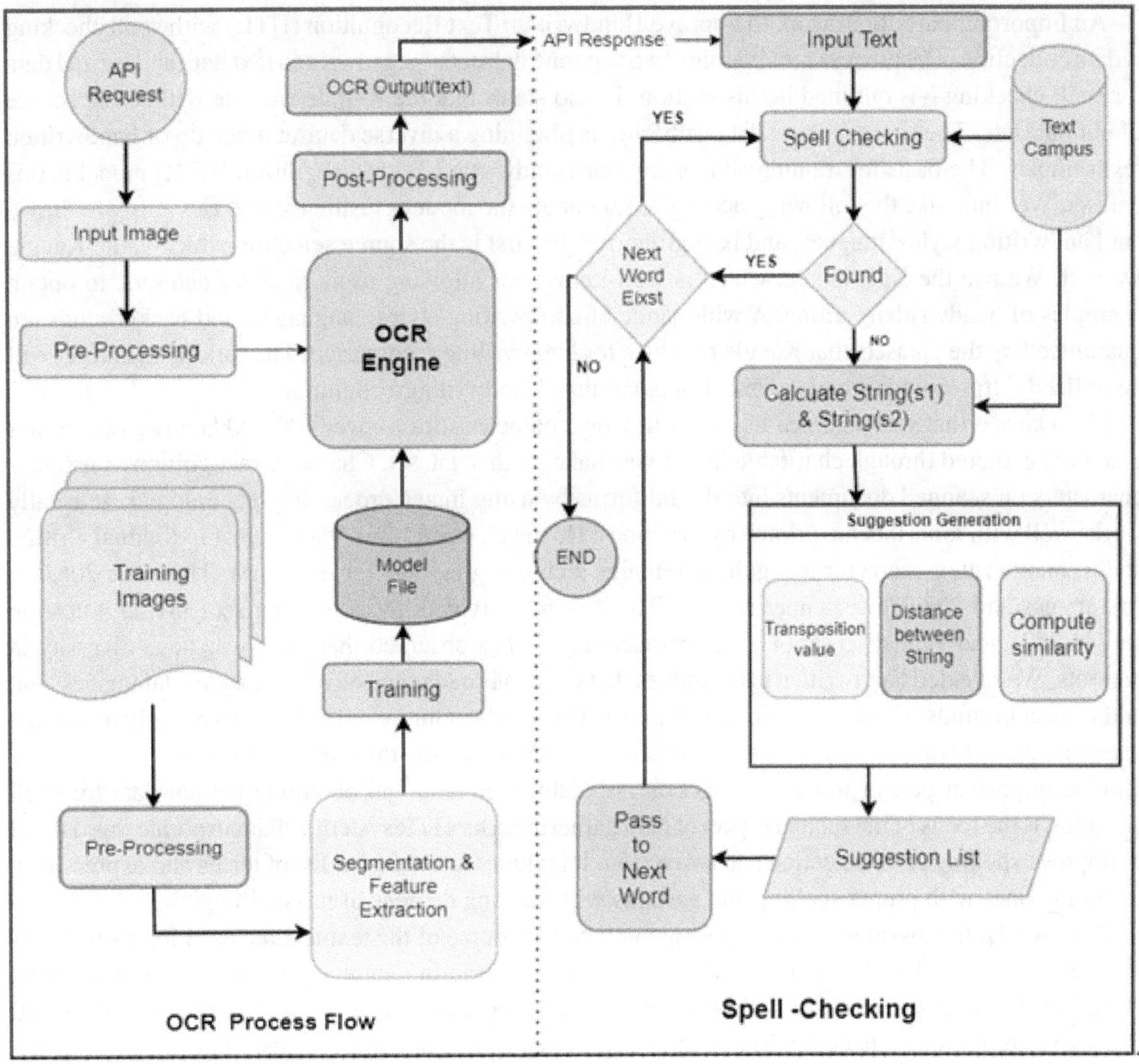

The project is structured into four distinct phases, each serving a crucial role in its overall development. The initial phase, Phase 1, focuses on data collection and pre-processing, establishing a solid foundation for subsequent stages. Following this, Phase 2 involves the integration of a Handwritten Text Recognition (HTR) model, a pivotal step in enhancing the system's ability to accurately interpret and transcribe handwritten text. Phase 3 introduces the integration of the Jaro-Winkler Algorithm, contributing to the project's sophistication by incorporating a powerful string matching algorithm used in spell checking. Finally, Phase 4 marks the culmination of efforts with the implementation of Enhanced Text Recognition and Spell Checking, aiming to refine and optimize the overall text recognition capabilities of the system. This phased approach ensures a systematic and comprehensive development process, addressing various aspects of the project to ultimately deliver a robust and efficient solution.

a) Data Collection and Pre-Processing

An important part of our work to improve Handwritten Text Recognition (HTR) with spell checking is data collection. The process for obtaining two separate datasets—handwritten text data and textual data for spell checking—is outlined in this section. It also states that the Kaggle website will be the source of our datasets. The first aspect of data gathering is obtaining a diverse dataset made up of handwritten text samples. The basis for training and testing our Handwritten Text Recognition (HTR) model is this dataset. We shall take the following actions to guarantee the model's resilience and flexibility to different handwriting styles, tongues, and backgrounds. The first is the source selection which is the Kaggle Dataset. We use the Kaggle site, which is well-known for allowing users to share datasets, to obtain examples of handwritten writing. A wide range of handwriting styles, languages, and backgrounds are guaranteed by the datasets that Kaggle provides for handwriting recognition. The following dataset will be utilized: https://www.kaggle.com/datasets/landlord/handwritingrecognition

The Dataset that was obtained has the following characteristics as over 400,000 handwritten names that were gathered through charitable initiatives make up this dataset. Character recognition transforms characters on scanned documents into digital forms by using image processing technologies. It usually works well with fonts that are printed by machines. However, due to the wide range of individual writing styles, handwritten character recognition remains a challenging task for machines. There are 206,799 first names and 207,024 surnames in total. The data was divided into a training set (331,059), testing set (41,382), and validation set (41,382) respectively. It was observed that there was huge diversity in datasets. We selected handwritten text samples that cover a broad range of writing styles, languages, and author backgrounds in order to build an extensive HTR model. Our model's ability to reliably transcribe handwritten text from any source or author is made possible by the diversity of datasets.

One important part of the data collection is handwritten data and obtaining textual data for spell checking is the focus of the second aspect of data gathering. Our HTR system will incorporate this dataset to improve spelling error detection and correction. It includes an extensive list of terms and expressions, including ones with proper spelling and variants with varying degrees of misspellings.

Just like the handwritten text data, Kaggle will be the source of the textual data used for spell checking. The vast textual data in Kaggle's datasets is ideal for training language models and putting spell checking algorithms to use. We will perform data cleaning and structuring in order to get the textual dataset ready for spell checking. The goal is to produce a well-organized dataset that works with our technology to improve spelling error detection and correction. The next step in Phase 1 is the pre-processing of data. Preparing the data for further stages of our research is essential, as it guarantees that the textual and handwritten data are in the right format. In order to improve the quality and consistency of the dataset—which is necessary for both training and assessing our Handwritten Text Recognition (HTR) model—pre-processing handwritten text data is crucial. Noise in handwritten text data, such as smudges, artefacts, and background interference, is common. Techniques for noise reduction will be used to lessen the effect of noise on the HTR model. Improving the clarity of handwritten text and guaranteeing accurate character recognition depend heavily on the quality of handwritten text images. We'll use image enhancement techniques to sharpen edges, adjust brightness, and improve contrast. For the textual data utilized in spell checking, pre-processing is essential to ensure dataset organization and the removal of unnecessary elements. This clean and structured dataset is integrated into our system to improve the recognition and correction of spelling errors. It involves special character and digit removal and whitespace handling.

b) Handwritten Text Recognition (HTR) Model Integration

Our research revolves around the creation and incorporation of a pre-trained Handwritten Text Recognition (HTR) model obtained via an online OCR API. The procedures for incorporating the OCR API-based HTR model into our project are described in this section. Carefully choosing an online OCR (Optical Character Recognition) API with a trained HTR model for handwritten text recognition will be our first step. The ability of the selected OCR API to identify different handwriting styles and languages will be evaluated. Next step will be API integration. Our project will seamlessly incorporate the chosen OCR API and its HTR model. This integration includes setting up API access, configuring the model, and implementing the required API calls in our system. Samples of handwritten text that need to be recognised will be sent in as input to the OCR API integrated. These samples could be digital text transcriptions from handwritten sources, scanned documents, or photos. The OCR API's output of recognised text will be retrieved and processed for our system's later spell checking and enhancement. As outlined in following phases, our spell checking component will be integrated with the recognised text that was obtained from the OCR API. The spell checking feature will improve text recognition accuracy and provide suggestions for spelling corrections. The performance of the OCR API-based HTR model and the integrated system will be evaluated using various metrics, including: Accuracy, Word Error Rate, Precision, Recall, and F1-score.

c) Jaro-Winkler Algorithm Integration

The incorporation of the Jaro-Winkler Algorithm is a crucial measure in improving our project's spell checking feature. A thorough explanation of the procedures for implementing the JaroWinkler Algorithm for enhanced spell checking and suggestion generation is given in this section. The initial discussion is on algorithm selection. We have chosen to compute string similarity using the Jaro-Winkler Algorithm. Because of its well-established effectiveness in comparing the similarity of two strings, the Jaro-Winkler Algorithm is a good choice for identifying similar words in the context of spell checking. Another thing to consider is the threshold setting. A similarity threshold will be defined to see if two words are similar enough for the spell checking feature to recommend a correction. The threshold will be empirically determined in accordance with the particular needs of the project, guaranteeing a suitable ratio of recall to precision.

d) Enhanced Text Recognition and Spell Checking

A fundamental aspect of our work is the combination of spell checking and Handwritten Text Recognition (HTR). The procedures for developing an integrated system that uses spell checking and HTR to improve spelling error detection and correction are described in this section. The input for the spell checking component will be the handwritten text recognition output from the HTR component. There could be typographical or factual errors in this text. The recognised text from the HTR component will be sent to the spell checking component, which will carry out the spell checking and correction tasks detailed in above phases. Error Recognition in order to find any spelling mistakes, the spell checking feature will examine the text that has been identified. To do this, it will employ Jaro-Winkler similarity, and dictionary comparison. Next we will carry out generation of suggestions. The spell checking feature will produce a list of suggestions for fixing the error when a spelling mistake is found. These recommendations will be determined by utilising the Jaro-Winkler Algorithm to compute similarity of correctly spelt words, vocabulary, and text context. The spell-checking feature will offer the user suggestions for corrections. According to their scores for similarity and relevance, the suggestions will be ranked. The suggested corrections can be accepted or rejected by the user. As new data becomes available, the spell checking component—which includes the Jaro-Winkler Algorithm and SLM—will be continuously trained and adjusted. This guarantees that the system will always be able to identify and fix spelling mistakes and stay current. A predetermined set of metrics, including accuracy, precision, recall, F1-score, and user satisfaction, will be used to assess the integrated system's work. The efficacy of the spell check and correction feature will be evaluated using these metrics. The user's feedback and experience will be a key component of assessing the integrated system. Usability testing and user satisfaction surveys will reveal how well the system functions in practical situations.

Algorithm

This section elaborated the Jaro Winkler Algorithm and how it is slightly modified to be used in our particular system.

Data Preparation:

1. Data Fetching:
    - The Jaro-Winkler algorithm takes two strings, s1 and s2, as input for comparison.
2. String Pre-processing:
    - Pre-processing steps can include converting the strings to lowercase and removing spaces or other non-alphanumeric characters, depending on your application.

Jaro Similarity Calculation:

3. String Length Comparison:
    - Calculate the length of both strings, denoted as n for s1 and m for s2.
4. Matching Characters:
    - For each character in s1, determine if there is a matching character in s2 within a certain range. The range is calculated as max (n, m) / 2 - 1.
5. Transpositions:
    - Count the number of character pairs that match but are out of order in both s1 and s2. This helps account for minor transpositions that might occur when two strings are similar.
6. Jaro Similarity Calculation:
    - Calculate the Jaro similarity, denoted as J, using the formula:

$$J = (1/3) * (m/n + m/m + (m - \text{transpositions}) / m)$$

- m is the number of matching characters between the two strings.
- n is the length of s1.
- m is the length of s2.
- transpositions is the number of transpositions.

Winkler Factor Calculation:

7. Scaling Factor (Winkler Factor):
   - The Jaro similarity score can be enhanced using a scaling factor called the Winkler factor. This factor is applied if the Jaro similarity is above a certain threshold (commonly 0.7).
8. Common Prefix Length (L):
   - Calculate the length of the common prefix (same characters at the beginning of both strings).
9. Winkler Factor Calculation:
   - Calculate the Winkler factor, denoted as P, using the formula:

$$P = J + (L * p * (1 - J))$$

   - p is a constant scaling factor, typically set to 0.1.

Final Result Prediction:

10. Jaro-Winkler Similarity Score:
    - The final Jaro-Winkler similarity score, denoted as JW, is calculated by adding the Jaro similarity score (J) and the Winkler factor (P).
11. Result Prediction:
    - The Jaro-Winkler similarity score, JW, can be interpreted as a measure of similarity between the two strings. You can define a threshold (commonly 0.8 or 0.9) to classify the result. If JW is greater than the threshold, you can predict that the two strings are similar; otherwise, they are not considered similar.

Recall, precision, and the F1-score for spelling error detection and correction are among the appropriate evaluation metrics that will be used to gauge how well the Jaro-Winkler Algorithm integration works. The results of this evaluation will show how the algorithm affects the functionality of the spell checking component. Any necessary fine-tuning or parameter adjustments will be implemented based on the evaluation results. This could entail changing the threshold for similarity, improving the system for ranking suggestions, or improving the suggestions' user interface.

5. EXPERIMENTAL RESULTS

In order to carry out spell checking on the handwritten text, first we need to recognize the text written in the ink format and convert it into a digital format so as to perform further operations on it. The system is capable of taking an image of handwritten text as input which it will utilize further by making use of the functions to extract useful information from the given input. The following figure depicts the sample input which is given to the system.

Figure 2. Handwritten text as sample input

Next step is to perform OCR on the input image in order to convert the handwritten text into digital text. We make use of an API call in order to achieve this particular task and then the obtained text from the image is saved in a text file format for further processing. The following figure demonstrates the intermediate output from the OCR as well as notifying about the creation of the output file.

Figure 3. Intermediate output from OCR

```
Output file created!
The obtained text is as follows:

####*********************####
####    fram works     ####
####*********************####
```

The following figure demonstrates the output from the OCR is saved in a text file which will be accessed by the Jaro Winkler Algorithm Java code. The contents of the above file which is the output from the OCR process are read and then treated as input to carry out spell checking process on it. After applying Jaro Winkler algorithm on the input the system is able to highlight whether the word is correctly spelled or not. If the word is not spelled correctly then the system is able to specify the mapped result which is the closest to the misspelled word along with the highest similarity score. It also lists the characters that are missing from the word and the summary of the result.

Figure 4. Output of JW algorithm

```
Input word: framworks
Mapped result: frameworks
Highest similarity: 0.98
Missing characters: [e]
Result summary: CLOSE_MATCH
```

The following table presents the performance metrics of different Optical Character Recognition (OCR) models across two datasets: IAM and CBC. The metrics include Accuracy and Character Error Rate (CER). The IAM database is an English sentence database for offline handwriting recognition. The IAM database contains 13,353 images of handwritten lines of text created by 657 writers. The other is the dataset of printed CBC images.

Table 1. Performance of different OCR models

Dataset	Metric	Amazon Textract	Google Vision	Pytesseract	Nanonets API
IAM	Accuracy	89.42%	88.53%	81.02%	95%
	CER	0.1403	0.1621	0.2650	0.1231
Document database	Accuracy	95%	90.3%	84.1%	96%
	CER	0.1082	0.1332	0.2231	0.1069
Chars74K Data	Accuracy	93%	87.3%	80.1%	94%
	CER	0.1282	0.1430	0.2022	0.1170

These results provide insights into the OCR models' effectiveness on different datasets, emphasizing the trade-offs between accuracy and character error rates. Nanonets API stands out for achieving both high accuracy and low CER, making it a strong performer across the evaluated datasets. The system includes assistive features including voice input assistance, dyslexia-friendly fonts, and text-to-speech to ensure inclusivity and make it usable for students with impairments. This project guarantees that educational institutions can successfully integrate OCR-based spell-checking without encountering technological obstacles by placing a high priority on usability, low infrastructure requirements, and adaptive learning capabilities.

The project incorporates multilingual and adaptive spell-checking, incorporating AI-powered language identification that automatically adapts for various scripts and dialects, to support a range of educational needs. This improves accuracy and decreases manual configuration, particularly for multilingual pupils. Furthermore, it is mobile-friendly and optimised for low-bandwidth contexts, allowing access on a variety of devices—including smartphones and tablets—without the need for expensive hardware. Because of infrastructure limits, financial constraints, and technical complexity, educational institutions frequently encounter difficulties while installing OCR-based spell-checking systems. This project provides both cloud-based and on-premise solutions to guarantee accessibility, giving institutions the option to select a lightweight local version for more privacy or an online model for environments with limited resources. Both teachers and students will find the system easy to use thanks to its straightforward and user-friendly design, which includes drag-and-drop text/image upload, easy-to-navigate menus, and real-time corrective feedback.

To evaluate our system we make use of various evaluation metrics such as accuracy, precision, recall and F1 score. To calculate accuracy, precision, recall, and F1 score, we need additional information which is the confusion matrix. The confusion matrix is a table that describes the performance of a classification model. It has four entries: true positives (TP), true negatives (TN), false positives (FP), and false negatives (FN). In this case:

- True Positives (TP): The number of correctly predicted positive instances.

- True Negatives (TN): The number of correctly predicted negative instances.
- False Positives (FP): The number of instances predicted as positive but are actually negative.
- False Negatives (FN): The number of instances predicted as negative but are actually positive.

Accuracy is a measure of overall correctness. Precision measures the accuracy of the positive predictions. Recall measures the ability of the model to capture all relevant instances of the positive class. The F1 Score is the harmonic mean of precision and recall. These metrics are calculated as follows:

Accuracy = ((True Positives + True Negatives) / (Total Instances)) * 100
Precision = True Positives / (True Positives + False Positives)
Recall = True Positives / (True Positives + False Negatives)
F1 Score = 2 * ((Precision * Recall) / (Precision + Recall))

The following table presents the performance metrics of our system Enhanced Handwritten Text Recognition model with integrated spell checking capabilities. The model's effectiveness is evaluated across key metrics, including Accuracy, Precision, Recall, and F1 Score.

Table 2. Performance of the system

	Accuracy	Precision	Recall	F1 Score
Jaro Winkler based Handwritten Text Recognition with Spell Checking	91.02%	0.95	0.95	0.78
Feed Forward NN	73.9%	77.6	60.8	0.512
Hill Climbing Algorithm	81.42%	0.75	0.833	0.494

These metrics collectively showcase the model's competency in accurately recognizing handwritten text, coupled with effective spell checking. While the model achieves a notable accuracy, the precision-recall balance, as indicated by the F1 Score, emphasizes its ability to maintain a harmonious trade-off between minimizing false positives and capturing relevant instances.

6. CONCLUSION

The use of optical character recognition (OCR) and the Jaro-Winkler algorithm for spell checking is presented in this paper, along with an analysis of how well it corrects errors and generates recommendations. The system outperforms current methods in both handwriting recognition and spell check, as demonstrated by the paper's comparison of the system's performance. The system's useful applications in a variety of fields, including document digitization, archives, and accessibility improvement, are covered in the paper. Finally, a reliable and precise solution for managing the difficulties posed by handwritten text has been produced by the application of Enhanced Handwritten Text Recognition (HTR) with spell checking, which makes use of a Small Language Model (SLM) and the Jaro-Winkler algorithm. The accuracy of recognition has been greatly enhanced by the synergistic combination of the contextual understanding offered by the SLM and the spell checking prowess of the Jaro-Winkler algorithm. This combination ensures a more thorough and contextually aware correction process in addition to correcting errors caused by handwriting variations. Enhancing the overall user experience, users can gain more confidence in the system's ability to accurately transcribe and correct handwritten text. Moreover, the system's versatility across various domains and writing styles highlights its pragmatic value. Many applications can benefit from the efficiency of the Jaro-Winkler algorithm in maintaining computational speed, which guarantees that spell checking does not impair real-time performance. In conclusion, even though the current implementation represents a significant breakthrough in HTR, more research and development work could look into improving the system even further and maybe adding more sophisticated algorithms to raise the accuracy and adaptability of handwritten text recognition systems even further. The paper proposes a novel approach to handwritten text recognition and spell checking using the JaroWinkler algorithm and big data analytics. This study shows that combining OCR with Jaro-Winkler similarity greatly increases handwriting recognition and spell-checking accuracy and usability. The Jaro-Winkler algorithm improves OCR output by improving text correction, particularly in situations of unclear or distorted handwriting. It is well-known for its effectiveness in managing slight spelling differences and phonetic similarities. The system outperforms conventional Levenshtein Distance and rule-based spell-checkers by integrating sophisticated image preprocessing, adaptive spell correction, and contextual error handling. It successfully handles script changes, misclassification, and segmentation mistakes.It is a more scalable and flexible solution than current methods since it excels in multilingual text processing, low-resource handwriting recognition, and educational accessibility

REFERENCES

Agbehadji, I. E., Yang, H., Fong, S., & Millham, R. (2018, August). The comparative analysis of Smith-Waterman algorithm with Jaro-Winkler algorithm for the detection of duplicate health related records. In 2018 International Conference on Advances in Big Data, Computing and Data Communication Systems (icABCD) (pp. 1-10). IEEE. DOI: 10.1109/ICABCD.2018.8465458

Anggoro, D. A., & Nurfadilah, I. (2022). Active Verb Spell Checking Mem-+ P in Indonesian Language Using the Jaro-Winkler Distance Algorithm. *Iraqi Journal of Science*, ●●●, 1811–1822. DOI: 10.24996/ijs.2022.63.4.38

Arora, S., Narayan, A., Chen, M. F., Orr, L., Guha, N., Bhatia, K., . . . Ré, C. (2022). Ask me anything: A simple strategy for prompting language models. arXiv preprint arXiv:2210.02441.

Brown, T., Mann, B., Ryder, N., Subbiah, M., Kaplan, J. D., Dhariwal, P., & Amodei, D. (2020). Language models are few-shot learners. *Advances in Neural Information Processing Systems, 33*, 1877–1901.

Callan, J., Connell, M., & Du, A. (1999). Automatic discovery of language models for text databases. *SIGMOD Record, 28*(2), 479–490. DOI: 10.1145/304181.304224

Fahda, A., & Purwarianti, A. (2017, November). A statistical and rule-based spelling and grammar checker for Indonesian text. In 2017 international on data and software engineering (icodse) (pp. 1-6). IEEE.

Gao, T., Fisch, A., & Chen, D. (2020). Making pre-trained language models better fewshot learners. arXiv preprint arXiv:2012.15723.

Jozefowicz, R., Vinyals, O., Schuster, M., Shazeer, N., & Wu, Y. (2016). Exploring the limits of language modeling. arXiv preprint arXiv:1602.02410.

Kaddour, J., Harris, J., Mozes, M., Bradley, H., Raileanu, R., & McHardy, R. (2023). Challenges and applications of large language models. arXiv preprint arXiv:2307.10169.

Kim, Y., Jernite, Y., Sontag, D., & Rush, A. (2016, March). Character-aware neural language models. In *Proceedings of the AAAI on artificial intelligence* (Vol. 30, No. 1).

Kumar, A., Singh, P., & Lata, K. "Comparative Study of Different Optical Character Recognition Models on Handwritten and Printed Medical Reports," *2023 International Conference on Innovative Data Communication Technologies and Application (ICIDCA)*, Uttarakhand, India, 2023, pp. 581-586, DOI: 10.1109/ICIDCA56705.2023.10100213

Manaf, K., Pitara, S. W., Subaeki, B., & Gunawan, R. (2019, October). Comparison of carp rabin algorithm and Jaro-Winkler distance to determine the equality of Sunda languages. In 2019 IEEE 13th international conference on telecommunication systems, services, and applications (TSSA) (pp. 77-81). IEEE. DOI: 10.1109/TSSA48701.2019.8985470

Melis, G., Dyer, C., & Blunsom, P. (2017). On the state of the art of evaluation in neural language models. arXiv preprint arXiv:1707.05589.

Nguyen, Q. D., Phan, N. M., Kromer, P., & Le, D. A. (2023). An Efficient Unsupervised Approach for OCR Error Correction of Vietnamese OCR Text. *IEEE Access : Practical Innovations, Open Solutions, 11*, 58406–58421. DOI: 10.1109/ACCESS.2023.3283340

Perez, E., Kiela, D., & Cho, K. (2021). True few-shot learning with language models. *Advances in Neural Information Processing Systems, 34*, 11054–11070.

Roark, B., Saraclar, M., & Collins, M. (2007). Discriminative n-gram language modeling. *Computer Speech & Language, 21*(2), 373–392. DOI: 10.1016/j.csl.2006.06.006

Schick, T., & Schütze, H. (2020). It's not just size that matters: Small language models are also few-shot learners. arXiv preprint arXiv:2009.07118.

Schick, T., & Schütze, H. (2021). Generating datasets with pretrained language models. arXiv preprint arXiv:2104.07540. DOI: 10.18653/v1/2021.emnlp-main.555

Shi, D., Wei, X., Li, L., Ren, Y., & Tan, W. (2022). End-to-end multi-person pose estimation with transformers. In *Proceedings of the IEEE/CVF conference on computer vision and pattern recognition* (pp. 11069-11078).

Ye, Y., Zhu, S., Wang, J., Du, Q., Yang, Y., Tu, D., & Luo, J. (2018, December). A unified scheme of text localization and structured data extraction for joint OCR and data mining. In 2018 IEEE on Big Data [IEEE.]. *Big Data*, •••, 2373–2382.

Zukarnain, N., Abbas, B. S., Wayan, S., Trisetyarso, A., & Kang, C. H. (2019, August). Spelling checker algorithm methods for many languages. In *2019 International Conference on Information Management and Technology (ICIMTech)* (Vol. 1, pp. 198-201). IEEE. DOI: 10.1109/ICIMTech.2019.8843801

Nguyen, Q. D., Phan, N. M., [illegible] (2023). An Efficient Unsupervised [illegible] OCR Error Correction of Vietnamese OCR Text. IEEE Access [illegible] Open Solutions, [illegible] DOI: 10.1109/ACCESS.2023.[illegible]

[illegible]

[illegible]

[illegible]

[illegible]

[illegible]

[illegible] (2014, December) [illegible] document structured data extraction based on OCR [illegible]. In 2014 IEEE [illegible] Big Data [illegible]

Zhang, [illegible] (2019, [illegible]) [illegible] In 2019 International Conference on Document Analysis and Recognition (ICDAR) (pp. [illegible]). IEEE. DOI: 10.1109/ICDAR.2019.[illegible]

Chapter 14
Long Short-Term Memory Models for High-Accuracy Chatbot Development: A Case Study for the NITH Website

Vijay Kumar
Dr. B.R. Ambedkar National Institute of Technology, Jalandhar, India

ABSTRACT

This chapter investigates the performance of Multilayer Perceptron (MLP) and Long-Short Term Memory (LSTM) models in the development of a high-accuracy chatbot for the NITH website. Tokenization and lemmatization are used for data preprocessing. LSTM model is used to interpret sequential data. MLP model used a 3-layer neural network with a bag-of-words technique for text representation. The experimental results reveal that the MLP model is more suitable for this specific application. The chatbot is successfully integrated with a web frontend using Flask and AJAX. The developed chatbot could respond to inquiries almost exactly like a human. Both models achieved over 97% accuracy on a dataset of predetermined patterns and responses.

INTRODUCTION

A prominent usage of artificial intelligence nowadays is chatbots, which provide a user interface for communication in natural language. Because these AI systems are meant to mimic human communication, users can engage with them just like they would with a human. Chatbots are designed to function without the assistance of human operators. They simulate human communication by providing natural language answers to questions. Technological developments in machine learning and natural language processing (NLP) have propelled the creation of chatbots (Kumar and Kumar, 2023). Chatbots can now comprehend and interpret human language more efficiently, producing more precise and appropriate responses for the given situation. Chatbots have become widely used in some industries in recent years, such as customer service, e-commerce, healthcare, and education. Chatbots offer practical means of boosting communication efficiency in learning environments, providing staff and students with prompt assistance, and enhancing the standard of the educational process as a whole (Ranoliya et al., 2017).

DOI: 10.4018/979-8-3693-7260-9.ch014

Aside from providing personalized study tools, chatbots can also suggest resources and provide basic subject-specific instruction to students. They can also encourage student participation by reminding them of important dates, deadlines, and tests (Jeon, 2024). Chatbots can also help with gathering employee and student feedback, which helps businesses to enhance their offers in terms of services and courses continuously. Chatbots can help educational institutions improve student support, communication effectiveness, and the responsiveness and interactive nature of the learning environment (Agarwal et al., 2021). The general AI Chatbot development methodology is shown in Figure 1 (Lokman & Ameedeen, 2019).

Developing chatbots that can successfully mimic human-like conversations is challenging since they must react with a high degree of accuracy, ideally near 100%. This requires sophisticated language production and comprehension abilities and the ability to maintain context during a conversation. According to Ayanwale and Ndlovu (2024), generative models, retrieval-based models, and rule-based systems are some of the approaches that have been studied in the process of creating chatbots.

Retrieval-founded models are among the broadly applied for chatbots since they deliver accurate, predefined responses to precise queries. Neural network architectures such as Long Short-Term Memory (LSTM) networks and Multilayer Perceptron (MLPs) have introduced the ability to improve chatbot performance (Patil et al., 2020). MLPs are responsible for text representation, such as a bag of words. However, LSTMs work well with consecutive data, which could serve to consider the context in conversations.

This study aims to evaluate the two integrated approaches, which are MLP and LSTM, to develop a chatbot that assists the educational institution's website. This new approach contributes to ongoing efforts to improve AI-powered communication systems in educational adjusts by evaluating their efficacy and integrating the chatbot implemented in a real application; this implementation provides the facility to quickly answer the user's queries frequently asked by the students and parents on the web application of NIT Hamirpur. Here, we have proposed an integrated framework of MLP and LSTM that analyzes the query of the students and others and gets the high accuracy of the model.

Figure 1. General framework for AI chatbot

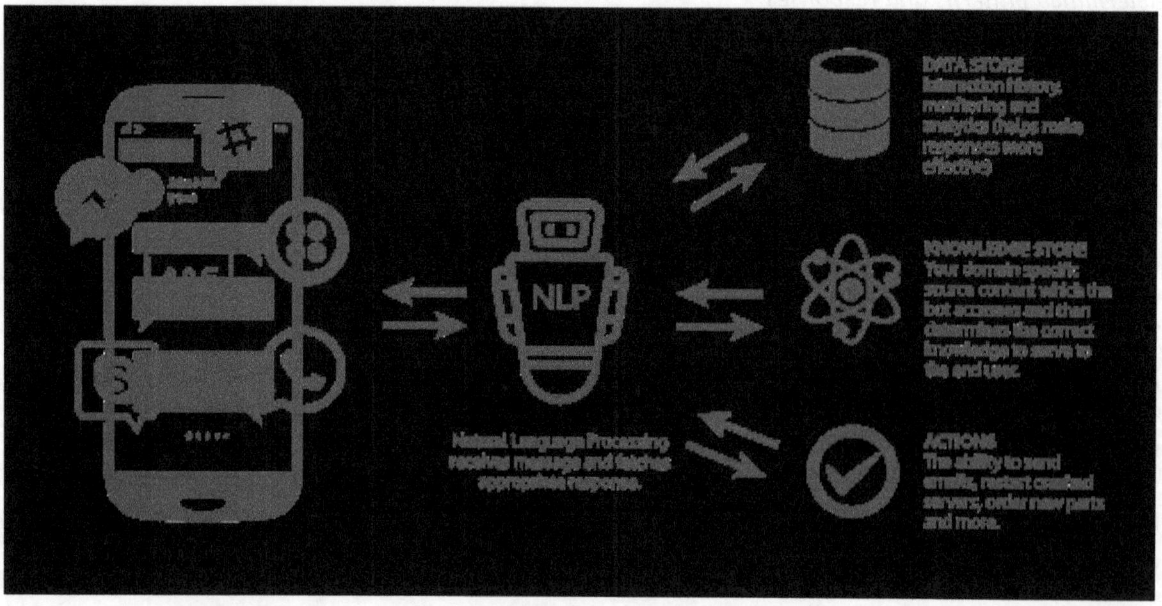

BACKGROUND

This section explores the fundamental concepts of Multilayer Perceptron (MLP) and Long-Short Term Memory (LSTM) models related work and how these approaches are implemented to develop chatbots. Software developed to mimic human-machine dialogue implemented natural language that is called chatbot. Chatbots have developed with AI technologies composite systems that can preserve context and facilitate real-time human communication *(Patil S. et al., 2020)*. In this process, natural language process, the sentence is segmented, vectorization, using TF and IF process to sentence analysis, the deep learning approaches were integrated, web crawling, and using the predicting hard-coded judgment to user determined. The researchers have applied MLP for classification, TF-IDF for feature extraction, and Jieba for word segmentation. They have attained 80% accuracy in the performance of the approach with the Facebook Chat dataset. These approaches effort to enhance intent recognition in chatbot systems (Liu, Y. T. et al., 2021). To progress context retention and prediction in chatbot software, this study presents a novel collaborative model that integrates Long Short-Term Memory (LSTM) networks with Multilayer Perceptron (MLP).

Multilayer Perceptron Model

A basic form of artificial neural network, the MLP model is majorly applied in AI applications, including chatbot creation (Popescu et al., 2009). This NITH website illustrates its versatility and effectiveness; construction is a major option for several practices. The MLP development comprises several tiers of interconnected nodes known as neurons, which modify arriving data to generate aspect outputs. This architecture consists of three layers: an input, an output, and a hidden layer. Getting the inputs, multiplying them by weights, adding them all up, and then transient the result via an activation function, each neuron in the network outputs the outcome. Pattern recognition, regression, and classification are the activities the network may practice because of its ability to discover complex patterns and relationships within the data (Mohamed, 2024). The universal approximation theorem contains the MLP, which evaluates the pattern and classification. These techniques can be applied in various contexts, including natural language processing which are required in chatbot development (Karlik & Olgac, 2011).

The researchers implemented the MLP model created in the chatbot. This model has a three-layer neural network using the well-known deep learning toolkit Keras sequence API. The first layer responsible for the input data and consists of 128 neurons that analyse the features; the second layer of neurons classifies the data in a training set and categorizes inputs. Rectified Linear Unit (ReLU) activation functions assist in analyzing the more complex pattern. Deep neural networks often suffer from the vanishing gradient problem, which is why ReLU is chosen despite its computing efficiency. This technique develops more resilient features by randomly deactivating a predetermined percentage of neurons during training. Here, the learning rate taken by the researchers was 0.01, and momentum 0.9 for optimizing the model with Stochastic Gradient Descent (Ciayandi in 2020). This optimization approach gives a faster convergence of the model and potentially progresses the local minimum.

Categorical cross-entropy is used as the loss function, which is highly effective for multi-class classification applications like chatbot intent recognition. The MLP model analyzes text using a bag-of-words strategy, which ignores word order and focuses on word occurrence. It creates a vocabulary of well-known keywords and counts their occurrence in the input. Using this strategy and the neural network design, the model can classify user inputs into defined intents and select appropriate responses for the chatbot.

A chatbot is developed based on AI techniques to mimic human dialogue and answer users' questions via text. The importance of chatbots in the medical field, where the NLP methodologies and MLP (ANN) enhance the chatbot performance, the model predicts the illness and delivers treatments to the patient. This gives early treatment, saves time and money, and reduces doctor visits, but the patient should visit the doctor for physical advice. That approach improves the efficiency of chatbot disease diagnosis by suggesting medications and asking follow-up questions for a deeper understanding (Ogirala M. K. et al., 2023). IoT, which lives outside the phone and computer connected, is penetrating homes with gadgets from security cameras to smart speakers, presenting discrete privacy and security challenges. Due to their technical limits and proximity to consumers, IoT devices are highly vulnerable to botnet attacks, among other infiltration attacks. Presenting MLP with ANN to categorize botnet activity utilizing Mirai and Bashlite-contaminated IoT gadgets, this exploration suggests an AI-encouraged technique for catching distinctive kinds of occurrence (Javed, Y., & Rajabi, N., 2020). Deciding on question categories for classifying the user requirements to get the most relevant questions and answers, and Question-Answering (QA) models in NLP with MLP provide an accurate process on how one question relates to what type of answer. Introducing a Thai conversational chatbot that combines MLP and BERT-based multilingual cases with a determined accuracy of 92.57%. The researchers present the integrated BERT-based methodology and MLP and present the Thai2Vec model and compare with SVM, NB, KN, and DTs machine learning algorithms and improve the accuracy with BERT-MLP technique performs regarding chatbot question classification (Thananukhun, K. et al., 2023).

Long-Short-Term Memory Model

Long-short memory (LSTM) models are a particular kind of Recurrent Neural Network (RNN) architecture designed to solve the difficulties of processing and forecasting time series data or sequential information. LSTM architecture was developed by Hochreiter and Schmidhuber (1997). They have worked on various deep neural network applications, such as time series analysis, speech recognition, and natural language processing. The LSTM models focused on overcoming the vanishing gradient problem that besets conventional RNNs by selectively retaining or forgetting information across extended sequences (Gers et al., 2002). For this reason, the features of the LSTM network are required for long-term context understanding, such as language translation, sentiment analysis, and, in this case, chatbot development for the NITH website.

The researchers in this study used the LSTM model, which is introduced with four interacting layers in each module: the input gate, the forget gate, the output gate, and the cell state. These layers connected to the cell state purposes as a conveyor belt of information that runs through the whole chain (Yu et al., 2019).

The LSTM model is developed as a three-layered neural network to process sequential data, including text inputs (Anki et al., 2021). The first LSTM layer receives a 2D matrix representing a padded word sequence, and these words are first encoded using One-Hot Encoding; each word is presented as a binary vector, and the output is sent to a Dense layer that activates ReLU, adding non-linearity, and enabling the network to recognize increasingly intricate patterns. Finally, a second Dense layer with softmax activation receives the output and generates a probability distribution across all potential output classes. So, the framework receives the query input in text from the users and completes the classification task needed to identify the chatbot's intent. The model's loss function is categorical cross-entropy, which works especially well for multi-class classification issues. The researchers discovered that a learning rate of 0.2 worked best during training. After 200 training epochs, the model attained good accuracy. This accuracy indicates that even with the intricacies of real language and the possibility of long-term dependencies in discussions, the LSTM model can comprehend and categorize user inputs.

In this study researchers implemented the LSTM model on the Cornell Movie Dialog Corpus dataset to develop a chatbot. They got the accuracy and performance in the various kinds of testing mythologies with parameter. An average accuracy of 99.49% was attained using the ideal parameters (size_layer 512, num_layers 2, embedded_size 256, learning_rate 0.001, batch_size 32, epoch 20). Having fine-tuned parameters related to LSTM can result in better accuracy of the chatbot, which is demonstrated by the results (Anki P. et al., 2021). Chatbots continually evolve to understand human language and respond meaningfully, fostering customer engagement while also serving business functions such as customer service and personal assistant. In response to the current limitations of existing chatbot models, this article details an enhanced mechanism of generating chatbot responses using LSTM combined with attention mechanisms in a Seq2Seq architecture, in addition to using Bag of Words (BOW) and beam search decoding. The model is trained on a dialog dataset, and the metric used to measure its performance is the BleuN algorithm, indicating higher accuracy in responding to users. This strategy is designed to improve chatbots' effectiveness and business impact (Choudhary, P., & Chauhan, S. (2023)). Focusing on the morphologically complex Lithuanian and English languages, this study investigates the evolution of generative seq2seq-based chatbots. The researchers embedded the three approaches: first founded architecture, the second BiLSTM, and the third BERT. The model implemented on the English dataset achieved BLEU BLEU scores (~0.513) than Lithuanian datasets (~0.488) (Kapočiūtė-Dzikienė, J., 2020).

Table 1. Models used with dataset for Chatbot applications

Year	Model	Application Domain	Dataset	Key Techniques	Accuracy	References
2020	MLP + LSTM	Chatbot for intent recognition	Facebook Chat data	Web crawling, TF-IDF, MLP for intent classification	80%	**Patil, S. et al.**
2009	MLP	General AI applications	-	MLP, ANN for pattern recognition	-	**Popescu et al.**
2020	MLP	Chatbot for intent classification	-	ReLU activation	-	**Ciayandi**
2020	MLP (ANN)	IoT security (Botnet traffic classification)	-	MLP for classifying botnet traffic		**Javed, Y., & Rajabi, N.**
2023	MLP + BERT	Thai conversational chatbot	Thai corpus	BERT-based multilingual, MLP for question classification	92.57%	**Thananukhun, K. et al.**
1997	LSTM	General NLP tasks	-	LSTM architecture,	-	**Hochreiter & Schmidhuber**
2021	LSTM	Chatbot for movie dialog			99.49%	**Anki P. et al.**
2023	LSTM + Attention	Chatbot (	Dialog dataset	LSTM, attention mechanisms,	a cumulative Bleu-4 score of 0.8537285	**Choudhary, P., & Chauhan, S.**
2020	LSTM, BiLSTM	Chatbot for Lithuanian & English	Small domain-specific datasets	LSTM, BiLSTM, BERT embeddings, seq2seq	BLEU score: ~0.513 (English), ~0.488 (Lithuanian)	**Kapočiūtė-Dzikienė, J.**

PROPOSED APPROACH

This study's proposed approach for putting the chatbot on the NITH website shows how web development, UI design, and machine learning are all thoroughly interwoven. This method produces a useful and intuitive chatbot system using contemporary web technology and artificial intelligence. The trained neural network model—the Multilayer Perceptron (MLP) or the Long Short-Term Memory (LSTM) model, depending on which was found to be more appropriate for the particular application—is the central component of this integrated approach. This model acts as the chatbot's brain, interpreting user input and selecting relevant responses based on prior experience.

The MLP model classifies the chats which contain four layers, where first is the input layer, which layer receives the tokenized and vectorized input (e.g., word embeddings or TF-IDF features), and there are two or more two hidden layers with the ReLU activation function, where the neurons work. The next layer is the dropout layer, which is implemented for regularization (e.g., 0.5) to prevent overfitting. The last layer is the output layer, which has neurons equal to the number of intents or classes; here, the activation function is the softmax activation function. So, the MLP model works with a fixed set of input features such as word frequencies or vectorized representations of text.

The integrated LSTM model aims to entail managing sequential data with long-term dependencies, such as preserving context after several conversational exchanges, go with the LSTM model. When a chatbot needs to comprehend the input's word sequence and provide pertinent answers, LSTM is the best option. Where we have applied the One-Hot encoding such as Word2Vec, FastText, or BERT, the input layer receives padded word index sequences. The LSTM layer manages the text's sequential structure and preserves context, adding one or more LSTM layers. So, the integrated chatbot architecture MLP with LSTM models produces the advantages of effective intent classification (via MLP), context retention, and sequence processing (through LSTM). Figure 2 represent the proposed approach with MLP and LSTM model. This approach enhances the chatbot's capacity to manage organized, one-turn inquiries and more intricate, multi-turn discussions, leading to more precise and responsive interactions.

Figure 2. An integrated framework of MLP and LSTM to develop chatbot.

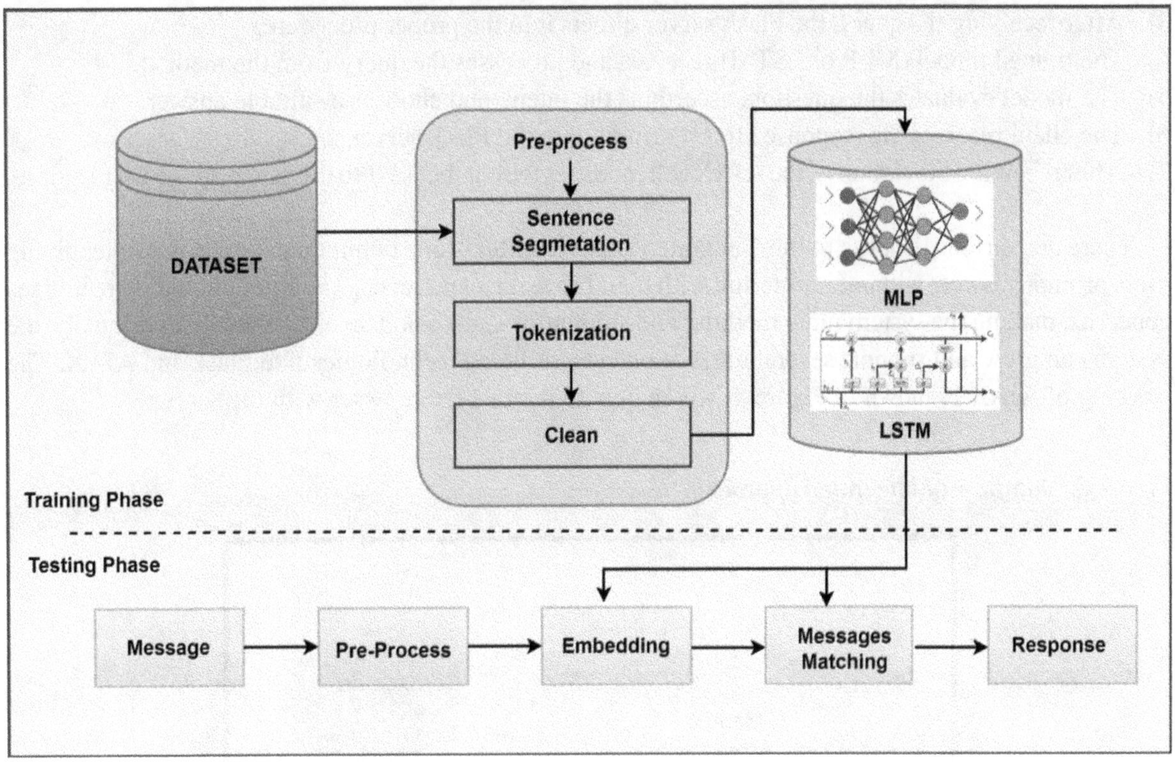

A popular design pattern in web development, Model-View-Controller (MVC) architecture, is followed in the integration process. Code that is better organized and easier to maintain is made possible by this architecture, which divides the application logic into three interconnected components:

1. Model: The trained neural network model serves as the database or data source in this instance. It has the reasoning behind answering questions and forecasting answers.
2. View: The chatbot's User Interface (UI) represents this on the client side. It is the system component that is directly incorporated into the NITH website and is used by users.
3. Controller: This part comprises the paths or techniques that decide how to handle requests and choose relevant answers. It serves as a go-between for the Model and the View.

A lightweight web framework for Python called Flask is used in the server-side implementation. Requests from the client are routed to the relevant backend methods via Flask. Upon receiving a query from a user via the chatbot interface, Flask forwards it to the trained model for further processing.

The NITH website has integrated the chatbot interface on the client side. The system uses AJAX (Asynchronous JavaScript and XML) technology to allow seamless, real-time interaction without page reloads. With AJAX, a web page can communicate asynchronously with a server and retrieve data without affecting how the website looks and functions.

Figure 2 shows the data flow of the integrated system. The steps are given below:

1) A user inputs a question into the NITH website's chatbot interface.
2) AJAX sends the query to the web server, enabling asynchronous communication.
3) After receiving the query, the Flask server directs it to the proper procedure.
4) The trained model (MLP or LSTM) receives and processes the query from the method.
5) The model evaluates the question, ascertains the intent, and chooses a suitable answer.
6) The client receives the response after returning it to the Flask server.
7) After receiving the response, the AJAX call modifies the chatbot's UI so the user may see the response.

There are various benefits to this integrated approach. Real-time communication is possible, giving users prompt answers without interfering with their browsing experience. The MVC architecture divides concerns, making the system more modular and straightforward to update or maintain. Additionally, the system can grow and support several users at once by utilizing technologies like Flask and AJAX. The working of AJAX is shown in Figure 4, where how to interact the browser with the server.

Figure 3. Dataflow of integrated approach.

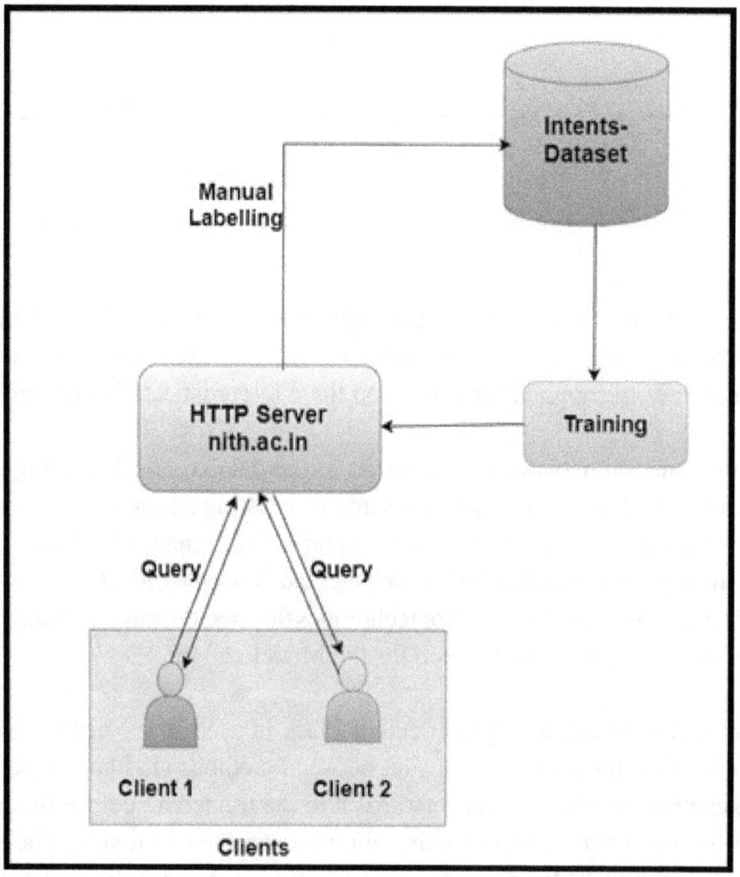

Figure 4. Working of AJAX.

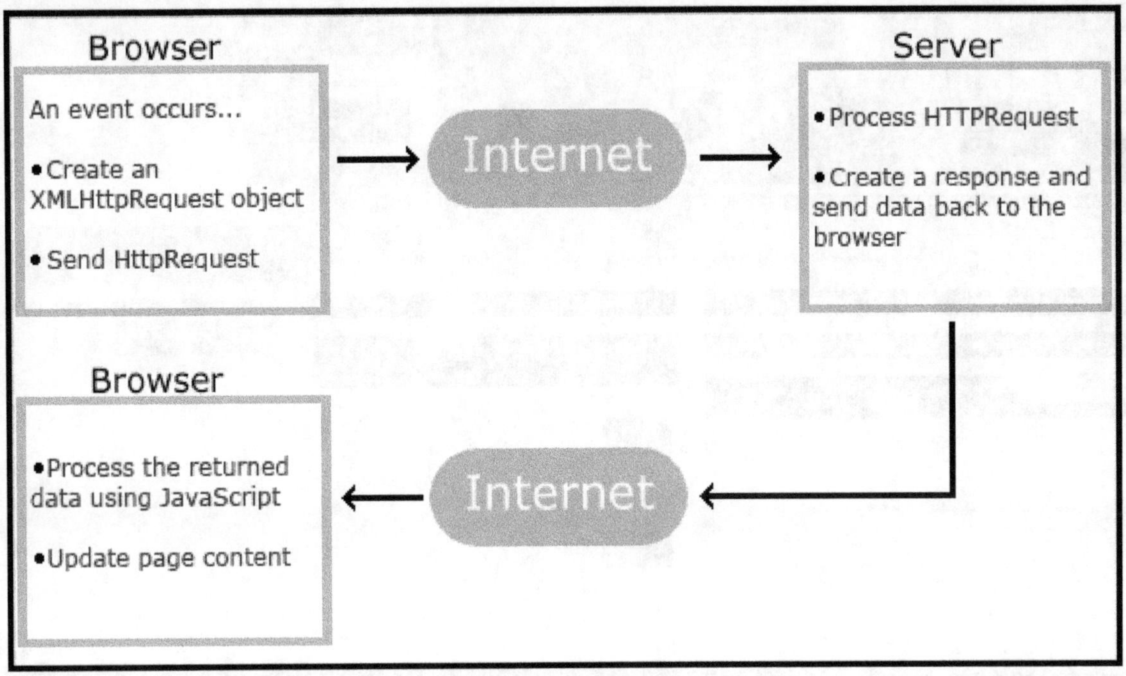

The chatbot's seamless integration into the NITH website serves as an example of how AI may be used to improve user experience on educational platforms. It demonstrates how machine learning models can be used to good effect in real-world situations, offering website users helpful support in the form of conversational information and answers to frequently asked queries. Figure 4 shows the finalized chatbot's working and integration with the NITH website.

Figure 5. The final chatbot of NITH.

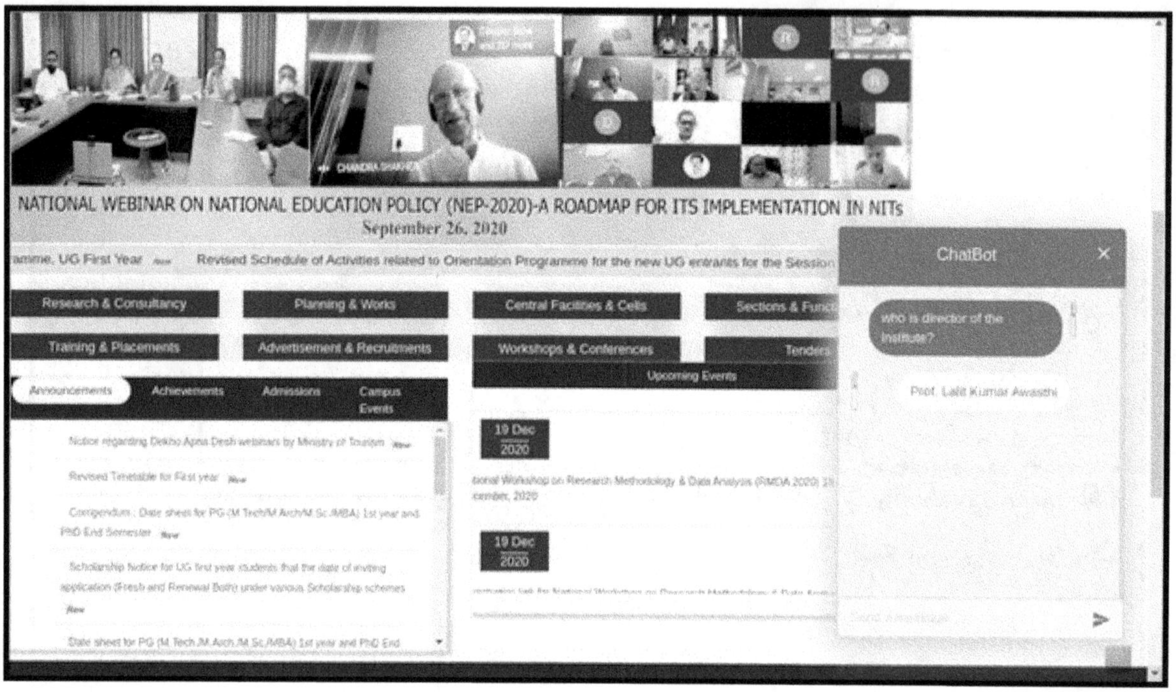

DISCUSSIONS

Figure 5 illustrates the accuracy and loss rates of the MLP model, which is employed in chatbot development. Two curves are displayed in this figure. The orange curve, the accuracy rate, approaches nearly 100%, showing that the model's predictions were made with a high degree of accuracy during training. The blue curve represents the loss rate or the model's prediction error. As it gets closer to zero, it indicates smaller errors. These findings imply that the MLP model learns from the training data efficiently, attaining high accuracy and low loss, which qualifies it for use in the NITH online chatbot application.

Figure 6. Accuracy and loss for MLP model.

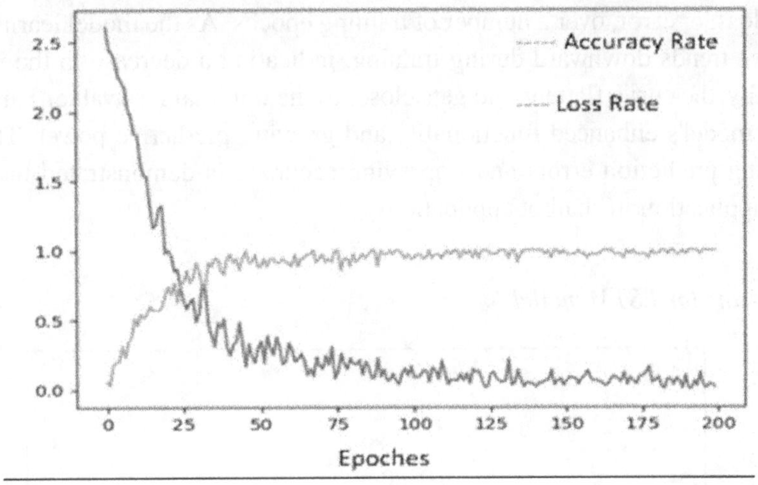

Figure 6 represents the accuracy of the model LSTM, performed on the chatbot, and the framework trained with several epochs displayed in the graph. The model is trained on 200 epochs, and the x-axis represents cycles across the entire training dataset. The proportion of accuracy is displayed on the y-axis. The accuracy curve has a notable rising trend over the training process, suggesting that the LSTM model gradually improves its prediction capabilities as it gains knowledge from the data. Here, the graph reached 97% accuracy, performing the model trained successfully and anticipating relevant replies. This figure demonstrates the LSTM model's capacity to handle sequential input and its effectiveness in procurement high accuracy, making it a feasible option for chatbot applications.

Figure 7. Accuracy for LSTM model

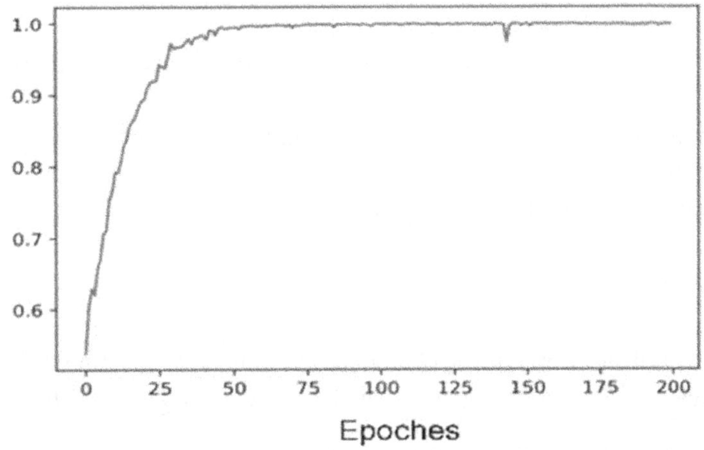

Figure 7 shows the loss rate graph for the LSTM model, which is employed in chatbot development. The y-axis shows the loss value, and the x-axis represents the number of training epochs. The graph displays the model's loss, or error, over a number of training epochs. As the model learns from the training data, the loss curve trends downward during training, indicating a decrease in the model's prediction mistakes. Eventually, the curve flattens and gets closer to the minimal loss value. This gradual decrease in loss shows the model's enhanced functionality and growing predictive power. The LSTM model's efficacy in reducing prediction errors and improving accuracy is demonstrated in this figure, hence corroborating its application in chatbot applications.

Figure 8. The loss rate for LSTM model

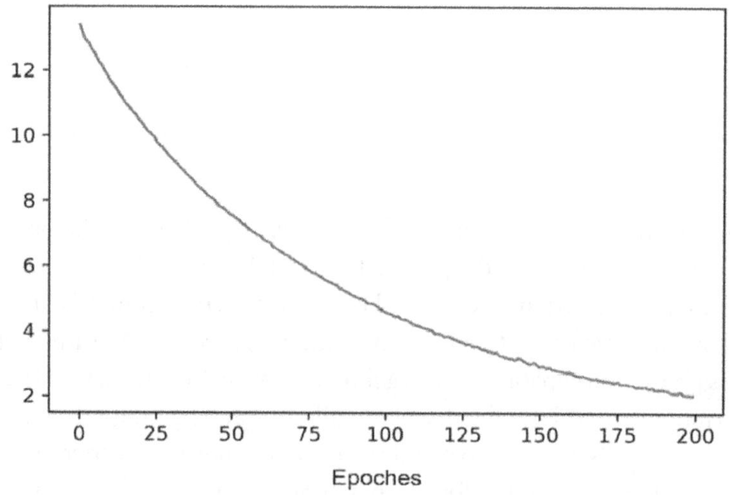

Merits of Chatbots

- **Efficiency:** Chatbots give the instance response, which enhances user experience and save expensive time
- **Cost-Effectiveness:** Chatbots reduce the need for human effort, which is cutting working costs.
- **Availability:** Operators provide the facility to the users 24/7 and ensure the response at any time.
- **Scalability:** Chatbot can handle several queries simultaneously.

Demerits of Chatbots

- **Limited Understanding:** Sometimes, chatbots can not be able to understand the user's query.
- **Language Barriers:** The performance of chatbot may be degrade with complex language and words.
- **Dependence on Data:** The model should be trained on large and diverse datset.
- **Security Concern:** The sensitive data can not be converse with chatbot since data can be breaches.

CONCLUSION

This chapter introduces the integrated MLP network and LSTM model framework and compares their efficacy. That approach can be implemented to develop a chatbot application for the NITH website; this may help the students and their parents resolve their inquiries and give quick responses in 24 hours. This approach was established in chatbot generation, and the framework achieved remarkable accuracy rates of over 97% on the training dataset. This outcome highlights the importance of empirical observations and model complexity to task specifications. The effective application of the proposed model in real-world scenarios is established by the chatbot's integration with the NITH website through AJAX and a Flask server.

This framework exemplifies the well-organized application of AI-driven chatbots to improve user experience and accessibility of information on learning websites. Responses to common FAQs were efficaciously provided by the retrieval-based technique, which used pre-established patterns and responses. This could lead to an improvement in the effectiveness of communication between the institution and its stakeholders.

Future research could make the chatbot even more helpful in educational settings by strengthening its capacity to manage trickier questions and keep context across longer exchanges.

REFERENCES

Agarwal, A., Sharma, S., Kumar, V., & Kaur, M. (2021). Effect of E-learning on public health and environment during COVID-19 lockdown. *Big Data Mining and Analytics*, *4*(2), 104–115. DOI: 10.26599/BDMA.2020.9020014

Anki, P., Bustamam, A., Al-Ash, H. S., & Sarwinda, D. (2021). Intelligent chatbot adapted from question and answer system using RNN-LSTM model. []). IOP Publishing.]. *Journal of Physics: Conference Series*, *1844*(1), 012001. DOI: 10.1088/1742-6596/1844/1/012001

Anki, P., Bustamam, A., Al-Ash, H. S., & Sarwinda, D. (2021, March). Intelligent chatbot adapted from question and answer system using RNN-LSTM model. []). IOP Publishing.]. *Journal of Physics: Conference Series*, *1844*(1), 012001. DOI: 10.1088/1742-6596/1844/1/012001

Ayanwale, M. A., & Ndlovu, M. (2024). Investigating factors of students' behavioral intentions to adopt chatbot technologies in higher education: Perspective from expanded diffusion theory of innovation. *Computers in Human Behavior Reports*, *14*, 100396. DOI: 10.1016/j.chbr.2024.100396

Choudhary, P., & Chauhan, S. (2023). An intelligent chatbot design and implementation model using long short-term memory with recurrent neural networks and attention mechanism. *Decision Analytics Journal*, *9*, 100359. DOI: 10.1016/j.dajour.2023.100359

Ciayandi, A., Mawardi, V. C., & Hendryli, J. (2020). Retrieval based chatbot on tarumanagara university with Multilayer Perceptron. []). IOP Publishing.]. *IOP Conference Series. Materials Science and Engineering*, *1007*(1), 012146. DOI: 10.1088/1757-899X/1007/1/012146

Gers, F. A., Schraudolph, N. N., & Schmidhuber, J. (2002). Learning precise timing with LSTM recurrent networks. *Journal of Machine Learning Research*, *3*(Aug), 115–143.

Hochreiter, S., & Schmidhuber, J. (1997). Long short-term memory. *Neural Computation*, *9*(8), 1735–1780. DOI: 10.1162/neco.1997.9.8.1735 PMID: 9377276

Javed, Y., & Rajabi, N. (2020). Multi-layer perceptron artificial neural network based IoT botnet traffic classification. In *Proceedings of the Future Technologies Conference (FTC) 2019: Volume 1* (pp. 973-984). Springer International Publishing. DOI: 10.1007/978-3-030-32520-6_69

Jeon, J. (2024). Exploring AI chatbot affordances in the EFL classroom: Young learners' experiences and perspectives. *Computer Assisted Language Learning*, *37*(1-2), 1–26. DOI: 10.1080/09588221.2021.2021241

Kapočiūtė-Dzikienė, J. (2020). A domain-specific generative chatbot trained from little data. *Applied Sciences (Basel, Switzerland)*, *10*(7), 2221. DOI: 10.3390/app10072221

Karlik, B., & Olgac, A. V. (2011). Performance analysis of various activation functions in generalized MLP architectures of neural networks. *International Journal of Artificial Intelligence and Expert Systems*, *1*(4), 111–122.

Kumar, Y., & Kumar, V. (2023). Security in IoT systems using natural language processing: Future challenges and directions. *Internet Technology Letters*, *6*(4), e411. DOI: 10.1002/itl2.411

Liu, Y. T., Hsih, M. H., & Hsieh, C. C. (2021, November). An Automatic Response System based on Multi-layer Perceptual Neural Network and Web Crawler. In *2021 International Conference on Technologies and Applications of Artificial Intelligence (TAAI)* (pp. 246-249). IEEE. DOI: 10.1109/TAAI54685.2021.00054

Lokman, A. S., & Ameedeen, M. A. (2019). Modern chatbot systems: A technical review. In *Proceedings of the Future Technologies Conference (FTC) 2018: Volume 2* (pp. 1012-1023). Springer International Publishing. DOI: 10.1007/978-3-030-02683-7_75

Mohamed, A. M. (2024). Exploring the potential of an AI-based Chatbot (ChatGPT) in enhancing English as a Foreign Language (EFL) teaching: Perceptions of EFL Faculty Members. *Education and Information Technologies, 29*(3), 3195–3217. DOI: 10.1007/s10639-023-11917-z

Ogirala, M. K., Tallapaneni, R., Chalamcharla, S. M., & Chinta, A. (2023, May). A Medical Diagnosis and Treatment Recommendation Chatbot using MLP. In *2023 2nd International Conference on Applied Artificial Intelligence and Computing (ICAAIC)* (pp. 495-500). IEEE. DOI: 10.1109/ICAAIC56838.2023.10141211

Patil, S., Mudaliar, V. M., Kamat, P., & Gite, S. (2020). LSTM based Ensemble Network to enhance the learning of long-term dependencies in chatbot. *International Journal for Simulation and Multidisciplinary Design Optimization, 11*, 25. DOI: 10.1051/smdo/2020019

Patil, S., Mudaliar, V. M., Kamat, P., & Gite, S. (2020). LSTM based Ensemble Network to enhance the learning of long-term dependencies in chatbot. *International Journal for Simulation and Multidisciplinary Design Optimization, 11*, 25. DOI: 10.1051/smdo/2020019

Popescu, M. C., Balas, V. E., Perescu-Popescu, L., & Mastorakis, N. (2009). Multilayer perceptron and neural networks. *WSEAS Transactions on Circuits and Systems, 8*(7), 579–588.

Ranoliya, B. R., Raghuwanshi, N., & Singh, S. (2017). Chatbot for university related FAQs. In *2017 International Conference on Advances in Computing, Communications and Informatics (ICACCI)* (pp. 1525-1530). IEEE. DOI: 10.1109/ICACCI.2017.8126057

Thananukhun, K., Jaiyen, S., Jitkajornwanich, K., & Hanskunatai, A. (2023, February). Question classification for thai conversational chatbots using artificial neural networks and multilingual bert models. In *2023 15th International Conference on Knowledge and Smart Technology (KST)* (pp. 1-4). IEEE. DOI: 10.1109/KST57286.2023.10086784

Wu, R., & Yu, Z. (2024). Do AI chatbots improve students learning outcomes? Evidence from a meta-analysis. *British Journal of Educational Technology, 55*(1), 10–33. DOI: 10.1111/bjet.13334

Yu, Y., Si, X., Hu, C., & Zhang, J. (2019). A review of recurrent neural networks: LSTM cells and network architectures. *Neural Computation, 31*(7), 1235–1270. DOI: 10.1162/neco_a_01199 PMID: 31113301

KEY TERMS AND DEFINITIONS

Chatbot: It is an artificial intelligence computer that uses digital platforms like websites, messaging apps, or phone systems to mimic human-like communication.

Multilayer Perceptron: It is an artificial neural network with numerous layers of connected nodes (neurons)

Long Short-Term Memory: It is a specific kind of recurrent neural network architecture to handle and forecast sequential data.

Chapter 15
Teaching AI to High School Students for Enhancing Argumentative Essay Writing Skills

Nguyen Le Ngoc Anh
Can Tho University, Vietnam

Pham Thanh Dieu
Bui Huu Nghia High School, Vietnam

ABSTRACT

This chapter explores the transformative impact of integrating artificial intelligence into writing instruction, emphasizing its potential to enhance students' writing performance. By utilizing artificial intelligence chatbots, educators can support specific sub-skills such as grammar, vocabulary, and sentence structure, while fostering creativity and engagement. However, the chapter cautions against over-reliance on artificial intelligence, advocating for a balanced approach that encourages critical thinking and discernment in evaluating AI-generated content. It underscores the importance of professional development for teachers to effectively incorporate these technologies while maintaining a focus on essential writing skills. Ultimately, this chapter argues that the thoughtful integration of artificial intelligence in high school education not only makes learning more relevant and engaging but also equips students with the necessary tools to navigate the evolving landscape of writing and communication in the digital age.

INTRODUCTION

High school students' writing proficiency remains a concern, as indicated by school reports and academic studies. Despite literacy education efforts, students struggle due to limited teaching time, large class sizes, and the intrinsic challenges of learning to write independently. Pokrivčáková (2019) stresses the need to rethink language instruction, particularly with AI's growing role in education. AI-powered

DOI: 10.4018/979-8-3693-7260-9.ch015

tools, like ChatGPT, offer solutions by providing real-time feedback, streamlining grading, and supplementing teacher instruction.

Time constraints in writing classes hinder individualized feedback. Overburdened teachers struggle to offer personalized guidance, leaving many students underprepared for complex writing tasks in higher education or the workforce. Vygotsky's scaffolding theory provides insight into addressing this issue (Barrs, 2022). Scaffolding, grounded in the zone of proximal development (ZPD), emphasizes the gradual transfer of responsibility from teacher to student, enabling learners to acquire skills beyond their independent capabilities. AI tools can serve as scaffolds, offering immediate feedback and step-by-step guidance, thus bridging the gap between traditional instruction and self-directed learning.

ChatGPT exemplifies AI-driven scaffolding by identifying grammatical errors, providing explanations, and suggesting revisions, ensuring that students receive timely and constructive feedback. Barrot (2023) highlights AI's benefits for second-language (L2) writing, where students require frequent input to develop accuracy and fluency. In classrooms where teachers cannot offer individualized support to every student, AI facilitates a guided learning process, gradually reducing dependence as students become more proficient writers.

Beyond feedback, AI enhances the grading process, a labor-intensive task for educators. Automated assessment tools evaluate writing, generate detailed explanations, and provide formative feedback. Mitra & Banerjee (2022) note that AI-supported ELT classrooms benefit from these technologies, as they alleviate teachers' workloads and allow them to focus on higher-order writing skills, such as argument development and coherence. Marr & Ward (2019) reinforce that AI's ability to handle routine tasks enables educators to devote more time to fostering critical thinking and creativity.

However, AI integration requires careful implementation to prevent overreliance. Barrot (2023) cautions against students becoming dependent on AI-generated content, which may hinder independent thinking. Effective scaffolding necessitates a balance between AI support and human instruction. In the classroom, educators can apply a gradual release model ("I do, We do, You do"), wherein AI initially models writing techniques, then assists students through guided practice, and finally encourages independent writing. This aligns with Vygotsky's principle of progressively reducing instructional support as students gain proficiency.

To optimize AI in writing instruction, teachers should tailor scaffolding strategies based on students' ZPD. Techniques such as pre-teaching vocabulary, using visual aids, and encouraging peer collaboration can enhance AI-assisted learning. Small group work, where proficient students guide peers, fosters collaborative engagement and reinforces learning. AI should complement, not replace, human feedback, ensuring students internalize writing principles rather than passively accepting AI-generated corrections.

A reimagined instructional approach integrating AI and Vygotskyan scaffolding can address the challenges of writing education. By leveraging AI for personalized feedback, structured guidance, and efficient grading, teachers can mitigate the limitations of large class sizes and time constraints. As education evolves, embracing AI as a scaffold rather than a substitute for instruction will be crucial in fostering proficient, independent writers.

BACKGROUND

Can Tho University and Bui Huu Nghia High School: A Collaborative Partnership

Can Tho University, a prominent public research institution located in the vibrant city of Can Tho, Vietnam, has a longstanding commitment to academic excellence and research innovation. With its focus on equipping students with the knowledge and skills necessary for success in today's competitive global market, the university has established itself as a leading educational institution in the region.

Bui Huu Nghia High School, a renowned educational institution named after the Vietnamese revolutionary Bui Huu Nghia, shares Can Tho University's dedication to fostering students' intellectual, social, and personal development. The school's emphasis on both academic achievement and character building equips its students for success in higher education and beyond.

Recognizing the potential for collaboration, Can Tho University and Bui Huu Nghia High School have formed a partnership aimed at enhancing the educational experiences of students from both institutions. One of the key initiatives stemming from this collaboration is the establishment of an English club at Bui Huu Nghia High School.

The English club, facilitated by experienced educators from Can Tho University, provides students with opportunities to improve their language skills, develop critical thinking abilities, and engage in cultural exchange. Through a variety of activities, including language practice, discussions, and creative writing exercises, the club aims to foster a love of learning and equip students with the tools they need to succeed in a globalized world.

A Case Study on Integrating AI in Writing Instruction: ChatGPT as a Learning Tool

Recognizing AI's potential in education, the English club at Bui Huu Nghia High School conducted an experimental study on ChatGPT's effectiveness in writing instruction. The study involved 123 students divided into an experimental group, which incorporated ChatGPT tools, and a control group using traditional methods. Data collection through pre-tests, post-tests, and semi-structured interviews assessed the AI's impact on writing skills, language proficiency, and learning attitudes.

Findings suggest that AI-supported instruction fosters student engagement and facilitates immediate, personalized feedback, which aligns with Vygotskyan scaffolding by guiding learners through their ZPD. AI serves as an interactive scaffold, modeling writing techniques before gradually encouraging independent application. This reflects the "I do, We do, You do" approach, ensuring a structured transition from teacher-led to autonomous learning.

Applying McMurry et al.'s (2016) evaluation framework, this study examined ChatGPT's usability, effectiveness, and impact on student writing. The framework's systematic approach—identifying the evaluand, engaging stakeholders, and employing qualitative and quantitative analysis—ensured a comprehensive assessment. Results indicated that ChatGPT effectively supplements traditional instruction by automating routine feedback, thus allowing educators to focus on higher-order writing skills like argumentation and coherence.

By integrating AI into TESOL writing instruction within a structured theoretical framework, educators can address challenges such as large class sizes and time constraints. ChatGPT and similar tools can support differentiated learning, provide targeted feedback, and enhance student autonomy. However, ongoing evaluation using established CALL assessment models is crucial to ensuring that AI remains a beneficial supplement rather than a replacement for teacher guidance. Through informed implementation, AI can serve as a powerful scaffold that empowers students to develop their writing skills in meaningful, interactive ways.

The Objectives

- Introduce emerging AI tools that can be effectively utilized in writing education, providing an overview of their capabilities and potential applications in the section titled 'Emerging AI Tools for Writing Education'.
- Explore implementation strategies for incorporating AI tools into existing writing programs, offering practical guidance and best practices in the section titled 'Integrating AI into Writing Programs'.
- Present a detailed case study that have successfully integrated AI into their writing instruction, highlighting the benefits, challenges, and lessons learned in the section titled 'Case Study of AI-Enhanced Writing Instruction'.
- Examine the ethical implications of AI in writing education, addressing concerns related to data privacy, plagiarism risks, over-reliance on AI, equity issues, teacher training, and the balance between AI use and critical thinking development in the section titled 'Ethical Considerations in AI-Powered Writing Education'.
- Provide recommendations for educators and institutions seeking to leverage AI to enhance writing instruction while maintaining ethical standards in the section titled 'Guidelines for Ethical and Effective AI Implementation in Writing Instruction'.

EMERGING AI TOOLS FOR WRITING EDUCATION

AI Tools for Research and Analysis

The integration of AI into research and analysis has transformed how educators and students access and interpret information. AI-powered search engines, such as Elicit and Semantic Scholar, refine research queries by using natural language processing to deliver more relevant academic resources efficiently. These tools enable users to process large amounts of data quickly, allowing educators and students to focus more on critical thinking and analysis rather than spending excessive time gathering materials (Pokrivčáková, 2019). By leveraging AI-enhanced search capabilities, students develop stronger research skills, learning to synthesize and evaluate multiple sources effectively.

AI has also reshaped data analysis in educational settings. Rather than relying solely on manual evaluation of student progress, AI-driven data models, such as Bayesian inference and mixed quantile regression, provide educators with predictive insights into student performance. These tools analyze past learning patterns and forecast future outcomes, helping instructors tailor their teaching strategies to individual needs (Chen Lin, 2024). In the realm of second language education, these AI-powered visualizations offer real-time tracking of language acquisition, providing educators with a clearer understanding of student progress and challenges. By automating data analysis, AI not only increases efficiency but also allows educators to implement timely interventions that foster academic success.

Additionally, AI plays a vital role in resource curation. Instead of manually sifting through databases, educators can rely on tools such as Research Rabbit to generate customized reading lists based on specific topics. AI-assisted curation not only saves time but also ensures that students engage with high-quality, relevant sources that align with their learning objectives. Marr & Ward (2019), cited in Mitra & Banerjee (2022), highlight how these AI applications promote deeper engagement with scholarly material by filtering out irrelevant or unreliable sources. This advancement is particularly useful in writing-intensive courses, where credible sources are critical for developing well-supported arguments and evidence-based essays.

AI-Assisted Writing Tools

AI-assisted writing tools enhance technical accuracy, improve writing style, and support creativity. Grammar and style checkers, such as Grammarly and Criterion, have become essential for students and educators by offering real-time corrections and suggestions for improving grammatical accuracy and stylistic consistency. These tools are particularly beneficial for second-language learners who may struggle with complex grammar rules (Korenev, 2024). By automating proofreading, educators can allocate more time to higher-order concerns, such as argument structure and critical thinking, ensuring that students develop comprehensive writing skills beyond surface-level corrections.

Beyond basic grammar checking, AI writing tools provide style analysis, helping students tailor their writing for different audiences and contexts. Tools such as Hemingway Editor analyze readability and suggest modifications that enhance clarity and conciseness (Mitra & Banerjee, 2022). Advanced AI-driven writing assistants like ChatGPT and Jasper take this functionality further by offering real-time feedback on structure, organization, and tone. Li (2024) emphasizes how these AI writing assistants act as brainstorming partners, guiding students through idea generation, organization, and revision. This capability helps students overcome writer's block, refine arguments, and develop stronger essay structures while maintaining their unique voice.

The integration of AI into writing support extends beyond correction and revision. AI-powered applications now assist students in the creative process itself, prompting them to explore new perspectives and refine their articulation of complex ideas. AI-generated writing prompts encourage students to think critically about their arguments and produce well-structured essays. However, Tseng & Warschauer (2023) caution that while AI can facilitate the writing process, it is essential for educators to guide students in evaluating AI-generated suggestions critically. Rather than passively accepting AI recommendations, students should be encouraged to use them as a starting point for deeper inquiry and refinement.

AI for Feedback and Assessment

AI-driven feedback and assessment systems are revolutionizing the way educators evaluate student writing. Automated grading platforms such as Criterion and Turnitin Revision Assistant provide instant, personalized feedback on essays, helping students identify weaknesses and areas for improvement. These tools analyze recurring errors, suggest targeted corrections, and enable students to refine their work iteratively (Stavytska et al., 2024). By reducing the time required for manual grading, teachers can focus on providing more nuanced feedback related to argumentation and content development.

AI feedback tools go beyond surface-level error correction by offering contextual explanations that improve students' understanding of writing mechanics. For instance, Write & Improve evaluates coherence and cohesion, guiding students in structuring their ideas more logically (Tseng & Warschauer, 2023). AI-powered assessment platforms also track discourse patterns, providing insights into how students develop arguments over multiple drafts. By integrating these tools into classroom practice, educators can create a more interactive and iterative learning process, where students receive continuous guidance rather than waiting for end-stage evaluations.

One challenge in AI-based assessment is ensuring that students engage meaningfully with AI-generated feedback rather than relying on it as a substitute for critical thinking. AI feedback should complement, rather than replace, teacher and peer reviews. Educators must teach students how to interpret and apply AI-generated suggestions effectively, ensuring that writing remains an intellectual and creative exercise rather than a purely mechanized process.

AI Detection Tools

As AI tools become more prevalent in writing education, concerns about over-reliance and academic integrity have emerged. The risk of students submitting AI-generated essays without proper attribution necessitates the use of AI detection tools. Platforms such as Turnitin's AI detection software help educators distinguish between student-generated and AI-assisted writing, ensuring that students engage authentically with their learning process (Tseng & Warschauer, 2023). However, reliance on AI detection also raises questions about false positives and the evolving sophistication of AI-generated content.

Bias in AI-generated feedback is another ethical concern. AI algorithms are trained on vast datasets, but these datasets may contain linguistic biases that disadvantage non-native English speakers or reinforce outdated writing conventions. McMurry et al. (2016) advocate for transparent evaluation frameworks, such as the CALL evaluation model, which help educators assess AI tools for fairness and inclusivity. By integrating a structured pedagogical approach to AI use, educators can ensure that students engage critically with AI-generated suggestions rather than accepting them without scrutiny.

Additionally, concerns about data privacy and security must be addressed. Many AI platforms collect user data to refine their models, but this raises ethical questions about data ownership and confidentiality. Educational institutions must implement clear policies on AI data usage, ensuring compliance with privacy regulations such as GDPR and FERPA (Stavytska et al., 2024). Students and educators should be informed about how AI tools store and process data to maintain transparency and protect sensitive information.

In short, AI is poised to play a transformative role in writing education, offering students and educators valuable tools for research, writing support, feedback, and assessment. However, its integration must be managed thoughtfully to balance efficiency with ethical responsibility. AI tools should enhance, rather than replace, critical thinking and creative engagement in the writing process. By incorporating AI into structured learning environments, educators can harness its benefits while mitigating risks related to over-reliance, academic integrity, and data privacy. As AI continues to evolve, ongoing research and responsible implementation will be essential to ensuring that AI serves as a tool for empowerment rather than a shortcut to learning (Akayoğlu, 2019).

INTEGRATING AI INTO WRITING PROGRAMS

Curriculum Design for AI-Integrated Writing Programs

The integration of AI tools into writing instruction requires a well-structured curriculum that aligns with traditional pedagogical approaches while leveraging AI's capabilities. AI should be incorporated into three critical stages of the writing process: pre-writing, drafting, and revision. Each stage offers opportunities to enhance student engagement, improve writing quality, and develop critical thinking skills through AI-supported interventions.

In the pre-writing stage, AI-powered brainstorming tools such as ChatGPT and Elicit assist students in generating thesis statements, structuring arguments, and exploring multiple perspectives. AI-enhanced brainstorming improves students' ability to develop well-supported arguments, helping them engage more effectively with their writing tasks (Li, 2024). Additionally, AI-driven search tools, such as Research Rabbit and Semantic Scholar, allow students to quickly gather relevant academic resources, refining their research process and enabling deeper engagement with scholarly material (Pokrivčáková, 2019).

During the drafting phase, AI can function as a co-writer by providing sentence starters, suggesting organizational improvements, and correcting basic errors. However, students must retain creative control over their work, ensuring AI-generated suggestions do not diminish originality. Tseng & Warschauer (2023) emphasize the importance of critical engagement with AI feedback, requiring students to evaluate, refine, and modify AI-generated text. Educators should guide students in using AI for support rather than as a primary writing tool, ensuring a balance between automation and independent thought.

The revision stage benefits significantly from AI tools such as Grammarly and Criterion, which provide real-time feedback on grammar, coherence, and structure. Stavytska et al. (2024) advocate for integrating AI-generated feedback with peer and teacher assessments to ensure students engage critically with suggested revisions. AI tools can help identify common grammatical errors and structural inconsistencies, but human assessment remains essential for evaluating argument quality, depth of analysis, and rhetorical effectiveness. By structuring AI integration within these stages, students progressively refine their writing skills while maintaining reflective engagement with technology.

Teacher Training and Professional Development

The successful integration of AI into writing instruction depends on comprehensive teacher training and professional development programs. Educators must develop AI literacy to understand AI tools' functionality, limitations, and ethical implications. AI literacy workshops should cover evaluating AI-generated content, recognizing biases, and guiding students in ethical AI use (McMurry et al., 2016). These training sessions help educators navigate AI's strengths and weaknesses while promoting responsible student engagement with AI-assisted writing.

Effective AI integration requires a balanced approach that supplements traditional teaching methods rather than replacing them. Teachers should adopt scaffolding techniques that incorporate AI in structured exercises, ensuring students develop independent writing skills rather than relying excessively on AI-generated text (Pokrivčáková, 2019). Moreover, ethical training is crucial in helping educators reinforce academic integrity principles. Plagiarism detection tools such as Turnitin play a pivotal role in ensuring that students use AI to refine their work rather than bypassing intellectual effort (Tseng & Warschauer, 2023).

Professional development programs should also focus on adaptive teaching strategies that accommodate diverse learning needs. AI provides opportunities for differentiated instruction, allowing educators to tailor feedback and writing exercises to individual students. However, teachers must be trained to interpret AI analytics effectively and integrate AI-generated insights into personalized learning plans. By equipping educators with the necessary skills, institutions can ensure that AI enhances rather than disrupts writing instruction.

AI Integration in Resource-Limited Settings

AI adoption in writing instruction should be accessible to all students, regardless of economic and technological disparities. Schools in resource-limited environments can still integrate AI tools effectively by utilizing cost-effective and accessible alternatives. Offline AI tools such as LanguageTool provide grammar and style feedback without requiring constant internet access, making them valuable in low-resource settings. Similarly, free versions of AI-powered applications such as Grammarly and Hemingway Editor offer essential writing analysis features, ensuring AI-driven feedback remains available to students from diverse backgrounds.

Collaborative learning strategies further optimize AI resources in constrained settings. Educators can implement AI in group activities, allowing students to collectively analyze AI-generated feedback and refine their writing. This approach not only maximizes the benefits of AI but also fosters peer learning and critical engagement. Additionally, schools can prioritize AI literacy workshops that equip students with strategies to leverage AI tools effectively while minimizing dependence on costly digital infrastructure.

Partnerships with universities and educational organizations can also enhance AI access in underfunded institutions. Many AI developers offer educational discounts or free trials for academic use, providing opportunities for schools to integrate AI without excessive financial burdens. Policymakers and educators must advocate for equitable AI adoption, ensuring that all students benefit from advancements in writing technology.

Best Practices for Integrating AI into Writing Instruction

To ensure effective AI integration, educators must adopt best practices that balance AI's benefits with traditional writing instruction. AI should be used as a supportive tool rather than a dominant force in the writing process. Students must critically engage with AI-generated suggestions rather than accepting them uncritically (Mitra & Banerjee, 2022). AI should complement, not replace, teacher and peer feedback, ensuring that students receive the efficiency of automated support alongside the depth of human assessment (Chen Lin, 2024).

An iterative learning approach is particularly effective for AI-assisted writing instruction. Students should engage in multiple drafts, initially using AI tools for preliminary suggestions before refining their work through human feedback. This iterative process reinforces both critical thinking and writing autonomy, allowing students to develop their writing skills progressively (Akayoğlu, 2019). Educators should design assignments that require students to document their AI interactions, explaining how they incorporated AI suggestions while maintaining original thought. This transparency ensures that AI serves as a tool for refinement rather than a shortcut to completing assignments.

Additionally, fostering ethical AI use is crucial in writing instruction. Educators should establish clear guidelines that define appropriate AI engagement, emphasizing that AI should enhance rather than replace human cognition. Schools should implement honor codes that outline responsible AI use, helping students develop a principled approach to AI-assisted learning. Ethical AI literacy programs can further reinforce these principles, equipping students with the skills to navigate AI tools responsibly while maintaining academic integrity.

In short, the integration of AI into writing instruction presents immense opportunities for enhancing writing proficiency, but its success depends on thoughtful and structured implementation. By aligning AI with structured writing stages, providing comprehensive teacher training, and ensuring accessibility in resource-limited settings, educators can create an environment where AI enhances student learning while maintaining pedagogical integrity. A balanced approach that fosters both technological proficiency and independent critical thinking empowers students to engage with AI meaningfully while developing strong writing skills. Through responsible AI use, the next generation of writers can harness technological advancements without compromising originality, creativity, or ethical standards.

CASE STUDY OF AI-ENHANCED WRITING INSTRUCTION

The integration of AI into writing instruction presents both opportunities and challenges for educators. This case study examines an experimental writing program that incorporated ChatGPT as a tool for self-assessment and revision. The study highlights the benefits, challenges, and long-term implications of using AI in writing instruction, while also addressing underexplored issues such as equity, cultural considerations, and teacher training.

Implementation of AI in Writing Instruction

The structured integration of AI tools into writing instruction follows a systematic process designed to enhance student engagement and writing proficiency. The first stage focuses on pre-writing activities where students brainstorm ideas, create outlines, and engage with AI to refine their thesis statements. AI-assisted brainstorming tools such as ChatGPT enable students to explore multiple perspectives, strengthening their argument development. However, disparities in digital literacy among students influenced their ability to navigate AI tools effectively, raising concerns about equity in access to technology. Educators play a vital role in bridging this gap by providing training on AI usage, ensuring that all students benefit from these advancements.

The next stage involves structured training for students on how to use AI tools such as ChatGPT for self-assessment. Teachers model AI interactions, demonstrating how to generate prompts that elicit meaningful feedback. This instructional phase is crucial in helping students understand AI's capabilities and limitations. Some students struggle with overly generic AI-generated feedback, necessitating additional teacher guidance to refine AI interactions and receive specific, relevant suggestions. Educators must ensure that students engage critically with AI-generated responses rather than accepting them passively.

Following the training sessions, students apply their AI knowledge independently by drafting and revising their essays. They submit their original drafts, ChatGPT interactions, and revised versions for teacher evaluation. This process allows educators to assess both the quality of student writing and their engagement with AI tools. The results indicate significant improvements in grammar, vocabulary diversity, and sentence structure. However, students continue to face challenges in maintaining logical flow and effectively meeting assignment requirements, highlighting the need for balanced AI-human intervention in writing instruction.

Step-by-Step Guide for Educators

The integration of AI in writing instruction follows a structured, multi-phase process, enabling educators to effectively incorporate AI into their teaching methods. This approach ensures that students receive comprehensive guidance while leveraging AI tools for writing development.

Pre-Writing Stage

Educators should introduce brainstorming tools and AI-generated idea prompts, ensuring that students engage critically with AI suggestions rather than relying on them uncritically. This phase helps students generate ideas, structure their arguments, and refine their thesis statements. To enhance this process, teachers should provide students with graphic organizers such as mind maps and outlines, guiding them in structuring their thoughts effectively.

AI Training Sessions

To maximize AI's potential, teachers must conduct AI training sessions where they model AI interactions, demonstrating how students can refine prompts to receive targeted feedback. Educators should guide students in distinguishing between relevant AI-generated suggestions and superficial corrections, helping them develop the skills needed to interact with AI meaningfully. These sessions should also address AI's limitations, ensuring that students remain critical users rather than passive recipients of AI feedback.

Drafting with AI Assistance

During the drafting phase, students should be encouraged to use AI tools for grammar and structure refinement while maintaining ownership of content and argumentation. AI should support, not replace, independent thought. Educators must design assignments that require students to integrate AI-assisted improvements while preserving their voice and critical thinking. AI can assist in generating varied sentence structures, offering stylistic improvements, and providing suggestions for better coherence and cohesion.

Revision through AI and Peer Review

AI-generated feedback should be paired with teacher and peer review, ensuring that students receive well-rounded insights. This combined approach helps students refine their work beyond AI's technical corrections, enabling them to strengthen their analytical and structural writing skills. Revision should not solely depend on AI-generated corrections but should incorporate peer discussions and teacher feedback to create a comprehensive revision process.

Assessment of AI Effectiveness

The effectiveness of AI-assisted writing instruction should be evaluated through structured assessment methods. Educators should require students to submit original drafts, AI interactions, and final revisions, allowing them to analyze AI's impact on writing improvements. By comparing these versions, teachers can track progress in writing proficiency and determine how well students integrate AI-assisted revisions into their work. This evaluation process helps refine instructional strategies, ensuring that AI is used as an enhancement tool rather than a substitute for critical engagement in writing.

The integration of AI into writing instruction underscores the importance of strategic implementation to ensure that AI tools enhance student learning rather than hinder independent skill development. The study revealed that while AI is effective in refining grammar, vocabulary, and sentence structures, higher-order writing skills such as argument development, logical consistency, and critical analysis still require teacher intervention. Thus, AI must be viewed as a supportive tool that complements, rather than replaces, human feedback.

Additionally, ensuring equity in AI accessibility remains a key challenge. Disparities in students' familiarity with AI tools indicate the need for structured digital literacy training. Schools must implement AI literacy programs to help students from diverse backgrounds engage meaningfully with AI tools. Furthermore, AI-driven instruction should be continuously refined through educator feedback and student performance tracking to ensure that technology enhances, rather than diminishes, student engagement in the writing process.

By adopting a structured, iterative approach to AI integration, educators can foster a balanced learning environment where AI tools empower students without compromising essential writing skills. The responsible use of AI in education ensures that students develop both technological proficiency and critical thinking, preparing them for an evolving academic and professional landscape.

The Outcomes

The implementation of ChatGPT as a writing support tool resulted in statistically significant improvements in student performance, particularly in technical aspects of writing. A series of t-tests conducted on the experimental and control groups provided robust empirical evidence of AI's effectiveness in enhancing specific writing skills. These results underscore the potential of AI to enhance technical writing skills, providing a structured and effective method for students to refine their grammar, vocabulary, and sentence structure. However, while AI demonstrated measurable benefits, its limitations in improving higher-order writing skills suggest that AI should be used in conjunction with teacher guidance to maximize effectiveness.

Independent Samples T-test Results: Pre-Test and Post-Test Performance

The statistical comparison between the experimental and control groups in both pre-test and post-test phases highlights a distinct difference in learning outcomes. Initially, the pre-test results showed no significant variance between the groups, with a Sig. (2-tailed) value of 0.713, confirming similar proficiency levels before AI intervention. However, the post-test results demonstrated a highly significant improvement in the experimental group's performance, with a Sig. (2-tailed) value of 0.000, strongly indicating that students who used ChatGPT performed significantly better than those who did not.

These results provide empirical support for the claim that AI-enhanced writing instruction can accelerate student improvement in technical writing elements. The stark contrast in post-test performance between the control and experimental groups suggests that AI-based writing tools effectively provide the necessary support to refine surface-level writing mechanics. However, while the AI-assisted group showed measurable gains, the data suggests that AI alone is not sufficient for improving deeper writing competencies such as critical thinking and argumentation.

Paired Samples T-test Results: Evaluating Growth in Writing Proficiency

A comparison within each group revealed further insights. The control group's pre-test and post-test scores yielded a Sig. (2-tailed) value of 0.340, showing no significant progress in writing skills over the course of the study. This result suggests that traditional methods alone were insufficient in substantially improving writing proficiency within the given timeframe.

Conversely, the experimental group exhibited a statistically significant improvement in their post-test scores compared to their pre-test results, with a Sig. (2-tailed) value of 0.038. This finding confirms that consistent use of ChatGPT for drafting, revision, and feedback led to measurable improvements in students' writing abilities. Students who engaged with AI tools demonstrated a more structured approach to revision, as they were able to refine grammar, vocabulary, and sentence structure more efficiently than their peers in the control group. These findings support the argument that AI can serve as a beneficial tool in streamlining technical aspects of the writing process while allowing educators to focus on more complex instruction such as argument development and logical coherence.

Skill-Specific Analysis: AI's Role in Writing Development

A deeper analysis of the experimental group's writing performance across various skill categories provided additional insights into AI's strengths and limitations. Several areas showed no significant improvement despite AI assistance, including understanding the assignment (Sig. 0.520), outlining the essay (Sig. 0.729), and maintaining logical flow and consistency (Sig. 0.433). These results suggest that while AI is effective in refining technical writing skills, it does not replace the need for human instruction in areas that require deeper cognitive processing, such as argument organization and conceptual clarity.

However, AI's effectiveness was evident in technical aspects of writing, with significant improvements observed in multiple skill areas, including: avoiding errors in spelling and word formation: Sig. (2-tailed) 0.000, using a wide range of vocabulary: Sig. (2-tailed) 0.036, avoiding grammar mistakes: Sig. (2-tailed) 0.026, using a variety of sentence structures: Sig. (2-tailed) 0.018, incorporating transitions and linking words: Sig. (2-tailed) 0.000. These findings indicate that AI tools such as ChatGPT provide immediate and precise feedback on mechanical and stylistic aspects of writing, leading to substantial gains in grammar, vocabulary use, and textual coherence. The ability of AI to highlight spelling, grammar, and transition-related errors in real time contributed to these statistically significant improvements in the experimental group. This suggests that AI functions as an effective real-time writing assistant, capable of reducing surface-level errors and improving fluency, which is particularly beneficial for second-language learners and students struggling with grammatical accuracy.

Additionally, the study findings highlight the differential impact of AI across various writing sub-skills. While AI proved highly effective in reducing spelling and grammatical errors, its capacity to assist in constructing logically structured arguments or maintaining coherence across paragraphs remained limited. This underscores the necessity for a hybrid approach where AI tools supplement traditional instruction but do not replace it entirely. Teachers remain integral to guiding students in structuring their ideas, crafting compelling arguments, and developing a coherent writing style.

The statistical evidence from this study strongly supports the notion that AI tools can play a crucial role in improving specific aspects of student writing. However, the findings also highlight key considerations for long-term AI integration in writing education. Structured AI training is essential to ensure that students engage critically with AI-generated feedback rather than passively accepting it. This aligns with McMurry et al. (2016), who emphasize the need for AI literacy in education. Additionally, while AI tools improve writing efficiency, they do not inherently foster higher-order writing skills such as argument construction and logical reasoning. Educators must implement AI-supported pedagogical approaches that encourage critical thinking alongside AI-generated recommendations. One potential strategy is to combine AI-based grammar and style corrections with teacher-led discussions that focus on content organization and thesis development. Such an approach would ensure that students benefit from AI's efficiency while also receiving the necessary cognitive challenges required for strong academic writing.

Students' Attitudes Toward ChatGPT Implementation

The feedback from students in the experimental group highlights a generally positive reception of ChatGPT as an AI-assisted writing tool. The majority of students found the tool beneficial for generating ideas, structuring their essays, and improving their technical writing skills. However, some limitations were also noted, particularly concerning ChatGPT's ability to help students fully grasp assignment requirements and maintain a consistent writing style. These insights align with broader discussions on AI-assisted learning, where AI has been shown to enhance surface-level writing skills while requiring human intervention for higher-order cognitive tasks.

A substantial number of students cited grammar correction as one of the most beneficial aspects of ChatGPT. According to student ST3, "ChatGPT has been a lifesaver for my grammar! It helps me identify and correct mistakes I never noticed before. My writing is definitely more polished now." This observation aligns with the statistical results, which showed a highly significant improvement in grammatical accuracy in the experimental group, with a Sig. (2-tailed) value of 0.026.

Similarly, several students noted improvements in their sentence structure and overall writing flow. Student ST8 commented, "ChatGPT has really improved my sentence structure. It shows me different ways to express the same idea, making my writing more interesting and engaging." This finding is supported by the statistical evidence, which indicates that students in the experimental group showed notable improvement in sentence variation and fluency (Sig. 2-tailed: 0.018).

These observations are consistent with findings from Li (2024), who reported that AI-driven writing assistants significantly enhance students' grammatical precision and sentence structuring in second-language learning environments. The ability of AI tools to provide immediate corrections on syntax and grammar appears to be one of the most tangible benefits for students.

Another frequently mentioned advantage of ChatGPT was its ability to enhance vocabulary usage. Student ST6 stated, "I've expanded my vocabulary so much thanks to ChatGPT. It suggests different word choices, and I've learned a lot of new words." Statistical analysis confirmed this trend, with the experimental group showing a significant increase in vocabulary range, as evidenced by a Sig. (2-tailed) value of 0.036.

This finding mirrors those of Stavytska et al. (2024), who observed that AI-assisted writing tools help students diversify their vocabulary and improve lexical accuracy. The immediate synonym suggestions provided by AI allow students to refine word choice, leading to more sophisticated and varied writing.

Students also found ChatGPT useful for improving coherence and transitions within their essays. ST10 noted, "ChatGPT helped me use more varied sentence structures and transitions. My writing flows much better now, and it's easier to read." The statistical findings support this claim, as the use of transitions and linking words showed a highly significant improvement, with a Sig. (2-tailed) value of 0.000.

This aligns with the conclusions of Tseng & Warschauer (2023), who argue that AI-generated feedback aids students in structuring their writing more coherently, especially when transitioning between ideas. The ability of AI tools to highlight areas requiring smoother transitions contributes to better text cohesion, making it easier for students to construct logical, well-connected arguments.

Despite these benefits, several students highlighted challenges associated with ChatGPT's use. One major issue was the tool's inability to fully convey assignment requirements. Student ST7 remarked, "While ChatGPT can be helpful for generating ideas, I found it difficult to use it to truly understand the requirement of the assignment. I still needed to rely on my teacher for clarification."

This concern was reflected in the statistical results, which showed no significant improvement in understanding assignment requirements (Sig. 2-tailed: 0.520). These findings suggest that AI tools, while effective in refining technical aspects of writing, are not as useful for guiding students in comprehending broader assignment expectations. Marr & Ward (2019) reached similar conclusions, arguing that AI cannot fully replace human instructors in clarifying complex instructions or nuanced essay prompts.

Another challenge noted by students was maintaining a consistent tone and style. Student ST11 stated, "I struggled to maintain a consistent tone and style in my writing when using ChatGPT. It felt like I was piecing together different parts without a clear overall direction."

This aligns with the statistical results, which showed no significant improvement in maintaining logical flow and consistency (Sig. 2-tailed: 0.433). The findings reinforce the argument made by Xie (2023), who cautioned that AI-generated text can sometimes lead to fragmented or disjointed writing, especially when students rely too heavily on it without careful revision.

Some students reported difficulties when using ChatGPT for outlining their essays. Student ST12 commented, "Creating an outline with ChatGPT was hit or miss. Sometimes it provided a good starting point, but other times it missed the main points of the assignment, leading to a disorganized essay." This aligns with the lack of statistical improvement in outlining skills (Sig. 2-tailed: 0.729), indicating that AI tools may not be sufficiently reliable in helping students structure their essays from the ground up.

These findings are consistent with McMurry et al. (2016), who emphasized that AI tools, while helpful in providing structural suggestions, still require human oversight to ensure logical organization. AI-generated outlines may serve as preliminary frameworks, but students must refine them through critical thinking and teacher feedback.

The results of this study align closely with previous research on AI-assisted writing instruction. Similar to Pokrivčáková (2019), the study confirms that AI significantly improves grammatical accuracy, vocabulary diversity, and sentence complexity. However, like McMurry et al. (2016), it also highlights AI's limitations in guiding students through higher-order writing processes such as argument development and assignment interpretation.

Moreover, the findings reinforce Mitra & Banerjee (2022), who emphasized that AI tools work best when combined with teacher feedback. The mixed results from this study suggest that AI should be used as a supplementary writing aid rather than a standalone instructional tool.

The integration of ChatGPT into the writing process yielded statistically significant improvements in grammar, vocabulary diversity, and sentence structure, as confirmed by t-test analyses. However, it showed no measurable impact on higher-order writing skills, such as outlining, logical flow, and assignment comprehension. These results align with existing research, reinforcing the notion that AI is most effective when used in tandem with teacher support.

Ultimately, while ChatGPT has proven to be a valuable asset in writing education, it should not replace traditional pedagogical methods. Instead, it should function as a complementary tool, helping students refine technical aspects of their writing while still relying on human instructors for deeper cognitive and analytical skills.

Challenges and Considerations

While AI integration yielded measurable benefits, it also introduced challenges that educators must navigate. Equity concerns emerged as students from lower socioeconomic backgrounds had limited access to AI tools outside the classroom. To address this, schools must provide AI access within educational settings to prevent disparities in learning outcomes.

Cultural considerations also played a role in AI's effectiveness. Some AI-generated feedback did not align with students' linguistic or rhetorical conventions, particularly for non-native English speakers. This highlights the need for culturally aware AI applications that consider linguistic diversity in writing instruction.

Teacher training proved essential in mitigating AI's limitations. Educators needed professional development to understand AI's functionality, limitations, and ethical implications. Without adequate training, teachers struggled to guide students effectively in AI interactions, reducing the potential benefits of AI-enhanced learning.

This case study underscores the importance of a balanced approach to AI integration in writing instruction. While AI tools effectively enhance technical writing skills, they do not replace the critical role of educators in fostering higher-order thinking and argumentation skills. Equity issues must be addressed by ensuring all students have access to AI tools, and AI models should be refined to accommodate diverse linguistic and cultural backgrounds. Additionally, continuous teacher training is necessary to optimize AI's benefits in educational settings.

The long-term implications of AI in education extend beyond writing instruction. As AI continues to evolve, its role in personalized learning and formative assessment will likely expand. However, its success depends on responsible implementation, ensuring that AI remains a supportive tool rather than a substitute for human instruction. By addressing its challenges and refining its applications, AI can serve as a valuable asset in writing education, empowering students to become more independent and proficient writers.

ETHICAL CONSIDERATIONS IN AI-POWERED WRITING EDUCATION

The rise of AI in writing education presents both opportunities and ethical challenges. While AI can enhance personalized learning and provide instant feedback, its integration into the educational landscape raises concerns regarding data privacy, plagiarism risks, over-reliance on AI, equity in access, teacher training, and the balance between AI use and critical thinking development. A thorough examination of these ethical dimensions is essential to ensure that AI serves as a tool that enhances rather than undermines educational integrity and fairness.

Data Privacy and Security Concerns

One of the primary ethical concerns in AI-powered writing education is the collection and management of student data. AI tools often require vast amounts of user input to provide personalized feedback, raising concerns about how this data is stored, who has access to it, and whether it is used for commercial purposes. Stavytska et al. (2024) highlight that without robust data security measures, student information could be vulnerable to breaches or unauthorized use. Ensuring compliance with data protection regulations, such as the General Data Protection Regulation (GDPR) and the Family Educational Rights and Privacy Act (FERPA), is essential to maintaining student trust and safeguarding their information.

Beyond regulatory compliance, educational institutions must adopt transparent policies regarding data collection and establish clear consent protocols, ensuring students and teachers understand how AI systems handle their information. Students should have the right to opt out of data collection or request the deletion of stored data to maintain control over their personal information. Additionally, AI developers should design systems that prioritize data minimization, storing only essential information and implementing encryption techniques to mitigate the risk of data breaches.

Plagiarism and Academic Integrity

The use of AI in writing instruction raises concerns about academic integrity and the potential for AI-assisted plagiarism. AI-powered writing tools can generate sophisticated text, allowing students to produce assignments with minimal effort, which may undermine the development of independent writing skills. While tools such as Turnitin and Grammarly offer plagiarism detection, they may not always detect AI-generated content effectively. Xie (2023) argues that educators must redefine what constitutes original work in an AI-assisted learning environment, encouraging students to use AI ethically as a tool for refinement rather than as a means to generate complete assignments.

Teachers should emphasize process-oriented writing, where students document their revisions and interactions with AI, ensuring transparency in how AI tools contribute to their learning process. Implementing writing logs, requiring students to submit drafts alongside AI-generated feedback, and encouraging reflective writing exercises can help ensure that AI supports, rather than replaces, student effort. Moreover, academic institutions should establish clear policies regarding AI use in coursework, distinguishing between acceptable AI-assisted writing and inappropriate dependence on AI-generated content.

Over-Reliance on AI and the Erosion of Critical Thinking

AI-driven writing tools, while effective for grammar correction and structural enhancements, risk fostering over-reliance among students, reducing their ability to develop independent writing skills. Stavytska et al. (2024) caution that AI cannot replace the depth of human guidance, particularly in fostering argumentation, originality, and critical thinking.

Educators must integrate AI in a way that supports rather than replaces cognitive engagement. Assignments should be designed to require students to engage in analysis, synthesis, and evaluation, ensuring that AI serves as a support mechanism rather than a substitute for intellectual effort. Furthermore, teachers should guide students in critically assessing AI-generated content, teaching them to discern inaccuracies and refine outputs rather than accepting AI-generated text at face value.

Recent studies have demonstrated that students who rely excessively on AI for drafting and revision often struggle with deeper analytical tasks. For example, research by Tseng & Warschauer (2023) found that while AI-assisted students improved their grammar and vocabulary, they did not show significant gains in developing arguments and logical coherence in their essays. These findings emphasize the necessity of structuring AI-assisted learning in a way that encourages critical engagement rather than passive acceptance of AI-generated suggestions.

Equity and Accessibility in AI Integration

The integration of AI tools in writing education poses significant equity challenges, particularly for schools with limited technological resources. AI-based education tools are often expensive, requiring high-speed internet, up-to-date devices, and institutional support, which may not be available in underfunded schools. This digital divide exacerbates existing educational inequalities, as students from privileged backgrounds benefit from AI-enhanced learning while those from low-income schools face barriers to access.

Xie (2023) emphasizes the need for policymakers and educational institutions to implement strategies that ensure equitable AI access. Solutions may include subsidizing AI tools for low-income schools, offering offline AI capabilities, and training teachers in resource-limited settings to use AI effectively with minimal infrastructure. Additionally, open-source AI tools that do not require extensive computing power should be developed to make AI-supported learning accessible to a broader range of students. Institutions must work toward minimizing the disparity in AI adoption to prevent further marginalization of underprivileged students.

Teacher Training and Professional Development

Successful AI integration in writing instruction depends on well-trained educators who understand both the capabilities and limitations of AI. However, many teachers lack formal training in AI literacy, leading to inconsistent and sometimes ineffective implementation. Professional development programs should focus on equipping teachers with the knowledge to guide students in ethical AI use, helping them navigate AI-generated feedback, and incorporating AI into lesson planning without compromising instructional depth.

Without sufficient training, educators may either underutilize AI or over-rely on it, diminishing its potential as a complementary teaching tool. Institutions must prioritize continuous professional development to ensure that AI enhances, rather than disrupts, pedagogical best practices. For example, workshops on AI integration should include hands-on experience in using AI tools, discussions on best practices for AI-assisted instruction, and strategies for addressing AI-related ethical concerns in the classroom.

The Balance Between AI and Human-Led Learning

AI should not replace the human elements of writing instruction, such as mentorship, feedback, and personal engagement. While AI tools can provide immediate corrections and suggestions, they lack the nuanced understanding, empathy, and contextual awareness that human teachers bring to education. Stavytska et al. (2024) argue that writing is not just a technical skill but also a process of self-expression and critical reasoning, requiring mentorship that AI cannot replicate.

A balanced approach involves integrating AI as a supplementary tool while maintaining student-teacher interactions that foster deeper learning. Teachers should design activities that encourage students to engage in peer reviews, discussions, and debates, ensuring that writing remains a reflective and interactive process. Research by Mitra & Banerjee (2022) supports this approach, demonstrating that students who engaged in AI-assisted learning combined with structured human feedback showed greater long-term retention of writing concepts than those who relied solely on AI tools.

Additionally, studies comparing AI-assisted writing programs with traditional writing instruction (Chen Lin, 2024) suggest that AI improves surface-level writing proficiency but does not contribute significantly to creative expression and deep analytical thinking. These findings reinforce the need for a hybrid approach where AI supports, rather than replaces, traditional instructional methods.

In short, AI-powered writing education presents promising advancements but also requires careful ethical consideration. Issues of data privacy, plagiarism, over-reliance on technology, equity in access, and the necessity of teacher training must be addressed to create an AI-enhanced learning environment that upholds academic integrity and fairness. Ensuring that AI remains a tool for support rather than a substitute for critical thinking and human instruction is essential.

By implementing robust data protection policies, promoting ethical AI use, prioritizing equity in access, and equipping teachers with AI literacy, educational institutions can leverage AI responsibly, enhancing student learning while maintaining ethical standards in writing education. The future of AI in writing instruction will depend on how effectively it is integrated into pedagogical frameworks that balance technological innovation with human-centered learning approaches. AI should be seen not as a replacement for traditional writing instruction but as a complement that enhances the learning experience while preserving the fundamental role of educators in shaping students' intellectual and creative development.

GUIDELINES FOR ETHICAL AND EFFECTIVE AI IMPLEMENTATION IN WRITING INSTRUCTION

As AI continues to shape writing instruction, educators and institutions must approach its integration with a critical and balanced perspective. While AI tools offer benefits such as automated feedback and real-time corrections, their use must be carefully managed to ensure that they enhance, rather than replace, essential elements of writing education. AI's role in education should be viewed as a supportive tool that fosters improvement in technical aspects of writing while preserving the cognitive and creative engagement that traditional instruction provides. This section outlines key recommendations for leveraging AI effectively while maintaining ethical standards and safeguarding pedagogical integrity.

Aligning AI with Pedagogical Objectives

Educators must ensure that AI tools align with instructional goals, serving as a supplement to writing instruction rather than a substitute for fundamental learning processes. While AI-powered applications can improve grammar, vocabulary, and coherence, they should not replace human oversight in fostering critical thinking and creativity. AI-generated content often lacks the depth, nuance, and originality that human instruction nurtures, making it essential for teachers to guide students in using AI as a constructive tool rather than a crutch (Stavytska et al., 2024). Institutions should integrate AI into structured lesson plans where students actively engage with AI outputs, critique suggestions, and refine their writing through informed decision-making.

Moreover, AI's ability to enhance personalization in learning should be leveraged to meet diverse student needs. AI-driven writing assistants can tailor feedback based on individual learning profiles, offering students a more adaptive and responsive writing experience. However, while AI provides efficiency in technical skill development, the cognitive and rhetorical aspects of writing require teacher intervention. Instructors should balance AI-generated feedback with guided discussions, peer collaboration, and interactive writing exercises to ensure that students develop comprehensive writing skills rather than focusing solely on mechanical accuracy.

Addressing Ethical Concerns in AI Use

The ethical use of AI in writing education requires institutions to establish clear policies on data privacy, academic integrity, and responsible AI usage. One pressing concern is data security, as AI tools often collect user data for optimization purposes. Ensuring compliance with data protection regulations such as GDPR and FERPA is necessary to safeguard students' personal information (Stavytska et al., 2024). Transparency is critical—educators must inform students about data collection practices, the risks associated with AI-generated content, and how their information is used in AI-based platforms.

Another critical issue is plagiarism and the potential misuse of AI to generate assignments without genuine intellectual effort. Xie (2023) warns that unregulated AI use may encourage students to submit work that lacks originality and depth. To mitigate this risk, educators must incorporate AI literacy training, teaching students how to engage with AI tools ethically by refining AI-generated drafts rather than relying on them for complete assignments. AI should be framed as a tool for enhancement, not for substitution. Assignments should require students to document their writing process, including AI interactions and revisions, ensuring accountability and originality. Institutions should also employ AI detection tools to monitor for academic dishonesty while emphasizing a learning culture that values process-oriented writing and independent thought.

Furthermore, AI models often reflect biases present in their training data, potentially influencing the writing style, content suggestions, and language structures they promote. Educators must train students to recognize and critically assess AI-generated biases, encouraging a reflective approach to writing that prioritizes inclusivity and diverse perspectives. Ethical AI literacy should be embedded into the curriculum to equip students with the skills necessary to navigate the evolving landscape of AI-powered writing education.

Ensuring Equitable Access to AI Technologies

Disparities in AI access pose a significant challenge in education, particularly for underfunded schools that lack the necessary technological infrastructure. AI-enhanced writing instruction should not widen the educational divide by benefiting only well-resourced institutions. Barrot (2023) emphasizes the need for inclusive AI implementation strategies that ensure equitable access to AI tools, including subsidized software programs, offline functionalities, and mobile-friendly applications. Schools should prioritize funding initiatives that equip all students with AI-enhanced learning opportunities, ensuring that technological advancements do not create further disparities in educational outcomes.

To address this issue, policymakers should explore public-private partnerships with AI developers to provide free or low-cost AI tools to schools with limited resources. Additionally, the development of AI tools that function with minimal internet bandwidth or offline capabilities can benefit students in rural or low-income areas. Training educators to use AI tools efficiently in resource-limited settings is also essential; even simple AI applications can significantly improve student writing when integrated effectively into instructional strategies.

Teacher Training and Professional Development

Successful AI integration hinges on educators' ability to use these tools effectively while maintaining instructional depth. Many teachers lack formal training in AI literacy, leading to inconsistent implementation and an overreliance on automated corrections. Pokrivčáková (2019) argues that teacher training programs must incorporate AI education, focusing on strategies for meaningful AI integration without compromising pedagogical goals. Workshops and continuous professional development should empower teachers to critically assess AI-generated content, guide students in refining AI-assisted writing, and address ethical concerns surrounding AI use. Institutions should foster collaborative learning environments where educators share best practices and refine AI-assisted teaching methodologies over time.

Additionally, professional development should emphasize adaptive learning strategies that incorporate AI effectively while maintaining pedagogical rigor. Educators should learn to differentiate between AI-assisted learning and AI-dependent learning, ensuring that students continue to engage in the cognitive processes essential for writing development. Training should also focus on AI bias recognition, ethical considerations, and techniques for integrating AI into formative assessment practices without diminishing the role of human evaluation.

Balancing AI Use with Critical Thinking Development

While AI can streamline technical aspects of writing, it must not overshadow the development of independent thought and analytical skills. Xie (2023) notes that AI-generated text, if used uncritically, can lead to formulaic writing that lacks depth and originality. Educators should design assignments that encourage students to question AI suggestions, compare multiple writing approaches, and integrate AI feedback selectively. Activities such as peer review, in-depth discussions, and reflective writing exercises can counterbalance AI's automation by reinforcing human creativity and analytical reasoning.

Moreover, critical thinking can be fostered through AI-interactive learning models, where students actively challenge and refine AI-generated content. For instance, educators can create assignments that require students to compare AI-generated essays with human-written counterparts, evaluating the strengths and weaknesses of each. By engaging in this analytical process, students develop deeper insights into writing mechanics, argument structure, and the importance of human creativity in effective communication.

Future Directions for AI in Writing Education

Looking ahead, AI's role in writing instruction will likely continue to evolve, necessitating ongoing research and policy development. Future advancements in AI writing tools should focus on enhancing critical thinking rather than simply automating grammar and syntax corrections. AI developers should work closely with educators to create tools that support deeper learning, such as AI-driven scaffolding techniques that guide students through complex writing processes rather than merely suggesting surface-level corrections.

Furthermore, interdisciplinary research between AI developers, educators, and cognitive scientists can provide insights into how AI can be designed to foster higher-order thinking skills. AI models that incorporate adaptive learning, personalized feedback loops, and cognitive engagement strategies could play a transformative role in education. Institutions should also encourage experimental approaches to AI integration, evaluating different pedagogical frameworks that maximize AI's potential while mitigating its limitations.

By implementing thoughtful policies and structured integration strategies, AI can be leveraged as a valuable educational tool without compromising the integrity of writing instruction. The future of AI in writing education depends on maintaining ethical standards, fostering inclusivity, and continually refining instructional methodologies to create a learning environment where technology enhances—rather than replaces—human intellect and creativity.

CONCLUSION

The integration of AI into teaching methods is transforming students' writing performance in significant ways. As educators explore the potential of AI tools, particularly chatbots like ChatGPT, they discover that these technologies can enhance various sub-skills critical to effective writing. For instance, AI chatbots provide immediate feedback on grammar, vocabulary usage, and sentence structure, enabling students to refine their writing skills in real time. This instantaneous support helps students identify errors they may not have recognized, fostering a more polished final product. Moreover, AI can assist in generating ideas, organizing thoughts, and even offering prompts that encourage creativity, which are essential components of the writing process.

However, while AI presents numerous advantages, teachers must remain vigilant regarding its limitations. It is essential for educators to approach the integration of AI with a balanced perspective, ensuring that students do not overly rely on these tools. For instance, AI can sometimes produce suggestions that lack context or relevance, leading to misunderstandings about the assignment or topic. Therefore, teachers should emphasize the importance of critical thinking and discernment when using AI-generated content. By guiding students in evaluating the suggestions provided by AI, educators can help them develop a more nuanced understanding of writing as a craft, rather than merely a series of technical tasks.

Additionally, the engagement of students with new technologies like AI is a notable aspect of this integration. High school students, often digital natives, are more inclined to participate actively in their learning when they can utilize tools that resonate with their experiences outside the classroom. Incorporating AI into writing instruction can make learning more dynamic and relatable, allowing students to explore topics of interest in ways that feel relevant and exciting. This increased engagement can lead to a more effective teaching process, as students are more motivated to invest time and effort into their writing assignments when they see the immediate benefits of using AI tools.

To maximize the effectiveness of AI in the classroom, educators must create a supportive environment that fosters experimentation and encourages students to embrace both the benefits and challenges of these technologies. Professional development for teachers should include training on how to effectively integrate AI into their teaching practices while maintaining a focus on the development of critical writing skills. By equipping teachers with the necessary skills and knowledge, schools can ensure a smooth transition to AI-enhanced writing instruction.

In conclusion, the integration of AI into teaching methods holds great promise for enhancing students' writing performance. By leveraging AI chatbots to target specific sub-skills, teachers can create a more engaging and effective writing curriculum. However, it is crucial for educators to remain aware of the limitations of AI and guide students in using these tools thoughtfully. As high school teaching evolves to incorporate innovative technologies, the potential for improved student engagement and writing proficiency becomes increasingly attainable.

REFERENCES

Akayoğlu, S. (2019). Theoretical frameworks used in CALL studies: A systematic review. *Teaching English with Technology*, *19*(4), 104–118.

Barrot, J. S. (2023). Using CHATGPT for Second language writing: Pitfalls and potentials. *Assessing Writing*, *57*, 100745. DOI: 10.1016/j.asw.2023.100745

Barrs, M. (2022). *Vygotsky the Teacher: A Companion to his Psychology for Teachers and Other Practitioners*. Routledge, Taylor & Francis Group.

Korenev, A. A. (2024). Strategies of using artificial intelligence for written corrective feedback in language education. *Moscow University Bulletin. Series 19. Linguistics and Intercultural Communication*, *27*(N°2_2024), 68–77. DOI: 10.55959/MSU-2074-1588-19-27-2-5

Li, Y. (2024). Usability of chatgpt in Second language acquisition: Capabilities, effectiveness, applications, challenges, and solutions. *Studies in Applied Linguistics and TESOL*, *24*(1). Advance online publication. DOI: 10.52214/salt.v24i1.12864

Lin, C. (2024). Research on innovative models of Second language teaching in the age of Artificial Intelligence. *Applied Mathematics and Nonlinear Sciences*, *9*(1), 20240760. Advance online publication. DOI: 10.2478/amns-2024-0760

Marr, B., & Ward, M. (2019). *Artificial Intelligence in practice: How 50 successful companies used artificial intelligence to solve problems*. Wiley.

McMurry, B. L., Williams, D. D., Rich, P. J., & Hartshorn, K. J. (2016). An Evaluation Framework for CALL. *The Electronic Journal for English as a Second Language*, 20(2).

Mitra, N., & Banerjee, A. (2022). A study on using AI in promoting English language learning. *Lecture Notes in Networks and Systems*, 287–297. DOI: 10.1007/978-981-19-4052-1_30

Pokrivcakova, S. (2019). Preparing teachers for the application of AI-powered technologies in Foreign Language Education. *Journal of Language and Cultural Education*, *7*(3), 135–153. DOI: 10.2478/jolace-2019-0025

Stavytska, I., Shalova, N., & Korbut, O. (2024). Exploring the impacts and techniques of teaching with Artificial Intelligence Tools. *Перспективи Та Інновації Науки*, (6(40)). Advance online publication. DOI: 10.52058/2786-4952-2024-6(40)-40-47

Tseng, W., & Warschauer, M. (2023). Ai-writing tools in education: If you can't beat them, join them. *Journal of China Computer-Assisted Language Learning*, *3*(2), 258–262. DOI: 10.1515/jccall-2023-0008

Xie, J. (2023). Opportunities and challenges brought by artificial intelligence to Second language teaching: A case study of international chinese language education. *Advances in Engineering Innovation*, *3*(1), None. Advance online publication. DOI: 10.54254/2977-3903/3/2023045

KEY TERMS AND DEFINITIONS

Artificial Intelligence: Technology that simulates human intelligence, allowing machines to perform tasks that typically require cognitive functions, such as understanding language and generating text.

Writing Performance: The ability of students to express ideas clearly and effectively through written communication, encompassing skills such as grammar, vocabulary usage, and coherence.

AI Chatbots: Interactive programs that use AI to simulate conversation with users, often employed in educational settings to provide instant feedback and support in writing tasks.

Sub-Skills of Writing: Specific components of writing proficiency, including grammar, vocabulary usage, structure, and coherence, that contribute to overall writing quality.

Student Engagement: The level of interest, motivation, and participation that students demonstrate in their learning activities, often enhanced by the integration of new technologies.

Feedback Mechanisms: Systems or processes used to provide students with information about their performance, including strengths and areas for improvement, which can be enhanced through AI tools.

Educational Technology: Tools and resources that use technology to facilitate learning and improve educational outcomes, including software, online platforms, and digital devices.

Compilation of References

Abburi, H., Roy, K., Suesserman, M., Pudota, N., Veeramani, B., Bowen, E., & Bhattacharya, S. (2023). *A Simple yet Efficient Ensemble Approach for AI-generated Text Detection* [Conference session]. roceedings of the Third Workshop on Natural Language Generation, Evaluation, and Metrics (GEM).

Abdul Rahman, N. A., Zulkornain, L. H., Che Mat, A., & Kustati, M. (2023). Assessing writing abilities using AI-powered writing evaluations. *Journal of ASIAN Behavioural Studies*, *8*(24), 1–17. DOI: 10.21834/jabs.v8i24.420

Abulibdeh, A., Zaidan, E., & Abulibdeh, R. (2024). Navigating the confluence of artificial intelligence and education for sustainable development in the era of industry 4.0: Challenges, opportunities, and ethical…. *Journal of Cleaner Production*, *437*, 140527. Advance online publication. DOI: 10.1016/j.jclepro.2023.140527

Ackermann, K., & Chen, Y. H. (2013). Developing the Academic Collocation List (ACL) - A corpus-driven and expert-judged approach. *Journal of English for Academic Purposes*, *12*(4), 235–247. DOI: 10.1016/j.jeap.2013.08.002

Aebersold, M., & Dunbar, D.-M. (2020). Virtual and Augmented Realities in Nursing Education: State of the Science. *Annual Review of Nursing Research*, *39*(1), 225–242. DOI: 10.1891/0739-6686.39.225 PMID: 33431644

Aeni, N., Khang, A., Al Yakin, A., Yunus, M., & Cardoso, L. (2024). Revolutionized teaching by incorporating artificial intelligence chatbot for higher education ecosystem. In *AI-Centric Modeling and Analytics* (pp. 43–76). CRC Press.

Afzal, A. M., Khan, S. A., Daud, S., Ahmad, Z., & Butt, A. (2023). Addressing the digital divide: Access and use of technology in education. *Journal of Social Sciences Review*, *3*(2), 883–895. DOI: 10.54183/jssr.v3i2.326

Agarwal, A., Sharma, S., Kumar, V., & Kaur, M. (2021). Effect of E-learning on public health and environment during COVID-19 lockdown. *Big Data Mining and Analytics*, *4*(2), 104–115. DOI: 10.26599/BDMA.2020.9020014

Agbehadji, I. E., Yang, H., Fong, S., & Millham, R. (2018, August). The comparative analysis of Smith-Waterman algorithm with Jaro-Winkler algorithm for the detection of duplicate health related records. In 2018 International Conference on Advances in Big Data, Computing and Data Communication Systems (icABCD) (pp. 1-10). IEEE. DOI: 10.1109/ICABCD.2018.8465458

Ahmad, K., Iqbal, W., Qadir, J., Benhaddou, D., Ayyash, M., & Al-Fuqaha, A. (2023). Data-Driven Artificial Intelligence in Education: A Comprehensive Review. *IEEE Transactions on Learning Technologies*, *•••*, 17.

Ahmad, S. F., Alam, M. M., Rahmat, M. K., Mubarik, M. S., & Hyder, S. I. (2022). Academic and Administrative Role of Artificial Intelligence in Education. *Sustainability (Basel)*, *14*(3), 1101. DOI: 10.3390/su14031101

Ahmad, S. F., Rahmat, M. K., Mubarik, M. S., Alam, M. M., & Hyder, S. I. (2021). Artificial Intelligence and Its Role in Education. *Sustainability (Basel)*, *13*(22), 12902. DOI: 10.3390/su132212902

Ahmad, Z., Rahim, S., Zubair, M., & Abdul-Ghafar, J. (2021). Artificial intelligence (AI) in medicine, current applications and future role with special emphasis on its potential and promise in pathology: Present and future impact.... *Diagnostic Pathology*, *16*(1), 24. Advance online publication. DOI: 10.1186/s13000-021-01085-4 PMID: 33731170

Aithal, P. S., & Aithal, S. (2023). Optimizing the Use of Artificial Intelligence-Powered GPTs as Teaching and Research Assistants by Professors in Higher Education Institutions: A Study on Smart Utilization. *International Journal of Management, Technology, and Social Sciences*, *8*(4), 368–401. DOI: 10.47992/IJMTS.2581.6012.0326

Ajeesh, A. K., & Rukmini, S. (2023). Posthuman perception of artificial intelligence in science fiction: An exploration of Kazuo Ishiguro's Klara and the Sun. *AI & Society*, *38*(2), 853–860. Advance online publication. DOI: 10.1007/s00146-022-01533-9

Akayoğlu, S. (2019). Theoretical frameworks used in CALL studies: A systematic review. *Teaching English with Technology*, *19*(4), 104–118.

Al Mahmud, F. (2023). Investigating EFL students' writing skills through artificial intelligence: Wordtune application as a tool. *Journal of Language Teaching and Research*, *14*(5), 1395–1404. DOI: 10.17507/jltr.1405.28

Alabi, M. (2023). Visual Learning: The Power of Visual Aids and Multimedia. *Technology and Visual Learning*, *9*(7).

Alakrash, H. M., & Abdul Razak, N. (2021). Technology-based language learning: Investigation of digital technology and digital literacy. *Sustainability (Basel)*, *13*(21), 12304. Advance online publication. DOI: 10.3390/su132112304

Alam, A. (2023). Data-Driven Instructional Practices: Using Behavior Detection and Model Assignment Techniques to Inform Teaching Strategies for School Education. *2023 International Conference on Quantum Technologies, Communications, Computing, Hardware and Embedded Systems Security (iQ-CCHESS)*, 1–8. DOI: 10.1109/iQ-CCHESS56596.2023.10391777

Alam, A. (2023). Harnessing the Power of AI to Create Intelligent Tutoring Systems for Enhanced Classroom Experience and Improved Learning Outcomes. In Rajakumar, G., Du, K.-L., & Rocha, Á. (Eds.), *Intelligent Communication Technologies and Virtual Mobile Networks* (Vol. 171, pp. 571–591). Springer Nature Singapore., DOI: 10.1007/978-981-99-1767-9_42

Alam, A., & Mohanty, A. (2024). Integrated constructive robotics in education (ICRE) model: A paradigmatic framework for transformative learning in educational ecosystem. *Cogent Education*, *11*(1), 2324487. Advance online publication. DOI: 10.1080/2331186X.2024.2324487

Alamri, H., Lowell, V., Watson, W., & Watson, S. L. (2020). Using personalized learning as an instructional approach to motivate learners in online higher education: Learner self-determination and intrinsic motivation. *Journal of Research on Technology in Education*, *52*(3), 322–352. DOI: 10.1080/15391523.2020.1728449

Aldebaran. (n.d.). *NAO*. https://www.aldebaran.com/en/nao

Aldoobie, N. (2015). ADDIE Model. *American International Journal of Contemporary Research*, *5*(6), 68–72.

Alenizi, M. A. K., Mohamed, A. M., & Shaaban, T. S. (2023). Revolutionizing EFL special education: How ChatGPT is transforming the way teachers approach language learning. Innoeduca. *International Journal of Technology and Educational Innovation*, *9*(2), 5–23. DOI: 10.24310/innoeduca.2023.v9i2.16774

Alhaisoni, E. (2016). EFL teachers' and students' perceptions of dictionary use and preferences. *International Journal of Linguistics*, *8*(6), 31. DOI: 10.5296/ijl.v8i6.10267

Alhalangy, A., & AbdAlgane, M. (2023). Exploring the impact of AI on the EFL context: A case study of Saudi universities. *Journal of Intercultural Communication*, *23*(2), 41–49. DOI: 10.36923/jicc.v23i2.125

Alharbi, M. A. (2020). Exploring the potential of Google Doc in facilitating innovative teaching and learning practices in an EFL writing course. *Innovation in Language Learning and Teaching*, *14*(3), 227–242. DOI: 10.1080/17501229.2019.1572157

Alharbi, W. (2023). AI in the foreign language classroom: A pedagogical overview of automated writing assistance tools. *Education Research International*, *2023*, 1–15. Advance online publication. DOI: 10.1155/2023/4253331

Ali, Y. K., Mammadova, M., Geyis, A. J., & Mehdiyeva, G. B. (2024). Enhancing esl education with ai: Innovations in teaching methods and au-thentic materials. *International Journal of Membrane Science and Technology*, *11*(1), 497–505. DOI: 10.15379/ijmst.v11i1.3687

Ali, Z. (2020, February). Artificial intelligence (AI): A review of its uses in language teaching and learning. [). IOP Publishing.]. *IOP Conference Series. Materials Science and Engineering*, *769*(1), 012043. DOI: 10.1088/1757-899X/769/1/012043

Aljedaani, W., Aljedaani, M., AlOmar, E. A., Mkaouer, M. W., Ludi, S., & Khalaf, Y. B. (2021). I cannot see you—the perspectives of deaf students to online learning during covid-19 pandemic: Saudi arabia case study. *Education Sciences*, *11*(11), 712. DOI: 10.3390/educsci11110712

Aljuaid, H. (2024). The impact of artificial intelligence tools on academic writing instruction in higher education: A systematic review. *Arab World English Journal*, *1*(1), 26–55. DOI: 10.24093/awej/ChatGPT.2

Allouch, M., Azaria, A., & Azoulay, R. (2021). Conversational agents: Goals, technologies, vision and challenges. *Sensors (Basel)*, *21*(24), 8448. Advance online publication. DOI: 10.3390/s21248448 PMID: 34960538

Almohesh, A. R. I. (2024). AI Application (ChATGPT) and Saudi Arabian Primary School students' autonomy in online classes: Exploring students and teachers' perceptions. *International Review of Research in Open and Distance Learning*, *25*(3), 1–18. DOI: 10.19173/irrodl.v25i3.7641

Almufareh, M. F., Kausar, S., Humayun, M., & Tehsin, S. (2024). A conceptual model for inclusive technology: Advancing disability inclusion through artificial intelligence. *Journal of Disability Research*, *3*(1), 20230060. DOI: 10.57197/JDR-2023-0060

Almurtadha, Y. (2019). LABEEB: Intelligent Conversational Agent Approach to Enhance Course Teaching and Allied Learning Outcomes Attainment. *Journal of Applied Computer Science & Mathematics*, *13*(27), 9–12. DOI: 10.4316/JACSM.201901001

Alotaibi, E. (2023). The Impact Of AI-Powered Grammarly on Enhancing Grammar Proficiency Among Saudi EFL Students. Remittances Review, 8(4). https://remittancesreview.com/menu-script/index.php/remittances/article/view/1105

Alqahtani, T., Badreldin, H. A., Alrashed, M., Alshaya, A. I., Alghamdi, S. S., Bin Saleh, K., Alowais, S. A., Alshaya, O. A., Rahman, I., Al Yami, M. S., & Albekairy, A. M. (2023). The emergent role of artificial intelligence, natural learning processing, and large language models in higher education and research. *Research in Social & Administrative Pharmacy*, *19*(8), 1236–1242. DOI: 10.1016/j.sapharm.2023.05.016 PMID: 37321925

Al-Shallakh, M. A. I. (2024). Embedding artificial intelligent applications in higher educational institutions to improve students' pronunciation performance. *Theory and Practice in Language Studies*, *14*(6), 1897–1906. DOI: 10.17507/tpls.1406.31

Alshemali, B., & Kalita, J. (2020). Improving the reliability of deep neural networks in NLP: A review. *Knowledge-Based Systems*, *191*, 105210. Advance online publication. DOI: 10.1016/j.knosys.2019.105210

Alshriedeh, A. (2021). The Effect of an Artificial Intelligence Program on EFL Students on Reading Skill. *Ilkogretim Online*, *20*(5), 1727. DOI: 10.17051/ilkonline.2021.05.190

Altamimi, D., & Ab Rashid, R. (2019). Spelling Problems and Causes among Saudi English Language Undergraduates. *Arab World English Journal*, *10*(3), 178–191. DOI: 10.24093/awej/vol10no3.12

Alzahrani, N. M. (2020). Augmented reality: A systematic review of its benefits and challenges in e-learning contexts. *Applied Sciences (Basel, Switzerland)*, *10*(16), 5660. Advance online publication. DOI: 10.3390/app10165660

Alzubaidi, L., Al-Sabaawi, A., Bai, J., Dukhan, A., Alkenani, A. H., Al-Asadi, A., Alwzwazy, H. A., Manoufali, M., Fadhel, M. A., Albahri, A. S., Moreira, C., Ouyang, C., Zhang, J., Santamaría, J., Salhi, A., Hollman, F., Gupta, A., Duan, Y., Rabczuk, T., & Gu, Y. (2023). Towards Risk-Free Trustworthy Artificial Intelligence: Significance and Requirements. *International Journal of Intelligent Systems*, *2023*(1), 4459198. DOI: 10.1155/2023/4459198

Amanbekqyzy, A. A., Serikovna, N. A., & Erlanovna, A. A. (2021). AI-Enhanced Educational Content Creation. *Endless Light in Science*, *5*(3).

Amelia, M. D. (2022). *The effectiveness of Grammarly application on students' accuracy in writing.* Education Thesis. Pendidikan Bahasa Inggris, STKIP PGRI Bangkalan.

Amelia, R., & Irham, M. (2021). Exploring Teachers' and Students' Perceptions on Using Grammarly as a Tool for Enhancing Students' Writing Quality. *Journal of English Language Teaching and Linguistics, 6*(1), 1–15. DOI: 10.21462/jeltl.v6i1.286

Amirjalili, F., Neysani, M., & Nikbakht, A. (2024). Exploring the boundaries of authorship: A comparative analysis of AI-generated text and human academic writing in English literature. *Frontiers in Education, 9*, 1347421. Advance online publication. DOI: 10.3389/feduc.2024.1347421

Andersen, C., Jacobsen, S., Uvebrant, K., Griffin, J. F.IV, Vonk, L. A., Walters, M., Berg, L. C., Lundgren-Åkerlund, E., & Lindegaard, C. (2023). Integrin α10β1-selected mesenchymal stem cells reduce pain and cartilage degradation and increase immunomodulation in an equine osteoarthritis model. *Cartilage, 19476035231209402*, 19476035231209402. Advance online publication. DOI: 10.1177/19476035231209402 PMID: 37990503

Anderson, T., & Shattuck, J. (2012). Design-Based Research: A Decade of Progress in Education Research? *Educational Researcher, 41*(1), 16–25. DOI: 10.3102/0013189X11428813

An, F., Xi, L., & Yu, J. (2023). The relationship between technology acceptance and self-regulated learning: The mediation roles of intrinsic motivation and learning engagement. *Education and Information Technologies, 29*(3), 2605–2623. DOI: 10.1007/s10639-023-11959-3 PMID: 37361728

Anggita, D., Sumarni, S., Darmahusni, D., & Sulistyaningrum, S. D. (2023). A systematic review of online grammar checker for EFL learners: Potential and limitations for English self-directed learning. *Proceedings of EEIC, 3*, 30–39.

Anggoro, D. A., & Nurfadilah, I. (2022). Active Verb Spell Checking Mem-+ P in Indonesian Language Using the Jaro-Winkler Distance Algorithm. *Iraqi Journal of Science*, •••, 1811–1822. DOI: 10.24996/ijs.2022.63.4.38

Anki, P., Bustamam, A., Al-Ash, H. S., & Sarwinda, D. (2021). Intelligent chatbot adapted from question and answer system using RNN-LSTM model. []. IOP Publishing.]. *Journal of Physics: Conference Series, 1844*(1), 012001. DOI: 10.1088/1742-6596/1844/1/012001

Annamalai, N., Ab Rashid, R., Hashmi, U. M., Mohamed, M., Alqaryouti, M. H., & Sadeq, A. E. (2023). Using chatbots for English language learning in higher education. *Computers and Education: Artificial Intelligence, 5*, 100153. DOI: 10.1016/j.caeai.2023.100153

Anoop, K., Gangan, M. P., Deepak, P., & Lajish, V. L. (2022). Towards an enhanced understanding of bias in pre-trained neural language models: A survey with special emphasis on affective bias. In Responsible Data Science: Select Proceedings of ICDSE 2021 (pp. 13-45). Singapore: Springer Nature Singapore. [PDF] DOI: 10.1007/978-981-19-4453-6_2

Anson, C. M. (2022). AI-Based Text Generation and the Social Construction of "Fraudulent Authorship": A Revisitation. *Composition Studies, 50*(1), 37–46. https://eric.ed.gov/?id=EJ1361686

An, X., Chai, C. S., Li, Y., Zhou, Y., Shen, X., Zheng, C., & Chen, M. (2023). Modeling English teachers' behavioral intention to use artificial intelligence in middle schools. *Education and Information Technologies, 28*(5), 5187–5208. DOI: 10.1007/s10639-022-11286-z

An, X., Chai, C. S., Li, Y., Zhou, Y., & Yang, B. (2023). Modeling students' perceptions of artificial intelligence assisted language learning. *Computer Assisted Language Learning*, •••, 1–22. DOI: 10.1080/09588221.2023.2246519

Ardhy, A. A. S., Waris, A. M., & Kryati, L. (2023). Students' Perception of The Use of The Grammarly Application in Their Writing. *ETERNAL (English, Teaching, Learning, and Research Journal), 9*(02), 221-243. DOI: 10.24252/Eternal.V92.2023.A4

Arifin, M. N., Heriyanto, E., Kurniadi, D., & Arvianti, I. (2024). Analyzing grammar errors among HelloTalk users and proposing effective correction strategies. *English Learning Innovation, 5*(1), 26–37. DOI: 10.22219/englie.v5i1.31569

Arora, S., Narayan, A., Chen, M. F., Orr, L., Guha, N., Bhatia, K., . . . Ré, C. (2022). Ask me anything: A simple strategy for prompting language models. arXiv preprint arXiv:2210.02441.

Artino, A. R.Jr, & Stephens, J. M. (2009). Academic motivation and self-regulation: A comparative analysis of undergraduate and graduate students learning online. *The Internet and Higher Education, 12*(3), 146–151. DOI: 10.1016/j.iheduc.2009.02.001

Asmail, A. (2024). The impact of employing the "Reading Progress" tool based on artificial intelligence analyzes via the Microsoft Teams platform on developing reading skills among primary school students. *Artificial Intelligence Information Security*, 2(3), 79–167.

Aspers, P., & Corte, U. (2019). What is Qualitative in Qualitative Research. *Qualitative Sociology, 42*(2), 139–160. DOI: 10.1007/s11133-019-9413-7 PMID: 31105362

Assaly, I. R., & Smadi, O. M. (2015). Using Bloom's Taxonomy to Evaluate the Cognitive Levels of Master Class Textbook's Questions. *English Language Teaching, 8*(5), 100–110. DOI: 10.5539/elt.v8n5p100

Astuti, D., Darmahusni, D., Sumarni, S., & Suseno, M. (2023, June). The use of Grammarly in the academic writing of undergraduate students: Advantages, weaknesses, and challenges (systematic review). In English Language and Literature International Conference (ELLiC). *Proceedings, 6*, 593–607.

Atlas, S. (2023). *ChatGPT for higher education and professional development: A guide to conversational AI.* The University of Rhode Island. Retrieved from https://digitalcommons.uri.edu/cba_facpubs/548

Attali, Y., & Burstein, J. (2004). Automated Essay Scoring With E-Rater® V.2.0. *ETS Research Report Series, 2004*(2). DOI: 10.1002/j.2333-8504.2004.tb01972.x

Aung, Y. Y. M., Wong, D. C. S., & Ting, D. S. W. (2021). The promise of artificial intelligence: A review of the opportunities and challenges of artificial intelligence in healthcare. *British Medical Bulletin, 139*(1), 4–15. DOI: 10.1093/bmb/ldab016 PMID: 34405854

Ayanwale, M. A., & Ndlovu, M. (2024). Investigating factors of students' behavioral intentions to adopt chatbot technologies in higher education: Perspective from expanded diffusion theory of innovation. *Computers in Human Behavior Reports, 14*, 100396. DOI: 10.1016/j.chbr.2024.100396

Ayedoun, E., Hayashi, Y., & Seta, K. (2019). Adding communicative and affective strategies to an embodied conversational agent to enhance second language learners' willingness to communicate. *International Journal of Artificial Intelligence in Education, 29*(1), 29–57. DOI: 10.1007/s40593-018-0171-6

Ayoub, A., Amin, R., & Wani, Z. A. (2020). Contribution of developed countries towards MOOCs: An exploration and assessment from a representative platform Coursera. *Asian Association of Open Universities Journal, 15*(2), 251–262. DOI: 10.1108/AAOUJ-03-2020-0016

Baha, T. A., Hajji, M. E., Es-Saady, Y., & Fadili, H. (2023). The impact of educational chatbot on student learning experience. *Education and Information Technologies, 29*(8), 10153–10176. DOI: 10.1007/s10639-023-12166-w

Bahns, J., & Eldaw, M. (1993). Should we teach EFL students collocations? *System, 21*(1), 101–114. DOI: 10.1016/0346-251X(93)90010-E

Bahri, H., & Mahadi, T. S. T. (2016). Google translate as a supplementary tool for learning Malay: A case study at Universiti Sains Malaysia. *Advances in Language and Literary Studies, 7*(3), 161–167. https://files.eric.ed.gov/fulltext/EJ1127217.pdf

Baidoo-Anu, D., & Ansah, L. O. (2023). Education in the Era of Generative Artificial Intelligence (AI): Understanding the Potential Benefits of ChatGPT in Promoting Teaching and Learning. *Journal of AI, 7*(1), 52–62. DOI: 10.61969/jai.1337500

Bai, L., Liu, X., & Su, J. (2023). ChatGPT: The cognitive effects on learning and memory. *Brain-X, 1*(3), 1–9. DOI: 10.1002/brx2.30

Bailey, D., & Lee, A. R. (2020). An Exploratory Study of Grammarly in the Language Learning Context: An Analysis of Test-Based, Textbook-Based and Facebook Corpora. *TESOL International Journal, 15*(2), 4–27. https://files.eric.ed.gov/fulltext/EJ1268470.pdf

Bandyopadhyay, S., Bardhan, A., Dey, P., Bhattacharyya, S., Bandyopadhyay, S., Bardhan, A., ... & Bhattacharyya, S. (2021). Education Ecosystem: A Chronological Perspective. Bridging the Education Divide Using Social Technologies: Explorations in Rural India, 43-75. https://doi.org/DOI: 10.1007/978-981-33-6738-8_3

Barnes, E., & Hutson, J. (2024). Navigating the ethical terrain of ai in higher education: Strategies for mitigating bias and promoting fairness. *Forum for Education Studies, 2*(2), 1229. DOI: 10.59400/fes.v2i2.1229

Baron, N. S. (2001). Commas and canaries: The role of punctuation in speech and writing. *Language Sciences, 23*(1), 15–67. DOI: 10.1016/S0388-0001(00)00027-9

Baron, P. (2024). Are AI detection and plagiarism similarity scores worthwhile in the age of ChatGPT and other generative AI? *Scholarship of Teaching and Learning in the South, 8*(2), 151–179. DOI: 10.36615/sotls.v8i2.411

Barrett, A., & Pack, A. (2023). Not quite eye to A.I.: Student and teacher perspectives on the use of generative artificial intelligence in the writing process. *International Journal of Educational Technology in Higher Education, 61*(20), 59. DOI: 10.1186/s41239-023-00427-0

Barrot, J. S. (2022). Integrating technology into ESL/EFL writing through Grammarly. *RELC Journal, 53*(3), 764–768. DOI: 10.1177/0033688220966632

Barrot, J. S. (2023). Using ChatGPT for second language writing: Pitfalls and potentials. *Assessing Writing, 57*, 100745. DOI: 10.1016/j.asw.2023.100745

Barrs, M. (2022). *Vygotsky the Teacher: A Companion to his Psychology for Teachers and Other Practitioners.* Routledge, Taylor & Francis Group.

Belda-Medina, J. & Calvo-Ferrer, J. R. (2022). Using chatbots as AI conversational partners in language learning. Applied Sciences. mdpi.com

Belligoni, S., Stevens, K. A., Hasan, S., & Yu, H. (2023). Privacy and security concerns with passively collected location data for digital contact tracing among US college students. *PLoS One, 18*(11), e0294419. DOI: 10.1371/journal.pone.0294419 PMID: 37992048

Benaiche, M. (2023). *The Effectiveness of Using Grammarly in the Writing Process.* Master Thesis in Language and Culture, Department of Letters and English Language, University of 8 Mai 1945 Guelma. http://dspace.univguelma.dz/jspui/handle/ 123456789/15398

Beninghof, A. M. (2020). Co-teaching that works: Structures and strategies for maximizing student learning. tesl-ej.org

Benson, M., Benson, E., & Elson, R. (1997). *The BBI dictionary of English word combinations.* John Benjamins. DOI: 10.1075/z.bbi1(2nd)

Benson, M., Benson, E., & Ilson, R. F. (1986). *The BBI Combinatory Dictionary of English: A guide to word combinations.* John Benjamins Publishing Company. DOI: 10.1075/z.bbi1(1st)

Bentley, S. V., Naughtin, C. K., McGrath, M. J., Irons, J. L., & Cooper, P. S. (2024). The digital divide in action: How experiences of digital technology shape future relationships with artificial intelligence. *AI and Ethics, 2024*(4), 901–915. Advance online publication. DOI: 10.1007/s43681-024-00452-3

Bermudez-Contreras, E., Clark, B. J., & Wilber, A. (2020). The neuroscience of spatial navigation and the relationship to artificial intelligence. [frontiersin.org]. *Frontiers in Computational Neuroscience, 14*, 523744. DOI: 10.3389/fncom.2020.00063 PMID: 32848684

Beuls, K., & Van Eecke, P. (2023). Construction Grammar and Artificial Intelligence. arXiv. https://arxiv.org/pdf/2309.00135

Bhatti, I., Mohi-U-din, S. F., Hayat, Y., & Tariq, M. (2024). Artificial intelligence applications for students with learning disabilities: A systematic review. European Journal of Science. *Innovation and Technology, 4*(2), 40–56.

Bhirud, N. S. (2017). Grammar checkers for natural languages: a review. International Journal on Natural Language Computing (IJNLC), 6.

Bhutoria, A. (2022). Personalized education and artificial intelligence in the United States, China, and India: A systematic review using a human-in-the-loop model. Computers and Education: Artificial Intelligence. sciencedirect.com

Bick, M., Breaugh, J., Dong, C. W., Pina, G., & Waldner, C. (2023). *AI and the future of academic writing: Insights from the ESCP Business School Prompt-o-thon workshop in Berlin*. ESCP Business School, Berlin Campus.

Blewitt, C., O'connor, A., Morris, H., Nolan, A., Mousa, A., Green, R., Ifanti, A., Jackson, K., & Skouteris, H. (2021). "It's embedded in what we do for every child": A qualitative exploration of early childhood educators' perspectives on supporting Children's social and emotional learning. [mdpi.com]. *International Journal of Environmental Research and Public Health*, *18*(4), 1530. DOI: 10.3390/ijerph18041530 PMID: 33562768

Bloom, B. S., Englehart, M. D., Furst, E. J., Hill, W. H., & Krathwohl, D. R. (1956). *Taxonomy of Educational Objectives. The Classification of Educational Goals*. Longmans, Green and Co Ltd., Retrieved from https://web.archive.org/web/20201212072520id_/https://www.uky.edu/~rsand1/china2018/texts/Bloom%20et%20al%20-Taxonomy%20of%20Educational%20Objectives.pdf

Bok, E., & Cho, Y. (2023). Examining Korean EFL college students' experiences and perceptions of using ChatGPT as a writing revision tool. *Journal of English Teaching through Movies and Media, 24*(4), 15-27. DOI: https://doi.org/DOI: 10.16875/stem.2023.24.4.15

Borger, J. G., Ng, A. P., Anderton, H., Ashdown, G. W., Auld, M., Blewitt, M. E., Brown, D. V., Call, M. J., Collins, P., Freytag, S., Harrison, L. C., Hesping, E., Hoysted, J., Johnston, A., McInneny, A., Tang, P., Whitehead, L., Jex, A., & Naik, S. H. (2023). Artificial intelligence takes center stage: Exploring the capabilities and implications of ChatGPT and other AI-assisted technologies in scientific research and education. [wiley.com]. *Immunology and Cell Biology*, *101*(10), 923–935. DOI: 10.1111/imcb.12689 PMID: 37721869

Bouranta, N., Chitiris, L., & Paravantis, J. (2009). The relationship between internal and external service quality. *International Journal of Contemporary Hospitality Management*, *21*(3), 275–293. DOI: 10.1108/09596110910948297

Bozkurt, A., Karadeniz, A., Baneres, D., Guerrero-Roldán, A. E., & Rodríguez, M. E. (2021). Artificial intelligence and reflections from educational landscape: A review of AI Studies in half a century. [mdpi.com]. *Sustainability (Basel)*, *13*(2), 800. DOI: 10.3390/su13020800

Brandtzaeg, P. B., & Følstad, A. (2018). Chatbots: Changing user needs and motivations. *Interactions (New York, N.Y.)*, *25*(5), 38–43. DOI: 10.1145/3236669

Bransen, D., & Govaerts, M. J. (2020). How to conceptualise self-regulated learning: Implications for measurement. *Medical Education*, *54*(8), 684–686. DOI: 10.1111/medu.14183 PMID: 32311141

Brena, R. F., Zuvirie, E., Preciado, A., Valdiviezo, A., Gonzalez-Mendoza, M., & Zozaya-Gorostiza, C. (2021). Automated evaluation of foreign language speaking performance with machine learning. [IJIDeM]. *International Journal on Interactive Design and Manufacturing*, *15*(2), 317–331. DOI: 10.1007/s12008-021-00759-z

Brian, L. F., & ChatGPT. (2023). Should Using an AI Text Generator to Produce Academic Writing Be Plagiarism? *FORDHAM INTELL. PROP. MEDIA & ENT. L.J, XXIII*(947-969).

Brown, L. E., & Kauchak, D. (2013). Educational Advances in Artificial Intelligence. *AI Magazine*, *34*(4), 127–127. DOI: 10.1609/aimag.v34i4.2508

Brown, T., Mann, B., Ryder, N., Subbiah, M., Kaplan, J. D., Dhariwal, P., & Amodei, D. (2020). Language models are few-shot learners. *Advances in Neural Information Processing Systems*, *33*, 1877–1901.

BSSS. (2023). *Student Guide: AI and Academic Integrity*. chrome-extension://efaidnbmnnnibpcajpcglclefindmkaj/https://www.bsss.act.edu.au/__data/assets/pdf_file/0005/571721/BSSS_Student_Guide_AI_and_Academic_Integrity.pdf

BTEC. (2024). *BTEC Centre Guide to Plagiarism 2024 - 2025*. chrome-extension://efaidnbmnnnibpcajpcglclefindmkaj/https://qualifications.pearson.com/content/dam/pdf/Support/Quality%20Assurance/btec-centre-guide-to-plagiarism.pdf

Bui, T., Boers, F., & Coxhead, A. (2020). Extracting multiword expressions from texts with the aid of online resources. *ITL International Journal of Applied Linguistics*, *171*(2), 221–252. DOI: 10.1075/itl.18033.bui

Burk, S., & Miner, G. D. (2020). *It's All Analytics!: The Foundations of Al*. Big Data and Data Science Landscape for Professionals in Healthcare, Business, and Government. [HTML] DOI: 10.4324/9780429343988

Cachat-Rosset, G. & Klarsfeld, A. (2023). Diversity, equity, and inclusion in artificial intelligence: an evaluation of guidelines. Applied Artificial Intelligence. tandfonline.com

Callan, J., Connell, M., & Du, A. (1999). Automatic discovery of language models for text databases. *SIGMOD Record*, *28*(2), 479–490. DOI: 10.1145/304181.304224

Calma, A., Cotronei-Baird, V., & Chia, A. (2022). Grammarly: An instructional intervention for writing enhancement in management education. *International Journal of Management Education*, *20*(3), 36–75. DOI: 10.1016/j.ijme.2022.100704

Calp, M. H., & Akcayol, M. A. (2015). The importance of human-computer interaction in the development process of software projects. *Global Journal of Information Technology: Emerging Technologies*, *5*(1), 48–54. DOI: 10.18844/gjit.v0i0.114

Canella, V. B., D, M., Batista, A. G. C., & N. A., Aacute, N. A., D, U. S. T., Sousa, E., Rocha, M. L. S., & Canella, L. B. (. (2025). Necessary skills for teachers towards digital information and communication technologies in the current era. *International Journal of Education Economics and Development*, *16*(1/2), 62–77. DOI: 10.1504/IJEED.2025.143605

Cano, P., Mayne, J., Catiggay, L., Michael, J., Florida, M., Mathew, J., Pua, R., Jane, M., & Samonte, C.Paulo Miguel A. Cano. (2024). Natural Language Processing of Grammar Checker Tools for Academic Writing: A Systematic Literature Review. *Journal of Electrical Systems*, *20*(7), 1151–1156. https://media.proquest.com/media/hms/PFT/1/uizFZ. DOI: 10.52783/jes.3611

Cao, D. T. P. (2018). *The effect of an online collocation dictionary on advanced learners' use of collocations in L2 writing* [Doctoral dissertation, University of Leeds]. https://etheses.whiterose.ac.uk/22829/

Carayannopoulos, S. (2018). Using chatbots to aid transition. *The International Journal of Information and Learning Technology*, *35*(2), 118–129. DOI: 10.1108/IJILT-10-2017-0097

Casal, J. E., & Kessler, M. (2023). Can linguists distinguish between ChatGPT/AI and human writing?: A study of research ethics and academic publishing. *Research Methods in Applied Linguistics*, *2*(3), 100068. DOI: 10.1016/j.rmal.2023.100068

Cavaleri, M. R., & Dianati, S. (2016). You want me to check your grammar again? The usefulness of an online grammar checker as perceived by students. *Journal of Academic Language and Learning*, *10*(1), A223–A236. https://journal.aall.org.au/index.php/jall/article/view/393

Celik, I. (2023). Towards Intelligent-TPACK: An empirical study on teachers' professional knowledge to ethically integrate artificial intelligence (AI)-based tools into education. *Computers in Human Behavior*, *138*, 107468. DOI: 10.1016/j.chb.2022.107468

Celik, I., Dindar, M., Muukkonen, H., & Jarvela, S. (2022). The promises and challenges of artificial intelligence for teachers: A systematic review of research. *TechTrends*, *66*(4), 616–630. DOI: 10.1007/s11528-022-00715-y

Chaipidech, P., Srisawasdi, N., Kajornmanee, T., & Chaipah, K. (2022). A personalized learning system-supported professional training model for teachers' TPACK development. *Computers and Education: Artificial Intelligence*, *3*, 100064. DOI: 10.1016/j.caeai.2022.100064

Chan, C. K. (2024). Students' perceptions of 'AI-giarism': Investigating changes in understandings of academic misconduct. *Education and Information Technologies*. Advance online publication. DOI: 10.1007/s10639-024-13151-7

Chan, C. K. Y. (2023). A comprehensive AI policy education framework for university teaching and learning. [springer.com]. *International Journal of Educational Technology in Higher Education*, *20*(1), 38. DOI: 10.1186/s41239-023-00408-3

Chang, D. H., Lin, M. P. C., Hajian, S., & Wang, Q. Q. (2023). Educational design principles of using AI chatbot that supports self-regulated learning in education: Goal setting, feedback, and personalization. Sustainability. mdpi.com

Chan, K. Y. C., & Hu, W. (2023). Students' voices on generative AI: Perceptions, benefits, and challenges in higher education. *International Journal of Educational Technology in Higher Education*, *20*(43), 43. Advance online publication. DOI: 10.1186/s41239-023-00411-8

Chen, L. C., & Chang, K. H. A novel frequency-range analysis (FRA) method for determining critical words among English high-stakes tests. Journal of Intelligent & Fuzzy Systems, (Preprint), 1-16.

Chen, Y. (2024, May). Enhancing Language Acquisition: The Role of AI in Facilitating Effective Language Learning. In 2024 3rd International Conference on Humanities, Wisdom Education and Service Management (HWESM 2024) (pp. 593-600). Atlantis Press. atlantis-press.com

Chen, B., Bao, L., Zhang, R., Zhang, J., Liu, F., Wang, S., & Li, M. (2024). A multi-strategy computer-assisted EFL writing learning system with deep learning incorporated and its effects on learning: A writing feedback perspective. *Journal of Educational Computing Research*, *61*(8), 60–102. DOI: 10.1177/07356331231189294

Chen, C. M., & Huang, Y. M., & Kinshuk. (2018). Effects of an intelligent tutoring system on students' learning outcomes and attitudes in the context of English as a foreign language. *Journal of Computer Assisted Learning*, *34*(4), 376–393.

Cheng, K., He, Y., Li, C., Xie, R., Lu, Y., Gu, S., & Wu, H. (2023). Talk with ChatGPT about the outbreak of Mpox in 2022: Reflections and suggestions from AI dimensions. *Annals of Biomedical Engineering*, *51*(5), 870–874. DOI: 10.1007/s10439-023-03196-z PMID: 37031289

Cheng, L., Han, J., & Nasirov, J. (2024). Ethical considerations related to personal data collection and reuse: Trust and transparency in language and speech technologies. *International Journal of Legal Discourse*, *9*(2), 217–235. DOI: 10.1515/ijld-2024-2010

Chen, L., Chen, P., & Lin, Z. (2020). Artificial Intelligence in Education: A Review. *IEEE Access : Practical Innovations, Open Solutions*, *8*, 75264–75278. DOI: 10.1109/ACCESS.2020.2988510

Chen, M. P., Wang, L. C., Zou, D., Lin, S. Y., & Xie, H. (2019). Effects of caption and gender on junior high students' EFL learning from iMap-enhanced contextualized learning. *Computers & Education*, *140*, 103602. DOI: 10.1016/j.compedu.2019.103602

Chen, M.-R. A., & Lin, Y.-H. (2023). AI Chatbot-Supported Grammar Tense Learning on EFL Students Learning Effectiveness. INTED Proceedings. DOI: 10.21125/inted.2023.0353

Chen, T. J. (2023). ChatGPT and other artificial intelligence applications speed up scientific writing. *Journal of the Chinese Medical Association*, *10*(4), 1097. DOI: 10.1097/JCMA.0000000000000900 PMID: 36791246

Chen, X., Zou, D., Xie, H., & Cheng, G. (2021). Twenty years of personalized language learning. *Journal of Educational Technology & Society*, *24*(1), 205–222.

Chen, X., Zou, D., Xie, H., Cheng, G., & Liu, C. (2022). Two decades of artificial intelligence in education. *Journal of Educational Technology & Society*, *25*(1), 28–47. https://www.jstor.org/stable/48647028

Chen, Y., Jensen, S., Albert, L. J., Gupta, S., & Lee, T. (2023). Artificial intelligence (AI) student assistants in the classroom: Designing chatbots to support student success. [HTML]. *Information Systems Frontiers*, *25*(1), 161–182. DOI: 10.1007/s10796-022-10291-4

Chien, S.-P., Wu, H.-K., & Wu, P.-H. (2018). Teachers' Beliefs About, Attitudes Toward, and Intention to Use Technology-Based Assessments: A Structural Equation Modeling Approach. *Eurasia Journal of Mathematics, Science and Technology Education*, *14*(10). Advance online publication. DOI: 10.29333/ejmste/93379

Chinnasamy, P., Rani, R. M., Ayyasamy, R. K., Sujithra, L. R., Mounika, T., & Cherukuvada, S. (2025). Transforming Education With AI-Driven Intelligent Tutoring Systems: In T. Murugan, K. P., & A. M. Abirami (Eds.), *Driving Quality Education Through AI and Data Science* (pp. 239–258). IGI Global. DOI: 10.4018/979-8-3693-8292-9.ch011

Chinta, S. V., Wang, Z., Yin, Z., Hoang, N., Gonzalez, M., Quy, T. L., & Zhang, W. (2024). *FairAIED: Navigating Fairness, Bias, and Ethics in Educational AI Applications* (arXiv:2407.18745). arXiv. https://doi.org//arXiv.2407.18745DOI: 10.48550

Chiu, T. K. (2024). A classification tool to foster self-regulated learning with generative artificial intelligence by applying self-determination theory: A case of ChatGPT. *Educational Technology Research and Development*, *72*(4), 1–16. DOI: 10.1007/s11423-024-10366-w

Chiu, T. K. F. (2021). A holistic approach to the design of artificial intelligence (AI) education for K-12 schools. *TechTrends*, *65*(5), 796–807. DOI: 10.1007/s11528-021-00637-1

Chiu, T. K. F., Meng, H., Chai, C.-S., King, I., Wong, S., & Yam, Y. (2022). Creation and Evaluation of a Pretertiary Artificial Intelligence (AI) Curriculum. *IEEE Transactions on Education*, *65*(1), 30–39. DOI: 10.1109/TE.2021.3085878

Chiu, T. K. F., Moorhouse, B. L., Chai, C. S., & Ismailov, M. (2022). Teacher support and student motivation to learn with artificial intelligence (AI) based chatbot. *Interactive Learning Environments*, •••, 1–17. DOI: 10.1080/10494820.2022.2129392

Chiu, T. K., Xia, Q., Zhou, X., Chai, C. S., & Cheng, M. (2023). Systematic literature review on opportunities, challenges, and future research recommendations of artificial intelligence in education. *Computers and Education: Artificial Intelligence*, *4*, 100118. DOI: 10.1016/j.caeai.2022.100118

Chomphooyod, P., Suchato, A., Tuaycharoen, N., & Punyabukkana, P. (2023). English grammar multiple-choice question generation using Text-to-Text Transfer Transformer. *Computers and Education Artificial Intelligence*, *5*, 100158. DOI: 10.1016/j.caeai.2023.100158

Chopra, A., Patel, H., Rajput, D. S., & Bansal, N. (2024). Empowering Inclusive Education: Leveraging AI-ML and Innovative Tech Stacks to Support Students with Learning Disabilities in Higher Education. In Applied Assistive Technologies and Informatics for Students with Disabilities (pp. 255-275). Singapore: Springer Nature Singapore. [HTML]

Choudhary, P., & Chauhan, S. (2023). An intelligent chatbot design and implementation model using long short-term memory with recurrent neural networks and attention mechanism. *Decision Analytics Journal*, *9*, 100359. DOI: 10.1016/j.dajour.2023.100359

Chow, C. S., Zhan, G., Wang, H. F., & He, M. (2023). Artificial Intelligence (AI) Adoption: An Extended Compensatory Level of Acceptance. *Journal of Electronic Commerce Research*, *2*(1).

Ciayandi, A., Mawardi, V. C., & Hendryli, J. (2020). Retrieval based chatbot on tarumanagara university with Multilayer Perceptron. [). IOP Publishing.]. *IOP Conference Series. Materials Science and Engineering*, *1007*(1), 012146. DOI: 10.1088/1757-899X/1007/1/012146

CMI. (2024). *CMI Plagiarism, Collusion and Artificial Intelligence (AI) Statement*. chrome-extension://efaidnbmnnnibpcajpcglclefindmkaj/https://www.managers.org.uk/wp-content/uploads/2023/12/cmi-plagiarism-collusion-and-ai-misuse-statement.pdf

Cohen, S., Mompelat, L., Mann, A., & Connors, L. (2024). The linguistic leap: Understanding, evaluating, and integrating ai in language education. *Tydskrif vir Taalonderrig*, *4*(2), 23–31. DOI: 10.54475/jlt.2024.012

ComonLit, & Quill. (2024). *A Toolkit for Addressing AI Plagiarism in the Classroom*. chrome-extension://efaidnbmnnnibpcajpcglclefindmkaj/https://s3.amazonaws.com/quill-image-uploads/uploads/files/A_Toolkit_for_Addressing_AI_Plagiarism_in_the_Classroom_2747.pdf

Cornell University Center for Teaching Innovation. (2024). Ethical AI for teaching and learning. https://teaching.cornell.edu/generative-artificial-intelligence/ethical-ai-teaching-and-learning

Cota-Rivera, E. I., González Correa, M. E., Bernal Marín, L. A., Marquez Montenegro, M. Y., Herrera, A. M., & Martinez Martinez, M. A. (2024). Transforming Education With the Power of Artificial Intelligence: Case Studies. In Demir, Ş., & Demir, M. (Eds.), *Enhancing Higher Education and Research With OpenAI Models* (pp. 113–140). IGI Global Scientific Publishing., DOI: 10.4018/979-8-3693-1666-5.ch006

Cotton, D. R., Cotton, P. A., & Shipway, J. R. (2024). Chatting and cheating: Ensuring academic integrity in the era of ChatGPT. *Innovations in Education and Teaching International*, *61*(2), 228–239. DOI: 10.1080/14703297.2023.2190148

Crawford, J., Cowling, M., & Allen, K. A. (2023). Leadership is needed for ethical ChatGPT: Character, assessment, and learning using artificial intelligence (AI). Journal of University Teaching & Learning Practice, 20(3), 02.

Črček, N., & Patekar, J. (2023). Writing with AI: University students' use of ChatGPT. *Journal of Language and Education*, *9*(4), 128–138. DOI: 10.17323/jle.2023.17379

Creely, E. (2024). Exploring the role of generative ai in enhancing language learning: opportunities and challenges. *International Journal of Changes in Education*, 1-10. DOI: 10.47852/bonviewIJCE42022495

Crompton, H., Edmett, A., Ichaporia, N., & Burke, D. (2024). AI and English language teaching: Affordances and challenges. *British Journal of Educational Technology*, *55*(6), 2503–2529. DOI: 10.1111/bjet.13460

Crompton, H., Jones, M. V., & Burke, D. (2024). Affordances and challenges of artificial intelligence in K-12 education: A systematic review. *Journal of Research on Technology in Education*, *56*(3), 248–268. DOI: 10.1080/15391523.2022.2121344

Csizér, K. & Kontra, E. H. (2020). Foreign language learning characteristics of deaf and severely hard-of-hearing students. The Modern Language Journal. wiley.com

Curtis, N. (2023). To ChatGPT or not to ChatGPT? The impact of artificial intelligence on academic publishing. *The Pediatric Infectious Disease Journal*, *42*(4), 275. DOI: 10.1097/INF.0000000000003852 PMID: 36757192

Dai, Y., Liu, A., & Lim, C. P. (2023). Reconceptualizing ChatGPT and generative AI as a student-driven innovation in higher education. Procedia CIRP. sciencedirect.com

Daneshvar, E., & Rahimi, A. (2013). Written Corrective Feedback and Teaching Grammar. *Procedia: Social and Behavioral Sciences*, •••, 136.

Dang, T. H. N. (2024). EFL Students' Perceptions of Peer Feedback in Writing Classes at a University in HCM City. *International Journal of Language Instruction*, *3*(2), 18–28. DOI: 10.54855/ijli.24322

Daniels, P., & Leslie, D. (2013). Grammar software ready for EFL writers. *OnCue Journal, 9*(4), 391-401. https://jaltcue.org/files/OnCUE/OCJ9.4/OCJ9.4_pp391_401_AC_Daniels_Leslie.pdf

Darvishi, A., Khosravi, H., Sadiq, S., & Gašević, D. (2022). Incorporating AI and learning analytics to build trustworthy peer assessment systems. [wiley.com]. *British Journal of Educational Technology, 53*(4), 844–875. DOI: 10.1111/bjet.13233

Darvishi, A., Khosravi, H., Sadiq, S., Gašević, D., & Siemens, G. (2024). Impact of ai assistance on student agency. *Computers & Education, 210*, 104967. DOI: 10.1016/j.compedu.2023.104967

Darwin, R., Rusdin, D., Mukminatien, N., Suryati, N., Laksmi, E. D., & Marzuki, . (2024). Critical thinking in the AI era: An exploration of EFL students' perceptions, benefits, and limitations. *Cogent Education, 11*(1), 2290342. DOI: 10.1080/2331186X.2023.2290342

Davies, J., & Graff, M. (2005). Performance in e-learning: Online participation and student grades. *British Journal of Educational Technology, 36*(4), 657–663. DOI: 10.1111/j.1467-8535.2005.00542.x

Davis, F. D. (1989). Perceived usefulness, perceived ease of use, and user acceptance of Information Technology. *Management Information Systems Quarterly, 13*(3), 319. DOI: 10.2307/249008

Dawson, P., Henderson, M., Ryan, T., Mahoney, P., Boud, D., Phillips, M., & Molloy, E. (2023). Technology and feedback design. In J. M. Spector, B.B., Lockee, & M. D. Childress (Eds), *Learning, design, and technology,* (pp. 695-739). Springer. DOI: 10.1007/978-3-319-17461-7_124

De Angelis, L., Baglivo, F., Arzilli, G., Privitera, G. P., Ferragina, P., Tozzi, A. E., & Rizzo, C. (2023). ChatGPT and the rise of large language models: The new AI-driven infodemic threat in public health. [frontiersin.org]. *Frontiers in Public Health, 11*, 1166120. DOI: 10.3389/fpubh.2023.1166120 PMID: 37181697

Dede, C. (2009). Immersive Interfaces for Engagement and Learning. *Science, 323*(5910), 66–69. DOI: 10.1126/science.1167311 PMID: 19119219

Deepak, P. (2020). Ethical considerations in data-driven fake news detection. Journal: Data Science for Fake News The Information Retrieval Series, 205-232. [HTML]

Dehouche, N. (2021). Plagiarism in the age of massive generative pre-trained transformers (GPT-3). *Ethics in Science and Environmental Politics, 2*, 17–23. DOI: 10.3354/esep00195

Dembsey, J. (2017). Closing the Grammarly® gaps: A study of claims and feedback from an online grammar program. *Writing Center Journal, 36*(1), 63–100. https://www.jstor.org/stable/44252638. DOI: 10.7771/2832-9414.1815

Deng, X. & Yu, Z. (2022). A systematic review of machine-translation-assisted language learning for sustainable education. Sustainability. mdpi.com

Devlin, M. (2005). *Higher Education Avoiding plagiarism and cheating A guide for students at Swinburne University of Technology*. Swinburne University of Technology.

Dewi, N. A. (2019). *The Effectiveness of Grammarly Checker towards Students' Writing Quality of the Fourth Semester of English Department at IAIN Tulungagung*. IAIN Tulungagung. http://repo.uinsatu.ac.id/12020/

Dhiraj, A., & Kumar, P. D. S. (2023). Impact of E-learning on the Higher Education Sector during the COVID-19 pandemic through Pedagogy tools: An observational Study. *Revista de Educación y Derecho, 27*(27). Advance online publication. DOI: 10.1344/REYD2023.27.40935

Díaz-Rodríguez, N., Del Ser, J., Coeckelbergh, M., de Prado, M. L., Herrera-Viedma, E., & Herrera, F. (2023). Connecting the dots in trustworthy Artificial Intelligence: From AI principles, ethics, and key requirements to responsible AI systems and regulation. [sciencedirect.com]. *Information Fusion, 99*, 101896. DOI: 10.1016/j.inffus.2023.101896

Dieker, L. A., & Rodriguez, J. A., Lignugaris/Kraft, B., Hynes, M. C., & Hughes, C. E. (. (2014). The Potential of Simulated Environments in Teacher Education: Current and Future Possibilities. *Teacher Education and Special Education: The Journal of the Teacher Education Division of the Council for Exceptional Children, 37*(1), 21–33. DOI: 10.1177/0888406413512683

Dignum, V. (2023). Responsible artificial intelligence: recommendations and lessons learned. In Eke, D. O., Wakunuma, K., & Akintoye, S. (Eds.), *Responsible AI in Africa: Challenges and opportunities* (pp. 195–214). Springer.

Dimitriadou, E., & Lanitis, A. (2023). A critical evaluation, challenges, and future perspectives of using artificial intelligence and emerging technologies in smart classrooms. *Smart Learning Environments, 10*(1), 12. DOI: 10.1186/s40561-023-00231-3

Dinh, A. D., & Pham, N. M. C. (2024). A Qualitative Study into How Non-English Major Students Emotionally Respond to Teacher-Written Feedback. *International Journal of TESOL & Education, 4*(3), 62–77. DOI: 10.54855/ijte.24434

Dodigovic, M., & Tovmasyan, A. (2021). Automated Writing Evaluation: The Accuracy of Grammarly's Feedback on Form. *International Journal of TESOL Studies, 3*(2), 71–88. https://www.tesolunion.org/journal/details/info/8MTEw3LjM3/Automated-Writing-Evaluation:-The-Accuracy-of-Grammarly's-Feedback-on-Form

Dokukina, I. & Gumanova, J. (2020). The rise of chatbots–new personal assistants in foreign language learning. Procedia Computer Science. sciencedirect.com

Domeij, R., Knutsson, O., & Eklundh, K. S. (2002). Different ways of evaluating a Swedish grammar checker. *Paper presented at Association for Computational Linguistics, 3*(1), 262-267.

Domínguez Figaredo, D. (2020). Data-driven educational algorithms pedagogical framing. *RIED.Revista Iberoamericana de Educación a Distancia, 23*(2), 65. DOI: 10.5944/ried.23.2.26470

Dong, L. (2024). "Brave New World" or not?: A mixed-methods study of the relationship between second language writing learners' perceptions of ChatGPT, behaviors of using ChatGPT, and writing proficiency. *Current Psychology (New Brunswick, N.J.), 43*(21), 1–15. DOI: 10.1007/s12144-024-05728-9

Dorobantu, M., & Wilks, Y. (2019). MORAL ORTHOSES: A NEW APPROACH TO HUMAN AND MACHINE ETHICS: with Fraser Watts, "Mutual Enhancement between Science and Religion: In the Footsteps of the Epiphany Philosophers"; William H. Beharrell, "Transformation and the Waking Body: A Return to Truth via Our Bodies"; Marius Dorobantu and Yorick Wilks, "Moral Orthoses: A New Approach to Human and Machine Ethics"; Galen Watts, "Religion, Science, and Disenchantment in Late Modernity"; and Rowan Williams, "Epiphany Philosophers: Afterword.". *Zygon*, *54*(4), 1004–1021. DOI: 10.1111/zygo.12560

Du Boulay, B. (2016). Artificial Intelligence as an Effective Classroom Assistant. *IEEE Intelligent Systems*, *31*(6), 76–81. DOI: 10.1109/MIS.2016.93

du Preez, V., Bennet, S., Byrne, M., Couloumy, A., Das, A., Dessain, J., Galbraith, R., King, P., Mutanga, V., Schiller, F., Zaaiman, S., Moehrke, P., & van Heerden, L. (2024). From bias to black boxes: Understanding and managing the risks of ai – an actuarial perspective. *British Actuarial Journal*, *29*, e6. Advance online publication. DOI: 10.1017/S1357321724000060

Du, J., & Alm, A. (2024). The Impact of ChatGPT on English for Academic Purposes (EAP) Students' Language Learning Experience: A Self-Determination Theory Perspective. *Education Sciences*, *14*(7), 1–17. DOI: 10.3390/educsci14070726

Duong, P. T., Perez, M. M., Desmet, P., & Peters, E. (2021). Differential effects of input based and output-based tasks on L2 vocabulary learning. *Canadian Journal of Applied Linguistics*, *24*(3), 120–144. DOI: 10.37213/cjal.2021.31183

Duong, T. K. H., & Le, T. T. H. (2024). Utilizing artificial intelligence in writing feedback: Benefits and challenges forfFirst-year students at Hanoi University of Industry. *Proceedings of the AsiaCALL International Conference, 6*, 238-249. DOI: DOI: 10.54855/paic.24617

Durrant, P. (2009). Investigating the viability of a collocation list for students of English for academic purposes. *English for Specific Purposes*, *28*(3), 157–169. DOI: 10.1016/j.esp.2009.02.002

Dwivedi, Y. K., ... (2203). Opinion Paper: "So what if ChatGPT wrote it?" Multidisciplinary perspectives on opportunities, challenges and implications of generative conversational AI for research, practice and policy. *International Journal of Information Management, 71*, https://doi.org/DOI: 10.1007/978-3-031-08215-3_9

Eaton, S. E. (2023). Postplagiarism: Transdisciplinary ethics and integrity in the age of artificial intelligence and neurotechnology. *International Journal for Educational Integrity*, *19*(1), 23. Advance online publication. DOI: 10.1007/s40979-023-00144-1

Ebadi, S., Gholami, M., & Vakili, S. (2022). Investigating the effects of using Grammarly in EFL writing of articles. *Interdisciplinary Journal of Practice. Theory and Applied Research*, *40*(1), 85–105. DOI: 10.1080/07380569.2022.2150067

El Naggar, A., Gaad, E., & Inocencio, S. A. M. (2024). Enhancing inclusive education in the UAE: Integrating AI for diverse learning needs. *Research in Developmental Disabilities*, *147*, 104685–104685. DOI: 10.1016/j.ridd.2024.104685 PMID: 38330845

El Shazly, R. (2021). Effects of artificial intelligence on English speaking anxiety and speaking performance: A case study. *Expert Systems: International Journal of Knowledge Engineering and Neural Networks*, *38*(3), e12667. DOI: 10.1111/exsy.12667

Elkhatat, A. M., Elsaid, K., & Almeer, S. (2023). Evaluating the efficacy of AI content detection tools in differentiating between human and AI-generated text. *International Journal for Educational Integrity*, *19*(1), 17. Advance online publication. DOI: 10.1007/s40979-023-00140-5

ElSayary, A. (2023). An investigation of teachers' perceptions of using ChatGPT as a supporting tool for teaching and learning in the Digital Era. *Journal of Computer Assisted Learning*, *40*(3), 931–945. DOI: 10.1111/jcal.12926

Embarak, O. H., & Hawarna, S. (2024). Automated AI-driven System for Early Detection of At-risk Students. *Procedia Computer Science*, *231*, 151–160. DOI: 10.1016/j.procs.2023.12.187

Escamilla, K., Hopewell, S., & Slavick, J. (2021). Teaching (bi) multilingual learners: Connecting languages. [HTML]. *The Reading Teacher*, *75*(3), 363–371. DOI: 10.1002/trtr.2044

Espejel, J. L., Ettifouri, E. H., Alassan, M. S. Y., Chouham, E. M., & Dahhane, W. (2023). GPT-3.5, GPT-4, or BARD? Evaluating LLMs reasoning ability in zero-shot setting and performance boosting through prompts. *Natural Language Processing Journal*, *5*, 100032. DOI: 10.1016/j.nlp.2023.100032

Essa, S. G., Celik, T., & Human-Hendricks, N. E. (2023). Personalized Adaptive Learning Technologies Based on Machine Learning Techniques to Identify Learning Styles: A Systematic Literature Review. *IEEE Access : Practical Innovations, Open Solutions*, *11*, 48392–48409. DOI: 10.1109/ACCESS.2023.3276439

Eyong, E. I. (2022). Grammarly Plagiarism Checker in Promoting Quality. *Journal of Research in Multidisciplinary Methods and Applications*, *1*(4), 01220104003. http://www.satursonpublishing.com/jrmma/article/view/a01220104003

Fahda, A., & Purwarianti, A. (2017, November). A statistical and rule-based spelling and grammar checker for Indonesian text. In 2017 international on data and software engineering (icodse) (pp. 1-6). IEEE.

Fahd, K., Venkatraman, S., Miah, S. J., & Ahmed, K. (2022). Application of machine learning in higher education to assess student academic performance, at-risk, and attrition: A meta-analysis of literature. *Education and Information Technologies*, *27*(3), 3743–3775. DOI: 10.1007/s10639-021-10741-7

Famaye, T., Irgens, G. A., & Adisa, I. (2024). Shifting roles and slow research: Children's roles in participatory co-design of critical machine learning activities and technologies. [clemson.edu]. *Behaviour & Information Technology*, •••, 1–22.

Familoni, B. T., & Onyebuchi, N.Babajide Tolulope FamiloniNneamaka Chisom Onyebuchi. (2024). Advancements and challenges in AI integration for technical literacy: A systematic review. *Engineering Science & Technology Journal*, *5*(4), 1415–1430. Advance online publication. DOI: 10.51594/estj.v5i4.1042

Fan, M., Antle, A. N., & Warren, J. L. (2020). Augmented reality for early language learning: A systematic review of augmented reality application design, instructional strategies, and evaluation outcomes. [HTML]. *Journal of Educational Computing Research*, *58*(6), 1059–1100. DOI: 10.1177/0735633120927489

Faturoti, B. (). Online learning during COVID19 and beyond: A human right based approach to internet access in Africa. International Review of Law. tandfonline.com

Fedele, A., Punzi, C., & Tramacere, S. (2024). The ALTAI checklist as a tool to assess ethical and legal implications for a trustworthy AI development in education. Computer Law & Security Review. sciencedirect.com

Feijóo, C., Kwon, Y., Bauer, J. M., Bohlin, E., Howell, B., Jain, R., Potgieter, P., Vu, K., Whalley, J., & Xia, J. (2020). Harnessing artificial intelligence (AI) to increase wellbeing for all: The case for a new technology diplomacy. [sciencedirect.com]. *Telecommunications Policy*, *44*(6), 101988. DOI: 10.1016/j.telpol.2020.101988 PMID: 32377031

Feng, Y., Han, J., & Lan, X. (2024). After one year of ChatGPT's launch: Reflections on artificial intelligence in scientific writing. *European Journal of Nuclear Medicine and Molecular Imaging*, *51*(5), 1203–1204. DOI: 10.1007/s00259-023-06579-5 PMID: 38236428

Ferguson, C., van den Broek, E. L., & van Oostendorp, H. (2022). AI-Induced guidance: Preserving the optimal Zone of Proximal Development. *Computers and Education. Artificial Intelligence, 3*, 100089-. DOI: 10.1016/j.caeai.2022.100089

Ferguson-Patrick, K. (2020). Cooperative learning in Swedish classrooms: Engagement and relationships as a focus for culturally diverse students. Education Sciences. mdpi.com

Ferrara, E. (2023). Fairness and bias in artificial intelligence: A brief survey of sources, impacts, and mitigation strategies. Sci. mdpi.com

Fithriani, R. (2023). Utilizing artificial intelligence-based paraphrasing tool in EFL writing class: A focus on Indonesian university students' perceptions. *Scope: Journal of English Language Teaching*, *7*(2), 210–218. DOI: 10.30998/scope.v7i2.14882

Fitria, R. A. (2021). *Students' perceptions of the use of grammarly in undergraduate thesis writing at iain Palangka Raya*. IAIN Palangka Raya.

Fitria, R. A., Sabarun, S., & Miftah, M. Z. (2022). Students' perception of the use of grammarly in undergraduate thesis writing. PROJECT (Professional Journal of English Education), 5(2), 366-371.

Flavián, C., & Casaló, L. V. (2021). Artificial intelligence in services: Current trends, benefits and challenges. *Service Industries Journal*, *41*(13-14), 853–859. DOI: 10.1080/02642069.2021.1989177

Fletcher, R. R., Nakeshimana, A., & Olubeko, O. (2021). Addressing fairness, bias, and appropriate use of artificial intelligence and machine learning in global health. [frontiersin.org]. *Frontiers in Artificial Intelligence*, *3*, 561802. DOI: 10.3389/frai.2020.561802 PMID: 33981989

Fosso Wamba, S., Guthrie, C., Queiroz, M. M., & Minner, S. (2024). ChatGPT and generative artificial intelligence: An exploratory study of key benefits and challenges in operations and supply chain management. *International Journal of Production Research*, *62*(16), 5676–5696. DOI: 10.1080/00207543.2023.2294116

Fowler, J. (2007). Thinking and Writing at Masters Level: A Reflective Passage. *British Journal of Nursing (Mark Allen Publishing)*, *16*(14), 887–890. DOI: 10.12968/bjon.2007.16.14.24332 PMID: 17851352

Frankenberg-Garcia, A. (2020). Combining user needs, lexicographic data and digital writing environments. *Language Teaching*, *53*(1), 29–43. DOI: 10.1017/S0261444818000277

Fryer, L. K., Ainley, M., Thompson, A., Gibson, A., & Sherlock, Z. (2017). Stimulating and sustaining interest in a language course: An experimental comparison of Chatbot and Human task partners. *Computers in Human Behavior*, *75*, 461–468. DOI: 10.1016/j.chb.2017.05.045

Fryer, L. K., Nakao, K., & Thompson, A. (2019). Chatbot learning partners: Connecting learning experiences, interest and competence. *Computers in Human Behavior*, *93*, 279–289. DOI: 10.1016/j.chb.2018.12.023

Fu, Y., & Lee, J. (2023). The role of AI in language learning: Perspectives from EFL teachers. *Journal of Educational Technology Development and Exchange*, *16*(3), 205–221.

Gain, A., Rao, M., & Bhat, S. K. (2019). Usage of grammarly–online grammar and spelling checker tool at the health sciences Library, Manipal Academy of Higher Education, Manipal: A study. *Library Philosophy and Practice, 26*(10), 1–13.

Gao, T., Fisch, A., & Chen, D. (2020). Making pre-trained language models better fewshot learners. arXiv preprint arXiv:2012.15723.

Garrote Jurado, R., Pettersson, T., & Zwierewicz, M. (2023). Students' attitudes to the use of artificial intelligence. *ICERI Proceedings, 1*, 514-519. https://doi.org/DOI: 10.21125/iceri.2023.0191

Gayed, J. M., Carlon, M. K. J., Oriola, A. M., & Cross, J. S. (2022). Exploring an AI-based writing Assistant's impact on English language learners. [sciencedirect.com]. *Computers and Education: Artificial Intelligence*, *3*, 100055. DOI: 10.1016/j.caeai.2022.100055

GenApe AI. (2024, June 19). *What are the differences between Poe and ChatGPT? –GenApe AI*. https://www.genape.ai/blogs/poe-chatbot/

Geng, H., & Li, Y. (2023). The impact of AI on vocabulary acquisition in EFL contexts. *Language Learning & Technology*, *27*(2), 89–105.

Gers, F. A., Schraudolph, N. N., & Schmidhuber, J. (2002). Learning precise timing with LSTM recurrent networks. *Journal of Machine Learning Research*, *3*(Aug), 115–143.

Ghamrawi, N., Shal, T., & Ghamrawi, N. A. R. (2023). Exploring the impact of AI on teacher leadership: Regressing or expanding? *Education and Information Technologies*, *29*(7), 8415–8433. DOI: 10.1007/s10639-023-12174-w

Ghasemi, E., & Karami, H. (2024). Evaluating AI-driven adaptive learning systems for EFL learners. *Journal of Computer Assisted Learning*, *40*(1), 123–140.

Ghimire, P. R., Neupane, B. P., & Dahal, N. (2024). Generative AI and AI Tools in English Language Teaching and Learning. *An Exploratory Research*, *9*(1-2), 30–40. DOI: 10.3126/eltp.v9i1-2.68716

Ghosh, S. S. (2024). Nurturing Sustainable and Inclusive Learning Ecosystems: A Glimpse Into the Future of Indian Education. In Preparing Students for the Future Educational Paradigm (pp. 256-277). IGI Global. [HTML] DOI: 10.4018/979-8-3693-1536-1.ch011

Gill, S. S., Xu, M., Ottaviani, C., Patros, P., Bahsoon, R., Shaghaghi, A., Golec, M., Stankovski, V., Wu, H., Abraham, A., Singh, M., Mehta, H., Ghosh, S. K., Baker, T., Parlikad, A. K., Lutfiyya, H., Kanhere, S. S., Sakellariou, R., Dustdar, S., & Uhlig, S. (2022). AI for next generation computing: Emerging trends and future directions. [PDF]. *Internet of Things : Engineering Cyber Physical Human Systems*, *19*, 100514. DOI: 10.1016/j.iot.2022.100514

Giri, A. (2024). Revolutionizing Student Evaluation: The Power of AI-Powered Assessment. In Moreira, F. T., & Teles, R. O. (Eds.), (pp. 333–362). Advances in Educational Technologies and Instructional Design. IGI Global., DOI: 10.4018/979-8-3693-6170-2.ch012

Gkonou, C. & Miller, E. R. (2021). An exploration of language teacher reflection, emotion labor, and emotional capital. Tesol Quarterly. wiley.com

Golan, R., Reddy, R., Muthigi, A., & Ramasamy, R. (2023). Artificial intelligence in academic writing: A paradigm-shifting technological advance. *Nature Reviews. Urology*, *20*(6), 327–328. DOI: 10.1038/s41585-023-00746-x PMID: 36829078

Goldsmith, J., Burton, E., Dueber, D. M., Goldstein, B., Sampson, S., & Toland, M. D. (2020). Assessing Ethical Thinking about AI. *Proceedings of the AAAI Conference on Artificial Intelligence*, *34*(09), 13525–13528. DOI: 10.1609/aaai.v34i09.7075

Golub, T. P., Kovalenko, O. O., Zhygzhytova, L. M., & Kotkovets, A. L. (2024). Ai-powered pedagogy: foreign language study in higher education. *Академічні Студії. Серія «педагогіка»*, *4*, 50-56. DOI: 10.52726/as.pedagogy/2023.4.7

Good, R. (1987). Artificial intelligence and science education. *Journal of Research in Science Teaching*, *24*(4), 325–342. DOI: 10.1002/tea.3660240406

Graesser, A. C., Sabatini, J. P., & Li, H. (2022). Educational Psychology Is Evolving to Accommodate Technology, Multiple Disciplines, and Twenty-First-Century Skills. *Annual Review of Psychology*, *73*(1), 547–574. DOI: 10.1146/annurev-psych-020821-113042 PMID: 34587781

Graham, S., & Perin, D. (2007). A Meta-analysis of writing instruction for adolescent students. *Journal of Educational Psychology*, *99*(3), 445–476. DOI: 10.1037/0022-0663.99.3.445

Grammarly. (2019). *Grammarly.Edu.* Available at: https://www.grammarly.com

Grammarly. (2020). *Grammarly: free online writing assistant.* Available at: https://www.grammarly.com/

Guerin, F. (2011). Learning like a baby: A survey of artificial intelligence approaches. *The Knowledge Engineering Review*, *26*(2), 209–236. DOI: 10.1017/S0269888911000038

Gul, M. I., Khan, I. A., Shah, S., & El-Affendi, M. (2023). Can Nonliterates Interact as Easily as Literates with a Virtual Reality System? A Usability Evaluation of VR Interaction Modalities. Systems. mdpi.com

Gulati, S. (2008). Technology-Enhanced Learning in Developing Nations: A review. *International Review of Research in Open and Distance Learning*, *9*(1). Advance online publication. DOI: 10.19173/irrodl.v9i1.477

Guo, J., Bai, L., Yu, Z., Zhao, Z., & Wan, B. (2021). An AI-Application-Oriented In-Class Teaching Evaluation Model by Using Statistical Modeling and Ensemble Learning. *Sensors (Basel), 21*(1), 241. DOI: 10.3390/s21010241 PMID: 33401482

Gupta, M., Parra, C. M., & Dennehy, D. (2021). Questing racial and gender bias in AI-based recommendations: Do espoused national cultural values matter? *Information Systems Frontiers, 24,* 1465.1481. https://link.springer.com/article/10.1007/s10796-021-10156-2

Gupta, R., & Singh, P. (2023). AI-based language learning tools: Benefits and challenges in EFL education. *International Journal of Emerging Technologies in Learning*, *18*(5), 45–60.

Gupta, V., Liao, W. K., Choudhary, A., & Agrawal, A. (2023). Evolution of artificial intelligence for application in contemporary materials science. *MRS Communications*, *13*(5), 754–763. DOI: 10.1557/s43579-023-00433-3

Ha, T. T. A. (2023). *Exploring the impact of Grammarly on grammatical accuracy in second language writing of fifth-grade students in Vietnam: A mixed- methods case study*. Bachelor in TESOL, University of Techonology and Education, Ho Chi Minh, Vietnam.

Habibi, A., Riady, Y., Samed Al-Adwan, A., & Awni Albelbisi, N. (2023). Beliefs and Knowledge for Pre-Service Teachers' Technology Integration during Teaching Practice: An Extended Theory of Planned Behavior. *Computers in the Schools*, *40*(2), 107–132. DOI: 10.1080/07380569.2022.2124752

Habibzadeh, F. (2023). GPTZero performance in identifying artificial intelligence-generated medical texts: A preliminary study. *Journal of Korean Medical Science*, *38*(38), e319. Advance online publication. DOI: 10.3346/jkms.2023.38.e319 PMID: 37750374

Haddad, C. R., Nakić, V., Bergek, A., & Hellsmark, H. (2022). Transformative innovation policy: A systematic review. [sciencedirect.com]. *Environmental Innovation and Societal Transitions*, *43*, 14–40. DOI: 10.1016/j.eist.2022.03.002

Hadi Mogavi, R., Deng, C., Juho Kim, J., Zhou, P., & Kwon, D., Y., Hosny Saleh Metwally, A., Tlili, A., Bassanelli, S., Bucchiarone, A., Gujar, S., Nacke, L. E., & Hui, P. (. (2024). ChatGPT in education: A blessing or a curse? A qualitative study exploring early adopters' utilization and perceptions. *Computers in Human Behavior: Artificial Humans*, *2*(1), 100027. DOI: 10.1016/j.chbah.2023.100027

Haider, M. Z., & Yasmin, S. (2023). AI in EFL learning: A study on ChatGPT's impact on students' writing performance. *Journal of Educational Technology & Society*, *26*(3), 312–327.

Hakiki, G. N. R. (2021). Perception of EFL students on the use Grammarly application in writing class. *Eduvelop: Journal of English Education and Development*, *4*(2), 99–106. DOI: 10.31605/eduvelop.v4i2.891

Halbert, J. D., DiMatteo-Gibson, D., Cabrera, M., Mazurowski, T., & Ingram, M. (2024). Artificial intelligence's role in student plagiarism: A graduate University's model of best practices. *Journal of Leadership, Accountability and Ethics*, *21*(3). Advance online publication. DOI: 10.33423/jlae.v21i3.7208

Hamal, O., El Faddouli, N.-E., Harouni, M. H. A., & Lu, J. (2022). Artificial Intelligent in Education. *Sustainability (Basel)*, *14*(5), 2862. DOI: 10.3390/su14052862

Hamidi, H., & Hatami, J. (2023). Analyzing the use of AI in language learning: Insights from Iranian EFL learners. *Interactive Learning Environments, 31*(5), 615–630.

Hampton University. (2024). *Directing The Ethical Landscape: Challenges In Addressing The Ethical Usage Of Generative Artificial Intelligence (Ai) And Academic Dishonesty* [PPT].

Hamuddin, B., Julita, K., Rahman, F., & Derin, T. (2020). Artificial Intelligence in EFL Context: Rising Students' Speaking Performance with Lyra Virtual Assistance. *International Journal of Advanced Science and Technology, 29*(5), 6735–6741. https://repository.unilak.ac.id/1512/1/Artificial%20Intelligence%20in%20EFL%20Context-%20Rising%20Students%E2%80%99%20Speaking%20Performance%20with%20Lyra%20Virtual%20Assistance2.pdf

Hareesh, P. (2024, August 23). *Battle of the AI content detectors: ZeroGPT vs GPTZero*. ZeroGPT - Free ChatGPT Detector (AI Plagiarism Checker). https://zerogpt.tools/zerogpt-vs-gptzero

Haristiani, N. (2019). Artificial intelligence (AI) chatbot as language learning medium: An inquiry. *Journal of Physics: Conference Series, 1387*(1), 2020. DOI: 10.1088/1742-6596/1387/1/012020

Haristiani, N., Danuwijaya, A. A., Rifai, M. M., & Sarila, H. (2019). Gengobot: A chatbot-based grammar application on mobile instant messaging as language learning medium. *Journal of Engineering Science and Technology, 14*(6), 3158–3173.

Harmsen, E. (2024). A Future Perspective on the Digitalised Work Environment: Understanding the Role of Artificial Intelligence and Social Robots in Future Work Environments. diva-portal.org

Harvey-Jordan, S., & Long, S. (2001). The process and the pitfalls of semi-structured interviews. *Community Practitioner, 74*(6), 219.

Hassani, H., Huang, X., & Silva, E. (2021). The human digitalisation journey: Technology first at the expense of humans?. Information. mdpi.com

Hassanipour, S., Nayak, S., Bozorgi, A., Keivanlou, M., Dave, T., Alotaibi, A., Joukar, F., Mellatdoust, P., Bakhshi, A., Kuriyakose, D., Polisetty, L. D., Chimpiri, M., & Amini-Salehi, E. (2024). The ability of ChatGPT in paraphrasing texts and reducing plagiarism: A descriptive analysis. *JMIR Medical Education, 10*, e53308–e53308. DOI: 10.2196/53308 PMID: 38989841

Hassija, V., Chamola, V., Mahapatra, A., Singal, A., Goel, D., Huang, K., Scardapane, S., Spinelli, I., Mahmud, M., & Hussain, A. (2023). Interpreting black-box models: A review on explainable artificial intelligence. *Cognitive Computation, 16*(1), 45–74. DOI: 10.1007/s12559-023-10179-8

Hausmann, F. J. (1989). Le dictionnaire de collocations. In Hausmann, F. J., Reichmann, O., Wiegand, H. E., & Zgusta, L. (Eds.), *Wörterbücher: ein internationales Handbuch zur Lexikographie. Dictionaries. Dictionnaires* (pp. 1010–1019). Mouton De Gruyter. DOI: 10.1515/9783110095852.1.7.1010

Heckert, A., Forsythe, L. P., Carman, K. L., Frank, L., Hemphill, R., Elstad, E. A., Esmail, L., & Lesch, J. K. (2020). Researchers, patients, and other stakeholders' perspectives on challenges to and strategies for engagement. [springer.com]. *Research Involvement and Engagement, 6*(1), 1–18. DOI: 10.1186/s40900-020-00227-0 PMID: 33042576

Helander, M. G. (Ed.). (2014). *Handbook of human-computer interaction*. Elsevier.

Hendricson, W. D., Andrieu, S. C., Chadwick, D. G., Chmar, J. E., Cole, J. R., George, M. C., Glickman, G. N., Glover, J. F., Goldberg, J. S., Haden, N. K., Meyerowitz, C., Neumann, L., Pyle, M., Tedesco, L. A., Valachovic, R. W., Weaver, R. G., Winder, R. L., Young, S. K., & Kalkwarf, K. L.ADEA Commission on Change and Innovation in Dental Education. (2006). Educational Strategies Associated with Development of Problem-Solving, Critical Thinking, and Self-Directed Learning. *Journal of Dental Education*, *70*(9), 925–936. DOI: 10.1002/j.0022-0337.2006.70.9.tb04163.x PMID: 16954414

Hern, A. (2022, December 31). *AI-assisted plagiarism? ChatGPT bot says it has an answer for that.* the Guardian. https://www.theguardian.com/technology/2022/dec/31/ai-assisted-plagiarism-chatgpt-bot-says-it-has-an-answer-for-that

He, Y., & Zhu, H. (2024). AI-powered feedback and its effects on EFL learners' writing skills. *Language Learning Journal*, *52*(1), 12–29.

Hickman, S. E., Baxter, G. C., & Gilbert, F. J. (2021). Adoption of artificial intelligence in breast imaging: Evaluation, ethical constraints and limitations. *British Journal of Cancer*, *125*(1), 15–22. DOI: 10.1038/s41416-021-01333-w PMID: 33772149

High, S. (2022). A fruitless exercise? The political struggle to compel corporations to justify factory closures in Canada. [HTML]. *Labor History*, *63*(3), 297–315. DOI: 10.1080/0023656X.2022.2098261

Hill, J., Ford, W. R., & Farreras, I. G. (2015). Real conversations with artificial intelligence: A comparison between human–human online conversations and human–chatbot conversations. *Computers in Human Behavior*, *49*, 245–250. DOI: 10.1016/j.chb.2015.02.026

Hochreiter, S., & Schmidhuber, J. (1997). Long short-term memory. *Neural Computation*, *9*(8), 1735–1780. DOI: 10.1162/neco.1997.9.8.1735 PMID: 9377276

Hofstetter, J. S., De Marchi, V., Sarkis, J., Govindan, K., Klassen, R., Ometto, A. R., Spraul, K. S., Bocken, N., Ashton, W. S., Sharma, S., Jaeger-Erben, M., Jensen, C., Dewick, P., Schröder, P., Sinkovics, N., Ibrahim, S. E., Fiske, L., Goerzen, A., & Vazquez-Brust, D. (2021). From sustainable global value chains to circular economy—Different silos, different perspectives, but many opportunities to build bridges. [springer.com]. *Circular Economy and Sustainability*, *1*(1), 21–47. DOI: 10.1007/s43615-021-00015-2 PMID: 34888550

Holmes, W., & Luckin, R. (2016). *Intelligence unleashed: An argument for AI in education*. Pearson : UCL Knowledge Lab.

Hong, W. C. H. (2023). The impact of ChatGPT on foreign language teaching and learning: Opportunities in education and research. *Journal of Educational Technology and Innovation*, *5*(1). Advance online publication. DOI: 10.61414/jeti.v5i1.103

Hooda, M., Rana, C., Dahiya, O., Rizwan, A., & Hossain, M. S. (2022). Artificial Intelligence for Assessment and Feedback to Enhance Student Success in Higher Education. *Mathematical Problems in Engineering*, *2022*, 1–19. DOI: 10.1155/2022/5215722

Ho, P. X. P. (2024). Using ChatGPT in English Language Learning: A Study on I.T. Students' Attitudes, Habits, and Perceptions. *International Journal of TESOL & Education*, *4*(1), 55–68. DOI: 10.54855/ijte.24414

Hopster, J. (2021). What are socially disruptive technologies?. Technology in Society. sciencedirect.com

Hossain, M. A., & Rahman, M. (2023). AI in EFL contexts: Enhancing reading comprehension through technology. *Journal of Language and Linguistic Studies*, *19*(2), 132–150.

Ho, T. L. U. (2024). Problems with Academic Writing Encountered by EFL Postgraduate Students at a University in the Mekong Delta. *International Journal of Language Instruction*, *3*(1), 1–16. DOI: 10.54855/ijli.24311

Howard, S. K., Swist, T., Gasevic, D., Bartimote, K., Knight, S., Gulson, K., Apps, T., Peloche, J., Hutchinson, N., & Selwyn, N. (2022). Educational data journeys: Where are we going, what are we taking and making for AI? *Computers and Education: Artificial Intelligence*, *3*, 100073. DOI: 10.1016/j.caeai.2022.100073

Huang, W., Hew, K. F., & Fryer, L. K. (2022). Chatbots for language learning—Are they really useful? A systematic review of chatbot-supported language learning. *Journal of Computer Assisted Learning*. John Wiley and Sons Inc. DOI: 10.1111/jcal.12610

Huang, X., Zou, D., Cheng, G., Chen, X., & Xie, H. (2023). Trends, Research Issues and Applications of Artificial Intelligence in Language Education. *Educational Technology & Society, 26*(1), 112–131. JSTOR. https://doi.org/DOI: 10.2307/48707971

Huang, C., & Wang, J. (2023). Integrating AI in EFL classrooms: Teacher perceptions and challenges. *Journal of Computer Assisted Learning*, *39*(1), 76–90.

Huang, X., Zhou, D., Cheng, G., Chen, X., & Xie, H. (2023). Trends, research issues, and applications of artificial intelligence in language education. *Journal of Educational Technology & Society*, *26*(1), 112–131. https://www.jstor.org/stable/4870797

Huang, Y., Richter, E., Kleickmann, T., & Richter, D. (2023). Virtual Reality in Teacher Education from 2010 to 2020: A Review of Program Implementation, Intended Outcomes, and Effectiveness Measures. In Scheiter, K., & Gogolin, I. (Eds.), *Bildung für eine digitale Zukunft* (Vol. 15, pp. 399–441). Springer Fachmedien Wiesbaden., DOI: 10.1007/978-3-658-37895-0_16

Hudson, A. D., Finn, E., & Wylie, R. (2023). What can science fiction tell us about the future of artificial intelligence policy?. AI & SOCIETY. springer.com

Hung, J., & Chen, J. (2023). The benefits, risks and regulation of using ChatGPT in Chinese academia: A content analysis. *Social Sciences (Basel, Switzerland)*, *12*(7), 380. DOI: 10.3390/socsci12070380

Hutson, J. (2024). Rethinking plagiarism in the era of generative AI. *Journal of International Communication*, *4*(1). Advance online publication. DOI: 10.54963/jic.v4i1.220

Hu, Z., & Zhang, W. (2024). The impact of AI-based pronunciation tools on EFL learners. *Journal of Second Language Pronunciation*, *10*(2), 115–130.

Hwang, G. J., Xie, H., Wah, B. W., & Gašević, D. (2020). Vision, challenges, roles and research issues of Artificial Intelligence in Education. [sciencedirect.com]. *Computers and Education: Artificial Intelligence*, *1*, 100001. DOI: 10.1016/j.caeai.2020.100001

Ifenthaler, D., Gibson, D., Prasse, D., Shimada, A., & Yamada, M. (2021). Putting learning back into learning analytics: Actions for policy makers, researchers, and practitioners. [springer.com]. *Educational Technology Research and Development*, *69*(4), 2131–2150. DOI: 10.1007/s11423-020-09909-8

Igbokwe, I. C. (2023). Application of Artificial Intelligence (AI) in Educational Management. *International Journal of Scientific and Research Publications*, *13*(3). Advance online publication. DOI: 10.29322/IJSRP.13.03.2023.p13536

Imran, M., & Almusharraf, N. (2023). Analyzing the role of ChatGPT as a writing assistant at higher education level: A systematic review of the literature. *Contemporary Educational Technology*, *15*(4), ep464. DOI: 10.30935/cedtech/13605

İnci Kavak, V., Evis, D., & Ekinci, A. (2024). *The use of chatgpt in language education*. Experimental and Applied Medical Science., DOI: 10.46871/eams.1461578

Iqbal, S., & Anwar, N. (2024). AI-enhanced EFL learning: Student engagement and motivation. *International Journal of Educational Technology in Higher Education*, *21*(1), 203–222.

Irvin, L. L. (2010). What Is "Academic" Writing? *Writing spaces. Reading and Writing*, •••, 3–17. https://wac.colostate.edu/docs/books/writingspaces1/irvin--what-is-academic-writing.pdf

Ismail, A. A. (2024). *Over-Reliance Of AI Tools In Academic Writing Tasks: The Malaysian Tertiary Level Context*. In *E-Prosiding Persidangan Antarabangsa Sains Sosial & Kemanusiaan kali ke-9 (PASAK9 2024)* (pp. 218-224). PASAK 9.

Jafari, D., & Shaterzadeh-Yazdi, Z. (2024). Transforming Education with AI: The Development of a Personalized Learning Algorithm for Individual Learning Styles. *Journal of Algorithms and Computation*, *56*(2).

Jafari, K., & Chalak, A. (2023). The effectiveness of AI chatbots in improving EFL learners' speaking abilities. *Journal of Language Teaching and Research*, *14*(1), 110–125.

Janet, T. (2024, May 15). *5 reasons to avoid using AI for academic writing*. LinkedIn. https://www.linkedin.com/pulse/5-reasons-avoid-using-ai-academic-writing-janet-tumulty-k2mye

Jansen, R. S., van Leeuwen, A., Janssen, J., & Kester, L. (2022). Exploring the link between self-regulated learning and learner behaviour in a massive open online course. *Journal of Computer Assisted Learning*, *38*(4), 993–1004. DOI: 10.1111/jcal.12675

Japoshvili-Ghvinashvili, M., & Suleman, N. (2023). Assisting ELT teachers: Designing activities for the use of ChatGPT in teaching and learning. *Pakistan Journal of Multidisciplinary Innovation*, *2*(1), 24–35. DOI: 10.59075/pjmi.v2i1.219

Jarrah, A. M., Wardat, Y., & Fidalgo, P. (2023). Using ChatGPT in academic writing is (not) a form of plagiarism: What does the literature say? *Online Journal of Communication and Media Technologies*, *13*(4), e202346. DOI: 10.30935/ojcmt/13572

Javed, Y., & Rajabi, N. (2020). Multi-layer perceptron artificial neural network based IoT botnet traffic classification. In *Proceedings of the Future Technologies Conference (FTC) 2019: Volume 1* (pp. 973-984). Springer International Publishing. DOI: 10.1007/978-3-030-32520-6_69

Jędrejko, K., Lazarev, A., Jędrejko, M., & Muszyńska, B. (2023). Ergogenic properties, safety evaluation and regulations of selected ingredients in testosterone booster dietary supplements. [tandfonline.com]. *Food Reviews International*, •••, 1–29.

Jeon, J. (2024). Exploring AI chatbot affordances in the EFL classroom: Young learners' experiences and perspectives. *Computer Assisted Language Learning*, *37*(1), 1–26. DOI: 10.1080/09588221.2021.2021241

Jia, J., & Ruan, M. (2008). Use chatbot CSIEC to facilitate the individual learning in English instruction: A case study. In *Lecture Notes in Computer Science (including* subseries Lecture Notes in Artificial Intelligence and Lecture Notes in *Bioinformatics)* (Vol. 5091 LNCS, pp. 706–708). Springer Verlag. DOI: 10.1007/978-3-540-69132-7_84

Jia, J., Chen, Y., Ding, Z., & Ruan, M. (2012). Effects of a vocabulary acquisition and assessment system on students' performance in a blended learning class for English subject. *Computers & Education*, *58*(1), 63–76. DOI: 10.1016/j.compedu.2011.08.002

Ji, H., Han, I., & Ko, Y. (2023). A systematic review of conversational AI in language education: Focusing on the collaboration with human teachers. *Journal of Research on Technology in Education*, *55*(1), 48–63. DOI: 10.1080/15391523.2022.2142873

John Benjamins. Nguyen, C. D. (2016). Creating spaces for constructing practice and identity: Innovations of teachers of English language to young learners in Vietnam. *Research Papers in Education*, *32*(1), 56–70. DOI: 10.1080/02671522.2015.1129644

John, K. S., Hussin, S. N., Mohd Yusoff, R., Mohd Rocky, N. A., Mohd Nawi, M. N., Syed Hussain, S. S., & Mohd Mutalip, S. S. (2024). Mini review on the ethical use of AI bots in academic writing. *International. The Journal of Learning in Higher Education*, *19*(2), 65–72. DOI: 10.24191/ijelhe.v19n2.1924

Johnson, S., Owens, E., Menendez, H., & Kim, D. (2024). Using chatgpt-generated essays in library instruction. *Journal of Academic Librarianship*, *50*(2), 102863. DOI: 10.1016/j.acalib.2024.102863

Jozefowicz, R., Vinyals, O., Schuster, M., Shazeer, N., & Wu, Y. (2016). Exploring the limits of language modeling. arXiv preprint arXiv:1602.02410.

Junaidi, J. (2020). Artificial intelligence in EFL context: Rising students' speaking performance with Lyra virtual assistance. *International Journal of Advanced Science and Technology*, *29*(5), 6735–6741.

Kabilan, M. K., & Khan, M. A. (2012). Assessing pre-service English language teachers' learning using e-portfolios: Benefits, challenges and competencies gained. *Computers & Education*, *58*(4), 1007–1020. DOI: 10.1016/j.compedu.2011.11.011

Kaddour, J., Harris, J., Mozes, M., Bradley, H., Raileanu, R., & McHardy, R. (2023). Challenges and applications of large language models. arXiv preprint arXiv:2307.10169.

Kang, H. (2022). Effects of artificial intelligence and native speaker interlocutors on ESL learners' speaking ability and affective aspects. *Multimedia-Assisted Language Learning*, *25*, 9–43. DOI: 10.15702/mall.2022.25

Kannan, J., & Munday, P. (2018). New trends in second language learning and teaching through the lens of ICT, networked learning, and artificial intelligence.

Kapočiūtė-Dzikienė, J. (2020). A domain-specific generative chatbot trained from little data. *Applied Sciences (Basel, Switzerland)*, *10*(7), 2221. DOI: 10.3390/app10072221

Karaca, O., Çalışkan, S. A., & Demir, K. (2021). Medical artificial intelligence readiness scale for medical students (MAIRS-MS)–development, validity and reliability study. BMC medical education. springer.com

Karan, B., & Angadi, G. R. (2023). Artificial Intelligence Integration into School Education: A Review of Indian and Foreign Perspectives. *Millennial Asia*, *09763996231158229*. Advance online publication. DOI: 10.1177/09763996231158229

Karanikola, Z., & Panagiotopoulos, G. (2023). Adult Education and Globally Engaged Trainers: The Case of Vocational Training Institutes. *Education Sciences*, *13*(4), 362. DOI: 10.3390/educsci13040362

Karataş, F., Eriçok, B., & Tanrikulu, L. (2025). Reshaping curriculum adaptation in the age of artificial intelligence: Mapping teachers' driven curriculum adaptation patterns. *British Educational Research Journal*, *51*(1), 154–180. DOI: 10.1002/berj.4068

Kardefelt-Winther, D. (2014). A conceptual and methodological critique of internet addiction research: Towards a model of compensatory internet use. *Computers in Human Behavior*, *31*, 351–354. DOI: 10.1016/j.chb.2013.10.059

Kardefelt-Winther, D. (2017). Conceptualizing Internet use disorders: Addiction or coping process? *Psychiatry and Clinical Neurosciences*, *71*(7), 459–466. DOI: 10.1111/pcn.12413 PMID: 27278653

Karlik, B., & Olgac, A. V. (2011). Performance analysis of various activation functions in generalized MLP architectures of neural networks. *International Journal of Artificial Intelligence and Expert Systems*, *1*(4), 111–122.

Karyuatry, L. (2018). Grammarly as a tool to improve students' writing quality: Free online-proofreader across the boundaries. [Jurnal Sains Sosial Dan Humaniora]. *JSSH*, *2*(1), 83–89. DOI: 10.30595/jssh.v2i1.2297

Kasneci, E., Seßler, K., Küchemann, S., Bannert, M., Dementieva, D., Fischer, F., Gasser, U., Groh, G., Günnemann, S., Hüllermeier, E., Krusche, S., Kutyniok, G., Michaeli, T., Nerdel, C., Pfeffer, J., Poquet, O., Sailer, M., Schmidt, A., Seidel, T., & Kasneci, G. (2023). ChatGPT for good? On opportunities and challenges of large language models for education. *Learning and Individual Differences*, *103*, 102274. Advance online publication. DOI: 10.1016/j.lindif.2023.102274

Kassem, M. A., & Al-Awadhi, A. (2024). AI in language learning: A review of current applications and future trends. *Educational Technology Review*, *52*(1), 87–105.

Kataev, M., Bulysheva, L., & Mosiaev, A. (2022). Application of artificial intelligence methods in the school educational process. *Systems Research and Behavioral Science*, *39*(3), 531–541. DOI: 10.1002/sres.2873

Katznelson, G., & Gerke, S. (2021). The need for health AI ethics in medical school education. *Advances in Health Sciences Education : Theory and Practice*, *26*(4), 1447–1458. DOI: 10.1007/s10459-021-10040-3 PMID: 33655433

Kayaalp, M. E., Ollivier, M., Winkler, P. W., Dahmen, J., Musahl, V., Hirschmann, M. T., & Karlsson, J. (2023). Embrace responsible ChatGPT usage to overcome language barriers in academic writing. *Knee Surgery, Sports Traumatology, Arthroscopy : Official Journal of the ESSKA, 32*(1), 5–9. DOI: 10.1002/ksa.12014 PMID: 38226673

Kessler, G. (2018). Technology and the future of language teaching. *Foreign Language Annals, 51*(1), 205–218. DOI: 10.1111/flan.12318

Kessler, M. (2023). Supplementing mobile-assisted language learning with reflective journal writing: A case study of Duolingo users' metacognitive awareness. *Computer Assisted Language Learning, 36*(5-6), 1040–1063. DOI: 10.1080/09588221.2021.1968914

Keyue, X. (2023). Papers Concealing Usage of ChatGPT to be Rejected or Withdrawn. *Global Times.* Retrieved from https://www.globaltimes.cn/page/202302/1285398.shtml

Khalaf, M. A. (2024a). Aigiarism: The New Form of Plagiarism in the Era of ArtificialIntelligence. *Short Communication*, 1.

Khalaf, M. A. (2024b). Does attitude towards plagiarism predict aigiarism using ChatGPT? *AI and Ethics*. Advance online publication. DOI: 10.1007/s43681-024-00426-5

Khalifa, M., & Albadawy, M. (2024). Using Artificial Intelligence in Academic Writing and Research: An Essential Productivity Tool. *Computer Methods and Programs in Biomedicine Update, 5*, 100145. DOI: 10.1016/j.cmpbup.2024.100145

Khan, A., Khan, S., & Turi, S. (2019). An exploratory study focusing on teaching and learning practices at the tertiary level in Pakistan: A case study of a public sector university. *International Journal of Educational Development, 65*, 106–114. DOI: 10.1016/j.ijedudev.2017.08.008

Khan, M. O., Nazim, M., & Alzubi, A. A. F. (2024). Exploring Arab EFL Learners' Attitudes: Is Grammarly a Game -Changer in Academic Writing Classes? *Educational Administration: Theory And Practice, 30*(4), 1365–1371. DOI: 10.53555/kuey.v30i4.1612

Khanna, T., Washington, J. N., Tyers, F. M., Bayatlı, S., Swanson, D. G., Pirinen, T. A., Tang, I., & Alos i Font, H. (2021). Recent advances in Apertium, a free/open-source rule-based machine translation platform for low-resource languages. [springer.com]. *Machine Translation, 35*(4), 475–502. DOI: 10.1007/s10590-021-09260-6

Khanzode, K. C. A., & Sarode, R. D. (2020). Advantages and disadvantages of artificial intelligence and machine learning: A literature review. [IJLIS]. *International Journal of Library and Information Science, 9*(1), 3.

Kharbat, F. F., Alshawabkeh, A., & Woolsey, M. L. (2021). Identifying gaps in using artificial intelligence to support students with intellectual disabilities from education and health perspectives. [HTML]. *Aslib Journal of Information Management, 73*(1), 101–128. DOI: 10.1108/AJIM-02-2020-0054

Khor, E. T., & Mutthulakshmi, M. (2023). A systematic review of the role of learning analytics in supporting personalized learning. *Education Sciences, 14*(1), 51. DOI: 10.3390/educsci14010051

Khosravi, H., Shum, S. B., Chen, G., Conati, C., Tsai, Y. S., Kay, J., & Gašević, D. (2022). Explainable artificial intelligence in education. [sciencedirect.com]. *Computers and Education: Artificial Intelligence*, *3*, 100074.

Khurana, D., Koli, A., Khatter, K., & Singh, S. (2023). Natural language processing: state of the art, current trends and challenges. Multimedia tools and applications. springer.com

Kim, E. (2024). A study on using ai learning for elementary school students struggling with english. The Korea Association of Primary English Education, 30(2), 81-104. DOI: 10.25231/pee.2024.30.2.81

Kim, J. (2014). The effectiveness of automated essay scoring in an EFL college classroom. *Multimedia-Assisted Language Learning*, *17*(3), 11–36. DOI: 10.15702/mall.2014.17.3.11

Kim, J. (2020). Learning and teaching online during Covid-19: Experiences of student teachers in an early childhood education practicum. *International Journal of Early Childhood*, *52*(2), 145–158. DOI: 10.1007/s13158-020-00272-6 PMID: 32836369

Kim, J. (2023). Leading teachers' perspective on teacher-AI collaboration in education. *Education and Information Technologies*, *29*(7), 8693–8724. DOI: 10.1007/s10639-023-12109-5

Kim, J., Lee, H., & Cho, Y. H. (2022). Learning design to support student-AI collaboration: Perspectives of leading teachers for AI in education. *Education and Information Technologies*, *27*(5), 6069–6104. DOI: 10.1007/s10639-021-10831-6

Kim, J., Yu, S., Detrick, R., & Li, N. (2024). Exploring students' perspectives on generative AI-assisted academic writing. *Education and Information Technologies*. Advance online publication. DOI: 10.1007/s10639-024-12878-7

Kim, N.-Y. (2016). Effects of voice chat on EFL learners' speaking ability according to proficiency levels. *Multimedia-Assisted Language Learning*, *19*(4), 63–88.

Kim, N.-Y. (2018). A study on chatbots for developing Korean college students' English listening and reading skills. *Journal of Digital Convergence*, *16*(8), 19–26.

Kim, N.-Y. (2019). A Study on the Use of Artificial Intelligence Chatbots for Improving English Grammar Skills. *Journal of Digital Convergence*, *17*(8), 37–46. DOI: 10.14400/jdc.2019.17.8.037

Kim, S., & Park, J. (2023). AI-driven personalized learning in EFL education: A case study in South Korea. *Journal of Educational Computing Research*, *59*(5), 1111–1128.

Kim, Y., Jernite, Y., Sontag, D., & Rush, A. (2016, March). Character-aware neural language models. In *Proceedings of the AAAI on artificial intelligence* (Vol. 30, No. 1).

Kinshuk, C., Chen, N.-S., Cheng, I.-L., & Chew, S. W. (2016). Evolution Is not enough: Revolutionizing Current Learning Environments to Smart Learning Environments. *International Journal of Artificial Intelligence in Education*, *26*(2), 561–581. DOI: 10.1007/s40593-016-0108-x

Kirschner, P., Strijbos, J.-W., Kreijns, K., & Beers, P. J. (2004). Designing electronic collaborative learning environments. *Educational Technology Research and Development*, *52*(3), 47–66. DOI: 10.1007/BF02504675

Kishore, H. S., Solomon Paul Raj, D., & Senthilkumar, K. R. (2024). AI for Accessibility: A Case Study of Enhancing Library Services for Users With Disabilities. In Senthilkumar, K., & Jagajeevan, R. (Eds.), *Improving Library Systems with AI: Applications, Approaches, and Bibliometric Insights* (pp. 214–225). IGI Global Scientific Publishing. DOI: 10.4018/979-8-3693-5593-0.ch015

Kisnanto, Y. (2016). The Effect of Written Corrective Feedback on Higher Education Students' Writing Accuracy. *Jurnal Pendidikan dan Bahasa, 16*(2). Retrieved from DOI: 10.17509/bs_jpbsv.vl6i2.4476

Klimova, B., Pikhart, M., & Kacetl, J. (2023). Ethical issues of the use of AI-driven mobile apps for education. Frontiers in Public Health. frontiersin.org

Knezek, G. A., & Christensen, R. (2014). Tools for Analyzing Quantitative Data. In Spector, J. M., Merrill, M. D., Elen, J., & Bishop, M. J. (Eds.), *Handbook of Research on Educational Communications and Technology* (pp. 203–220). Springer New York., DOI: 10.1007/978-1-4614-3185-5_17

Koehler, M. J., & Mishra, P. (2008). Introducing TPCK. In AACTE Committee on Innovation and Technology (Ed.), *Handbook of technological pedagogical content knowledge (TPCK) for educators* (pp. 3–29). Routledge.

Koehler, M. J., Mishra, P., & Cain, W. (2013). What is Technological Pedagogical Content Knowledge (TPACK)? *Journal of Education, 193*(3), 13–19. DOI: 10.1177/002205741319300303

Kohl, K., Hopkins, C., Barth, M., Michelsen, G., Dlouhá, J., Razak, D. A., Abidin Bin Sanusi, Z., & Toman, I. (2022). A whole-institution approach towards sustainability: A crucial aspect of higher education's individual and collective engagement with the SDGs and beyond. [emerald.com]. *International Journal of Sustainability in Higher Education, 23*(2), 218–236. DOI: 10.1108/IJSHE-10-2020-0398

Kohnke, L., Moorhouse, B. L., & Zou, D. (2023). ChatGPT for language teaching and learning. *RELC Journal,* •••, 00336882231162868.

Kohnke, L., Moorhouse, B. L., & Zou, D. (2023). ChatGPT for Language Teaching and Learning. *RELC Journal, 54*(2), 537–550. DOI: 10.1177/00336882231162868

Kohnke, L., Moorhouse, B. L., & Zou, D. (2023). Exploring generative artificial intelligence preparedness among university language instructors: A case study. *Computers and Education Artificial Intelligence, 5*, 100156–100156. DOI: 10.1016/j.caeai.2023.100156

Koltovskaia, S. (2022). Postsecondary L2 writing teachers' use and perceptions of Grammarly as a complement to their feedback. *ReCALL (Cambridge, England),* 1-15. DOI: 10.1017/S0958344022000179

Koltovskaia, S. (2020). Student engagement with automated written corrective feedback (AWCF) provided by Grammarly: A multiple case study. *Assessing Writing, 44*(3), 100450. DOI: 10.1016/j.asw.2020.100450

Koltovskaia, S. (2020). Student engagement with automated written corrective feedback (AWCF): An exploratory study. *Journal of Language and Linguistic Studies, 16*(2), 468–479.

Korenev, A. A. (2024). Strategies of using artificial intelligence for written corrective feedback in language education. *Moscow University Bulletin. Series 19. Linguistics and Intercultural Communication, 27*(N°2_2024), 68–77. DOI: 10.55959/MSU-2074-1588-19-27-2-5

Krathwohl, D. R. (2002). A revision of Bloom's taxonomy: An overview. *Theory into Practice*, *41*(4), 212–218. DOI: 10.1207/s15430421tip4104_2

Kuddus, K. (2022). *Artificial intelligence in language learning: Practices and prospects*. Advanced Analytics and Deep Learning Models. [HTML]

Kukulska-Hulme, A., & Lee, H. (2020). Intelligent assistants in language learning: analysis of features and limitations. CALL for widening participation: short papers from EUROCALL 2020, 1(1), 172-176.

Kulkov, I., Kulkova, J., Rohrbeck, R., Menvielle, L., Kaartemo, V., & Makkonen, H. (2024). Artificial intelligence-driven sustainable development: Examining organizational, technical, and processing approaches to achieving global goals. [wiley.com]. *Sustainable Development (Bradford)*, *32*(3), 2253–2267. DOI: 10.1002/sd.2773

Kumar, A., Singh, P., & Lata, K. "Comparative Study of Different Optical Character Recognition Models on Handwritten and Printed Medical Reports," *2023 International Conference on Innovative Data Communication Technologies and Application (ICIDCA)*, Uttarakhand, India, 2023, pp. 581-586, DOI: 10.1109/ICIDCA56705.2023.10100213

Kumar, S. (2024a). Impact of Assessment on Childhood Education Theories and Practice. In Badea, M., & Suditu, M. (Eds.), *Advances in Early Childhood and K-12 Education* (pp. 84–101). IGI Global., DOI: 10.4018/979-8-3693-0956-8.ch004

Kumar, S. (2024b). The Role of Digital Marketing on Customer Engagement in the Hospitality Industry. In Bansal, R., Ngah, A. H., Chakir, A., & Pruthi, N. (Eds.), (pp. 177–191). Advances in Business Information Systems and Analytics. IGI Global., DOI: 10.4018/979-8-3693-0815-8.ch010

Kumar, Y., & Kumar, V. (2023). Security in IoT systems using natural language processing: Future challenges and directions. *Internet Technology Letters*, *6*(4), e411. DOI: 10.1002/itl2.411

Kumi-Yeboah, A., Kim, Y., Yankson, B., Aikins, S., & Dadson, Y. A. (2023). Diverse students' perspectives on privacy and technology integration in higher education. *British Journal of Educational Technology*, *54*(6), 1671–1692. DOI: 10.1111/bjet.13386

Kuppuswamy, P., Ansari, M. D., Mohan, M., & Al Khalidi, S. Q. (2024). Data Mining for Predictive Analytics. Intelligent Techniques for Predictive Data Analytics, 1-24. [HTML]

Kwong, T., Wong, E., & Yue, K. (2017). Bringing Abstract Academic Integrity and Ethical Concepts into Real-Life Situations. *Technology. Knowledge and Learning*, *22*(3), 353–368. DOI: 10.1007/s10758-017-9315-2

Lahiri, A. (2024). Sociological implications of the digital divide: Exploring access to information and social inequality in the age of artificial intelligence and automation. RESEARCH REVIEW. *International Journal of Multidisciplinary*, *9*(1), 156–167. DOI: 10.31305/rrijm.2024.v09.n01.019

Lai, Y., Saab, N., & Admiraal, W. (2022). Learning strategies in self-directed language learning using mobile technology in higher education: A systematic scoping review. Education and Information Technologies. springer.com

Lai, J. W., & Cheong, K. H. (2022). Educational Opportunities and Challenges in Augmented Reality: Featuring Implementations in Physics Education. *IEEE Access : Practical Innovations, Open Solutions, 10*, 43143–43158. DOI: 10.1109/ACCESS.2022.3166478

Lameras, P. (2022). A Vision of Teaching and Learning with AI. *2022 IEEE Global Engineering Education Conference (EDUCON)*, 1796–1803. DOI: 10.1109/EDUCON52537.2022.9766718

Lanke, M. M., Porwal, M. A., Sarolkar, M. S., Palaskar, M. G., & Kakad, S. (2022). AI based student's assignments plagiarism detector. *International Journal for Research in Applied Science and Engineering Technology, 10*(12), 991–999. DOI: 10.22214/ijraset.2022.48080

Lara, F. (2021). Why a Virtual Assistant for Moral Enhancement When We Could have a Socrates? *Science and Engineering Ethics, 27*(4), 42. DOI: 10.1007/s11948-021-00318-5 PMID: 34189623

Latif. E., Zhai. X., Liu, L.. (2023). AI Gender Bias, Disparities, and Fairness: Does Training Data Matter?. arXiv.org, abs/2312.10833 DOI: 10.48550/arxiv.2312.10833

Lazic, D., Thompson, A., Pritchard, T., & Tsuji, S. (2020). Student preferences: using Grammarly to help EFL writers with paraphrasing, summarizing, and synthesizing. In *CALL for widening participation: short papers from EUROCALL 2020* (pp. 183-189). Research-publishing.net. DOI: 10.14705/rpnet.2020.48.1186

Lee, D., Huh, Y., Lin, C.-Y., & Reigeluth, C. M. (2022). Personalized Learning Practice in U.S. Learner-Centered Schools. *Contemporary Educational Technology, 14*(4), ep385. DOI: 10.30935/cedtech/12330

Lee, K. (2017). Rethinking the accessibility of online higher education: A historical review. *The Internet and Higher Education, 33*, 15–23. DOI: 10.1016/j.iheduc.2017.01.001

Lee, S. M. (2023). The effectiveness of machine translation in foreign language education: A systematic review and meta-analysis. [HTML]. *Computer Assisted Language Learning, 36*(1-2), 103–125. DOI: 10.1080/09588221.2021.1901745

Leona, N. L., van Koert, M. J., van der Molen, M. W., Rispens, J. E., Tijms, J., & Snellings, P. (2021). Explaining individual differences in young English language learners' vocabulary knowledge: The role of Extramural English Exposure and motivation. [sciencedirect.com]. *System, 96*, 102402. DOI: 10.1016/j.system.2020.102402

Le, T. B. N., & Ngo, V. G. (2024). Difficulties of first-year students of English Language at Hanoi University when writing paragraphs in academic English. *Journal of Education, 24*(11), 47–52. https://tcgd.tapchigiaoduc.edu.vn/index.php/tapchi/article/view/1908

Le, T. M., & Duc, N. H. (2024). The impact of AI-based tools on EFL learners' writing performance and motivation. *Language Learning & Technology, 28*(2), 123–144.

Le, T. T. H. (2020). English non-major students' difficulties in writing academic essays and some suggested solutions. *Vietnam Journal of Educational Science, 30*, 42–48. http://lib.yhn.edu.vn/bitstream/YHN/5131/1/N385.pdf

Le-Thi, D., Rodgers, M., & Pellicer-Sánchez, A. (2018). Teaching formulaic sequences in an English-language class: The effects of explicit instruction versus coursebook instruction. *TESL Canada Journal, 34*(3), 111–139. DOI: 10.18806/tesl.v34i3.1276

Lewis, M. (1997). *Implementing the Lexical Approach: Putting theory into practice.* http://ci.nii.ac.jp/ncid/BA35070833

Lewis, A., & Stoyanovich, J. (2022). Teaching Responsible Data Science: Charting New Pedagogical Territory. *International Journal of Artificial Intelligence in Education, 32*(3), 783–807. DOI: 10.1007/s40593-021-00241-7 PMID: 33880114

Lew, R., & Doroszewska, J. (2009). Electronic dictionary entries with animated pictures: Lookup preferences and word retention. *International Journal of Lexicography, 22*(3), 239–257. DOI: 10.1093/ijl/ecp022

Li, L., Gow, A. D. I., & Zhou, J. (). The role of positive emotions in education: A neuroscience perspective. Mind. [HTML]

Li, Z. & Li, J. (2022). Using the flipped classroom to promote learner engagement for the sustainable development of language skills: A mixed-methods study. Sustainability. mdpi.com

Li, Z., Dhruv, A., & Jain, V. (2024). Ethical considerations in the use of ai for higher education: a comprehensive guide. In *2024 IEEE 18th International Conference on Semantic Computing (ICSC).* DOI: 10.1109/ICSC59802.2024.00041

Liang, J. C., Hwang, G. J., Chen, M. R. A., & Darmawansah, D. (2023). Roles and research foci of artificial intelligence in language education: An integrated bibliographic analysis and systematic review approach. *Interactive Learning Environments, 31*(7), 4270–4296. DOI: 10.1080/10494820.2021.1958348

Liang, X., & Luo, J. (2024). Integration of ChatGPT into Project-based Learning: A Course Design Framework. *International Journal of Chinese Language Teaching, 5*(1). Advance online publication. DOI: 10.46451/ijclt.20240104

Li, G., Liu, F., Sharma, A., Khalaf, O. I., Alotaibi, Y., Alsufyani, A., & Alghamdi, S. (2021). Research on the natural language recognition method based on cluster analysis using neural network. [wiley.com]. *Mathematical Problems in Engineering, 2021*(1), 9982305. DOI: 10.1155/2021/9982305

Lin, C. (2024). Research on innovative models of Second language teaching in the age of Artificial Intelligence. *Applied Mathematics and Nonlinear Sciences, 9*(1), 20240760. Advance online publication. DOI: 10.2478/amns-2024-0760

Lin, C. C., Huang, A. Y., & Lu, O. H. (2023). Artificial intelligence in intelligent tutoring systems toward sustainable education: A systematic review. *Smart Learning Environments, 10*(1), 41. DOI: 10.1186/s40561-023-00260-y

Lin, C. J., & Mubarok, H. (2021). Learning analytics for investigating the mind map-guided AI chatbot approach in an EFL flipped speaking classroom. *Journal of Educational Technology & Society, 24*(4), 16–35. https://www.jstor.org/stable/48629242

Liu, G. L., Darvin, R., & Ma, C. (2024). Exploring AI-mediated informal digital learning of English (AI-IDLE): A mixed-method investigation of Chinese EFL learners' AI adoption and experiences. *Computer Assisted Language Learning*, •••, 1–29. DOI: 10.1080/09588221.2024.2310288

Liu, Y. T., Hsih, M. H., & Hsieh, C. C. (2021, November). An Automatic Response System based on Multi-layer Perceptual Neural Network and Web Crawler. In *2021 International Conference on Technologies and Applications of Artificial Intelligence (TAAI)* (pp. 246-249). IEEE. DOI: 10.1109/TAAI54685.2021.00054

Liu, Y., & Chen, H. (2024). A study on the effect of AI-assisted vocabulary learning on EFL learners. *International Journal of Emerging Technologies in Learning*, *19*(7), 124–138.

Livberber, T., & Ayvaz, S. (2023). The impact of artificial intelligence in academia: Views of Turkish academics on ChatGPT. *Heliyon*, *9*(9), e19688. DOI: 10.1016/j.heliyon.2023.e19688 PMID: 37809772

Li, X., & Xie, H. (2023). Investigating the effectiveness of AI-based feedback on EFL learners' writing. *Journal of Language Teaching and Research*, *14*(4), 859–874.

Li, Y. (2024). Usability of chatgpt in Second language acquisition: Capabilities, effectiveness, applications, challenges, and solutions. *Studies in Applied Linguistics and TESOL*, *24*(1). Advance online publication. DOI: 10.52214/salt.v24i1.12864

Lodge, J. M., De Barba, P., & Broadbent, J. (2024). Learning with generative artificial intelligence within a network of co-regulation. *Journal of University Teaching & Learning Practice*, *20*(7). Advance online publication. DOI: 10.53761/1.20.7.02

Lodge, J. M., Thompson, K., & Corrin, L. (2023). Mapping out a research agenda for generative artificial intelligence in tertiary education. *Australasian Journal of Educational Technology*, *39*(1), 1–8. DOI: 10.14742/ajet.8695

Loewen, S. (2012). The role of feedback. In Gass, S., & Mackey, A. (Eds.), *The Routledge handbook of second language acquisition* (pp. 24–41). Routledge.

Lokman, A. S., & Ameedeen, M. A. (2019). Modern chatbot systems: A technical review. In *Proceedings of the Future Technologies Conference (FTC) 2018: Volume 2* (pp. 1012-1023). Springer International Publishing. DOI: 10.1007/978-3-030-02683-7_75

Long, D., & Magerko, B. (2020). What is AI Literacy? Competencies and Design Considerations. *Proceedings of the 2020 CHI Conference on Human Factors in Computing Systems*, 1–16. DOI: 10.1145/3313831.3376727

Lori, S., Stephanie, F., & Benjamin, B. (2024). *Evaluating the Effectiveness of Turnitin's AI Writing Indicator Model.* chrome-extension://efaidnbmnnnibpcajpcglclefindmkaj/https://teaching.temple.edu/sites/teaching/files/media/document/Evaluating%20the%20Effectiveness%20of%20Turnitin%E2%80%99s%20AI%20Writing%20Indicator%20Model_0.pdf

Luan, H., Geczy, P., Lai, H., Gobert, J., Yang, S. J. H., Ogata, H., Baltes, J., Guerra, R., Li, P., & Tsai, C.-C. (2020). Challenges and Future Directions of Big Data and Artificial Intelligence in Education. *Frontiers in Psychology*, *11*, 580820. DOI: 10.3389/fpsyg.2020.580820 PMID: 33192896

Lucía, R. (2023, November 20). *2023: An intelligent learning Odyssey*. International Bar Association I International Bar Association. https://www.ibanet.org/2023-an-intelligent-learning-odyssey

Luckin, R., Cukurova, M., Kent, C., & du Boulay, B. (2022). Empowering educators to be AI-ready. *Computers and Education: Artificial Intelligence*, *3*, 100076. Advance online publication. DOI: 10.1016/j.caeai.2022.100076

Luo, J., & Qiu, L. (2024). Review of artificial intelligence-based tools in EFL classroom. *Arts. Culture and Language*, *1*(7), 1–5. DOI: 10.61173/s266nr95

Lu, X. (2012). The relationship of lexical richness to the quality of ESL learners' oral narratives. *Modern Language Journal*, *96*(2), 190–208. DOI: 10.1111/j.1540-4781.2011.01232_1.x

Lu, Y. (2019). Artificial intelligence: A survey on evolution, models, applications and future trends. *Journal of Management Analytics*, *6*(1), 1–29. DOI: 10.1080/23270012.2019.1570365

Machusky, J. A., & Herbert-Berger, K. G. (2022). Understanding online learning infrastructure in US K-12 schools: A review of challenges and emerging trends. [HTML]. *International Journal of Educational Research*, *114*, 101993. DOI: 10.1016/j.ijer.2022.101993

Madonna University. (2023). *Generative AI and Academic Writing Tasks What*. chrome-extension://efaidnbmnnnibpcajpcglclefindmkaj/https://madonna.edu/resources/writing-center/online-tutoring/ChatGPTandAcademicWritingTasksRevised.pdf

Mageira, K., Pittou, D., Papasalouros, A., Kotis, K., Zangogianni, P., & Daradoumis, A. (2022). Educational AI Chatbots for Content and Language Integrated Learning. *Applied Sciences (Basel, Switzerland)*, *12*(7), 3239. DOI: 10.3390/app12073239

Maguraushe, K., da Veiga, A., & Martins, N. (2024). A personal information privacy perceptions model for university students. *Information Security Journal: A Global Perspective*, 33(4), 394-424. DOI: 10.1080/19393555.2024.2329554

Makeleni, S., Mutongoza, B. H., & Linake, M. A. (2023). Language Education and Artificial Intelligence: An Exploration of Challenges Confronting Academics in Global South Universities. *Journal of Culture and Values in Education*, *6*(2), 158–171. DOI: 10.46303/jcve.2023.14

Maleki, N., Padmanabhan, B., & Dutta, K. (2024). AI hallucinations: A misnomer worth clarifying. *2024 IEEE Conference on Artificial Intelligence (CAI)*. https://doi.org/DOI: 10.1109/CAI59869.2024.00033

Malik, A. R., Pratiwi, Y., Andajani, K., Numertayasa, I. W., Suharti, S., Darwis, A., & Marzuki, . (2023). Exploring artificial intelligence in academic essay: Higher education student's perspective. *International Journal of Educational Research Open*, *5*, 100296. DOI: 10.1016/j.ijedro.2023.100296

Malik, M. A., Amjad, A. I., Aslam, S., & Fakhrou, A. (2024). Global insights: ChatGPT's influence on academic and research writing, creativity, and plagiarism policies. *Frontiers in Research Metrics and Analytics*, *9*, 1486832. Advance online publication. DOI: 10.3389/frma.2024.1486832 PMID: 39583913

Malon, J. C., Virtudazo, J., Vallente, W., Ayop, L., & Malon, M. F. (2024). Expressing ideas: AI-integrated paraphrasing to students' writing skills. *International Journal of Educational Methodology, volume-10-2024*(volume-10-issue-4-november-2024), 531-542. https://doi.org/DOI: 10.12973/ijem.10.4.531

Manaf, K., Pitara, S. W., Subaeki, B., & Gunawan, R. (2019, October). Comparison of carp rabin algorithm and Jaro-Winkler distance to determine the equality of Sunda languages. In 2019 IEEE 13th international conference on telecommunication systems, services, and applications (TSSA) (pp. 77-81). IEEE. DOI: 10.1109/TSSA48701.2019.8985470

Mansilla, V. B., & Wilson, D. (2020). What is global competence, and what might it look like in Chinese schools? [sagepub.com]. *Journal of Research in International Education, 19*(1), 3–22. DOI: 10.1177/1475240920914089

Maphoto, K. B., Sevnarayan, K., Mohale, N. E., Suliman, Z., Ntsopi, T. J., & Mokoena, D. (2024). Advancing students' academic excellence in distance education: Exploring the potential of generative AI integration to improve academic writing skills. *Open Praxis, 16*(2), 142–159. DOI: 10.55982/openpraxis.16.2.649

Markauskaite, L., Marrone, R., Poquet, O., Knight, S., Martinez-Maldonado, R., Howard, S., Tondeur, J., De Laat, M., Shum, S. B., Basevic, D., & Siemens, G. Rethinking the entwinement between artificial intelligence and human learning: What capabilities do learners need for a world with AI? *Computers and Education: Artificial Intelligence, 3.*https://doi.org/DOI: 10.1016/j.caeai.2022.100056

Marks, B., & Thomas, J. (2022). Adoption of virtual reality technology in higher education: An evaluation of five teaching semesters in a purpose-designed laboratory. *Education and Information Technologies, 27*(1), 1287–1305. DOI: 10.1007/s10639-021-10653-6 PMID: 34257511

Marr, B., & Ward, M. (2019). *Artificial Intelligence in practice: How 50 successful companies used artificial intelligence to solve problems.* Wiley.

Marzuki, U., Rusdin, D., & Indrawati, I. (2023). The impact of AI writing tools on the content and organization of students' writing: EFL teachers' perspective. *Cogent Education, 10*(2), 2236469. Advance online publication. DOI: 10.1080/2331186X.2023.2236469

Masters, K. (2023). Ethical use of Artificial Intelligence in Health Professions Education: AMEE Guide No. 158. *Medical Teacher, 45*(6), 574–584. DOI: 10.1080/0142159X.2023.2186203 PMID: 36912253

Mauranen, A. (2023). *Reflexively speaking: Metadiscourse in English as a lingua Franca* (p. 236). de Gruyter.

Mazikana, A. T. (2023). *The Good Part of Using a Questionnaire: Advantages and Disadvantages.* Available at *SSRN*: DOI: 10.2139/ssrn.4386399

McLaren, B. M., Sosnovsky, S., & Aleven, V. (2014). Preface - Emerging Technologies and Landmark Systems for Learning Mathematics and Science: Dedicated to the Memory of Erica Melis - Part 1. *International Journal of Artificial Intelligence in Education, 24*(3), 211–215. DOI: 10.1007/s40593-014-0021-0

McMurry, B. L., Williams, D. D., Rich, P. J., & Hartshorn, K. J. (2016). An Evaluation Framework for CALL. *The Electronic Journal for English as a Second Language*, 20(2).

McNamara, D. S., Crossley, S. A., & McCarthy, P. M. (2010). Linguistic Features of Writing Quality. *Written Communication, 27*(1), 57–86. DOI: 10.1177/0741088309351547

Meace-Williams, S. (2024). *Conceptualising Welsh Secondary School Teachers' Pedagogic Use of Technology: A Case Study*. 5725652 Bytes. DOI: 10.25401/CARDIFFMET.26177323.V1

Mehta, P., Chillarge, G. R., Sapkal, S. D., Shinde, G. R., & Kshirsagar, P. S. (2023). Inclusion of Children With Special Needs in the Educational System, Artificial Intelligence (AI). In AI-Assisted Special Education for Students With Exceptional Needs (pp. 156-185). IGI Global. [HTML]

Mejeh, M., & Rehm, M. (2024). Taking adaptive learning in educational settings to the next level: Leveraging natural language processing for improved personalization. *Educational Technology Research and Development*, *72*(3), 1597–1621. DOI: 10.1007/s11423-024-10345-1

Meletiou-Mavrotheris, M., & Paparistodemou, E. (2024). Sustaining Teacher Professional Learning in STEM: Lessons Learned from an 18-Year-Long Journey into TPACK-Guided Professional Development. *Education Sciences*, *14*(4), 402. DOI: 10.3390/educsci14040402

Melis, G., Dyer, C., & Blunsom, P. (2017). On the state of the art of evaluation in neural language models. arXiv preprint arXiv:1707.05589.

Menabò, L., Skrzypiec, G., Sansavini, A., Brighi, A., & Guarini, A. (2022). Distance Education among Italian Teachers: Differences and Experiences. *Education and Information Technologies*, *27*(7), 9263–9292. DOI: 10.1007/s10639-022-11008-5 PMID: 35370442

Merriam, S. B. (2009). Qualitative research. A guide to design and implementation, (2nd e.d.). San Francisco, CA: Jossey-Bass.

Mhlanga, D. (2023). Open AI in education, the responsible and ethical use of ChatGPT towards lifelong learning. In *FinTech and artificial intelligence for sustainable development: The role of smart technologies in achieving development goals* (pp. 387–409). Springer Nature Switzerland., DOI: 10.1007/978-3-031-37776-1_17

Miao, J., Thongprayoon, C., Suppadungsuk, S., Garcia Valencia, O. A., Qureshi, F., & Cheungpasitporn, W. (2023). Ethical dilemmas in using AI for academic writing and an example framework for peer review in nephrology academia: A narrative review. *Clinics and Practice*, *14*(1), 89–105. DOI: 10.3390/clinpract14010008 PMID: 38248432

Ming, Y., & Yang, Y. (2024). The role of AI in language learning: A systematic review. *Journal of Computer Assisted Learning*, *40*(2), 222–234.

Minn, S. (2022). AI-assisted knowledge assessment techniques for adaptive learning environments. *Computers and Education: Artificial Intelligence*, *3*, 100050. DOI: 10.1016/j.caeai.2022.100050

Mitchell, M. (2021). Abstraction and analogy-making in artificial intelligence. [PDF]. *Annals of the New York Academy of Sciences*, *1505*(1), 79–101. DOI: 10.1111/nyas.14619 PMID: 34173249

Mitchell, M. (2023). Abstraction and analogy in AI. [HTML]. *Annals of the New York Academy of Sciences*, *1524*(1), 17–21. DOI: 10.1111/nyas.14995 PMID: 37014085

Mitra, N., & Banerjee, A. (2022). A study on using AI in promoting English language learning. *Lecture Notes in Networks and Systems*, 287–297. DOI: 10.1007/978-981-19-4052-1_30

Mitra, S., Lakshmi, D., & Govindaraj, V. (2023). Data analysis and machine learning in AI-assisted special education for students with exceptional needs. In *AI-Assisted Special Education for Students With Exceptional Needs* (pp. 67–109). IGI Global. [HTML] DOI: 10.4018/979-8-3693-0378-8.ch004

Mohamed, A. M. (2024). Exploring the potential of an AI-based Chatbot (ChatGPT) in enhancing English as a Foreign Language (EFL) teaching: Perceptions of EFL Faculty Members. *Education and Information Technologies, 29*(3), 3195–3217. DOI: 10.1007/s10639-023-11917-z

Mohammed Taher Qutub, M., Bukhari, S. S. F., Ali Fadel, S., & Sulaiman Abdulkader Aljuhan, H. (2023). The Future of English as a Foreign Language Teaching and Learning in View of the Fourth Industrial Revolution in the MENA Region. SSRN *Electronic Journal*. DOI: 10.2139/ssrn.4534567

Mohammed, P. S., & Watson, E. (2019). Towards inclusive education in the age of artificial intelligence: Perspectives, challenges, and opportunities. In J. Knox, Y. Wang, & M. Gallagher, M. (Eds) A*rtificial intelligence and inclusive education. perspectives on rethinking and reforming education*. Springer. https://doi.org/DOI: 10.1007/978-981-13-8161-4_2

Motz, B. A., Carvalho, P. F., De Leeuw, J. R., & Goldstone, R. L. (2018). Embedding Experiments: Staking Causal Inference in Authentic Educational Contexts. *Journal of Learning Analytics, 5*(2). Advance online publication. DOI: 10.18608/jla.2018.52.4

Moustaghfir, S., & Brigui, H. (2024). Navigating critical thinking in the digital era: An informative exploration. *International Journal of Linguistics. Literature and Translation, 7*(1), 137–143. DOI: 10.32996/ijllt.2024.7.1.11x

Mouta, A., Torrecilla-Sánchez, E. M., & Pinto-Llorente, A. M. (2023). Design of a future scenarios toolkit for an ethical implementation of artificial intelligence in education. *Education and Information Technologies, 29*(9), 10473–10498. DOI: 10.1007/s10639-023-12229-y

Munawwaroh, K. (2017). Using Mind Mapping to Improve Students' Skill in Descriptive Writing at Semester Two of Batanghari. *Jurnal Ilmiah Dikdaya, 7*(1), 26–33. DOI: 10.33087/dikdaya.v7i1.27

Munir, H., Vogel, B., & Jacobsson, A. (2022). Artificial Intelligence and Machine Learning Approaches in Digital Education: A Systematic Revision. *Information (Basel), 13*(4), 203. DOI: 10.3390/info13040203

Murtaza, M., Ahmed, Y., Shamsi, J. A., Sherwani, F., & Usman, M. (2022). AI-Based Personalized E-Learning Systems: Issues, Challenges, and Solutions. *IEEE Access : Practical Innovations, Open Solutions, 10*, 81323–81342. DOI: 10.1109/ACCESS.2022.3193938

Mystakidis, S., Fragkaki, M., & Filippousis, G. (2021). Ready Teacher One: Virtual and Augmented Reality Online Professional Development for K-12 School Teachers. *Computers, 10*(10), 134. DOI: 10.3390/computers10100134

Nader, N., & Khedri, S. (2024). The role of artificial intelligence in promoting EFL learning outcomes: A systematic review. *International Journal of Educational Research, 103*, 101682.

Nagao, K. (2019). Artificial Intelligence in Education. In K. Nagao, *Artificial Intelligence Accelerates Human Learning* (pp. 1–17). Springer Singapore. DOI: 10.1007/978-981-13-6175-3_1

Naseer, F., Khalid, M. U., Ayub, N., Rasool, A., Abbas, T., & Afzal, M. W. (2024). Automated Assessment and Feedback in Higher Education Using Generative AI. In Transforming Education With Generative AI: Prompt Engineering and Synthetic Content Creation (pp. 433-461). IGI Global. [HTML] DOI: 10.4018/979-8-3693-1351-0.ch021

Naseer, F., Khan, M. N., Tahir, M., Addas, A., & Aejaz, S. M. H. (2024). Integrating deep learning techniques for personalized learning pathways in higher education. *Heliyon*, *10*(11), e32628. DOI: 10.1016/j.heliyon.2024.e32628 PMID: 38961899

Navarro, D., & Henshaw, J. (2024). ChatGPT as a tool for teaching English writing: Exploring its potential and limitations. *Journal of English for Academic Purposes*, *64*, 101123.

Nazaretsky, T., Ariely, M., Cukurova, M., & Alexandron, G. (2022). Teachers' trust in AI-powered educational technology and a professional development program to improve it. *British Journal of Educational Technology*, *53*(4), 914–931. DOI: 10.1111/bjet.13232

Nazari, N., Shabbir, M. S., & Setiawan, R. (2021). Application of Artificial Intelligence powered digital writing assistant in higher education: Randomized controlled trial. *Heliyon*, *7*(5), 1–9. DOI: 10.1016/j.heliyon.2021.e07014 PMID: 34027198

Neha, K., Kumar, R., & Sankat, M. (2024). AI Wizards: Pioneering Assistive Technologies for Higher Education Inclusion of Students with Learning Disabilities. In Applied Assistive Technologies and Informatics for Students with Disabilities (pp. 59-70). Singapore: Springer Nature Singapore. [HTML]

Neji, W., Boughattas, N., & Ziadi, F. (2023). Exploring new AI-based technologies to enhance students' motivation. *Issues in Informing Science & Information Technology*, *20*, 95–110. DOI: 10.28945/5149

Nesselhauf, N. (2005). *Collocations in a learner corpus.*

Nesselhauf, N. (2003). The use of collocations by advanced learners of English and some implications for teaching. *Applied Linguistics*, *24*(2), 223–242. DOI: 10.1093/applin/24.2.223

Newton, P. M., Da Silva, A., & Peters, L. G. (2020). A pragmatic master list of action verbs for Bloom's taxonomy. *Frontiers in Education*, *5*, 1–6. DOI: 10.3389/feduc.2020.00107

Ng, S. Z. (2024). *The Effects Of Ai Tools On Undergraduates' Academic Writing Proficiency In Malaysia* [Unpublished doctoral dissertation]. Universiti Tunku Abdul Rahman.

Ngo, T. V., Nguyen, P. T., Nguyen, V. V., Ha, T. L., & Nguyen, L. M. (2022). An Efficient Method for Generating Synthetic Data for Low-Resource Machine Translation: An empirical study of Chinese, Japanese to Vietnamese Neural Machine Translation. [tandfonline.com]. *Applied Artificial Intelligence*, *36*(1), 2101755. DOI: 10.1080/08839514.2022.2101755

Nguyen, Q. H. (2023). *AI and Plagiarism: Opinion from Teachers, Administrators and Policymakers*. In *Proceedings of the AsiaCALL International Conference*. PAIC. https://doi.org/DOI: 10.54855/paic.2346

Nguyen, T. T. H., & Hoang, T. T. H. (2023). Exploring the use of adaptive learning technology in higher education writing classes: Students' perspectives. *VNU Journal of Foreign Studies, 39*(4), 16-38. https://jfs.ulis.vnu.edu.vn/index.php/fs/article/view/5082/4460

Nguyen, A., Ngo, H. N., Hong, Y., Dang, B., & Nguyen, B. P. T. (2023). Ethical principles for artificial intelligence in education. [springer.com]. *Education and Information Technologies, 28*(4), 4221–4241. DOI: 10.1007/s10639-022-11316-w PMID: 36254344

Nguyen, C., & Boers, F. (2018). The effect of content retelling on vocabulary uptake from a TED talk. *TESOL Quarterly, 53*(1), 5–29. DOI: 10.1002/tesq.441

Nguyen, L. Q. (2022). Learners' satisfaction of courses on Coursera as a massive open online course platform: A case study. *Frontiers in Education, 7*, 1086170. DOI: 10.3389/feduc.2022.1086170

Nguyen, Q. D., Phan, N. M., Kromer, P., & Le, D. A. (2023). An Efficient Unsupervised Approach for OCR Error Correction of Vietnamese OCR Text. *IEEE Access : Practical Innovations, Open Solutions, 11*, 58406–58421. DOI: 10.1109/ACCESS.2023.3283340

Nguyen, T. H., & Tran, T. H. (2023). AI-powered learning and EFL: Implications for teaching and learning. *Computer Applications in Engineering Education, 31*(2), 345–356.

Nguyen, T. T. H. (2023). EFL Teachers' Perspectives toward the Use of ChatGPT in Writing Classes: A Case Study at Van Lang University. *International Journal of Language Instruction, 2*(3), 1–47. DOI: 10.54855/ijli.23231

Nguyen, T. T. H., Do, T. T. Y., & Vu, V. P. (2021). The effects of web-based technology Quizizz on EFL students' vocabulary achievement. *Journal of Inquiry into Languages and Cultures, 5*(3), 245–254.

Niemi, H. (2021). AI in learning: Preparing grounds for future learning. Journal of Pacific Rim Psychology. sagepub.com

Nova, M. (2018). Utilizing Grammarly in evaluating academic writing: A narrative research on EFL students' experience. *Premise: Journal of English Education and Applied Linguistics, 7*(1), 80–96. DOI: 10.24127/pj.v7i1.1332

Nunan, D. (2003). The impact of English as a global language on educational policies and practices in the Asia-Pacific region. *TESOL Quarterly, 37*(4), 589. DOI: 10.2307/3588214

Nurmayanti, N., & Suryadi, S. (2023). The Effectiveness of Using Quillbot in Improving Writing For Students Of English Education Study Program. *Jurnal Teknologi Pendidikan: Jurnal Penelitian dan Pengembangan Pembelajaran, 8*(1), 32-40. DOI: https://doi.org/DOI: 10.33394/jtp.v8i1.6392

Nwohiri, A., JODA, O., & Ajayi, O. (2021). AI-powered plagiarism detection: Leveraging forensic linguistics and natural language processing. *Fudma Journal Of Sciences, 5*(3), 207-218. https://doi.org/DOI: 10.33003/fjs-2021-0503-700

Nye, B. D. (2016). ITS, The End of the World as We Know It: Transitioning AIED into a Service-Oriented Ecosystem. *International Journal of Artificial Intelligence in Education, 26*(2), 756–770. DOI: 10.1007/s40593-016-0098-8

OECD. (2019). *Artificial Intelligence in Society*. https://www.oecd.org/en/publications/2019/06/artificial-intelligence-in-society_c0054fa1.html

Office of Educational Technology. (2023). *Artificial Intelligence and the Future of Teaching and Learning Insights and Recommendations*. chrome-extension://efaidnbmnnnibpcajpcglclefindmkaj/https://www.ed.gov/sites/ed/files/documents/ai-report/ai-report.pdf

Ogirala, M. K., Tallapaneni, R., Chalamcharla, S. M., & Chinta, A. (2023, May). A Medical Diagnosis and Treatment Recommendation Chatbot using MLP. In *2023 2nd International Conference on Applied Artificial Intelligence and Computing (ICAAIC)* (pp. 495-500). IEEE. DOI: 10.1109/ICAAIC56838.2023.10141211

Okoye, K., Hussein, H., Arrona-Palacios, A., Quintero, H. N., Ortega, L. O. P., Sanchez, A. L., Ortiz, E. A., Escamilla, J., & Hosseini, S. (2023). Impact of digital technologies upon teaching and learning in higher education in Latin America: An outlook on the reach, barriers, and bottlenecks. [springer.com]. *Education and Information Technologies*, *28*(2), 2291–2360. DOI: 10.1007/s10639-022-11214-1 PMID: 35992366

Omar, N., Haris, S. S., Hassan, R., Arshad, H., Rahmat, M., Zainal, N. F. A., & Zulkifli, R. (2012). Automated analysis of exam questions according to Bloom's taxonomy. *Procedia: Social and Behavioral Sciences*, *59*(7), 297–303. https://reader.elsevier.com/reader/sd/pii/S1877042812037263?token=6B2AC3430535A2B0AD0FBE49E8D873D4AC811B8638C4B9174025393B65885F9F213F4AE64D2D1D4482B682CCABEC4D66&originRegion=eu-west-1&originCreation=20230520140845. DOI: 10.1016/j.sbspro.2012.09.278

ONeill, R., & Russell, A.ONeill. (2019). Stop! Grammar time: University students' perceptions of the automated feedback program Grammarly. *Australasian Journal of Educational Technology*, *35*(1). Advance online publication. DOI: 10.14742/ajet.3795

Onesi-Ozigagun, O., Ololade, Y. J., Eyo-Udo, N. L., & Ogundipe, D. L. (2024). Revolutionizing education through ai: A comprehensive review of enhancing learning experiences. *International Journal of Applied Research in Social Sciences*, *6*(4), 589–607. DOI: 10.51594/ijarss.v6i4.1011

Open, A. I. (2023). What learning benefits can ChatGPT provide to students? What are the risks of using ChatGPT in academic environment? Retrieved from https://chat.openai.com/

Orji, R. U. (2023). Artificial intelligence and EFL learning: Opportunities and challenges for learners. *Educational Technology Research and Development*, *71*(4), 1229–1247.

Osawa, H., Miyamoto, D., Hase, S., Saijo, R., Fukuchi, K., & Miyake, Y. (2022). Visions of Artificial Intelligence and Robots in Science Fiction: A computational analysis. [springer.com]. *International Journal of Social Robotics*, *14*(10), 2123–2133. DOI: 10.1007/s12369-022-00876-z PMID: 35874175

Osman, Z., Ahmad Khan, B. N., Ismail, M. N., Yusoff, Y., Alwi, N. H., & Mohamad Jodi, K. H. (2023). Artificial intelligence usage in higher education: Academicians' perspective. *International Journal of Academic Research in Accounting. Finance and Management Sciences*, *13*(4). Advance online publication. DOI: 10.6007/IJARAFMS/v13-i4/19391

Ottenbreit-Leftwich, A., Glazewski, K., Jeon, M., Jantaraweragul, K., Hmelo-Silver, C., Scribner, A., Lee, S., Mott, B., & Lester, J. (2022). Principles for AI Education for Elementary Grades Students. *Proceedings of the 27th ACM Conference on on Innovation and Technology in Computer Science Education* Vol. 2, 627–627. DOI: 10.1145/3502717.3532143

Owan, V. J., Abang, K. B., Idika, D. O., Etta, E. O., & Bassey, B. A. (2023). Exploring the potential of artificial intelligence tools in educational measurement and assessment. *Eurasia Journal of Mathematics, Science and Technology Education, 19*(3), em2307. Advance online publication. DOI: 10.29333/ejmste/13428

Oxford, R. L. (2006). Task-based language teaching and learning: An overview. *Asian EFL journal, 8*(3), 94-121. ISSN 1738-1460

Ozdilek, Z. (2024). ChatGPT in EFL classrooms: Impacts on students' reading comprehension and motivation. *Journal of Computer Assisted Learning, 40*(2), 102–116.

Ozfidan, B., El-Dakhs, D. A. S., & Alsalim, L. A. (2024). The use of AI tools in English academic writing by Saudi undergraduates. *Contemporary Educational Technology, 16*(4), ep527. DOI: 10.30935/cedtech/15013

Pablos, P. O., & Parra, D. C. (2023). ChatGPT and English teaching: Perceptions of teachers and students. *International Journal of Educational Research, 122*, 102335.

Pahuja, A., Kaur, S., Budhraja, K., & Kathuria, S. (2024). Examining the Impact of AI on Education: Ethical, Psychological, and Pedagogical Perspectives. In Saluja, S., Nayyar, V., Rojhe, K., & Sharma, S. (Eds.), *Ethical AI and Data Management Strategies in Marketing* (pp. 208–225). IGI Global Scientific Publishing., DOI: 10.4018/979-8-3693-6660-8.ch015

Pajares, M. F. (1992). Teachers' Beliefs and Educational Research: Cleaning Up a Messy Construct. *Review of Educational Research, 62*(3), 307–332. DOI: 10.3102/00346543062003307

Paludi, M. (2024). Safeguarding Privacy and Data Protection Rights in AI- Enhanced Education and Learning Analytics: An Interdisciplinary Approach in Secondary High School Educational Settings. *Proceedings of the Doctoral Consortium of the 19th European Conference on Technology Enhanced Learning,* 56.

Panadero, E. (2017). A review of self-regulated learning: Six models and four directions for research. *Frontiers in Psychology, 8*, 422. DOI: 10.3389/fpsyg.2017.00422 PMID: 28503157

Panagiotis, P., Krystalli, P., & Arvanitis, P. (2023). Technology as a motivational factor in foreign language learning. *European Journal of Education, 6*(1), 69–84. https://revistia.org/files/articles/ejed_v6_i1_23/Panagiotidis.pdf. DOI: 10.2478/ejed-2023-0007

Pan, X. (2020). Technology Acceptance, Technological Self-Efficacy, and Attitude Toward Technology-Based Self-Directed Learning: Learning Motivation as a Mediator. *Frontiers in Psychology, 11*, 564294. Advance online publication. DOI: 10.3389/fpsyg.2020.564294 PMID: 33192838

Papagiannidis, S., & Davlembayeva, D. (2022). Bringing Smart Home Technology to Peer-to-Peer Accommodation: Exploring the Drivers of Intention to Stay in Smart Accommodation. *Information Systems Frontiers*, *24*(4), 1189–1208. DOI: 10.1007/s10796-021-10227-4 PMID: 34899040

Papastratis, I., Chatzikonstantinou, C., Konstantinidis, D., Dimitropoulos, K., & Daras, P. (2021). Artificial intelligence technologies for sign language. [mdpi.com]. *Sensors (Basel)*, *21*(17), 5843. DOI: 10.3390/s21175843 PMID: 34502733

PapersOwl. (2024). *Free plagiarism checker online for students - PapersOwl.* Write My Essay For Me | Essay Writing Service by PapersOwl.com. https://papersowl.com/free-plagiarism-checker

Parashar, B., Sharma, R., Parashar, V., Rana, G., Nayyar, A., & Harish, V. (2023). An Overview of the Accessibility and Need of AI Animation Tools for Specially Abled Students. AI-Assisted Special Education for Students With Exceptional Needs, 1-22. [HTML]

Pardamean, B., Suparyanto, T., Cenggoro, T. W., Sudigyo, D., & Anugrahana, A. (2022). AI-Based Learning Style Prediction in Online Learning for Primary Education. *IEEE Access : Practical Innovations, Open Solutions*, *10*, 35725–35735. DOI: 10.1109/ACCESS.2022.3160177

Parker, L., Carter, C., Karakas, A., Loper, A. J., & Sokkar, A. (2024). Graduate instructors navigating the AI frontier: The role of ChatGPT in higher education. *Computers and Education Open*, *6*, 100166. DOI: 10.1016/j.caeo.2024.100166

Parmaxi, A. (2020). Virtual reality in language learning: A systematic review and implications for research and practice. *Interactive Learning Environments*, *31*(1), 172–184. DOI: 10.1080/10494820.2020.1765392

Parycek, P., Schmid, V., & Novak, A.-S. (2023). Artificial Intelligence (AI) and Automation in Administrative Procedures: Potentials, Limitations, and Framework Conditions. *Journal of the Knowledge Economy*, *15*(2), 8390–8415. DOI: 10.1007/s13132-023-01433-3

Paschal, M. J., & Melly, I. K. (2023). Ethical Guidelines on the Use of AI in Education. In Keengwe, J. (Ed.), *Creative AI Tools and Ethical Implications in Teaching and Learning* (pp. 230–245). IGI Global Scientific Publishing., DOI: 10.4018/979-8-3693-0205-7.ch013

Patil, S., Mudaliar, V. M., Kamat, P., & Gite, S. (2020). LSTM based Ensemble Network to enhance the learning of long-term dependencies in chatbot. *International Journal for Simulation and Multidisciplinary Design Optimization*, *11*, 25. DOI: 10.1051/smdo/2020019

Paullet, K., Pinchot, J., Kinney, E., & Stewart, T. (2024). Can gptzero detect if students are using artificial intelligence to create assignments? *Issues in Information Systems*, *25*(3), 165–174. DOI: 10.48009/3_iis_2024_113

Paul, R., & Elder, L. (1992). Critical thinking: What, why, and how. *New Directions for Community Colleges*, *77*(2), 3–24. https://web.iitd.ac.in/~nkurur/2014-15/IIsem/cyl565/CriticalThinking.pdf. DOI: 10.1002/cc.36819927703

Pavelieva, T. Y. (2024). Platforms for teaching grammar with the help of artificial intelligence: Prospects and problems. International Journal of Advanced Studies in Education and Sociology, 7(1), 13–17. http://sic-publ.press/index.php/es/article/view/194

Peng, T., Luo, Y., & Liu, Y. (2022). AI-Based Equipment Optimization of the Design on Intelligent Education Curriculum System. *Wireless Communications and Mobile Computing*, *2022*, 1–13. DOI: 10.1155/2022/3614883

Perdana, I., & Farida, M. (2019). Online grammar checkers and their use for EFL writing. *Journal of English Teaching* [JETALL]. *Applied Linguistics and Literatures*, *2*(2), 67–76. DOI: 10.20527/jetall.v2i2.7332

Perez, E., Kiela, D., & Cho, K. (2021). True few-shot learning with language models. *Advances in Neural Information Processing Systems*, *34*, 11054–11070.

Perry, N. E., Yee, N., Mazabel, S., Lisaingo, S., & Maatta, E. (2017). Using self-regulated learning for creating inclusive classrooms for ethnically and linguistically diverse in Canada. In Cabrera, N. J., & Leyendecker, B. (Eds.), *Handbook of positive development of minority and youth* (pp. 361–385). Springer. DOI: 10.1007/978-3-319-43645-6_22

Pham, V. P. H. (2024). Vietnamese Graduate Students' Perspectives on the Use of ChatGPT. In Bui, H. P., Namaziandost, E. (eds) *Innovations in Technologies for Language Teaching and Learning*. Studies in Computational Intelligence, vol 1159. Springer, Cham. DOI: https://doi.org/DOI: 10.1007/978-3-031-63447-5_9

Pham, V. P. H., & Nguyen, M. T. (2024). ChatGPT va hoat đong giang day: Cac thach thuc moi cua giang vien. *Tap Chi Khoa hoc va Cong nghe Dai hoc Cong nghe Dong Nai*, No. 01-2024, 115-123. Retrieved from https://vjol.info.vn/index.php/dntu/article/view/91869

Pham, Q. H., & Vu, K. P. (2024). Leveraging lecturers' intelligence for student engagement enrichment in blended learning courses. *Cogent Education*, *11*(1), 2334930. DOI: 10.1080/2331186X.2024.2334930

Pham, V. P. H., & Le, A. Q. (2024). ChatGPT in Language Learning: Perspectives from Vietnamese Students in Vietnam and the USA. *International Journal of Language Instruction*, *3*(2), 59–72. DOI: 10.54855/ijli.24325

Phan, T., & Nguy n, V. (2023). Application of ChatGPT in Teaching, Research, and Management at the University Level. *Scientific Journal of Tan Trao University*, *9*(3), 170–182. DOI: 10.51453/2354-1431/2023/974

Pijls, F., Daelemans, W., & Kempen, G. (1987). Artificial intelligence tools for grammar and spelling instruction. *Instructional Science*, *16*(4), 319–336. DOI: 10.1007/BF00117750

Plotnikova, V., Dumas, M., & Milani, F. P. (2022). Applying the CRISP-DM data mining process in the financial services industry: Elicitation of adaptation requirements. [HTML]. *Data & Knowledge Engineering*, *139*, 102013. DOI: 10.1016/j.datak.2022.102013

Pokrivcakova, S. (2019). Preparing teachers for the application of AI-powered technologies in foreign language education. *Sciendo*, *7*(3), 135–153. DOI: 10.2478/jolace-2019-0025

Poon, A. I. F., & Sung, J. J. Y. (2021). Opening the black box of AI-Medicine. *Journal of Gastroenterology and Hepatology*, *36*(3), 581–584. DOI: 10.1111/jgh.15384 PMID: 33709609

Popescu, M. C., Balas, V. E., Perescu-Popescu, L., & Mastorakis, N. (2009). Multilayer perceptron and neural networks. *WSEAS Transactions on Circuits and Systems*, *8*(7), 579–588.

Porter, B., & Grippa, F. (2020). A platform for AI-enabled real-time feedback to promote digital collaboration. *Sustainability (Basel)*, *12*(24), 10243. DOI: 10.3390/su122410243

Prasetya, R. E., & Raharjo, D. H. (2023). Enhancing English Language Writing Skills: An Evaluation of the Efficacy of Grammarly Application. *Journal of English Language & Studies*, *8*(2), 320–338. DOI: 10.30870/jels.v8i2.19294

Prasse-Freeman, E. (2023). Reassessing reification: ethnicity amidst "failed" governmentality in Burma and India. Comparative Studies in Society and History. cambridge.org

Pregowska, A., Masztalerz, K., Garlińska, M., & Osial, M. (2021). A worldwide journey through distance education—from the post office to virtual, augmented and mixed realities, and education during the COVID-19 pandemic. Education Sciences. mdpi.com

Price, G., & Sakellarios, D., M. (. (2023). The effectiveness of free software for detecting AI-generated writing. *International Journal of Teaching. Learning and Education*, *2*(6), 31–38. DOI: 10.22161/ijtle.2.6.4

Privitera, A. J., Ng, S. H. S., Kong, A. P. H., & Weekes, B. S. (2024). AI and Aphasia in the Digital Age: A Critical Review. Brain Sciences. mdpi.com

Qassemzadeh, A., & Soleimani, H. (2016). The impact of feedback provision by Grammarly software and teachers on learning passive structures by Iranian EFL learners. *Theory and Practice in Language Studies*, *6*(9), 1884–1894. DOI: 10.17507/tpls.0609.23

Qiao, H., & Zhao, A. (2023). Artificial intelligence-based learning: Illuminating the impact of speaking skills and self-regulation in Chinese EFL context. *Frontiers in Psychology*.https://www.ncbi.nlm.nih.gov/pmc/articles/PMC10652775/

Qin, Y., Luo, Y., & Zhai, Y. (2023). French error type annotation for dictation: A platform with automatic error type annotation for French dictation exercises. Frontiers in Psychology. frontiersin.org

Qiu, Z., & Zhang, J. (2023). Exploring the integration of AI in English language education: Benefits and barriers. *Journal of Computer Assisted Learning*, *39*(2), 208–225.

Rad, H. S., Alipour, R., & Jafarpour, A. (2023). Using artificial intelligence to foster students' writing feedback literacy, engagement, and outcome: A case of Wordtune application. *Interactive Learning Environments*, *32*(9), 5020–5040. DOI: 10.1080/10494820.2023.2208170

Ragas, I. M., Pontillas, P. V., & Comon, J. D. (2024). Skills and Roles of Teachers in 21st Century Teaching: Basis for Professional Development Plan. *European Modern Studies Journal*, *8*(4), 344–370. DOI: 10.59573/emsj.8(4).2024.15

Rahimi, M., & Momeni, G. (2012). The effect of teaching collocations on English language proficiency. *Procedia: Social and Behavioral Sciences*, *31*, 37–42. DOI: 10.1016/j.sbspro.2011.12.013

Rahman, S., Irfan, M., Raza, M., Moyeezullah Ghori, K., Yaqoob, S., & Awais, M. (2020). Performance analysis of boosting classifiers in recognizing activities of daily living. [mdpi.com]. *International Journal of Environmental Research and Public Health, 17*(3), 1082. DOI: 10.3390/ijerph17031082 PMID: 32046302

Raiaan, M. A. K., Mukta, M. S. H., Fatema, K., Fahad, N. M., Sakib, S., Mim, M. M. J., ... & Azam, S. (2024). A review on large Language Models: Architectures, applications, taxonomies, open issues and challenges. IEEE Access. ieee.org

Rakhmonov, I. U., & Kurbonova, R. S. (2023). The pedagogical principles and effectiveness of utilizing ChatGPT for language learning. *Research in Education, 2*(9), 226–243. https://researchedu.org/index.php/re/article/view/4899

Ranalli, J. (2018). Automated written corrective feedback: How well can students make use of it? *Computer Assisted Language Learning, 31*(7), 653–674. DOI: 10.1080/09588221.2018.1428994

Rana, S., Sheshadri, T., Malhotra, N., & Mahabub Basha, S. (2024). Creating Digital Learning Environments: Tools and Technologies for Success. In Kumar, R., Ong, E. T., Anggoro, S., Toh, T. L., & Fukui, M. (Eds.), (pp. 1–21). Advances in Educational Technologies and Instructional Design. IGI Global., DOI: 10.4018/979-8-3693-8217-2.ch001

Ranoliya, B. R., Raghuwanshi, N., & Singh, S. (2017). Chatbot for university related FAQs. In *2017 International Conference on Advances in Computing, Communications and Informatics (ICACCI)* (pp. 1525-1530). IEEE. DOI: 10.1109/ICACCI.2017.8126057

Rasti-Behbahani, A. (2021). Why digital games can be advantageous in vocabulary learning. *Theory and Practice in Language Studies, 11*(2), 111–118. DOI: 10.17507/tpls.1102.01

Raza, S., Garg, M., Reji, D. J., Bashir, S. R., & Ding, C. (2024). Nbias: A natural language processing framework for BIAS identification in text. [PDF]. *Expert Systems with Applications, 237*, 121542. DOI: 10.1016/j.eswa.2023.121542

Read, J. (2010). The place of vocabulary in language assessment. In *Assessing Vocabulary*. Cambridge University Press., DOI: 10.1017/CBO9780511732942.002

Regie, B. B., Janet, C. R., Leah, C. S., Leo, J. M., Norlie, G. A., & Marjorie, C. A. (2024). Perceptions and Extent of Utilization of Generative Artificial Intelligence (AI) among Filipino Students. *International Journal of Education and Research, 12*(7), 107–126.

Reimann, P., & Niegemann, H. M. (2023). The influence of adaptive learning systems on EFL vocabulary retention. *Language Teaching Research, 27*(2), 273–290.

Renandya, W. A., & Widodo, H. P. (2024). AI for English language learning: Teachers' beliefs and practices in Asian contexts. *RELC Journal, 55*(1), 3–21.

Renz, A., & Hilbig, R. (2020). Prerequisites for artificial intelligence in further education: Identification of drivers, barriers, and business models of educational technology companies. [springer.com]. *International Journal of Educational Technology in Higher Education, 17*(1), 14. DOI: 10.1186/s41239-020-00193-3

Ricardo, P., Ingrid, W. R., Vania, R. U., & Neri, D. S. (2023). *SEMEAD 2023.*

Rizvi, M. (2023). Investigating AI-Powered Tutoring Systems that Adapt to Individual Student Needs, Providing Personalized Guidance and Assessments. *The Eurasia Proceedings of Educational and Social Sciences, 31*, 67–73. DOI: 10.55549/epess.1381518

Roark, B., Saraclar, M., & Collins, M. (2007). Discriminative n-gram language modeling. *Computer Speech & Language, 21*(2), 373–392. DOI: 10.1016/j.csl.2006.06.006

Rogalska-Chodecka, K. (2019). The Role of Interaction in Language Evolution. Evidence from Two Iterated Learning Experiments with Human Participants. *Theoria et Historia Scientiarum, 16*, 115. DOI: 10.12775/ths.2019.007

Rogerson-Revell, P. M. (2021). Computer-assisted pronunciation training (CAPT): Current issues and future directions. Relc Journal. sagepub.com

Roohani, A., & Asiabani, S. (2015). Effects of self-regulated strategy development on EFL learners' reading comprehension and metacognition. *GEMA Online Journal of Language Studies, 15*(3), 31–49. ISSN 1675-8021.

Rudolph, J., Tan, S., & Tan, S. (2023). ChatGPT: Bullshit Spewer or the End of Traditional Assessments in Higher Education? *Journal of Applied Learning and Teaching, 6*(1), 9–18. DOI: 10.37074/j

Rusmiyanto, R., Huriati, N., Fitriani, N., Tyas, N. K., Rofi'I, A., & Sari, M. N. (2023). The role of artificial intelligence (AI) in developing English language learner's communication skills. *Journal of Education, 6*(1), 750–757. Advance online publication. DOI: 10.31004/joe.v6i1.2990

Sabarun, S. (2019). The influence of different types of feedbacks on learners' writing performance at higher education. *Proceedings of International Conference on English Language Teaching (INACELT), 3*(1), 205–226.

Sabzalieva, E., & Valentini, A. (2023). *ChatGPT and artificial intelligence in higher education: quick start guide.* United Nations Educational, Scientific and Cultural Organization. Retrieved from https://eduq.info/xmlui/handle/11515/38828

Sabzalieva, E., & Valentini, A. (2023). *ChatGPT and Artificial Intelligence in higher education: Quick start guide.* United Nations Educational, Scientific and Cultural Organization.

Sadji Evenddy, S. (2024). Investigating AI's automated feedback in english language learning. *FLIP Foreign Language Instruction Probe, 3*(1), 76–87. DOI: 10.54213/flip.v3i1.401

Sako, T. (2024). Enhancing critical thinking through ai-assisted collaborative task-based learning: A case study of prospective teachers in Japan. *Journal of English Language Teaching and Linguistics, 9*(2), 157. DOI: 10.21462/jeltl.v9i2.1319

Salas-Pilco, S., Xiao, K., & Hu, X. (2022). Artificial Intelligence and Learning Analytics in Teacher Education: A Systematic Review. *Education Sciences, 12*(8), 569. DOI: 10.3390/educsci12080569

Salvagno, M., Taccone, F. S., & Gerli, A. G. (2023). Artifcial intelligence hallucinations. *Critical Care, 27*(180), 1–2. DOI: 10.1186/s13054-023-04473-y PMID: 37165401

Sanabria-Navarro, J.-R., Silveira-Pérez, Y., Pérez-Bravo, D.-D., & de-Jesús-Cortina-Núñez, M. (2023). Incidences of artificial intelligence in contemporary education. *Comunicar*, *31*(77). Advance online publication. DOI: 10.3916/C77-2023-08

Sandhu, R., Channi, H. K., Ghai, D., Cheema, G. S., & Kaur, M. (2024). An Introduction to Generative AI Tools for Education 2030. In Doshi, R., Dadhich, M., Poddar, S., & Hiran, K. (Eds.), *Integrating Generative AI in Education to Achieve Sustainable Development Goals* (pp. 1–28). IGI Global Scientific Publishing. DOI: 10.4018/979-8-3693-2440-0.ch001

Sannino, A. (). Transformative agency as warping: How collectives accomplish change amidst uncertainty. Pedagogy. tandfonline.com

Sari, A. N. (2024). Exploring the Potential of Using AI Language Models in Democratising Global Language Test Preparation. *International Journal of TESOL & Education*, *4*(4), 111–126. DOI: 10.54855/ijte.24447

Sari, N. E., & Megawati, F. (2020). Grammarly as an alternative assessment tool for EFL writing: Students' perceptions. *Journal of English Language Teaching and Linguistics*, *5*(2), 219–229. DOI: 10.21462/jeltl.v5i2.403

Sarker, I. H. (2022). AI-based modeling: techniques, applications and research issues towards automation, intelligent and smart systems. SN Computer Science. springer.com

Sayed, W. S., Noeman, A. M., Abdellatif, A., Abdelrazek, M., Badawy, M. G., Hamed, A., & El-Tantawy, S. (2023). AI-based adaptive personalized content presentation and exercises navigation for an effective and engaging E-learning platform. *Multimedia Tools and Applications*, *82*(3), 3303–3333. DOI: 10.1007/s11042-022-13076-8 PMID: 35789938

Sayyadnejad, M. M., Asgari, A., Sami, A., & Tahyori, H. (2024). Exploring the black box: analyzing explainable ai challenges and best practices through stack exchange discussions. 23 April 2024, PREPRINT (Version 1) available at Research Square DOI: 10.21203/rs.3.rs-4304124/v1

Schiavo, G., Businaro, S., & Zancanaro, M. (2024). Comprehension, apprehension, and acceptance: Understanding the influence of literacy and anxiety on acceptance of artificial intelligence. *Technology in Society*, *77*, 102537. Advance online publication. DOI: 10.1016/j.techsoc.2024.102537

Schick, T., & Schütze, H. (2020). It's not just size that matters: Small language models are also few-shot learners. arXiv preprint arXiv:2009.07118.

Schick, T., & Schütze, H. (2021). Generating datasets with pretrained language models. arXiv preprint arXiv:2104.07540. DOI: 10.18653/v1/2021.emnlp-main.555

Schmulian, A., & Coetzee, S. A. (2019). The development of messenger bots for teaching and learning and accounting students' experience of the use thereof. *British Journal of Educational Technology*, *50*(5), 2751–2777. DOI: 10.1111/bjet.12723

Schneiderman, B. (2020). Bridging the gap between ethics and practice: Guidelines for reliable, safe, and trustworthy human-centered AI systems. *ACM Transactions on Interactive Intelligent Systems*, *10*(4), 1–31. DOI: 10.1145/3419764

Schofield, J. W., Evans-Rhodes, D., & Huber, B. R. (1990). Artificial Intelligence in the Classroom: The Impact of a Computer-Based Tutor on Teachers and Students. *Social Science Computer Review, 8*(1), 24–41. DOI: 10.1177/089443939000800104

Schunk, D. H., & Zimmerman, B. J. (2007). Influencing children's self-efficacy and self-regulation of reading and writing through modeling. *Reading & Writing Quarterly, 23*(1), 7–25. DOI: 10.1080/10573560600837578

Scientific Foresight Unit. (2020). *The ethics of artificial intelligence: Issues and initiatives.* EPRS European Parliamentary Research Service.

Sciolette, F., Giovannetti, E., & Marchi, S. (2023). LexicO: an Italian Computational Lexicon derived from Parole-Simple-Clips. Umanistica Digitale. unibo.it

SCISPACE. (2024). *Academic AI Detector.* AI Chat for scientific PDFs | SciSpace. https://typeset.io/

Scott, C., Yu, T., Choi, J. S., Langdon, H., & Wesley, M. (2024). *Plagiarism Detection Using Keystroke Logs.* In *Proceedings of EDM2024.*

SDSU. University Library. (2024, December 9). *Research by subject: AI at SDSU: AI citation and plagiarism.* Research by Subject at San Diego State University. https://libguides.sdsu.edu/AI4Students/citation

Secretariat Malaysia, S. E. A. M. E. O. (2021). *Education In Malaysia In The AI and Digital Era.* https://chrome-extension://efaidnbmnnnibpcajpcglclefindmkaj/www.internship.seameo.org/images/Library/GBM/RETRAC/2023/Educational%20Forum/Malaysia.pdf

Šedlbauer, J., Činčera, J., Slavík, M., & Hartlová, A. (2024). Students' reflections on their experience with ChatGPT. *Journal of Computer Assisted Learning, 40*(2), 1–9. DOI: 10.1111/jcal.12967

Selvanathan, B., & Narayanan, S. (2024). Chatgpt in higher education Malaysia: An opportunity or threat to the education system? *International Journal of Academic Research in Progressive Education and Development, 13*(3). Advance online publication. DOI: 10.6007/IJARPED/v13-i3/21455

Seo, K., Tang, J., Roll, I., Fels, S., & Yoon, D. (2021). The impact of artificial intelligence on learner–instructor interaction in online learning. *International Journal of Educational Technology in Higher Education, 18*(1), 54. DOI: 10.1186/s41239-021-00292-9 PMID: 34778540

Shadiev, R., & Yu, J. (2024). Review of research on computer-assisted language learning with a focus on intercultural education. *Computer Assisted Language Learning, 37*(4), 841–871. DOI: 10.1080/09588221.2022.2056616

Shah, A. A., Gong, Z., Pal, I., Sun, R., Ullah, W., & Wani, G. F. (2020). Disaster risk management insight on school emergency preparedness–a case study of Khyber Pakhtunkhwa, Pakistan. [HTML]. *International Journal of Disaster Risk Reduction, 51*, 101805. DOI: 10.1016/j.ijdrr.2020.101805

Shahbudin, M. H. (2024). The Role And Influence Of Artificial Intelligence (Ai) In Novel Writing In Malaysia. *American Journal of Humanities and Social Sciences Research, 8*(7), 100–105.

Shaik, T., Tao, X., Li, Y., Dann, C., McDonald, J., Redmond, P., & Galligan, L. (2022). A Review of the Trends and Challenges in Adopting Natural Language Processing Methods for Education Feedback Analysis. *IEEE Access : Practical Innovations, Open Solutions*, *10*, 56720–56739. DOI: 10.1109/ACCESS.2022.3177752

Sharma, A., Sharma, V., Jaiswal, M., Wang, H. C., Jayakody, D. N. K., Basnayaka, C. M. W., & Muthanna, A. (2022). Recent trends in AI-based intelligent sensing. [mdpi.com]. *Electronics (Basel)*, *11*(10), 1661. DOI: 10.3390/electronics11101661

Sharma, R., & Mohan, M. (2022). Artificial Intelligence and E-Learning: Best Practices Across the Globe. In Singh, S. (Ed.), (pp. 1–25). Advances in Marketing, Customer Relationship Management, and E-Services. IGI Global., DOI: 10.4018/978-1-7998-7959-6.ch001

Shi, D., Wei, X., Li, L., Ren, Y., & Tan, W. (2022). End-to-end multi-person pose estimation with transformers. In *Proceedings of the IEEE/CVF conference on computer vision and pattern recognition* (pp. 11069-11078).

Shintani, N., Ellis, R., & Suzuki, W. (2014). Effects of written feedback and revision on learners' accuracy in using two English grammatical structures. *Language Learning*, *64*(1), 103–131. DOI: 10.1111/lang.12029

Shin, Y., & Kang, H. (2023). AI chatbots in language learning: A study on user satisfaction and learning outcomes. *Language Learning & Technology*, *27*(1), 101–118.

Shofiah, N., Putera, Z. F., & Solichah, N. (2023). Challenges and opportunities in the use of artificial intelligence in education for academic writing: A scoping review. In *Conference Psychology and Flourishing Humanity (PFH 2023)* (pp. 174-193). Atlantis Press. DOI: https://doi.org/DOI: 10.2991/978-2-38476-188-3_20

Shrivastava, S. K., & Shrivastava, C. (2022). The Impact of Digitalization in Higher Educational Institutions. [IJSCE]. *International Journal of Soft Computing and Engineering*, *11*(2), 7–11. DOI: 10.35940/ijsce.B3536.0111222

Shuford, J. (2024). Examining ethical aspects of ai: Addressing bias and equity in the discipline. [JAIGS]. *Journal of Artificial Intelligence General Science*, *3*(1), 262–280. DOI: 10.60087/jaigs.v3i1.119

Siemens, G. (2013). Learning Analytics: The Emergence of a Discipline. *The American Behavioral Scientist*, *57*(10), 1380–1400. DOI: 10.1177/0002764213498851

Simms, R. C. (2024). Work with ChatGPT, not against: 3 teaching strategies that harness the power of artificial intelligence. *Nurse Educator, 49*(3), 158-. DOI: 10.1097/NNE.0000000000001634

Sinclair, J. M. (1991). *Corpus, concordance, collocation*. Oxford University Press.

Singer, J. B., Báez, J. C., & Rios, J. A. (2023). AI creates the message: Integrating ai language learning models into social work education and practice. *Journal of Social Work Education*, *59*(2), 294–302. DOI: 10.1080/10437797.2023.2189878

Sioux, M. (2024). A Closer Look at Plagiarism within the Context of Student Academic Writing in an Era of Generative Artificial Intelligence. *Briefly Speaking Council on Higher Education*, 1-10.

Smutny, P., & Schreiberova, P. (2020). Chatbots for learning: A review of educational chatbots for the Facebook Messenger. *Computers & Education, 151*, 103862. Advance online publication. DOI: 10.1016/j.compedu.2020.103862

SOAS. (2024). *Recommendations for students on use of Generative AI (e.g., Open AI's 'Chat GPT').* chrome-extension://efaidnbmnnnibpcajpcglclefindmkaj/https://www.soas.ac.uk/sites/default/files/2023-07/ChatGPT%20and%20generative%20AI%20%E2%80%93%20a%20guide%20for%20students.pdf

Soelistiono, S. & Wahidin. (2023). Educational Technology Innovation: AI-Integrated Learning System Design in AILS-Based Education. *INFLUENCE: INTERNATIONAL JOURNAL OF SCIENCE REVIEW, 5*(2), 470–480. DOI: 10.54783/influencejournal.v5i2.175

Solak, E. (2024). Revolutionizing language learning: How ChatGPT and AI are changing the way we learn languages. [IJTE]. *International Journal of Technology in Education, 7*(2), 353–372. DOI: 10.46328/ijte.732

Song, C. & Song, Y. (2023). Enhancing academic writing skills and motivation: assessing the efficacy of ChatGPT in AI-assisted language learning for EFL students. Frontiers in Psychology. frontiersin.org

Song, C., & Song, Y. (2023). Enhancing academic writing skills and motivation: Assessing the efficacy of ChatGPT in AI-assisted language learning for EFL learners. *Frontiers in Psychology, 14*, 1260843. Advance online publication. DOI: 10.3389/fpsyg.2023.1260843 PMID: 38162975

Sorin, V., Barash, Y., Konen, E., & Klang, E. (2020). Deep learning for natural language processing in radiology—Fundamentals and a systematic review. [HTML]. *Journal of the American College of Radiology, 17*(5), 639–648. DOI: 10.1016/j.jacr.2019.12.026 PMID: 32004480

Srinivasa, K. G., Kurni, M., & Saritha, K. (2022). Harnessing the Power of AI to Education. In *Learning, teaching, and assessment methods for contemporary learners: pedagogy for the digital generation* (pp. 311–342). Springer Nature Singapore. [HTML] DOI: 10.1007/978-981-19-6734-4_13

Srinivasan, V., & Murthy, H. (2021). Improving reading and comprehension in K-12: Evidence from a large-scale AI technology intervention in India. *Computers and Education: Artificial Intelligence, 2*, 100019. Advance online publication. DOI: 10.1016/j.caeai.2021.100019

Stapleton, P., & Kin, B. L. K. (2019). Assessing the accuracy and teachers' impressions of Google Translate: A study of primary L2 writers in Hong Kong. *English for Specific Purposes, 56*, 18–34. DOI: 10.1016/j.esp.2019.07.001

Starks, A. C., & Reich, S. M. (2023). "What about special ed?": Barriers and enablers for teaching with technology in special education. Computers & Education. sciencedirect.com

Stavytska, I., Shalova, N., & Korbut, O. (2024). Exploring the impacts and techniques of teaching with Artificial Intelligence Tools. *Перспективи Та Інновації Науки*, (6(40)). Advance online publication. DOI: 10.52058/2786-4952-2024-6(40)-40-47

Stavytska, I., Shalova, N., & Korbut, O. (2024). Exploring the impacts and techniques of teaching with artificial intelligence tools. *Перспективи Та Інновації Науки, 6*(40), 40–48. DOI: 10.52058/2786-4952-2023-16(34)

Stephan, K. D., & Klima, G. (2021). Artificial intelligence and its natural limits. *AI & Society*, *36*(1), 9–18. DOI: 10.1007/s00146-020-00995-z

Steponenaite, A., & Barakat, B. (2023). Plagiarism in AI Empowered World. In Antona, M., & Stephanidis, C. (Eds.), Lecture Notes in Computer Science: Vol. 14021. *Universal Access in Human-Computer Interaction. HCII 2023*. Springer., DOI: 10.1007/978-3-031-35897-5_31

Stokel-Walker, C. (2022). AI bot ChatGPT writes smart essays-should academics worry? *Nature*, *12*. Advance online publication. DOI: 10.1038/d41586-022-04397-7 PMID: 36494443

Stracqualursi, L. & Agati, P. (2024). Twitter users perceptions of AI-based e-learning technologies. Scientific Reports. nature.com

Strohm, L., Hehakaya, C., Ranschaert, E. R., Boon, W. P., & Moors, E. H. (2020). Implementation of artificial intelligence (AI) applications in radiology: Hindering and facilitating factors. [springer.com]. *European Radiology*, *30*(10), 5525–5532. DOI: 10.1007/s00330-020-06946-y PMID: 32458173

Su ( ), J., & Yang ( ), W. (2023). Unlocking the Power of ChatGPT: A Framework for Applying Generative AI in Education. *ECNU Review of Education*, *6*(3), 355-366. https://doi.org/DOI: 10.1177/20965311231168423

Su, A. A. T., & Tran, T. H. N. (2024). The Benefits and Weaknesses of ChatGPT on Students' Learning Writing. *International Journal of AI in Language Education*, *1*(1), 20–28. DOI: 10.54855/ijaile.24112

Su, F., & Zou, D. (2020). Technology-enhanced collaborative language learning: Theoretical foundations, technologies, and implications. *Computer Assisted Language Learning*, *35*(8), 1754–1788. DOI: 10.1080/09588221.2020.1831545

Su, L., & Wu, X. (2024). A study on the effects of AI-based listening tools on EFL learners. *Journal of English Language Teaching and Linguistics*, *9*(1), 35–52.

Šumak, B., Heričko, M., & Pušnik, M. (2011). A meta-analysis of e-learning technology acceptance: The role of user types and e-learning technology types. *Computers in Human Behavior*, *27*(6), 2067–2077. DOI: 10.1016/j.chb.2011.08.005

Sumakul, D. T., Hamied, F. A., & Sukyadi, D. (2022). Artificial intelligence in EFL classrooms: Friend or foe. *LEARN Journal*, *15*(1), 232-256. https://so04.tci-thaijo.org/index.php/LEARN/article/view/256723

Sun, Y., Sheng, D., Zhou, Z., & Wu, Y. (2024). AI hallucination: Towards a comprehensive classification of distorted information in artificial intelligence-generated content. *Humanities & Social Sciences Communications*, *11*(1), 1278. Advance online publication. DOI: 10.1057/s41599-024-03811-x

Sun, Y., & Zhao, Z. (2024). AI-based translation tools in EFL writing: Enhancing accuracy and coherence. *Journal of Second Language Writing*, *35*, 100939.

Sun, Z., Anbarasan, M., & Praveen Kumar, D. J. C. I. (2021). Design of online intelligent English teaching platform based on artificial intelligence techniques. [HTML]. *Computational Intelligence*, *37*(3), 1166–1180. DOI: 10.1111/coin.12351

Suta, P., Lan, X., Wu, B., Mongkolnam, P., & Chan, J. H. (2020). An Overview of Machine Learning in Chatbots. *International Journal of Mechanical Engineering and Robotics Research*, •••, 502–510. DOI: 10.18178/ijmerr.9.4.502-510

Sweller, J. (1988). Cognitive load during problem solving: Effects on learning. *Cognitive Science*, *12*(2), 257–285. DOI: 10.1207/s15516709cog1202_4

Sweller, J. (2016). Cognitive Load Theory, Evolutionary Educational Psychology, and Instructional Design. In Geary, D., & Berch, D. (Eds.), *Evolutionary Perspectives on Child Development and Education. Evolutionary Psychology*. Springer., DOI: 10.1007/978-3-319-29986-0_12

Sweller, J., Ayres, P., & Kalyuga, S. (2011). Cognitive load theory in perspective. In *Cognitive load theory* (pp. 237–242). Springer., DOI: 10.1007/978-1-4419-8126-4_18

Taher, B., & Chaaban, Y. (2023). AI-enhanced grammar learning: A case study of Syrian EFL learners. *TESOL Quarterly*, *57*(2), 333–354.

Talukder, M. B., Farhana, N., & Salsabil, I. T. (2025). Enhancing Tourism Through AI-Driven Professional Development of ESL Teachers in Bangladesh. In Ali, M. M., Anwar, M. N., Fazal, S., & Ayyaz, S. (Eds.), (pp. 195–222). Advances in Computational Intelligence and Robotics. IGI Global., DOI: 10.4018/979-8-3693-9077-1.ch009

Tambunan, A. R. S., Andayani, W., Sari, W. S., & Lubis, F. K. (2022). Investigating EFL students' linguistic problems using Grammarly as automated writing evaluation feedback. *Indonesian Journal of Applied Linguistics*, *12*(1), 16–27. https://ejournal.upi.edu/index.php/IJAL/article/view/46428. DOI: 10.17509/ijal.v12i1.46428

Tang, B. L. (2024). AIgiarism is plagiarism: Artificial intelligence can (be perceived to) plagiarize and can also be plagiarized. *Science Editing*. Advance online publication. DOI: 10.6087/kcse.346

Tang, L., & Su, Y. (2024). Ethical implications and principles using artifical intelligence models in the classroom: A systemic literature review. *International Journal of Interactive Multimedia and Artificial Intelligence*, *8*(5), 25–36. DOI: 10.9781/ijimai.2024.02.010

Tapalova, O., & Zhiyenbayeva, N. (2022). Artificial Intelligence in Education: AIEd for Personalised Learning Pathways. *Electronic Journal of e-Learning*, *20*(5), 639–653. DOI: 10.34190/ejel.20.5.2597

Taylor, G. (2009). *A student's writing guide: How to plan and write successful essays*. Cambridge University Press. DOI: 10.1017/CBO9780511609749

Tegos, S., Demetriadis, S., & Tsiatsos, T. (2014). A configurable conversational agent to trigger students' productive dialogue: A pilot study in the CALL domain. *International Journal of Artificial Intelligence in Education*, *24*(1), 62–91. DOI: 10.1007/s40593-013-0007-3

Teräs, H. (2016). Collaborative online professional development for teachers in higher education. *Professional Development in Education*, *42*(2), 258–275. DOI: 10.1080/19415257.2014.961094

Thananukhun, K., Jaiyen, S., Jitkajornwanich, K., & Hanskunatai, A. (2023, February). Question classification for thai conversational chatbots using artificial neural networks and multilingual bert models. In *2023 15th International Conference on Knowledge and Smart Technology (KST)* (pp. 1-4). IEEE. DOI: 10.1109/KST57286.2023.10086784

Thanh, T. D. (2024). AI's Impact on Academic Writing and Mitigating Challenges in the Digital Era. *International Academic Journal of Education & Literature*, *5*(1), 1–7. DOI: 10.47310/iajel.2023.v05i01.002

The Open University. (2024). *Generative AI and plagiarism*. Distance Learning Courses and Adult Education - The Open University. https://www.open.ac.uk/libraryservices/beingdigital/activity/XK1383#page1

Thorp, H. H. (2023). ChatGPT is fun, but not an author. *Science*, *379*(6630), 313. DOI: 10.1126/science.adg7879 PMID: 36701446

Tiulkanov, A. (2023). AI and Data Policy Lawyer.

Torralba, K. D., Jose, D., & Byrne, J. (2020). Psychological safety, the hidden curriculum, and ambiguity in medicine. *Clinical Rheumatology*, *39*(3), 667–671. DOI: 10.1007/s10067-019-04889-4 PMID: 31902031

Tossell, C. C., Tenhundfeld, N. L., Momen, A., Cooley, K., & De Visser, E. J. (2024). Student perceptions of ChatGPT use in a college essay assignment: Implications for learning, grading, and trust in artificial intelligence. *IEEE Transactions on Learning Technologies*, *17*, 1069–1081. DOI: 10.1109/TLT.2024.3355015

Tosuntaş, Ş. B., Çubukçu, Z., & İnci, T. (2019). A Holistic View to Barriers to Technology Integration in Education. *Turkish Online Journal of Qualitative Inquiry*, 349–371. DOI: 10.17569/tojqi.613969

Tran, T. T. L., & Bui, T. O. (2023). The effectiveness of using Grammarly software to improve foreign language learners' writing skills. *Journal of educational equipment. Applied Research*, *1*(302), 37–39. https://vjol.info.vn/index.php/tctbgd/article/view/92218/78055

Trattner, C., Jannach, D., Motta, E., Costera Meijer, I., Diakopoulos, N., Elahi, M., Opdahl, A. L., Tessem, B., Borch, N., Fjeld, M., Øvrelid, L., De Smedt, K., & Moe, H. (2022). Responsible media technology and AI: Challenges and research directions. [springer.com]. *AI and Ethics*, *2*(4), 585–594. DOI: 10.1007/s43681-021-00126-4

Trinh, T. H., Nguyen, M. N., & Tran, T. T. H. (2022). Teachers and students' perceptions of using digital games in improving vocabulary at non-English-majored class. *AsiaCALL Online Journal*, *13*(5), 112–131. DOI: 10.54855/acoj.221358

Trinh, T. L. A., Tran, T. K. N., Vo, T. B. N., & Huynh, T. T. S. (2021). The difference effects of paper dictionaries vs. online dictionaries. *AsiaCALL Online Journal*, *12*(3), 28–38.

Truscott, J. (1996). The case against grammar correction in L2 writing classes. *Language Learning*, *46*(2), 327–369. DOI: 10.1111/j.1467-1770.1996.tb01238.x

Tseng, W., & Warschauer, M. (2023). Ai-writing tools in education: If you can't beat them, join them. *Journal of China Computer-Assisted Language Learning*, *3*(2), 258–262. DOI: 10.1515/jccall-2023-0008

Tumiran, M. A., Mohammad, N., & Bahri, S. (2024). Implications of leveraging AI in students' academic writing: A review analysis. [MJSSH]. *Malaysian Journal of Social Sciences and Humanities*, *9*(8), e002954. DOI: 10.47405/mjssh.v9i8.2954

Turnitin. (2024). *AI writing detection in the classic report view*. https://guides.turnitin.com/hc/en-us/articles/28457596598925-AI-writing-detection-in-the-classic-report-view

Tuyen, T., Ha, N. D. N., & Loc, N. (2024). Exploring The Relationship Between ChatGPT and Task-based Approach: Opportunities and Challenges. In *20th International Conference of the Asia Association of Computer-Assisted Language Learning (AsiaCALL 2023)* (pp. 22-36). Atlantis Press. DOI: https://doi.org/DOI: 10.2991/978-94-6463-396-2_3

Umali, J. N. D. (2024). Artificial Intelligence Technology Management of Teachers, Learners Motivation and Challenges Encountered. Educational Research (IJMCER). ijmcer.com

Umar, U. (2024). Advancements in English language teaching: Harnessing the power of artificial intelligence. *FLIP Foreign Language Instruction Probe*, *3*(1), 29–42. DOI: 10.54213/flip.v3i1.402

UMPSA. (2024). *Guidelines For Using Generative Artificial Intelligence At Universiti Malaysia Pahang Al-Sultan Abdullah*. chrome-extension://efaidnbmnnnibpcajpcglclefindmkaj/https://caic.umpsa.edu.my/media/attachments/2024/05/21/ai-bi-garis-panduan-kecerdasan-buatan-generatif_translation-bi.pdf

Universiti Teknologi Malaysia. (2024). *Guidelines for the Use of Generative Artificial Intelligence in Teaching and Learning Universiti Teknologi Malaysia*. chrome-extension://efaidnbmnnnibpcajpcglclefindmkaj/https://fke.utm.my/wp-content/uploads/2024/11/Guidelines-for-the-Use-of-Generative-Artificial-Intelligence-in-Teaching-and-Learning-UTM-1.pdf

University of Liverpool. (2024). *CODE OF PRACTICE ON ASSESSMENT APPENDIX L Academic Integrity Policy 2024-25 Applicable to all cohorts*. chrome-extension://efaidnbmnnnibpcajpcglclefindmkaj/https://www.liverpool.ac.uk/media/livacuk/tqsd/code-of-practice-on-assessment/appendix_L_cop_assess.pdf

Vafadar, D., & Qomi, H. (2023). AI in EFL assessment: A review of tools and techniques. *Language Assessment Quarterly*, *20*(2), 187–204.

Vall, R. R., & Araya, F. G. (2023). Exploring the benefits and challenges of AI-language learning tools. *International Journal of Social Science and Humanities Invention*, *10*(1), 7569–7576. https://valleyinternational.net/index.php/theijsshi. DOI: 10.18535/ijsshi/v10i01.02

VanLehn, C., Banerjee, F. M., & Wetzel, M. J. (2020). Teaching algebraic model construction: A tutoring system, lessons learned and an evaluation. *International Journal of Artificial Intelligence in Education*, *30*(3), 459–480. DOI: 10.1007/s40593-020-00205-3

VanLEHN, K. U. R. T.VanLEHN. (2011). The Relative Effectiveness of Human Tutoring, Intelligent Tutoring Systems, and Other Tutoring Systems. *Educational Psychologist*, *46*(4), 197–221. DOI: 10.1080/00461520.2011.611369

Varona, D. & Suárez, J. L. (2022). Discrimination, bias, fairness, and trustworthy AI. Applied Sciences. mdpi.com

Vellinga, N. E. (2024). Rethinking compensation in light of the development of AI. *International Review of Law Computers & Technology*, *38*(3), 391–412. DOI: 10.1080/13600869.2024.2324554

Vitalis, T., Antonius, K., & Arnoldus, H. (2021). Students' Perception Towards the Application of Grammarly: The Automatic Grammar Checker In Writing Narrative Text In The Third Semester At Stkip Ypup Makassar. [Jurnal Inovasi Pendidikan Dasar]. *JIPD*, *5*(2), 123–133. DOI: 10.36928/jipd.v5i2.858

Vo, H. K. N., & Nguyen, T. Q. (2021). Applying Grammarly as an Online Grammar Checker Tool to Enhance Writing Skills for English-Major Students. *Proceedings of The 9th OpenTESOL International Conference 2021, Language Education in Challenging Times: Designing Digital Transformations*, 454-467, Publishing House of Economics, Ho Chi Minh City.

Vo, T. K. A. (2015). Using E-Learning as a tool to support writing skill development at the Faculty of English, Danang University of Foreign Languages. *Journal of Science and Technology, Danang University, 4*(89), 1-5. https://jst-ud.vn/jst-ud/article/view/2386

Voudoukis, N., & Pagiatakis, G. (2022). Massive Open Online Courses (MOOCs): Practices, Trends, and Challenges for the Higher Education. *European Journal of Education and Pedagogy*, *3*(3), 288–295. DOI: 10.24018/ejedu.2022.3.3.365

Vu, D. V., & Peters, E. (2021). Incidental learning of collocations from meaning input: A longitudinal study into three reading modes and factors that affect learning. *Studies in Second Language Acquisition*, *44*(3), 685–707. DOI: 10.1017/S0272263121000462

Vu, D. V., & Peters, E. (2022). Learning vocabulary from reading-only, reading-while listening, and reading with textual input enhancement: Insights from Vietnamese EFL learners. *RELC Journal*, *53*(1), 85–100. DOI: 10.1177/0033688220911485

Vygotsky, L. S. (1978). *Mind in society: The development of higher psychological processes*. Harvard University Press.

Walkington, C. A. (2013). Using adaptive learning technologies to personalize instruction to student interests: The impact of relevant contexts on performance and learning outcomes. *Journal of Educational Psychology*, *105*(4), 932–945. DOI: 10.1037/a0031882

Wan Ismail, W. S., Awang, N. A., & Mohd Pauzi, N. (2024). An overview of the use of artificial intelligence (AI) tools in higher education. *International. The Journal of Learning in Higher Education*, *19*(3), 27–40. DOI: 10.24191/ijelhe.v19n3.1932

Wang, H. (2022). An Analytical Study Based on Computer-Assisted Language Teaching. In Pei, Y., Chang, J.-W., & Hung, J. C. (Eds.), *Innovative Computing* (Vol. 935, pp. 897–902). Springer Nature Singapore., DOI: 10.1007/978-981-19-4132-0_118

Wang, L., & Zhang, Q. (2024). AI-based tools for EFL learning: An exploration of teachers' perspectives. *Journal of Language Teaching and Research*, *15*(1), 22–35.

Wang, T., Lund, B. D., Marengo, A., Pagano, A., Mannuru, N. R., Teel, Z. A., & Pange, J. (2023). Exploring the potential impact of artificial intelligence (AI) on international students in higher education: Generative AI, chatbots, analytics, and international student success. [mdpi.com]. *Applied Sciences (Basel, Switzerland)*, *13*(11), 6716. DOI: 10.3390/app13116716

Wang, X., He, X., Wei, J., Liu, J., Li, Y., & Liu, X. (2023). Application of artificial intelligence to the public health education. *Frontiers in Public Health*, *10*, 1087174. DOI: 10.3389/fpubh.2022.1087174 PMID: 36703852

Wang, X., Liu, Q., Pang, H., Tan, S. C., Lei, J., Wallace, M. P., & Li, L. (2023). What matters in AI-supported learning: A study of human-AI interactions in language learning using cluster analysis and epistemic network analysis. *Computers & Education*, *194*, 104703. Advance online publication. DOI: 10.1016/j.compedu.2022.104703

Wang, X., Pang, H., Wallace, M. P., Wang, Q., & Chen, W. (2022). Learners' perceived AI presences in AI-supported language learning: A study of AI as a humanized agent from community of inquiry. *Computer Assisted Language Learning*. Advance online publication. DOI: 10.1080/09588221.2022.2056203

Wang, Y. F., Petrina, S., & Feng, F. (2017). VILLAGE—Virtual immersive language learning and gaming environment: Immersion and presence. *British Journal of Educational Technology*, *48*(2), 431–450. DOI: 10.1111/bjet.12388

Wang, Y.-J., Shang, H.-F., & Briody, P. (2013). Exploring the impact of using automated writing evaluation in English as a foreign language university students' writing. *Computer Assisted Language Learning*, *26*(3), 234–257. DOI: 10.1080/09588221.2012.655300

Wardatin, N. K. (2022). *Investigating EFL students' perception of Grammarly Premium as an automatic writing evaluation in the aspects of writing: A narrative inquiry*. Degree of Sarjana in English language education, Islamic University of Malang.

Wardatin, F. N., Setiawan, S., Mustofa, A., & Nugroho, H. A. (2022). Integrating self-directed learning in facilitating writers engagement through Grammarly: Exploring the perceptions of premium users. *EnJourMe (English Journal of Merdeka). Culture, Language, and Teaching of English*, *7*(1), 32–46. DOI: 10.26905/enjourme.v7i1.6580

Wei, L. (2023). Artificial intelligence in language instruction: impact on English learning achievement, L2 motivation, and self-regulated learning. Frontiers in Psychology. frontiersin.org

Weidman, A. C., Fernandez, K. C., Levinson, C. A., Augustine, A. A., Larsen, R. J., & Rodebaugh, T. L. (2012). Compensatory internet use among individuals higher in social anxiety and its implications for well-being. *Personality and Individual Differences*, *53*(3), 191–195. DOI: 10.1016/j.paid.2012.03.003 PMID: 22791928

White, J., & Stevens, K. (2024). Ethics of digital education. In *Edward Elgar Publishing eBooks* (pp. 252–289). DOI: 10.4337/9781803928241.00019

Williamson, B. & Eynon, R. (). Historical threads, missing links, and future directions in AI in education. Learning. tandfonline.com

Williamson, S. M. & Prybutok, V. (2024). Balancing privacy and progress: a review of privacy challenges, systemic oversight, and patient perceptions in AI-driven healthcare. Applied Sciences. mdpi.com

Willis, J. (1996). *A framework for task-based learning*. Addison Wesley.

Wilson, E. (2005). Powerful pedagogical strategies in initial teacher education. *Teachers and Teaching, 11*(4), 359–378. DOI: 10.1080/13450600500137141

Winkler, R., & Soellner, M. (2018). Unleashing the Potential of Chatbots in Education: A State-Of-The-Art Analysis. *Proceedings - Academy of Management, 2018*(1), 15903. DOI: 10.5465/AMBPP.2018.15903abstract

Woo, J. H., & Choi, H. (2021). Systematic Review for AI-based Language Learning Tools. *Diji'teol Kontencheu Haghoe Nonmunji/Dijiteol Kontencheu Hakoe Nonmunji, 22*(11), 1783–1792. DOI: 10.9728/dcs.2021.22.11.1783

Woodward, J. P., & Carnine, D. W. (1988). Antecedent Knowledge and Intelligent Computer Assisted Instruction. *Journal of Learning Disabilities, 21*(3), 131–139. DOI: 10.1177/002221948802100302 PMID: 3280714

Wu, R., & Yu, Z. (2024). Do AI chatbots improve students learning outcomes? Evidence from a meta-analysis. *British Journal of Educational Technology, 55*(1), 10–33. DOI: 10.1111/bjet.13334

Wu, T. T., Lee, H. Y., Li, P. H., Huang, C. N., & Huang, Y. M. (2024). Promoting Self-Regulation Progress and Knowledge Construction in Blended Learning via ChatGPT-Based Learning Aid. *Journal of Educational Computing Research, 61*(8), 3–31. DOI: 10.1177/07356331231191125

Xia, Y., Shin, S.-Y., & Kim, J.-C. (2024). Cross-Cultural Intelligent Language Learning System (CILS): Leveraging AI to facilitate language learning strategies in cross-cultural communication. *Applied Sciences, 14*(13), 5651-. DOI: 10.3390/app14135651

Xia, L., & Wang, Y. (2023). AI-supported collaborative learning in EFL contexts: Teacher and student perspectives. *Educational Technology Research and Development, 71*(3), 1123–1139.

Xiao, Y., Chatterjee, S., & Gehringer, E. (2022). A new era of plagiarism the danger of cheating using AI. *2022 20th International Conference on Information Technology Based Higher Education and Training (ITHET)*, 1-6. https://doi.org/DOI: 10.1109/ITHET56107.2022.10031827

Xiao, Y., & Zhi, Y. (2023). An exploratory study of EFL learners' use of ChatGPT for language learning tasks: Experience and perceptions. *Languages (Basel, Switzerland), 8*(3), 212–224. DOI: 10.3390/languages8030212

Xia, Q., Chiu, T. K. F., Chai, C. S., & Xie, K. (2023). The mediating effects of needs satisfaction on the relationships between prior knowledge and self-regulated learning through artificial intelligence chatbot. *British Journal of Educational Technology, 54*(4), 967–986. DOI: 10.1111/bjet.13305

Xie, J. (2023). Opportunities and challenges brought by artificial intelligence to Second language teaching: A case study of international chinese language education. *Advances in Engineering Innovation, 3*(1), None. Advance online publication. DOI: 10.54254/2977-3903/3/2023045

Xu, Y., Liu, X., Cao, X., Huang, C., Liu, E., Qian, S., ... & Zhang, J. (2021). Artificial intelligence: A powerful paradigm for scientific research. The Innovation, 2(4). cell.com

Xu, W., & Ouyang, F. (2022). A systematic review of AI role in the educational system based on a proposed conceptual framework. *Education and Information Technologies*, *27*(3), 4195–4223. DOI: 10.1007/s10639-021-10774-y

Xu, X., Hong, W. C. H., Zhang, Y., Jiang, H., & Liu, J. (2023). Learning paths design in personal learning environments: The impact on postgraduates' cognitive achievements and satisfaction. *Innovations in Education and Teaching International*. Advance online publication. DOI: 10.1080/14703297.2023.2189603

Xu, Y., Wang, D., Collins, P., Lee, H., & Warschauer, M. (2021). Same benefits, different communication patterns: Comparing children's reading with a conversational agent vs. a human partner. *Computers & Education*, *161*, 4059. DOI: 10.1016/j.compedu.2020.104059

Yan, D. (2023). How ChatGPT's automatic text generation impact on learners in a L2 writing practicum: An exploratory investigation. https://doi.org/DOI: 10.35542/osf.io/s4nfz

Yang, A. (2024). Challenges and Opportunities for Foreign Language Teachers in the Era of Artificial Intelligence. *International Journal of Education and Humanities*, *4*(1), 39–50. DOI: 10.58557/(ijeh).v4i1.202

Yang, C. C. Y., & Ogata, H. (2023). Personalized learning analytics intervention approach for enhancing student learning achievement and behavior engagement in blended learning. *Education and Information Technologies*, *28*(3), 2509–2528. DOI: 10.1007/s10639-022-11291-2

Yang, H., & Kyun, S. (2022). The current research trend of artificial intelligence in language learning: A systematic empirical literature review from an active theory perspective. *Australasian Journal of Educational Technology*, *38*(5), 180–210. DOI: 10.14742/ajet.7492

Yang, Z., & Li, L. (2023). AI-powered language learning platforms: An empirical study on student engagement. *Computers & Education*, *182*, 104455.

Yeliena, P., Rashmi, G., & Hayri, U. (2024). The Use of AI Chatbots In Higher Education: The Problem of Plagiarism. *Review of Artificial Intelligence in Education*, *5*, 1–8. DOI: 10.37497/rev.artif.intell.educ.v5i00.31

Yetkin, R., & Özer-Altınkaya, Z. (2024). AI in the language classroom: Insights from pre-service English teachers. *E-Learning and Digital Media*, *0*(0), 20427530241267011. Advance online publication. DOI: 10.1177/20427530241267011

Ye, Y., Zhu, S., Wang, J., Du, Q., Yang, Y., Tu, D., & Luo, J. (2018, December). A unified scheme of text localization and structured data extraction for joint OCR and data mining. In 2018 IEEE on Big Data [IEEE.]. *Big Data*, •••, 2373–2382.

Yuan, Y., Li, H., & Sawaengdist, A. (2024). The impact of ChatGPT on learners in English academic writing: Opportunities and challenges in education. *Language Learning in Higher Education*, *14*(1), 41–56. DOI: 10.1515/cercles-2023-0006

Yu-Ching, T., & Lin, Y. (2024). Enhancing English as a foreign language (EFL) learners' writing with ChatGPT: A university-level course design: EJEL. *Electronic Journal of e-Learning*, *22*(2), 78–97. DOI: 10.34190/ejel.21.5.3329

Yuen, C. L., & Schlote, N. (2024). Learner Experiences of Mobile Apps and Artificial Intelligence to Support Additional Language Learning in Education. [sagepub.com]. *Journal of Educational Technology Systems*, *52*(4), 00472395241238693. DOI: 10.1177/00472395241238693

Yulianti, E. (2018). Utilizing Grammarly in Teaching Writing Recount Text Through Genre Based Approach. *International Journal of Science. Technology in Society*, *6*(1), 1–5. DOI: 10.11648/j.ijsts.20180601.11

Yu, Y., Si, X., Hu, C., & Zhang, J. (2019). A review of recurrent neural networks: LSTM cells and network architectures. *Neural Computation*, *31*(7), 1235–1270. DOI: 10.1162/neco_a_01199 PMID: 31113301

Zachia Raiza, J. B. (2024). Integrating Artificial Intelligence in Academic Writing. *International Multidisciplinary Journal of Research for Innovation, Sustainability and Excellence, 1*(8), 280-293. https://risejournals.org/index.php/imjrise/article/view/637#:~:text=AI%20can%20automate%20routine%20tasks,for%20over%2Dreliance%20on%20AI

Zafari, M., Bazargani, J. S., Sadeghi-Niaraki, A., & Choi, S.-M. (2022). Artificial Intelligence Applications in K-12 Education: A Systematic Literature Review. *IEEE Access : Practical Innovations, Open Solutions*, *10*, 61905–61921. DOI: 10.1109/ACCESS.2022.3179356

Zardiashvili, L. & Fosch-Villaronga, E. (2020). "Oh, dignity too?" said the robot: human dignity as the basis for the governance of robotics. Minds and Machines. springer.com

Zawacki-Richter, O., Marín, V. I., Bond, M., & Gouverneur, F. (2019). Systematic review of research on artificial intelligence applications in higher education – where are the educators? *International Journal of Educational Technology in Higher Education*, *16*(1), 39. DOI: 10.1186/s41239-019-0171-0

Zdravkova, K. (2022). The potential of artificial intelligence for assistive technology in education. In Handbook on Intelligent Techniques in the Educational Process: Vol 1 Recent Advances and Case Studies (pp. 61-85). Cham: Springer International Publishing. [HTML] DOI: 10.1007/978-3-031-04662-9_4

Zdravkova, K. (2023). Personalized Education for Sustainable Development. *Sustainability (Basel)*, *15*(8), 6901. DOI: 10.3390/su15086901

Zeb, A., Ullah, R., & Karim, R. (2024). Exploring the role of ChatGPT in higher education: Opportunities, challenges and ethical considerations. *The International Journal of Information and Learning Technology*, *41*(1), 99–111. DOI: 10.1108/IJILT-04-2023-0046

Zhai, C. & Wibowo, S. (2023). A systematic review on artificial intelligence dialogue systems for enhancing English as foreign language students' interactional competence in the university. Computers and Education: Artificial Intelligence. sciencedirect.com

Zhai, X. (2023). ChatGPT: Artificial Intelligence for Education. *International Journal of Scientific and Research Publications*, *13*(2).

Zhai, X., Chu, X., Chai, C. S., Jong, M. S. Y., Istenic, A., Spector, M., Liu, J.-B., Yuan, J., & Li, Y. (2021). A Review of Artificial Intelligence (AI) in Education from 2010 to 2020. *Complexity, 2021*(1), 8812542. DOI: 10.1155/2021/8812542

Zhang, B., & Liu, J. (2024). AI-based speaking practice for EFL learners: A comparative study. *Journal of English for Academic Purposes, 57*, 101140.

Zhang, B., Zhu, J., & Su, H. (2023). Toward the third generation artificial intelligence. *Science China. Information Sciences, 66*(2), 121101. DOI: 10.1007/s11432-021-3449-x

Zhang, J., & Tao, D. (2021). Empowering Things With Intelligence: A Survey of the Progress, Challenges, and Opportunities in Artificial Intelligence of Things. *IEEE Internet of Things Journal, 8*(10), 7789–7817. DOI: 10.1109/JIOT.2020.3039359

Zhang, J., & Zhang, Z. (2024). AI in teacher education: Unlocking new dimensions in teaching support, inclusive learning, and digital literacy. *Journal of Computer Assisted Learning, 40*(4), 1871–1885. DOI: 10.1111/jcal.12988

Zhang, R., & Zou, D. (2022). Self-regulated second language learning: A review of types of benefits of strategies, modes of teacher support, and pedagogical implications. *Computer Assisted Language Learning, 37*(4), 720–765. DOI: 10.1080/09588221.2022.2055081

Zhang, R., & Zou, D. (2022). Types, purposes, and effectiveness of state-of-the-art technologies for second and foreign language learning. *Computer Assisted Language Learning, 35*(4), 696–742. DOI: 10.1080/09588221.2020.1744666

Zhang, Y., Peng, J., & Zheng, Y. (2024). Teachers' perceptions of implementing digital multimodal composing in tertiary classrooms: Voices from Chinese EFL teachers. *International Journal of Applied Linguistics, 34*(4), 1265–1282. DOI: 10.1111/ijal.12560

Zhan, Z., Tong, Y., Lan, X., & Zhong, B. (2024). A systematic literature review of game-based learning in Artificial Intelligence education. *Interactive Learning Environments, 32*(3), 1137–1158. DOI: 10.1080/10494820.2022.2115077

Zhao, Y., & Huang, X. (2024). The impact of AI tools on EFL learners' reading skills and motivation. *Journal of Language Teaching and Research, 15*(3), 305–318.

Zheng, L., Long, M., Zhong, L., & Gyasi, J. F. (2022). The effectiveness of technology-facilitated personalized learning on learning achievements and learning perceptions: A meta-analysis. *Education and Information Technologies, 27*(8), 11807–11830. DOI: 10.1007/s10639-022-11092-7

Zhou, M. Y., & Lawless, W. F. (2014). An Overview of Artificial Intelligence in Education. In Khosrow-Pour, D. B. A. (Ed.), *M* (pp. 2445–2452). Advances in Information Quality and Management. IGI Global., DOI: 10.4018/978-1-4666-5888-2.ch237

Zimmerman, B. J. (2002). Becoming a self-regulated learner: An overview. *Theory into Practice, 41*(2), 64–70. DOI: 10.1207/s15430421tip4102_2

Zinkevich, N. A., & Ledeneva, T. V. (2021). Using Grammarly to Enhance Students' Academic Writing Skills. *Professional Discourse & Communication, 3*(4), 51–63. DOI: 10.24833/2687-0126-2021-3-4-51-63

Zirar, A. (2023). Exploring the impact of language models, such as ChatGPT, on student learning and assessment. *Review of Education*, *11*(3), e3433. Advance online publication. DOI: 10.1002/rev3.3433

Zou, M., & Huang, L. (2023). The impact of ChatGPT on L2 writing and expected responses: Voice from doctoral students. *Education and Information Technologies*, *29*(11), 13201–13219. DOI: 10.1007/s10639-023-12397-x

Zukarnain, N., Abbas, B. S., Wayan, S., Trisetyarso, A., & Kang, C. H. (2019, August). Spelling checker algorithm methods for many languages. In *2019 International Conference on Information Management and Technology (ICIMTech)* (Vol. 1, pp. 198-201). IEEE. DOI: 10.1109/ICIMTech.2019.8843801

About the Contributors

Pham Vu Phi Ho, Faculty of Foreign Languages, Industrial University of Ho Chi Minh City, Vietnam, used to be a Vice-President of Ba Ria – Vung Tau University and Vice-President at Van Hien University, Vietnam. Pham has published more than 70 research articles in both local and International Journals, such as Computer-Assisted language Learning, SAGE Open, System, and Journal of Psycholinguist Research (17 Scopus/14 ISI), and 10 books and course-books, 3-course books. He is the Vice President for Administrative Affairs of AsiaCALL. He is now the Editor-in-chief of the International Journal of TESOL & Education. He is an editor of an Edited Book published by Springer, and an Edited Book entitled "Empowering Educators: Integrating AI Tools for Personalized Language Instruction", which will be published by Springer Nature.

***

Alagesan Ambikapathy holds a Doctor of Philosophy from the University of Malaya, Malaysia, in the field of Instructional Technology; a Master of Science (Pedagogy) from Universiti Putra Malaysia; and a Bachelor of Arts (Indian Studies & Anthropology & Sociology) from the University of Malaya. He has served as a lecturer at Universiti Pendidikan Sultan Idris, Malaysia, for 10 years. He has also worked as a part-time lecturer at Universiti Tunku Abdul Rahman for three semesters. Currently, he works as a business development associate at Uma Publications Sdn. Bhd. He is interested and involved in various research and publication activities, especially in the field of Tamil Language Education and Pedagogy, Teaching and Learning Strategies, and Tamil Language Teaching and Learning, which focuses on teaching methods, ICT applications in teaching and learning, and using the Fuzzy Delphi Method in module and model development.

Mansour Amini is an interdisciplinary researcher and a senior lecturer from the School of Languages, Literacies, and Translation, Universiti Sains Malaysia (USM). He has a Diploma in Mathematics and Physics, a B.A. in English Language and Literature, an M.A. in English Language Teaching, and a PhD in Translation Studies. He has published articles in Translation, Education, Humanities, and Social Sciences, and is the principal investigator of several research projects. He has conducted workshops, seminars, and talks on Thesis Writing and Research Methodology in Malaysia, Thailand, Indonesia, Iran, and China. Dr. Mansour Amini is a reviewer, editing manager, and editorial board member of several academic journals. He has tried to link research with teaching practice by applying the lessons learned from authentic research outputs to teaching scenarios.

Andi Asrifan, S.Pd, M.Pd, a distinguished figure in the realm of education, particularly in English Language Education, has made significant contributions through his extensive research, teaching, and leadership roles. As the Head of the Institute for Cooperation and International Affairs at Universitas Muhammadiyah Sidenreng Rappang, Dr. Asrifan's academic journey is marked by a rich tapestry of achievements, including a Doctor of Education in English Language Education. His work spans various facets of education, language, and technology, reflecting the diverse topics covered in his publications and research endeavors. These include, but are not limited to, the impact of the COVID-19 pandemic on educational practices, methodologies in English as a Foreign Language (EFL) classrooms, and the integration of technology in teaching and learning processes. Dr. Asrifan's commitment to advancing educational standards and practices is further evidenced by his active participation in international conferences, webinars, and workshops across countries like India, the Philippines, and Pakistan. These events, organized by various institutions and associations, underscore his role as a global educator and thought leader. His dedication to professional development is also highlighted through his involvement in numerous courses and certifications in personal branding, public speaking, and literacy teaching. Moreover, Dr. Asrifan's leadership extends beyond academia into organizational and educational development, where he has served in various capacities, including as an external examiner for Ph.D. dissertations and a reviewer for scientific journals. His accolades, memberships in professional organizations, and roles as an ambassador for international associations speak volumes of his influence and commitment to fostering educational excellence and sustainable development goals globally.

Arsad Bahri, S.Pd. M.Pd. is a distinguished educator and researcher currently chairing the Institute for Educational Development and Quality Assurance at Universitas Negeri Makassar (UNM). He has built a robust academic career with a strong foundation in Biology Education, holding degrees from Universitas Negeri Makassar and Universitas Negeri Malang. With extensive teaching experience across various biology courses, he is a respected Professor and functional academic with significant research contributions, boasting an H-Index of 21 on Google Scholar. His work spans multiple domains, including developing innovative learning strategies, environmental studies, and implementing ICT in education. Prof. Bahri has received numerous accolades and holds several intellectual property rights for his educational models and tools. He actively participates in national and international seminars, contributing to modern educational practices and policy discourse. His prolific research output includes articles in high-impact journals and numerous funded projects to enhance educational quality and student engagement through problem-based learning and technology integration. Prof. Bahri's dedication to education is further evidenced by his involvement in community service projects and professional organizations, cementing his leadership in Biology Education.

Pham Thanh Dieu is a teacher in Bui Huu Nghia High School, Can Tho City. Her main research interests are teaching methods for learning English. She has been an English teacher for more than three years.

Malini Ganapathy is a lecturer at the School of Languages, Literacies and Translation, Universiti Sains Malaysia, Penang. She has a Certificate of Education (TESL), B.A. (Hons.) in English Language and Literature Studies, M.A. and Ph.D in Applied Linguistics from Universiti Sains Malaysia. She has 18 years of teaching experience at secondary schools, prior to joining Universiti Sains Malaysia in 2014. Her research interests include English Language Teaching (ELT), Literacy (Multiliteracies, Multimodality, New Literacies) and Writing. She has published numerous research articles focusing on her area of research, both in international and local journals.

Ramratan Guru, Assistant Professor Level III, School of Design, Mody University of Science and Technology, Lakshmangarh- 332311, Rajasthan,India. Research and Academic Experience: He has more than 10 Years of experience in academics and research. Research Area: His areas of interest include nonwovens, clothing comfort, medical textile, sewing thread/garment, biodegradables, plastic recycling, nanotechnology, sustainable materials and high-performance fibers and Fashion Merchandising.Number of Published papers: He has contributed more than 95 Research papers in referred journals and 51 research papers in International Conferences of repute. He has contributed 12 book chapters published by Intech UK, B P International UK, and Woodhead Publications. He has applied for more than T30 Indian/ International Patents and also 06 books published. Appreciate his research work to U.K., Canada, Australia and U.S.A. Government, Europe, Brazil etc.

Sajed S. Ingilan is Associate Professor V at the University of Southeastern Philippines, where he teaches linguistics and Mindanao studies. He is the Chief Editor of the Southeastern Philippines Journal of Research and Development, a Scopus-indexed journal. He is a certified writer and editor by the National Book Development Board-Philippines and an associate member of the National Research Council of the Philippines.

Vidhi Jalan is currently serving as an Assistant Professor in Corporate Communication at the Institute of Business Management, GLA University, Mathura. She holds a Ph.D. in English Literature from Dayalbagh Educational Institute, awarded in 2023. Vidhi is an accomplished educator specializing in business communication and business etiquette. She has designed and taught practical communication courses for MBA and BBA students, focusing on professional communication and preparing students for placement drives. Her academic journey includes the completion of a Master of Arts in English and clearing the UGC NET-JRF in 2017. Vidhi has also contributed significantly to academic research, with publications in peer-reviewed journals and presentations at national and international conferences. Her work engages with topics ranging from business communication to aesthetic literature. Vidhi's dedication to education extends beyond the classroom, as she actively participates in faculty development programs and organizes value-added courses for students.

Mohamed Khaldi is Professor of Higher Education of the Department of computer Science and management at Ecole Normale Supérieure Tétouan of the University Abdelmalek Essaadi where he has been since 1987. From 2011 to 2014, he served as coordinator of the Specialized Master in Computerized Management for the company. He was a member of advisory board of dozen of international congress in the field of computer science. He received a B.S from Mohamed V University in 1982, and a 3rd cycle diploma from ENS Rabat in 1986. He received his PhD in Didactics, Information and Communication Technology from the Faculty of Science Ben MSik in 2001. And the Academic habilitation in 2003, from the Faculty of Science Ben MSik.

Khadizatul Kobra has been a lecturer in the Department of English and Modern Languages under the College of Arts and Sciences (CAAS) at the International University of Business Agriculture and Technology (IUBAT), Dhaka, Bangladesh, since September 2023. She was born and brought up in Sirajganj, Bangladesh. Khadiza completed her BA (Honors) in English in 2021 and her MA in English Language Teaching and Applied Linguistics (ELTAL) in 2022 from the Department of English, Bangladesh University of Professionals. She commenced her teaching career in March 2023 at the Department of English, Shanto-Mariam University of Creative Technology (SMUCT), Dhaka, Bangladesh.

Sanjeev Kumar is a Professor in Lovely Professional University Punjab India. He received Undergraduate in Hotel Management from Osmania University, Postgraduate in Tourism Management from Madurai Kamaraj University. He completed Doctor of Philosophy in Hospitality Management in 2019 from Amity University Jaipur India. His research areas lies in food Service Industry, his research focuses on Alcoholic beverages, Event management and Sustainable Management Practices, Metaverse, AI Machine Learning and Artificial Intelligence. He published more than 60 research papers, articles and chapters in Scopus Indexed, UGC Approved and peer reviewed Journals and books. Dr. Sanjeev Kumar participated and acted as resource person in various National and International conferences, seminars, session chair, research workshops and industry talks and his work has been widely cited. Dr. Sanjeev also edited more than 12 books with various International Publishers such as IGI Global, Cambridge Scholars, Emerald, CABI, Bentham Science, Taylor & Francis. Dr Sanjeev is an active researcher and has published numerous research articles in prestigious national and international journals and books.

Vijay Kumar is Associate Professor in Information Technology Department, Dr B R Ambedkar NIT Jalandhar, Punjab. He received his Ph.D. degree from NIT Kuruksherta. Previously, he received M.Tech. and B.Tech. degrees from GJUS&T, Hisar and Kurukshetra University Kurukshetra, respectively. He has more than 3 years of teaching and research experience at NIT Hamirpur. Prior, he had 12 years of teaching experience in various reputed institutes like Manipal University Jaipur and Thapar University Patiala. He completed 2 DST SERB and 1 CSIR-sponsored research projects. He has published more than 180 research papers in International Journals/Conferences. He has many book chapters in international repute publishers. He has supervised many Ph.D. and M.Tech. thesis on Metaheuristics, Image Mining, and Data Clustering. He is the reviewer of several reputed SCI journals. He is member of ACM, CSI, International Association of Engineers, International Association of Computer Science and Information Technology, Singapore. His current research area is Soft Computing, Data Mining, Deep Learning, Steganography, and Pattern Recognition.

Yoke Lian Lau graduated from Universiti Malaya in 2009 with a Master of Modern Language and Mokpo National University Korea with a Master of Arts in 2011. In addition, she earned a Bachelor of Arts from Universiti Malaya in 2006 and a Certificate in Korean Language and Culture from Chongju University. Presently, she holds the position of lecturer at Universiti Malaysia Sabah's Centre for the Promotion of Knowledge and Language Learning. The scope of her research encompasses translations, AI, Chinese learning and teaching, Chinese languages, and linguistics.

Nguyen Le Ngoc Anh is the lecturer in School of Social Sciences and Humanities, Can Tho University. Her main research interests are teaching methods and the importance of the library in learning English. She has been an English teacher for more than seven years.

Nguyen Hong Nhung obtained a Bachelor's degree in TESOL at Saigon University and a Master's degree in English Language Studies at Van Lang University. Now, she is teaching English at Lam Son Secondary School in Vietnam. Her research interests mainly cover Cognitive Linguistics, Contrastive Linguistics, Teaching English Language Skills and Vocabulary, and CALL.

Himani Oberai is working as an Associate Professor in GLA University, Mathura. Also, she is the Area Chair in Business Communication Domain. She is having 15+ years of rich teaching and research experience. Her area of interest is Organizational Behavior, Sustainable Development, Workplace Adversity and Human Resource Management. She earned her Ph.D. in the area of Workplace Adversity from GLA University. She completed her Master's in Business Administration with distinction in the area of Human Resource Management from Banasthali University, Rajasthan. She has published many research papers in SCOPUS, ABDC-B, Web of Science, Journals. She completed two Projects under Ministry of Education where she developed the course content and recorded lectures for management students for DTH channel 13 for online education of Swayam Prabha. She is also an Adjunct Faculty on Thesis Supervisor Role at Liverpool John Moore Business School UK through UPGRAD.

Phan Thi Ngoc Le is currently an English lecturer at VNU University of Languages and International Studies, Hanoi. Her research interests include English Linguistics, World Englishes, L1 transfer to L2, English as a medium of instruction, English for specific purposes, and Computer-assisted language learning. She has contributed to numerous publications covering diverse topics with her works appearing in various journals such as Interdisciplinary Journal of Problem-based Learning, Journal of Mekong Societies, Rupkatha Journal on Interdisciplinary Studies in Humanities, Journal of Indian and Asian Studies, among others.

Widya Rizky Pratiwi, S.Pd., MM is an Assistant Professor in the Master Program of English Education at the School of Graduate Program, Universitas Terbuka, Indonesia. She completed her doctoral degree at Universitas Negeri Makassar in the English Education Study Program under the Indonesian Lecturer Excellence Scholarship (BUDI-DN). She was a visiting researcher at the University of Newcastle in 2019, Australia, under the Ministry of Education, Culture, Research, and Technology (Kemendikbudristek) scholarship. Her research interest is TEFL, teaching innovation, learning strategies, immersion programs, and ODL. .

Ankit Saxena is currently working as associate professor at Institute of Business Management, GLA University, Mathura. He is a Director Medalist from Dayalbagh Educational Institute, Agra. He qualified NET-JRF (UGC). He has excellent academic background and a rich experience of 17 years in research and academics. He has published number of research papers and contemporary business case studies. His area of interest comprises Strategic Financial Management and behavior of market participants.

Shafa, an accomplished academic with a robust educational background, earned his S1 from IAIN/UIN Alauddin Makassar in 2004, S2 from Universitas Negeri Makassar in 2007, and S3 from the same institution in 2021. Currently serving as a lecturer at the Faculty of Tarbiyah and Teacher Training at UIN Sultan Aji Muhammad Idris Samarinda, Dr. Shafa has held numerous academic positions, including Assistant Lecturer at IAIN Alauddin Makassar, Lecturer at STITEK Bontang, and Coordinator of English at STAIN Samarinda. His professional experience extends to roles such as secretary at LP2M STAIN Samarinda and Vice Dean at UINSI. Actively engaged in various organizations in Samarinda, Dr. Shafa has also contributed significantly to academic conferences and workshops, both as a participant and presenter. His publications cover a range of topics from linguistic theory to multicultural education, highlighting his diverse research interests and commitment to advancing educational practices.

Muh Ibnu Sholeh, S.HI., M.Pd.I., is a prominent figure in Islamic education and business management, born on December 25, 1984, in Trenggalek. He currently serves as a lecturer in the Islamic Education Management Study Program at STAI KH Muhammad Ali Sodiq Tulungagung. He completed his undergraduate studies in Muamalah Sharia Law at STAIN Tulungagung in 2005, followed by a Master's Degree in Islamic Education Management from IAIN Tulungagung in 2008. He pursued further studies and earned a Doctoral Degree in Management of Islamic Education from UIN Sayyid Ali Rahmatullah Tulungagung. Muh. Ibnu Sholeh, S.HI., M.Pd.I., has authored numerous scholarly articles in the field of Islamic education management. By 2023, he had published 60 articles in national journals indexed by Sinta 2 to Sinta 6, and in Scopus-indexed Q2 journals. In 2024, he expanded his publication record with works in international journals indexed by Scopus Q1 and Q4. Some of his notable publications include "Islamic Education Management" and "HR Management for Islamic Education". In addition to his role as a prolific writer, Muh. Ibnu Sholeh is actively engaged as a young lecturer at STAI KH Muhammad Ali Sodiq Tulungagung. He also serves as the Chair of the Journal Management for the Islamic Education Management Study Program and teaches at various Islamic and general educational institutions across Indonesia. His previous educational roles include teaching positions at SDN Ngubalan 01 Tulungagung, SDN Salakkembang Tulungagung, SMPI Trenggalek, and Muhammadiyah Tourism Vocational School Tulungagung. He has also held administrative positions such as Deputy Principal for Curriculum and teaching staff at MA Al-Furqon Trenggalek. Muh. Ibnu Sholeh is widely recognized as an experienced expert in Islamic education and business management, making significant contributions to the education sector in Indonesia. He stands out as a leading figure in the field of Islamic education management and business in the country.

Sri Rahmadhani Siregar, M.Pd., born on May 6, 1986, in Arse Jae Dolok, has established a distinguished academic and professional career. She completed her elementary education at SD N 142806 in Bunga Bondar in 1998, followed by junior high at SMP N 1 in Sipirok in 2001, and senior high at SMA N 2 Plus Sipirok in 2004. Pursuing higher education, she earned her Bachelor's degree in English Literature from North Sumatra University (USU) in Medan in 2008. Furthering her academic credentials, she obtained a Master of Education in English Education from the State University of Padang (UNP) in 2014. Sri Rahmadhani began her teaching career in February 2009 at STKIP Tapanuli Selatan and Adzkia Course, demonstrating her dedication to education from the onset. In 2014, she joined the English Education Department at UIN Syekh Ali Hasan Ahmad Addary Padangsidimpuan, where she has since been instrumental in shaping the curriculum and pedagogy. Her scholarly contributions include three significant research studies on teaching English as a foreign language, all sponsored by BOPTN UIN Syekh Ali Hasan Ahmad Addary Padangsidimpuan. These studies underscore her commitment to advancing methodologies in English language teaching, cementing her reputation as an academic leader in her field. Sri Rahmadhani's work continues to influence and inspire both her peers and students, contributing to the broader discourse on English education in Indonesia.

Aubrey Statti, Ed.D. earned a Bachelor of Arts in Political Science and Spanish from the University of Florida and a Master's of Professional Counseling and a Doctorate of Education from Liberty University. She has worked in higher education for 13 years and has taught at the undergraduate, graduate, and post-graduate levels in areas of psychology, counseling, education, and research. Additionally, she has worked in the Florida public schools as both a high school teacher and a school counselor. Dr. Statti is currently a professor for The Chicago School of Professional Psychology's (TCSPP) Educational

Psychology and Technology program, primarily teaching research and ethics courses. She also serves as a Dissertation Chair and reader on doctoral student's dissertations. Her research interests in the areas of educational technology include K-12 education, online education, early childhood education, digital storytelling, mentorship, and rural education. Dr. Statti has served as a reviewer for the Contemporary Issues in Technology and Teacher Education journal and is currently on the development committee of TCSPP's International Journal of Educational Psychology and Technology.

Mohammad Badruddoza Talukder is an Associate Professor, College of Tourism and Hospitality Management, IUBAT - International University of Business Agriculture and Technology, Dhaka-1230, Bangladesh. He holds PhD in Hotel Management from Lovely Professional University, India. He has been teaching various courses in the Department of Tourism and Hospitality at various universities in Bangladesh since 2008. His research areas include tourism management, hotel management, hospitality management, food & beverage management, and accommodation management, where he has published research papers in well-known journals in Bangladesh and abroad. Mr. Talukder is one of the executive members of the Tourism Educators Association of Bangladesh. He has led training and consulting for a wide range of hospitality organizations in Bangladesh. He just became an honorary facilitator at the Bangladesh Tourism Board's Bangabandhu international tourism and hospitality training institution.

Tan Jee Chin currently a Mandarin Language Teacher in Centre for the Promotion of Knowledge and Language Learning, University of Sabah Malaysia. His academic research focuses on Chinese Literature, Cultural Studies and Mandarin Language Teaching.

Kelly M. Torres, Ph.D. is the Department Chair of the Educational Psychology and Technology program at The Chicago School. Her research interests are focused on international education, teacher certification programs, innovative technologies, and online learning.

Yong Hui Wen is a language teacher of Mandarin at Universiti Malaysia Sabah (UMS). She earned her Master Degree in Teaching Chinese to Speakers of Other Languages (TCSOL) from East China Normal University in 2023, where her work focuses on the teaching methods in teaching Mandarin language as foreign languages. Yong Hui Wen's academic interests include the teaching materials, new era teaching methods, and teaching skills.

Ali Zahabi has a Phd in Applied Linguistics from Universiti Sains Malaysia. He is a lecturer at the School of Liberal Arts, King Mongkut's University of Technology Thonburi, Thailand.

Index

A

C

E

M

O

P

www.ingramcontent.com/pod-product-compliance
Lightning Source LLC
LaVergne TN
LVHW062112300926
849161LV00010B/2443